D1277397

BLOOD ON MY HANDS

Craig Jurisevic was born in Adelaide, South
Australia in 1965 and is married with
three children.

He is a cardiothoracic and trauma surgeon and has
worked in many conflict zones including Israel and
Gaza (1992–93), Albania and Kosovo (1999), and
with the Royal Australian Army Medical Corps
in East Timor (2006) and Afghanistan (2008).

Craig works full-time as a surgeon in Adelaide and
is a Senior Lecturer at the University of Adelaide.
He is a member of the International Humanitarian
Law Committee of the Australian Red Cross.

CRAIG JURISEVIC
BLOOD ON MY HANDS

A SURGEON AT WAR

WILD
DINGO
PRESS

Published by Wild Dingo Press
Melbourne Australia
books@wilddingopress.com.au
www.wilddingopress.com.au

First published by Wild Dingo Press in 2010, reprinted 2010

Text copyright © Craig Jurisevic 2010

The moral right of the author has been asserted.

Except as permitted under the Australian Copyright Act 1968, no part of this
book may be reproduced, stored in a retrieval system, or transmitted in any
form or by any means, electronic, mechanical, photocopying, recording,
or otherwise without prior written permission of the copyright owner and
the above publisher of this book.

Cover design: Grant Slaney
Maps: Dimitrios Propokis
Editing: Janice Bird
Printed in Poland by Hussar Books.

National Library of Australia
Cataloguing-in-Publication data

Jurisevic, Craig, 1965-
Blood on my hands : a surgeon at war / Craig Jurisevic.

ISBN: 9780980757002 (pbk.)

Jurisevic, Craig, 1965- ; International Medical Corps; Surgeons--Australia—
Biography; Surgeons--Kosovo (Republic)—Biography; Volunteer workers in
medical care—Kosovo (Republic)—Biography; Kosovo War, 1998-1999—
Medical care; Kosovo War, 1998-1999—Personal narratives, Australian.

617.0232092

Acknowledgements

I would like to thank all those people who have assisted in bringing this book to fruition.

Firstly, special thanks to Robert Hillman for working with my detailed memoir to develop the narrative momentum of this book. I greatly appreciate his ability and experience as a writer and I thank him for his invaluable work. He played a vital role in helping to craft this memoir into its current form.

Thank you to my wife Donna – you have lived through your own, and my, experiences of this war and patiently supported me with equanimity and love during the aftermath – including the demands of the writing and publishing processes.

To my friend and editor, Dr Bob Rich, thanks for setting everything in motion by passing on my original memoir, *They Sleep With Me*, to Catherine Lewis, my publisher. Catherine took up this project with great passion and has devoted much time and care developing the manuscript – her suggestions, sensitivity and commitment to accuracy are all greatly appreciated.

This book is a tribute to all of those who died in this war – the young and idealistic people who thought such a bright future would be theirs and who fought so valiantly.

Most importantly this book is a plea for peace; it aims to expose the corrupting nature of such conflicts and the needless suffering of so many innocents as well as the horrors of the injuries that modern warfare invariably inflicts, especially on civilian populations.

Finally, to those who worked on the various elements of this book and to the many unnamed supporters of this project, I express my deep gratitude and heartfelt thanks.

✢ ✢ ✢

Robert Hillman is a Victorian-based writer whose biographies include *The Rugmaker of Mazar-e-Sharif*, *My Life as a Traitor* (shortlisted for the 2008 Prime Minister's Literary Award), his memoir *The Boy in the Green Suit* (winner of the 2005 Australian National Biography Award); and his novels include *The Deepest Part of the Lake* and *The Hour of Disguise*.

MAP 1 – EUROPE

MAP 2 – THE FORMER YUGOSLAVIA

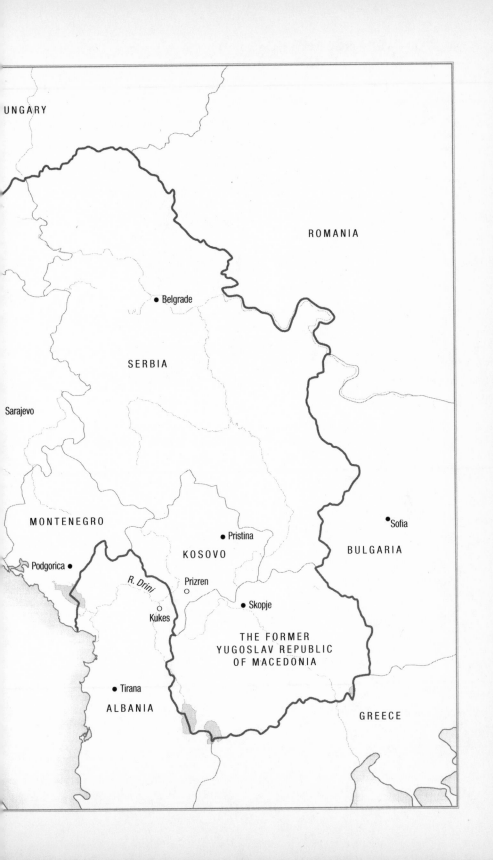

MAP 3 – ALBANIA AND KOSOVO

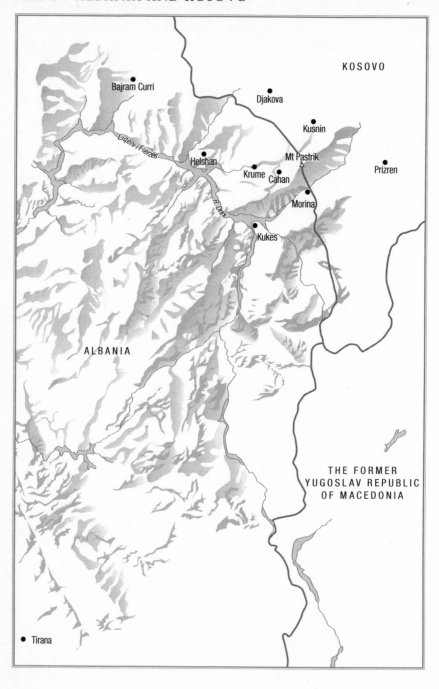

DISCLAIMER

The story told here is factual. Every care has been taken to verify names, dates and details throughout this book, but as much is reliant on memory, some unintentional errors may have occurred. On occasions, real names have been replaced with substitute names to protect people who remain in danger of recrimination. The behaviour and speech of each person in the book is accurate, regardless of any prudent disguise.

The Publishers assume no legal liability or responsibility for inaccuracies; they do, however, welcome any information that will redress them.

With shards from hell, they cry and die,
  young lives now damned and lost.
Their thoughts, their dreams,
  their hopes once bright,
  now lie beneath these rocks.
My angel's love, her thoughts, her
  dreams, stay with me day and night.
This love, the strength I draw upon,
  to help them in their plight.

Craig Jurisevic, 5 June 1999

Written in the cave at the front line,
Mount Pastrik, Kosovo.

Part One
THE JOURNEY

Chapter 1

It's not a well-known part of the world, Kosovo, but in the northern hemisphere autumn of 1998 this mountainous region of the Balkans has become the backdrop to television news bulletins everywhere. Something appalling is happening in Kosovo; something that generates images of the sort that people in the West associate with the unruly republics of the Third World. Columns of refugees, despair etched on their faces, shuffle along roads littered with burning vehicles; broken bodies lie in ditches, corpse stacked on corpse, mouths open in the rictus of the violently slain.

Fifteen thousand kilometres away on the other side of the world, in sleepy Adelaide, Australia, dinner with friends stalls while we wander into the living room to see the latest images from Kosovo on the seven o'clock news. Someone murmurs, 'Is this really happening?' and we shake our heads and experience that mixture of impotence and disgust that news journalism and the telephoto lens have made so familiar to middle-class folk like ourselves ever since the Vietnam war. A fresh hell is being created before our eyes, and it is hardly to be credited that the enlightened nations of Europe are allowing this new hell to grow and grow only sixty minutes by jet from Paris and London.

And it is in Kosovo that the term 'ethnic cleansing' has developed a currency that reminds me and millions like me of the hideous events of the mid-twentieth century, when a newly triumphant European power began the systematic extermination of a race. For the Nazis also spoke of 'cleansing' when they meant mass murder, and it occurs to me as I gaze at my television screen that whenever national leaders start applying metaphors of ablution and disinfection to human beings, you can expect killing on a large scale to follow. The Serbian leaders who are promoting this 'cleansing' of Kosovo are equally attracted to rationalising murder by talking of cancer and infection, of scalpels and surgical intervention.

These metaphors – disinfection, surgical excision – become so compelling to those who employ them that they overwhelm all other considerations. If you talk of people as pollutants, then cleansing means getting rid of the polluting children as well; if you talk about people as a disease, then cutting out the malignancy means the kids have to be cut out too. I have a child of my own, a five-year-old son. While I'm watching the news, he's drifting off to sleep in his bedroom. In another time and another place, he might be thought a pollutant, and so might my wife, so might I. It is in the choice of metaphors we apply to the people who share our planet that we express our humanity, or lack of it.

What I see and hear of the war in Kosovo makes me consider a surgical intervention of my own, but in my case no metaphor is involved. I am a trainee cardiothoracic surgeon at the Royal Adelaide Hospital, but earlier in my medical career I had daily experience of the type of wounds being inflicted in Kosovo; wounds caused by automatic and semi-automatic weapons fire; by the explosion of anti-personnel mines, hand grenades, mortar rounds and artillery shells.

It was in Southern Israel during the first Intifada of 1992 and 1993 that I'd witnessed what bullets and shrapnel could do to the human body, and where I'd learnt how effective modern surgery could sometimes be in restoring the wounded to the world. I was a member of an Israeli MEDEVAC team making runs into Gaza to retrieve injured Israeli soldiers and Palestinian civilians. Most retrievals in such situations are made under fire, and so this experience and training has prepared me for work in a war zone. Based in Ashkelon, near the border with the Gaza strip, I volunteered to help in a MEDEVAC team attached to the hospital in which I was working. The attraction of the battlefield, where rapid surgical intervention is especially crucial – and in many cases life-saving – was too hard for this young surgeon to resist.

Saddened and sickened though I am by the images of war swarming on my television screen, I've no clear path to involvement. I mooch about, discontented, until I hear of calls from United Nations member states for volunteer field medical staff. My visceral response is, 'I'll go to Kosovo'. But in the way we do, I run one of those internal debates in the parliament of my skull and listen to voices arguing that I can't hope to make much difference in Kosovo, that it isn't really my war, that I have a beloved wife and adored child to care for here in Adelaide. Arguing back and forth with myself in this way is really a type of sham; I know exactly what I intend to do; I intend to go to Kosovo. My own Slovenian grandfather on my mother's side survived Dachau and Mauthausen. If I can't feel roused to action by Milosevic's concentration camps, it will be a betrayal of my memories of that gentle and compassionate man.

And then there is a question of skill and training. Not everybody can negotiate the surgical treatment of blast injuries to the chest, abdomen, limbs of a human being, close the wounds and supervise post-operative care. But I can. And I can do so under less than ideal conditions, in the field, in the back of a jeep if I have to. And knowing that I can, makes it seem that I should.

Perhaps this phoney debate I've conducted in silence is really a preparation for the rowdier one that may break out when I tell my wife that I want to go to Kosovo. Donna, however, is surprisingly reasonable in her point of view: she would never obstruct my path to something that is dear to my heart. She knows what drives me. She knows that is who I am. She sees my point of view but she's also standing up for home and hearth. After all, there was nothing in our marriage vows about me running off to a war zone four months into our domestic life. Her concern also lies with the effect this could have on my young son Jackson, who is still adjusting to the demise of my previous marriage. A woman taking on a man who has been married before feels that her husband will try especially hard to get it right this time. Surely I know better these days.

I do know better in certain ways, but in other ways my experience of life since my time in Israel, in Gaza has made it more difficult to say no to Kosovo. This will sound perverse, but it's the very fact that my life has become more satisfyingly settled that has made going to Kosovo so imperative; it's the thrill of watching Jackson growing up; the joy of being loved and understood by Donna; the promise of a rich and rewarding life stretching before us. Each day I awake to security; each month my delight in being alive is enhanced. And my home town is Adelaide, tranquil Adelaide, the most civilised city in Australia.

I am not a person who sees in his mind's eye a beacon on a distant hilltop that signals the ultimate destination of the human race. Every community harbours its complement of thugs, bullies, egomaniacs, sociopaths, just as surely as it includes a great many people of genuine goodwill, people who accept the guidance of their better angels. In some communities – in the Australian community, for example – the worst impulses of people are restrained by tested institutions and by the rule of civilising laws. But I do have a spiritual reverence for justice. I don't want to fight the Serbs, but I do want to take a couple of months out of my life to undo some of their harm.

By the time I'm ready to leave on 27 April 1999, I have Donna's blessing, up to a point. She is, after all, as sickened by what is happening in Kosovo as I am. She says, 'I knew you'd go before you knew yourself. But take care. I want you back in one piece.'

Packing my bags, kissing Donna and Jackson goodbye, I'm not in anything like one piece. Guilt and remorse wrestle with conviction. I say what people heading towards harm always say to those they love: 'I'll be fine, don't worry.' But you can't know that with certainty. Many times in Gaza, I could easily have come to grief. I say it again in the car on the way to the airport, and maybe twice more before I reach the departure lounge. 'I'll be fine, absolutely. Don't worry about a thing.'

Her eyes now brimming with tears, she asks, 'Who are you trying to convince?'

Chapter 2

Arriving at Tirana airport in the Albanian capital, I expect disorder, frenzy, evidence of this former Communist state's endemic poverty, but nothing on the scale that I encounter here. The terminal is a seething mass of refugees, soldiers, media janissaries, mangy dogs, skinny cats and down-at-heel chickens. I stand smiling in the midst of it, fascinated by the motion and mayhem, the shouting and struggling, even the stink. It's late April – spring here in the northern hemisphere – and pretty warm, ripening the reek. A dog that has never seen a minute's affection in its life makes its way to my feet through the mad jumble and sniffs my shoes. I reach down and pat him, murmuring, 'God, you're ugly,' and he gives a yawn and moves on.

Journalists appear to outnumber every other category of visitor to the terminal by a margin of about three to one, and no wonder: this is the world's biggest story, the renewal of fascism in Europe, and news editors everywhere, I imagine, are demanding accounts of atrocities, massacres, rape, torture. Anyone who looks like a refugee or appears to be heading for the front line – mercenaries prepared to fight against the Serbs, for example – is set upon by the journalists, in the manner of Harpies. A German reporter from Deutsche Welle Radio thrusts me against a wall next to the utilitarian toilet block, tells me that I'm a soldier of fortune and invokes the Right of the People to know all about my plans.

'I'm a tourist,' I tell him.

'A tourist?'

'Yes.'

'You're lying!'

'Do you think so?'

He dismisses me with a gesture of disgust and hurries off to accost a refugee.

I'm standing around in this idle way because no one has turned up to meet me. It was agreed that I'd be welcomed by a representative of the IMC (International Medical Corps) under whose auspices I'll be working in Kosovo, but other than the German reporter and an ugly dog, I'm not attracting much interest. I study the famished chickens in a desultory way for a time then give up waiting and wander out to an open area near the main runway. Various non-governmental organisations – the Red Cross and UNHCR (the UN Refugee Agency), amongst others – have set up shop here in shipping containers. It's a curious fact that anywhere in the world where people are busily killing each other you find shipping containers used as improvised offices, prison cells, torture chambers. You could almost index international bloodletting by placing a marker on a map wherever these yellow and orange crates are employed in this vernacular fashion. In the container that houses the UNHCR I pick out the rowdy woman in charge and ask where I'll find the shipping container of the IMC. She introduces herself as Debra Mohl, tells me she's never heard of the IMC and, without breaking stride, offers to put me up in her apartment-cum-office in the city if I want to hang around for a bit. She has that brusquely unsentimental manner of many non-military professionals in war zones; people who've been sickened by the things they've seen; who've lived through years of lies and propaganda and seen so many good intentions wither and die. All that they can do is roll up their sleeves and get on with it, and all they hope for is that they'll come across someone every now and then who says, 'Yes, I can do that,' and who actually does it.

Driving from the airport to Tirana with Debra, I have to shake my head in disbelief at the panorama of poverty.

'Not pretty, is it?' says Debra. 'Gets worse the longer you stay. You notice more.'

I'm thinking, 'Is this really Europe we're in?' Crossing a border or two will take you to Boulevard Saint Germain, the Via Veneto, Regent Street, places where people saunter along magnificent boulevards and shop for designer attire at stratospheric prices. And here? The roads are goat tracks, the people are dressed in clothing one step up from rags and I see the glitter of hunger in every set of eyes that turns towards us as we pass. I've worked in a number of chaotic conflict zones and the thing that pulls at my emotions most is not the battlefield wounds, but the sheer wretchedness of the innocents caught up in the mess – in this case, the Kosovar refugees. If a man with a lower leg dangling by a few strips of skin and tendon is writhing on my operating table, I can do something for him with drugs and surgical instruments, but about the grinding wretchedness of ten thousand people forced onto the road, there's not a damned thing I can do. They want to feed their children, but there's nothing to eat. They want to sleep, and there's nowhere but the mud on the roadside. They want to rest but some sociopath with an automatic rifle is threatening to put a bullet in them if they stop even for a minute. All they have to live for is the prospect that sometime, somewhere, a house like the one they used to live in will miraculously be found for them and that it will be safe, secure from a repeat of the horrors already visited upon them. The epitaph for nearly all the refugees you see in places like this is going to read, 'Died waiting'. Still, I'm not here to find a solution to this crisis, this ethnic cleansing. It's not my role, it's not my place. I can, however, do something that will ease the suffering of at least a few. That's what I'm trained to do and that's what my years of experience will enable me to do.

A weird feature of the Albanian landscape we're speeding through is the dome-shaped bunkers set a little back from the roadside, a great many of them. Some stand alone in the midst of the debris-strewn fields; others are shoved up against ramshackle houses.

'Why are there so many bunkers around the place?' I ask Debra, and she refers me to our driver, Fadil, a sardonic little fellow with a three-day growth of stubble and a Camel hanging from his lips.

'Fadil, tell Craig about the bunkers.'

'The bunkers?' says Fadil, without removing his cigarette. 'The bunkers are very interesting. They are a gift. A gift from Enver Hoxha.'

'Your ex-leader?' I say. I know a bit about Albania's Marxist dictator, who ruled until his death in 1985.

'He was the boss for forty years. This is what he left us. Concrete bunkers.'

Fadil goes on to explain that Hoxha had around seven hundred and fifty thousand of these concrete bunkers built up and down Albania, in every village, almost every field, all over the major cities and towns. He says that Hoxha held onto power by making Albanians believe that their country was forever on the brink of being invaded either by Western European powers, urged on by America, or by Yugoslavia, with the encouragement of Moscow. His Propaganda Bureau painted lurid word pictures of what the average Albanian could expect when the invasion started (bombing, strafing, shelling) then made people believe that their salvation depended on these dome-shaped bunkers he was building. Meanwhile, Hoxha stuffed his personal bank accounts with every penny he could squeeze out of the populace, and out of his patrons – the Russians at one time, then the Chinese. Same old same old, I think as Fadil tells his story. Would anyone be surprised to learn that Hoxha ran a vicious state security bureau, known as the Sigurimi? That all dissent was forbidden? That by the end of his forty-year rule, Albania was an economically crippled and psychologically traumatised basket case? This is Fadil's take on Hoxha's rule, but I know that the full story is more complex; Hoxha's regime did in fact provide some material and social advances for Albanians. But at what cost? Does anyone anywhere need more evidence from the twentieth century's catalogue of political disasters before conceding that rigid ideology makes for disastrous government?

When you fly off to some God-forsaken disaster zone hoping to do some good, you've put your head in a peculiar place. If I were coming here as a tourist, I'd be thinking right now, 'What on earth have I done?' because it's awful, Tirana; it's everything you want to avoid in a travel destination; depressing architecture, littered streets, the people on the pavements unsmiling and suspicious. But I can't let what I'm looking at register in the normal way; I can't think, 'What a dump!' and shake my head in disgust and disappointment. All I can think is, 'This is where the people who are getting shot to bits live, or nearby at least; the aesthetics of the place are irrelevant.' And that's true, but from the very start of this mercy dash, I'm getting rid of impressions and censoring observations that don't help me, that don't feed into the mission. Otherwise I'd be saying to the driver, to Debra, 'Okay, let's say the Albanians and the Kosovars get their way and boot the Serbs out – the place is still going to be a dump, they're not fighting for Venice or Portofino, are they?' But that's the thing, isn't it? If you're fighting injustice for the right to live by your own rules in the worst suburb of the poorest country on earth, you're still going to fight.

We weave through the darkening streets, dodging beaten-up cars and motorcycles, and pull up at a dowdy apartment block. Debra, the driver and I head down a dank alley to the front entrance. I'm thinking of Donna and talking to her silently, affectionately, maybe also a little apologetically, 'It isn't exactly the quest for glory you were imagining, it really isn't …' The conversation is terminated abruptly when a battered Volkswagen Golf roars out of the gloom of the alley, the rear passenger firing a pistol at us from no more than three metres away. I've flattened myself against the wall and can't say just this moment whether I'm dead but still standing, or not dead and still standing, or still standing but about to drop dead. Fadil, exuding cool, shrugs and makes a gesture of dismissal.

'Happens all the time,' he says. 'Gangs. After dark, it gets dangerous.'

'Yes, but why were they shooting at us?' I ask, which seems to me the overwhelmingly pertinent point.

'Who knows? Nothing personal. Big city, bad things happen.'

Debra also seems unexercised, so I pick up my bag and return to my heart-to-heart with Donna. 'Sorry about the interruption my darling – just life in the big city. Wasn't as spooky as it looked. Love you.'

A fitful night's sleep on an aged three-seater vinyl sofa in Debra's apartment. A fluoro tube overhead flickers constantly. The cabbagy stink of food prepared in an unventilated kitchen hangs in the air. In the light of early morning, I go to the window and gaze out at Tirana floating in soot and smog. I know how I got here, I know why I came, I've seen sights more lowering to the spirits than Tirana in the grainy light of early morning, but the question that keeps repeating itself in my head is, 'What the hell have I done?' At the same time, I'm sort of amused. What did I expect? Emporiums, glittering towers of glass and steel? At this moment I find myself subconsciously pressing the reset button, switching to conflict zone mode, putting emotions and preconceptions on hold. I'm ready.

The IMC people have turned up this morning to take me to a security briefing at the airfield. Later, a UNHCR helicopter will fly the small group of recently arrived medical volunteers (including me) to the town of Kukes, a couple of hundred kilometres northeast of Tirana, closer to the front line of the Serbian advance. The security briefing is handled by people from both IMC and UNHCR and the tone of what's being said is intended to strike a balance between frightening truth and mild reassurance. People don't travel by road in the rural areas of Albania, we're told. Bandits own the countryside and, so far as the bandits are concerned, the people who've come to Albania to help out – doctors, aid workers, drivers, administrative staff – are a valuable resource, capable of being kidnapped and sold back. Or murdered, if things don't work out. But not to worry; Albanian police units now escort most supply convoys. Organised crime is Albania's only growth industry, the IMC official tells us; the government is hopeless, basic infrastructure barely exists, most local and regional government posts are the sovereign property of well-connected thugs. The soothing words, 'Don't worry, we'll cope,' return like a chorus whenever the bleak facts threaten to overwhelm us.

Five of us climb aboard the chopper that will fly us to Kukes – three UNHCR officials and a couple of Albanians involved in refugee affairs in some way I don't quite understand. We all shake hands and smile, but it's the pilot and co-pilot I'm paying most attention to. I like to see a little evidence of competency in any pilot of a small aircraft becoming airborne, and I'm relieved to see them run through standard safety checks. It would be humiliating to be killed in a crash before I've even stepped into a surgical gown.

The flight takes us over a landscape that may have looked much as it does now a thousand years ago: patchwork fields, shining rivers, towering mountains. No sites of industry, nothing approaching a developed road network. From above, God's view of the earth, it all looks placid, but that of course is the great shortcoming of God's view of the earth; the truth about our planet is only revealed when you're close enough to see faces and the joy or despair in people's eyes. Confirming this, the scale of the disaster into which I'm descending becomes evident an hour later when the chopper dips and turns towards Kukes and the refugee camps on the outskirts of the town. Above the throb of the chopper's rotor, one of the UNHCR officials tells me that the camps house a community much larger than the town's.

'A hundred thousand! More stream in each day.'

'From Kosovo?' I ask.

'Sure, from Kosovo. They either make it to the border or die on the way. Very bad news, Kosovo!'

We land in an arid field on the edge of Camp Italia, run by the Italian Red Cross, home to forty thousand Kosovars. The border lies only ten kilometres to the east, placing it in easy range of Serbian missiles and heavy artillery. Even though we are still in Albania, nobody I speak to doubts that the Serbs would bombard the camps if it were strategically worth their while to do so; if they wanted to push the camps further away from the border, for example. For the time being, it suits the Serbs to simply get the Muslim population (and Kosovo is overwhelmingly Muslim, the legacy of the Ottoman Turk occupation of centuries past) out of Kosovo so that the whole region can be included in the Greater Serbia of Milosevic's Slavophile dreams.

We're driven through Camp Italia on our way to the provincial city of Kukes, which will be my base for the whole of the time I'm in Albania. Roads, tracks, boulevards of khaki tents draped with washing, a few toys scattered about at the entrances, the kids themselves playing and gambolling in the manner of children everywhere, clusters of mothers trading news and gossip, men with guarded expressions sharing a quiet smoke, vehicles on missions of one sort and another raising clouds of dust; the smell of disinfectant from makeshift toilets, of diesel from the exhausts of trucks, of a thousand meals being prepared. Not much immediate evidence of despair and psychological trauma, but it'll be there, I'm sure of that.

I can easily imagine the range of responses amongst these thousands, thrown out of their homeland; I've been amongst people who've endured a blitzkrieg of injustice such as the one that descended on these Kosovars. Many will be hoping and praying that NATO will fix everything; others will be nursing heartache, recalling ten times an hour the homes they've fled, the family members they've seen killed, yearning for what they used to think of as a normal day, and some, mostly men, will be bitterly formulating strategies of revenge on the Serbs, itching for the day when it will be their boots on the necks of their enemies.

And what about my response? The sight before me fills me with horror. I am appalled by the grotesque nationalist fantasies that lead to the creation of these cities of the homeless and those toxic grievances that can never be assuaged by anything but a burst from a Kalashnikov at close range. I hate knowing that some of the young men in this camp will live and breathe vengeance for the rest of their lives, and that the Serbs ten kilometres away will train their artillery on these desperate people in seconds, if ordered to do so. But I want to get to work. I've come with years of training and field experience behind me, and I want to use it. Just thinking of getting down to work restores my spirits.

The refugees glance at us in our 4-wheel drive as we make our slow way to Kukes, the children sometimes smiling, sometimes waving, but the older people betraying little. We stop briefly to let pedestrians pass and I'm arrested by the steady gaze of one old woman who seems to be studying my face in a way that makes me feel nakedly exposed. She must be asking herself what this fair-haired boy expects to achieve here with his big smile. I can almost read her thoughts in her dark gaze: Is he going to save us from the Serbs, is that what he thinks? Well, best of luck to him, whatever he is here for. Best of luck when he sees the things that I have seen.

Chapter 3

Kukes is awful; loveless and unloved, as bleak as a broken heart. The architecture expresses the bare essentials of function, and everything that a city government would normally spend money on doesn't get spent here. Footpaths, lighting, parks, roads – all crumbling or broken or hopelessly neglected. Cows, goats and sheep are herded along the pavements, mingling with refugees, beggars. Milaim, an IMC translator driving with us into town, explains to me as we negotiate the rowdy traffic that local criminals own the town and that nothing gets done unless money is paid. I ask him about the traffic; the clutter on the roads seems too much for a backwater like Kukes.

'The press!' he shouts, raising his voice above the din like the guy in the chopper. 'Everybody's here: BBC, ABC, CNN, all the big newspapers. They want the story!'

'And what is the story?'

'How many dead!'

I think of the German reporter at the airport, of how avid he was for a scoop. A war like this is a catastrophe for the

Kosovars but a godsend to news editors. Milosevic's ethnic cleansing has tapped into the public's appetite for horror stories, for moral outrage.

'The town doesn't look as if it can support all these news people!' I call to Milaim. 'Where do they stay? What do they eat?'

'You know something? In Kukes, you can hardly find any food, but if you want a Kalashnikov, if you want ten grams of coke, no problem!'

Our accommodation is one star at most, just an apartment in a dilapidated block that five of us are supposed to share, but I wasn't expecting anything flash. My immediate task is to inspect the local hospital, assess its surgical capability and get down to work. My eyes and ears are taking in so much that's demoralising that once again, I yearn to be in a situation that I can control. I'm a good surgeon, an adaptable surgeon. I can provide a few successes in this environment of failure once I find my bearings, learn the lie of the land and start using my tools of trade.

But the hospital – it's a nightmare. The building itself is a decaying ruin, windows smashed, gates hanging from broken hinges, medical and general refuse scattered around the grounds. From well before I enter the front door with Milaim the stench of gangrenous wounds, of suppuration left untreated, acts on my gorge like a plateful of putrefying meat. A number of small barricades lie between the gate and the main entrance; what their function is I don't know, unless it's to prevent a car full of explosives from driving into the lobby. About thirty refugees are waiting outside the Emergency Room, in the baking sun, none of them looking in the least bit hopeful. A few metres from this group the rotting corpse of a cow with its limbs hacked off is stretched out on the ground. Flies and ants swarm around the animal's drying flesh to complete this picture of fetid decay. Milaim says that a couple of days ago a group of refugees searching for food and medical attention found a way into the hospital grounds. They were refused treatment, refused food. They fell on the cow and chopped off its legs for sustenance. I can't be sure from this description that the cow was dead before it parted with its legs. I ask Milaim what on earth the cow was doing here to start with.

'Maybe looking for food, same as the refugees.'

'Looking for food?'

Milaim shrugs and smiles. 'The cow didn't know it was a hospital. You will have to forgive the poor beast.'

At the invitation of the hospital director, Dr Cena, I wander over to get a close look at the Emergency Room, passing today's group of sorrowing refugees on the way. I take a glance through the doors then make my way in and sit in a corner with Milaim to observe the proceedings. Ten or more badly injured refugees lie on the bare floor, some semiconscious, one possibly dead. I've had enough experience with combat casualties to identify the wounds as grenade and landmine injuries and old, poorly treated gunshot wounds. Some of the wounded are whimpering; others have that glazed expression you see on the faces of people in pain who have lost their will to groan or who no longer have the strength for it. Two orderlies in filthy white coats move amongst the wounded. They ignore the injuries, intent instead on picking through the scant belongings of these suffering people, hissing in disdain when they find nothing of value. Cena steps between us and the wounded and gestures for Milaim and me to follow him.

'It's not what you are used to in your country, Dr Jurisevic. But we are "snowed under" – is that what you say, "snowed under"? Like an avalanche?'

'Yes, that's what we say.'

'We do our best.'

'I'm sure you do.'

'You look shocked.'

'Do I? No, I'm not shocked. Just taking it all in.'

And in fact that's perfectly true; I'm not shocked by the injuries I'm seeing but I am appalled by the obvious abuse and neglect of defenceless, highly traumatised patients.

I want to say, 'Why is no one attending these patients? What the hell are those orderlies doing?' but I hold my tongue. I've just arrived, I'm just observing, gauging the lie of the land. I don't know enough yet and don't want to be the arrogant, know-all newcomer alienating everyone in my path. At least, not quite yet.

Cena has his own armed bodyguard, a vile-looking thug with an eye patch, an ill-fitting tan leather jacket, dress pants and snakeskin boots. Armed with an AK-47 he'd be perfect as a henchman in an old James Bond film.

Why the hospital director needs an armed guard is a mystery to me; maybe this will become clearer in due course.

I'm led into a cubicle off to one side of the ER where a doctor and a nurse are treating a boy, six or seven years old, with a mangled hand. Cena must be trying to demonstrate to me that surgery does actually occur in his hospital, the negligence back in the Emergency Room notwithstanding.

Observing the doctor at work I see that surgery *is* occurring, but it is surgery the likes of which I've never witnessed before. The doctor is hacking away at the exposed muscle and tendons of the blast-injured hand with a pair of blunt scissors as the nurse holds the boy down, slapping his face whenever the pain causes him to scream and writhe.

'Serbs,' Cena murmurs in my ear. 'They remove the detonators from grenades and paint them in bright colours, scatter them around villages. The kids pick them up and play with them. This is what happens.'

I nod in understanding, but this is not what I'm focused on. The child's agonised screams tear at my heart, and I use all my reserves of self-control to stop myself from ripping the scissors from the doctor's hands. If he were deliberately torturing the boy he couldn't possibly produce a more violent display. I can't watch any longer and raise my voice to ask the doctor exactly what he's trying to achieve

'What's it look like?' he replies sarcastically.

'Are you using any anaesthetic? This child's in pain.'

'We only use anaesthetic for big operations.'

'Do you mind if I help?'

'Please yourself.'

Not particularly bothered by my thinly disguised criticism of his surgical ability, he hands me the scissors and stands back.

I can see unopened boxes of the local anaesthetic Marcaine in the supply cupboard on the wall, each box stamped with the Red Cross emblem. I reassure the boy as best I can and grab a few ampoules of anaesthetic. I inject the boy's hand with enough Marcaine to relieve the pain quickly, while the doctor looks on glowering.

'What's the point of this?' he wants to know. 'A couple of fingers! It's nothing!'

'Yes, I know, but all the same ...'

Cena and his bodyguard are sitting in the corner, both of them chuckling softly, amused by the surgeon who wears his heart on his sleeve. They're thinking I'm the delicate surgeon from some comfortable haven overseas, shocked at their rough and ready medical procedures. If that's what amuses them, they've got it wrong. I'm not easily shocked, but I'm easily disgusted by a complete disregard for the suffering of a child. I've witnessed hellish scenes in my time, and I've been in surgical teams dealing with one medical basket case after another, never betraying emotions by so much as a tremor in our voices. To the uninitiated, we could have looked coldly detached, maybe harsh, and we weren't above joking to relieve the tension. But we never lost the natural human empathy for a patient in pain, never saw the slightest hilarity in hacking a kid's hand up with blunt scissors.

All the same, I ought to step back a bit. When I become self-righteous, I don't like myself. Now that the child's hand is anaesthetised and pain-free, I glance at Cena and the surgeon, smile, and step away. I hate myself for doing it but in the long run I'll achieve more by hanging loose than by looking down my nose at these people.

I have to break off my hospital tour to meet with IMC and UNHCR officials in Kukes. I'm still hoping that what I've seen so far has nothing to do with the way the hospital is run generally, just an aberration. Maybe the callous surgeon with the blunt scissors is an exception but it's difficult to make myself believe this when the hospital director himself unashamedly appeared to take such pleasure in another's suffering.

The meeting with the IMC and UNHCR people is brief and to the point. It's recommended that, as I am independent of the various surgical units, I should be offered the post of surgical co-ordinator for the refugee camps. If this comes about, I'll have responsibility for co-ordinating medical staff and logistics needed to cater for over a hundred thousand refugees. Considering the condition of the refugees, that's like being put in charge of all the surgical arrangements for a sizable city.

It's a rowdy, bustling sort of place, the IMC apartment, like a dormitory in a backpackers' hostel. If you get a chance to eat, take it, and if the racket of people passing through eases off for a period, grab that time to sleep.

I don't know anyone here. I get introduced in a blur to someone called Bob, and the next time I see him I have no idea who he is. Men and women appear for five minutes then disappear into their sleeping bags. Someone calls out, 'Hi, chief!' and before I can answer another fellow heading the opposite way says, 'Gotta go, great to meet you!'

Most of those living here are IMC doctors but during the afternoon and evening translators and drivers and refugees looking for work and money drift in and out.

'Excuse me sir, you need a driver? Best driver, very cheap!'

'No, I have a driver, but thanks for ...'

'You need a Walkman?'

'No, I'm pretty much set for everything.'

'Rolex?'

'No.'

'Special Colombian sugar, you want some? You need hashish? Moroccan Gold?'

'No. Nothing.'

I wolf down cheese and bread, pour my third cup of coffee, await my turn on the satellite telephone for a call to Donna. At this time of the year back in Adelaide – it's now 29 April – it's still warm enough for a walk along Brighton beach in the evening. Donna is herself a doctor, and when our rosters align that's the very sort of thing we do – walk through the froth of the receding waves at sunset like one of those improbable couples in a Club Med advertisement. One of the things I'm missing so much now is the sharing of experiences that is such a feature of my life with Donna. Not that being here is such a rich and rewarding thing (at least, not visually) that I long to share it with her, but I value the way in which we have created that crucial flow between us of things seen, things recalled, things that act on your heart. As I think this, reality hits, and I'm relieved that she's not here to witness the distressing events just passed. Brighton beach at sunset will do. I'll hold that thought.

Not everyone is capable of being woken from a deep sleep by the muffled sound of distant gunfire, but I am. It's not the decibel level of gunfire reports that wake you – rifle and small-arms fire at a distance are rarely as ear-splitting as in the movies – but more the quality of the sound and the intervals between shots; you know it's gunfire. And that's the sound that wakes me in the early hours of this first morning in Kukes. I run down the stairs and at the bottom find a boy of about ten writhing in a pool of blood and screaming for his mother. He's been shot in the lower abdomen. Our translator, Milaim, and some of the other doctors in the apartment have been roused by the gunshots too, and it's Milaim who helps me carry the boy across the road to the hospital and straight to the operating suite. While we're waiting for assistance, Milaim tells me that he heard raised voices just before the boy was shot.

'Gang people,' he says. 'They wanted money from him. He's ten. How much money do they think he would have? He had none, so they shot him.'

Milaim says the boy is an orphan from Kosovo, living with a host family in the same apartment block as us. He says there's very little sympathy amongst most Albanians for Kosovars. Same people ethnically, speak the same language, very similar heritage but the Albanians have a seething resentment of the Kosovars going back to the days before Yugoslavia fractured.

'Albanians think the Kosovars had it easy under Tito,' Milaim tells me. 'Easy compared to what Albania endured under Hoxha. They resent the Kosovars. The Kosovars had more money, a little more liberty. Albanians, many of them, think the Kosovars are getting what they deserve. It's insane, but that's the way it is. The refugees who come here are treated like dogs.'

A doctor arrives, Ylber Vata, the hospital's general surgeon: tall, big frame, well into his forties. After my experience with Cena, I'm concerned that this boy is going to be subjected to the same barbaric treatment as the boy with the mangled hand, but Vata seems different. He's sympathetic, at least. He strokes the boy's head and speaks to him in a gentle, crooning manner. 'He's telling him that he'll make him better and return him to his mother,' Milaim whispers. Then he translates the boy's response: 'He's saying that his mother, father and brothers are all dead.'

We move the boy carefully onto the operating table, anaesthetise him, and hastily open his abdomen. The bullets, fired at point-blank range, have shattered his liver. Vata and I try everything to stem the torrential haemorrhage, but he dies on the operating table. Vata makes a gesture of what seems to be frustration or even despair, murmurs something rapidly, a prayer perhaps, and on the verge of tears, hurries from the theatre. The nurse assisting us shrouds the dead boy's face with the blood-soaked drape that had been covering his legs. She whispers something to Milaim before she, too, hurries off.

'She said that Dr Vata has lost a large number of children lately. She asks you to understand how upset he is.'

Understanding such distress is easy. Trying to understand Cena and that butcher at work on the other boy yesterday – no, I won't be putting any effort at all into that.

I'm left at a loose end, wishing with all my heart to get back to work but not knowing how to go about it. I stand around in my surgical gown reading what appears to be a list of names written in chalk on an old blackboard above the anaesthetic machine. I can't work out what the names represent until Vata returns. Dry-eyed now, he shakes my hand and asks me to forgive his emotional display at the death of the boy.

He points at the blackboard.

'These names, Dr Jurisevic, they are the Kosovars who were admitted last night and early this morning. Refugees. Twenty-four hours ago, they were all in Kosovo. You see beside each name I've written the age and also the type of operation I propose. Most of them have penetrating gunshot wounds or shrapnel wounds. So what can be done? Do you have the time to help me with these people? Please say no if you are too tired.'

Vata is speaking in a way intended to show me that he's a solid surgeon, not normally inclined to lose control. Surgeons don't usually cry. That's the rule, not an illogical one; we see so much that could make us wail – and not only in combat zones – that a culture of detachment has evolved. But I would rather be working with a surgeon who can throw this rule overboard on occasions than with one who has taken the culture of cool so completely to heart that he or she can't shed a tear when kids die in such a futile way as this. And it is futile, this child's death. Ten years old – what did they expect to thieve from him? A yoyo?

We operate for sixteen hours straight. The first patient is a girl of eleven, torn apart by a Serb rocket. She's still bleeding from a jagged wound behind one knee and has lost skin, sections of her popliteal artery, fat, hamstring, tendons. Four of the fingers of her right hand are gone, also the muscle and nerves of her upper right arm. Her left breast is mutilated and her right eye ruptured. This is what shrapnel fragments moving at high velocity do to the human body. Refinements are being developed in weapons' laboratories all the time. Some shells and rockets are designed to inflict wrenching injury more than death, the idea being that the wounded tie up more medical and military personnel than a corpse. We're an inventive species.

I amputate the girl's right leg above the knee and her right arm above the elbow. I have to enucleate her ruptured eye, remove it; it can't be saved. What sort of life she'll lead after all this I can't dwell on; I simply want this poor girl to live, and I think she will. Her wounds are less horrendous than those of some of the other patients Vata and I attend, more horrendous than others.

We're working at such speed that I miss the entry wound of a small shrapnel fragment in a man whose lower leg I amputated earlier and have to hasten to the ward to open his abdomen. His liver is haemorrhaging. While I'm attending to him I'm also struggling to fashion a schedule for the remaining patients. I'll have to let the unsalvageable die, but painlessly and in whatever comfort this hospital can provide. I hate doing this, but if we devote time to the doomed, those we can save will expire before we reach them. This is the brutality of triage in a war zone.

I wanted to get down to work, and I have. Think hard about what you wish for, because you'll get it in time, as the saying goes. Vata and I are surviving on adrenaline and coffee, a fabulous cocktail, certain to keep you alert unless it kills you. I'm full of admiration for Vata. He's candid about his limitations, confessing that his skills are being stretched, but he works with the will of a zealot and without a hint of complaint. I've come from the comfort of an affluent country, a world away from the oppressive stress of labouring under a corrupt hospital administration and living cheek-by-jowl with thugs and crooks and drug hounds. For Vata, whenever he raises his gaze from the operating table, he sees Kukes; that's all there is: Kukes in all its squalor. He must have his private sources of delight, even in this town, but God knows what they are.

We operate on nine patients over the sixteen hours. Eight survive. Eight is good. Eight pulses. A number of limbs have been lost, but if I can get a patient off the operating table with a healthy pulse, I'm pleased.

At two in the morning, I check on the last of today's patients in the recovery wards then leave the hospital and stroll under the stars to the apartment block. I'm completely spent, but I have that contented buzz of feeling that I am finally doing the work I came here to do. I'm not even thinking of the war and its hideousness just for the moment. I'm thinking of the eight pulses, wishing it had been nine and a clean sweep.

I pause under the stars, enjoying the stillness, the quiet. A picture of my wife surfaces in my mind. I know exactly where this image comes from. I was meeting Donna outside a restaurant in Adelaide, a year ago it would have been. She'd arrived before me and when I first glimpsed her she was standing on the footpath seeking me in the passing parade on Rundle Street. She wasn't looking in the direction from which I was approaching, so I stood still in the balmy air of the spring evening, just as I am now, and gazed at her with a type of awe and reverence and a deep gratitude that this wonderful woman was waiting for me, searching for my face out of all the faces in my city. I remember the richness of that feeling, the gladness that filled my heart. If this season of surgery in Albania ends badly for me – stray rocket, madman with a handgun, whatever – I'll awake in the hereafter crazed with disappointment. You only get so many chances in life to relish the conviction of being with the right person, travelling the right path.

I walk the last thirty metres to the apartment block fashioning phrases of a promise to myself, but settle for three simple words: Don't die, idiot.

Wonderful sleep, what there was of it, but a monster of a headache on waking, thanks to all the coffee. And what's the cure for a caffeine headache? More caffeine, and a kilogram of Paracetamol, down the hatch.

I want to get back to the hospital, want to visit yesterday's patients and take a more detailed look at equipment and facilities. Within half an hour of waking I'm standing in the operating theatre murmuring, 'Bloody hell!' like a profane mantra to ward off despair. I hadn't paid much attention while Vata and I were cutting and sawing and clamping, but the theatre is feculent. I let my gaze take it all in. A greenish-grey mould has colonised the whole place and one wall is daubed in dried blood, from the floor up to the height of a metre, as if the theatre were the site of a massacre. And the operating table itself is wooden, rickety and incapable of being properly disinfected. The instruments – the tools of trade that gave me satisfaction yesterday – are pitted with rust; I was working so rapidly that I'd simply employed what was slapped into my hand. Here in the sterilisation room, used gauze swabs and wound packs that should have been thrown out have been washed and hung up to dry for re-use.

The two nurses rostered for duty in the operating theatre this morning saunter in. They barely register my presence. Both of them complement perfectly the dismaying condition of the theatre. One is obviously drunk, the other can't keep her eyes open, her arms patterned with syringe tracks.

At this stage of the Kosovo crisis, after so much publicity, there must be a mountain of donated surgical supplies somewhere. I search through cupboards, open doors, pry into sealed cartons. And in a way that feverish searches of this sort are hardly ever rewarded, I actually do find sparkling new and up-to-date surgical equipment: forceps, retractors, amputation saws. Everything is still packed in the styrofoam moulds in which they were transported. So why were we using those rusty old farm tools yesterday? Is it that Vata and his fellow surgeons are simply more comfortable with the old, well-worn tools – shying away from the modern? It's exasperating, but even more exasperating is the fact that I'm ferreting around the hospital in this way. I came here to perform surgery, not to go snooping about in cupboards and cartons. And those nurses – don't they care about what their patients are enduring? And what hope is there for a country in which people are treated in this callous, uncaring way?

The tolerably happy surgeon is now the thoroughly irritated surgeon.

I take myself off to the wards to follow up on our patients of yesterday and last night, hoping that they haven't been thrown into a rubbish skip and carted away. From what I've seen, it's not out of the question. But before I enter the wards I have to administer some advice to myself. I didn't come to Kukes to study World's Best Practice medical care. I didn't come here to swan about the corridors of this place issuing congratulatory smiles and offering little bursts of applause for jobs well done. It's Albania! People here have been swimming against a tide of ordure for decades at least, and maybe centuries. They're traumatised, some are brutalised, but they didn't choose this life for themselves, did they? If those two nurses need alcohol and drugs to get by, then they do.

The wards are an abyss of suffering and stench. Frightened faces turn to me as I pick my way along the narrow aisles. Has everyone in Kosovo decamped to here? It's like Dante's Inferno, except that these people are not being punished for their sins but merely for being in a certain place at a time when an artillery shell or a rocket landed nearby, or when a Serb cadre cheerfully let loose with a burst from a

Kalashnikov. Bed after bed of festering wounds; bed after bed of pain and despair. The wards are almost gloomy and airless. Oh, this is a version of hell, all right. This is about as bad as it gets.

I'm now standing by a bed in which a boy of about four is staring back at me, his left leg amputated below the knee and his right arm amputated below the shoulder. Beneath the bed, a woman I take to be his mother is cradling the dead body of a child younger still than the boy above her, perhaps a year and a half old. Must have died in the night. Maybe she doesn't even know her child's dead. Or perhaps she knows but has lost the ability to react. And what of my own ability to react? I came here as a surgeon, but I can't limit my response to what I do in the operating theatre. I'm gazing at the most elemental of human tragedies, a mother clutching the body of her dead child, and my response is one of pity, mere pity. It feels inadequate. I feel inadequate.

I'm able to find all but four of my patients. The mother of a boy who'd undergone a lower-leg amputation tells me that he is 'shumë mirë', (very good). He's asleep at the moment, which is what I would wish for him. Other patients are sleeping or resting. I'm amazed at the tolerance of pain that these people display. They've had one, sometimes two doses of morphine in the previous twelve hours. A single dose can keep a patient relatively content for maybe two hours. At a maximum these people have had four hours of relief in the past twelve. Six hours of almost insupportable pain would be considered barbaric in Adelaide. In Kukes, expectations of solace are low. Expectations of anything at all are low, I'd imagine; of sympathy, of mercy, of deliverance. These people simply endure, for as long as they can.

But where are my missing four patients? I collar a nurse, one of the very few about. She appears to be only in her twenties yet her hair is thin and already greying. Politely but with obvious concern in my voice, I ask her what has become of the four. The poor woman doesn't know what to tell me.

At last she says, 'They have gone.'

Gone? That can't possibly be true. Three of the four had undergone amputations and, for each, major chest or abdominal surgery compounded their conditions.

'Are you sure?' I ask her.

'Yes. Gone.'

'But that's . . . that's completely irresponsible. These people need days on end of close medical attention.'

'Gone.'

She's distressed; I shouldn't press her. Out on the street ten hours after major surgery? This is grotesque.

I ask her their condition when they left, a ludicrous question since I know that their condition would have been bloody awful.

'One is dead,' she answers uncomfortably.

'Which one?'

She can't give me a name, but from the description she provides I realise that it is the young girl, the double amputee. Four hours Vata and I worked on her. I want to protest to someone, demand that my patients be returned to the ward. And to whom should I protest? Cena, the hospital director? A man who is entertained by the screams of an unanaesthetised child undergoing surgery? Maybe I'd been overly optimistic about that girl's chances of survival, but with half-decent post-operative care she would have survived. As I scan the wards searching for Vata, hoping he's now turned up, I have to concede that it would have been a torment for the girl had she survived. An arm, a leg and an eye gone forever – imagine the wretchedness of the life she would have led.

Surgery is what might be called wet mechanics; the human body approximates a machine in so many respects that it can seem as if the patient is on a hoist in a motor workshop having various malfunctioning parts repaired, replaced, reconditioned. Clamps, retractors, power saws, electric drills, angle-grinders – versions of the tools of a surgeon's trade can be located in any mechanic's workshop. And when I'm at work in the operating theatre, the patient immobile, anaesthetised, is not a creature that has issued from the imagination of God on High, but an extraordinarily clever machine that, for one reason or another, requires maintenance. I don't find myself studying the patient's eyes, wondering what sort of personality animates them each day; or what dreams and delights and acts of love and generosity or villainy the patient is known for. I am completely focused on maintenance, on getting the extraordinarily clever machine back into the traffic of life.

And yet, and yet … Well, the mechanical metaphor is useful, without being sufficient. A human being, or almost any living creature, is always more than the sum of its mechanical parts. When a patient of mine dies, I don't think of a mechanism that has expired, incapable of any further self-driven motion, but of the extinction of a speck of some mysterious and maybe even divine agent of life.

Milaim appears ahead of me as I continue searching for Vata in this vast dormitory of the doomed and suffering. While I've been looking for Vata, Milaim has been searching for me. The look on his face is a question to which he already knows the answer: 'Seen enough?' I tell him I want to go back to the apartment. I need to get away from all this despair and horror for a short time. I need coffee and food. As we pass through the last ward on our way to the exit we hear a shriek louder than the background groaning and weeping. I stop and look around. On the far side of the ward a boy with a wounded leg is being slapped about by a nurse. The nurse is really laying into the child; she intends to inflict pain. I glance at Milaim and he's dead white. Whatever barbarity is being enacted here, it's not something that makes him think of intervention.

'We must leave now,' he whispers. 'We have to go.' I don't know what the hell to do. I look at Milaim again and make a gesture of frustration, raising my hands, asking him to let me step in and sort this vile nurse out. He says again, 'We must leave, Craig. We must go now.' The mother of the boy – I take her to be his mother – has been imploring the nurse to stop but now takes the law into her own hands and leaps onto the nurse's back. An armed security guard enters the ward, takes one look at what's happening, runs full tilt to the scene of the struggle and manhandles the boy's mother to the floor. He raises his rifle and sinks the butt into her back. I must have let out an involuntary yell because the guard turns quickly toward us, lifts his rifle to his shoulder and takes aim. I'm not conscious of any distinct reaction; but I'm standing perfectly still though resisting Milaim's restraining tug at my sleeve. The security guard moves the barrel of the rifle toward the exit sign above the door to the ward and shouts something in Albanian.

'What'd he say?' I ask Milaim as he silently bustles me out of the ward.

'He said, "Fuck off!"'

'What's the story with the boy?'

'I do not know. We have to get out of here.'

'Does this go on all the time? Doctors and nurses abusing patients? Does it?'

'Maybe. I don't know.'

'But it does go on all the time, doesn't it?'

'I don't know.'

Milaim doesn't seem the sort of man who spooks easily. He must have believed that the security guard was capable of shooting us. He still has that haunted look when we cross the open stretch between the hospital and the apartment block. I doubt I look as pale as Milaim. I'm too enraged and annoyed for that. In my eternal optimism I put this event and its characters down to an obstacle. An obstacle to delivering the care that these refugees need. Some obstacles are surmountable; some best avoided, another path taken. I still believe that a hospital is a sanctuary. People inside do the best with what they've got. But if I have to work in a place where injured kids have the daylights belted out of them, I don't know how I'm supposed to keep my cool. I'm sure there's a way, but just at the moment I'm too sick at heart to imagine what it might be.

Chapter 4

On this third day in Kukes, 30 April, the moral geography of the catastrophe I've flown into is taking shape in my mind. In every direction: corruption, brutality, homicide, insatiable appetites for revenge, international conventions for the conduct of war and the treatment of refugees dismissed with scorn. But I have to concede that I've fashioned this map with a broad brush. I've relied on impressions. I simply don't have the time to sit down and study the conflict in any dispassionate way. And I don't know that I want to.

Word comes through that the Serb forces have completed 'cleansing' (there's that euphemism again) the city of Prizren in Kosovo, twenty-five kilometres northeast of Kukes. Thousands of refugees are pouring along every track and road towards the Albanian border at Morina. The IMC has made a mobile surgery unit available and it's to be moved up to the border immediately.

The road we take from Kukes hugs the southern bank of the Drini, the river that rises in the mountains of Western

Kosovo near Pec and crosses the Albania-Kosovo border at Morina. Beyond the river the Pastrik mountains stand against the sky as captivating as a big, gorgeous poster in the window of a travel agency. Look at the smiles. The stunning scenery all around has us murmuring, 'Wow!' and 'Oooh!' like tourists on a Kontiki tour ('See magical Kosovo!').

Fifteen kilometres along the road we round a corner and all smiles disappear. From a slight promontory we gaze down on a vast panorama of human misery, Kosovars in their thousands lurching and hobbling towards the convoy of trucks and buses waiting to transport them to the refugee camps of Kukes. Their faces are haggard with fatigue and fear, as if they've spent the entire journey from Prizren looking over their shoulders. Most of these thousands are on foot but the frailest amongst them are being carried in trailers pulled by horses or tractors, some pushed along in wheelbarrows. It takes us only a couple of minutes to notice something that we should have expected: almost no young men, only old men, women and children. The young men would have been detained or murdered. That's what 'cleansing' is all about; the elimination of those who might fight back, or who might in the future father children. This isn't a war; it's a civilian-targeted campaign of terrorism.

Once amongst the refugees it becomes evident that we will be dealing with a great many wounded. Most of these people are malnourished and dehydrated. The exodus from Prizren and its surrounds would have followed days of siege and bombardment. Only when the Serbs had gathered together all of the young men would they have driven the kids and women and elderly out. These people are traumatised.

Something about the river, the Drini, puzzles me at first. At the crossing the water is a deep blue, but looking upstream it's the colour of rust. Milaim explains that the Serbs have dumped scores of bloodied corpses in the river. I can now make out a great many bodies lolling in the water where the meander slows on a bend, some of them snagged in reeds, some bobbing face down. It's an advertisement. It's the Serbs saying, 'Stand here and watch and your son will float past, your husband, your father. We did this. You have much to fear.' These bodies will, in time, be carried down into Albania and some might make it all the way to the Adriatic. Everyone who sees them will dread the Serbs that much more; dread them and loathe them. There's an appalling, primitive logic to this kind of savagery. It's related to the strategy of Tamburlaine, the Mongol warrior chief of the fourteenth century who piled up the heads of captives then sent those he'd spared to spread the word of his barbarity. And at the same time that they advertise themselves in this way – irony is black in wartime – the Serbs are content to euphemise murder as 'cleansing'.

We've established the mobile unit on a bare patch of ground close to a small stone bridge that crosses a tributary of the Drini and carries all the traffic of this exodus. The number of people struggling to cross the bridge is so great that it becomes clogged and the moving line of refugees stretching kilometres back into Kosovo frequently comes to a halt. We're dealing with gunshot and shrapnel wounds primarily, many of them fresh enough to have been inflicted within the past hour or two. Whenever I glance down the line of refugees, I notice the distant shapes of the stragglers breaking from the line and falling to the ground, as if too exhausted to continue. We can't go over into Kosovo to help them. We have to rely on them somehow getting back on their feet and reaching the crossing. At the very moment that I'm trying to imagine how these exhausted stragglers can be assisted, a young man – one of the very few amongst the refugees – grabs me by my arm and implores me in English to come with him. I'm already overwhelmed by the wounded arriving at the mobile unit but I can't refuse this man. He has horror and despair written all over his face. I follow him at a run up the small promontory behind the mobile unit and Milaim chases along behind. The young man hands me a small pair of binoculars and stutters out the words, 'Look! Look what is happening!' I train the binoculars in the direction he's pointing and immediately the figures and even the faces of Serb soldiers half a kilometre away grow distinct. And now I understand that the stragglers are not falling from exhaustion. Serbs snipers on a hill facing down on the column are picking them off. I murmur, 'Oh Jesus!' to myself, but what can I say to this young man? 'I'll put a stop to this!' – something as fatuous as that?

'Milaim, is there anything we can do?'

Milaim lifts his shoulders and lets them fall. 'If any of them survive, you can treat their wounds.'

'That's all?'

Milaim gives his trademark shrug once more. It's not a shrug of indifference, but helplessness.

'Craig, if we go over the bridge to help them, the Serbs will shoot us. I'm sure you understand that.'

'Yes, but all the same …'

'Craig, listen to me. The Serbs could have shot these people kilometres away, before they even reached the river. They shoot them now so that we can see. And they think, 'Okay, you want to help these people? Go ahead!' It gives them pleasure, Craig. You can do nothing.'

The young man, meanwhile, is trembling in his distress, hoping that Milaim and I have some miracle solution we can call on.

'I'm terribly sorry,' is all I can say.

The young man nods, his face running with tears. He touches my arm, as if to convey his thanks. He keeps nodding, even as his gaze takes in the awful scene across the border.

Before I gather my thoughts and formulate something more to say to this poor man, the sound of three dull blasts in quick succession echo down the river. From this vantage point I can see smoke rising two hundred metres along the line of refugees on the Kosovo side of the border. People are flattened on the ground, some dead or wounded, some attempting to find shelter where there is no shelter. The explosions were mortar strikes – I'm familiar with the heavy clump of a mortar shell detonating – and there could be more to come. We've got media people galore here, most mingling with the refugees just as they cross the border. Many now run towards the bridge hoping to get footage of the chaos, unable to see much as they jostle with the crowds. I can see the Serb soldiers who fired the mortar rounds dancing a heinous jig of celebration.

The refugees around the site of the mortar strikes are climbing back to their feet, those who can. The whole line is beginning to move again. It shocks me to see that these people of the exodus have become so habituated to the savagery of the Serbs that they barely wait to check if they have all their limbs before resuming the trudging march to what they hope will be safety. Is this what people do when there is nothing they can do? They just keep going and pray that the next bullet or the next mortar shell won't kill them? Is this just another day in Kosovo to them?

We treat scores of wounded refugees at the mobile unit over the next six hours; stabilise them, load them into tractors, ambulances and trucks bound for local hospitals and medical facilities. I've moved further up the line of catastrophe. I started out two days ago shaking my head over the number of wounded in the hospital at Kukes; yesterday I was up to my elbows in blood in the operating theatre, and today I'm closer to the point at which it all begins. I've seen the Serbs inflicting the wounds that I treat. And I've seen once more what I saw in Gaza; the complete breakdown of civilising restraint. War is said to be hell, but it is really a series of hells; and when you think you've seen the worst of them a new one sickens you all over again.

As light fades in the late afternoon, the last of this day's refugees make their way across the bridge at the border. At the rear of this final group comes a boy of about eighteen in a heavy black overcoat and jeans, carrying a girl in his arms, a frail little thing, her face as white as bone. I help the pair into the mobile unit. The boy has gaunt cheeks, a great shock of dark hair and the unnaturally red lips of the half-starved. His sister, maybe fifteen or sixteen, is dark-haired too and would probably be pretty if she weren't reduced to skin and bones by illness. Her afflictions have spared her teeth, which are a brilliant white and perfectly formed. It's an odd thing, but surgeons, like ambulance drivers, develop an acute, one-glance awareness of the nearness of mortality after a few years in the trade and right now, looking down at this once-pretty girl, I know that it's only the last of her life looking back at me. She has a high fever, brought on by an infection which has entered her bloodstream, septicaemia. She lifts her hand and thrusts a balled-up wad of white paper towards me. I open it out and find a handwritten note in fractured English, signed by a doctor at the hospital in Prizren. The girl watches my face as I read. It advises whoever reads this note that the young woman, Lule, has been undergoing treatment for leukaemia and makes recommendations for continued care. Although it's been written rapidly, the doctor has been conscientious and detailed in his suggestions for ongoing treatment. At the very end comes a plea: 'Please help this girl. I have done everything possible. God help her and the others!' I fold the crumpled paper and slip it into my pocket. I doubt that this poor girl will require any further treatment for her leukaemia; she's not going to last that long.

I ask the boy for his name. Milaim translates.

'His name is Liridian. He's her brother.'

I shake the boy's hand.

'I'm Craig. I'm a doctor from Australia. Good to meet you, Liridian.' I add hastily, 'Except for the circumstances, of course ...'

'He says thank you for coming here from Australia.'

'What's their story? Ask him what happened.'

Milaim talks quietly, making rapid gestures with his hands. Liridian answers in his soft way, glancing down at his sister constantly, as if she might die while his attention is elsewhere.

'He says the Serbs expelled everyone from the hospital in Prizren, told them to get out. He says it was very sudden. Even those who were very sick were made to leave the hospital.'

Now the girl, Lule, begins talking in a faltering way. Milaim listens intently, nodding as he takes in her story.

'She says that the soldiers were paramilitaries. They beat many of the patients before throwing them out of the hospital.

46

Some they shot. Her doctor was a Serb, but the soldiers attacked him anyway. He stood by her side, refused to leave her to the soldiers' mercy. She says he was a hero. She says he was a very good man and a hero.'

Lule has utterly exhausted herself with this account of the doctor's courage and compassion. It is obviously very important to her to tell us of her doctor's dedication, but she hasn't the strength to add a single further sentence. Liridian takes up where his sister finished and Milaim translates for me while I do what I can to stabilise her. The two voices, Liridian's and Milaim's, both soft and earnest, are interrupted now and again by murmurs of agreement from Lule.

'Everything was chaos, shouting, shooting, the soldiers in a frenzy. The Serb doctor and this young fellow managed to get her away from the soldiers and down to the front entrance of the hospital. The doctor put the note into Lule's hand and went back into the hospital. The boy here was carrying his sister along in a stream of patients trying to escape. Many patients were being helped by family members. When Liridian was just beyond the main gates he heard gun shots. He looked back and saw two soldiers dragging the body of the doctor, feet first, out of the main entrance. They dumped the body outside the gates.'

I shake my head every few seconds, seeing in my mind's eye the stark details of the horror these young people are reliving. But the surgeon in me is struggling to imagine what sort of care we can offer this girl; I make a mental note to reflect later on the heroism of the murdered doctor. I organise an intravenous fluid regime for Lule and a course of broad-spectrum antibiotics to arrest the septicaemia, but I'm still listening to Milaim and Liridian even as I issue orders to nurses and other personnel.

The girl will die, I know that. Her Serb doctor gave up his life to save her; her brother has carried her an astonishing twenty-five kilometres to get her to safety, but she will die. She is valued here, in this mobile unit, valued by Liridian, by me, by the medical staff, by Milaim. And she would be valued in many other countries in the world. Doctors would do their utmost to keep her alive; the rule of law would prevent soldiers from dragging her from her bed and throwing her onto the street. But she found herself in a place where she was not valued; where her life was held in contempt; where no law could protect her. She's going to die of misfortune and politics.

And she does. When I return to Kukes in the evening I hear, from a nurse who was accompanying the wounded and ill, that she died on the way to hospital.

I ask Milaim where she will be buried. He says, 'In a pit with many others.'

I call Donna on the satellite phone later in the evening. The signal reception is only occasionally good enough to get through. I surprise myself by speaking of what I've seen today in a fairly dispassionate way; I'd thought I would be more vehement about the tactics of the Serbs. Maybe it's because I've already debriefed, told my tale to other doctors here at the apartment, listened to their stories, all of them as harrowing as my own. Maybe the years of experience have hardened me, prepared me. I don't know.

Donna asks how old Lule was.

'Maybe sixteen. Very frail.'

'That's so sad. I know her brother got her all the way to you, but in that state her leukaemia had such a poor prognosis that she would have died anyway. Craig, you did your best. You know that's all you could do.'

I change the subject abruptly, emotion creeping into my voice.

'Is Kosovo still in the news in Australia?' I ask.

'It's about all that's on at the moment. I watch the BBC and CNN reports whenever I'm not at work. Everyone here is glued to their screens hoping to catch a glimpse of you. In fact, your brother called me yesterday to tell me that you're alive and well. He saw you on a CNN news report carrying a stretcher in one of the camps. It looks truly miserable there, all those families streaming across the border. They must be in a terrible state.'

She pauses, and then asks, 'Are you close to the fighting?'

'No, no. Nowhere near it. It's very safe where we are.'

'I worry all the time. But I'm proud of what you're doing. Not happy, but very proud. They're so fortunate to have you there. But do take care, my love.'

'I will.'

Chapter 5

It's early morning, I'm still in bed, and my ears are full of the sounds of children riotously at play. Such a carefree chorus in this grim sector of a loveless city seems so unlikely that I expect to be mistaken. After a further five minutes of concentration I'm convinced that the voices are those of children. Only kids sound like kids.

I wriggle my way out of my sleeping bag still fully dressed; I didn't have the strength to strip off the previous night. Unshaven and coated in two day's sweat and grime, I make a rapid mental list of the tasks I'll have to attend to if I'm going to become presentable once more – shower, shave, brush my teeth, put on a fresh T-shirt. I can't look a mess in front of my patients. I make myself a mug of coffee and wander downstairs to find out why children are laughing in the middle of Kukes – because they shouldn't be, surely, with so much around to make them weep.

The sun has just come up. The shadows still have that hard-edge intensity of early morning. The cold air is more bracing than chilling. And yes, children are playing, a dozen or more, all about six or seven years old. They're over in the empty wasteland between the hospital and the apartment house – the area across which Milaim and I carried the boy with the shattered liver the morning before last. The children are kicking a soccer ball about, dodging and weaving and feinting and sprinting. The ball appears to be only half-inflated but that's not inhibiting their enjoyment. I stand in the sunshine, smiling between sips of coffee. This is one of the great things in life, isn't it, watching kids at play? I do this sort of thing with my own son, kick a ball about in the sunshine, my heart soaring, delighted by his delight. God I miss that. I miss him.

A woman of about fifty is supervising the children, grey-haired, too old to be their mother. I wander over and she greets me in Albanian then becomes aware that I'm not a local and switches to English.

'American?'

'Australian.'

'Australian!'

'Craig Jurisevic. Nice to meet you.'

My offered hand is accepted, but with a puzzled frown.

'A Serb name, Jurisevic.'

'Slovenian. My grandfather.'

'Ah!'

She reflects for a time, as if the oddness of a fair-haired stranger from Australia with a Slovenian grandfather deserves some study.

'My name is Edona,' she says at last.

'And who do the children belong to?'

Edona lights up a cigarette and takes a long drag before nodding towards the apartment block next to mine. 'Orphans,' she says. 'They live with us. My family, other families. One day they go back to Kosovo. Maybe.'

On the surface, at least, the children seem fine. Deeper down, who knows. Becoming an orphan would be devastating even if your parents died in their sleep with smiles on their faces. But the parents of these kids wouldn't have died in any comfortable way, I'm sure of that, and some may have died in full view of their children.

I ask Edona about a little girl with long brown hair sitting all by herself on the fringe of the empty lot. She's gazing expressionlessly at the other kids. Edona tells me that it's only two weeks since the girl's parents were killed in a village near the town of Suhareka in Eastern Kosovo. 'She saw her mother and father killed, and her sister,' says Edona. 'The Serbs maybe would have killed her too but she hid herself in a cupboard.'

We watch the kids for a few minutes longer. My gaze keeps returning to the silent little girl on the fringe of the playground. What's happening behind that mask? Is she attempting to understand what's happened and why, or is it beyond her? Perhaps she's simply baffled most of the time, nursing her pain in the way that you'd nurse a bruise, doing everything possible to prevent the bruise being struck again.

Edona says she's going to take the children inside for breakfast and she asks me if I'd like to come along. The kids line up at the entrance to the apartment block, remove their shoes and carry them in their hands. I say, 'You've trained them well,' but Edona shakes her head. 'Not me. In the camps they teach them to do that.'

Edona's son, a boy of twelve who speaks faultless English, offers me a cup of coffee. I glance around the apartment as

I sip, impressed by the order and cleanliness of the place. I imagine one of the reasons Edona invited me in is to show how well these children are cared for; she's proud of that. Certainly puts the dump in which I'm living to shame.

While the children are eating, Edona shows me the drawings and paintings that they produce. When children of six and seven in Adelaide are given the opportunity to use pencils and paints and crayons, the results are no doubt cheerful representations of trees, blue skies, cows, shiny cars, TV stars, dolls and superheroes, also a smiling mum, a smiling dad. There's nothing subtle about the subjects children choose to put on paper; whatever's dominating their thoughts at the time comes pouring out. What comes pouring out of these kids from Kosovo is death, overwhelmingly; pictures of bodies spreadeagled in vast lakes of blood, of soldiers firing rifles, of tanks, of explosions, of houses ablaze, of children weeping long chains of tears. A common image is a child standing beside a dead body. Edona says, 'That is the orphan, and that is the parent.' She goes on to tell me that trauma art of this sort helps the children sleep at night.

I stay with Edona and the kids for as long as I can, but finally I have to leave for a morning catch-up with the other doctors in my apartment. I offer Edona my contact details, should she need me in a medical emergency. She thanks me and all of the foreigners who've come to Albania to help, calling us heroes. What I might say is, 'I'll be back in Adelaide in a couple of months, Edona – it's limited-tenure heroism.' But I don't.

Nothing immediately distinguishes the type of doctor who packs a bag for Kosovo or Ethiopia or Gaza to put in a couple of months in a combat zone. I have colleagues here on the downhill side of fifty, others in their twenties, people who fret constantly, optimists, depressives, thrill-seekers. The motives for being here are just as various as personality type, or age: religious conviction, pacifism, the desire to make recompense for some past failing, humanism, profound disgust, a need to address over-privilege, Samaritanism, or simply an urgent desire to stand between the victim and his suffering, her suffering. But I haven't met anyone here who believes that he or she could achieve anything sensational. No messiahs, no egomaniacs. Once you take a look around, you know within minutes that the guys with the guns and mortars are the ones who make the biggest difference in people's lives; a couple of accurate mortar strikes, limbs and death everywhere. If you're not humble when you get here, you'll certainly catch on.

Or maybe there is one thing that most of my colleagues have in common: nationality, because most are Americans: Larry Stock from Los Angeles, Frank Tyler from Boston and Brenda Vittachi from San Diego; Steve McRae and George Seminov from somewhere or other in California. All terrifically competent. But the fellow I'm most impressed by is Roger Lake, a Canadian GP – humble, yes, but in an extroverted way. Roger embraces life with a grip like a grizzly bear. Medicine gave him a structure for his energy, but if he hadn't become a doctor he could have been happy as a boulevardier, an adventurer, a raconteur, a bon vivant, or simply as a delightful ratbag. He's in his fifties, has a couple of grown-up children and also a new wife much younger than he is – which, if you're in your fifties, probably gives life a certain golden glow. When I'm on the other side of fifty, I hope with all my heart that I still have the relish for life and the belief in my fellow human beings that Roger displays. Because it can wear out – I've noticed that.

Roger is with me when we head off to the daily UN briefing, held in a crowded, smoke-filled room on the first floor of a municipal building in the middle of Kukes. These meetings can be tedious. We hear of water-purification projects, food supply logistics, refugee movements in the region. The NATO security briefing that follows commands more attention. Serb artillery is zeroing in on areas pretty close to us and there's nothing to prevent the Serbs shelling the camps, shelling Kukes itself, unleashing their Katyusha rockets if they're in a particularly vicious mood – and they're always in a particularly vicious mood.

At the end of the meeting, I'm approached by a couple of UNHCR folk and asked if I'd accept the office of surgical co-ordinator and surgeon on call for the camps in the Kukes area. This is an appointment that was mooted a couple of days ago and one that fits my experience, passions and energy for the organisation of large and complex teams and deployment of resources. I'm flattered to be asked and agree on the spot.

'You do appreciate how much work is involved, Dr Jurisevic?'

'Yes. Absolutely.'

'It won't be too great a burden?'

'No, absolutely not. That's why I'm here.'

Back at the apartment, I get to work fashioning a thorough triage and primary treatment plan for all the surgical services in the Kukes camps. I want the facilities we have here employed to the maximum benefit for the short time I and the refugees are here.

The largesse of the UNHCR has extended to providing me with a radio, a Land Cruiser and a driver. I take a break from planning in the afternoon to tour the refugee camps and familiarise myself with the medical facilities. The most impressive of all are the two inflatable surgical and intensive care units of the United Arab Emirates' contingent, set up in the camp they oversee beside a thousand-metre-long runway built to accommodate Hercules C-130 transports. The units are fabulously well equipped. Lieutenant colonel Mahmoudi from the UAE armed forces is in charge and shows me over the facility. This mission is the highlight of his life, he says.

'Why am I so proud of what we are doing here? I will tell you. We are doing God's will, that is why. We are doing God's will by caring for our Muslim brothers and sisters.'

I'm guessing that Mahmoudi has never seen the inside of the Kukes hospital, where his Muslim brothers and sisters have all the comfort and care you'd associate with an abattoir.

The Camp Italia Military Surgical Unit, run by the Italian Red Cross, is also pretty impressive but not quite of the glittering standard of the UAE unit. I immediately take to the vascular surgeon here, Colonel Toccafundi, who is very proud of what his people are doing.

The Médecins Sans Frontières (MSF) people have a rudimentary surgical facility, too. The MSF has to get by on the seat of its pants; it's almost entirely funded by private donors, but it does a fine job within limitations. I'm amused at the way in which each team's emergency vehicles index the image it wants to convey. It's Mercedes for the stylish Italians; showy Humvee behemoths for the well-funded UAE contingent – while MSF has workaday Toyotas.

I set aside my work on the treatment plan at regular intervals to gown-up in the operating theatre at Kukes hospital. So many amputations! Reports of casualties don't fully convey what war does to people. Imagine if I were to give a weekly surgeon's report to the news services and display the limbs that had been lost, the metres of bowel discarded, the eyes blinded.

The warnings of invasion are coming in thick and fast from UNHCR envoys and NATO officers, and not only at the daily briefings; these alarms are in the air now. The main UNHCR envoy, a fellow by the name of McNamara, tells me that an invasion could happen at any time.

'The Serbs are massing in Kosovo. If they invade, they won't be stopped.'

'Are you saying that the Serbs could cross the border and enter Kukes itself?'

My question sounds naïve, but I hadn't contemplated a Serb escalation of the war into Albania. What would be the point? The Serb strategy is to force all Muslim Kosovars into Albania. So, the Serbs might hit out of sheer malice? Is that what McNamara is saying?

'You have to plan for evacuation,' he says.

'Are you serious? One hundred and forty thousand refugees? Evacuate them all?'

'If necessary, yes. Evacuate them all.'

I happen to know that we have about a hundred transport vehicles and that a third of those are off the road. Another twenty have been brazenly commandeered by municipal officials in league with the Kukes mafia. It would be utterly impossible to move one hundred and forty thousand refugees half a kilometre down the road with the vehicles available, let alone fifty kilometres out of harm's way.

'I doubt that would be feasible.'

'Nevertheless,' says McNamara.

Is there something I don't know about the situation here? Some covert plan that will only be revealed once the Serbs hit Kukes? Because everything I do know leaves me baffled by the way the UNHCR and NATO people shrug off the logistical impossibility of moving so many refugees at short notice. It doesn't seem to worry them in the way that it worries me. Maybe the UNHCR has already factored in a huge loss of life following an invasion and, having made that assessment, they delude themselves that they're on top of the problem. It's a paper war to many of them; something that's dealt with in communiqués and press releases. The NATO people probably expect the war to be settled in some place a long way from Kukes; in Belgrade maybe, after enough damage has been inflicted on that city's infrastructure by the bombing campaign. Is it possible that NATO's strategists and the UNHCR envoys employ bean-counters in the same fashion as big corporations? People who write out a projected profit-and-loss report before a shot's been fired? I get the feeling that some of the NATO and UNHCR people I talk to have never actually seen a refugee, except at a distance. One thing I'm sure of is this: the NATO forces will never commit ground troops to a place like the Kukes border. They might send in some air strikes, but they're not going to put flesh-and-blood soldiers in the path of the Serbs.

Late in the afternoon, weary of paperwork, the apartment empty, I stand at the window chewing on a crust of bread.

The heat of the day has turned the air in the apartment to a lukewarm soup; breathing is like imbibing something slightly toxic. I hum pop songs in a desultory way, check the refrigerator for things I'm not going to find in there – a block of chocolate, cold pizza, a Farmer's Union iced coffee. Mostly I want to talk to Milaim about the invasion rumours, because I don't have a lot of confidence in McNamara's take on the whole thing. But I have no idea where to find Milaim. Maybe if I called in at every coffee bar in central Kukes? Can I be bothered?

I wander up along the streets and lanes, passing people who give me a mildly curious glance, one more player in the mysterious drama that's overtaken them. There are lots of children about – you always see hordes of kids in these poor communities. Nearly all of them look as if they've been dressed from a Target clearance sale: cheap sneakers and bomber tops, trackies, T-shirts bearing the emblems that the vast Chinese factories that manufacture them believe will appeal to Western children: stylised spaceships, speeding cars, Disney rip-offs, Michael Jackson moonwalk silhouettes, soccer heroes from the big European leagues. The younger kids look and behave like kids everywhere, but I notice that the older ones have developed a more guarded look, as if they've heard things that make them think of the world as a very menacing place. Some women wear headscarves, but by no means all. This is a Muslim country with a Turkish influence; women enjoy a more relaxed dress code, particularly the younger ones.

I know a bit about Kukes from the reading I did on the flight from Sydney to Rome. I know, for example, that the town of Kukes is not really the town of Kukes. The real Kukes lies drowned at the bottom of the huge artificial lake that laps against this new version of the city. When Enver Hoxha lost the friendship of the Russians in the early 1970s he embraced the Chinese, who were only too glad to have a friend on the European continent. The Chinese expressed their friendship in the accepted communist way: they built massive dams and hydroelectric plants for Hoxha up and down the country. No environmental studies; they just dug the holes, laid the pipes, and sent delegations to applaud when the ribbons were cut. A number of towns up this way were drowned, just as Old Kukes was. If you dived down to the bottom of the lake, you'd see empty streets, fish swimming in and out of the arches of ancient mosques, the buildings of the old bazaar coated in slime. The whole of Albania was once the Roman province of Illyria; the ruins of that period are ruins for a second time.

It's barely fifteen years old, this town of New Kukes, but poverty has aged it prematurely, in the way that smoking can make a human look fifty at the age of thirty-five. And yet, and yet ... well, New Kukes has a sort of homely charm, a charm that was completely lost on me on the drive in from the landing strip three days ago. It's as if the town is declaring that it is what it is: unlovely yes, but candid in its lack of beauty. The people I come across, they're just playing the cards they've been dealt – very unpromising hands, definitely, but they're not complaining. I stop in the town square by the municipal offices and watch mums with toddlers in old fold-up pushers. Another set of mothers, those in my gleaming suburb of Adelaide, steering ritzy strollers with pneumatic tyres and adjustable suspensions, would look askance at these dated contraptions. One mother has a baby in her arms, a little child in a pusher and a couple of others under five to cope with, and the sun beating down on her head – and not too much spare change in her purse for icy poles, I'll bet. She has that versatile look of young mums who've taught themselves, out of necessity, to keep an eye on a dozen things at once.

I can't find Milaim in the coffee shops. I ought to try the American Bar just across the way, next to the municipal block. I've heard a bit about this fabled dive. The home-brew is meant to be pretty potent stuff. In a Muslim state, you're not going to find a bar every hundred metres along the boulevard as you might in New York or Sydney or even Adelaide. The American Bar is Kukes' only true watering hole and is said to attract every sinner in the city and quite a few angels on a break. It looks harmless enough from the outside, with its moulded plastic chairs and tables covered in red-and-white checked tablecloths, but inside it seethes. There must be a hundred people crammed into the bar area, more in a small dining room to the left. A dense blue cloud of cigarette smoke floats above the heads of the patrons, pungent enough to get me coughing before I'm a metre inside the door. Three or four drinkers at the bar turn and gaze at me disinterestedly – noting, however, my newcomer status. The rowdiness of the place – music issuing from three or four different sources, conversations amplified to compensate for the din – makes it almost impossible for me to ask the guys at the bar if they've seen Milaim.

'I'm looking for my interpreter!'

'For what?'

'My interpreter! Milaim!'

'You want a beer?'

'No, no! Milaim! He works for IMC!'

'I'll get you a beer!'

I've heard Milaim say that the American Bar is the hub of the town. Deals of all sorts are done here; some that benefit the refugees who stream into Kukes, and a lot that benefit the bad guys. Winding my way through the smoke with the beer in my hand that I didn't really want, I can identify a few of the doctors I've met in my three days here, but they're outnumbered by journalists and the cadres of the local mafia.

I eventually find Milaim, hunched over a scotch on a sofa in the corner with a couple of his Albanian friends.

'Craig! Sit down! Finish your beer, I get you another one.'

'One's enough, but thanks.'

'You are looking for me?'

'I am. I'm concerned about this invasion everybody's talking about.'

'Invasion? What invasion?'

'Haven't you heard people talking about it?'

'It's just talk. Forget it. Invasion, evacuation, all of that. Just crazy stuff.'

'So I shouldn't be worried?'

'These people, UN, NATO, they get scared easily. Ever since they come to Kukes, they are talking about invasions.'

'Is that what it is?'

'Better to relax.'

'And the Serbs won't invade? They won't shell the camps?'

'I don't know. They might.'

'You're about as reassuring as a drunk pilot!'

'Serbs are insane. Who can say?'

This is Milaim's way: he tells you to chill, then gives you a few good reasons why you shouldn't, then tells you to relax again. Milaim has translated my concerns to his two friends.

They look at me and shake their heads, 'No, no,' they say, 'no Serbs come.'

'I'm glad to hear it.'

I think I have to accept that nobody has the faintest idea about what the Serbs will or won't do. I drink my beer and relax into conversation with Milaim and his friends. The smoke and the noise aside, it is possible to enjoy this place. It has a pulse, I have to concede that.

I lean back on the sofa, watch the passing parade of bad guys and good guys, calmly contemplating the apocalypse.

Chapter 6

The border crossing at Morina has become a haemorrhage over these first seven days in May. I'm travelling up there from Kukes each day now with the IMC team. The Serb regulars pound a target with artillery, then the paramilitaries have free rein to take over the cities, towns and villages, leaving the streets littered with corpses. They're like a medieval plague, the paramilitaries; like the Black Death. And every massacre reinforces Milosevic's message to Kosovo: 'We can do what we like. Nothing can save you.'

Certain features of the Serb campaign, ugly as they all are, retain a savage logic. The scheme of scattering brightly painted grenades and detonators in soccer fields and playgrounds goes beyond mere malice; the Serbs know that the locals will come to dread what their children might bend down and pick up and rather than wait for the worst, they will head for Albania. Other tactics make no sense unless you factor in sheer, primitive sadism. The escape routes down from the hills heading west and south to the Albanian border have been mined and booby-trapped, so the Serbs are inflicting appalling wounds on the people they have already frightened into flight. Where is the strategic sense in that? When Milaim says that the Serbs are insane, I think he means 'insane' in a particular way. He means that they're crazed with a lust for blood, like ravening wolves.

I have days when I'm troubled by the contempt seething inside me. It's natural to be sickened by the savagery of the Serbs, but at times I'm dwelling more on retaliation than I ought. I'm not the sort of person who can find a balm for disgust in moral philosophy.

But I don't want to become the prisoner of my disgust. I came here with the sole purpose of patching up victims of war. I shouldn't concern myself with motives, with politics. Yes, the Serbs are inflicting indescribable horrors on the Albanian Kosovars, but they are doing so with hatred in their hearts for similar horrors inflicted on them over the centuries. Most recently, Serbs endured genocide and forced expatriation from Kosovo during World War II under the Axis occupation.

The ratio of ethnic Albanians to Serbs in Kosovo has flowed back and forth, each turn of the tide leaving thousands of corpses and refugees. Rationalising in this way eases the sting of my contempt, but only just.

As I'm preparing for today's journey to the border, I'm called to a meeting with the UNHCR medical director, Daniel Endres, and Lieutenant Colonel Mahmoudi of the UAE contingent. Endres looks grim.

'Craig, the UAE facility is going to have to close for a week.'

'What! Why?'

This is going to punch a huge hole in our capacity to deliver the primary treatment plan I have worked on, to get urgently needed medical care to the ongoing avalanche of refugees arriving daily.

Mahmoudi says, in his formal way, 'Unforeseen difficulties of a technical nature.'

We'll have to send more patients than we should to Kukes hospital, which is very like inviting them to die.

Unforeseen difficulties of a technical nature, again.

I tell Endres and Mahmoudi that I'll redraft the treatment plan, but I'm very concerned. On the one hand, we've got people here with their guts held in by field dressings and, on the other, a multimillion-dollar surgical facility sitting there like a Ferrari with a dud ignition. This is really a scandalous situation. Something is amiss and yet, right now, there is not a thing I can do about it.

I'm heading north today with the IMC team to Bajram Curri, a sizeable town only a few kilometres west of the Serbian border near a mountain with the fascinating name of Bjeshkët e Nemuna – 'Accursed Mountains'. A number of small camps have been established up there for the refugees crossing from Kosovo, but so far the people in the camps haven't had access to medical facilities. We'll make assessments and return with those in dire need of surgery to Kukes.

As we lurch along the unpaved roads of the mountains that straddle the Albanian-Serbian frontier, the superb scenery unfolding around us is truly breathtaking. To the south, the rivers of the region feed into an elongated lake, Liqeni i Fierzës, created by industrial damming further downstream. The rising waters of the lake have crept up the slopes of the lower foothills, inundating the natural flood plain. The banks of Liqeni i Fierzës are now the slopes of the hills, rising almost sheer from the waters. I reflect in an idle way on the possibility of coming back to this lovely part of the world with Donna and Jackson one fine day to spend a few tourist dollars. But really, how likely is that? The beauty of the landscape is now saturated with the stuff of nightmares.

Another good reason for studying the scenery is to take my mind off the danger we're in. A convoy of ambulances provides a target for artillery and mortar that I can barely imagine the Serbs being able to resist. In warfare of the sort Milosevic is waging, the line is drawn exactly nowhere. The Serbs might incinerate a couple of ambulances, then claim that the vehicles were not displaying Red Cross identification (and ours are not, in fact; a bad mistake). Or they mightn't even bother with excuses. At this stage in the war, Milosevic would be counting on unwavering Russian support in the UN Security Council: the Grand Brotherhood of Slavs, because the Russians want Milosevic to prosper. A friendly regime governing a Greater Serbia on the Balkan Peninsula would suit them nicely.

We're only a few kilometres from Bajram Curri when an artillery strike ahead brings the convoy to an abrupt halt.

'Shit! That's only about five hundred metres away!' There's no way we can tell if we're the target.

'Fuck me!' exclaims Milaim.

'Are they aiming at us?'

'No,' says Milaim, 'at the village.'

'What village?'

'Don't know the name.'

'On this side of the border?'

'Yes, this side.'

'Why?' I ask Milaim. It's a ridiculous question, but it jumps out.

'To kill people,' he says.

We wait silently. There'll be no warning if an artillery round takes us out; alive one second, soggy fragments the next. I free a tiny part of my brain from paralysis to apologise to Donna: 'Sorry, my darling.'

The order is given somewhere up ahead for the convoy to advance. The lurching of the Land Cruiser is comforting; being jolted from side to side at least confirms that we're alive.

In the village that has suffered the strike we come upon a playground next to a small kindergarten, where the smoke and stench of the artillery strike still hang in the air. From the window of the Land Cruiser I can make out body parts strewn all over the scorched grass and dry earth.

'Many dead here,' says Milaim.

'That's an understatement. It's a bloody mess.'

'Many,' he says again. 'I think children.'

'Oh Christ!'

Out of the vehicle and amongst the debris of the strike, I stride about in search of survivors, glancing only for a second at those who are obviously beyond help. I'm unable to find a torso for a pair of small legs and when I do find one I don't know which legs belong to it; so many limbs, so many hands and arms, and feet still in their boots. I stop beside the headless body of a girl, her doll, undamaged, soaking up her blood beside her. I'd like to vomit or tear my teeth out or shut my eyes and fall to my knees, but there's no time; five children who might yet be saved are identified. The shouting of the paramedics for stretchers, IVs, dressings and morphine combines with the shrieking of the people from the village as they gaze on the bodies and body parts of their children. The head paramedic takes me along to those he thinks are salvageable. I am the only doctor on the scene and I must triage the survivors quickly. I don't dare meet the eyes of the mothers just for the moment because there's nothing, simply nothing, that I can convey that would comfort them other than sympathy and it makes me feel wretched. I join the organised turmoil of the struggle to save the surviving children.

We can't save all of the five children. When the last child dies – a small girl – the mother, who's been watching and hoping and praying, reaches over and places her hand on top of mine. She is young and strikingly beautiful with lustrous brown eyes. She lifts my hand and kisses it, tears running down her cheeks. She has accepted that her daughter's life is over, and she has accepted that we struggled to save the girl; struggled tenaciously. With the one gesture, she conveys her grief and her gratitude. She places my hand on her daughter's face, like a final benediction, then takes the girl up in her arms and walks away with her.

We spend the night in the town of Bajram Curri, our original destination when we set off from Kukes this morning. In the evening, I listen to stories from refugees who've fled the Serb advance. Something I notice in these stories is that the refugees see nothing to choose between the behaviour of the Serb regulars and Serb paramilitaries. Militias supporting regular troops tend to attract hobby sadists; young men who would never wish to subject themselves to the discipline, regulation and tedium of a long stint in the armed services but yearn to arm themselves with semi-automatics and frock-up in battle camouflage and act out fantasies of domination. In this war, the regulars are just as likely to get filthy as the militia boys. This contradicts my experience in the past with regulars and militias. Regular troops usually take pride in their professionalism. They experience more of the sorrow and pity of warfare, and it's fairly common for them to develop a degree of grudging respect for the bravery of their enemies. Militias are often saved for the despicable side of things; terrorism, torture, brutalising unarmed civilians, programmed rape. In Kosovo, the thrill of sadistic reprisal seems to have permeated the entire Serbian armed forces. It must come from the top.

I sit talking with an old man who had survived the razing of his village inside Kosovo. The village was lightly defended by Kosovo Liberation Army cadres but they were quickly swept aside by Serb regulars. When the regulars moved on, the village was left in the hands of paramilitaries. In such situations, a paramilitary commander will often seek out a way to impress his followers, to reinforce their esteem, initiate them in a ritual way into the enchantment of torture. The paramilitary commander in this village allowed his men to drink themselves stupid and then, to show what a devil of a fellow he was, he seized a small child, held the boy aloft by the neck then skewered him through the abdomen with his knife. A blade wound to the abdomen will usually take a while to kill the victim; a minute, a few minutes, sometimes longer. And so it did in this case, according to the old man. The mother was forced to watch as her impaled child screamed himself to death. The old man tells me, too, of his neighbours being forced from their homes in the middle of a freezing night, held at gunpoint in their sleeping attire until the more vulnerable – some of the elderly, some of the infants – had shivered themselves into the terminal torpor of hypothermia.

I don't welcome these stories of atrocity. I don't seek them out. Each tale stains my sleep. But in listening to the victims of the Serb advance tell their tales, I make sure that I hear them out if they seem needful of a sympathetic audience. Their stories matter to them almost as much as the medical care I'm here to provide; they can't rest until someone from the world outside the house of horrors they inhabit has been told. It's as if I'm being made their witness. 'Maybe we won't survive', they seem to be saying, 'but you will. Tell our story.'

Chapter 7

Tens of thousands of people around me, but I doubt I've ever felt lonelier in my life. The gaze of so many eyes follow me as I walk about the camps, some of them imploring, many dull with fatigue. None of these people are asking for miracles; just some message of hope from me, from any of the doctors or UNHCR officials. They seem to be asking, 'The worst is over, is that true?' I try to give an impression of brisk confidence, but in my heart of hearts I'm maddened by a sense of not doing enough. What can I promise with a clear conscience? That the Serbs won't invade Albania and tear the camps to pieces? I wish I could promise that. I wish I could say, 'We will save you, we will guard you, your suffering is at an end.'

I rely on Roger for an example of a man who has stared down into the abyss of human misery without losing his geniality. And I rely on my fellow surgeons, Toccafundi, the Italian, and Ylber Vata, for sane conversation. Occasionally I'm in the operating theatre with Toccafundi or with Ylber, but usually I operate alone. Today, for one reason or another, I have a great need to chatter away with Ylber, listen to what he has to say about the politics of the region. Everything I know about the Balkan States is abstract and theoretical, but Ylber lives the mayhem of Balkan politics every day of his life.

I find him in the operating theatre at Kukes Hospital well into a below-knee amputation. I scrub in to help out, but from the moment I look my friend in the face I can see that something is amiss. He looks ill at ease and keeps nodding in a fugitive way towards a guy on a chair in the corner of the theatre, a big scowling fellow with a shaven scalp who doesn't have any evident function in the room.

The amputation Ylber is involved in looks wrong, too. The leg is infected and should have been taken off days earlier. Why the delay? Every time I try to ask a polite question or two, Ylber glances towards the corner and to me with a slight shake of his head. I have to wait until the leg is off and Ylber and I have left the theatre before I can get any sense out of him.

'What the hell was that all about?'

'Not here,' says Ylber, and hustles me away, down the corridor to a little out-of-the-way nook. His hand is trembling as he lights up a cigarette. He's not about to tell me anything until he's exhaled a long stream of smoke.

'Mafia, Craig.'

'What, that guy in the corner?'

'Yes, that guy in the corner.'

'What the hell is the Mafia doing in the theatre?'

Ylber takes another drag and then another before replying. 'Craig, all is not as it seems.'

'Really? In what way?'

Ylber shakes his head and makes a gesture of resignation. 'That man is Mafia, okay? And Cena is like this with the Mafia, okay?'

Ylber stubs out his cigarette and clasps his two hands tightly together.

'Cena is in the Mafia? The hospital director?'

'No, but he works with them. In this hospital, you only get help if you pay Cena. And Cena pays the Mafia. You understand?'

'What, everyone has to pay Cena? Even the refugees?'

'Especially the refugees. Everything in their pockets goes into his pockets. This patient we just finished with – he has no money, he can't pay. But I operated in any case. The Mafia man, he doesn't like it. He wanted me to stop. So, this.'

Ylber shows me his hand. It's still trembling.

I'm struggling to take it all in. The hospital is the private extortion racket of the director? I've come here from Adelaide to help Cena buy an apartment in Monte Carlo?

I shake my head in disgust. Rage is finding its way up into my chest, painfully.

'Ylber, this is terrible!'

'Yes. Shameful. Exactly.'

'What now? What will they do next? Shoot you?'

'Perhaps. I don't know.'

'Jesus, Ylber. Do the UN people know?'

Ylber lights up a second cigarette. His hand is finally steady.

'Craig, what do you think? You are an intelligent man. You have eyes. If the UN doesn't want to know about something, they don't see it.'

A nurse walks past the door and darts us a quick suspicious glance. Ylber's fatigued face takes on renewed anxiety.

'Is she a stooge?' I ask.

'What is "stooge"?'

'A spy.'

'Yes, she is a spy. Come with me.'

Ylber ushers me along the corridor and out of the hospital altogether. He indicates a coffee place just across the street from the hospital and doesn't say another word until we're huddled in a corner of the shop. In the relative security of this dingy place, he pours out the full story of Cena's racket. He tells me that a number of his colleagues in the hospital are involved, and names names. He says that the patients who can't pay are removed from the hospital under cover of night and dumped in dark alleys or open fields outside the town. And he has a special warning for me.

'Me? What's Cena got against me?'

'Your treatment plan, Craig. You've been sending patients to the Italians and the UAE. Every patient you send somewhere else, you take money from Cena. He thinks you are an evil influence.'

I could make light of what Ylber is telling me about the danger I'm in; I don't have as much cause to fear Cena as all that. I mean, he's not going to kneecap an IMC surgeon without opening up his rackets to scrutiny. But I can see that Ylber is sincerely concerned. And I can see, too, that he is appealing to me in a certain way. He can't seize me by the shirt and plead for help, but yes, he does want me to intervene if I can. He explains that it is not only he himself who stands in danger of reprisals by Cena, but his family too; his wife and children. He wants to clear out of Kukes with his family, work for UNHCR or IMC somewhere beyond the reach of Cena.

'I must do this, Craig. Cena will not think twice if he decides to have me killed. This is Albania. Murder is a normal way of doing business.'

'Ylber, of course I'll help. Of course. But how have you survived here so long? Surely Cena is onto you by now?'

Ylber opens his hands in a gesture of helplessness. 'These are my people. They have nothing. How can I leave them? But now it is too dangerous for my family, Craig. Too dangerous. Maybe Cena thought I would join him. Maybe he was being patient. And you know, Craig, if I stay here, I could end up like the others who do what he wants them to do. Any man can use up his courage. It is not like a well that never dries up.'

Ylber has to return to the hospital. I remain in the corner of the coffee shop, wrestling with my rage. My emotional response to injustice always consumes me in the way that it's doing now. A red mist hangs before my eyes like a gauze curtain. I head for the American Bar, march straight up to the barman and call for a shot of whisky. This will be only the second or third whisky I've downed in the past five years – a couple of beers usually does me – but I need something to restore my cool.

'Sure you want whisky?' asks the barman.

What's he talking about?

'Yes. Whisky.'

The barman leans towards me and gestures with his finger for me to lean close to him.

'Something has upset you,' he says.

'Damn right!'

'You are a doctor?'

How does he know that?

'Yes, I'm a doctor.'

'Call me Danny. Pleased to meet you.'

We shake hands, and I offer my name.

'I'm going to give you something that I keep for special occasions,' says Danny. 'My very special, eighty-proof scotch. Home-made.'

He has reached under the bar for a bottle and is already pouring.

'Best thing in Albania for when you are upset, okay? Best thing except for heroin and coke. You don't want heroin or coke?'

'God no!'

'Of course not. Here. Drink this.'

And I do. In two gulps. But hell! – it's like lava.

'Another one?' says Danny.

'Yes. No. Maybe. Okay.'

'You're not so sure? Better you don't.'

'One more,' I tell him.

'Okay. This one, you drink slowly, my friend. In two, three minutes, everything is okay again.'

I take the second shot with me to a dilapidated sofa at the back of the bar. The seething in my chest and guts diminishes.

At a table close by, a couple of Americans are complaining about the lack of printable stories in Kukes. Journalists, evidently working for *The Stars and Stripes*, the US Services' newspaper. *The Stars and Stripes* sends its correspondents everywhere the US military is serving.

I think, 'You need a story, guys? I could give you a story!'

And if I want to expose Cena's racket, I get the opportunity within minutes, because one of the Americans takes his leave and the remaining one, in the manner of journalists everywhere, strikes up a conversation with me just in case

I know something or someone, or something about someone, which would make good copy.

'Jon Anderson, *The Stars and Stripes*,' he says. Even as I'm chatting with Jon about things that have nothing to do with Cena's racket, I'm turning over the idea of giving him the story. But I should restrain myself. I have no proof, and even with proof, would it help Ylber or make things worse for him?

'Here to cover the NATO campaign,' says Jon, 'but what's to tell? It's all flyboy stuff, bombing raids from twenty thousand feet up. You know the real story? The real story is Kukes, the refugee exodus, the biggest enforced migration in Europe since the Nazis. Got anything for me, Craig?'

'No. Nothing at this stage, but I'll keep you posted.'

'You sure? You've got the look of a man with something up his sleeve.'

'No. Not a thing.'

He doesn't entirely believe me, and that's okay. Another time, I might let it all out. We bond over our scotch, talk sport and politics and journalism.

'Here's my biggest beef,' says Jon. 'Censorship. I sniff something out, my copy goes upstairs to NATO Command, Wesley Clark's boys take a look and say, "No, no, that's too sensitive, can't let you print that." Clark's in charge of the whole NATO thing. Jesus, the stories I could tell! You know what Albania is? Albania is the Corleones. Biggest business in this country is organised crime. Absolutely.'

'Tell me about it.'

'You've seen the Corleones at work, right?'

'Maybe.'

'You're holding out on me, Craig! Come on, tell me what you've got.'

My beeper goes off. The text says I'm wanted at the Italian Red Cross surgical unit.

'Another time, Jon.'

'I'll be here every day at ten, after the media briefing. Okay?'

'Right.'

As I head for the door Jon calls after me, 'I'll buy you a special – that's a promise! You're not going to hold out on me forever!'

I take my Land Cruiser at a snail's pace through the camps to Italia. There's too much haphazard driving here, with so many children about. Last week I was called to an accident at the German camp, Camp Anamur. A four-year-old boy had been ground into the mud under the wheel of a reversing truck, the driver having paid too little heed to the children playing around him. When we freed him he was dead, his face torn from his skull. As the boy was unidentifiable, mothers raced around frantically to account for their own, each in desperate fear that he was one of theirs. I left before his mother came. I'll take what comes when I'm dealing with the Serbs, but there's something too sickening altogether about children making it to these camps only to be killed or maimed by reckless drivers.

I arrive at the Italia surgical unit in time to see three bulky guys in ill-fitting suits leaving the camp commander's tent. All three are wearing the conspicuous silver badges that distinguish local government officials. Anyone from local government in the camps is a worry. I doubt there's one of them who gives a damn about the refugees. So when I see the camp commander emerge from his tent with a face like thunder, I can guess that this wasn't a social visit. I know the Italian commander. He's a conscientious man, a committed guy, he's proud of what his people achieve here. I've spent time with him over a coffee and I've never seen him upset in the way he is now. He's hissing Italian curses, stamping his boots on the ground. When he catches sight of me, he throws his arms up and gestures for me to follow him. He obviously wants to put some distance between himself and the local officials. Around the back of his tent, he lights up a cigarette, just as Ylber had earlier when he was distressed. And like Ylber, he needs a couple of drags before he can get his emotions under control.

'Craig, Craig, Craig,' he says. 'What do you think, Craig? What do you think those idiots wanted? You saw those people? The three of them?'

'I saw them. Local government, weren't they?'

'No more operations at our unit, that's what they told me. No more surgery.'

'But that's absurd! You're not serious?'

'Look at me! Am I joking? No more surgery! Imbeciles!'

I ask imploringly, 'But why?' and the question is no sooner out of my mouth than I know the answer. This is all Cena. This is all to do with getting the refugees back into Kukes hospital. This is a Cena business decision.

'Why?' says the commander. 'God knows! They say that all refugees crossing the border have to go to the hospital if they need surgery. All of them!'

'But can't you tell them that this is impossible? Kukes can't handle what it gets now. People are going to die like flies.'

'Craig, if I tell them to fuck off, they shut me down. They are criminals!'

The commander is using 'criminals' metaphorically; he doesn't know that he should be using the word literally. Maybe he suspects that there's some benefit to some group or the other in shutting down the Italia surgical unit, but exactly what that benefit is, he hasn't yet realised. I could tell him, but what good would it do? The Italians are here on Albanian soil as guests. If the commander makes a big deal of the closure of his unit, he'll be an unwelcome guest. His superiors will chastise him, perhaps recall him.

'What about the UAE people?' I ask him. 'What about Mahmoudi? When he gets up and running again, does he have to send all his surgical cases to Kukes, too?'

'That's where those bastards are going now!' says the commander. 'To tell Mahmoudi he's finished! We're all finished, Craig. Look at me. I'm almost weeping.'

There's something dangerous working in me. But I don't want to run to the hospital and kick Cena's arse up and down the corridor. The frustration of being obstructed at every turn has taken me into a new zone altogether. I hunker down at the IMC apartment and think the whole situation over. One thing I know without any reflection at all is that I won't walk away from all this shit. I'll find some way to stay here and make the sort of difference that motivated me in the beginning. I've put my life on the line, I've caused Donna God knows how much anguish, I've left my son baffled at his father's absence and, after all this, I'm not going to take up some allocated role in Cena's business plan. And more than anything, what about the Kosovars? They endure hell on earth at the hands of the Serbs, and then fall into the hands of this criminal, Cena, who wants to mint coin from their misery. No, the hell with it,

I'm going to fight back. If the foreign medical teams are a problem for Cena, we're about to become a bigger problem still. And yes, I know that egotism and altruism are close cousins; I know that do-gooders like me are partly motivated by a sense that the world can't do without us, that we're needed, but whatever it takes, I'm staying.

I toss and turn fitfully for the first part of the night, but when I finally fall asleep it's fabulous – rich and deep and nourishing. I wake in the morning with an exultant feeling pulsing through me. It's like the first day of spring.

Chapter 8

The apartment was empty when I went to bed but by the morning the other doctors have found their way home. I muster them for a meeting in the living room. We look pretty raggedy. Difficult to imagine us saving a family of guinea pigs from a dose of rodent flu, let alone some thousands of Kosovo refugees from high-impact ballistic trauma. Roger asks me to speak my mind, and I tell my tale of woe – Cena's racket, the Mafia thugs roaming the hospital, the motive behind the closing down of the Italian surgical unit.

'You're sure about this?' I'm asked.

'Yes, I'm sure. I've witnessed the intimidation. Cena's making a grab for the whole refugee intake so he can fleece them.'

Another colleague nods and endorses the claims I'm making. 'I've seen it too. I didn't want to believe it. Craig's right.'

'Oh, there's no question, he's right!' Roger exclaims. 'I've heard of patients bleeding to death because they couldn't pay two hundred deutschmarks to the Albanian doctors. Believe me, this place is as twisted as Craig says.'

After another half-hour of desultory discussion, most of the doctors leave to catch up on sleep or for another stint at the remaining medical units. Roger and I have been drafted to establish the path ahead.

The immediate path ahead leads to the American Bar and a decision, ultimately, to go to the UNHCR people and spill the beans about Cena and his associates. Roger in his bustling way is more exercised about the whole grotesque business than I am. I've chilled off a little out of necessity. I'm not like Roger; I don't have a headlong way of throwing myself into a fray. I'm more of a strategist.

We've missed this morning's briefing but we fashion a plan to make our case at tomorrow's briefing. Roger has a commitment at the IMC medical depot in Kukes hospital to distribute drug packages and medical equipment, and I have a commitment to more sleep. I promise to meet him at the hospital later in the afternoon.

Two hours later I'm feeling better for the snooze. I top up with coffee and Oreos then stroll across the barren patch between the apartment block and the hospital to meet up with Roger again. Even from a distance, I can see that something weird is unfolding at the IMC depot. Roger is pacing up and down outside the gates in an agitated way; three or four other members of the IMC team are standing behind him like sentinels. As I get closer, I see that the expression on Roger's face is as remote as it could be from the geniality that he's known for. He looks like an attack dog in a ferocious mood.

'What's happening?'

'Good thing you're here, Craig. Might need you. Those thieving arseholes tried to –'

'Whoa! Who are we talking about?'

'From the hospital! Doctors, nurses! Can you believe it? They tried to break into the depot. Take the drugs and equipment and sell everything on the black market. Over my fucking dead body! They had guns, Craig! Even the women! Pistols, Kalashnikovs. Arseholes!'

'Jesus Christ! Where are they now?'

Roger gives a short laugh, like a baritone bark.

'Stripped down to my jocks and ran straight at 'em, screaming like a lunatic. Frightened the hell out of 'em! Boy, did they scatter!'

'You stripped to your jocks? Are you nuts?'

'Craig, sometimes you just have to do what your mojo tells you to do.'

'They could have shot you!'

'Could've. But they didn't.'

We leave the local IMC staff to guard the depot and get some coffee into Roger at the hospital cafeteria. He's still fulminating when I excuse myself and go looking for Ylber. If I end up handing Jon Anderson the story of Cena's scam I'll need to give Ylber fair warning. Along the way I glance into the Emergency Room. Twenty or so untreated patients have been left whimpering, moaning, bleeding. I grab two Albanian doctors and demand that they provide some treatment. They comply, with bad grace.

I find Ylber offering sympathy to the relatives of a patient who has just died. I bide my time until he's finished then tell him in an urgent whisper all about the siege of the IMC depot. Ylber listens quietly, but the furrows in his face seem to me to have deepened over the past two days. I decide against raising the possibility of putting the story in *The Stars and Stripes*.

'I'll let the UNHCR officials know about Cena's scam, at the briefing tomorrow morning. That's a promise,' I tell him. Ylber leans closer.

'Scam?'

'Cena's racket. You know, ripping money off the refugees. Stealing. The Mafia connection. All of it.'

'Craig, I thank you for this. With all my heart. If nothing is done, we are no better than the Serbs. But you must take care. Cena hates you.'

Ylber insists on giving me the contact details of some honest local officials and some KLA muscle boys in Kukes who could come to my aid if I needed extra security. 'Honest local officials' sounds like a contradiction in terms, but I accept the details gratefully. Ylber's final request is one that he raises with evident sorrow. He says that we should break off contact with each other for the time being. 'It's my family, Craig. Cena will look for a way to put pressure on both of us if he believes that I'm giving you information. I don't want a knife held to the throat of my children. My friend, I hope you will forgive me. You have told me that you have a son?'

'Yes, Ylber. Very young. Only five years old.'

'Then you understand?'

'Perfectly.'

We shake hands, briefly, surreptitiously. Losing Ylber in this way, for however long, deprives me of a great source of consolation. Our friendship has become collateral damage in Cena's cowardly war on the refugees. Why it should be, I don't know, but as I slowly walk back to the IMC apartment I have an uneasy feeling around my heart – a kind of heaviness, of foreboding.

The foreboding and unease is relieved as soon as I walk through the door of the apartment. Roger greets me in his animated way and tells me that he has good news. He's secured details of a tour of the camps around Kukes tomorrow by none other than Kofi Annan, the UN Secretary General. He has a copy of Annan's schedule that tells us exactly where he will be and at exactly what time. We can ambush him and highlight our disgust with the refugee racket. This is Kofi Annan, the Big Boss! Cena can't touch him. I can barely contain my glee. A host of media people the size of the Serb army will be following Annan about, avid for something more than the sort of anodyne expressions of hope and goodwill that you get on these occasions.

But this needs planning. We can't jump out of the crowd and shriek a few slogans like students dressed as gum leaves at a G8 summit. What we need is a refugee whose story exemplifies the callousness with which many of the Kosovars are treated in Kukes. Not to put it too indelicately, we need a prop if this drama we're plotting is going to work.

Roger and I drive down to Camp Italia in search of the best possible horror story. With the assistance of Colonel Toccafundi, we find the ideal refugee in the Médecins Sans Frontières camp – if 'ideal' is not too tactless a word in this context. Arjana is in her mid-twenties. What she has endured is so appalling that I repent of the jaunty way in which I sat down to listen to her story, hoping that she could provide enough nightmarish detail to send a jolt through the jaded press corps.

I outline our plan to Arjana, trying hard not to sound as if I'm involving her in a dangerous conspiracy. She has no objections. She listens with the trusting expression of a person to whom tricks and dodges are completely alien. She nods every so often as my words are translated. She's even able to make me a gift of a soft smile.

'We want your story to touch the heart of Kofi Annan. We want him to take action against the criminals.'

'Yes, that would be good.'

'Everything we say will be the truth.'

'Yes, the truth. Good.'

The sorrow in Arjana's eyes is so deep that I almost want to lift her in my arms and hug her. She has seen her children die, but there isn't a hint of hatred in her demeanour for those who killed her kids. I limit myself to holding her hand in both of mine. Her expression recalls those that painters of the Renaissance strove to render on the face of the Virgin Mary cradling the body of her son. When I leave her, she nods and rewards me with another gentle smile.

I wish I had the leisure to spend a full day reflecting on the morality of what I'm doing, but I don't. Am I being insensitive here? Does the fact that I might be exploiting her story in a good cause mitigate my offence, if it is an offence?

I spend the evening scripting what I'll say tomorrow. Extemporaneity has its place, but not in a situation like this. We'll only get one shot at attracting attention. I write an initial draft, refine it, try out a second draft, rehearse it.

❖ ❖ ❖

Arjana is a 24-year-old Kosovar from a village near Kusnin, 10 kilometres over the border. Her village had been attacked by a Serb paramilitary unit: her husband and two children, a boy aged three and a girl aged five, murdered in front of their house as she watched on. Heavily pregnant at the time, she escaped into the mountains with several other villagers, including her mother. While on the run, she gave birth to a girl, Besijana, her only surviving child. Two days later, in a forest near the front line, she and her group were caught in the crossfire between Serb and KLA forces. She was shot in the right ankle, sustaining a compound fracture and, after walking for two days with the help of her mother, safely reached the border crossing at Morina. From there she was taken directly to the Kukes Hospital. Here the staff demanded money and, unable to pay, she was denied treatment and discharged. She was then taken to the Italia Camp where she had surgery and subsequently made a rapid recovery.

✧ ✧ ✧

The crucial sentence is, 'Here the staff demanded money and, unable to pay, she was denied treatment and discharged.' Should I emphasise more than I have the culpability of the Kukes hospital staff? Because I want Annan to pick up on what I'm saying. This is a *J'accuse!* thing, not mere data. And another thing: am I hoping for too much from Annan? He doesn't have a reputation as a human dynamo; on television, he always seems to me a little zombie-like. The UN is a vast bureaucracy, after all. In any big bureaucracy (like the medical bureaucracies I deal with in Adelaide) the great priority of the bureaucrats is not to fling themselves about in strenuous endeavour but rather to watch their backs. They form alliances of mutual interest, one scratches another's back knowing that the owner of the back he is scratching will be obliged to reciprocate.

The enemy of all bureaucrats is activity, because activity can lead to change, to innovation. Inactivity is the safer option. The head of the vast bureaucracy of the UN is the Bureaucrat-in-Chief, Kofi Annan, and he certainly would not have been elected to that position if he were likely to rock the boat. He would have to be utterly predictable; he would have to have demonstrated a capacity for minting platitudes without ever showing the slightest embarrassment over using a hundred words to say nothing whatever. Is this guy really going to spring into action when I take the stage and make a relatively mild attack on people who really should be tried as war criminals? Maybe I should go for the jugular. Or would I just be dismissed as a hothead, a nutcase? Hell, I don't know. I'll stick with the script I've got and hope for the best.

We've scheduled our ambush for Annan's 2p.m. visit to the MSF camp, but I also attend the 8a.m. UNHCR meeting. It's a sit-down event. I take a seat next to an Austrian guy I've glimpsed about the camps, a senior aide to Daniel Endres, the Chief Emergency Co-ordinator. I introduce myself, mention that I'm the surgical co-ordinator.

'Nice to meet you. How are things going?'

I'm not always alert to the message-within-the-message when I'm talking with bureaucrats. I take it that this pleasant Austrian really wants to know how things are going but it's soon apparent that his real message is, 'Tell me that everything is going as well as can be expected and then be quiet.' I give him a rapid summary of the grotesque state of affairs in the camps and tell him that the corruption makes me sick. A look of panic takes hold of his features; his eyes widen, his lips tighten. He glances quickly over his shoulder at an Albanian official seated behind us then leans close to me. 'You should not concern yourself with these issues. Not at all. Things are very complicated here. We are guests of the Albanians. Do not get involved.'

'What do you mean? I am involved.'

'Listen to me. Do not get involved. Please don't mention this to me again.'

I draw back and study the diplomat with what I hope looks like disdain. Don't get involved? I've just told him that people – actual human beings! – are dying in Kukes hospital because of hideous neglect and he wants me to pipe down? As if my concerns were in poor taste? I'd been thinking that UNHCR officials would stick up for me when I come out with my scripted *J'accuse!* this afternoon. Am I being too optimistic? I glance around the room at the audience, searching for the glitter of rage in another set of eyes. Surely I'm not the only person here who's both worried and angry?

After the briefing I take a shift in the emergency room at Kukes hospital, but even as I'm working I'm coping with the disappointment of the senior aide's response. Because this is the way that the atrocities we read about in newspapers are perpetuated: mediating organisations such as the UN cease to think of human beings as human beings, but rather as part of a problem that can be addressed with meetings and communiqués. Think of Gaza, of Rwanda, of Srebrenica, of a dozen other places. People were blown to pieces, hacked to pieces, burned to cinders, and all that we know of the flesh and blood beings who suffered so badly is the tally of dead buried in some long-forgotten report in the UN archives. But each person who died had a story to tell of the ordinary things that people do – cook, eat, care for a household, bear children, work in the fields or in a factory. And each ordinary story ended in horror. Don't these officials understand what human beings experience when they have a foot blown off? It's not like stubbing your toe: the agony is unspeakable; bones are shattered, flesh torn apart. In the grip of trauma like that, most people would choose death in a heartbeat if it would end the pain. And then there's the stuff that gets into the heads of people in a war like this one. Arjana saw her two children murdered. That's a boy of three and a girl of five. And her husband, murdered at the same time. Think of what she had invested in those three lives; the care, the love, the sheer hard work of running a family. They didn't die of an illness or in an accident: soldiers came to her village, to her house and applied knives and guns to the flesh of the people she loved. We can't always stop murder of that sort; we can't outlaw the passions that lead to murder. But we can do more than whisper in an anxious voice, 'Don't get involved.'

I meet up again with Arjana at the MSF camp early in the afternoon and run through the script. She murmurs her approval from the stretcher on which she lies, and her thanks. Arjana's no firebrand. Her sorrow is evident in her every expression, in every sentence she speaks. My intensity and urgency and anger would give an onlooker the impression that *I* am the one who has been betrayed and abused; that *I* am about to raise my hands to heaven and demand justice. But if that onlooker looked more closely, he or she would see the depth of suffering in Arjana's dark eyes, such as could never be discovered in my privileged blue eyes.

An MSF doctor joins us as we wait for the Secretary General to arrive. Angela's her name – I've met her before.

She's as motivated as I am, and as sick of the corruption. She speaks gently to Arjana, promises her that we will achieve something here today. Arjana is courteous in her response, but I don't detect any anticipation in her manner. It may be that she has done away with hoping and believing and is simply going along with our theatrics so as not to hurt our feelings. Jesus, I couldn't blame her if she found it difficult to imagine justice rising above the hills like a new dawn. But maybe she'll get a surprise today. Maybe.

At 2p.m. on the dot, the tent flap swings open and in strides Kofi Annan followed by a grand entourage numbering twenty – local officials, Albanian federal officials, bodyguards, UNHCR envoys. Kofi's eyes give the impression of being lidless – a little bit disconcerting. Three other bedridden refugees have been carried into the tent on stretchers to receive the benediction of the Secretary General, and they get it, a few words in Annan's West African accented English, in which the final 'g' is dropped from verbs in the continuous tense.

And now it's our turn. The Secretary General turns his lidless gaze on Arjana and on me. He bows slightly in order to offer his hand to Arjana, then shakes my hand.

'And what can you tell me of this young woman's situation?' he says.

Without any preamble, I leap into my scripted response. 'Arjana is a twenty-four-year-old Kosovar from a town near Kusnin . . .'

The Secretary General listens attentively. Required as I am to get the words right, I don't have the chance to study the response amongst the Albanian officials. But there are certain tell-tale signs that any speaker addressing an audience picks up in split-second glimpses; somebody glancing at a watch or a clock on the wall; another person frowning. My unanalysed impression is of growing displeasure amongst the Albanian officials. And I can't be sure, but Kofi Annan's gaze seems to be suggesting that my short speech is not quite short enough to win his approval. 'From there, she was taken directly to the Kukes hospital. Here the staff demanded money and because Arjana was unable to pay – she had no money at all – she was denied treatment and discharged. Her ankle was shattered; she was in terrible pain – but nothing. Denied treatment, discharged.'

It's quiet, except for the shuffling of feet, a few embarrassed coughs. The media people with their microphones and tape recorders and cameras are waiting for some response from the Secretary General. I don't know what's going on in Annan's head, but he doesn't look all that moved to me. He takes a step towards Arjana, glances at her for two seconds, then at me for less than that. The media bustles forward, hoping for a denunciation of the local Mafia maybe, or a promise to take matters in hand. 'This was a terrible tragedy,' says the Secretary General, and moves away with his entourage without a backward glance. Twenty seconds after my speech ends, the tent is emptying. Angela bounds to her feet and shrieks at the retreating entourage, 'Arseholes! Stupid arseholes!' Cena is here, embedded in the official party. As he passes me, he gives me the look of a barracuda circling a school of sardines. Another of the Albanian officials whispers in the ear of Cena's bodyguard, and the bodyguard gives me a quick, appraising glance.

My hands have formed fists without my knowing. God knows what the expression on my face suggests, but Arjana feels the need to intervene. We have an interpreter on hand; it was our hope that Kofi Annan would address a few questions to Arjana – a futile hope as it turns out. Arjana speaks softly to the interpreter and her words are relayed to me.

'Craig, do not be angry. I knew nothing would happen. It's all right.'

'I'm sorry, Arjana. I'm terribly sorry.'

'No, no. Don't be upset. I am not an important person.'

Arjana is carried away on her stretcher. Angela and I exchange looks of despair.

'Not an important person,' says Angela. 'That sums it up. If anything is to be done, Craig, it must come from us.'

'Obviously.'

'Keep in touch with me, Craig.'

'Of course.'

The only way ahead is to get the story of the Kukes hospital scandal into *The Stars and Stripes*. And that's what I intend to do. I'll contact Jon Anderson. But oh God, the look on Arjana's face when she was carried out of the tent. Not despair, just resignation; acceptance. She never expected anything from our theatre stunt. She was being kind to us, allowing us to exercise our moral outrage, but she herself is a long, long way past moral outrage. How many years of peace and justice and decent government would it take for Arjana to develop a sense of entitlement again?

Chapter 9

It's mid-May now and I'm well into my third week here, spending as much time as I can personally reviewing the incoming patients at Kukes hospital. I have no alternative. Without deutschmarks or dollars, you could arrive at Emergency carrying your guts in a plastic bucket and get turned away. I've been shuffling the worst cases to the back door in a stealthy manner and conveying them to the Camp Italia surgical unit. For the time being, the camp commander at Italia is ignoring the Albanian officials who want to shut him down.

I spirited a sixty-two-year old Kosovar with a gangrenous leg across to Italia this morning and amputated in the afternoon. He's going to make it. The crooks at Kukes had denied him treatment. You can sell coke and smack and speed right out in the open, while Cena's thugs fleece refugees with the blessing of the police. Meanwhile, I'm sneaking out of back doors and looking over my shoulder to save innocent lives. What a world.

Late in the afternoon I meet a Kosovar television cameraman, Milaim Seka, who's nursing a shrapnel wound from a Serb mortar. He was filming a KLA training camp inside Kosovo. His injuries are no big deal; I attend to him back at the apartment. Once he's patched up, he asks me if he can use the satellite phone to call his wife in Sweden. Hearing his wife's voice reduces him to tears; I'm watching him tremble as the emotion surges through him and all at once I'm missing Donna again, comparing my motives in being here with Seka's. Kosovo is his country. His emotional investment has a great deal more gravity than mine.

A belief in the sanctity of universal human rights is why I'm here. Seka has no option but to be here, and no option but to weep for the life he's missing out on back in Sweden. Me, I've left Donna wondering whether she'll ever see me again. And then there's Jackson. If I wanted to be unambiguously noble, maybe I should be standing beside that boy and being a proper father.

The luxury of introspection is snatched from me by a request to report to the Morina border crossing where thousands more refugees are emerging from the forests and stumbling towards safety. The Morina crossing is like one of those creeks in the outback of Australia that flood only when there's a catastrophic downpour hundreds of kilometres away. When the Serbs are enjoying one of their festivals of homicide further upstream, the refugees in torrents swell what in other times is a trickle at the crossing. So once again we go lurching along the track to Morina – Land Cruisers and ambulances – and once again each of us sequestered in a private dread that some Serb commander might amuse himself by taking out our convoy with artillery.

Spring at this latitude and height above sea level can become very warm, although the nights are often freezing. Today it's hot, like Adelaide in the same season; a perfect environment for infections. I'm expecting limbs tumid with gangrene, I'm expecting amputations galore. Our first sight of the refugees as we approach the bridge is of women and children wrapped up in blankets even though it's thirty-five degrees Celsius. Absurd. It's explained to me that they are carrying everything they were permitted to leave with, all their clothing, every scrap of bed covering. The most efficient way of doing this is to wear all they own.

Beneath the blankets are the inevitable wounds, mostly shrapnel and gunshot and the occasional infant who has died in transit from suffocation or dehydration. This wave of refugees is from the Suhareka region. The whole area has been under fierce attack by Serb regulars and paramilitaries for the past two days. The stories I'm told as I organise the surgical teams and ambulance evacuation are all versions of those I've heard before.

And as before, I'm moved by the need of the refugees to tell their stories to someone from the broader world; to see them preserved. When an old man, who gives his name as Musli Jaagh from the village of Slapuzane, speaks in a halting way of what happened in his town, I realise that this is perhaps the first of many, many times he will need to put into words what he witnessed. As his story is translated, I offer very few comments other than those that show that I believe him and that I am listening closely. I doubt that he wants to reduce me to tears or shock me. He wants me to hear. As he speaks, I write down his words in my notebook under the date, 21 May.

'They killed fourteen from my village. Three were children. They shot the children first so that their fathers and their mothers could see. They shot the parents of these children with some others of my village. I don't know why they chose those three children. I don't know why they chose any of us. Only God can say. The one who was the commander said it was punishment. He said we allowed three men of the KLA to stay in Slapuzane.

'The three men of the KLA they kept somewhere else. When they brought them out, they could not stand on their legs. They had blood and marks on their bodies. I think they were kept away from us while the Serbs punished them. The commander told his soldiers to pour diesel fuel on the three men of the KLA. The men were tied and could not run. The soldiers set fire to them. We were not permitted to cover our eyes and our ears. We were made to watch and listen. My tears are for those men and for the three children and the people of my village who were shot.'

Fifteen hundred of the eight thousand Kosovars who crossed the border today are men released by the Serbs from prisons and detention camps. Why the Serbs have chosen to release these men is not at all clear. One possibility is that detaining a large number of men ties up Serb soldiers and paramilitaries. Another is that the Serbs – or the particular commanders in this region – can now see the distinct chance of the NATO bombing eventually forcing a Serb withdrawal from Kosovo, and the alternative to releasing the men – that is, killing them – would require the speedy disposal of fifteen hundred bodies. Everything I have witnessed here inclines me to think that the Serbs would have no hesitation in murdering fifteen hundred Kosovars, or fifteen thousand, if they thought they could conceal the killings. Whatever the Serbs' motives, mercy is not amongst them.

Many of the Kosovar men released from detention show signs of gross physical trauma. Even without the corroboration of the men themselves, I would say that the blade wounds and overlaid bruising (bruises on top of other bruises in patterns associated with repeated contusion) are the result of torture. Fractured and amputated fingers are also common amongst these men. Damaging the hands of men of fighting age in this way is a trademark of the Serb paramilitaries. A badly fractured hand will be an impediment to using a weapon for life; a lost finger or two or three, even more so.

It's after nine at night by the time the border is finally closed. I'm exhausted, body and brain. But I can't do what I desperately want to do and climb into my sleeping bag when we get back to Kukes because even more than sleep, I want to find Jon Anderson and get the story of Cena's rotten trade into *The Stars and Stripes*.

Kukes is no hive of activity after nightfall. Except for dealers moving smack on the pavements, what commerce there is in the city is closed. But the American Bar is open, as it has to be, because there are a lot of people needing a beer or a scotch or a Danny's Special after a day like this one. And Jon Anderson is here. When he sees me, he knows in an instant by the look on my face that whatever I was holding back from him is not going to be held back any longer. I don't even bother to order a drink before I sit down with Jon, but a beer is brought to our table while I'm speaking.

'Okay, listen – you said I had a story in me,' I tell Jon. 'Are you ready?'

'Am I ready? Craig buddy, I'm your property. Let's hear it.'

Jon flips open his notebook and writes the date, May 22, at the top of a blank page; the story comes flowing out of me. He nods, he lets out little exclamations of astonishment, sometimes he grunts in disgust at what he's hearing. But he only lets eye contact with me lapse for a few seconds at a time as he writes. He doesn't want me to stop, or become sidetracked, or surrender to the balm of the beer and grow drowsy. He knows that this is the story he sensed was in me; he knows that his patience is paying off.

'Okay, here's the story,' he says. 'Lots of bad guys in the hospital here. Albanian doctors and nurses won't do a damned thing for the refugees who check in unless they get money. Doesn't matter what sort of injuries the refugees have – no money, no surgery, no medicine, no nothing. Okay?'

'Not every Albanian doctor and nurse. Some. I know one Albanian doctor who's put his life on the line to treat refugees without asking for a cent.'

'Okay, most then – can I say most?'

'Maybe half. No, more than half.'

'Right, fifty percent is what we'll go with. Could be sixty, seventy, but we'll play it safe and say fifty. And the guy behind this whole racket, that's Cena, right? The hospital director?'

'That's right.'

'And Cena, he has ties to the Mafia? He pays them a cut?'

'He probably has to,' I say. 'Nothing bent can happen in Kukes without the Mafia taking a cut. That's what my Albanian doctor friend tells me.'

'Craig, here's the thing. I need pictures, I need to see the bad guys at work myself. A story like this, my chief has to know that the reporter who wrote it saw things with his own eyes. He's going to demand a really, really high standard of accuracy. We can't say our Albanian allies are full of shit without being sure. See what I'm saying, Craig?'

'You want to walk around the wards taking pictures? I can't see Cena agreeing to that.'

'I need those pictures, Craig.'

I nurse my beer and think about it. Jon is entirely in the right to demand proof, but if he's going into the hospital, we'll have to do it in a cloak-and-dagger way.

'I'll kit you out as a doctor,' I tell him. 'White coat, give you a badge of some sort, drape a stethoscope around your neck. Will you be taking the pictures?'

'No way. I'll bring a photographer.'

'You realise that, if Cena's boys spot you, they might shoot you?'

Jon grinned. 'Small price to pay. This is a huge story.'

So next day we costume up and get to work. We go briskly about the hospital as if we're way too busy to bother with anything like scams and extortion, but Jon and his photographer see everything they need to see. Cena and his boys are so farcically blatant in their rottenness that the whole racket could be seen as comical if it were not so tragic.

Jon writes the story up and sends it to Wesley Clark's team at NATO headquarters a couple of hours after our tour of the hospital. He's been careful to describe only what he's seen, or to quote me as a witness to things he hasn't seen. Against the odds the Chief of Staff, Wesley Clark, gives his approval for the story to run. The next day, *The Stars and Stripes* publishes the story on the front page.

Monday 24 May 1999

REFUGEE DEATH TRAP

Surgeon says hospital uses 'ethnic and monetary triage'

Jon R. Anderson, Staff writer
KUKES, Albania

At the old, rundown hospital in Kukes, people are dying – not for the lack of doctors or medical supplies. Instead, they are dying because local officials are extorting what money they can from the refugees, who are pouring into Kukes and leaving those who can't pay to languish, foreign physicians say.

"The Kukes Hospital is a death trap," said Craig Jurisevic, an Australian surgeon working in Kukes.

At the same time, local authorities refuse to allow those who can't afford care to be evacuated into medical facilities set up at refugee camps, he said.

"The Albanian Health Ministry demands that all operations be done at the Kukes Hospital," Jurisevic said. "But if they can't pay for it, they don't get treated." A Canadian emergency room physician, Dr Roger Lake, also said the poor were going untreated. "They have invented two new forms of triage here; ethnic and monetary triage," said Lake, who works with Jurisevic at the Kukes Hospital.

An Albanian government official denied the allegations Sunday. "I called the hospital in Kukes, and they said there is no problem up there," Musa Ulqini, a spokesman for the Albanian Ministry of Information said to an interpreter.

But the doctor said at least three people have died because they could not pay:

- One 60-year-old Kosovar who managed to crawl across the border after being shot in the chest died without treatment because he had no money, Jurisevic said. "The doctors here refused to operate on him. He just bled to death," he said.

- An 18-month-old Kosovar baby died of pneumonia two weeks ago after local doctors refused to give it antibiotics and oxygen.

- A 25-year-old Albanian man also died from sniper wounds after doctors learnt that he had no money.

Lake said he thinks part of the problem is that Albanian doctors only make about $80 a month. With a huge influx of refugees, the doctors' workload has skyrocketed as well.

"So they feel like they shouldn't have to work more if they are not going to get paid more," Lake said. "This is the end of the world here. It's the lowest of the low. I see a lot of my job as just getting people out of here."

Kukes, in Albania's rugged northern frontier with Yugoslavia, has exploded with refugees in the two months since NATO began its air campaign against Slobodan Milosevic's forces. More than 100,000 Kosovars have found sanctuary here living with host families in the large refugee centres.

The camps have set up hospitals to treat the sick and wounded. But Albanian officials are refusing to allow the camps to treat critical care patients there. "They say they want to ensure the patients are getting the best possible care," Jurisevic said.

But this policy keeps them from getting that care, he said. The United Arab Emirates camp "has a $1 million US-built mobile emergency medical facility that can't be used because the local officials are trying to make money from these people," Jurisevic said.

The Italians have a similar facility at another refugee camp.

Jurisevic is the senior regional medical coordinator in the area for the International Medical Corps, which helps manage the 30 international physicians working at refugee camps in Kukes.

The dirty two-story 240-bed hospital in Kukes, plaster walls crumbling onto dirty floors, is already filled with patients who receive little attention from the staff. Those without family to take care of them lie in their own urine and faeces for days and sometimes weeks. Nurses say it's not their job to do that kind of clean-up work. There is usually no running water. A dead cow rotted in front of the hospital for two days recently before being carved up by refugees who left only its four hooves behind.

"If this were the United States, these people would be put in jail for second-degree murder once a week," Jurisevic said of the hospital staff. "They're worse than the Serbs."

Jurisevic has appealed to U.N. officials for help, but explained, "Their hands are tied. They can't force the Albanians to do anything."

So, instead, Jurisevic is appealing to NATO for help. "We need the military to lean on these people. If the Albanian Government will listen to anybody, it will be NATO," he said.

Lt. Col Andy Williams, a spokesman for NATO Albania Force Headquarters in the central coastal city of Durres, said on Sunday that NATO plans to press the issue.

In the meantime, Jurisevic and his colleagues in Kukes sneak some patients out to refugee camps for treatment, or conduct operations by themselves on the sly.

"We had one man lie in the emergency room for three days, slowly bleeding to death", Jurisevic said. "The Albanian doctors wouldn't treat him. When one of our doctors found him, we were able to sneak him out to the Italian Camp and get him evacuated."

Those who were treated by the Albanians are often little better off, he said. "The first day I got here, three weeks ago, I saw a little boy whose hand had been blown apart by a hand grenade detonator. They were cutting away his flesh and tendons with scissors without any anaesthetic." On Saturday afternoon Jurisevic amputated the leg of an elderly man whose foot had turned gangrenous from improper care. He had to perform the operation while the hospital director was out of town for the day.

Bones could be seen protruding out the blackened flesh before Jurisevic sawed the leg off below the knee. "The Albanian doctors said he just needed bandages," he said.

(Volume 58, Number 37)

✢ ✢ ✢

We meet at the bar on the morning of publication, Jon and I. Reading through the piece thrills me in a complex way. Having the story out there is fabulous, but I'm also enjoying the thought of Cena reading it, giving orders to have a horse's head left in my sleeping bag.

'Hope you're proud of yourself,' says Jon.

'Very.'

'They're going to cut your throat, Craig.'

'Small price to pay, as a dauntless reporter once said to me.'

But Cena's not going to cut my throat. The story's in *The Stars and Stripes*. It's a message from Wesley Clark. If NATO didn't want to take Cena on, the story would never have seen the light of day.

Chapter 10

This is fantastic. I'm listening to a NATO media officer at the morning briefing informing all of us here that, 'certain new arrangements will apply to the management of medical treatment for refugees crossing the border into Albania from Kosovo.' From now on, the NATO guy says, all refugees in need of medical care, including surgery, will be directed to the facilities of Camp Italia and the surgical unit of the UAE.

Two days from the publication of the article Cena's scam comes to an end.

I shake Jon's hand and congratulate all those involved. We head off to an eatery in the centre of Kukes for chicken and a bottle of beer to celebrate. Jon leans over and asks, 'Craig, have you heard of the term, "exit strategy"?'

'I have indeed. Why do you ask?'

'I'm going to Tirana tomorrow. Cena's not going to shoot us, but some Mafia guy would be happy to plug both of us for a hundred bucks and taxi fare.'

This seems unlikely to me – or it does until I chat with a local by the name of Fadil, a friend of an Albanian doctor I know from one of the IMC clinics in Kukes. He says the word on the street is that Cena and the Mafia are homicidal about *The Stars and Stripes* story. The new arrangements are going to ruin their racket, sure, but their fury goes further than that. They're taking the whole thing personally.

'No Albanian would do what you have done, Craig. We know how things work. If you get in the way of business, the people in the gangs never forget. Better for you if you get out of Kukes.'

'You're serious?'

'Very serious, Craig.'

'But where can I go? This is Kukes, it isn't London, or somewhere. There isn't an infinite number of alternatives.'

'Into one of the camps,' says Fadil. 'That would be best. It's much harder for them to kill you in a camp.'

I'm getting a bit exasperated with the whole thing. I'm not ready for the Apocalypse, as it turns out. All I did was pass on what I knew to a journalist.

'Fadil, I want to be sure that you really believe this is necessary. I don't want to go carting my sleeping bag all over Albania unless this revenge thing is real.'

Fadil looks at me in that intense, unblinking way that people rely on when they're either telling you the absolute truth, or a carefully composed lie.

'Craig, trust me. I am Albanian, you are from somewhere else. Where are you from?'

'Australia.'

'Australia. Okay. Australians are nice people, sure, but about Albania, nice Australian people know nothing. Listen to me. Cena thinks you are a thief. He thinks you are stealing money from his business. You see?'

'Yes, I see.'

'In Albania when someone steals from us, we don't go to the police. The police are themselves thieves. In Albania when someone steals from us, we find a gun and shoot him. Okay? You are a thief. They will shoot you. Okay?'

'Got it.'

'There's a man you must meet. An important man. Have you got time to come with me now?'

The meeting place Fadil has in mind is the American Bar. We find a table in a corner away from the crowd. I'm glancing around, wondering who it is I'm supposed to be meeting, unable to pick out anyone amongst the chattering boozers whom I haven't noticed in the past. Or maybe a few, but nobody with any mystery about him commensurate with the spookiness of Fadil's build-up. Five minutes pass, nothing eventful happens. Fadil isn't saying a word. He's sitting over his beer, the same as me, looking as bland as he possibly can. Then out of the crowd emerges a tall, balding fellow, unremarkable in appearance. Without introducing himself, he sits at our table. I take my cue from Fadil and react as if this new arrival is someone we've known for years who happened to be passing by.

'Good morning, Dr Jurisevic. Pleased to make your acquaintance.'

This man's flawless English immediately impresses me. It suggests that he's well educated, and I am culturally conditioned to trust the well educated. It's rubbish, of course; Cena, certifiably subhuman, has degrees and diplomas, no doubt.

'Likewise,' I say, and reach my hand over the table. This unprepossessing fellow tells me that his name is Hosnje

Hoxha, and that he is a thoracic physician. He'd been practising in Kosovo, in Prizren, until a few months ago when he was compelled to flee to Kukes. He trained in Germany and the US.

'I read the story in the newspaper,' he says. 'I congratulate you. It was a very brave thing to do. A great service to my countrymen and women. A very great service.'

'Thank you. I'm glad it's done some good.'

'Yes, it has done some good. And now in return, I hope to do you some good, Dr Jurisevic.'

'Craig,' I say. 'How do you mean?'

'They will kill you, Craig. You understand that?'

'Yes, I understand that,' I say with a sigh. 'Fadil has made the same point. But here's what I don't understand. How is killing me going to help Cena and the Mafia? NATO's all over his racket now. Things are not going to get better for Cena just because I'm dead, surely?'

Hoxha shakes his head and smiles, not exactly in a patronising way, but almost. He can see that I will need instruction.

'If this goes as far as criminal prosecution, Craig, you will find it difficult to testify against these people if you are dead. At a trial, NATO might enter a deposition based on the story. But without you in court, the defence would claim that the story was fabricated. A quest for glory. Something that you and the writer cooked up. You see?'

'And for that they'd risk killing me?'

Hoxha holds my gaze. 'Dr Jurisevic – Craig – the risk for them is not in killing you. The risk is not to kill you. That is the sad truth about Albania, I'm afraid. Killing somebody is cheap insurance.'

He lets this warning have its effect on me – and it does convince me in a way that nothing has before, that my life is genuinely in danger – then he tells me, quietly, and still holding my gaze, that he is a KLA commander.

'Is that so?'

I lean back in my chair and study Hoxha with what I have to say is enhanced respect. The perfect English and the medical qualifications impressed me, as I've said, but the combat credentials stir something deeper in me. Is my response to do with this wretched feeling of impotence that comes over me every so often – the feeling of not doing enough? Is there something working in me that makes me think of a Kalashnikov as a more effective utensil of intervention than a surgical kit? Just at this moment, gazing back at Hoxha, I'm more aware than ever that I am not a pacifist by temperament. My abhorrence of injustice explains why I am here much more than any philosophical conviction about peace. In the simplest possible terms, I hate to see the bad guys get away with murder. But if the bad guys get clobbered on the battlefield, I can accommodate that. I'd still patch up the wounded, but I would do so without the smouldering anger I experience when I'm patching up people who had no opportunity to fight back.

'There's a KLA recruitment place here in Kukes. Are you associated with that?'

'Yes, I am.'

'And how are the recruitments faring? Are men joining up?'

'More than you can imagine. Hundreds every week. And why would they not? Are they to sit in camps listening to stories of murder every day? Just listen and never retaliate?

Never fight for their rights as human beings, as citizens of Kosovo?'

'No, of course not.'

'You know, Craig, I have seen doctors come and go from Kukes – doctors from America, from Britain, Canada, France – and the work they do is splendid. Splendid. We are grateful to them. But I have never seen anyone do what you did. And so now I tell you that it is very important to move into a camp where we can protect you. A camp closer to the front line where we have the men to keep you safe. Will you come?'

'I'll have to think about it.'

Hoxha nods, accepting my caution as reasonable.

'I'll hope to see you under our protection, then,' he says.

At that moment, the BBC World Service news bulletin commences on the television screen above the bar. Someone reaches up and turns the volume to full so the presenter can be heard above the shouting and laughter. The BBC news is our only source of reliable information about what's happening right here in our backyard. The briefings we get from Jamie O'Shea, the NATO media officer, are always maddeningly circumlocutious and end up revealing nothing whatever.

What the BBC presenter has to say is brief: the Serbs have ordered the closure of all border crossings with Albania, to take effect over the next twenty-four hours. The presenter goes on to say that NATO air strikes have been targeting Serb positions near the Kosovo-Albania border for two days now. No connection between the two items is offered, but Hoxha touches my arm to get my attention and tells me that the Serbs are regrouping after suffering heavy losses in a significant clash with KLA forces in the Has region around Mount Pastrik.

'They have to use their troops to fight us. They can't spare any to clear the towns. They close the borders in retaliation.'

It strikes me that Fadil and Hoxha are now talking as if I am one of them. They would not talk in this way to someone who was impartial, someone whose sole task was to patch up the wounded. They take it for granted that I have a partisan interest in a KLA victory. Now, I have never conceded that I am on the side of the KLA and I'm not comfortable with the assumption. But I'm even more uncomfortable with the prospect of having my head shot off by a Mafia hitman.

'I'll get back to you about moving into a camp,' I say, and get to my feet. Hoxha shakes my hand.

'We know about the people in the hospital who are exploiting the refugees,' he says quietly. 'They will be dealt with.'

There's a steely menace in Hoxha's voice. I'm left in no doubt that he and his people will do exactly what he says. The KLA people are the good guys in the broader scenario being played out here, but amongst them there are killers as proficient and ruthless as any Serb paramilitary, I'm sure of that.

I take my leave. I need to think my way through the proposition. How would I explain this one to Donna? 'This nice man from the KLA wants me to move in with his men, but I'm sure he'll respect my non-partisan status. Oh, and I should also mention that some homicidal thugs are trying to murder me. Love you!'

Chapter 11

Talking to Fadil and Hoxha and learning how likely it is that I'd be shot, I had it in the back of my mind that I might simply take Jon Anderson's advice and split; fly back to Tirana, fly to London, fly to Adelaide, kiss Donna, kiss Jackson, go to bed for a month. But back at the IMC apartment I'm told that NATO has imposed a no-fly zone over Albania and much of Kosovo; could be weeks or months before it's lifted. At the same time, road traffic between Kukes and Tirana has just about stopped dead. The colourful Albanian folk custom of stopping cars and trucks on the road and perforating the drivers and passengers with automatic weapons fire has developed into a joyous, nationwide festival. You take a car to Tirana, you die, maybe. So my options for staying alive have been reduced to taking up Hoxha's offer and moving into a camp near the front line. The camp he has in mind is probably Helshan near Mount Pastrik, where the fighting is at its heaviest.

If I go, I'm no longer an IMC surgeon on a mission of mercy. I'll be a KLA recruit, for all intents and purposes. I won't be able to travel back to the UAE unit or to Camp Italia and do the work I signed on for. But if I go, at least I'll be using my skills as a surgeon. Does it really matter if I'm patching and stitching up near Mount Pastrik rather than in Camp Italia or Kukes hospital? It's the same blood and bone and flesh. I'm going. What I'll tell Donna I have no idea. Something anodyne. It's not lying. It's not deceit. I would never lie to Donna. I have no option but to leave Kukes. It's something that's been forced on me.

I can't drop out of the IMC without providing it with a summary of the events that led me to quit. And that is to be my chore for this evening. I want to make it detailed and dispassionate, a level-headed professional assessment.

Summary of Recent Events
Kukes Hospital Issue
20/05/99 – 24/05/99

To follow is a summary of the issues that resulted in my recent discussions with *The Stars and Stripes* newspaper (subsequently published on 24/05/99).

From my initial assessment of the Kukes hospital and regional surgical services, it was apparent that corruption and nepotism influenced the great majority of issues pertaining to patient care. Corruption at the highest level was evident within the Kukes Hospital (namely that instigated by Dr Cena, Hospital Director) and at all levels within the hospital network. A summary of this organised corruption is given below.

Dr Cena exploits the hospital linen laundering services as a profitable venture by allowing his wife to use the facility to launder for several large NGO relief organisations.

Dr Mustafi and Dr Shagir (surgeons) openly demand monetary payment from patients in return for their surgical services; failure or inability to pay results in refusal of these two surgeons to operate on these patients. There are several pertinent examples of this criminal malpractice.

A 28-year-old male Kosovar refugee with a shrapnel injury to the left upper arm resulting in a compound comminute fracture of the humerus with brachial artery involvement was refused surgery by the orthopaedic surgeon as the patient had insufficient funds. Despite my pleas with this doctor, and my availability to perform the vascular surgical procedure required, the patient remained in the emergency department for three days without treatment. I eventually had the patient transferred to the Italia 1 field hospital where he was stabilised and transferred to the Mother Teresa Hospital for appropriate management.

A 24-year-old female Kosovar refugee with a gunshot wound to the left ankle (resulting in a compound talar fracture) was denied operative and antibiotic treatment by the orthopaedic surgeon as she had insufficient funds (having being robbed by Serb paramilitary forces two days prior). This patient was subsequently transferred to the Italia 1 field hospital where she was managed appropriately.

A 60-year-old male Kosovar refugee with a right haemopneumothorax secondary to a gunshot wound sustained whilst fleeing Serb forces one day previously, was refused treatment by Dr Mustafi (orthopaedic surgeon) because of his inability to pay. The patient died two days subsequently.

A 61-year-old male Albanian citizen with a gangrenous left forefoot (secondary to atherosclerotic peripheral vascular disease) was refused a below-the-knee amputation by Dr Mustafi as he had insufficient funds. I subsequently performed the operation with the permission of Dr Ylber Vata (general surgeon).

These are just a few of many such incidents witnessed by me and other IMC workers at the Kukes Hospital which made it impossible for me as a surgeon to ethically treat or refer patients to this institution. As Surgical Co-ordinator for the Kukes region, I made the decision to refer all surgical patients from both camps and the region to the Italia 1 Field Surgical Unit for appropriate management. This facility is of a high standard with two general surgeons, an orthopaedic surgeon, a vascular surgeon and a full complement of anaesthetic and intensive care personnel on staff. This system was instituted and functioned well until 20/05/99 when an Albanian Health Ministry official informed the Italia 1 Field Surgical Unit staff and the UNHCR Emergency Officer that all surgical procedures were to be performed at the Kukes Hospital.

This was an unworkable, untenable and, from my point of view as an Australian surgeon, unethical situation. I tried on several occasions to amend this situation through meetings with both UNHCR and Albanian Health Ministry officials; however this was to no avail.

As my only remaining option, I decided to work through channels that I felt would achieve my aim, that is, Health Ministry approval for the use of the Italia 1 surgical facility. Through several unnamed sources I was informed that the only way to achieve this was via notification of the relevant NATO officials. This I achieved by giving a detailed report to a journalist working for The Stars and Stripes *newspaper (the official publication of the US Armed Forces).*

This is an accurate account of events between 20/05/99 and 25/05/99 and can act as a record of my activities during this period.

And now the resignation. I really don't like doing this.

26/05/99
Re: Letter of Resignation
To: IMC Director, Albania

Dear Sir / Madam

As of today (26/05/99) I withdraw my service as a volunteer surgeon with the IMC. Please accept this as a formal notice of my resignation from the International Medical Corps.

Yours sincerely,
Dr Craig Jurisevic

I've packed what little I'm taking with me to Helshan – a couple of changes of underwear, three pairs of socks, a few other garments, a couple of books. This is what my life has been reduced to: a single backpack. Sitting here on the sofa and staring at it gives me a shudder. It's as if I've blundered into a time warp and I'm now a teenager again, nothing to my name, washing my socks in the evening so that I have something to wear the next day, and my social life reduced to knocking back the occasional foreign beer in a seedy bar. Owning nothing is all well and good, so long as the carefree confidence of youth complements it. But I'm way past the carefree chapters of my life. I'm into my second marriage, I have a child, a mortgage, professional obligations. Just for the moment, this whole venture seems a little bit immature, as if it's the expression of an adolescent hunger for stirring times in exotic climes that some of my friends in Adelaide suggest. Was it really necessary to get up Cena's nose in that way? At my age, shouldn't I have learnt how to control the sort of fury his racket has provoked in me?

Roger has ordered a couple of IMC Land Cruisers to take us to the camp. Roger himself is coming up to the camp with me, although without resigning from the IMC, and with the intention of returning to Kukes. We need two Land Cruisers because we are about to – well, what word should I use here? – we're about to 'requisition' the entire contents of the IMC medical store at Kukes hospital. If we leave all that stuff behind, Cena will have it on the black market within hours. Our requisition is theft, maybe (if I'm scrupulously honest), but it's theft in a good cause. I have enough energy and wherewithal to support good causes, but not enough to mount a detailed argument just at this moment defending the morality of expedient theft. But I'm comfortable with it.

I have no idea what's going to happen up at Helshan. I have only a tenuous grasp on what I'm doing. At times during the morning I've felt sick at heart about the whole thing. And it's best if I call Donna on the satellite phone (our use of it is strictly rationed) while I still have my dread of what I'm doing under some sort of control.

'Donna? It's me.'

'Craig. It's so good to hear your voice. I miss you. Are you OK?'

'Yes, I am.'

'I haven't heard from you for a while – is something wrong?

'We're only allowed to use this phone once in a blue moon. Sorry about that, my darling.'

'But there is something wrong, isn't there? I can hear it in your voice.'

'Everything's . . . everything's fine. I've just got a really heavy workload.'

'That's not it. I know that voice. You're being evasive.'

'Evasive? No! Not at all. And I'm fine.'

Donna knows I'm squirming, even over a crappy satellite link. And when I try to be especially cheery and reassuring, I sound even more as if I'm dissembling. It's an exasperating thing about Donna. Once she picks up that slight hollowness in my tone or that pause that lasts a second too long, I'm gone. As soon as I ring off I'm flooded with guilt. This is a woman of character and depth; and a woman who loves me with all her heart. Being only half-honest with her is a type of betrayal. I feel ashamed of myself and angry with Cena for putting me in this position. But then I also hate the sort of self-serving rationalisation that makes me blame Cena for the lies I'm telling my wife. What the hell can I say? If Donna knew what I was up to, she'd be horrified, and she'd be sleeping even less than she is already. God, I worry about her, working long shifts in the intensive care unit, sitting up by the phone all night expecting a call to say I'm injured, or worse.

But while I have the use of the phone, I should talk to Jackson. I call his home, where he lives with his mother. I can relax more talking to a five-year-old who has no idea where Albania is, or why I'm here. I could be in Melbourne eating pancakes for all he knows, or in Sydney. And children have a limited appetite for affectionate phrases. They enjoy feeling loved, but probably think that twenty expressions of love in three minutes is a little bizarre and just a tiny bit tedious. When I hear that distracted note in Jackson's voice, I wind it up quickly. His last words over the phone are, 'Love you too, Daddy. See you tomorrow!'

I'm in that state when the love you feel for wife, for child mounts to such an intensity that it becomes an unlocalised pain, bruises everywhere, like the aftermath of a beating. The distance between here and Adelaide seems to have increased from thousands of kilometres to hundreds of thousands. This is love doing me harm.

It's 27 May 1999. Maybe I'll look back on this date as the commencement of a catastrophic blunder. I'm taking off into unknown territory, so to speak.

The two Land Cruisers arrive early in the morning. Roger and I make our raid on the IMC medical depot then pick up a couple more doctors – Brenda Vittachi, who wants to make an assessment of the medical situation up at Helshan, and Mehmet, an Albanian who is said to be one of the honest doctors who avoids all contact with Cena. Mehmet chats to me in the vehicle before we get underway, about his family, his hopes for a better Albania, for a liberated Kosovo. He actually lives in Helshan and is coming along to check on his family. He says that his son recently joined the KLA and he's anxious about the boy. I feel like shouting at Mehmet, 'Anxious? You let your boy join the KLA when you know what the Serbs will do to him if he's captured?' But isn't what I'm doing tantamount to joining the KLA? So I keep my mouth shut.

Leaving Kukes, we bump along a goat track for an hour and a half before we reach Helshan, perched on the side of a hill. It's a farming village, from a distance the sort of charming little place that tourists would see pictured on the internet then search the site for a darling B&B. But it's not charming. It's a town where subsistence farmers have toiled for centuries to keep the wolf from the door. It's a town so exposed to artillery attack that a couple of Serb dropkicks with a mortar could wipe the place off the map with half a dozen accurate rounds. As we climb the road to Mehmet's home, three truckloads of KLA fighters bounce past us on their way to join other fighters at the front. Mostly teenagers and young men. We smile and wave but what I'm saying to myself is, 'Please God, if these kids have to die, make it quick'. I can't bear to think of them tethered and tortured. Roger gives me a glance that shows he's sharing my thoughts.

Mehmet's house is pretty modest, in keeping with his reputation for honesty; I can't imagine that he benefits from Cena's racket. To his great relief, his son runs out to greet him; the boy wasn't amongst the troops who passed us on the way here. Mehmet, in his joy, invites us in for lunch. We sit down at the kitchen table to home-baked bread, olives and lamb. Mehmet stands with his wine glass raised and toasts his son. 'Success!' he says, beaming. The boy smiles back proudly.

After lunch, Mehmet takes us on a tour of his small farm. Nice olive grove, maybe twenty goats and sheep. At the top of a prominence that forms the highest point of his property, he invites us to gaze down on the tents of the KLA base in the valley below.

'They are on my land,' he says. 'I am proud to support my fighting brothers and sisters.' I smile at Mehmet and say, 'Yes, wonderful'. Roger says, 'Hmm' and Brenda asks if it's not a little risky, having the KLA on your land.

'I mean, they could take it out on you, couldn't they?'

Mehmet shrugs, as if this is a circumstance that might trouble a woman, but not a man. Well, I'm a man, and I can see so many ways in which things could go dreadfully wrong for Mehmet and his family. At the same time, I'm moved by the courage of father and son. They know even better than I what sort of venom they can expect from the Serbs if there's an invasion. In fact, it wouldn't even have to be an invasion. The Serbs regard the border between Kosovo and Albania as arbitrary; if it became important enough to them, they could shell the base, send over a force of regulars and paramilitaries, crucify Mehmet's family and return to Kosovo in time for breakfast. We don't know – and by 'we' I mean the UN, NATO, and anyone who wishes the Kosovars well – just how far the Serbs are prepared to go. The rabid nationalism that drives the Serbs is like a massive, daily whack of adrenaline. It's not inconceivable that they could torch the border regions of northern Albania to create a broad no-man's-land, pushing the KLA bases further back into Albania. The Serbs see this war as a golden opportunity to establish themselves as the kingmakers of the whole Balkan region. They believe that the Russians will back them every step of the way. And I think they also believe that the West will never go all-out to support a new Muslim state in the Balkans, and that's what an independent Kosovo would be – a de facto Muslim state, sitting beside another de facto Muslim state in Albania. The Serbs will bank on that fear. And there's another racist factor at work here, I think. Milosevic and his ultra-nationalist supporters regard the Muslim Kosovars as subhuman, and they can't credit that Americans and Europeans are going to get all that distressed about Muslims being slaughtered in the way they would if the Kosovars were a race of fair-haired Christians. They are seeing the evidence now of their miscalculation; NATO is conducting a bombing campaign which is devastating infrastructure in and around Belgrade as well as military targets in Kosovo. And that miscalculation enrages them.

Looking down on the KLA camp with Mehmet smiling all over his face, I ask myself if there is any way I would see Jackson off to war at age eighteen, with a wave and a smile; whether there's any circumstance that would make me speak with pride of my son fighting in a makeshift guerrilla army against a well-equipped foe who enact sadistic punishments on their prisoners. No, there isn't any circumstance that would make me swell with pride at seeing Jackson kitted out in battle fatigues with an automatic rifle in his hands. I might see the necessity in certain situations; I might honour his courage, I might even manage a wan smile as I said goodbye. But my heart would be full of ash and despair and dread. And when I toasted him, I would not say, 'Success!' I would say, 'Dear son, I beg you not to take any foolish risks, I beg you to keep your eyes peeled, I beg you to come back unscathed, alive, and never do such a thing ever again in your life.'

Chapter 12

We leave Mehmet with his family after an inordinate number of handshakes and hugs and slaps on the back and expressions of thanks to Mehmet's wife and to his children. Mehmet makes us promise that we will come back one day and enjoy his hospitality all over again. In the way that you do, we make a promise we probably can't keep.

The base is no great distance away by goat track. At the guarded entrance to the base the driver stops the vehicle while we wait to be called in. Within the compound, troops in combat camouflage hurry purposefully about the place. The Kosovo Liberation Army seems to be made up of men and women in a ratio of about three to one. The Muslims of the Balkan Peninsula, with their Turkish legacy, must have adopted a more enlightened approach to the rights of women than their fellow Muslims in certain regions of the Middle East. The Kosovar women have the right to shoot people, so it appears.

The recruits smile at us and wave as we enter the base, and their smiles move me in the way that certain poems and song lyrics catch at your heart. They're up against some of the most accomplished butchers in the world but they could almost be the cheerful and motivated members of a youth organisation, enjoying a camping adventure.

The first person we meet inside is Hosnje Hoxha, looking every inch the soldier that he is in his Commander's uniform. He's more in his element kitted out in KLA gear than in his civvies at the American Bar in Kukes. He shakes our hands, a big welcoming grin spilling across his face. I could say, 'Well, mate, you wanted me and now you've got me, much joy may it bring you.' But I don't. I've been just slightly manipulated into this fix I'm in, I know it, but I'm a big grown-up boy and I made my own choice. In a fashion.

'Dr Jurisevic, it is my honour to greet you. And you, Dr Lake, Dr Vittachi.'

Beyond Hoxha's shoulder on a big parade ground flanked by tents, hundreds of KLA soldiers, male and female, are busily boarding buses. Hoxha notices the direction of my gaze.

'They are going to the front,' he says, nodding towards the buses. 'Krume is ten kilometres south of here. They will pass through Krume and into Kosovo.'

Hoxha is making a point of giving us detailed information, as if to confirm that he considers us on his side now.

'If you'll wait here for a short time, I'll tell the base commander of your arrival.'

While Hoxha is away, a couple of young KLA cadres invite us to sit at a table under a big birch in full foliage. We're served coffee and cake. It's a little absurd, isn't it? Good manners, green valley, the breeze whispering in the leaves of the tree, cheerful young people heading off to war in buses. As Roger and Brenda and I sip from our cups, we acknowledge with brief, satiric smiles the comic aspect of our situation.

'Your tea is to your liking, Dr Jurisevic?' says Roger.

'Thank you for asking, Dr Lake. It's most refreshing. And yours, Dr Vittachi?'

'Yeah, great,' says Brenda. 'You know what you're doing, Craig? You're in the army now, hope you realise.'

'Looks like it.'

Hoxha returns with a tall, bulky, uniformed man in his fifties, a little on the rumpled side, a pipe in his mouth. We stand to shake his hand.

'May I introduce you to Ajvet Misini, Commander of the 123rd UCK Brigade,' says Hoxha. 'The Commander doesn't speak English, so with your permission, I'll translate. Shall we take a tour of the base?'

We form a walking cluster around the central figure of Misini as he commences to tell us in an animated, almost jovial way exactly what goes on at the base. Hoxha expertly transforms the rapid patter of the Commander's Albanian into Cambridge English.

'Camp Helshan is a base of tents and semi-rigid buildings attached to the edge of the village of Helshan, as you can see. It accommodates four to five hundred KLA soldiers at any one time. The base is what you might call a 'jump-station' for the rapid deployment of KLA forces across the border to the front line in the Has region around Mount Pastrik. You witnessed just a short time ago some of our soldiers boarding transports to Has, and I think you might have seen some more of our soldiers on the road on your way?'

'Yes, in trucks,' I confirm.

'It's a busy time.'

Every so often, Misini provides an affectionate pat on the shoulder for each of us; first Roger, then Brenda, then me. He can hardly contain his high spirits. It occurs to me that he's enjoying the war, although not in the psychotic way that the Serbs are enjoying it; Misini is the Happy Warrior, the man whose talents find their ideal expression in combat situations. I've met such men before in war zones; men who were born to be soldiers; who relish the rough-and-tumble of camp life, of combat logistics; next to fearless. And on top of all that, he no doubt believes in the justice of his cause and anticipates eventual victory. But so do the Serbs.

'The Commander has made a joke,' says Hoxha. 'He says you must be a Serbian spy, Craig, with a name like Jurisevic.'

I could explain that my father's surname is McLachlan, and that I adopted my mother's maiden name many years ago at a time of strained relations between my father and myself. I could tell him that my father, with whom I have long since reconciled, is a fourth-generation Australian of Scottish and Irish descent, and that he served in the Australian Army. But why spoil the joke?

'No, I'm not a spy,' I reply with a grin on my face. 'I'm a friend'.

The Commander likes this. He turns to me with a huge smile, although with his pipe still gripped in his teeth, and says something that's obviously heartfelt.

'The Commander says that he knows you are a friend to Kosovo,' Hoxha translates. 'He has heard all about your bravery and your great service to the patients in the hospital. He honours you and Dr Lake. The Commander is also impressed by the speed at which you are learning to speak Albanian.'

'Well, thanks for that,' I say, perfectly aware that I am being overrated; I've picked up a few phrases of Albanian, but not enough to be considered a wizard of languages. The tour concludes at the surgical tent. Misini asks me to call in at his tent for a longer chat later in the afternoon. Roger, Brenda and I have our hands shaken in hearty fashion one more time, then we're left to ourselves. We set to work unloading the medical supplies from the Land Cruisers into the surgical tent. My own skinny backpack of belongings I toss into the tent that Hoxha indicated during our tour would be my home for the next – the next what? Month? God alone knows.

And now the slightly awkward parting. Roger won't be staying – I knew that – and Brenda, of course, was only here for the day.

'Would've loved to keep you company, Craig,' says Roger, 'but hell, I'm too old to rough it. Could've once, when I was a kid like you.'

'Not a problem, granddad.'

'I'd be more of a burden than anything.'

'I'm sure you wouldn't, but I understand.'

'Take care of yourself.'

'Don't worry, I will.'

We hugged, shook hands.

'Same from me,' Brenda says, tears in her eyes. Her hug has a degree of matronly concern about it.

I see them into the Land Cruiser, then wait for Roger's parting line, because there will definitely be a parting line.

'Take it easy,' he calls above the hum of the engine, 'but take it!'

I stand alone, orphaned, hands in my pockets, and with no clearer idea of what I'm doing than I had when we first arrived. The dull thuds of Serb artillery and mortar strikes sound in the distance. On the vivid blue sheet of the sky, the vapour trails of NATO's high-altitude bombers leave long white welts, lengthening at one end, fading at the other. Soldiers, from the youngest to those in middle age, all brimming with zeal, attend to their various tasks in readiness for combat; packing field kits, cleaning weapons, forming into squads. I feel bereft, but this is not the place to display any attitude other than solid commitment. I wander back to my tent to unpack.

So it's come to this, Dr Craig! A tent on the border of two of the least-desirable countries in the world to visit at this time, a change of undies, a couple of books. I stand inside the humid tent, breathing in the canvas aroma, a rueful smile spreading over my face. It's come to this!

I spend the rest of the day wandering about the camp like a conscientious tourist, chatting with the locals. And like an earnest tourist, I become educated. All but a very few of the soldiers I talk to speak a pretty good brand of English and most are fluent in a widely spoken alternative to Albanian, such as German or Italian. And it comes as a surprise to me to learn that the majority of these volunteers have made their way here from America, Canada, Germany, Britain, Italy; they haven't wandered across the border from Kosovo or hiked here from some Albanian village. There's a huge diaspora of Kosovars and Albanians spread all through Europe and North America – people who fled from Serbian oppression in Kosovo after Milosevic's rise to power in Belgrade in 1989, or the barbarity of the post-Hoxha gangster scene in Albania in the early 1990s. This diaspora, contrary to common knowledge, is not comprised of Muslims alone. A significant number are Catholic and Albanian Orthodox, along with a fair number of agnostics. The expatriate Kosovar and Albanian communities have rallied to the cause of independence for Kosovo, raising funds and encouraging young men and women to get in there and fight. The money that flows in from the expatriates isn't chicken feed, either: about half a million US dollars each week.

Amongst the volunteers, there's a significant minority who'd never seen Albania or Kosovo before the outbreak of the war a few months ago. Young Americans, Brits and Germans have turned up here to help out. I haven't met a large enough number of these outsiders to develop an opinion about their motives but, going on past experience in combat zones, I'd expect the international complement to be made up of a mixture of sincere well-wishers, ratbags, would-be Rambos, psychotics and thrill-seekers. We've even got a small number of ex-Mujaheddin from Afghanistan who fought the Russians in the 1980–1988 Afghan civil war, here to support their Muslim brothers.

I learn something of the KLA's history too; bits and pieces that I can put together with what I already knew about the organisation before I came here. The volunteers, even up to officer rank, are very candid about their little army; I don't get much impression of bland or self-serving official clichés. The armed struggle against Serbian rule in Kosovo amounted, I'm told, to a ragtag hobby militia armed with rubbishy weaponry before Milosevic revealed his Greater Serbia strategy in the early 1990s; a strategy that didn't accommodate Kosovar ambitions for autonomy in the least. Milosevic's savage anti-Muslim prejudice, so evident in the Bosnian campaigns of the mid-1990s, put the writing on the wall. Kosovars with a little savvy could foresee the ethnic cleansing that was to come. Advocacy for Kosovar autonomy turned to armed struggle in 1996 when the KLA announced its formation with a series of nuisance attacks on Serb-manned police stations and Serb-dominated administrative centres in Western Kosovo. The Serbian authorities denounced the KLA as a terrorist organisation and came down on the non-Serb majority in Kosovo with a wrath so fierce that it had the unintended effect of commending the fledgling KLA to the ethnic-Albanian diaspora. Over the years leading up to the crisis of 1999, the KLA continued with its small-scale hit-and-run attacks on Serbian forces and police units within Kosovo without ever posing a serious threat to Serb control. There may or may not have been some abuses by KLA fighters against Kosovar Serbs during this period – the soldiers filling me in don't think such abuses are out of the question, and nor do I – but there's no doubt that Milosevic exaggerated them hugely to justify his invasion. It was probably a version of the three-card trick: the Serbs cut a large number of Muslim throats, the KLA in retaliation cuts a few Serb throats, then the Serbs in a state of feverish moral outrage shout, 'Look! Look! Those Muslim arseholes are cutting throats!' and then no Muslim throat is safe.

Kosovar Albanians and their neighbours in Albania itself are an eclectic mix of Muslims, Catholics, Orthodox and agnostics. This recurring reference to Kosovar Muslims (rather than Kosovar Albanians) has been an effective propaganda tool of the Milosevic regime. It worked in Bosnia, imparting an irrational fear of those following the Islamic faith amongst the Serbs in all the former states of Yugoslavia. The term 'Kosovar Albanian' eventually came to imply 'Kosovar Muslim', this misrepresentation filtering into Western conscience through clever manipulation by the Serbian media apparatus.

I'm making an earnest attempt to keep my wits about me as I stroll around. It will do me no good at all to think of everything I hear as the gospel truth. I'm in the heart of a camp of partisans: I'm not about to hear a meticulously objective account of the origins of the war. Over in the Serb bases across the border, maybe there's some newly drafted surgeon from Belgrade wandering about listening to stories of Kosovar atrocities and developing a potent conviction about the justice of the Serbian cause. I don't want to shove aside everything I've ever learned about the fragility of truth in combat zones. But I have to concede that I like these people, these volunteers, these men and women. I don't hear anything venomous from them; no fantasies of revenge, just a calm determination. I like the camaraderie that lights their faces, and the unforced equality of male and female; I like the way they greet me, the way they ask me about my background in the casual manner you'd expect in a pub or at a party. And I like, very much, the fact that I've been permitted to amble about without a minder; allowed to chat in an unmediated way with whomever I please. I haven't exactly been seduced by the friendliness of these young men and women, but some of the doubts I had about being here have diminished.

My stroll finally brings me to the base commander's office. Misini rises from his desk to shake my hand for the third time that day. Hoxha must be occupied elsewhere, because Misini calls for an interpreter. The fellow we get is an eager junior officer who appears delighted to have his translating skills put to use by his commander. Very enthusiastic people in the KLA, I must say.

Misini's manner has changed since our tour of the base earlier in the day. He's less jovial. Perhaps he wants to impress on me how seriously he takes his position, or maybe it's just that I'm here now, I'm living in the camp, I don't have to be courted any longer. He tells me that he himself is a refugee; that most of his family is still over the border in Kosovo.

'Dr Jurisevic, I must be honest with you. I don't know much about the refugee situation over there. Many, many Kosovars try to reach the border, this I do know. But they die on the way. The Serbs kill them. They step on landmines. Many die. How many, we can't be sure.'

Puzzlingly, Misini looks away for a moment. I wait for him to continue, then I realise that he's attempting to control his emotions; that there are tears in his eyes. I avert my gaze.

'These things distress me,' he says through his interpreter. 'You must excuse me. Let me tell you about our soldiers. We have three battalions stationed here. We call the biggest one the German Battalion. All the soldiers are Kosovars who went to Germany and other countries in Europe some time ago to escape from the Serbs. Now they have come back. Then we have a smaller battalion of refugees who have come across the border over the past three months. You saw our women soldiers? They are in this battalion. Their husbands have been killed. They are very good soldiers. Amongst my best. We use them in our Special Forces units. You know Special Forces? Like commandos. Very good soldiers. Of course, they give me great cause for concern. I am sure you know why. If they are captured, terrible things will be done to them. Terrible things. But they are very brave.'

Misini pauses again, once more struggling with his emotions. Again, I avert my gaze.

'We have a third battalion, Doctor. The smallest. They make a lot of noise. We call this the Atlantic Battalion. Men from America, Kosovars and Albanians. They have come to fight for their homeland. Some were born in America. They come from New York and the state they call Massachusetts. Do you know this place, Massachusetts?'

'Yes I do. Boston is the capital.'

'Boston, yes. These who come from New York and Massachusetts are very noisy, as I said. They make jokes. They shout all the time. A bit crazy. But good soldiers, I promise you.'

'I met many of your soldiers on the way here. They all seem very committed.'

'That is the right word. Committed. We have very committed soldiers. Now I want to talk to you about medicine, Dr Jurisevic. We have a surgical unit here. You would have noticed the unit?'

'Yes, I did. We brought you a lot of medical supplies and left them there.'

'I know you did. I was told. I thank you with all my heart. Now that we have this facility, we will bring soldiers from the front line in the east to be treated here in the camp. Of course, we had the facility before, but we didn't have a surgeon. You have changed all that, Dr Jurisevic.'

I think, 'Hmm'. And realise all over again that I have been just a tiny, tiny bit manipulated. Possibly. Did Hoxha overstate the danger I was in if I'd remained in Kukes?

'Here is what I'd like you to do,' says Misini. 'I'd like you to look over the surgical unit closely. Anything you need, you can write it on a list and we will get it for you. Equipment, supplies, personnel. Anything you require. Will you do that?'

'Of course.'

'Dr Jurisevic, I give thanks to God for your safe arrival amongst us.'

I leave Misini and head for the surgical unit. I have to forget about this whole manipulation business. They wanted me, they got me, maybe it was sleight of hand, maybe I jumped in too readily. I am sure my better judgement has been clouded by compassion for the plight of the innocent victims of this God-forsaken war. I can't dwell on that too much. Am I going to pretend that I still maintain my impartiality as a non-combatant? You're in the KLA, mate, you'd better face it.

Part Two
THE MOUNTAIN

Chapter 13

Over the next three days I continue my goodwill/fact-finding tour of the base, dropping in to chat with the troops as if I were the Minister of Defence hunting down photo opportunities. I start with the surgical unit, which is spick-and-span, beautifully equipped, and has never seen a combat casualty. This close to the front? Unheard of. And odd. There are fixed and portable anaesthetic machines, brand new overhead operating lights, a portable operating table, and more spotless surgical instruments than you'd find in a Surgeon's Emporium. Also – and this is superb! – a portable oxygen concentrator. Lovely, all of it – but a bit suss too. Just consider. These KLA soldiers are very likely to get killed the minute they come into contact with the Serbs. The Serbs are battle-hardened, rigorously trained, brilliantly equipped. So by rights, every incursion over the border by the KLA should result in a bloodbath and dozens of candidates for a stint in this very theatre. But it's never been used. It's not even staffed.

I go looking for some relief from my bafflement. In a tent not far from the surgical unit I happen on three Kosovar-

Albanian doctors (so I'm assuming) in ill-fitting camouflage gear under short white coats. They're sitting around a fold-up card table drinking coffee, chain-smoking and playing cards.

The doctors look up from their game as I saunter in. I introduce myself and am invited with a gesture to take a seat at the table.

'What's the game?'

'Yes?'

'Does anyone speak English?'

Two of the doctors glance at the third, who doesn't commit himself either way just for the moment.

'What are you playing?' I mime a fanned hand of cards. 'What game?'

'Blackjack,' says the third guy, ready to communicate now. 'Will you play?'

'Sure.'

I'm dealt my two opening cards and as I consider my strategy, I try out a few questions.

'Had much to do here? In the surgical unit?'

'A little.'

'Casualties?'

'Very few. Not serious.'

'Any require surgery?'

'No. We are not trained for surgery.'

'But there must be quite a number of combat casualties?'

'Yes. Sure. But they die before they get here.'

'That's a shame.'

'Yes.'

'Have any of you been up to the front? You know, to help with the combat casualties?'

'No. Not yet.'

'Any plans to move the unit closer to the front?'

'Maybe.'

The English speaker seems uncomfortable, and his unease is taken up by his colleagues. I'm thinking, 'What the hell?', but I go on with the game, picking up one rubbish hand after another before I finally fold and drop out. My geniality notwithstanding, the three blackjack specialists are relieved to see me go.

I met some of the men of the Atlantic Battalion in ones and twos on my first day here, but now I've met them in numbers and I'm a worried man. Well, I've been a worried man for weeks but my disquiet has increased. The Atlantic battalion soldiers, for instance, are terrific, very gung-ho, full of passion for the cause, but on the whole, appallingly undertrained. They handle their weapons like kids playing with toys; they know next to nothing about combat and are completely naïve as to the formidable capability of their enemy. I meet them as they drink coffee in their tent, belting out 'American Pie'. And that's fine, soldiers everywhere sing, not usually as badly as the Atlantics maybe, but it's okay. It's just that the abandon of this session, taken with their laxness and disdain for the high combat readiness of the Serbs reinforces my impression of the KLA as hopelessly amateur. I watch them in horror flinging their weapons about, a round in the chamber, safety off, set to semi-automatic or automatic, not the slightest regard for what a loaded weapon can do, the injuries it can inflict. I use guns regularly – I'm a recreational shooter back home – and I've handled weapons in combat zones in the way that competent instructors train you to handle them. You can gauge the capability of a combat unit just by looking at the way the individual members care for their weapons; the way they know at any instant where the muzzle of their firearm is pointing, whether or not there's a round in the chamber. The more experience you have with firearms, the more combat you see, the greater your concern for safety. And that goes double for combat-zone surgeons. Soldiers see other soldiers bleeding on the battlefield, certainly, but surgeons see the close-up detail of high-calibre weapon wounds; the severed arteries, shredded tissue, splintered bones. The soldier should come to think of his weapon as a great friend who has to be treated with respect every minute of every day. The respect lapses, your friend doesn't like it. Somebody gets hurt.

They're from New York, these Atlantics, as Commander Misini had said. From Brooklyn and the Bronx, where ethnic Albanians gather in ghettoes. They exhibit that cockiness and confidence that comes from thinking that they live in the greatest city on earth, even if it's a city they've adopted. I'm welcomed to the group with such back-slapping heartiness that you'd think I was the best friend that Kosovo has in the world. The Atlantics already know that I'm a surgeon, that I'm an Aussie, that I left Kukes with the Mafia after my head. I'm sure that contributes to the lustiness of my reception. Maybe they think of me as one hell of a fellow, fearless and full of cheek, but nothing could be further from the truth. I'm by nature a cautious man; I like rules, intelligent rules, and I follow them. The whole Cena confrontation gives a false impression, and it won't be too long before these Atlantics realise their mistake because I'm going to hammer away at safety until they're sick of the sight of me.

From the raucous camaraderie of the Atlantic recruits, I assume they share the same background, similar work. But no, their occupations are highly various. They're pizza-bar owners, lawyers, stockbrokers, restaurateurs, house painters, police officers. The camaraderie is the natural expression of a common cause and also a shared feeling – this is my guess – that they're up to their eyebrows in a great big adventure. Never underestimate the attraction of a battlefield to young men. The life of a pizza-bar owner or a lawyer provides very limited scope for adventure, surely. Looked at in a certain way – and I'm not being critical – going to war is an escapist thing for many of these men.

A couple of the soldiers in the tent aren't Albanians at all. This is consistent with what I'd been told a couple of days ago about a small number of the volunteers being enthusiasts for the cause rather than partisans. Listening to their stories – Andy Feeney's, Alan Kelly's: an Irishman, an Englishman, both ex-British Army – I ask myself with a figurative raised eyebrow whether their motives are more to do with battlefield fantasies than with a passion for justice. But the moment I start querying motives in that way, I get that familiar twinge of doubt about my own.

This, I'm sure, is just what Donna frets over – that I'm turned on by the thrill of it all, that I want to get myself kitted out as a Hero for Humanity, to cover myself in glory. If I want Donna to believe in my sincerity when I say I'm not looking for glory, I'd better accept Alan and Andy's reasons at face value: they saw scenes of atrocity on television and thought they should pitch in. If they'd been surgeons rather than one-time professional soldiers, they would've come here as doctors. What's the matter with that? The tradition of signing on to fight someone else's battle has a long and noble history, after all.

In the embrace of the Atlantics, I begin to get over my prissy disdain for their slack weapons savvy and chat with them like a normal human being. Or maybe it's just the much-needed coffee? The pizza-bar proprietor, Ylli Bytyci, wants me to know that he and his two brothers, Agron and Mehmet, make the best pizza in New York City – the best, understand? And he wants me to come to his place on Long Island and stay with him – that's Donna and me and Jackson. With his arms draped around my shoulder and his big, friendly face hovering in front of me, I tell him I'll come and stay, absolutely, but he wants me to swear an oath.

'I swear.'

'After we get rid of the Serbs, okay?'

'After we get rid of the Serbs.' I repeat in a less than convincing tone.

'You'll love it, my dear friend.'

'I'm sure I will.'

'You'll say, "Ylli, this is the best pizza I ever had in my life!" Do you believe me?'

'I believe you.'

'First we get rid of the Serbs.'

'Definitely.'

I'd feel more confident about meeting Ylli after the war if he'd experienced some combat training. Few of the volunteers in any of the battalions, I now realise, have ever been put through the hoops, been made to sweat, or fired a shot in anger. 'First we get rid of the Serbs'? Without the NATO bombing, the Serbs would put the KLA to the sword within a month, and that's the truth. But listen, Craig – just shut up. If these boys are guilty of taking the Serbs too lightly, they'll pay for it; they don't have to watch you wagging your finger.

ABOVE
The countryside around Kukes, with the town in the distance.

BELOW
Refugees crossing into Albania at the Morina border crossing. With little more than plastic sheeting to shield them from the elements, many have travelled like this for over a week. Most refugees were from farming communities. They would carry as much of their livestock as could fit on their tractor-trailers when fleeing the attacking Serb troops.

ABOVE
An avenue of tents housing refugees in the UAE camp.

BELOW
Two Kosovar refugee boys living in a park near the hospital
along with their livestock.

ABOVE
The view from the
IMC apartment. The
Kukes hospital is in
the background with
apartment blocks and
intervening wasteland
in between.

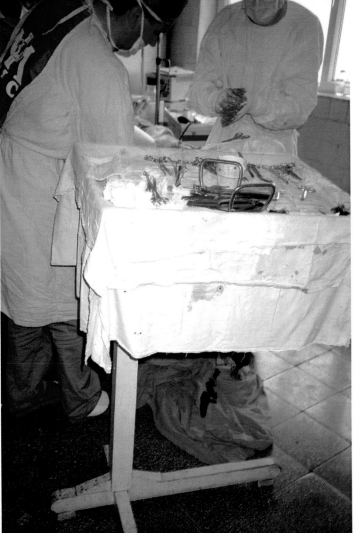

LEFT
Dr Ylber Vata and
I removing a leg.
Notice the dirty
trolley, stained
surgical drapes and
scant equipment.

ABOVE
Colonel Toccafundi and I at the Italian Military Surgical Unit.

BELOW LEFT
Kofi Annan with entourage at
the MSF camp in Kukes as
I present the case of Arjana.

BELOW RIGHT
Angela (Italian MSF doctor), Arjana
with baby and I just before the arrival
of Kofi Annan.

RIGHT
Mentor (a male nurse who assisted me in the cave) and I at the base at Cahan. We are carrying medical and other supplies back to the cave some 2000 metres up Mt. Pastrik (in the background). Often taking more than three hours, I made this trip nine times.

BELOW
The cave surgical unit. My surgical equipment to the left, the operating stretcher in the middle, my rifle against the wall. The sleeping bags on the far right were used as 'body-bags'.

ABOVE

On the front line at the top of Mt. Pastrik: a soldier melting the snow and boiling water for a morning coffee. Fetching fresh water from the spring put us in extreme danger from sniper fire. Improvisation was required to avoid dehydration.

BELOW

Soldiers carrying an injured comrade down from the cave to Cahan on a daytime retrieval run. This required 6–8 men, and the going was slow and dangerous. Each run could take up to four hours depending on the intensity of incoming fire. Many men died during these retrievals.

ABOVE
A booby-trapped front door in a village near Kusnin. Serbian troops placed these devices in recently ransacked villages to ensure that any rescuers would either be killed or suffer horrendous injuries. The wire would be obscured by shoes and foliage, the clearing of which by patrol members often had fatal consequences. We learned quickly from the mistakes of others.

BELOW
Dusk retrieval. The heavy loss of life with patrols necessitated night movement. By this stage of the war I was underweight and exhausted. I am on the right at the front.

RIGHT & BELOW
My IMC identity badge and
KLA (UCK) certificate. The KLA
provided me with this certificate
on my return to Kukes.

QEVERIA E PËRKOHËSHME E KOSOVËS
SEKTORI I SHËNDETËSISË
USHTRIA ÇLIRIMTARE E KOSOVËS

Vërtetim

Vërtetohet se CRAIG JURISEVIC
me profesion Kirurg — kardiolog
është anëtar/e i/e ekipit mjekësor të operacioneve

Dt. 10. VI. 1999
Kukës

Shefi i operacioneve
të Shërbimit Mjekësor
Dr. Durak Zyrapi

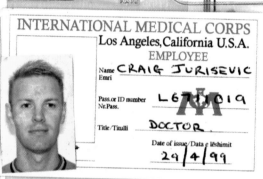

INTERNATIONAL MEDICAL CORPS
Los Angeles, California U.S.A.
EMPLOYEE
Name CRAIG JURISEVIC
Emri
Pass.or ID number L 6711019
Nr.Pass.
Title/Titulli DOCTOR
Date of issue/Data e lëshimit
29/4/99

BELOW
Article from *The Stars and
Stripes* where I exposed the
extortion racket taking place
at Kukes hospital.

The STARS and STRIPES

Vol. 58, No. 37   Monday, May 24, 1999   50¢ Daily • 75¢ Sunday

Refugee 'death trap'

By JON R. ANDERSON
Staff writer

KUKES, Albania – At the old, run-down hospital in Kukes, people are dying – not for lack of doctors or medical supplies.

Instead, they are dying because local officials are extorting what money they can from the refugees who are pouring into Kukes and leaving those who can't pay to languish, foreign physicians say.

"The Kukes hospital is a death trap," said Craig Jurisevic, an Australian surgeon working in Kukes.

At the same time, local authorities refuse to allow those

Surgeon says hospital uses 'ethnic and monetary triage'

who can't afford care to be evacuated into medical facilities set up at nearby refugee camps, he said.

The "Albanian Health Ministry demands that all operations be done at the Kukes hospital," Jurisevic said. "But if they can't pay for it, they don't get treated."

A Canadian emergency room physician, Dr. Roger Lake, also said the poor were going untreated.

"They've invented two new forms of triage here: Ethnic

and monetary triage," said Lake, who works with Jurisevic at the Kukes hospital.

An Albanian government official denied the allegations Sunday.

"I called the hospital in Kukes, and they said there is no problem up there," Musa Ulqini, a spokesman for the Albanian Ministry of Information, said through an interpreter.

But the doctors said at least three people have died because they could not pay:

■ One 60-year-old Kosovar who managed to crawl

See TRIAGE on Page 5

Shining Hope gets a break

Warehouses filling up with food, supplies

By CORY LANCASTER
Staff writer

I accept another coffee and let my nice-guy smile become set in place. I respond to the jokes, tell some of my own, accept the embrace of one Atlantic after another, listen to the bragging and banter, breathe in the cigarette smoke and avoid coughing to be polite. I can enjoy this sort of scene when I'm in the mood, and I'm earnestly striving to be in the mood, but the Serbs are going to mince these guys. Over the next few weeks – I can tell – the arms around my shoulders will be holding on grimly as I administer morphine and the laughter will have disappeared. I don't want these Atlantics or any of the other volunteers to die before my eyes, but it's going to happen and it makes me sick and very, very sad.

I leave the Atlantics after another half-hour to keep an appointment with Misini. He wants to talk about troop movements and medical evacuation procedures. I accept his handshake and yet another expression of gratitude, take a seat with his desk between us, maps on the wall behind. He's looking enormously cheerful once more. He must have had some good news. I refrain from telling him that his volunteers are pitiably ill-prepared for war.

With his pipe stuck in the corner of his mouth like a Balkan Popeye, Misini tells me through his interpreter that two KLA divisions of twelve hundred men had made a successful advance into Serb-controlled territory fifteen kilometres from Helshan.

'We have two fronts, Craig, five kilometres wide, at Mount Pastrik and Morina. We're ten kilometres inside Kosovo in some places. We do this with NATO. You understand? NATO has been bombing the Serb positions near to Mount Pastrik. Very serious bombing. You know what we call the B-52s,

Craig? "Clinton's Angels". Ha! Clinton is a great friend of Kosovo. He is a great president for America.'

'Unless you're a Serb,' I say with a tinge of sarcasm.

'Ha! Unless you're a Serb! Very good! But listen to me, Craig. Listen.' Misini leans across his desk. There's a twinkle in his eye. 'We will be in Pristina in two days, three days. In Pristina.'

In the capital of Kosovo in two or three days. That's what Misini is saying. He expects me to be impressed. I force a smile and nod, not wishing to seem sceptical. And I'm not sceptical, in fact. I'm somewhere between flabbergasted and dumbfounded. In Pristina?

Recovering, I keep my smile intact, but the despair I experienced listening to the foolish bragging of the Atlantic guys a short time ago is exacerbated by what Misini is saying. There is not the slightest prospect of the KLA reaching Pristina in two or three days, or two or three weeks, or two or three anything – not unless NATO sends in ten divisions, and NATO will not send in a single foot soldier, not one. Bombing from ten kilometres above Kosovo, above Yugoslavia, yes. But not one foot soldier. If Clinton bombs Belgrade into total submission and the Serb army withdraws, then an unopposed KLA division could maybe walk into Pristina. But while the Serbs are fighting back? No, absolutely not.

'Well, that's – that's excellent. Excellent.'

'In Pristina!'

'Indeed.'

'Ha!'

Misini has much more to say about the impending victory of the KLA in Kosovo and every word he utters bubbles with optimism. I contribute little phrases of endorsement and congratulations now and again, but mostly I'm quiet, scared to say anything with multiple clauses because I won't be able to keep the frustration out of my tone. It's only when we get onto the subject of medical evacuation that I can trust myself to open up, and that's by keeping the discussion entirely logistical.

When Misini and I part I hurry back to my tent, put my hands over my face and groan. It's not that I think Misini is deliberately exaggerating the KLA's wherewithal; no, I'm sure he genuinely believes that his men will be in Pristina for breakfast in three days. But surely he knows what I know, what every reasonably alert observer of this conflict knows? The forces amassed against the KLA in southwestern Kosovo place the Serbs in an entirely different league from the KLA. The Yugoslav Army (Vojska Jugoslavije – VJ) has nearly nine thousand troops in the area around Mount Pastrik and Morina alone. And those troops belong to the Pristina Corps of the Third Army, as tough a pack of bastards as any fighting force in Europe, possibly, in the world. Under the command of Major General Vladimir Lazarevic, the Pristina Corps has all but wiped out the KLA in the southern part of Kosovo. The Corps is said to have forty artillery pieces at its disposal; twelve mortar batteries; six Katyusha multiple rocket launchers; twenty armoured vehicles and a SAM-6 surface-to-air missile unit. Against what? Pizza-bar proprietors? Lawyers? Some are skilled soldiers and a few will make good field commanders, but many would have to think for ten minutes before they could distinguish the butt of an automatic rifle from the business end.

But that's not all. Apart from the VJ regulars, the Serbian Ministry of Internal Affairs has fifteen hundred secret police and paramilitary soldiers operating in the region, according to NATO intelligence. Their job is to carry out covert activities monitoring and harassing ethnic Albanian civilians and the KLA. The Interior Ministry has also deployed its special operations unit, the JSO (Jedinica za Specijalne Operacije), aka the Red Berets, aka 'Frenki's Boys' (after Frenki Simatovic, the homicidal maniac who founded the group, so it's said). Those guys are made-for-the-job barbarians; they draw the line exactly nowhere; if they were ordered to eat the brains of living infants, they'd do it, and we know they would because they've already committed atrocities you don't want to dwell on if you're going to get to sleep at night.

The numerical superiority of the Serbs is only part of the story. The VJ regulars and the paramilitaries are by far the most combat-experienced troops in Europe. Most of the senior VJ and paramilitary commanders and many of the soldiers served in the conflicts in Croatia and Bosnia-Herzegovina, some continuously from as far back as 1991. They're battle-hardened and they're experts in guerrilla warfare and counter-insurgency tactics. Consummate killers.

And now we come to the Serb Secret Weapons, except that they're not so secret after the years of fighting in the Balkans. Such simple weapons, so cheap, so effective: alcohol and amphetamines. The VJ regulars and the paramilitaries are stoked to the eyeballs when they step into the ring. It's not always that easy for a commander anywhere to get his troops to cut the throats of children, burn captives alive, spend a few hours blazing away with automatic rifles at men tethered in a pit. In my experience, most soldiers don't exactly relish murdering unarmed civilians; it's not your classical hero stuff celebrated in song and legend, is it? They'll do it, sure, but will they enjoy it? Or will they become remorseful and depressed and reluctant to back up for a second and third and fourth massacre? The amphetamines and the booze cut right through any qualms your troops might ordinarily express. Murder on tap.

Chapter 14

Bastard of a place to get any sleep. NATO starts bombing at dusk and keeps it up until dawn. The Serbs get busy with an exhaustive day-long barrage of artillery fire, mortars and Katyusha rockets about ten minutes after the last B-52 heads for its home base in Italy. The NATO commanders don't want their aircraft in the skies in daylight hours as they become much easier targets for Serb anti-aircraft fire. Forget sleeping.

In that state of light delirium that comes over you in the small hours of the morning on a sleepless night, images of Adelaide play through my mind. This is the Adelaide that's now in another galaxy, a dreamland, as if Albania and Kosovo existed in a grubbier, coarser world. I'm climbing out of bed in the morning knowing that the shower will work, then I'm shaving and afterwards wandering into the kitchen in bare feet. I'm making my breakfast, choosing between coffee and English Breakfast tea, between toast and muffins, jam and Nutella. Look at me puzzling, this is the trivial dilemma facing me in the first waking hour of the day. On the radio, an especially cheerful person is running through details of the weather around the nation and the cheerful weather man is followed by a cheerful traffic man advising me to avoid the Anzac Highway–South Road merge because a truck has lost its load. In the day that awaits me, my plans could be interrupted by a flat tyre, but I won't have to worry about a mortar attack. A man in combat camouflage will not use his boot on my front door, force me to my knees, place a gun muzzle against the nape of my neck. In Kosovo and these border regions of Albania, every vile thing is possible; the thing you most fear could happen; demons and goblins could emerge from the forest and carry you off to hell itself. But the curious thing is that it is Adelaide that seems unreal, seems a fantasy, as if peace and order and predictability, and milky light and toast and muffins, and the cup of coffee I prepare for my wife and carry up to the bedroom, and the good-morning kiss I give her, have less gravity than manifestations of evil. Why should this be? Why should we ever think of peace and love and beauty as fleeting things compared with barbarity? It takes a great deal more heart and soul and discipline and sheer hard work to create a morning in Adelaide than to construct a morning in a ravaged Kosovo village, in a Serb concentration camp. It should be manifestations of love that have the greater gravity.

Following this line of thought, I picture my grandfather, Franc, who spent a good part of World War II in Mauthausen and Dachau. I love my grandfather's story; I love the liberty of thought that he held dear, a liberty that he refused to curb no matter the cost. He was living in a small town just outside Trieste in the early years of the war, a city under Italian control at that time. He worked for the Istrian Water Board as a supervisor with responsibility for a whole region, but he and my grandmother, Marija, also kept what we would call a pub in the main street of Golac; a humble little place, two storeys, a dwelling above. Five children and Franc and Marija in that small apartment, but my mother – Danica – their first child, says that it was a happy place.

The Nazis marched in early in the war, enjoying the co-operation of a significant number of Mussolini's local fascists, but partisan groups formed to harass them as they did in occupied nations all over Europe. There were grotesque reprisals by the Germans, and deportations to labour camps, and summary executions; an efficient network of informers was established, and the Gestapo got to work. Here's the thing that always gets to me when I think of my grandfather: with a good job and a thriving pub and a big, beloved, boisterous family, he nevertheless joined the partisans and assisted in the sabotage of water infrastructure; pipelines and storage facilities. His pub had been a partisan meeting place for some time. Franc would, with reluctance, serve the Germans beer up until a certain hour, then close the doors until the partisans arrived for their turn at the bar. He put himself in harm's way with everything to lose. Whenever my mother told me tales of my grandfather, she knew that I grasped the significance of Franc's commitment; she knew that I realised what he was risking. She thought of him as a hero, and she wanted us all to think of him in the same way. And we did.

Grandfather Franc paid for his commitment when a workmate informed on him. After his arrest the SS sent him initially to Mauthausen in Austria, then to Dachau, north-east of Munich. Mauthausen and Dachau were labour camps, not extermination camps, but a sentence served in a Nazi labour camp was a sentence served in squalor and pain and misery, often ending in death. Dachau had its own busy crematorium, its execution yard, its centre for 'medical research'. There was a popular ditty at the time, sung in secret by Germans who had reason to fear arrest and detention – Catholic and Lutheran dissenters, communists, intellectuals: 'I ask, Dear God, to be made dumb, that I may not to Dachau come.'

My grandfather survived long enough to see Dachau liberated by the Americans in April 1945. He was a big man, very tall, but when he was liberated he weighed as much as a skinny kid in his early teens; the sort of hellhole survivor of whom it was said that you could count their ribs from fifty metres away. He made his way back to his home village of Golac using his wits and what remained of his exceptional physical strength. He wore a coat from the camp with a big yellow cross on the back – the distinguishing insignia for political prisoners, corresponding to the yellow star the Nazis forced Jews to wear. His family was intact, thanks to the resourcefulness of my grandmother, Marija, a tiny woman in stature but with the engine of a big heart driving her along. Marija and the children – my mother Danica, her sisters Rezika, Lilijana, Verica and her little brother, Pino – had to accept, with difficulty, that this shuffling skeleton was Franc; a man who before he'd gone off in the custody of the SS had stood bold and erect, his face full of humour and affection, and who now, fresh from hell, could manage tears but not yet his famous smile.

The smile returned, in time. He found work, the pub continued to subsidise their income, the children thrived. But he couldn't keep quiet about corruption and injustice, even after the hiding he'd endured in Dachau. He admired Tito greatly, but the petty communist officials of the newly created state of Yugoslavia irritated him, and he lampooned them in public and lampooned, too, the claims of the state to be the great benefactor of the Yugoslavian people. He wouldn't keep quiet. My mother said he despised lies and dishonesty and injustice in a way that made his disdain a handicap to him. No doubt about it: if you can't learn to turn a blind eye in a totalitarian state, you're going to be punished sooner or later. So he endured harassment, endured setbacks, endured ferocious flashbacks to his time in Dachau. On one occasion early after his return, as my mother tells it, he ran upstairs screaming, machine gun in hand, involuntarily overcome by the worst of these memories. From that day on, until his death, he said not a word of the camps, nor outwardly gave a sign of the horrors that tormented him.

I saw him once when he visited us in Australia, and once when we visited him in Golac. The first thing I noticed about him was the amused look on his face – a look that found its way to the surface through webs of wrinkles. He was a man who gave affection freely, and he took to me straight away; held me, patted my head of fair hair, called me 'Kennedy' after his favourite American president. It was the Americans who'd freed him from the nightmare that was Dachau, and his gratitude to the Americans was undying – also a little embarrassing, for they could do no wrong so far as he was concerned. Were he given another chance at life, he said, he would come back as an American soldier.

That look of amusement in his eyes, that humour that fashioned his wrinkles into smile lines! Yes, that's a hero worth the name. No bitterness, no excoriating resentment. If I've inherited anything from Grandfather Franc, I'd rather it be that amusement in the face of calamity than anything else. But I don't know. I find it impossible to be amused by what goes on around here.

I'm up at the hour that birds usually devote to singing, and they may well be singing now but who the hell can hear them above the bombing? And what on earth would a bird in this part of the world have to sing about?

I wake myself with a splash of cold water from my water bottle, brush my teeth and wander down to the mess tent. A number of the Atlantics are breakfasting here; also a few of the German Battalion recruits. Some of these Atlantics were the ones singing 'American Pie' at the session yesterday. Everybody knows the refrain of the song: 'This'll be the day that I die'. This collection of men and women will be moving up to the Mount Pastrik front line within the hour. All the bravado of yesterday is gone. They look edgy, anxious. Some will die. It's only in war zones and cancer wards that you get the unwelcome opportunity to look at the people around you knowing that two or three or more are spending their last day on earth. You can't help wondering which ones will be chosen. Amongst this nervous group I notice five or six who are young enough to be in high school. I'll bet that the ones who look most worried are not primarily concerned with losing their lives. No, they're frightened that they mightn't measure up; frightened that they'll let their comrades down; frightened that they may not have what it takes. That's the great fear of young men and boys in situations like this – that you will scream, that you won't be able to control the shaking of your hands, that you will start sobbing, run away, shame yourself. Compared to fears of that sort, the prospect of being shot is easy to handle.

As they leave the tent, getting ready to kit-up and climb into the transports, I wish them luck. 'Hey, keep your heads down, okay? Don't do anything crazy.'

I take a second mug of coffee down to the surgical tent. Although last night's air strikes targeted the Serb positions, there would have been ground combat around Mount Pastrik. I'm anticipating casualties. But there are no customers at the surgical unit; it remains as virginal as ever, the sleek new operating table gleaming in the sun that floods in through the tent flaps.

I occupy myself by checking the surgical equipment again and fiddling with the controls on the anaesthetic machine. When are we going to get the chance to use the damned thing? I feel as if I'm running a Sony outlet in the middle of the Simpson Desert; fabulous stuff on offer, but not a customer in sight.

Misini and his second-in-command, Fadil, make an appearance mid-morning. I've already told Misini that the set-up here is terrific and that I have enough supplies for twenty major ops, but he asks me again if everything is hunky-dory.

'Everything's fine.'

'Good. That is very good.'

Misini shapes to say cheerio, but I stall him by raising the possibility of moving the unit much closer to the front line.

'You know, we'd need maybe a platoon of your guys to move it. Say ten guys. In twelve hours, we could have it up and running. Here, it's no use as a primary trauma facility. We need to be closer.'

Fadil did the translation, but in a nonchalant way, as if I'd made a curiously amusing observation. Misini gives a great hoot of a laugh and slaps me on the shoulder.

'No need, Craig! No need! We have a new hospital at the front. Brand new!'

'Really?'

'In Krume.'

'Where's that?'

'At the bottom of Mount Pastrik. Seven kilometres from the front. Brand new. Excellent. We run it with some Norwegians. Nice people. They paid for it. All of our soldiers are getting excellent care. Excellent!'

In fact, seven kilometres from the front is not excellent. It's deadly. Moving the wounded manually over seven kilometres of rugged terrain would take maybe three, four hours. The first sixty minutes, from the moment of a wound's infliction to its treatment on the operating table, is crucial in the management of trauma. Surgeons and emergency physicians call this 'the Golden Hour', beyond which time the casualty has little chance of survival. A surgical unit that's going to be of any use has to be just out in the backyard of the battlefield; say ten minutes away. Movement over such rugged terrain is fraught with the danger of increased injury and trauma. The survival rate of soldiers wounded in battle improves dramatically when you evacuate quickly. The rapid evacuation helicopters of the Vietnam War saved tens of thousands of American and Vietnamese lives. But the KLA can't call in MEDEVAC choppers.

Misini's back-slapping heartiness conveys – as it is meant to – a subsidiary message. He wants me to feel appreciated but he also wants me to pipe down. I'm not at all confident that this great camaraderie he has with me is to do with anything more than show. Is it possible that he enjoys telling people that he has a first-class surgical unit here at Helshan and a wonderful surgeon to run it, without worrying about whether the overall set-up makes any sense? Am I a sort of trophy surgeon?

But since the facility up at Krume is at least closer to the action than this unit here at Helshan, that's where I should be. And that's what I request – a transfer to the Krume unit. Misini listens patiently to the translation.

'You wish to go to Krume?'

'Yes, I do.'

A spasm of irritation passes over his features.

'No, you cannot go to Pastrik.'

'Look, I'd be so much more use there. Let's face it – I'm doing nothing here.'

Misini says, 'No.'

And that's the end of the discussion. I get a big smile, somewhat forced, and Misini and Fadil head off. But Misini stops and turns to face me, as if he's worried that he's been too categorical. I am, after all, his wonderful trophy doctor. He doesn't want me to get sulky and go about pouting.

'Come back and see me in a few days, Dr Jurisevic. We'll discuss this matter again.'

I hang around the surgical unit hoping for a customer or two in the grim way that surgeons do, but there's not a major trauma victim to be had here for love or money. I saunter about the camp muttering to myself in frustration, watch the arrival of two hundred fresh recruits in four buses – more young people of the Albanian and Kosovar diaspora, this lot from Germany and Belgium. I mingle with them, say a few kind words, ask how much training they've had. Two weeks is the answer. Great. Two weeks. That's about enough time to train them to jump out of bed at reveille, turn off their Walkmans and get to the parade ground.

'Any of you had any military experience before you signed up?' I ask one of the recruits.

'No. This is the first time in uniform for us.'

Bloody marvellous. Two weeks. It's a war crime.

As the last bus is emptying, the muffled crack of a gunshot echoes down from the northern end of the camp. Some of the new recruits duck their heads; others look about in alarm. I'm gazing in the direction of the shot at the very moment that a soldier comes sprinting into view screaming hysterically, his face wet with tears. I ask one of the new recruits what the hell he's saying.

'He says someone's been shot. He says he's bleeding badly, bleeding everywhere.'

I sprint down to the resuscitation tent to set up intravenous fluids and the equipment I'll need. Five minutes pass; no sign of the casualty. It's approaching ten minutes from the shot when the stretcher detail finally arrives. The guy's dead, blood dripping down an arm that protrudes from under the blanket covering him. I lift the blanket, open the blood-soaked shirt, find the bullet entry wound to the midline of his left nipple. I check for a pulse even though I can see clearly that he's dead. It's just a thing you do. A reflex.

The guys of the stretcher team huddle over me as I examine the body. One of the Albanian doctors and an assistant are sobbing outside the tent.

'What the hell happened?' I ask as I cut the shirt from the body.

'A woman,' one of the stretcher team answers.

'What do you mean?'

'An argument about a woman. A bad argument. She is a soldier. Very young. The other one shot this one.'

'The other one is a recruit?'

'No. He is in the camp police.'

'Where is he now? Is he in custody?'

'No.'

'Why not?'

'He is an officer.'

'Is he really? And what's his name?'

'I am not permitted to say.'

'You're not permitted to say?'

'No.'

I turn the body over. The exit wound is horrendous, the size of my hand, the edges jagged with shattered rib fragments and muscle. Half his left lung and a large portion of his heart have been blown through. Now, this was no heat-of-the-moment thing. The guns in the hands of the soldiers here are AK-47s and SKSs and both chamber the same 7.62 x 39mm full metal jacket round. At point blank range it would be impossible for a round like that to produce such a hideous exit wound. A full metal jacket bullet travels so fast that it penetrates the body like a rapier thrust – small entry wound, small exit wound. A hollow-point, soft-tipped round, on the other hand, would fragment on impact causing major bone and soft tissue damage and a formidable exit wound. Hunters and snipers choose this type of fragmenting round. I knew of only one guy on the base who used the type of weapon and soft-tipped rounds capable of making the sort of mess I was now probing with my latex-gloved fingers. And I also knew that whoever fired the gun intended the shot to blow this young man apart. In other words, this was premeditated murder.

Nazmi Isufi walks in, the police commander for the base. He gives a cursory glance at the corpse on the stretcher then turns a quietly menacing gaze on the Albanian doctors and medics gathered around. Judging by the averted eyes, the nervous shuffling of feet and the general air of anxiety, Isufi can be pretty confident that there'll be no awkward questions asked by any Albanian or Kosovar here. I'm another matter.

'Dr Jurisevic, are you okay?'

'Of course.'

I meet Isufi's stare, which is meant to be intimidating. When he asks me if I am 'okay', what he's really asking is whether I am capable of mentioning nothing more about how the corpse on the stretcher came to be a corpse. I'm not about to quiver and cower and make some grovelling gesture of obeisance, but nor am I about to get on my high horse and demand an explanation.

'Good. Do you need anything?'

'Such as?'

'I'm sure you know what to do.'

'Yes, I do.'

Isufi addresses a few rapid phrases in Albanian to the doctors and medics – perhaps, 'You saw nothing, you know nothing' – then briskly leaves the resuscitation tent.

I'll have the body cleaned before his friends see him; wipe away the blood, close the wounds, cover the chest with a clean uniform. I think I can safely say there'll be no autopsy and nothing of the nature of a coronial investigation here.

Chapter 15

Things have changed. It's 29 May, I've been in Albania a full month and, with the approval of Fadil, the second-in-command here, I'm now training the recruits for combat, or at least showing them how to avoid the sort of mistakes that can cost an arm or a leg or a life. With my years of experience as a shooter and hunter, and of combat retrievals in Gaza, I feel a moral obligation to help train these men and women. I organise the recruits into units of five or six, men and women together, then take them out to a makeshift practice range set up at the far end of the base perimeter, one group at a time. I teach them how to care for their weapons. I teach them how to care for themselves. I teach them how to survive.

What I'm doing has nothing to do with surgery. It has nothing to do with the IMC. And it has nothing to do with the desire to help the Kosovars that took hold of me when I saw bodies heaped in ditches on my television screen in Adelaide. It is partly to do with my impatience with idleness, my inability to stay still and wait for customers in my shining surgical tent while Kosovars are dying in great numbers just over the border. I have never been able to sit still for long periods, not as a boy, not as a man.

The first group includes four men and a girl in her late teens. I walk them down to the range then introduce myself through translators in German and Albanian. The recruits listen attentively. This may be the first time that anyone who sincerely cares for their welfare has spoken to them since they enlisted. They've heard KLA people telling them that they're doing something of significance for their country, but that's a different thing, and a lesser thing; that's merely the sort of patriotic baby food that men and women like this are fed in armies everywhere. It's one thing to tell your recruits how brave they are; it's quite another to tell them that their country will benefit more if they survive the war than if they leave their entrails in a paddock somewhere. I have no interest in firing them up for battle; I just want them to survive.

'I'm going to talk to you about your weapons, principally about your rifles. I'm going to teach you how to keep your rifle working so that it doesn't blow up in your face. Please believe me when I tell you that your rifle was not created by a magician but by a mechanical engineer. If you want it to function properly, treat it as a mechanical apparatus. But it is a mechanical apparatus that is also your friend. Clean it, oil it, cherish it.'

They listen as if I am an expert combat instructor who also dabbles in surgery, not a surgeon who also dabbles in combat instruction. I am no expert, but the lessons I impart can only improve their chance of survival. I maintain an air of paternalistic confidence and self-assuredness, as any hint of doubt in my voice will lose them. I want them attentive and focused.

'I'm going to set up six targets down-range. One target for each of you. I want you to take a prone position on the ground with your weapon resting safely in front of you. Remember, I said "safely". Okay, go to it.'

The targets are images of Milosevic. This is not my choice.

'Very well. Now let me ask you a question. Is your weapon unsafe? Tell me if your weapon is unsafe.'

They are all puzzled by the question. I repeat it. They believe their weapons are safe. I walk over to the first recruit, a boy in his teens. He smiles up at me like a puppy. If he had a tail, it would be wagging. I put his rifle to my shoulder, squeeze the trigger and empty half the magazine of thirty rounds at the target. Then the gun jams. Astonished at the noise of the discharge, they throw their hands over their ears.

The fellow whose gun I fired looks both baffled and embarrassed.

'Okay,' I say. 'The gun was supposed to be safe. You said it was safe, didn't you?'

The translation comes back: 'Yes. I am sorry.'

'Sorry is okay, dead is not okay. The safety wasn't on, the mechanism was dirty. I fired fifteen rounds. In combat, the first fifteen rounds may not be the most effective. You're looking for cover, there go five rounds. You're tracking a target, another five rounds. Your target takes cover, you pin him down, another five rounds. Now you're set to take out the target when he appears. The gun jams, the VJ can see you, they know your weapon is useless, and they shoot you. You know why? Because the VJ guns don't jam. The VJ guns are clean. The VJ guy, if his gun is dirty, he gets his arse kicked. Don't you laugh at your comrade here. I could pick up any weapon and I'd probably get the same result.'

I tell them all to unload their weapons and put the safety levers on. I run through the procedure for correcting stoppages (jamming), show them how to field-strip their weapons. I make them repeat, in English, what I've taught them: 'Magazine off, clear chamber, cleaning rod out, recoil spring out, bolt out, gas piston out. Reassemble!'

It's a hot day. The sun is sitting right overhead now in a clean blue sheet of sky. I'm sweating, the soldiers are sweating. But by the end of the first hour each can fix any common jam and strip and reassemble his or her weapon confidently. I don't have to tell them again the value of what they're learning. They know they were about to go into combat without any knowledge of how to service a jammed firearm. They know they're better off for what we're doing here. No complaints about the intensity of the lesson, no complaints about the stinking heat.

'Listen to me now. What you've been learning is only part of what you need to know. It's also important that you use your weapons intelligently. What you're going to do now is learn how to zero your weapons – how to aim, how to maintain effective fire, how to avoid spraying bullets all over the shop. This will take some time, then we move onto fire-and-movement drills. You won't be lying down on a comfortable shooting range when you take your first angry shot. The type of fighting you'll be involved in is not trench warfare. You'll be in motion, you'll be walking or running when you fire, the VJ will be running at you. You have to hit a target when you're walking, running or stationary. Can you see the importance of this? Say yes or no.'

Yes, yes, yes, they all respond, yes, we understand that it's important, and they mean it. I don't want to shriek and bark but it's vital that they believe everything I'm telling them. I maintain a tone of supreme confidence because they'll detect any hesitation, any self-consciousness. Certainly I have a fair amount of experience under my belt as a recreational hunter and as a medical officer in other conflict zones, but I am no world-class combat instructor. I can, however, impart enough knowledge to give them fair odds on the battlefield, and that's the best I can hope for. With two larger groups to instruct after this one, I have a long day ahead of me.

After three hours, I can say with great confidence that some of these men and women are slightly less likely to get their heads shot off over the border than they were earlier in the day. Ah, but my heart aches as I watch them go merrily back to base, calling out, 'Thank you, sir, thank you Doc for teaching us!' Each one is probably convinced he or she is now a match for the VJ. And sadly, that's not true. But that's as much as I can do.

The last two sessions go as well as can be expected. In each session I rely on the approach I employed in the first: listen or you'll die. There's no need to modify what I have to say because all the groups are equally naïve and equally ill-prepared. I'm exhausted by the time the last group goes off in a chirruping chorus of thanks.

Packing up, I find myself brooding on the turn of events – me, the surgeon, actively training recruits. Although it's not much more than basic training, I'm still teaching them the art of killing, and of killing effectively – and searching for an acceptable justification. It's not in my nature to think of taking the life of another or to encourage others to do so. On the contrary, my whole sense of being is driven by the need to prevent death and to ease suffering. But I need a justification for what I am doing. My conscience needs one. Preventative medicine is what I'm going to call it. 'Preventative medicine' is one of those euphemistic phrases that health professionals employ to explain programs that minimise bad health outcomes by reducing risk factors. In this case, the major bad outcomes are injury and death. The major risk factors are the Serb forces and the various ordnance they fire at us or leave in the ground for us to stumble on. I can't change that. But other risk factors can be reduced. Poor weapons skills, situational unawareness on the battlefield and lack of attention to detail can all be remedied up to a point with elbow grease and competent instruction. So that's it. Minimise the risk factors and avoid poor health outcomes. Preventative medicine at work! Not a flawless justification, but it'll have to do to ease an already troubled conscience. Bassanio says in *The Merchant of Venice*, 'To do a great right, do a little wrong.' I'll accept that as an amendment to the Hippocratic oath: 'First, do no harm.'

It's dusk by the time I join the Atlantics at their tent for dinner. The fierce heat of the day has fled and it's now cold, and getting colder. Dinner is field rations donated by the boys of the Royal Dutch Army, God bless 'em. Lasagne or beef stew; an improvement on bread and cheese, which is what I've been sustaining myself on for the last little while. But even sitting around and trying to relax, I notice yet another potentially deadly faux pas and can't stop myself mounting the pulpit to give one further sermon on safety. On their caps, emblazoned in bright yellow and red, is the patch of the UCK (Ushtria Çlirimtare e Kosovës – Kosovo Liberation Army), and on their left shoulders, a vivid US flag patch to honour their new home in America. The girls favour stars-and-stripes headbands and bandanas, and also shiny necklaces. This is what makes a sniper's mouth water – an advertisement shouting, 'Shoot me!' I try to keep quiet, I try very hard, but it's no good. I stand up, mount my pulpit, and rail against the sin of bright technicolour insignia.

'But come on, Craig, come on. What do you want us to do now?'

'This,' I say, and pick up a handful of dirt and spit in it, seize the nearest offender and smear the mud over the badges. 'Okay?'

They don't like it. Particularly the girls. Most agree to do what I'm suggesting, but with begrudging reluctance. I realise then that they will only really believe what I'm saying when they hear a soft thud and look around to see their comrade dead on the ground with a gaping hole in his head.

I have to go to bed.

'Goodnight, Craig.'

'Goodnight, Doc.'

'Hey, Doc, have a good sleep. Maybe relax, okay?'

As I lie in my sleeping bag, mulling over the events of the day, I run over my new rationalisation. Preventative medicine; risk factor reduction. 'To do a great right, do a little wrong.' God bless William Shakespeare.

Chapter 16

Not every recruit here at Helshan is so full of the lust for adventure that he fails to see the reality of his situation.

Fatmir, the fellow who runs the pizza bar in Brooklyn, is one of those compulsive clowns who can't look at a gathering without thinking, 'audience'. He's an accomplished comedian. He could have a career in stand-up comedy if he were prepared to live on a small part of what a pizza-bar brings in. I listen in on his banter in the evenings around the fire. My own compulsion – safety, safety, safety – has me instructing recruits in weapons handling even as they're enjoying Fatmir's antics. My protective parental instinct overrides the temptation to sit back and enjoy the show. But I know enough to smile and keep quiet. Then Fatmir surprises me. Maybe his comic's instincts help him see through my smile. He sits beside me once I've finished lecturing, and for once he's not smiling.

'I agree,' he says.

'Agree with what?'

'I agree with what you're thinking, Doc.'

'You agree with what I'm thinking? What am I thinking?'

'You're thinking, "This guy, this Fatmir, he thinks it's all a big joke." Right?'

'Sort of. But not entirely. I do have a sense of humour, Fatmir.'

'Sure. But I'm right, aren't I? You want these guys to stay on the ball when you're doing your safety thing?'

'Well. Naturally.'

'Okay, here's the thing, Doc. I'm back in Brooklyn, okay? Never fought in a war, only thing I know is pizza. And all I'm hearing all day, all night, is Milosevic, Greater Serbia, all that shit. Places my parents speak about, little towns, his buddies are burning them to the ground. Better I get my head shot off than go on like that. It's the same for most of these guys. Worse than getting shot is doing nothing. We love your safety thing. You care, and that's great. But you see what I'm saying, Doc? We get it.'

'I know I can be intense, Fatmir, but that's how I get the message through.'

'You know what they call you, Doc?'

'I'm frightened to ask.'

'The Safety Nazi.'

I go off to bed with that title occupying my thoughts. The Safety Nazi. Actually, I like it. I might get a patch made to sew onto my shirt. 'Craig Jurisevic, Safety Nazi.' If being a pain in the arse gets just one of these recruits through the war with his limbs intact, it'll be worth the ridicule.

Listening in bed to the bombs falling across the border, I'm aware of a tingle at the base of my brain. If I had to come up with a diagnosis, I'd say it was stress. It's not the stress of listening to bombs exploding ten kilometres away. It's the stress of being neither fish nor fowl nor good roast beef. Working in war zones, I'm used to knowing exactly what I'm supposed to do and when I'm supposed to do it. Nobody on a battlefield or anywhere near it has a more distinct grasp of tasks and duties than a surgeon. Even soldiers are often in the dark as to what they're supposed to achieve. Not only does the bigger picture elude them; the smaller picture is usually blurry too. They follow orders. For a surgeon, it couldn't be clearer. Stem the bleeding from the casualty's neck; get him evacuated; make yourself busy in the surgical unit with the tools of your trade. The patient could die, only he doesn't, because you've done what you're here to do. But at Helshan, I'm making it up as I go along. This tingling, this sense of waste. I know it's a callous way to look at things but for me, right now, happiness would be three or four casualties to get to work on. I'd gladly give the rest of the night to it. In the morning you'd find me in blood-stained scrubs, exhausted, and smiling from ear to ear. A happy surgeon is a busy surgeon – I can't stand this inaction.

I turn this way and that in my camp bed, hungry for oblivion. The bombs fall in an irregular cadence. My brain in its idleness plays with stray fragments of sounds that drift in from the camp. A voice calls, then lapses into silence, then calls again. A truck door slams. Distantly, up at the farm, a dog barks once, twice, again. I'm fraying. I whisper the name of my wife over and over, as if chanting the words of a hymn to ward off harm.

At dawn, I awake from half an hour of something that resembles sleep but is more like a daze. The sounds have changed. The camp is beginning to rouse. Voices call more frequently. Fatigue coats me like a grey slurry of sweat. I lie still and wait, and wait a little longer, and then it starts, the dull thud of Serb artillery in the distance. How many of these shells make their mark; how many lives are shattered? No benefit in thinking in this way. I run my hands over my face, give a sigh and rouse myself.

In the middle of the morning a convoy of trucks pulls up at the main entrance to the camp. The trucks are escorted by four shining Toyota 4WDs. Nothing has been said of a convoy. I join in the speculation of the recruits. Maybe the trucks have brought proper food. That is the great hope – proper food. I like the idea of good food, but I'd prefer to see medical supplies for the front. It always thrills me to see cartons of medical equipment stacked high. It's like great wealth; like treasure. With all the right supplies, you can do anything.

The guard at the gate raises the boom and the convoy crawls heavily into the camp. Isufi, the intimidating police commander, is waiting with a group of recruits. When the trucks are unloaded – a great many wooden crates – I wander over to the quartermaster to get a closer look at the delivery. One of the opened crates contains ten Barrett bolt-action .50 calibre sniper rifles with high-powered telescopic sights attached. Beside them are five similarly packed LAR 'Grizzly' .50 calibre sniper rifles. The Grizzlys and Barretts are designed to hit human targets at up to two-and-a-half kilometres away, and to disable armoured vehicles at closer range. Next to this is a box containing several thousand rounds of ammunition for the rifles, some armour-piercing, others explosive-tipped. I wander over to the second stack of crates where recruits are unpacking hundreds of Kalashnikov (AK-47) and SKS automatic and semi-automatic assault rifles, Dragunov 7.62 x 54mm semi-automatic sniper rifles, and a variety of Czech CZ 9mm pistols. A third stack of cartons is packed with camouflage uniforms, boots, socks, gloves and other kit items. We also have grenades, rocket-propelled grenade launchers (RPGs), antipersonnel and anti-tank mines, and a dozen heavy machine guns, including four 7.62 x 54mm Gorjunov SGMs; a couple of DUSHKAs (DShK .50 calibre anti-aircraft/antipersonnel guns, a true monster of a weapon) and tens of thousands of rounds of ammunition in metal boxes stacked two metres high under the shade of an elm, like presents under a Christmas tree.

Isufi, the recruits and the quartermaster are ecstatic. I know what they're thinking: 'Milosevic, your goose is cooked.' But other than the Barretts and Grizzlys, the weapons on display are second-hand, their mechanisms very likely to be worn out; assault rifles are employed by their initial owners until they are of little more use. And look, I have to say it – the consignment of heavy sniper rifles is just plain whacky. Who's going to use them? Training a sniper takes years of patient instruction. To make effective use of a Grizzly or a Barrett, a sniper has to be a master of smaller calibre, lighter rifles; a master of stealth, a fantastic marksman; he has to be capable of judging the influence of wind, rain, heat and snow on a long-distance shot; he has the most patient temperament in the army, prepared to wriggle a metre an hour on his belly, if needs be, to get within range of a target. The Barretts and the Grizzlys are weapons for a super-sophisticated fighting force. The DUSHKAs and Gorjunovs are not toys for the novice; there's no way on earth the men and women here at Helshan could handle them. And the RPGs? We're going to have grenades going up like a fireworks display with the training these recruits have had.

Misini emerges from his office with the guy who'd been in the lead vehicle of the convoy. Misini introduces the convoy leader to me as 'Mister Steve'. Mister Steve addresses me as 'Sir', in the American way. He's not in uniform, Mister Steve. He could be CIA, he could be a weapons trader. He's taking notes as Misini talks to him on the way back to the Toyotas.

Once the convoy departs, Misini calls me over and explains through his interpreter that all this weaponry and ammunition has been paid for and delivered by 'his friends in America.'

'Sit with us, Dr Jurisevic. Let us celebrate.'

It's explained to me that the finance for the arms comes from expatriate Kosovar and Albanian businessmen in New York and Chicago. The weapons themselves were purchased in the US and Eastern Europe, then transported to Albania by sea and road. The CIA, US consular staff in New York, Rome and Tirana, and US Special Forces operatives in Albania arranged transport from point of purchase to the base at Helshan.

According to Misini, the individual who did more than anyone else to raise the money for the weaponry is a certain Florin Krasniqi, a Kosovar immigrant who runs a flourishing roofing business in Brooklyn. He amassed more than thirty million dollars through his network of contacts in the expatriate community. He also scooped up millions more in donations from fundraising events organised by state and federal politicians, Democrats and Republicans alike. With the money in a big brown bag (figuratively) he and his mates purchased much of the high-end weaponry in those US states where gun laws are so liberal that a teenager in high school can wander in and buy a sub machine gun. They also attended Eastern European Kalashnikov Karnivals: thriving arms bazaars held under the noses of police and government officials. The sellers at these bazaars would hand over an elephant gun to Osama Bin Laden if he had the cash.

'What do you think, Dr Jurisevic? Are we a step closer to winning this war?'

'Looks like it.'

'You don't seem convinced.'

'No, no. It's wonderful.'

'Yes?'

'Wonderful.'

'Good.'

The delirious smiles and self-congratulation are a little lowering to the spirits. Fatmir is right: I don't get it. I haven't hungered for my nation's liberty over a couple of centuries. I haven't dreamed of raising the Kosovar flag over Pristina, or sworn oaths of vengeance against the occupying Serbs. I want justice for the Kosovars, but that's not the same as living each day with the passion of a Misini, or a Fatmir. On the other hand, wars are not won by passion. A battle here and there, maybe, but not the whole war. You need those who can channel this passion into a steely determination; this only comes from cold, hard training and experience under fire.

I leave all the happy people, the high-fivers, and wander back to my tent. It's a few hours yet to dinner. I read, pause, count the artillery strikes, go back to my reading. I'm suffering from the feeling of foreboding that has troubled me off and on in Albania. It comes over me at dawn and at nightfall. What's the matter with me? Am I about to start believing in visions and voodoo? This is a part of the world where superstition is the reigning faith; there are gypsies up in the hills who deal in potions for warding off evil spirits.

I go back to my book until it's time to sit around the fire with the Atlantic Battalion.

'Hey, Craig,' one of the Atlantics calls to me, 'teach us how to use those DUSHKAs! What do you say?'

'You learn how to use your Kalashnikov first. You can't walk before you can crawl.'

'He's calling me a baby! The Safety Nazi's calling me a baby!'

'You're all babies.'

'Now he's saying we're all babies!'

Back in my tent, I wrestle with my sheets again, count up the number of days that have passed without me doing any surgery at all. I must have fallen into a light sleep sometime before midnight because I'm conscious of waking from a dream. Voices are raised in the camp. I climb out of bed, pick up my torch. I search through the darkened camp until I find a group of recruits huddled in the cold outside two of the tents. They glance at me with the expressions of chastened children. Some have wet cheeks.

'What's happened?'

'An accident.'

'Anyone hurt?'

'Two. Two are dead.'

'Two! How? Gunshots?'

'One shot. An accident.'

'One shot killed two people?'

'Two people.'

In the first tent, under the light of a naked bulb, a recruit of about twenty is lying spreadeagled. His T-shirt has been pulled up to his neck revealing an entry wound in his chest. He's obviously dead, but I check his pulse anyway.

'Where's the other one?' I ask.

The recruits and officers pressing around me compete to explain.

'One at a time. Are you saying the other one is in the next tent?'

'Yes, yes, the next tent.'

The body in the second tent has taken a bullet in the head. Both of these guys would have died instantly. The recruits insist that it was indeed only one shot that did all this damage. The bullet passed through the chest of the guy in the first tent, then into the brain of the second guy. It was a freakish thing. Looking at the trajectory, and the positions of the dead, I'd say the first was sleeping on his side, facing the boy with the gun.

'And where is the soldier who fired the gun? I know it was an accident, but where is he?'

I'm told that he ran away, taking his gun with him.

'Is anyone looking for him?'

'Yes. They will find him. He was screaming. It was his friend he shot.'

I return to my tent shaking my head and sighing with the pity of it all. I feel for the boy who's run off. His friend and the other man died without knowing a thing, but he's out there somewhere, suffering. He has his gun with him. I mutter a brief prayer, asking God to let the boy live. But I fear he won't. I fear he will do himself harm.

In the morning, one of the recruits I'd seen in the night comes to tell me that the boy has been found, outside the camp, dead. He'd shot himself through the face.

Chapter 17

The camp is sombre after the deaths of the previous night. Recruits I've instructed in weapons safety over the past week avert their eyes when I pass, conceding in their embarrassed way that all I'd said was true. I hope to God I haven't got some sort of vindicated look in my face. It's certainly not what I feel.

I'm on my way to see Misini. I've allowed twenty-four hours to pass since the arrival of the weapons shipment that so delighted him. He may now be ready to listen to reason when I tell him that his recruits will need a lot of help if they are to make use of the weapons in any sensible way. I want to put together a small unit of instructors for the task. If they're willing, I'll ask for Alan Kelly and Andy Feeney, and also for Arber Muriqi, a New Yorker in his late thirties who spent a year on the other side as a draftee in the Yugoslav Army in the mid-1980s. I only came across Arber recently and don't know him terribly well, but I'm sure he'd be willing to help train these recruits. And Sherifedin Dema, another New Yorker, in his early fifties, I think; he'd help, surely. He also served in the Yugoslav Army in the early 1980s then went off to Afghanistan to fight with the Mujaheddin during the Soviet occupation. Sherifedin (he's known, inevitably, as 'the Sheriff') still wears the long beard he'd cultivated in Afghanistan. When I first chatted with him, I assumed that he was a practising Muslim, and conscientiously questioned him about Islam and the importance of his beliefs. After a short time, he interrupted me politely to explain that he was not a particularly observant Muslim and only wore the beard as a mark of respect for the more devout Mujaheddin comrades he'd lost years before.

And then, problematically, there's Nazmi Isufi, the military police commander for Helshan. He has the experience this training unit will require. He lived in Germany for many years and completed eighteen months in the German army attached to an infantry unit as a sniper. A keen hunter in his spare time, he managed to bring his scoped Walther hunting rifle with him to Albania. More than a week ago he showed me, proudly, the high-powered hollow-point rounds he employed, designed to cause maximal soft tissue damage on impact. I've seen what such rounds can do to soft tissue. I've seen a boy with a hole in his back the size of a football; a boy who'd been shot with a Walther hunting rifle. Nonetheless, I'm going to ask for Isufi.

I sit over the desk from Misini and tell him that his newly arrived weapons are beautiful. He gives a modest little shrug of satisfaction, as if to say, 'Craig, please! You are being too kind!' Then I add, 'But ...' and pause, and Misini grimaces.

'But what, Dr Jurisevic?'

But his recruits will only get the best out of these weapons with good instruction. I tell him that the weapons themselves will have to be zeroed-in, which is to say adjusted in various important ways so that they shoot straight. I watch for signs of impatience, but Misini seems at least to be listening.

I suggest that I put together a training unit, and run through my list of preferred personnel. I promote the idea of the recruits we train becoming the new snipers and heavy gunners of the KLA.

'You will have a force that the Serbs will fear. They will shake in their boots.'

Misini studies me through a haze of blue-grey pipe smoke, perhaps trying to judge if I am implying any criticism of him for not realising this himself. Eventually he says, 'Okay'.

'And I can have the men I mentioned? To take charge of the training?'

'Okay. Take whoever you want.'

'You'll give me time to make these recruits proficient before they go up to the front line? I don't want to start their training, then have them taken from me. I'll need a couple of days. Believe me, if I'm given the time, these recruits will be a hundred percent more effective.'

'Okay. Sure.'

I thank him, and take my leave. I don't say anything about the fact that we were supposed to be in Pristina by this time, according to his claim of a week ago. And Misini doesn't say anything about the fact that I started out in Albania as an IMC surgeon and converted myself into an all-purpose combat impresario. It's a tacit agreement. I don't embarrass him, he doesn't embarrass me.

I'm in a hurry. I look around for the various members I'd like to make up the training team. I come across Isufi early in the piece, but he is too preoccupied with policing and other duties (including trysts with some of the young female recruits) to be of assistance when I need him. And I need him now. The others I'd hoped to second for training are scattered across the base in various stages of preparation to move out. In fact, the Atlantic Battalion, as I learn, will be at the front within forty-eight hours. So I'll have to handle the whole training regime alone. It's a pain in the arse in one way; in another way, I get to please myself, to work at the rapid pace that suits me. It streamlines things. I'd never call myself a loner; I enjoy working closely with people of real competence. But if the commitment of the people I'm supposed to work with is half-hearted, then yes, I'd rather just rely on myself.

The recruits I've chosen to be the snipers and heavy-gunners are delighted. I've selected those with at least some military or firearms experience to ensure that they aren't too daunted by the new tools of their trade. They throw themselves into the training with the sort of zeal you only encounter amongst the young and optimistic. I have to remind them that the guns they are learning to handle may make them seem indomitable, but that the VJ has the same weaponry. They nod their heads solemnly, but I know they don't really believe me. I'm reminded once more that the best preparation for combat is combat itself. All the real lessons are learnt on the battlefield. Good training helps, but training tested in real combat is the gold standard. These men and women don't have the luxury of a gradual introduction into combat situations, of being eased into battle. Would that they did! Because the battlefield is not like anything that they would have experienced in their lives. Nobody who hasn't gone through the struggle of staying alive under enemy fire, and of responding to that fire in an effective way can learn the more crucial things from mere exercises. A soldier on a battlefield under fire has to learn to quickly overcome the sheer shock of what's happening. People want to kill him; they're *striving* to kill him. All at once, and incredibly, you are a target; you're marked for death. It can cause a reaction of wild panic in some soldiers, almost as if they're thinking, 'But this is unfair, it shouldn't be permitted! I'm not ready for this yet!' Certain lessons will help, though; certain specific behaviours will help the raw recruit to live long enough to overcome the shock, to adjust to this elemental reality of the battlefield. And that's what I hope to achieve. I want these recruits to live long enough to make intelligent decisions under fire. I have to concede that at this stage I don't care about the right and wrong of what I'm doing with these recruits. My energies are channelled powerfully into getting the vital points across. It's preventive medicine, risk factor reduction at work and I go at it with missionary zeal.

One of the recruits I've chosen for the new sniper brigade is a girl by the name of Besjana, just seventeen. She's from Pej, in Kosovo. Her father taught her how to shoot – her father who is now dead, killed by the Serbs six months ago. She's a hell of a shot, I can tell you; hits target after target, with a variety of weapons at up to nearly a thousand metres. Her preferred weapon (and mine) is the light and nimble Dragunov semi-automatic sniper rifle, accurate at up to six hundred metres in the right hands, and Besjana's hands are definitely the right hands. She can also handle the Barrett with aplomb, despite its heavy weight and jackhammer recoil. There's a rage burning inside her, but a good, slow rage, nothing volcanic; she'll channel her anger into her new occupation of skilled killer.

I tell Besjana through an interpreter that she's very, very good at what she's doing. I feel the need to single her out in this way, as if my compliments might mitigate just a little the awful grief she lives with.

'Thank you for telling me,' she says. She doesn't look giddy with delight or anything like that. She's just being courteous. She knows she's good without me saying a thing. She's carrying a splinter of ice in her heart. It will never thaw. Her gaze is dark and steady.

'It's a fine weapon, isn't it?'

She looks down briefly at the Barrett. The briefest flicker of a smile passes across her face. It's gone in a split second.

'It is a very good weapon,' she says. 'Very good. Thank you.'

I nod and let her go. The other things I might say – 'You'll get your revenge, don't worry about that, you'll kill plenty of the enemy – seem tasteless. And she doesn't need to be spoken to in that way. At seventeen, she has something of the veteran's steely preference for plain talking.

These two days of training take us almost to the end of May. The weather is hotter, the sky an even more intense blue. Sweat has been running off me in streams. There's something I want from Misini, and it's something I've earned. At the end of this second day of training, I go to Misini even before cleaning myself up and ask him to let me move closer to the front, to Krume. It's a fair reward; Misini knows it. He says through his interpreter that he'll consider the request.

'But when?'

'Soon,' he says.

'I'd count it as a favour if you'd consider it now.'

Misini sits back and ponders my obstinacy. He smiles after a minute or so and says something to the interpreter, who laughs.

'I have a proposition for you,' says Misini. 'Will you hear it?'

'Of course.'

'We will wrestle,' he says. 'If you win, you have access to all front-line positions. Everything. If you lose, you stay here.'

'Wrestle? You want to wrestle me?'

Misini is a big guy, but he's way past the first bloom of youth. Unless he's got something up his sleeve, I'll cream him.

'Arm wrestle,' he says. 'You understand arm wrestling? You know what I am talking about?'

As he says this, he unbuttons the cuff of his tunic and pulls up his left sleeve. Then he unbuttons his right cuff, and pulls up that sleeve. He displays his forearms. He has Popeye's pipe, and he has Popeye's arms; they look like Christmas hams.

'All right,' I say.

'Yes?'

'Absolutely.'

'You don't wish to think about it first? Remember if you lose, you stay here. No more requests to go to the front, Doctor.'

'Suits me,' I tell him, and I'm stripping off my jacket even as I speak. I enjoy arm wrestling and I've had some success. I'm nowhere near as big as Misini, but I'm lean and strong, with years of training. More importantly, I cheat.

We take up our positions on either side of an old wooden table, fetched to Misini's tent for the purpose. We start with our left arms. Since Misini's left arm is his natural, he has the advantage and he wins in thirty seconds. I then suggest that a draw should be counted as a win for me, since he's so much bigger. Misini, with every reason to feel confident, agrees without hesitation. But when we position our arms for the right-arm bout, I make sure that the fleshy part of his elbow, where the ulnar nerve or 'funny bone' is situated, rests on a bulge in the table's surface. I apply pressure in such a way that his ulnar is fiercely compressed, and within a minute and a half, the pain overcomes him and he concedes.

'You are winner!' he says in English, and adds something in Albanian, probably along the lines of, 'You skinny little cheating rat!' Entirely justified, if that's what he said.

Misini's offsider Fadil leads me off to get kitted out at the weapons store. I pick out a Chinese AK-47, a Yugoslav 7.65 semi-automatic pistol, a gas mask and combat fatigues. I'm going with the Chinese rifle because they're renowned for their reliability, especially the older models. This one is stamped '1966', perfect. I check its barrel, bolt, gas unit. It's a weapon that could have once been in the hands of a Viet Cong cadre, or a North Vietnamese soldier. It could have been used against my fellow Australians in Vietnam, or against Americans. A rifle like this has a history, and now it comes down to me. It'll have a further history. I can sense it.

'And when do I head off?' I ask Fadil.

'First thing tomorrow morning.'

'You're joking!'

I'd expected a certain amount of procrastination from Misini while he explored a few devious alternatives of his own, but no – he wants to do this properly. Fadil goes on to say that I'll be driven to Krume in the commander's personal jeep.

'Really?'

'The commander expected to win, Craig. But since he didn't, he wants to do you honour.'

'Did you expect the commander to win?'

'Of course. He is much stronger than you.'

'But not as sneaky?'

'No, Craig, not as sneaky.'

It's approaching midnight before I return to my tent after dinner on this day of dubious accomplishment. I look down at my camouflage gear, my pistol and Kalashnikov on my bed. I confess that I'm pleased and excited, but at the same time apprehensive. The memories of Gaza, always in the background, feed my apprehension, dull any momentary excitement. An image of Donna comes to life in my mind's eye. It's an image from the scene in our living room months earlier, when I was in the full flight of my justification for going to Kosovo.

'But Craig, do you really know what you're doing? I mean, do you really know?'

'I'm saving lives. That's what I'll be doing. Saving lives. I can't just do nothing. I can't just let it all go by. I'll be saving lives.'

'Are you sure? Are you absolutely sure of that?'

'I couldn't be more certain. Trust me.'

Chapter 18

I awake from scattered half-hours of sleep on the morning of my thirty-fourth birthday: 30 May. The Serb artillery is pounding away in the background. I remain in bed with my arm across my face and ask myself if there's anything about a thirty-fourth birthday that I should consider significant. But there isn't. It's a nothing birthday. You look back on a few significant years of establishing yourself in a profession, in a marriage, in fatherhood, and if you haven't yet mastered adult life, not to worry, there's plenty of time left. Plenty of time. The path that stretches before you goes all the way to the horizon.

Except that I'm no longer on a path. This is the wilderness. I can always return to the path and be the husband I was once again, and the father I was, and the surgeon I was, so long as I can find it. Just for the moment, it's lost. The foreboding I'm now so familiar with at dawn and nightfall sits like a bruise over my heart. The images in my mind retain their dark borders. But the foreboding will abate once I get to my feet, pull on my boots and grab my rifle. I'll begin to talk to myself in a no-nonsense way. I'll give myself therapy. I'll say, 'Craig, don't let your guard down. Hold the anxiety at bay. Just for the time being, you can't be just a surgeon. You're a combatant; you'll have to use your experience and instincts to achieve your objective – saving life and limb. When the time comes, you'll leave all this behind, you'll leave Albania behind, Kosovo, the VJ, the KLA, the artillery, the bombing – all of it, you'll leave it behind and fly back to Adelaide and become once more a husband, a father, a surgeon. No big deal. It will pass, soon a distant memory.'

Misini knows it's my birthday. He treats me to a breakfast of eggs, unidentifiable processed meat and warm beer – truly disgusting but, you know, fabulous at the same time.

'You have been as welcome here as a brother in the struggle,' says Misini through his interpreter. 'I am sorry you are going.'

The jeep is ready to take me to Krume. Misini, Fadil and a dozen of the young men and women I've trained over the past few weeks stand to attention in the parade ground as I walk to the vehicle. I couldn't be more moved if they'd played 'Advance Australia Fair' or 'The Last Post' on Anzac day. At the same time, glancing along the line of recruits, shielding my blushes, I have to suppress a strong surge of sadness. Some of these men and women will be dead before long.

The road to Krume is the road to anywhere in Albania. The horizon is always dominated by mountains, the countryside is always primitively agricultural, and one's expectation is always of the next pothole being a true bastard that will catapult you through the windscreen. Apart from the apprehension of killer potholes, the mood that pervades the countryside is one of peace and mild contentment; of a lazy unfolding of days that are like every other day. The war seems remote. I chat with the driver cheerfully, listening to his equally cheerful responses. He's more like a tour guide than a soldier taking me to a destination a little more deadly than the place I've just left.

Krume, as it turns out, is a marginally more attractive town than Kukes. Or maybe it's just that my expectations of a frontier hellhole don't match the reality. Mid morning, and mums are pushing little ones through the streets in strollers. Children are off to school with *Star Wars* backpacks over their shoulders. The traffic isn't as chaotic as it is in Kukes, fewer cars, fewer cows. Even the architecture is an improvement. The old part of the town almost deserves a walking tour with a guide book. Mosques, new and old. The Soviet-era brutalist bunkers, actually apartment blocks of unrelieved concrete monotony – dominate parts of the town, certainly, but there's enough here to persuade a visitor like me that the war is a long way off. Very few clusters of refugees, so I comment to my driver, and I'm told that most of those who struggle over the border are speedily transported to the camps outside Kukes.

'And not many refugees lately,' says the driver. 'Too much fighting. Too dangerous for them to cross. They hide in the forests.'

We pull up in front of a fairly modern mosque with a beige two-storey building attached, a rather odd structure with truncated wings at each end, crenulations along the roof line and tall, arched windows. A green canvas awning extends out from the entrance and runs down to each wing. We're on the western side of Krume, I would judge. Mount Pastrik looms above us. The driver says the hall of the mosque is a hospital donated for the duration of the conflict by the local imam. The front gate of the compound is set between two flagpoles, one flying the Norwegian and the other the Albanian flag. The gate is guarded by an armed KLA soldier.

I learn from the driver that the hospital is a combined KLA and NORWAC (Norwegian Aid Committee) facility. It has the reputation of being the best surgical unit in Albania. I learned earlier, back in Helshan, that NORWAC has as its brief the provision of emergency medical aid and long-term health planning in areas of conflict. Its first project, going back sixteen years, involved the establishment of an emergency facility in southern Lebanon in the wake of the Israeli invasion. In the mid-1980s, the NORWAC folk extended their work to projects in Syria, Egypt, Sudan and in the mid-1990s to Bosnia-Herzegovina. At the end of the Kosovo conflict they assisted in the re-establishment of services at several hospitals that had been destroyed or severely damaged in the fighting.

The organisation is funded by the Norwegian Government and voluntary donations. In combat zones, you never know who you'll be saying thank you to; here it's the Norwegians; in other zones it could be the Swiss or the Danes, the Germans, Swedes, even the Australians. It's easy to think of these sorts of facilities as examples of the rich folk doing a little moral therapy, relieving the guilt of having so much to spend and so little to worry about, by setting up shiny medical units at the bleaker outposts of civilisation. But they do a lot of good, whatever the motivation. If you took away at a stroke every humanitarian project in the world sponsored by international governments, NGOs or charities, the sum of misery and wretchedness on earth would increase catastrophically.

I'm greeted in the hospital by its boss, Dr Erik Fosse, a Norwegian cardiothoracic and trauma surgeon. He's just emerged from theatre in a blood-spattered gown. He's tall and fair in the Nordic way, perhaps in his early forties, and he radiates confidence and competence. I like him immediately. Fosse apologises for not being in a position to give me a tour of the hospital straight away; he's got a theatre schedule to complete.

'Could you help, by any chance?'

'I most certainly can!'

I drop off my gear and weapons in the sleeping quarters on the first floor, gown-up then get right into it. And, oh God, the relief! Just to be a surgeon again! The unwelcome foreboding that I struggle with is banished. The ambiguity is way, way over the horizon. Oh, this is the absolute best; my hands are tingling, my brain is buzzing. And yes, I'm full of sympathy for the patients, I'm distressed that this patient's leg has to come off, that this other guy is going to have to get by with less than the entire complement of internal organs he was born with, but more than anything, I'm thinking 'Thank God for scalpels, saws and sutures. I'm home!'

Ten hours of operating. By nightfall the operating room stinks to high heaven of fetid body parts. No chance at all to talk to Fosse, of course, but ample opportunity for me to appreciate the exemplary way in which the unit is fitted out: world-class surgical and anaesthetic equipment, the full gamut of modern portable X-ray gear, and a seemingly endless supply of medications, surgical instruments, dressings and the like. Even a supply of expensive state-of-the-art disposable operating drapes and gowns for the surgeons and team members; you wouldn't always get that in a lot of the hospitals I know back home!

In addition to Fosse, the medical director and chief surgeon, we have a general surgeon, an anaesthetist, several operating room and intensive care nurses, and two medical technicians who keep the anaesthetic machines and medical equipment running effectively. Beautiful.

Late in the evening over coffee, I sit with Erik and his team to talk about the situation in and around Kosovo. I have to harness my delight at being back at work and listen soberly to what Erik has to say. He's not all that happy, as a matter of fact.

'We've lost many men and women in the past twenty-four hours, Craig. They had salvageable injuries, each of them, but by the time they reached us it was too late. We're too far from the front. Too far.'

He explains that the front line runs along the peak of Mount Pastrik, two thousand metres high. It takes three to four hours to evacuate a casualty to the hospital. This is what I was afraid of when Misini, back at Helshan, spoke of the hospital of which he was so proud.

'We should be much, much closer,' says Fosse. 'We should be on the mountain.'

'Then why aren't we?'

'Why aren't we? You will see the reason for yourself in the morning. You will see KLA doctors and commanders out the front of the hospital. You will see them talking and smoking and laughing. Doing nothing. Killing time.'

'But why is that?'

Fosse shakes his head and runs a hand over his fatigued face.

'I shouldn't say this, but I have to. They are afraid.'

'Of the Serbs? The VJ?'

'Of the Serbs, yes. They go up to the front line, they stay one day, maybe two, then they come back down. The soldiers remain, of course. But not the commanders, and not the KLA doctors. That is something I hate to see. They won't move us up to the front line because they themselves don't want to be there. My team here – sure, we will go, we'd love to. But the KLA doctors won't stay. My team can't man the unit all day and night, seven days a week.'

'They think the Serbs will advance and overcome them?'

'Absolutely. This war is the Americans in the air against the VJ on the ground. Without the bombs, the whole thing is over in a week, the VJ win, end of story. The KLA know the Serbs can come over the mountain anytime they like.'

I have more sympathy for the KLA doctors than Fosse does. They're novices, drafted from small towns and villages, with no military training, zero combat experience. And they know what awaits them if they're captured. Any European doctor who gets captured, maybe they'd shoot us, more likely we'd become prisoners of war. But the Serbs would unleash all the venom of their loathing if they captured a Kosovar doctor.

That's something you always have to keep in mind when you're a nice white boy from Adelaide.

Erik drags his exhausted frame off to his sleeping bag upstairs. I make myself comfortable in a sleeping bag on a nest of wound dressing packs and theatre drapes. The NATO bombardment is closer than ever now that I'm up here in Krume, but it doesn't keep me awake. I knew that my enforced stint as a combat trainer was acting as a burden, but I didn't know just how much of a burden until I lie down to sleep. I haven't told Erik and the team of my involvement in training the recruits at Helshan. I imagine they think I'm some wacky Aussie out for a thrill. I'm a little ashamed, almost embarrassed, this part of me out of place in Erik's hospital. I put this burden behind me as I near the point of sleep, thoughts of having helped as a surgeon today lifting my mood. Tonight when I whisper my endearments to Donna and Jackson, there's a smile on my face.

And the smile is still there when I wake in the morning. I'm buoyant with a sense of vindication. It was the right thing to do, moving on from Helshan. I greet Fosse at breakfast with my eager-beaver grin and all but offer a high five when he suggests that we start our ward check of the patients we attended yesterday.

My high spirits diminish, however, as Fosse and I make our rounds. Fosse warned me that I would be hearing stories of betrayal. Our patients are all young men in their formative years, naïve to war, not a senior commander amongst them. Through our interpreters, they sketch a picture of bleak neglect up on Mount Pastrik. They know what's going on. They know they're being left in the lurch by their commanders. One young soldier tells me of the guilt he feels at the death of his friends. He survived, and he feels bad about that. Other soldiers are bitter. A Kosovar boy from Germany calls out to us in a voice strangled with rage, '*Herr Doktor! Kommandanten sind Feiglinge!*' Fosse and I make our way through the crowded ward to placate him.

'You think commanders are cowards?' says Fosse, at the same time inspecting the dressings on the kid's below-knee amputation.

'Ja! Feiglinge! Feiglinge!'

Fosse makes a soothing sound, nodding as if to show understanding, perhaps even agreement. I know enough German to follow what the boy is saying. He says he is *der Glückliche*, 'the lucky one', as he had only lost his leg. He describes how four friends in his squad were left to bleed to death from what sounds like relatively simple penetrating upper and lower limb wounds. He points at two Kosovar doctors on their rounds.

'We die, those bastards sit down here and drink coffee!'

The doctors, who must be able to hear all this, act as if they're deaf.

'Many here feel the same,' says Fosse as we move on to other patients, other stories. 'Not all of them are so vocal.'

We inspect the arm wound of a teenage soldier from yesterday's operating list. We'd hoped to save the limb, but he's sustained such horrendous loss of nerve and muscle tissue that his arm – and this is only apparent now – will never function again. It will have to come off before gangrene takes hold. Blast injuries are deceptively extensive, unforgiving. The poor boy must have thought that he was going to keep the arm and he's inconsolable as Fosse and I explain the need for the amputation. He sobs and shakes his head and touches his arm and looks imploringly at us, as if hoping that his fear and misery will change our diagnosis. Eventually, he says, 'Yes, yes . . .', tears falling off his cheeks. He has no alternative.

He is only thinking of his immediate situation – eighteen years old, minus an arm – but God, his situation a little further down the road will be dire, as I well know. If a free and independent Kosovo emerges from all this carnage, it's going to be an impoverished state. We're not talking about a country that sits on top of fabulous oil reserves. It has no flourishing tourism industry, no foreign investment and nothing even remotely akin to a functioning economy. Sheep, goats, cows, sorghum – that's it. An amputation requires years of rehabilitative care – this soldier's not going to get ten minutes of rehabilitation. Oh, he can join in the singing when the Kosovar flag is raised over Pristina, sure; but the next day is another thing.

When the ward rounds are done, I seek out the local Kosovar doctors to ask them about this whole front-line disaster. I want to hear their version. As I say, I'm not without sympathy for their situation. It's just that the sight of so many young men and women abandoned to the fortunes of war is beginning to work on my mind in a way that demands relief.

I find a whole gaggle of the local medics out the back of the hospital, trying to keep well away from me and from Fosse.

'These soldiers in the ward, they're saying you people won't stay up at the front for more than a day or two. They say their commanders leave them up there on Pastrik to fend for themselves.'

The doctors cough and look away and scratch their heads and generally give the impression of wishing that I would fall through a hole in the ground and never reappear.

'Well?'

'No, no. Is bullshit.'

This one doctor, middle-aged, greying, an English speaker, is apparently going to be the voice of the group.

'Really?'

'Sure. Is bullshit.'

'Okay, but there are how many of you here? Six, seven, eight. How many up on Pastrik?'

'Now? Not so many.'

'Yes, but how many?'

'Now?'

'Yes, now.'

'None.'

'That's what I thought. You know what this is? This is an absolute disgrace. Shameful.'

I refrain from openly losing my temper any more than is already apparent. If their conscience hasn't driven them to the front then I can hardly expect that a few angry words from a foreigner will. It's not worth the effort.

I turn and stride away, looking for a place away from the public gaze where I can curse and rant. Because I can't bear it. I really can't. I know what decent officers mean to soldiers in combat. It makes the world of difference if there's someone in command they can respect. These soldiers haven't got any idea of what's going on at any given time. Nobody explains the mission, the strategy. Nobody shows them a map or invites them to give their opinion, their input. There's no one to provide the guidance and support that even well-trained soldiers need before and during a mission. They're like children, in many ways, young recruits like the ones in the ward, the ones up on the mountain. Every squad, every section, every platoon needs a leader. Condescending as it sounds, they need a father figure, one with experience to guide them to their objective. Imagine what it's like to look over your shoulder after a burst of automatic fire and see your friend who signed up with you and drank beer with you and chased girls with you writhing in the mud with his guts in his hands. You need someone saying, 'Get your head down, son. I'll have your friend evacuated. Now stop howling, get up and keep fighting. You'll be fine!' What the commanders are doing is abandoning children in the woods where much worse fates than being chased by bears or wolves await them. These young guys aren't stupid. They know that they are ill-prepared for what will face them, yet they fight on. Their bravery is admirable, humbling.

I find a private place after a search and turn the air blue with cursing. It gives me momentary relief from the sense of futility I thought I'd done away with only last night. If these people don't care enough about their own, how can anyone expect us to care? But we do. Erik does, NORWAC does, the thousands of overseas volunteers do. We shouldn't feel embarrassed by our willingness to stick our necks out, whatever the motivation. Better off dead with no regrets, than alive and racked with guilt I say. Before I realise it my conscience has booked the next stage of the journey. It's packed my backpack with surgical kits and supplies and dropped me at the front. It's made plans to leave the sanctuary of NORWAC and Krume and head to the front. Maybe I can't do any good up there, maybe I'll be more use down here, but who am I kidding. I'm going. And in good conscience.

Then I remember Donna's distress. I remember her saying, 'Are you really sure?' For the first time since I left Adelaide, I understand what she means. She wasn't saying, 'You just want an adventure, you're just a boy looking for a chance to show how brave he is, how good he is.' No, she was saying, in effect, 'Craig, I know you, I know your mind and I know your heart. You won't stop. Your drive for justice is an obsession. Unless this war you're talking about is fought in the way you want it fought, you'll go crazy and get yourself killed.' She's right. I can't bear to think of these naïve young people being ripped to shreds by the Serbs without a commander to lead them or a surgeon to save them. They signed up in a passion of conviction and that passion was applauded by the KLA leadership – applauded and encouraged. But the real test for leaders and commanders is not how much passion they can conjure in their followers, but how much care and direction they show; and how willing they are to sacrifice themselves. If a father raved about his love for his children but wouldn't rouse himself to look for them if they went missing, if they were out after dark, no one would take his expressions of affection seriously again, including the kids.

I feel that by being here, I'm a bad father. That is my sacrifice. But I'm here now and I won't be a bad surgeon, I won't be a bad leader. There has to be some redemption in that.

Chapter 19

I operate with Erik the entire day and into the evening without saying a word about my plans to go up the mountain. When I finally do have the chance to tell him, over dinner, he puts his head in his hands and groans, then looks at me and sighs.

'I began to feel you would want to do this,' he says. 'Then I thought, "No, he's not that crazy". But you are that crazy, aren't you?'

'Yes, I'm that crazy.'

'You know what I want to say? I want to say, "What can you hope to achieve?"'

'Are you going to say that?'

'No. No, I'm not going to say that. I know what you can achieve. If I were younger, I would go myself. We should be on the mountain. I get sick to my stomach when I think of what we could do if we were up on Pastrik. Do you think I'm just saying that? Do you think I am boasting when I say I would go if I were younger?'

'No, Erik. I know you would go.'

'Yes, I would.'

Piert, the hospital's general surgeon, also says he wants to go up the mountain. But it's out of the question. The hospital can't spare a general surgeon.

'What will you take?' says Erik.

'As much as I can.'

'Any preliminary care you can give will make a world of difference to us here.'

'That's what I figure.'

'But Craig, it's dangerous. You know that, I'm sure.'

'I'm not a thrill-seeker, Erik. I'll keep my head down.'

'Your wife knows?'

'Not exactly.'

'I didn't think so.'

I go to the storeroom and fill my backpack with supplies. I know the type of injuries I'm going to encounter up on the mountain. I can negotiate preliminary damage control surgery with fairly basic stuff. Ketamine will be important. It's an anaesthetic agent and a potent analgesic (for sale, as a matter of fact, on the streets of Australian cities as the recreational drug Special K). With Ketamine the patients are fully anaesthetised but still breathing spontaneously, on their own. This is perfect in the field setting as it allows me to operate without the need for an anaesthetist to ventilate the patient. I cram as many boxes of Ketamine as possible into my backpack, as well as morphine, basic surgical kits, chest drainage tubes, sutures and Betadine antiseptic.

The medicine taken care of, I turn my attention to my weapon. I strip my Kalashnikov, clean it, reassemble it, strap a couple of magazines side-to-side, inverted, giving me sixty rounds close at hand. If I'm a target as soon as I get to the front line, I want to return fire immediately. I don't want a jam, and I definitely don't want to be caught short of ammunition.

It's midnight when I crawl into my sleeping bag. I gaze out the window at the black bulk of the mountain looming above the hospital. I've been in an uneasy state the whole evening and the mountain's silhouette acts on me like an omen of disaster. I'm experiencing images that flash in and out of my mind; brief, vivid pictures of how I would look should parts of my living body encounter a projectile travelling at high velocity. The human body, though resilient in the civilian world, is a shockingly soft and vulnerable thing in war; it's really designed for a world in which there are no sharp edges. I've seen bodies with cavernous gouges torn into them; I've seen them full of bright red holes; I've seen limbs sheared away neatly and limbs torn away untidily, as if by the jaws of a frenzied lion. I've seen bodies with white bone exposed in half a dozen places; bodies split lengthways, bodies burned crisp like the crackling on a leg of pork. The fragments of my body could be sent back to Adelaide in a zippered bag. These images plaguing me come from nowhere. Or maybe not from nowhere. Maybe it's the task of the human mind to remind us at certain intervals exactly what can happen when we put ourselves in harm's way. I consider myself reasonably brave and resilient, yet I lie frozen throughout the demonstration, soaked in sweat, technicolour gore oozing everywhere. I want to scream, 'Enough! I get it!' but my jaw is locked in dread.

And then the images are gone. The lesson is over. I'm limp with relief. This bout is over. My mind drifts. Now I'm craving the quiet, smiling streets of Adelaide, not this evil place. I want to gaze at green lawns and the garden Donna and I have created in our corner of paradise. I'm craving an ice-cold beer at Alfresco's, my regular little haunt, and for the reassuring smiles of friends and family. I want to see all this just before I return to bed and lie in my wife's arms. I want her to whisper, 'That's the end, isn't it? You'll never go away again?'

It's arranged that I'll be picked up by a convoy at six in the morning and taken up to the front line on Mount Pastrik. In the event, the convoy arrives early, at five, and I have to scramble to make it. Erik is still asleep. I don't wake him to say goodbye.

I'm travelling with a couple of young soldiers in a little Pinzgauer medical evacuation vehicle. I sit in the back and accept a cup of coffee from the thermos of one of the soldiers, a cheerful, grinning guy who speaks perfect, American-accented English.

'How long will it take?' I ask him.

'An hour maybe.'

'And how far?'

'Four kilometres.'

'Four kilometres? One hour to go four kilometres?'

'It's rough all the way. And listen, Doc. You better take off your jacket and sit on it. The suspension is wrecked.'

A little way up the track we're stopped at a checkpoint by a couple of soldiers. It's a media checkpoint. No television crews and reporters are permitted up at the front line, and every non-military vehicle is searched for cameras. It's not hard to see why the KLA top brass wants to keep the media away from the action. This is supposed to be a war in which plucky little good guys are standing up to the bullying big bad guys. The little guys are the good guys, the big guys are the bad guys. If the world sees the little guys abandoned on the mountain by their commanders, it's not going to look good.

The two soldiers in the Pinzgauer with me exchange banter with the checkpoint soldiers, they share a smoke. Then the English speaker bursts into laughter.

'What's the joke?' I ask him, but he's convulsed and can't reply. One of the soldiers outside is telling a story.

'They're saying that an American television crew came up here yesterday. You know Tex Jackson? He has a show on cable in America. It was him. And these guys tell him, "You can't go up there, too dangerous." So he asks these clowns to help him out. He says, "Crawl up that ditch there with your rifles, we want to film you, look like you're under fire". So these guys are crawling in the ditch and acting like they're shit scared, like the whole Serb army is on their ass, and the crew films them. Then he interviews them.'

'And these guys didn't mind? They were happy to go along with it?'

'Of course! They want to be on television!'

'But it's bullshit!'

'Hey Doc, war is bullshit. What's the matter with you?'

After a further kilometre or so there's enough light in the sky for me to notice that the track is barely wider than the Pinzgauer and that the drop to the right is just about sheer. If my comrade in the driver's seat miscalculates, we're dead.

'Hey Doc, you don't like heights?'

'Normally, no problem. Right now – not a fan!'

'We're going to look after you. No problem.'

'Oh, right. Could you keep your eyes on the road?'

'Hey Doc, I'd like you to tell me something. You're from Australia, right?'

'From Australia, yes. Could you watch what you're doing? Please?'

'No problem. You've got those kangaroos in Australia. How high can they jump, those kangaroos?'

'About twenty metres.'

'Fuck me! Twenty metres!'

'Big ones, maybe thirty.'

'You're shitting me!'

'It's true.'

'Thirty metres?'

'They can jump over a two-storey house. Sometimes they land on your roof. They do a load of damage.'

We veer to the right, my side dipping suddenly.

'Be careful!'

'No problem. You're kidding me, aren't you Doc? Thirty metres! You promise that's true?'

'I promise.'

My comrades are still marvelling at the leaping prowess of the Australian kangaroo when an almighty blast just ahead of us sends an eruption of debris over the vehicle. The driver manages to keep control of the Pinzgauer and brings it to a halt before we blunder into the blast site. A metre-wide crater has opened in the middle of the track, smoke still rising from it. Three more blasts down the slope have us shielding our ears from the painful roar and blast waves of the detonations. I think they're missile explosions – Katyushas or maybe heavy mortars. It's hard to tell. We stay in the Pinzgauer, waiting for whatever we're waiting for – a direct hit, instant annihilation, whatever. When missiles or mortars are exploding around you, you're no better off in one place than another unless you're being directly targeted. There's no way that our small vehicle could be the target of this bombardment, so leaving the Pinzgauer and running for cover is just as dangerous as sitting tight. I've experienced first-hand the effects of grenades and petrol bombs at close range in Gaza, but never anything like this. I'm reminded all over again of what boys and young men must have endured in the trenches of the Western Front. A lot of them went mad, but the wonder is that they didn't all lose their minds.

We wait until the blasts move away, then leave the Pinzgauer cautiously to check the damage. The windscreen is shattered and the rear-vision mirrors torn from their mounts. But the tyres are still inflated and the radiator intact. The engine, we assume, is undamaged.

'What's that noise?' I ask the other two. I'm talking about an agonised bellowing and screaming coming up from the valley.

'Animals,' says the soldier with the thermos. He's standing on the side of the track staring down into the valley. 'Look.'

One or more of the blasts has strewn the pasture further down with the carcasses of sheep and goats. A number are still alive, thrashing about in pain. Some are smouldering as they frantically try to walk. Others run off dazed, entrails falling from split bellies.

'I'm going down to shoot them. We can't leave them like this.'

'No, no! You can't go down there, Doc. Toe-poppers everywhere.'

'Toe-poppers?'

'Mines. Many, many mines.'

'On this side of the border?'

'The Albanians. Border police. They take money from the Serbs, the Serbs come in and lay the mines. Arseholes.'

'Oh shit!' I'm surprised, but not shocked. This is Albania after all.

'Tell me about it.'

I'd initially intended to shoot the injured sheep and goats at close range with my pistol. But since I can't go down to them, I'm compelled to shoot them with my rifle from the track. Five shots, five hapless animals unburdened of their pain.

But the hush that follows is as bad as the bellowing itself.

Back in the Pinzgauer, we come to a halt every time we see a mound on the track, then climb out and inspect it gingerly. The mounds are just mounds, but the thermos guy takes the opportunity to educate me about the antipersonnel mines dotting the slopes down in the valley. They are laid to blow the feet off KLA cadres attempting to come up the mountain under the cover of darkness, so no great effort is made to conceal them from the dawn light. I'm told which mines are detonated by the weight on the trigger plate; which ones make use of trip-wires; where they're typically laid; how much damage each type does. Large anti-vehicle mines, small improvised Russian anti-personnel mines, and a selection of Chinese titbits. I appreciate the teacher's insistence that I listen carefully. I don't want to become a legless surgeon, swinging myself along on a couple of crutches back in Adelaide.

The closer we get to the base at Cahan, the more the scene comes to resemble Goya's *Disasters of War* etchings; pictures I first saw in my teens. Goya's art expressed his horror and revulsion at what war does to men, and my own horror and revulsion is growing minute by minute. The track and the embankments are now an open graveyard of dead animals –

goats, cows, sheep – putrefying in the summer heat. Down in the valley, the body of a shepherd lies across one of his sheep, also dead. The shepherd's dog is sorrowing at his side. It's possible that the shepherd isn't dead; he may have been knocked unconscious by the shock wave of a blast. But I can't go down and check without risking my limbs. It distresses me that we have to keep going.

'That guy down there, do you think he's dead?'

'Yeah, he's dead, Doc.'

'Are you sure?'

'I'm sure.'

'You don't want to risk coming down there with me to check?'

'No way!'

We pass on with me wondering if his family has any idea of what has become of him. Maybe his wife and kids still expect him to return. And when he doesn't return, what then? They go out searching? And glimpse what seems to be a human form from some distance away, and as they get closer, their dread mounts?

Two hours it takes us to reach the unguarded gate of the base at Cahan. A big farmhouse occupies the centre of the compound. One of the smaller farm buildings off to the east – maybe a milking shed – is fiercely ablaze. Soldiers are running everywhere, shouting and screaming, trying to carry water to throw on the flames in anything that will serve. Two dead soldiers lie on the ground near the blazing building; other soldiers are dragging and carrying the wounded to a farm shed way over on the western side of the compound. Once we're inside the base, we leap out of the Pinzgauer at the medical hut and run to help with the wounded. This carnage and mayhem is evidently the result of the Katyusha attack we experienced way down the track. The rockets that scared the shit out of us were strays; this is where the majority of the barrage landed. It's unusual for a relatively old-fashioned device like a Katyusha launcher to score a direct hit on a target; more commonly, the missiles land on the fringes of what's being aimed at and do some secondary damage. This is a Serbian fantasy – half a dozen rockets right on top of the main KLA base on the mountain.

Inside the hut it's like a scene from a World War I wound-dressing station. A couple of medics are working frantically amidst the screaming and weeping and groaning. The thing I'm most aware of as I stand in the doorway is the stink of seared flesh, clotted blood, sweat. Soldiers lie on a concrete floor awash with fluxive blood. The medics themselves are screaming. I'm trying to work out who's in charge – hoping that there is someone in charge, but there's not. I can see that the injuries are mostly to the groin and lower limbs, as if the rocket blasts had sent out a waist-high field of flame and shrapnel. The look in the eyes of the wounded in places like this index all the versions of dread and frenzy that war throws up. Some of the eyes are wide open in helpless panic; others are squeezing out tears of pain, or casting about wildly for someone who will work a miracle and make all that's happening seem no more than a frightful dream. The look that I always dread is that of glazed resignation, because it is succeeded by the motionless stare of death. One of the casualties, slumped against the wall behind the door, has just that look and I now notice that blood is seeping from his left groin. I grab him and lay him flat on his back and stick my knee into his groin to stem the flow of blood. I have to get to my backpack and to the surgical kits but if I release the pressure on his groin he'll be dead within a minute; his face, staring up at me, is already greyish-white. And now a baffled expression comes over him; he'd accepted the end and can't work out what all this frantic activity is about. I shout at the two medics and show them how to take over the compression of the groin wound while I fetch my surgical kit. They grasp what I'm saying and follow instructions. I make a ten-centimetre incision in the shrapnel wound and clamp the femoral artery. My guess is that everything I'm doing is exactly what wasn't done up here at Cahan until now. This is what made the patients down at the hospital in Krume so bitter: a comrade bleeding to death, and no one in sight to apply the basic principles of compression and clamping.

I repair the tear in the artery with nylon suture, not with any great finesse I must say, but rapidly. Speed is of the essence in these massive blood-loss situations, the poor ambient light and chaos all around me rendering finesse the least of my concerns. The bleeding is stopped. Lapsing in and out of consciousness he looks up at me and smiles. He'll have to be evacuated to the NORWAC hospital at Krume. If he survives the journey, it'll be up to Erik to keep him alive.

I do what I can for the other soldiers with the help of the two medics, a young man and woman in their early twenties. Most of the casualties have wounds less immediately life-threatening than the soldier with the groin wound. The thing you have to get used to when you have a dozen casualties screaming their heads off in pain and fear is to overcome your natural desire to offer relief to those who are screaming the loudest and look for the one person who isn't making a murmur. If you can scream, you've got enough cardio-pulmonary function to survive.

After two hours of mayhem, I sit with the two medics and sip hot coffee. Shkumbin, the guy, and Rukije the girl display a closeness that transcends the grimness of this place. As they chat, they hold hands and glance at each other with quiet affection. Shkumbin is twenty-two years old and Rukije twenty. They speak with bubbling enthusiasm in their fluent English of plans to study in the United States when the war is over. Shkumbin has his heart set on medicine, and Rukije on nursing. So attractive, each of them, with a tender radiance in their dark eyes. They're passionate about the cause of their people, but at no time do they express any hatred of the Serbs. The thing that strikes me above all is how much in love they are. It's more than the puppy love that is common at their age, and it seems all the more profound for having flourished in an environment so inimical to all the tender things in life. And their bravery – that's as moving as their affection. Married only six weeks earlier while on the run from Serb forces, they could have continued running to the relative safety of the camps in Albania. Instead they made a pact to stay together and help at the front, come what may, with the hope that they would survive the war and prosper together in better times. All they know is basic first aid, but they want to put the little they do know to the best possible use. If the Serbs take over the base, a bullet in the back of the head will be the most merciful death they can hope for. Their more senior colleagues have all fled back to Krume, but they've remained. I'd expect them to be demoralised, but they're brimming with optimism.

'The war will not last forever,' says Shkumbin. 'One morning we will wake up and it will be finished.'

'When that happens we will have to find a way to be friends with the Serbs,' says Rukije.

'And you think you can do that?' I ask.

'Yes, we can do that. Of course we can. I have known Serbs who hate the war as much as we do.'

As they speak, their hands twine and caress. That's true love for you; it 'builds a Heaven in Hell's despair', as William Blake said.

Chapter 20

I see to the evacuation of the most serious cases from the Katyusha strike, then sit with the remaining wounded, asking about the situation here and further up the mountain. I know the answer to the question I'm about to ask, but these damaged soldiers need to speak up, they want to speak up, and I might be the only one around they feel they can talk to. I try to appear calm as I'm chatting, but I'm not. If the Serbs can hit the base once with their Katyushas, they can do it again. And if they manage to zero in with mortars, we're screwed. It's likely that they will soon know the success of the strike, thanks to the bribes they pay to the Albanian border police.

'No KLA doctors up here?' I ask with mock innocence. 'Why is that?'

The hut erupts into catcalls and jeers and mirthless laughter. A couple of the English speakers contend for my attention.

'Because why? Because no balls!'

'You know where are the KLA doctors? Drinking coffee in Krume!'

'On holiday?'

'Sure, on holiday. You know when they take holidays? When the Serbs attack! No balls!'

'Only Shkumbin and Rukije stay here. Good people, they stay here. But we need proper doctors. You know? Like you. Proper doctors.'

'Well, I'm not planning a holiday. This is my holiday, don't worry.'

'Where are you from?'

'Where you are getting a Serb name?'

'Why you are wearing KLA uniform?'

I satisfy their curiosity and listen while they excoriate their negligent doctors and commanders. I would willingly have let them vent their anger for the rest of the day but more casualties from other sites on the mountain begin to arrive and I'm once again up to my elbows in blood.

Four of the new casualties are dead. The stretcher-bearers hadn't realised. The two-hour trek in the dark down the mountain to Cahan is so fraught with danger that the bearers had to focus on immediate threats and couldn't check the condition of those they were carting. So the soldiers silently bled to death along the way. We lose another three within half an hour. Two had sustained terrible wounds to their livers followed by such massive haemorrhaging that they were gone before anything could be done for them. Shrapnel had penetrated the left eye socket of the third and continued on into the brain. No hope after the long trek.

This hut is way too small to cater for all the casualties. I ask Shkumbin and Rukije and a couple of the less traumatised soldiers to help me carry the dead outside. We lay them under an olive tree as gently as possible, arms at their sides, legs

together. Ten dead all told. Of those, I think six could have
been saved if a basic surgical unit or even a competent medic
had been stationed further up the mountain. I ask Shkumbin
and Rukije to write the names of the dead on their arms with
a permanent marker, or if the arms are too injured, on their
chests. This will make it easier to identify them before burial.
I record the name and age of each of the dead soldiers in my
notebook, relying on their identity tags or wallet contents or,
if these are not available, then the personal knowledge of the
other soldiers. There's no professional obligation for me to
write out such a list, but I can't bring myself to write down
'Ten dead, all male' and leave it at that. It seems too casual.
They deserve more.

Z. Bytyci (39)

M. Shala (22)

G. Salli (21)

S. Salli (23)

R. Krasniqi (30)

J. Krasniqi (22)

M. Samakov (23)

S. Mackaj (22)

S. Berisha (29)

U. Mata (19)

At roll call yesterday, the soldiers who owned these names
would have replied, 'Here!' or 'Yes!' or 'Yo!' or whatever it is
they say on such occasions. Placing the bodies under the olive
tree satisfies some need in me to see the end of a life marked
by some sort of ritual, however makeshift. These soldiers were
all Muslim and according to the rites of the Islamic faith, they
should be buried before dusk tomorrow.

There won't be anything elaborate in the way of ceremony when they are laid to rest, and the burials certainly won't take place in a recognised Muslim cemetery. They'll be carried down to the valley and buried there.

I labour away with Shkumbin and Rukije in the medical hut, doing what I can for the casualties as they arrive. One above-knee and two below-knee amputations eat into the supplies of Ketamine and Tramadol I brought with me. I've taken to keeping what I have left for casualties that have a better than even chance of survival. And my supply of Gigli amputation wires is dwindling. The Giglis cut through bone in the manner of a cheese wire and are vital where other, more bulky surgical tools are not on hand. God knows, there'll be more amputations to come.

Our tally of operations for the day stops at fifteen. I'm spent – can't do another damned thing. Saved some, lost some. The casualties today were mostly young men, many eighteen, nineteen, twenty. They'd just come up to the front line. Barely had time to say their prayers before being hammered by the Serbs.

Shkumbin and Rukije sit with me against the wall of the medical hut watching the NATO bombardment. The detonations turn the night sky a strangely beautiful shade of orange, or not only orange but orange-vermillion and a golden yellow, all blurry, as if we're viewing the spectacle through uneven glass. We've got a small fire going, coffee brewing. From inside the hut we can hear the groans and whimpers and sobs of the soldiers we've been busy with. Some are simply coping with postoperative pain, some are calling for their mothers, some are bewildered and lonely. Even in the midst of the weeping and the suffering, Shkumbin and Rukije are at peace, somehow. They can hardly take their eyes off each other, hardly keep from reaching for each other's hands. In a moment of perfect quiet when the detonations pause and the soldiers in the hut are briefly silent, I gaze at them and redden with shame. Why am I not with the woman I love? Why am I not sitting with Donna, reaching for her hand? A third person in the presence of a loving couple feels an isolation that becomes an accusation. Isn't love, once you find it – and it's so hard to find – isn't love the force you should align yourself with, at all costs? That's what Shkumbin and Rukije have done. Why have I created this gulf between myself and the woman I love? What can I accomplish here to equal the force for good in the world that is created by faithful love?

I'm becoming maudlin. I should get some sleep. I ask Shkumbin and Rukije if they can stay awake and tend to the soldiers in the hut while I close my eyes for a couple of hours.

'Oh, no problem,' says Shkumbin. I could have said, 'Do you mind if I go to Paris and come back in a year or so?' and he'd still have said, 'No problem.' All he can think of is Rukije.

A little refreshed from my nap, I relieve the young couple and after checking on the wounded in the hut I sit once again with my back against the wall and stare at the dark shapes of the mountains under the glow of a fresh bombardment. I'm in a reverie, remembering Adelaide, replaying scenes of bliss with wife and son, humming tunes to myself. Then I detect movement further down the slope. I stiffen, and instinctively reach for my rifle, cock the action, safety off. The movement becomes a shape, then another. Three soldiers, struggling.

I can hear the gasp of their breathing. I'm still alert, still holding my rifle to my shoulder when the soldiers emerge from the gloom. Even before I recognise their faces I glimpse the badge of the Atlantic Battalion on their uniforms. The three of them stagger to where I'm crouching and collapse in front of me. I lower my rifle.

'Enver?' I say, 'Is that you?'

Enver lifts his head and stares at me.

'Dr Craig?'

'Yes, it's Craig. What happened to you? You look like shit.'

'Everything,' says Enver.

I brew coffee for the three of them, urge them to warm themselves by the fire. My last memory of these men was of broad smiles, hearty slaps on the back, jokes about my obsession with safety. That was – what? A week ago at Helshan? Less than a week? Now they look like wraiths. They've aged.

As Enver begins to feel the benefit of the coffee and the fire's warmth, he tells me the story of his unit's experience at the front, speaking for himself and his two comrades who nod in confirmation. The unit had been stranded at the front line with nearly a thousand other KLA soldiers, unable to move forward because of the incessant Serb shelling, twelve hours a day, every day, Enver says. There was no effective cover on top of the mountain and the KLA had suffered heavy casualties.

'It was madness, Craig. They put us into positions exposed to the Serb artillery, so we get the shit pounded out of us all day. Then they tell us we can't fire back. "Don't return fire, don't make any offensive move on the Serbs." What the fuck?

They don't want to make the Serbs angry. They don't want the Serbs to attack our lines with infantry. And these guys who tell us not to upset the Serbs, where the fuck are they? Back at Krume! They piss off and leave us to be slaughtered! Unbelievable!'

'I've heard the same story from the casualties I've been seeing,' I tell Enver. 'How many commanders stayed with you?'

'Three or four. Three or four out of twenty.'

One of his comrades shakes his head and holds up two fingers. 'Two,' he says.

'Two,' says Enver, correcting himself. 'And no doctors. The guys who didn't die straight away, they were dumped in these shepherds' huts up near the top of the mountain. No treatment, nothing. Screaming, Craig, screaming. Not medical huts, just huts for screaming. Guys screaming themselves to death.'

Enver stops to wipe his eyes. His two friends from the Atlantic Battalion look away, fighting back their own tears.

'What was the point of us going up there, Craig?' Enver says when he's regained control of himself. 'I mean, what was the fucking point? We're not allowed to fight back. We sit there shitting ourselves while the Serbs blast our heads off! What's the fucking point?

'I don't know, Enver. But tell me, how far over the border were you? How far inside Kosovo?'

Enver looks at the other two and asks their estimate.

'In the first four days nearly four kilometres. Now maybe five hundred metres,' says one, and the other nods.

'Five hundred metres!'

'About that. Not more. Maybe less.'

And Misini said that the KLA would be in Pristina within days. He said that a week ago. I thought it was foolish fantasising then, and now it's confirmed as something worse than fantasising; more like utter bullshit.

'Did any Serb infantry get through your lines?' I ask Enver. Maybe I shouldn't have asked, because he and his two friends drop their heads and stare at the ground.

'Yes, the Serbs came,' says Enver at last. 'Sometimes at dawn, sometimes just before nightfall. They took prisoners. I didn't see it, but others say that the Serbs torture them when they get back to their own lines. I didn't see it. But I believe it.'

Shkumbin and Rukije later told me that reports from other traumatised soldiers returning from the front confirmed what Enver feared.

We sit together without speaking, but not in silence; we can still hear the sobbing and groaning of the wounded in the hut, and the NATO bombardment has started up again. But it feels like silence, perhaps because of the weight settling on my heart. I know what Enver is going to suggest.

'Craig, you have to go up there,' he says quietly. 'You have to.'

'Do I?'

'Yes. You have to go.'

I don't reply. I resent deeply the negligence of the local surgeons and the KLA commanders. If they did their job, I wouldn't be under this pressure. I want to get them all together, the runaway commanders, the runaway surgeons, and shout at them. 'You said you wanted your own country. Well, do something about it, you feckless bastards!'

'Craig?'

'Yes?'

'Will you go?'

I don't say anything. I leave Shkumbin and Rukije to care for the Atlantic boys and head for my sleeping bag. The thought of saying, 'Yes, I'll go, sure,' and being thanked and slapped on the back and told what a great fellow I am makes me sick. I will go, but an irritation is working in me like a splinter. I'm going to get killed and there'll be a lovely little ceremony when they dump me in a shallow hole on the mountain, and a few people will wipe tears from their eyes and somebody will say, 'Dr Craig, he gave his life for the cause,' and it will all be drivel. I've got a country, I'm not here as a patriot. Yes, yes, it will be wonderful if these people end up with a free Kosovo, but what sort of free Kosovo is it going to be if the commanders and the doctors can't rouse themselves to help these poor, exploited men and boys trembling in their foxholes?

My fury at the hollow slogans of the KLA leadership makes me boil as I lie waiting futilely for sleep. These wretched soldiers up on the mountain are being butchered by slogans.

Chapter 21

I'm called on at four o'clock in the morning to tend to a new group of casualties. Two of the newly arrived are dead. One is a girl of just seventeen, but in death she looks older, as if what she experienced in the days before she died has aged her prematurely.

I pick out some of the most seriously wounded soldiers and have them loaded into a couple of Pinzgauers and a Jeep for the trip down to the NORWAC hospital at Krume.

I travel with them on a journey that takes almost two-and-a-half hours. The small convoy has to pause every so often so that I can move between vehicles and tend to the casualties. I notice that the body of the shepherd we saw on the way up is still sprawled in the field. It might be there in a month's time unless the NATO bombing causes the Serbs to think again about this invasion of Kosovo. 'Ethnic cleansing' – there's your cleansing: the rotting body of a shepherd in a green field.

At Krume, I move straight into the operating room with Erik and remain there for seven hours. As we operate Erik asks me brief questions about conditions on the mountain.

'It's as bad as we feared?'

'Every bit.'

'No doctors?'

'No. A couple of Albanians with a little first-aid training. A man and a woman. Lovely people.'

'It makes me weep.'

'Does it? I'm beyond weeping. It makes me puke.'

'You are very angry, Craig. I understand'

'Thanks Erik.' My anger eases as the list goes on.

When we complete the operating list, I head straight for the storeroom and fill a large trunk with drugs and surgical equipment. I'll take the next convoy back to Cahan, leave the supplies at the medical hut then find my way up to the front line. With the supplies at Cahan, I won't have to trek all the way back to Krume.

Heading up to Cahan once more in the early evening, I'm in a calmer state of mind. The anger has passed, replaced by a steely resolve. People in combat zones who become dominated by anger and disgust do reckless things and get killed. I've been imagining the sort of things that Donna and Jackson would be required to say if I were killed. 'My father? Well, he was a nice father and we played footy together and went to the beach and watched telly and he read me stories and loved me lots, but one day he went to Kosovo and got shot in the head.' And someone would say, 'But why did he go to Kosovo?' and Jackson would say, 'To help the sick people. Now I don't have a dad.' I don't want to get shot. Too much to lose. Too much explaining to do.

Reaching Cahan, I notice an American Humvee parked at the rear of the headquarters building.

'The KLA has come into some big money?' I ask Ljuli, the driver.

'You mean the Humvee? That's American Special Forces. They're based at Krume but they come up here twice a day to talk to the base commanders.'

'You mean the two or three commanders not drinking coffee down in Krume?'

'Those ones. The good ones. The Special Forces guys get information on Serb positions along the front and send it on to NATO headquarters. For the bombing. You know Craig, we're the only guerrilla army in the world with its own air force.'

'And one of the only armies in the world without doctors.'

I wander over to the headquarters building and ask one of the guards if I could speak to the commander. I want to tell him about the medical supplies I've brought, and of my plan to go further up the mountain. The guard, an American Kosovar in KLA uniform, shrugs and tells me to go right ahead.

The office of the commander is darkened and the air dense with cigarette smoke. A couple of KLA officers and three Americans in summer camouflage uniforms are huddled around a small table. The five men glance up from the maps spread on the table and study me with suspicion. But then the commander, whom I'd met briefly the day before in the medical hut, stands and strides across the room to shake my hand.

'This is the Australian surgeon I was telling you about. He saved many of my men yesterday.'

The Americans, still suspicious, offer the compromise of a handshake. One is an air force lieutenant, the other an air force sergeant, and the third an army specialist sergeant.

Only the army sergeant, a likeable guy of about thirty with an American smile of even white teeth, is prepared to divulge his name.

'Sonny,' he says, 'Sergeant Sonny Sonnenberg.'

'Dr Jurisevic, sit with us,' says the commander, and gestures toward a seat at the table. This makes the two Americans who kept their names to themselves distinctly uneasy.

'You sure about this?' says the lieutenant to the commander.

'Dr Jurisevic was at Helshan. Before that, at Kukes. He knows everything. We trust him.'

'Jurisevic?' says the lieutenant.

'I promise you, he is to be trusted.'

The air force lieutenant and the specialist sergeant glance at each other uncomfortably. Sonnenberg seems perfectly sanguine about the whole thing.

The discussion at the map table continues. The commander is pointing out sites at which Serb forces are concentrated. It appears to be a military map of the area judging by its division into square kilometre sectors. He says his patrols have gained good information on Serb troop movements over the past few days. Listening in, I think, 'Well, maybe'. From what I've seen and heard, there couldn't have been too many patrols up on the mountain sussing out Serb concentrations with any great accuracy. The commander is obviously not going to say, 'We have no idea where the Serbs are because my troops are sitting in foxholes waiting to be shredded by mortar strikes'.

The Americans move outside to discuss this latest intelligence. I take the opportunity to tell the commander that I intend to head right up to the front where I can do more for the casualties. Even as I'm speaking, I'm aware that I'm no longer making nice and dressing up my intention in the language of a request. I'm going and no one's going to stop me.

'You're certain you must go, Dr Jurisevic?'

'I'm certain.'

The KLA commander gazes at me steadily, and stalls momentarily, tears forming in his eyes.

'Forgive me,' he says. 'It always touches my heart when people come here to this place and put their lives in danger for us. I'm sure you know that we cannot always count on our own doctors. We thank you. All of us here, we thank you.'

He takes his pistol from its holster and hands it to me, together with a couple of magazines from one of his pockets.

'I want you to have this. You know why? Because it has always been lucky for me. I want it to be lucky for you.'

The pistol is a Beretta 92 model 9mm semi-automatic, a brand new American service pistol. I'm caught a little off-guard; I was preparing to argue my way to the front line, to dismiss any objections. And now this unforced approval, and this gift. Soldiers are superstitious about anything that they believe has given them good luck; items that act as talismans, warding off death or injury. The commander wouldn't have offered the gift lightly.

'I'm grateful, certainly,' I say, 'but I already have a pistol.'

I unclip my holster and show him the weapon. He shakes his head.

'That Yugoslav piece of shit? Here.'

The commander takes my pistol from its holster and slips in the Beretta.

'You know, Doctor, you might have to use this. You're aware of that?'

'Yes, I know.'

'If the Serbs capture you when you're armed, there's no way they will treat you like a noncombatant. You understand that? Remember, these VJ paramilitaries are animals. Wolves.'

'I'll be okay.'

'You are wearing a wedding ring. You have children?'

'A son. Five.'

'You carry my prayers, Doctor. Take whatever you need from the medical supplies. I'll have a squad take you up to the front line.'

I've been breathing in the potent fumes of cheap Albanian tobacco for the past hour and my head is throbbing. I wander about outside, filling my lungs with the crisp mountain air. I'm struck once more by the beauty of the place. The mountain peaks are largely treeless but covered in a skin of vivid summer grass. Further down the slopes, fingers of forest creep up toward the outcrops of rock that show through the pasture. The fresh air works on me like a tonic.

I find the three American Special Forces guys down by their Humvee and stroll over. The two who displayed so much professional caution in the commander's tent seem less guarded now. They're happy to chat about the war, and what a complete arsehole 'Herb the Serb' is, and about American football. I mention that I'm going up to the front with my cargo of medical supplies and this sweeps away the last vestiges of reserve. All three Americans are from military families, and mad keen to join in the fighting.

'No way we'd be allowed,' says Sonny, 'but boy, that'd be something. Unloading on those VJ and paramilitary bastards, I'd love that.'

'Well, I won't be unloading on anyone if I can help it,' I say.

'Are you kidding? Up there, you better be ready to fire back, Craig. They find you with that six-shooter strapped on, it's going to be high noon.'

'I'll fire back if I have to, don't worry.'

'You used a weapon before, Craig? Got off a few rounds in anger, maybe?'

'Yes I have. Not in anger. In self-defence!'

'Is that right! Man, I envy you. I really do.'

They inform me that they have to get back to Krume before dark. We part amicably, me promising not to exercise excessive restraint if the going gets hot, the Americans vowing that on their next trip there will be more Hersheys for me than I could eat in a year. Waving goodbye, I have to wonder briefly at the allure of battle that so animates these guys. Combat is absolutely bloody awful, except for a minute here and there, and maybe for a little while afterwards, if you're not wounded. I think of all those young men in America back in the 1960s, drafted into the military. Some were reluctant soldiers, but there were plenty who thought that they were off on the biggest, loudest, wildest turkey shoot imaginable. 'Hot damn, Vietnam!' One unforgiving bullet in the wrong place and all the excitement disappears in a flash. The frenzy and confusion of a fire-fight dispels any glamour in an instant. I learnt that in Gaza. The true story of combat is never recorded on cemetery headstones or on cenotaphs and other public memorials. A line that reads, 'Died gallantly' would tell a truer story, often, if it read, 'Died screaming'; and instead of the total number of troops who 'sacrificed' their lives, we might simply chisel onto a block of marble the number of limbs left on the battlefield or in hospitals, the number of body parts unaccounted for, missing in action. Such a memorial would be unthinkable, of course, and I must confess that even I would find it tasteless. But if you want the truth about war, you have to start and end with the screaming.

A couple of soldiers help me as I unload the trunk of surgical supplies and move it inside the medical hut. I find Shkumbin and Rukije inside, resting with their backs against a wall and looking unhappy.

'Too much, Craig,' says Shkumbin. 'Too much blood. It makes me sick to see it.'

I can tell that my two friends are suffering from the version of combat fatigue that affects surgeons and other medics. I've seen it before, and experienced it myself, the disgust and distress that takes hold of a doctor after days of mopping up blood and wrapping bandages around the raw stumps of legs and arms. You think, 'But there is no end to it!' and you want to go away and cry your eyes out when there is nowhere to go. You castigate yourself, saying, 'If you're sick to death of it all, imagine how the casualties feel! Shape up, damn you!' And you do shape up; you do keep going, and you never find the ten minutes you need for weeping. Eventually, of course, you toughen up to such an extent that you can take limbs off all morning, pronounce soldiers dead, look in surprise at the blood drenching your surgical gown, and then sit down to lunch with no compunctions at all.

I squat down with my two friends so that I'm at eye-level when I tell them that I'm going further up the mountain. Distress comes into Rukije's face instantly, and she grasps my arm.

'Oh, Craig, what you are doing is so dangerous,' she says. 'I don't want you to do this.'

'I'll be fine.'

'I don't think so. I don't think you will be fine. I think you will be killed.'

'Listen, I'll be back here drinking coffee with both of you. Believe me.'

'This is what all those who are now dead told to me,' says Shkumbin. He is as upset as his wife. 'They all said, "We see you soon!"'

'Well, when I say it, I mean it. I'll be back here, and you'll say, "Craig, will you have your coffee extra strong?" And I'll say, "Extra strong thanks, Rukije". Another thing – I want both of you to come to Australia one day.'

'To Australia?' says Rukije. She's smiling now.

'Absolutely. And I want you to bring your children. Okay?'

Rukije blushes, but her smile remains in place. She knows that I'm striving to reassure her, that I might be saying things I can't live up to, but she doesn't mind.

'You're going to have lots of kids, I'm sure,' I tell her. 'You know where I live in Australia? In the most beautiful of all the cities in Australia. It's called Adelaide.'

'Ad-lade?'

'Ad-el-aide. It's beautiful, believe me. And you two will meet my wife and my son and my new kids and we'll swim in the pool.'

'You have a swimming pool? Truly?'

'Well, no. Not yet. But by the time you come, I'll have a big, beautiful swimming pool. Olympic size. And you think this coffee is good? When you come to Australia, I'll show you real coffee. Believe me.'

I don't usually babble in this way. If I insist that they come to Australia, maybe I can cement in place this future visit; make it happen by saying it aloud. My friends fear for me, but I fear for them even more. I have experience of combat; I'm confident I can keep myself alive in most situations. But Rukije and Shkumbin? In a way they're like babes in the wood. If anything bad happens to them, I'll be devastated.

Later, just before I join the squad for the hike up the mountain, I check my weapons, check them again, make sure I've got sufficient ammunition and surgical supplies. Then I give Donna's contact details to Shkumbin.

Chapter 22

The commander promised a squad to escort me up the mountain, and at seven o'clock in the evening, five soldiers arrive. Two are Americans from the Atlantic Battalion, but not from amongst the Atlantics I'd known at Helshan. We shake hands sombrely then begin the trek along what must be an old goat track. I'm informed that the track is mined and to take great care each time I put a foot down. One of the Americans tells me that the goats have helped us by exploding a number of the strewn mines.

'Minesweepers,' he says, and grins.

'Good of them.'

'But still plenty of mines left.'

We walk in single file, five metres apart, three soldiers in front of me and the two Americans behind. After the first five hundred metres, the path begins to climb steeply, at the same time narrowing to no more than half a metre. The darkness all around us seems to deepen with each passing minute. The full moon above is obscured by thick cloud, and that's a good thing because it makes it difficult for Serb snipers to pick us off. The downside is – well, the downside: almost vertical cliffs dropping away on our left. Within half an hour of climbing, the drop-off has fallen away steeply, maybe a hundred metres deep. If I stumble, I'm dead.

Too much of my brain is devoted to caution for dread to settle in. I'm concentrating on finding a safe footfall each time I lift my legs. The ground is mostly hard and rocky and I try to avoid any spot where the soil is loose; any spot that might accommodate a mine.

I'm also conscious of how inviting a target we are for snipers every time we emerge from wooded areas. For long periods of time, we're nakedly exposed to the Serb positions below.

Concentrating in this way is exhausting. One's mind tires of the tension, and wants to think of other things; of the next meal, the next coffee, the plot of a movie seen years earlier, nonsense things.

The darkness is lit in brief episodes by the distant glow of NATO bombs and missiles as they strike targets in and around the towns of Prizren to the east and Djakova to the north. We remain motionless whenever light comes into the sky. The Serb snipers will know exactly where this track is, and they'll be watching.

I'm listening to the sometimes laboured breathing of the three guys in front of me and the two Atlantics behind. Fear tends to constrict respiration. All my companions are probably thinking what I'm thinking – that we're very like those ducks in shooting galleries that track across a painted background all in a line while excited customers shoot at them in an attempt to knock them over. I'd feel so much more comfortable if this goat highway was on the other side of the ridge where the Serbs couldn't see us. Those NATO bombs act on the spleen of the Serbs, I'm sure, rousing them to loathing. The Serbs know that they could win this war in a week if it were just a matter of destroying the KLA forces. They know that it's only NATO that stands in the way of victory. I can imagine the glee of their snipers when they pick out a line of enemy soldiers feeling their way along a mountain path. They must think, 'Revenge!'

We've been on the track for a little under an hour when two illumination flares burst above us throwing an intense white light over everything. It's like walking out of a dark night into the over-illuminated interior of a 7-Eleven. Our shadows are thrown in giant silhouettes against the cliff face to our right. For a split second as I drop flat on the ground, I glimpse the eerie pantomime of our frenzied shapes.

In the white glare we clutch the earth as if we're holding on for dear life to the wall of a precipice. I can still hear the traumatised breathing of the soldiers before me and behind. Do these guys know that they can on no account move a muscle? Do they know that? Has someone told them? Because the Serbs are sure to be watching through field binoculars. The snipers are waiting for the tiniest flicker of life. Even in this intense white light, they can't see us, our bodies flattened along the narrow path, but they believe we're here, somewhere. They're waiting for one of us to panic. They expect it. Their fingers are just barely touching their triggers. They are holding their breaths in half-expiration, ready to take a shot. Their excitement matches our terror. I'm praying silently for the men around me to hold their nerve. Even if an exploratory shot is fired, they must hold their nerve.

Then it comes, the moment I've been dreading. The soldier at the front abruptly leaps to his feet, intending to run to the cover of a wooded area up ahead. We can all see the wooded area, we all know we're safe if we reach it, we all know that thirty seconds running hard would deliver us from this suffocating fear, but it's a haven that has to be ignored, it's bait. I curse to myself, 'Shit shit shit!' The running guy in his panic trips and falls, climbs to his feet, sprints, trips again, crying out in his terror. Four flares are spreading their light over the mountainside now. The shadow of the panic-stricken guy rears up on the cliff face, arms waving as if dancing. He's in an ecstasy of fear; all he can think of is safety but every movement he makes shortens the time he has left to live.

Now the soldier in front of me is infected by the display of terror and attempts to get to his feet. I seize his ankle and pull him down.

'Stay still, idiot!'

'Let me go!'

'Stay fucking still!'

He kicks at me with his boot.

'Let me go!'

'You'll get us all killed. Stay still!'

Bright orange-yellow streaks of tracer rounds light up the path twenty metres in front of us, directed at the stumbling soldier ahead. This further inflames the poor guy's terror and he gets upright a third time, and the third time is the last time because two of the tracer rounds find their target. Three or four heavy rounds then slap into his side, the sound of the impact echoing off the cliff.

He's dead in an instant.

I keep a tight hold on the ankle of the guy in front of me. Surely to God he can see now that he was on the verge of being slaughtered. Surely he'll overcome his dread. I can feel the throb of his pulse through his tattered combat boot. If he moves, he'll die, and I'm so close that I'll be taken out, too.

'Don't move, don't move.'

He's emitting tiny squeaking sounds, like a child in tears who's been warned to stop crying or he'll be given something to cry about. Up ahead, light and heavy machine gun rounds are riddling the body of the soldier who panicked. The Serbs know he's dead but in their excitement they keep blasting away, tearing his corpse to pieces. It's like a feeding frenzy.

I can hear prayers being uttered in hoarse whispers. I risk raising my voice.

'Nobody move!'

The echoing thud of rounds striking the corpse ahead is losing its sickening quality. This is just mince being slapped around on a butcher's block. When the light of the last flare dies away, I repeat my warning. Any premature dash for cover will start the whole thing again.

Finally, I'm able to let go of the ankle I've been gripping like a vice. I tell the others to get to their feet, but carefully. When we reach the dead soldier, I stoop and attempt to retrieve his wallet from his pocket, but I can't grip it, it's been pounded into the pulp of his thigh.

'Help me carry him.'

Four of us hoist the body and carry it with as much haste as we can. The Serb patrol that butchered this poor bastard will be making their way up here to enjoy their kill, and it won't take them that long. I send two soldiers up ahead to the wooded area. The three of us with the body find a place where we can throw it down the cliff. Before we heave the body away, I ask if anyone knew who he was. Mutterings in the negative, a shaking of heads.

'He joined us this evening. We've never seen him before.'

The only consolation in all of this for the corpse and for us is that Serbs won't stand gloating over whoever it was. I know that the others are wishing that the body could be buried according to Muslim rites, but that just isn't possible. We all know this.

When we're all in the shelter of the trees, I tell the squad that we'll have to move fast even through the exposed areas, without exercising any sort of caution.

'We can't look for mines. The Serbs will be here very, very soon. If anyone stands on a mine, the rest keep going. The sound of the explosion will have the Serbs zeroing in from their positions down there. You agree with me? All of you?'

It takes us a further two-and-a-half hours to reach the KLA camp at the peak of the mountain. We're two thousand metres high now, and even though it's summer, patches of snow persist. It's bitterly cold.

The camp has been sited around a group of six shepherds' huts, strung out in a clearing along the stony ridge of the mountain. The huts are makeshift structures with steeply sloping shingled roofs designed to shed snow and low walls of loose limestone blocks. It's a desolate place, no trees, no cover. I know from what I've been told by the commander at Cahan that we are now only two hundred metres from the forward-most KLA position, which is itself only seven hundred metres from the Serb forward positions. The no-man's-land between the KLA and the Serbs is on the northern face of the mountain, sloping steeply down onto the plains of Kosovo. It is as open and as grim as the peak itself, swept by the frigid wind. I have no idea what the shepherds who would normally be camped here do to keep themselves sane. It's like a far outpost of the inhabited earth.

I ask the soldiers of the squad which of the huts serves as headquarters, but they have no idea. I leave them to hunker down while I try the first of the huts over on the southern side of the mountain. Within, ten men sit around a small fire in a state of misery and dejection. They gaze at me without the least curiosity.

'Anyone speak English?'

'Maybe.'

'Where can I find your commander?'

'Krume.'

'You're here alone? No commander?'

'No commander. Come and sit down. Get warm.'

'I'll keep looking.'

I try all the huts, believing without any good reason that I'll find someone with a bit of seniority. The last of the huts is a morgue, bodies in rows on the floor, faces covered, the air dense with the reek of congealed blood. Goya comes to mind again. I play the beam of my torch over the corpses, expecting to find massive wounds. There are no such wounds, just evidence of small penetrating shrapnel and bullet wounds. These soldiers all bled to death. If I'd been here twenty-four hours earlier, I could have saved some of them.

At the northern end of this naked area on the peak of Pastrik I locate what must be the base's main fighting force; about fifty soldiers pressed around a campfire, some sleeping, some hunched on the ground, some wandering about aimlessly with a blanket over their shoulders. Not one of them looks alert; not one gives any impression of having a sense of mission. Abandoned, demoralised, they are merely waiting for whatever happens next. Tired though I am, disgusted with the KLA leadership, I sorrow for these men who had come here with such high hopes, such an expectation of heroic deeds culminating in the liberty of their homeland.

'Anybody senior here?' I ask one of the soldiers ambling about. He stops and stares at me, clutching at the blanket draped around his neck.

'Anybody senior here? Commander?'

Uncomprehending, he lifts his shoulders in a half-hearted shrug.

I'll have to move up to the front-line positions in the northern zone. Maybe there I'll find someone with an overview of whatever the hell is happening here. I struggle through the darkness, pausing every few metres to get my bearings. I finally arrive at what must be the forward-most point of advance of the KLA forces. Soldiers are asleep in dugouts; small excavations, three metres long, one metre wide, a metre deep, dug by hand from the hard rocky ground. The dugouts are surrounded by a small wall of limestone rocks, reasonably good protection from incoming fire, unless you are unlucky enough to take a direct hit.

I locate a soldier with the Atlantic Battalion flash on his combat gear and in a whisper ask him if I'm likely to find a commander here, or anyone at all with seniority.

'No. No one. Don't waste your time.'

'How long have you been here?'

'Four days. It's mostly the 123rd Battalion here.'

'Much incoming artillery or mortar fire lately?' I ask knowing, but dreading, the answer.

'Shit yeah, man!'

'The Serbs are trying to blast you out?'

'Trying hard. We're barely hanging on. Lots of guys killed.'

I get myself into an empty dugout high up on a ledge with the plains of Kosovo stretched out below. Djakova, fifteen kilometres to the north, and Prizren, a dozen kilometres to the east are lit up by aerial bombardment. From this height and distance, the technicolour glows and flashes are morbidly compelling to watch. I find myself riveted by the display, wondering if and how anyone could survive such a ferocious assault. I pull myself out of my mesmerised state and settle into the dugout, slip into my sleeping bag and check my weapon before I go to sleep. As soon as I begin to drift off, mortar shells begin to land around my position. Not a full-on barrage, just a short burst of five or six scattered rounds, some no more than ten metres from me. I'm surprisingly calm, exhaustion providing a natural buffer to my fear. Once you're in a dugout you feel much more protected than you really are. The rounds landing so close could easily land right on top of me, but somehow I don't accept that they will. That's probably what the seventeen-year-old girl I saw at Cahan just yesterday believed; the girl who is now dead.

My eyes close, then open again, close and open. I'm in a state of deep fatigue and my body is craving sleep. The tingle of foreboding I have become so accustomed to is returning after a brief holiday, and it has an insistent, irritating voice accompanying it: 'This can't go on, your luck's running out, so many near misses, you're going to die, Craig, very soon you're going to die . . .' Cold and drained, I drift off.

My eyes fly open after what seems no more than ten minutes of sleep. Mortar rounds are exploding in a rapid series. I'm not properly aware of where I am, why I'm here, what I'm supposed to be doing. Albania? Kosovo? What's happening? I lift my head above the wall of limestone blocks. A weak, greyish-blue light has spread itself over the world. My waking confusion clears quickly.

I glance at my watch: 4.50a.m. Everything I was struggling to grasp comes rushing back. This is Pastrik. This is the war.

A mortar strike flings a hail of dirt and grit into my face. My limestone wall falters. I duck down again, ears ringing and throbbing with pain.

It was after midnight when I climbed into this hole. I've had maybe four hours' sleep, not ten minutes. My thinking's clearer, my sense of fear has returned.

I take a look above the fractured wall again and, dear God, the sheer ugliness of everything, the desolation! The mountain top has been hacked and chopped to pieces, the air is a choking mixture of smoke and stink. I'd thought there were no trees at all on the peak but I was wrong; a few pines still remain, scorched black and stripped of every needle.

The first strike of a new barrage throws earth and rock into the air further down the northern slope. I fling myself onto the floor of the dugout with my hands clamped over my ears. These are heavier mortars than last night, not 80mm, maybe 120mm, louder, more concussive. I count the blasts, at first believing that maybe five or six would end the attack. At twelve I'm almost hysterical. At twenty I'm somewhere beyond dread, unable to negotiate anything mentally, even something as basic as fear. I'm telling myself to hold on, hold on, and that's all I can manage. That and counting. At the twenty-fifth explosion I'm shouting, 'This is ridiculous!' as if the Serbs deserve to be castigated for the sheer profligacy of their assault.

Thirty explosions. And then silence. Silence broken only by the fierce ringing and pain in my ears.

Staying motionless, I'm still counting, as if I'd switched on a mechanism of survival that is reluctant to turn itself off.

'It's stopped,' I whisper to myself. 'You're okay, idiot. It's stopped.'

I get to my knees, aching all over from lying clenched in a wad, ears screaming. With great caution, I look out over the ruined mountain. Plumes of smoke hang over the area, mixed with the fine dust of superheated earth; this strange stink flowing over me in waves. Fifteen metres away, smoke issuing from a dugout like mine tells me that it has suffered a direct hit. I climb out of my hole clutching my rifle and run stooped over to the smoking dugout. I'm hoping that it's empty, but it's not. The soldier inside has been split apart, his torso gaping open, limbs ripped to pieces, his guts settling into a puddle in the well of the dugout. I wipe the sweat and dirt from my eyes, take a deep breath, and another. I gaze down into the dugout again, murmuring futilely, 'Poor bastard, poor bastard.'

Then I switch my gaze to the terrain of the peak and the northern slope. This is insane. The dugouts here have been sited in a position that could not possibly be more exposed to mortar fire from the Serb positions below. We're not firing back, so the Serbs have all the time in the world to adjust their trajectories and zero in on targets all over the peak. The soldiers here have been served up to the Serbs like a KLA smorgasbord. With field binoculars and a little patience, the Serbs could pick out an individual dugout and mortar it at their leisure. For all I know, that's exactly what they did to that poor devil in the smoking dugout.

I gather up my sleeping bag and backpack and head for the shepherd's huts, hoping against hope that I can find someone – anyone! – who can tell me what the plan is, why we're roosting here on an exposed mountain slope, what in fuck's name they're trying to achieve. I have a hunger for solid information more intense than the desire to eat and drink.

Soldiers have emerged from cover to start small cooking fires. Some are melting snow to make coffee. They look haggard, beaten, more like a crowd of refugees than a fighting force. They glance up at me as I pass but only a few can muster the will to lift a hand in greeting. None of the alertness you would normally find amongst soldiers on a battlefield is on show here. I don't see anyone who gives the impression of command. Are these guys simply waiting to die? Is that the only mission they have, to die when the time comes? Like a gathering of the damned?

At the hut clearing I come across fifty or sixty soldiers, men and women, some sitting slumped on the hard ground, others mooching along as they nurse a mug of coffee. I introduce myself to one of these exhausted figures after another, sometimes in English, sometimes in German, asking if anyone can point me in the right direction to find a commander.

'Hi, I'm the doctor. Who's in charge here? Is anyone in charge? Who gives you orders? Can you tell me where I can find the commander?'

They shake their heads, avert their eyes. It's as if they're ashamed to have to concede that there is no commander, that they're leaderless, unvalued. Then at last a young female soldier, speaking perfect German, tells me that the only commander she knows of has his headquarters in a small cave a little further down the mountain.

'Why do you want him?' she asks. 'Are you American? Are you Special Forces?'

'No, Australian. I'm a surgeon.'

'But you are armed.'

'Yes, but I'm a surgeon, I promise you.'

She smiles, and that's the first smile I've seen this morning. Maybe it's been a long time since a doctor made an appearance up here, or at least a doctor who doesn't look as if he hates being where he is. Maybe she takes it as a sign of things getting better. I smile back, happy to be able to display some warmth, some gladness.

'Come with me,' she says. 'I'll take you to the medical hut. It's very good that you've come here. Very, very good.'

The medical hut sits at the rear of the main group of huts, next to the ruined shell of another.

'That was the treatment centre before,' the girl says, pointing to the ruin. 'A mortar strike. All the injured soldiers inside were killed.'

Three lightly wounded soldiers are chatting and smoking inside the medical hut. And a medical attendant, by the looks of it. I introduce myself without getting much response. My weapons must make them think, as the girl thought, that I'm some foreign combat guru, some mercenary here on a flying visit.

'I'm a surgeon,' I tell the medical attendant. 'I'm here to set up a treatment station.'

And that does it. The wounded soldiers' faces break out in big smiles, and the medical attendant all but falls to his knees in front of me.

'A surgeon!' he cries, then as if he can't quite believe it he asks again, revealing a stammer, 'Are you a s-s-surgeon?'

'Yes, a surgeon.'

He throws his arms around me, sobbing with relief. 'A surgeon! It is good you have come! It is good!'

As it turns out, the stammering attendant is not a doctor but a pharmacist from Prizren. He's been treating the wounded here for weeks with a box of bandages and a bit of antiseptic. It's only an accident that he's here at all. His parents and his wife were killed by the Serbs in the 'cleansing' of Prizren and he fled across the Serb lines to Pastrik.

I tell the pharmacist that I have to leave him for a short time to locate the commander in the cave further down the mountain.

'A commander?' he says.

'Yes, your commander. This soldier says that the commander is in a cave down the mountain.'

The pharmacist looks doubtful. There's an exchange in Albanian between him and the female soldier. While it's going on, I think, 'If I get to that cave and find there's no commander I'll go back to Krume and lynch every senior officer I can find, so help me God!'

The soldier breaks off the debate and switches to German to address me again. 'It's okay,' she says. 'It's just that he doesn't want you to leave. You go down the track to the cave and I'm sure you will find the commander.'

I nod, but I haven't forgotten my vow. The poor wretched pharmacist, sleepless, haggard, tears welling in his eyes, lifts his hand in an unwilling gesture of farewell.

'Don't worry,' I tell him. 'I'm here to stay.' I don't add, 'As long as I find this phantom, cave-dwelling commander'.

Chapter 23

As we start walking toward the cave I ask the young soldier if she has a map of the area, a map of the front line. She stops, smiles, then turns to face me.

'I'm sorry, doctor, we have no maps but I will tell you. I will explain.'

With an authority beyond her years, she continues:

'That is north.'

She points toward the mountain peak.

'We are approximately three hundred metres east of the mountain peak. This clearing is where the shepherds come to rest. Front-line machine gun and sniper positions are situated at the northern reach of the mountain, maybe three hundred metres down from the peak.'

Impressed by her confidence, I nod and listen intently.

'The cave is located one hundred and fifty metres southeast from here,' she says, turning around to point in the direction from which we'd come.

'It is located on the side of the mountain facing southwest, away from incoming mortar and artillery fire.'

End of lesson. This is the most sense I have had from anyone in the past week.

I thank her and compliment her on her professionalism. She smiles, turns around and we continue down the narrow path as it descends steeply down the side of the mountain, our boots clattering on loose shale. It is not until I can see the opening of what does indeed appear to be a cave that I finally concede that it exists. A couple of soldiers emerge as I approach, and behind them an officer. Okay, I'm glad to have found the guy, but it means that I have to set aside my fantasy of mass murder by lynching in Krume, so that's a disappointment.

I thank the young soldier once more, telling her that I'll be fine now. She dips her head in a sort of salute and heads back up the path.

The officer steps forward and gestures for me to enter the cave. He doesn't speak English but he has a lieutenant who does.

'This is Commander Riza Imer Alija, of the 123rd Brigade from Djakova,' says the lieutenant. 'Please, he wishes to shake your hand.'

I shake the commander's hand, and the lieutenant's.

'The commander says he knew you had arrived. He sent some men up the mountain last night to find you and bring you down here. But they didn't see you.'

I refrain from telling them that they couldn't see me because I was in a dugout with mortar rounds exploding left, right and centre. We find places to sit in the cave while coffee is prepared for us – coffee being to Kosovars what a good stiff scotch is to those of us who haven't yet made any protracted study of the Koran. Glancing around, I have to concede that the 123rd commander, this Riza Imer Alija, has found himself the Taj Mahal of all improvised quarters. The walls are dense limestone, the floor plain earth, the roof high enough for men to walk about without stooping. Automatic weapons rest against the walls; boxes of ammunition. Somebody has driven a nail into the rock and hung his hat on it. Bedding is spread on the earthen floor. Pretty secure. Though the mouth of this small cave is widely exposed, its position means it can't take a direct hit. I wish the commander's boys had found me last night. My nerves are still stretched taut by the ordeal of the thirty-round mortar barrage this morning.

Sipping the coffee, I listen to Alija's lieutenant translating his commander's account of recent events. I hear of the commander's contempt for the officers who sprinted back to Krume when the going got bloody, and of his brigade's valour in pushing the Serbs off the mountain some weeks ago. I hear, once again, of the appalling order from KLA command to desist from 'aggravating' the Serbs. The commander says that such a craven scheme only succeeds in encouraging the enemy. He disregards the 'no engagement' order and sends patrols out whenever possible. The 123rd have beaten the Serbs once, he says, and could do it again if the commanders would only stay and fight. At the moment, without proper supplies, without doctors, without any commanders other than himself, he is restricted to holding the ground on top of Pastrik for as long as he can.

The commander launches into what appears to be a furious tirade of some sort, a big black cloud over his head. The lieutenant listens closely, nodding in agreement. 'Commander Alija says that the time will come when the war is over. At that time, he will name all the shameful officers who left their men on the mountain. Many men died, many women soldiers too because the officers were cowards. The commander says that he prays to God that he will be alive at the end of the war to do this important job.'

By this time, tears are running through the stubble on Alija's cheeks. Kosovars, I notice, are completely uninhibited about shedding tears in company, even war-hardened men like Alija.

'The commander says that his patrols find many wounded soldiers, many civilians trying to escape the enemy. But most of the soldiers die from their wounds before they get to a doctor. He says that most of the civilians are too old or too sick to climb the mountain. God knows what will become of them. Commander Alija himself is going into Kosovo in a few days to look for his family. God in His mercy will spare them. That is his hope.'

I ask Alija about the overall situation at the front – troop placement, defensive perimeter positions, chain of command. He confirms my own rapid assessment: bedlam.

A little bit of thought had gone into the placement of the fixed gun positions at the northernmost point of the front line, and that was it. Alija talks about the wholesale loss of life amongst his raw recruits, saying that casualties could have been reduced mightily if the KLA had the right sort of people in charge.

'Commander Alija says that the people who look at maps and give orders in Krume have never seen the front line. He says they have never seen it because they do not want to see it. He says his troops are like –'

Here the lieutenant pauses and consults Alija once more. They appear to be discussing the word Alija has used, or the metaphor; I can't tell. There is a certain amount of animated gesturing with hands and also, peculiarly, a fair bit of pointing at the mouth.

'His troops are like food for the Serb artillery,' says the lieutenant. 'You understand what this means? Like food?'

'Cannon fodder,' I say. 'That's what we would say in English.'

'Cannon fodder?'

'"Fodder" means food.'

'Fodder means food?'

'Yes.'

I think of the English soldier-poet of World War I, Wilfred Owen, who made it plainer in his verse than in the work of any other writer I know that foot soldiers are so often just that – cannon fodder: 'What passing bells for these who die like cattle . . .'

I ask the commander if I could use his cave to set up a small surgical unit. It would provide protection from the weather and its position facing away from incoming Serb artillery would make it a hell of a lot safer than the shepherds' huts in the clearance above us.

'The commander says he will clear the cave immediately. He says your arrival is a blessing from God.'

As the commander and two of his soldiers busy themselves clearing the cave, he keeps chatting to the lieutenant.

'Commander Alija asks if you will go inside Kosovo with his patrols. He hopes you will help the wounded villagers, and also his soldiers who are hurt on patrol.'

Ah, so here it is! I knew it was coming. It's as if my journey from Adelaide always had its destination inside Kosovo. I've pestered the KLA to allow me to work where

I can be of the most benefit, of course, but only because of their monumentally inadequate medical program. This is where the foreboding I've been plagued by originates: in the anticipation of fulfilling a role far removed from that of an unarmed surgeon. On patrol, I'll have to carry my AK-47, loaded, safety off. If the patrol is fired upon, I'll have to fire back. The wounds I'll be attending to amongst the KLA soldiers with me, I'll also be inflicting on the Serbs. There is irony and there is black irony, and a surgeon who shoots people in the morning and then operates in the afternoon has strayed into the black irony sphere.

I tell Alija that I will do as he hopes, but that my essential role will be to remain in the cave and man the surgical unit.

'Commander Alija asks me to tell you that he only makes this request because of the savage behaviour of the Serbs. They know that they will lose this war. The NATO bombing will make them ask for a cease-fire. But they want to kill as many of our people as they can before that happens. Commander Alija asks me to tell you that there have been many massacres in the villages along the road between Prizren and Djakova. His patrols have found many, many fresh graves.'

The lieutenant is interrupted by Alija and listens closely.

'Commander Alija asks me to say that our enemies want to cover up their crimes before NATO ground forces move in. You understand, doctor? Commander Alija with his own eyes has seen bodies on top of each other, many bodies, he has seen them burning. He weeps to see the people of his country killed and burned. It is for this reason that he asks for your help.'

I nod and give my tacit agreement. How could I not? But I'm left wondering if the next special request will be for me to parachute into Belgrade and personally assassinate Slobodan Milosevic. I know that Alija is completely sincere in his sorrow but I am approaching meltdown in my capacity to absorb all that is expected of me. Some part of me wants to say – not loudly, just insistently – 'Look, I know what the Serbs are capable of. I see so much blood and gore and horror and I don't need any further convincing. I'll do what you ask.'

Alija and the lieutenant leave me in possession of the cave after a final series of handshakes and expressions of thanks. I stand at the entrance, wondering how I can fashion this hole in the side of a mountain into a combination hospital ward and surgical theatre. I can see that I'll have to operate up here, at the mouth of the cave, where the light is the strongest. This leaves me exposed to artillery and mortar rounds exploding close by, maybe even to a direct hit by shrapnel, but without the light there can be no surgery. I'll sleep at the back of the cave and in between the sleeping section and the operating section I'll site stretchers and bedding for preoperative and postoperative nursing. I'll have to maintain a rapid turnover. As soon as patients are fit for travel, I'll have them moved down the mountain to Shkumbin and Rukije at Cahan, and then on to the NORWAC unit at Krume.

So this is a sort of dream come true, if I look at it in a certain way. I'm chief surgeon, director of surgery, hospital general manager, chief admissions officer, post-operative director and cleaner. What's to complain about? I'm the King of Rustic Surgeons.

With the surgical unit set up, I'm aching for rest, mind and body, but it's not going to happen. The first rocket of what will almost certainly be a barrage explodes fifty metres from the cave's entrance. From the cave mouth I witness the panic-stricken scattering of soldiers looking for cover up and down the mountainside. I'm cursing beneath my breath, 'Hurry! Jesus! Hurry!' The Katyushas are augmented by a mortar barrage and now the cave itself is shaking, dust falling from its ceiling. I'm still blaring my exhortations as I watch a soldier who's too exposed up on a ridge looking this way and that for shelter.

'Hit the ground, idiot!'

A split second later a mortar hits the ridge on which he was standing and he's in pieces, airborne.

I crouch inside the entrance to the cave, sheltered from the blasts and shock waves but not from my grief for the troops caught in the open. The Serbs must have a precise fix on the position – the barrage is extraordinarily accurate. Initially intense, it becomes more sporadic, and eventually subsides after ninety minutes. Amongst my volunteers is Mentor, a male nurse with broad experience. He's been working for years in the UK. Most of the other volunteers can only be employed carrying stretchers but Mentor is a genuine godsend. I tell him to prepare for the first casualties and, even as I'm speaking, they begin straggling in. Small shrapnel wounds, burns; we can cope with this low-level stuff – but there'll be another barrage soon, I can feel it coming, and after that we'll be struggling with much more serious casualties from further afield.

The aftermath of the next barrage is everything I feared it would be. The casualties are carried in screaming or moaning or bearing their wounds in stoic silence. Three of the wounded are bleeding badly from neck and abdominal injuries, all three under twenty years old, all three dead very quickly, in spite of my best efforts. One kid dies while I'm operating. The left side of his face is sheared away, carotid and jugular exposed. While I'm clamping the torn vessels he clutches the hand of a friend and says something over and over in Albanian, a prayer, a mantra, I don't know. I'm working desperately to stop the life ebbing from him but it's futile, the graveyard look is in his eyes, he's beyond fear, all but dead when he utters the final syllable of his chant.

I lean back on my knees and close my eyes just for two seconds, three seconds.

'What was he saying?' I ask his friend.

The friend can't respond. He's crying like a child, his grief so extravagant, perhaps they've been friends from the time they played soldiers as little children.

'What was he saying?' I ask Mentor. For some reason, I need to know.

'He was telling his friend to speak to his mother. He said, "Tell my mother I am sorry". That's all.'

'Sorry for being killed?'

'Yes, sorry for being killed.'

We have no blood, very little intravenous fluid, and only a small amount of Ketamine and, as on other occasions, I'm saving that for those soldiers who have a reasonable chance of survival. It feels callous, but economies like this are what I'm reduced to.

Corpses are carried into the cave, too. It's a hospital and morgue combined. I tell the volunteers to lay the dead shoulder to shoulder at the back, where I sleep.

I work alertly but with a sick sense of beginning a surgical list to which there will be no end. Two below-knee amputations are followed by three open abdominal procedures to stop bleeding from the liver, then an iliac artery clamping in the pelvis, a carotid artery repair, an open thoracotomy and a number of major wound clean-ups, debridements.

The shelling fluctuates throughout the day, sometimes intense, often in just ones and twos. I have to take advantage of the lulls to get the dead into the ground. I organise a party of volunteers to find an area of soft ground not so far from the cave, rapidly excavate a series of shallow graves, shovel the soil over the corpses and place limestone blocks as headstones, all the while expecting Serb snipers to spot us and pick us off. As we hurry back to the cave we pass the second burial detail carrying two more dead. I call out, 'Be quick!' because I know this lull could come to an end in seconds.

And that's exactly what happens. Four massive mortar strikes just as we reach the cave. I dive headlong inside, landing on top of the injured on their stretchers. I stay immobile for a count of ten, then look back praying that I won't see what I know I will see: four volunteers of the burial party all ripped to shreds; pieces of the corpses they were carrying and pieces of themselves strewn over the slope, the freshly killed mingling with the less freshly killed. I groan as I get myself off the top of the injured soldier I'd been smothering, and the injured soldier groans, and now the whole cave is echoing with groans and sobbing and cursing directed at the Serbs as soldiers sit up in the stretchers or from their bedding and gaze out on what is left of their comrades. One of the volunteers from the first burial party, the one I led, wants to run down the slope and retrieve the body of his friend who has just been killed. I seize his arm and wrench him back into the cave.

'You'll be killed! The snipers are watching!'

He struggles to free himself but I won't let go.

'Snipers!' I yell at him. 'Don't you understand? They're watching!'

The soldier relents. He subsides to the ground, heaving with sobs.

I can't spare the two or three minutes it would take to console him. This latest mortar strike means that there will be casualties waiting for us. I call out to my volunteers, all of them wracked with weeping, and tell them we'll have to go with stretchers and look for the injured. Without any diminishment of their grief, they nod their heads and prepare themselves for the open ground no more than five minutes after they've witnessed what can happen to them in the open. Their bravery would move me deeply if I had time for being moved.

I lead the stretcher teams up the track to the clearing where the shepherds' huts are sited. We hug the rock wall on one side but even so, snipers' rounds smack into the stone inches above our heads. Then mortar strikes break out, and it's as if the explosions are stalking us up the track, landing twenty metres behind us, covering us in dust and smoke. No shrapnel this time, thank God. The Serbs are good at this. Extremely good! They have us in their field glasses, and the mortar crews and snipers are working in close co-operation. It's a technique they've perfected in years of war in the Balkans.

The huts are still standing. That's something. Is it? I don't know. I think it is. Yes, it is something. Wake up, Doctor, of course it's good! Some of the huts are full of soldiers, most of them injured. A mortar shell on that hut would have turned the mountain top into an abattoir. I'm dazed in the head and sick in the heart. There's a limit to what anyone can stand when it comes to this kind of stress. If I get off this mountain alive, I'm going to be in the hands of trauma gurus and psycho-quacks for years to come. It's doing me harm but I haven't the time or inclination to dwell on that now. I take the opportunity to rest for a bit. I have to. The volume of adrenaline that's been flooding my arteries is going to leave me utterly spent when it abates. And I must find some rations to take back to the cave. What's the use of surviving mortar strikes and snipers only to die of thirst and starvation in a big limestone hole?

It's in the storage hut that I notice a man of about sixty who appears to know what's happening, issuing orders. I reach over and tap him on the shoulder.

'Listen, I need some rations to take down to a cave we've got set up as a hospital. What do you think?'

He leans back and studies me.

'You're an Aussie?'

'Yes. How did you know?'

'Where do you think I'm from?'

'No idea.'

'Australia, mate.'

'Really?'

'Rilind Bytyci. I've been living in Victoria for years. Originally from here.'

A great rush of relief washes through me just knowing that this man, this Rilind, is from Oz. I couldn't be more delighted if he were Hugh Jackman, or Paul Hogan, or Dame Edna!

We stand chatting for maybe half an hour, and every minute that passes replenishes me. It's a potent thing, a homeland, that sense of coming from somewhere. No wonder these Kosovars are prepared to leave their guts all over the place to secure the same sort of thing for themselves.

Rilind tells me that he has a son, Ilirian, also living in Victoria, whom he has ordered to stay put in Australia.

'I told him that I'll represent the family over here. You can see why I made him stay home, can't you? What's the life expectancy of a kid in a KLA uniform on this mountain?'

'About five minutes,' I say.

'I would have said three.'

Rilind and I shake hands and speak of catching up whenever possible. I begin looking for my stretcher crews out on the mountain. I see lots of smiles amongst the soldiers, lots of joshing. It's truly extraordinary how moods can change in combat zones. Half an hour ago, everyone was petrified, convinced it was their turn to die. Now, the sun is shining and you'd almost think that we were gathered for some sort of weekend sporting event, a Grand Final barbecue maybe. It's a survival mechanism. Smile while you can, even if the mountain top is strewn with bits of human flesh.

Chapter 24

I order a halt on our way back to the cave just before we descend down the exposed path near the entrance. If the Serbs are watching, their snipers will take advantage of the clear space. I order the soldiers, my volunteers, to strap their backpacks onto our two stretchers, then I position the first stretcher at the top of the slope, give it a shove and watch as it slides down the slope towards the cave mouth. My idea is to attract sniper fire with this dummy casualty, but nothing happens. Ever cautious, I send a second dummy casualty down the slope, again without attracting sniper fire. Then I slide down the slope on my arse, rifle above my head. The volunteers probably think I'm being excessively safety-conscious, but using a term like 'excessively' before 'safety-conscious' in a combat zone like Pastrik is a tribute to common sense.

Back in the cave, we have a problem with corpses. More soldiers have died while I've been away and the bodies are piling up. Pretty soon, being summer, they will attract flies and disease. We have to get them into the ground, but not until nightfall. It's madness risking the lives of the living to dispose of those who no longer have a life to lose.

I check the postoperative patients, expecting to find that they're all stable, or stable enough. But there's one soldier who's causing me grief, a chest wound patient I'd performed a thoracotomy on. He's beginning to bleed so much from the chest drainage tube I inserted that I'm concerned about his clotting. I think he's developed coagulopathy, a failure of the blood to clot. He'll have to be evacuated back to Krume. I have nothing in the way of blood and blood products up here, and this kid is going to need plenty, and soon.

With commanders so scarce, I'm in a position to exercise my seniority. After all, I'm wearing a KLA uniform and I'm almost old enough to be the father of the very youngest kids here. I've had more experience and training than any of these guys, and I can also rely on a good complement of mongrel common sense to boot. In any case, I'm way beyond any rarefied attempt at diplomacy, any apologetic, 'It's not up to me to issue orders' way of looking at things. I want this chest-wound guy down at Krume, so I simply pick a half-dozen soldiers on the basis of their knowledge of English or German and their combat experience and get started on the rocky track to Cahan. From there, if he lives, he can be evacuated to the NORWAC hospital at Krume.

There's a natural spring on the track not far down from the cave, the only water source on the whole mountain. We pass fifty or so KLA troops filling their water bottles at the spring and we join them to replenish our own canteens. I let my guys pause for a smoke, but I'm not best pleased to see so many soldiers in a clump and urge my men to make haste. We head off into a wooded area that provides a bit of cover and only just make it when mortars explode behind us, right in the middle of the soldiers at the spring. I'd thought that the Serbs would be attracted by a big gathering of KLA troops, but bloody hell, I didn't think they'd get close enough to lob mortars so accurately. I glance around, looking for the Serb patrol responsible. They have to be nearby. There! I spot them five hundred metres off, on a ridge. But even as I'm pointing, the patrol vanishes. I leave the chest-wound kid under cover then run back to the site of the carnage. Two soldiers are dead, another seven are injured, including a girl whose legs are badly cut up by shrapnel. I tell the soldiers to get the wounded up to the cave where Mentor can treat them, then turn back to the wooded area. When I glance back, the soldiers are still milling around the spring, not knowing what to do, not knowing where the mortar rounds came from.

'Move away from the fucking spring!' I yell, throwing my arms about to indicate the direction they should take. 'Get away from it!'

God, if ever an army needed commanders! In the Australian army, and all other modern military forces I'm sure, soldiers right down to the rank of private would know what to do in such a situation. If the more senior officers were dead or out of action in some way, the troops would do what they'd been taught and find cover. Here it's like children on their first day at school, looking at each other in confusion and fear.

Back on the downhill track, I bustle the soldiers along. We have to hope that the steady traffic of man and beast on the track has rid it of all the mines. I'm also worried about plain old-fashioned ankle injuries while moving along at this clip over uneven ground. Having to support a soldier with an injured ankle would hold us up badly.

We reach Cahan after a further two hours with no further emergencies. Our patient, still breathing, still conscious, is loaded up for evacuation to Krume. I fill my kit with supplies, give Shkumbin and Rukije an update on my movements and then head back up the track with a fresh team of soldiers. The sky is clear enough to navigate by moonlight.

An hour along the track, the NATO bombing commences. I can see a long way into Kosovo, the flashes of explosions around Prizren and Djakova; but we're getting some bombing closer to where we are, unusually, over on the hills to the west. Why the hell would NATO be targeting those hills? Nothing there but sheep and goats. My bafflement must be showing on my face because one of the soldiers slaps me on the back as we pause to watch the flashes.

'Bad night for the sheep,' he says.

'But why bomb over there?'

'Why? Good question. I'll tell you, Doc. The commanders in Krume and Cahan, they tell the Americans that the Serbs are over there. They put a cross on the map, they say, "Here! Many Serbs! Many tanks!" The Americans telephone the air base. "Hey, lots of Serbs in the west!" The airplanes come, kaboom! One hundred dead sheep, but no Serbs. You see?'

'But why do they tell the Americans that the Serbs are over there, when they have no idea?'

'Commanders? Commanders are shit. They don't want to say to the Americans, "Where are the Serbs? We don't know." So they put some marks on the map. You know something else? The Serbs use decoys. They make inflatable models of tanks and put them in the fields with the sheep. The Americans come along, "Hey, down there, twenty tanks!" Kaboom! The Serbs are laughing, laughing all day.'

264

We start our trek again, but I've lost my enthusiasm. I mean, I knew something dodgy was going on when I saw the commander down at Cahan marking the map for the Special Forces men with such confidence. And he was a good commander, one of the few prepared to get his arse up the mountain. So imagine what the rest are like. Thinking this, I can't help but ask myself if I've got rocks in my head. This isn't even my war, it's not Australia. I feel like a sucker. And what happens if I go back without a leg or a face? How the hell do I explain staying on when I have to admit to knowing all that I know? The only justification I can find is my feelings of pity for these poor bastards; these soldiers giving life and limb unquestioningly, these martyrs. Pity, that's it, nothing more. It's not a lot to hold on to.

We reach the cave close to nine at night. Mentor greets me warmly, telling me that we haven't had any further casualties while I've been away. I'm aching for sleep. The cave is full of the injured and the dead. It's the safest place to sleep, but I can't bring myself to stretch out beside the corpses at the back of the cave. They lie there, some with their eyes gazing toward the cave mouth as if they're studying the stars, others with grotesque sardonic expressions of death. I have to go. I just have to go. I leave the cave and wander about, chat with a couple of the Atlantic guys up at the northernmost machine gun emplacement. I settle into an empty dugout down from the emplacement and lie there, thinking. Those dead men in the cave, I can't get them out of my head, repulsion now replaced with guilt. I can't stay here, it doesn't feel right. I find myself back at the cave. I stare at the corpses and I'm suddenly engulfed by a terrible, wrenching sadness. The mothers of these men don't know that their sons are dead. Back in the towns they came from – maybe in Albania, maybe America, Germany, I don't know – but wherever their mothers are, they may be praying for their safety at this very moment, praying to Allah. I climb into my bedding and stretch out next to the bodies. I can't bear to abandon them to nothingness. This I owe their mothers.

Chapter 25

It's fairly brief, this experience of sleeping cheek-by-jowl with dead men. I'm woken at five in the morning by a soldier who wants to tell me that there's been a big Serb advance overnight. He's a little jittery and I try to calm him down.

'A big advance?'

'Very big. Many Serbs.'

'Did somebody send you to tell me this?'

'The squad leader sent me.'

'Really?'

I climb out of my sleeping bag, nod courteously towards the dead men, start cleaning my teeth. Through a mouthful of toothpaste, I ask the jittery soldier to tell me more. The Serb breakthrough is centred on the towns of Planeje and Gerozhup, he says. A KLA patrol witnessed Serb forces hustling civilians along at gunpoint in the smaller villages of the region. Volleys of rifle fire followed, which in all probability meant that Serb paramilitary death squads were going about their vile business. The KLA night patrol had itself been spotted, and had lost four men.

'Now they are sending out a patrol to see what has happened in the villages. The squad leader wants you to come with him.'

'What a surprise.'

'Pardon?'

'Nothing. Where is the squad waiting?'

'Where the machine gun is.'

'I'll be there in five minutes.'

I'm hoping very much that the patrol squad is experienced. I don't know that I'd be prepared to go behind Serb lines with some of the inexperienced troops I've seen up to now. The incident on the Cahan track when the panic-stricken guy almost had us all killed is vivid in my memory. Before making my way up to the machine-gun emplacement I fill my backpack with surgical equipment and some of the remaining Ketamine. Then I grab three extra loaded magazines and two grenades, in case I agree to go. Grappling with doubt, I make my way up the track to meet the squad.

The squad leader is a Kosovar named Garne, who speaks perfect English after a few years of playing soccer in Scotland, of all places. He says Commander Alija told him about me.

'And did he tell you I'm a surgeon, not a soldier?'

'Of course. But he says you have a great deal of experience, war experience. He says you know how to fire a rifle well.'

'Yes, I do. What about your soldiers? Do they know how to fire a rifle well?'

Garne gives a rueful smile. 'Maybe you have had some bad experiences. Don't worry, Doctor. This is the Eagle unit. All my soldiers have been in combat. They are Kosovars who have served in the VJ. They are not like the soldiers you have been with.'

As I'm talking I'm applying face paint, along with the other Eagle troops, which amounts to saying yes to Garne's proposal.

'Where are we heading?' I ask Garne.

'An area to the northeast. Five kilometres over the border.'

'And five kilometres behind Serb lines, I assume.'

'That would be correct.'

I take a deep breath, exhale, and in that act I accept whatever comes next. For all intents and purposes, I am now a soldier who can also practise surgery, rather than the other way round. I will have to fire at the enemy, perhaps fatally. The enemy will fire at me, perhaps fatally. All this I recognise and acknowledge. I've lost interest in finding rationalisations for what I'm doing. It's what I've become. I accept it.

The Eagle patrol makes its start on the trek into Kosovo after sunrise, but the light is not at all good. A dense mist hangs in the air above us and reaches right down into the valley below. The mist gives us cover, but it also gives the Serbs cover. If they hear us coming, we could wander straight into an ambush. But we'll be going through forested regions, and that will help. We can pick paths that keep the foliage screening us.

We're not taking stretchers. They would only slow us. We move down the path in a single staggered formation, one to the left and one to the right about five metres apart. I take up a position near the middle of the line as we descend into the mist. We're now in Kosovo, which means we're in enemy territory. We're walking in complete silence. Noise carries in mist further than normal. Four kilometres from the base of the mountain and three kilometres behind Serb lines, I can hear Serb artillery and mortar crews maybe only a kilometre to our north. I glance around, hoping to catch Garne's eye. My unspoken question will be, 'Do you know what the fuck you're doing?' I can't pick Garne out, but I have a certain amount of confidence in him. I assume he'll lead us away from the Serbs.

Suddenly Garne, up ahead, stops dead still with his arm raised as a signal to us to do the same. Then he gives a further signal and his soldiers move speedily and almost silently into the cover of a thicket. I follow the lead of the Eagle soldiers.

For two minutes by my count, nothing at all happens. I can't hear anything to suggest that we're in danger. I glance at the others in hiding with me but their expressions don't reveal much. Then the soldier nearest to me nods just once, indicating the direction from which the danger is arriving, whatever the danger is. I study the foliage downhill but can see nothing. Then I can. It's a Serb patrol a hundred and fifty metres off, paramilitaries, judging by their black uniforms. The Serbs are moving as silently and as stealthily as we were before we took cover. This is the first time I've seen the enemy up close. I don't feel anything, no special animosity. But if Garne intends to fire on the Serbs, I'll certainly join in, no compunction about that.

Garne lets the Serb patrol pass. A good thing. If we'd fired on it behind Serb lines, we would have been asking for very bad trouble. Now that we're clear, we head up a small path through an almond grove and finally to the edge of a hamlet of six houses somewhere between the towns of Planeje and Gerozhup. The mist is beginning to lift as the sun climbs higher in the east. Even here, near the hamlet, there's a big risk we'll be spotted by Serb patrols.

Still silent, we skirt the town, wary of an ambush. Garne points to bodies in the doorways of two of the houses. Keeping to the perimeter of the hamlet, we come across more bodies, a great many more. A few lie on the main path in attitudes of flight, but most are in the thicket that hems the place in. They'd been running for their lives. Fifteen bodies, some shot in the back of the skull when they fell over, most riddled by AK-47 rounds in the back, legs, arms and chest. Nine young women, three elderly women, three elderly men. Oh, this is heroic. Do the Serb paramilitaries consider this combat? Do they take pride in their courage? The faces of the other Eagle soldiers betray little. They would have seen this before. But I can imagine what's going on in their guts.

Nothing has been said. We're still waiting for the ambush. Fifteen minutes pass before Garne is prepared to raise his voice, telling us to break into two groups to search for survivors.

For some time we've heard the whimpering voice of a woman coming from a house at the far end of the hamlet. Two soldiers head that way to investigate while my group makes for the opposite end of the traversing path. Within a minute, maybe a little more, a great clout of an explosion comes from the direction from where the woman's cries had emanated. We all hurry to see what the hell has happened but I know before we reach the house that it's a booby trap. And there lie the two soldiers who went to investigate. One is torn in half, the other is missing an arm, a leg and a big part of his face. Both dead, absolutely dead, but I have to make sure and lean over the bodies feeling for the pulse that I will not find. I look into the house where the booby trap was set and see the remains of the woman, just as dead as her two would-be rescuers, finished off by the blast that killed the soldiers. The Serbs left the woman just alive enough to whimper, knowing that her cries would attract attention.

Garne issues orders rapidly. For my benefit, he switches to English. 'The Serbs will come. They heard the explosion.'

I return to the house I was originally heading towards. From this house, too, the weak cries of a woman issue. I signal for the soldiers with me to halt, and I'm very emphatic about it. The two soldiers killed in the booby-trap blast should have entered that house with far, far greater caution. I inspect the door's architrave as closely as if I were looking for microbes, blocking out the cries of the woman inside. I turn my attention to the hearth itself, to the pile of shoes at the base of the two steps. People in this part of Kosovo, in common with Muslim custom here, always leave their shoes at the door. And there it is, the tripwire, disguised by the placement of the shoes. The wire runs between two fragmentation grenades, one each side of the steps. These grenades have a phenomenal explosive force. The two dead soldiers at the other house must have kicked the shoes out of the way as they entered, tripping the wire. I kneel down and, with the utmost caution, lift the shoes away from the wire one by one. A soldier kneels beside me and cuts the wire with a pair of Leatherman pliers, one fast snip. It's possible to rig these booby traps so that the actual cutting of the trip-wire will detonate the grenades, but in this case that single snip of the Leatherman has rendered the grenades safe.

I enter the house first, trusting no one else on earth to exercise the degree of caution I demand when my flesh is at risk. I cast my glance left and right, high and low, still refusing to be rushed by the now shrill screams of the woman within. The Serb paramilitary squads include teams expert in the laying of booby traps. Even in my caution, I'm moved by the humbleness of this interior, the few pieces of furniture, the unadorned walls. It's just the farmhouse of a family living from hand to mouth.

The cries of the woman are coming from the room at the rear of the house. Only when I am absolutely certain that it's safe do I signal for the others to enter the house. I pass through the kitchen, the bedroom. I can see into the living room at the rear, I can even glimpse the woman within it. I pause before entering the room, reluctant to push the door open further since it may be rigged from the other side. But I have no choice other than to accept the risk and so I nudge the door further ajar and step in.

The woman, cradling a child in her arms, a boy of four or five, is sitting on the floor at the far end of the room with her back propped against the wall. Between where she sits and where I stand lies the body of a man, her husband I would think, his head resting in a pool of darkening blood. I step around the body and approach the woman, whose eyes are fixed on me. I don't think she knows whether I have come to help or to do more harm, but she is imploring me anyway. What she is asking me I don't know. The child in her lap is dead. He has been garrotted. The woman herself has been shot in both legs and is partially disembowelled. She is sitting in her own blood. The injuries to her legs are designed to prevent her moving. The wound to her lower abdomen is meant to cause enough pain to make her cry out without killing her too quickly. The scene confronts me more than any I have witnessed before. It cuts right to my core, my mind racing to comprehend the sheer horror, the depravity.

I kneel down beside her, because that seems to be what she's pleading for. She clutches my wrist with surprising force; she is, after all, only minutes from death. But the motion she makes in gripping me causes the boy to slide from her lap. She is attempting to speak, her voice a bare whisper now after all the exertion of crying out.

'What is she saying?' I ask one of the soldiers.

The soldier kneels and whispers to me, as if hush were the only remaining respect he could show the woman, 'She asks you to bury the child before the next day. It is our custom.'

'Tell her I will do that, with all my heart.'

The woman, now realising that I am not able to speak her language, addresses herself to the soldier. As he listens, he nods, his face now wet with tears.

'Doctor, she is asking us to kill her.'

'To kill her?'

'Yes. That is what she is saying. Doctor, I am sorry. I cannot do this.'

The soldier stands and steps away, covering his face with his hand.

I pick up the child gently and hand the body up to the soldier.

'Go outside,' I tell him. 'I will join you shortly.'

I gesture to a second soldier who has been standing further back to do the same thing. Each soldier nods. They leave me alone with the woman.

Her face is as pale as bone. The stress of her agony has aged her dreadfully. She whispers, '*Faleminderit shumë*,' meaning, 'Thank you very much.' What I intend to do I will have to do quickly. The Serbs will be back soon. If they find this woman still breathing, they will make her suffer a little more before death.

I move the woman as gently as I can and place her beside her dead husband. From the bedroom I fetch a thick blanket. I think she sees clearly enough what is to follow, and she nods and manages something like a smile. I turn her head to one side, gently place the blanket down on it, point the barrel of my pistol down and pull the trigger. I wait for a few seconds, then reach for the woman's wrist. The pulse has gone. I slide the pistol into its holster and take my leave.

Outside the house once more, the Eagle soldiers glance at me, then look away. They don't wish to intrude on what was a private agreement between me and the woman.

We retrieve the weapons from the two dead soldiers and remove all traces of identification. If the Serbs were to identify them, they would visit retribution on the dead soldiers' families. We can't take the bodies with us and can't afford the time to bury them.

I accept with all my heart the task of carrying the dead boy back to the mountain. I take the small body in my arms in the way one normally holds a living child. My rifle is slung over my shoulder. We start the long trek back to the front line, all of us distressed. My own sorrow is more piercing than any I have experienced before this day. I am in pain. I have carried a boy of this age in my arms, a living child, my son Jackson. I have carried him to bed when he was sound asleep and unresisting, when he was as still as this child of Kosovo. My thoughts of Jackson, his very image, have become merged with my thoughts of this boy, and when I look down at the face of the child I'm carrying, I see Jackson. This child's weight is no burden, but what his dead form conjures in me is a burden I can scarcely bear. The emotions at work in my heart are at moments like the shriek of a tempest, at other moments like a soft, low cry of sorrow and despair; a moaning.

As I carry the boy, I make the quick adjustments of movement that a parent would strive for when carrying a sleeping infant; the adjustments that spare the child any jolting, any sudden lurches that would cause him to wake. He cannot feel anything, I know that, but thinking of him and my son at the same time compels me to treat him with all the tenderness that I can provide. And the mother, that poor woman so savaged by the Serbs. I see her face and relive the moment when she accepted that I would keep my word and bury her child, the trust she conveyed in her gaze as she prepared for death. I cannot cry – the grief is beyond any such response. I pray to God that the mother of this boy took some final solace knowing that her son would not be left abandoned on the floor of that house.

For some of the Eagle soldiers, the most acute loss is that of their two comrades. The bond men form in combat is as deep as male comradeship can ever become. Compelled as the surviving soldiers are to leave the bodies behind is awful for them. They would have wished to stand over their graves and pray.

With the child in my arms, I pause on a hill overlooking the tiny town in which no living person remains. The morning sun shines brilliantly. The hamlet with its almond groves and glistening thickets looks peaceful, almost serene, as if it were mourning the dead in a calm and dignified way.

That afternoon, in accordance with the mother's wishes, we bury the boy. No tombstone, no epitaph, no name. We site his grave on the eastern side of the mountain, in a clearing from which one can see the entire valley below. The hamlet he grew up in is over that way.

Chapter 26

I return to the cave. Oh, the cave, the everlasting cave! The Serb bombardment has been so unrelenting that it is full of casualties and I have to toil nonstop with the pitiable and diminishing store of medicines available to me.

I have my wins and my losses, as usual. Abdurrahan, one of the soldiers I know by name, is one of the losses, and a piercing one. I glance up from an operation to see him carry an injured friend into the cave, stretch him out and hold his hand. I nod towards him, just to let him know that I'll be with him shortly. I see him slump over, and my assumption is that he's given way to exhaustion, as well he might, but when I ask him to let go of his friend's hand so that I can go to work, there's no response. I find a small shrapnel entry wound on his neck; not very obvious, but the shrapnel has pierced his carotid artery and he has quietly bled to death. It upsets me badly to discover that Abdurrahan is dead. It is as if death had acquired him by stealth, by trickery. I am used to death as a fairly open and honest sort of adversary. A man is carried in with only one arm remaining of his complement of four limbs and big hole in his chest, and it's as if death says, 'Doctor, I will be taking this one, that is only reasonable,' and I have to acknowledge the logic of what's being said. But every so often, I'm reminded that death can be a double-crossing, deceiving arsehole. And it's not as though I can address a complaint to a higher authority. Death is the highest authority.

I put on my empty pack, and make the trek down to Cahan, with the intention of going on further to Krume for more supplies, maybe some good food.

When I reach Cahan, I have a Pinzgauer loaded with casualties for the trip down the mountain to Krume. There's time for a coffee with Shkumbin and Rukije, but they're not about the place so I leave with a mental note to catch up with them as soon as I get back here. Because I will be coming back. I'm conscious of something inside me that's wearing out, or being eroded away. I don't know what to call it – something related to sanity. I've said that there is only so much horror and misery that a human being can endure, and a voice is telling me that I've almost reached my limit. But not quite.

Three hours later I'm in the operating theatre at NORWAC in Krume, assisting Erik Fosse with amputations. Hell, I've seen so many amputations! I could happily go for the rest of my life without seeing or performing even one more. But there's a reward after this stint with Erik. A beer, a meal, uninterrupted sleep. The most nourishing of these is the sleep. When I wake and glance at my watch, six hours have passed since my head hit the pillow. Oh, this is fabulous! Six hours. God knows how long it's been since I enjoyed a sleep like this. All night I dreamed of Donna and Jackson. I lie back for a few minutes just to luxuriate in the memory of those dreams.

I restock my backpack with medical supplies and as much food as I can carry in preparation for my return to the front. I don't want to go, but at the same time I do. I have a potent feeling of needing to be up the mountain. It's as if this thing's not finished yet; as if I'm somehow required to go right down to the wire. It's a peculiar thing to feel when I know that I could leave for Tirana right now, take a ferry to Italy, fly home to Adelaide. That wouldn't seem right, but exactly why it wouldn't I can't quite fathom. I'll go along with my instincts. It would plague me forever, this feeling, if I ignored it.

The trip back up the mountain is uneventful. What I'm looking forward to is sitting with Shkumbin and Rukije in Cahan over a cup of coffee and enjoying the buzz they create. True love on the battlefield. It's a delight for me to be in their company. They're more like Buddhists than anything else – no hatred of the Serbs, just a very quiet determination to do good. I maintain a small pantheon of heroes from my time here, people I think of for solace in the very bad times. Ylber, the hospital surgeon in Kukes, who resisted the corrupt regime of Cena; the Serbian doctor in Prizren who wouldn't leave his patients when the paramilitary killing squad invaded the hospital and paid for his dedication with his life. And Shkumbin and Rukije.

But Shkumbin and Rukije are still nowhere to be found when I reach Cahan. I make enquiries and I'm told that they'd volunteered to take supplies up to the cave. I hate the sound of this. They've offered in the past to bring supplies up the mountain, but I gave the strictest possible instruction to them to remain in Cahan. An uneasiness spreads through me like the chill from an icy wind.

'You're sure about this?' I ask the soldier who brought the news.

'No,' he says. 'Not sure. I heard them talking. They said they might go up to the top of the mountain with supplies. That's all.'

'But you didn't actually see them go?'

'No. I didn't see them.'

I hold onto the hope that they will emerge from somewhere or other and smile and open their arms to embrace me. This is something I do not want, Shkumbin and Rukije in harm's way. One of the reasons I was so adamant that they stay in Cahan is because I knew I would not be able to bear finding them dead on the mountain. Something good and fine must survive this war, and I want the love of those two to be that thing; I want them to flourish and fill Kosovo with children of their temperament and character. I want a fairytale. But, oh God, this shitty feeling! Something's happened to them. Something. I'm more fearful than I was on patrol yesterday when the Serbs passed so close, and I feel almost as sick as I did when looking down at the bodies of the two soldiers blown apart by the booby trap.

We continue on our way up the mountain. Near the halfway mark, I stop abruptly. I can glimpse a cluster of uniformed bodies fifty metres down the hillside, motionless, all obviously dead. I look away from the bodies to a series of mortar craters on and around the path ahead of us; big craters, gouged by 120mm shells. The bodies down the slope would have been blasted from the path by a near-direct hit, then rolled and tumbled to where they now lie. Further along the path we find the impact site littered with shredded limbs, packs and weapons. The debris forms a trail that continues down the slope. Above us in the branches of the trees unwound bandages hang like streamers in the sun's rays. It is the bandages that make me let out an involuntary cry. Who would be carrying a load of bandages up this path? Surely Shkumbin and Rukije are amongst those corpses. I peer at the bodies, trying to see more detail. One is a woman, yes, but her face is turned from me. She is slumped over a male body with a missing arm. I can't see the face of the male body, either. It is as if I am being teased in the most callous possible way. I can't go down the slope to turn the faces toward me and see if what I dread is true. Any path I took down the slope would be mined, and snipers will be watching from below. If the woman is Rukije, she may have been attempting to help Shkumbin and been shot by a sniper in that act. I can't know for certain if my friends are down there. I prefer the uncertainty. I will hope to meet them up at the cave. I don't know that I believe myself when I whisper, 'It's not certain', but I'm not ready to give Rukije and Shkumbin up. I can't.

At the top of the mountain, no sign of them. No one has seen them, no one knows a thing about them.

It's being whispered and muttered that the Serbs are planning a fresh offensive sometime over the next twenty-four hours. Rumours of advances are not an everyday thing; something must have happened to cause this much uneasiness. There's not a soldier up here who would be feeling anything other than sick. We cannot resist a big Serb sweep up the mountain. It will be preceded, no doubt, by the mother of all rocket, artillery and mortar bombardments. The ache in my heart for the loss of Shkumbin and Rukije – not that I'm conceding anything – contends for dominance with a rotten feeling in my guts at the prospect of a sudden Serb assault. If the Serbs come, they will first move into positions close to our front line before any barrage, then they'll order a halt to the shelling and storm the mountain top. The only warning we'll get is movement amongst the Serbs down at their bases right at this moment. I need that warning. I'm sure as hell not going to die here after what I've been through. I know all about the charming ironies of the battlefield, like the death of Wilfred Owen, my war poet of choice, blown up on the Western Front a week from the end of a futile and fatuous war that he abhorred.

I take a .50 calibre Barrett sniper's rifle with me to a dugout overlooking the Serb positions and use its powerful telescopic sight to study the camps below, searching for the first signs of preparation for an assault. I hate to say it, but I can't rest easy unless I do the checking myself. In the state I'm in – a very bad state, a hyper-vigilant state – it would drive me mad if I gave the task to someone else only to have it messed up. I'm paranoid, I know that, but paranoia I can live with; a smiling Serb standing over me with a Kalashnikov aimed at my head – no, that I can't live with. If we're overrun, it will be by Serb paramilitaries. A bullet through the head is one thing, but dying slowly for the amusement of the enemy, there I draw the line. Call me fussy if you like.

For the next three nights, I sleep in that dugout. I keep an eye on Serb movements to give myself the earliest possible warning of an advance up the mountain to our positions. I am convinced that I would miss the early warning signs were I tucked away in the cave. I position myself such that I can keep an eye on the enemy myself – don't trust the others! It's freezing cold and a night wind works its way into every little nook and cranny of my body. At close intervals I study the Serb positions, my nerves drawn taut. I can see armoured units and artillery positions quite clearly. They dot the foothills at the base of the mountain not far from where our patrol passed a few days earlier. During the day, when the positions below are more distinct, I mark them on a detailed map of the area that Sonnenberg gave me – well, not quite gave me. I snatched it from the rear of the Humvee, thinking it might come in handy sometime. With my field compass and protractor I record the sector and co-ordinates on the map, and then transcribe them into my notebook in case the map should be damaged or lost. From where I am, however, I can only see some of the Serb positions, and I can only estimate the co-ordinates to a six-digit grid reference – accurate to within one hundred metres. This is reasonably accurate but if I were closer I could do better, eight digits and accurate to within ten metres. I'm obsessing now, I know it.

Today, the third day of my paranoid vigil, a small crowd gathers behind me as I mark the map and record the coordinates. I don't pay much attention at first, but when the crowd starts spilling down into my dugout I ask them what the fuck they're doing. One of the soldiers, a German speaker, puts the question back to me.

'We don't know what this is about, Doctor. What are you writing?'

'Are you serious?'

'Oh yes, I am serious.'

'Haven't you ever done this yourselves?'

'Pardon me, Doctor – done what ourselves?'

'This! Marked a map and written out co-ordinates!'

'No. No, never.'

The soldier turned to the others, watching on in puzzlement. 'Anyone here done this with the maps?' he asks in Albanian (I can speak enough of the local language now to follow him). 'Anyone?'

Heads are shaken, followed by a little chorus of replies in the negative.

'No, Doctor. No one here can do this.'

I'm dumbfounded. I'd come to realise, of course, that the commanders at the bases – at Cahan and Krume – simply invented the sites of Serb concentrations that they passed onto Sonnenberg's Special Forces team. But I'd always assumed that the coordinates that were provided by the soldiers up on the mountain – soldiers who could look down the slope and see the Serbs and their armoured vehicles and artillery – were kosher. But no. No. These soldiers couldn't even read a map. I sit shaking my head as my audience smiles in bafflement, not knowing what's got into old Dr Craig. I mean, what bloody hope is there? The war is a farce. We're getting the living shit shelled out of us by Serb guns that could have been destroyed weeks ago if just one soldier here had known how to read a map.

'Okay, piss off now,' I tell the audience with an agitated gesture. The soldiers amble off, still puzzled at my mood. Cheerful Dr Craig, usually so stoic and positive. What's that about?

I treat casualties in my cave-hospital for the rest of the day, my mood still jaundiced. At five in the afternoon, craving sleep, I return to my front-line dugout and climb into my sleeping bag. I'll be kipping and waking all through the night, keeping watch on the Serbs. But just as my drowsiness is about to became total unconsciousness, a soldier clambers down into my dugout and asks me to come with him on the night patrol. He says he's the squad leader and he's hoping that I'll be able to do something for the civilian casualties the patrol is bound to find in the villages behind the Serb lines.

'I have heard how valuable you were with the other patrol, Doctor. You would be doing us a great service.'

I want to scream at the top of my voice, 'Leave me alone! I need some fucking sleep!' But I don't. I grunt and nod and get to my feet. It's not this man's fault. He doesn't know what a wreck I am. And after all, he's risking his life to check on the villages. But Christ, I'm near the end of my tether.

It's a clear night, no cloud cover, a three-quarter moon. A hunting night. I hope to God these guys I'll be patrolling with know the rudiments of the game. If I see one soldier standing against the skyline making a lovely silhouette for a sniper, I'll shoot him myself.

We take a more easterly route than the first patrol. After an hour we reach a small village near the town of Kusnin, just south of the road between Prizren and Djakova. We keep ourselves back two hundred metres from the village, sheltered by the embankment of a small road on its eastern edge. The dirt road has an elevated embankment on the right side and a gentle downward slope on its left. The village looks utterly deserted. No lights, no smell of smoke from wood fires. We reduce the distance to the village by degrees to a hundred metres, then to fifty. Still not the faintest sign of life in the place. This can mean only that all the villagers are dead, or that they've been taken somewhere to be massacred later.

I suppose there's some small chance that they all ran into the forest when they heard the Serbs coming, but that's not likely. The Serbs arrive in a hell of a hurry. Their meticulous training has prepared them perfectly for the wholesale murder of undefended Kosovars.

I'm getting my head ready for something appalling when, without warning, automatic rifle rounds are slapping into the embankment to our right. I spin around, looking for cover. On our left flank, about seventy-five metres away, I can see a Serb patrol of maybe nine or ten, could be more. We are too exposed to fight it out from the present position. I join two other soldiers in a headlong sprint down the side of the road toward the Serbs, taking cover in a shallow ditch twenty-five metres from them. The Serbs fired on us before they were in a covered position – a mistake that contradicts their training – and so we've reached the ditch while the Serbs are still exposed. The three of us roll out of the ditch, two to the right, me to the left and fire into the clustered Serbs. The range is so close that our fire kills four of the Serb patrol instantly. The other soldiers in our patrol have moved quickly to the Serbs' left flank and opened up, killing a further three. The last of the Serbs take to their heels, heading north and away from the village.

All of this has taken no more than two minutes. Adrenaline has powered me into a state of hyper-arousal. I think I'd be able to hear a cricket a kilometre away, my senses are that alert.

We wait in the hush, hoping that our fire hasn't drawn more Serbs to us.

'Anyone hit?' I call, and two of our men, Jetadeshai and Degut Krasniqi, brothers, call back to me. I abandon cover to check their wounds, but neither is seriously hurt and attention turns to stripping the dead Serbs of their weapons and ammunition. Five of the seven are regular VJ soldiers, but the remaining two are dressed in the black uniforms of the Special Police Unit – the unit that plans the massacres that the paramilitaries prosecute. No feelings of regret for killing them.

The village is empty, just as we'd anticipated. No bodies, no blood. We have to restrict the time we spend searching because more Serb patrols will be here shortly. We change our route and head south at a slow jog to dodge any Serb forces arriving from the west. This route will take us through two or three little villages or hamlets before we swing back and head for the mountain.

Thirty minutes later, we reach the outskirts of a smallish village about a kilometre from the larger town of Kusnin. Keeping ourselves concealed, we creep closer, coming to a complete halt when we're near enough to see clearly what's going on in the village centre. A couple of trucks and an M980 armoured vehicle are parked there, forming a circle. The headlights of the trucks and the M980 blaze in the darkness. I can see Serb soldiers milling about, unhurried. They're smoking, talking; I catch a few peals of laughter. Then I notice that other Serbs are moving in and out of the village houses. Three prisoners are bustled into the glare of the headlights. These people must be the last of those remaining in the houses. The other villagers will be in the forest hiding, or held somewhere out of sight. But just as I'm thinking this, a volley of rifle shots ring out and less than a minute later, people come running into the illuminated clearing. Those not running fast enough, including three children, are shoved along by the

Serb soldiers. I can now count thirteen or fourteen villagers huddled in the light. They keep still, bunched together, obeying shouted commands. The Serbs in their combat gear look so much taller and bulkier than the villagers. The sense of menace they convey must be overwhelming.

The people huddled in the illuminated clearing are going to be murdered. I know it; the others in the patrol know it. I would judge that twenty or thirty Serbs are holding the village; far too many for us to attack. We will be compelled to wait where we are, out of sight, like an audience beyond the footlights, and watch the killing. Glancing left and right, I see the tension in the faces of my companions. They want to attack the Serbs no matter what the cost. I lift my hand with the fingers splayed, hoping to convey with the stop-sign gesture that we must remain motionless. The horror I will be experiencing within minutes is already mounting in my guts, in my chest. Nothing can save these people. What solace would it be to them to know that their murders will be witnessed by those who desired with all their heart to save them? No solace at all.

The Serb soldiers begin pushing their prisoners to the ground. The prisoners struggle up to their knees. A woman attempts to stand and is thrown down again roughly. The Serbs accompany the shoving with loud shouts that I take to be curses. From one of the buildings in the village, unbelievably, the sound of singing breaks out, raucous singing, the rowdy singing of drunks.

Three Serb soldiers form a semicircle around the prisoners. I can tell from their stance and the position in which they are holding their rifles that they are about to start shooting. Two of the soldiers reach down to their weapons in a manner I recognise; they are switching the mechanism to fully automatic. The prisoners, some of them, are crying out, perhaps praying, perhaps giving voice to a final lament. I can see the mist of the soldiers' breath rising into the darkness above the glare of the headlights.

Now all of the women and children amongst the prisoners have taken up the laments and the sobbing and the anguished cries of those first two or three who broke down.

The shooting, even though anticipated, comes as a great shock to me. It's as if I were hoping for a miracle, knowing absolutely that no miracle would come. The soldiers move the barrels of their guns in a sweeping motion back and forth over the huddled shapes. A shriek here and there signifies that a few prisoners have not been killed with the first rounds. The soldiers rapidly fit new magazines and continue sweeping the shapes with fully automatic fire.

With two full magazines per soldier emptied into the prisoners, there is a pause. I think the soldiers are listening for any last sounds of life, but the only sound to be heard is that of the drunken singing. Then, accepting that every prisoner is dead, the soldiers break out into laughter and head away from the site towards the house from which the singing is coming.

Thirteen or fourteen prisoners may not be the total for a village of this size. The Serbs might be holding more in the houses. I know from reports by survivors of such massacres as this that the Serbs enjoy spreading the killing around. The three soldiers who killed this group of prisoners will be replaced by another three, who will kill the next batch. Killings like these are used sometimes as an initiation for soldiers, and also as a bonding rite.

The soldiers in our patrol are struggling with might and main to control their rage. The patrol leader and I whisper exhortations for calm, or if not calm then discipline. I jab a finger in the direction of the armoured vehicle, the M980 at the Serbs' disposal.

'There will be more killed, more are waiting!' one of the soldiers whispers at me.

'I know. We have to go.'

'And leave them? No!'

'Yes!'

'I cannot!'

'Yes you can! Right now!'

Within two hours we are back at our positions at the front. At eleven that night, I climb into my dugout and stare out at the orange flashes of the NATO bombing. It might have been amusing a week ago to joke about the NATO war on the sheep and goats of Kosovo. But not now. Not any more. I don't know if a heart can break unless it's caused by love, but my heart feels broken. It feels well and truly broken. Those poor, poor people, murdered before my eyes. Between the throbs of pain in my chest, a piercing loathing for the Serbs shakes me like a fit. I don't want to feel the heartbreak, and I don't want to feel the loathing. But I have no say.

Chapter 27

A cease-fire agreement of sorts came into effect yesterday, 5 June. It means nothing to us. The shelling today is the heaviest of the war, heavier than yesterday, and yesterday was heavier than the day before. In Belgrade, yes, the ceasefire means something. In Belgrade, I imagine, they are growing agitated about the power stations being bombed, and the water supply being interrupted. They are uncomfortable in Belgrade. Milosevic did not believe that his brother Slavs in Russia would permit NATO to bomb Belgrade, but the Russians have apparently said, 'Slobodan, this will disappoint you, but we are not going to initiate World War III so that you can create your Greater Serbia.' Frustrating for poor old Slobodan. I think he dreamed of the day when every Muslim in Kosovo would be hanging from a tree.

I'm bitter. The massacre in the village has done it for me. I'm sick at heart, sick in my very soul. I saw the aftermath of massacres in the hospital at Kukes on my first day there, and I've seen the wounds of survivors on dozens of occasions since. I've listened to an old man with tears running off his cheeks and chin telling me that he saw family members shot in front of him by the Serbs; seen children slaughtered. I've counted the bodies of villagers left behind when the Serb murder squads moved on. I knew all about the killings. But I hadn't seen a massacre with my own eyes. I hadn't sat helplessly and watched prisoners being shot. Now I've seen it and it has left me half mad. Bitter and half mad.

Over these three days of heavy shelling, I've treated nearly a hundred casualties, mostly alone, sometimes with Mentor when he wasn't helping in the field. The numbers blur, I keep no notes any more. Too tired. I treat them either out in the field where they fall, or here in my palatial and expensively equipped hospital-cave. Some with minor injuries, others not so lucky. Thirty-five or so died more or less straight away, in the field, in their dugouts. I barely had time to take a pulse before they succumbed. Many died in the cave, while I was trying to stem the blood flowing from them in streams, draining them of life. Forty, however, I managed to save; forty are still breathing. For the time being.

The shelling doesn't bother me anymore, and that's a bad sign. When you stop caring about safety, it's not long before you die. Shells land nearby, and the shock wave knocks me off my feet. I get upright again and walk on muttering, 'Missed, you bastards.'

I hear screaming and shouting and groaning from down the track. A mortar shell has just exploded. I run down the track with my surgical kit and my rifle and find a squad of new recruits in a state of hysteria, some rolling about and shrieking, some standing dazed with blood and guts plastered all over them.

'Keep calm!' I shout. 'Keep calm, for God's sake!'

They ignore me, of course. They're beside themselves, panic stricken. I fire my Kalashnikov into the air.

'Shut up! Shut up and calm down! Jesus Christ!'

And they do. The rifle rounds act on them like a slap on the face. I look for wounds, rapidly scanning their chests and limbs. A few cuts, nothing that could account for the quantity of blood and raw flesh, and I'm thinking, 'What the hell?' Then I look further down the track and see the carcasses of half a dozen sheep and goats torn to pieces. The recruits have been coated in barnyard gore.

'You're not bleeding, idiot!' I shout at a soldier who can't get himself under control. I point at the dead animals. 'Look!'

'It's not me?' he asks.

'No, moron, it's not you!'

I leave him to work it out. Has anybody counted the sheep and goat casualties of this war? Must be astronomical.

I make two more trips down to the NORWAC hospital at Krume, both runs made at night. After weeks of shelling, the Serbs have us targeted here with shocking accuracy. If you step out into the open for a leak during daylight hours, you die. All movement at the front has ceased during the day, except for retrieval of the wounded and sprints down to the spring for water. June, and it's unbelievably hot. We can't live without replenishing our water supplies. We've lost five men on water runs and casualty retrievals. We draw straws now to see who goes for water. Morale is at rock bottom. Our supply lines have been cut and we're in the situation of Old Mother Hubbard's dog: the cupboard's bare.

Suicides are becoming more common. Soldiers get to feel so utterly at the mercy of the Serbs that they exercise the only possible method of escape. It's one of those hideous ironies of the battlefield: so scared of dying that you kill yourself. Nobody blames them. Nobody badmouths them. Nobody says anything.

I continue to operate in my cave during the day when the light is strong, but I'm down to the last of everything. I'm suturing wounds with packing twine and operating on horrendous injuries with a third of the dose of Ketamine I would be using if I had more of the stuff. Sometimes while I'm operating I look up from the patient and take in the wrecked landscape, the craters, the dugouts, the charred foliage of the bushes and I think, 'This is what hell is supposed to look like.' I get back to work, try to shake the hopelessness, the sense of futility. I'm not coping, boys! Dr Craig isn't coping! Dr Craig needs a big holiday.

And another thing. I'm wasting away. I never wanted to be fat, but Jesus, I'm gliding down to the opposite end of the spectrum. Another week and I'll look like my grandfather when he walked out of Dachau.

Get a grip, Craig. Get a grip.

I've just finished operating on a young soldier with a nightmarish chest wound. I've done a good job – chests are my specialty – but there's something I have to face up to right now. This man will die unless I get him evacuated down to Krume. The prospect of that trek down the mountain with Serbs crawling all over it makes me want to throw up. I have nothing in my stomach to spare so I fight the dread down, try to summon some strength. More than ever in my life, I need to think of my grandfather, Franc Jurisevic. There must have been a thousand occasions on which he thought it was all over, couldn't go on, but he kept going and he lived to walk out of that prison. He found his village and in the village he found his wife and kids. He had years and years of gladness left to him, and he stayed alive to make sure he enjoyed it. Same goes for me. Get this young man down the mountain, live to tell the tale. That's my mantra now: live to tell the tale.

I call to the soldiers gathered in the cave and they lift their heads from their chests to listen.

'I need a team. This soldier has to go down to Cahan so we can get him to the NORWAC hospital in Krume. Anyone doesn't want to come, that's okay. I understand, absolutely. But I need a team.'

Seven hands are raised within seconds.

'You're sure about this? The Serbs are all over the mountain, remember that.'

One of the soldiers shrugs and manages a smile.

'It's okay,' he says. 'You go, we go.'

'And you're sure?'

'Doc, will you shut up! We're sure.'

We load the injured man on the stretcher and move out, sprinting at first to make it harder for the snipers. We pass the spring, some one hundred and fifty metres from the cave, and then head toward the first of the many wooded areas along the path. The stretcher bearers almost drop our patient but we manage to make it to the trees where we should be safe for a time. We keep moving quickly, a steep descent to our right, an even steeper ascent to our left. I'm bustling the guys along, at the same time trying to stay alert, trying to remember everything I taught soldiers just like these in Helshan. Never underestimate the people who want to kill you, it makes them feel good if they kill you, they dearly want to kill you, remember to think like them. And just as I'm running through the safety checklist two monster explosions rip up the ground around us and we're knocked flat on our backs. Even before I hit the ground I know that the explosions were not mortars and not artillery; they were RPGs and that means whoever fired them is much, much closer than a mortar crew. Confirming these rapid thoughts, bullets slap into the mountainside to our left, fizzing over our heads. I glance up, taking in as much as I can within the two or three seconds I can allow myself to be exposed. It's a Serb patrol, down to the right, maybe a hundred metres away. 'Leave the kid and the stretcher where he is!' I shout. 'Leave him! Give him some covering fire! They might back off!'

But within seconds the Serbs open up with machine-gun fire and the man on the stretcher is hit again and again. Because he's strapped onto the stretcher his body doesn't move at all; the sickening thuds of impact are the only immediate signs of his fate.

I glance back up the path in the direction we came, hoping we might be able to backtrack. But if we do that, we're going to be exposed as soon as we're out of the wooded area. And if we stay where we are, we'll be dead within a couple of minutes. We have no choice but to rush the Serb patrol. We'll snatch a brief advantage if we descend downhill through the shelter of the trees while the Serbs will be compelled to take up defensive positions. It's better if only three of us make this downhill attack; three soldiers moving rapidly is a much more difficult target than eight soldiers clustered. The Serbs believe that they are the hunters; a sudden reversal of expectations might panic them. We'll be killed, very likely, but we're dead anyway.

'We're going to rush them. Not all of us, just three.'

A soldier who only twenty minutes ago put his hand up to make the run to Cahan with me indicates with a nod that he'll join me. Another soldier nods and I point to each of them in turn, meaning, 'Yes, you two.'

I hold my right hand up to indicate that we'll start our assault at my signal. Beneath my breath I count to three then drop my hand. We descend rapidly towards the enemy, firing as we duck behind trees for cover. The advantage I was hoping for is working out for us; the Serbs have left themselves exposed on the downward slope, taken by surprise by our aggressiveness. We kill three of them straight out, only narrowly escaping their frenzied return fire ourselves. The rest of the Serbs have to turn their backs on us to clamber downhill. They can't fire at us and retreat downhill at the same time. We fire another volley at the retreating patrol. The Serbs are in a headlong rout. I motion to my companions to pause in the assault. I unclip a grenade, slip the pin and heave it at the retreating shapes, and my two comrades do the same. We're each able to get away two grenades. Throwing downhill enhances the heft and accuracy of our barrage and it appears that we've knocked over another two or three of the patrol. We continue our advance downhill, taking great caution; we don't want to be surprised by a wounded Serb watching us approach.

The three Serbs who fell to our rifle fire we leave for the rest of our squad to strip of weapons.

I find two more dead Serbs in the woods, killed by our grenade detonations. And one wounded. All three are wearing the black uniforms of paramilitaries. The wounded guy is attempting to show that he has no intention of resisting. His weapon is well out of his reach. I pause only briefly to see him taken in hand by our guys then hurry on. I'm buoyed by a feeling of success, of our plan having worked. Combat is not thrilling, as a game can be thrilling, but you do feel the ebb and flow of fortune acutely.

Nearly a hundred metres down the hill and deep in the woods, I call off the assault. I think the Serb force numbered around twenty, so it has plenty of strength around which to regroup. These Serbs, although paramilitaries and very likely to have spent the war engaged in various subhuman activities, will nevertheless have the same feelings about retrieving their dead and wounded that we do. I want to be the hell out of here when they come back.

Two of my men have the wounded Serb pinned against a tree, beating the life out of him. The fury in their faces makes it pretty plain that I won't be able to prevail if I tell them to stop. It might be different if their prisoner were a VJ regular, but they see a paramilitary as a professional torturer. And the will to stop them beating him, to stop them killing him, even if they have some protracted method in mind, is just not in me. It just isn't. I don't know that I could even bring myself to provide medical treatment if he survives what my comrades have planned for him. It's a rotten thing to admit, but it's true. If I'd come upon a couple of KLA soldiers torturing a Serb prisoner weeks and weeks back when I first arrived, I would have jumped in and saved the guy and given a sermon as I did so. But not now. Not now.

Amazingly, none of our squad is injured. But the young man on the stretcher is dead, torn up by the machine-gun rounds. I'd spent ninety minutes operating on him. Down at NORWAC, he would have survived. He hasn't got a face any more, not a proper face, the one he started this journey with. I didn't know I had tears left in me, but I'm weeping over this piece of raw butchery as if he were a family member. I'm murmuring as my face grows wet, 'Fuck them, fuck them ...' I gaze back down the track to where the unfolding murder of the Serb prisoner is taking place. I'm waiting to see if some residual impulse comes to life in me; some desire to act the part of saviour. Nothing's happening. I ask a couple of the squad members to bring the body back to the cave on the stretcher, then head up the track myself.

I sit in the cave with dead bodies rotting at the back, their reek growing riper in the awful heat. In his 1918 poem 'Strange Meeting', Wilfred Owen writes of escaping from the battlefield through a tunnel that leads to hell, where the dead of the Great War live as wraiths. My cave, with its stacked corpses from the battlefield, has come to resemble that tunnel. I wish I had Owen's poems with me. I wish a lot of things.

I'm still gazing out over the valley when the other squad members return. No prisoner.

Later, at dusk, I pen a note to Donna in my journal. I write about love and longing. It's as if I need to remind myself that I stand for more than the horror and depravity of a day like this day. I can also love. I can cherish. I'm not a butcher.

I should have saved that wretched man. I know it. But sympathy is beyond me at this point.

I sign off my note with love, get into my sleeping bag beside the stack of corpses and wait for sleep to come.

Chapter 28

My medical mission here is just about at an end. I have five ampoules of Ketamine left, hardly any surgical sutures, next to no antiseptic solution. I'm cleaning my instruments with alcohol swabs.

I've stopped documenting the names of the dead. One body after another is stacked in the cave in an anonymous heap. And after yesterday's attempt to evacuate that kid, I've given up making the run down the mountain with casualties. The Serbs are everywhere. The only reason they haven't stormed into the camp and murdered us all is that the war is drawing to a close and they don't want to get themselves killed. They thought the shelling would get rid of us without any need to risk their necks. But if they do storm us, despite their concerns, they bloody well will lose some of their number. They'll lose as many as I can shoot, for one thing.

And where's Mentor? He's disappeared. I would have searched high and low for him a week ago, in the forest, down the track, up the track. I would've turned over rocks to find him. Now, I'm resigned. He's gone. I ask the soldiers, they know as little as me. Lately, it's become possible for people up here to simply vanish in the way Mentor has. The Serbs are so close. Mentor would not have abandoned us. He knew he was my only experienced medical aide. I think he's been shot. Or captured. God help him.

I have the wherewithal for one remaining roll of the dice, one remaining act of defiance, of revenge. I've been harbouring a plan in the back of my mind for days now, held back only by the fear of guilt, of remorse. That fear has passed. I'm going to take a small patrol down behind the Serb lines and map the co-ordinates of every piece of Serb armour, every piece of artillery, every troop concentration on the front line. Not six-digit grid references, but eight. This will amount to a refinement of the coordinates I've already recorded and allow targeting to within ten metres. Then I'll get the results to the US Special Forces guys at Cahan. What I intend to provide will be the only accurate co-ordinates NATO has ever received from this region. Sonny and his team will pass the co-ordinates on to NATO, and NATO – this is what I'm hoping for, this is what I want – will bomb the Serbs down the mountain. And the shelling will stop.

What I'm intending to do is wrong. I have no authority to circumvent the KLA chain of command. I have no authority to record co-ordinates. I have no right to pass anything on to Sonny. I'm a noncombatant, a volunteer medical officer. But I don't care about all that now. What I do care about is stopping those guns permanently. Precision bombing will catch the Serbs completely off guard. Up until now, they could, if they wished, play soccer in the open air, sunbake, gather around a barbie and roast lamb chops. They know that the NATO bombs will land kilometres away. So a precision bombing run based on accurate co-ordinates will result in wholesale slaughter.

And I shouldn't be involved in it. I should have strong enough moral convictions about my true role here to resist the urge. Certainly I've led patrols in my time here; certainly I've fired on the KLA's enemies; certainly I may have killed a small number of them. But that was circumstance, and the circumstances were such that my own life was in immediate danger. It could be argued – I always seem to be self-justifying – that I have only ever fired my weapon here in self-defence. I have not so far plotted the mass killing of Serb soldiers.

But I will do it. If I want justification, I will go back to my splendid and very helpful amendment to the Hippocratic oath: to do a great right, do a little wrong. Except that the 'wrong' in this case is not so little. But it is preventative medicine – it may save the lives of many of those around me.

The other three soldiers on the patrol with me I will select from the German-speaking 123rd Battalion. It's difficult to find three soldiers with experience of combat and more than a year or two out of high school who are able to speak English, so I'll rely on my German.

I don't employ any inspiring phrases when I tell the patrol members what we're up to. No, 'Men, this mission is designed to end the war in our region'. It is, after all, entirely possible that the Serbs have no intention of shelling us any longer. They may be packing up, getting ready to depart. I simply tell my men to follow my orders on every occasion, to keep close, to stay alive.

The patrol moves quickly. The three soldiers keep as close as I could ask. I expect every minute to run into a Serb patrol and end my mission and my life and my glorious career and my ambitions for a flourishing family life with Donna on the slopes of Mount Pastrik. But we don't see any patrols. It's as if the mission is blessed.

We locate a large garrison of Yugoslav Army and paramilitary forces two kilometres from the base of Mount Pastrik. Two to three hundred men, fifteen mortar and artillery pieces, two surface-to-air-missile launchers. The Serbs are using the camouflage of tree cover to hide all this stuff and it is easy to see how high altitude NATO bombers would have trouble spotting any of it. Not a single piece of this hardware has been damaged by the NATO bombardment, now into its seventy-seventh day. I can't see a single bomb or missile crater anywhere near the Serb positions. The bombing could go on for another seventy-seven days, another seventy-seven years and this equipment would still be in mint condition. The Serbs must spend most of each day laughing themselves silly.

'Laugh while you can, boys,' I murmur. And with patience and all the skill I can bring to bear, I record the exact position of everything. My companions remain absolutely silent while I write in my notebook, scan my map, check my compass bearings over and over again. Every so often I look up and nod, and they nod back. They can see I'm taking great pains to get this right. When I'm done, I give the same sort of nod I've been dispensing all along, and make a couple of gestures with my hand that these soldiers know the meaning of: 'Back to the camp, but carefully, carefully'.

On my return to the cave, I hand the map and my handwritten notes to two of the patrol members for delivery as speedily as possible to the US Special Forces team when they make their regular visit to Cahan.

'Take great care,' I tell them in German. 'I want this map and these notes to get through. Avoid engaging the Serbs, no matter what.'

'We will do exactly as you say,' says the guy I consider the more senior of the two.

'I know I don't have to tell you how important this is, but I'm going to. It's very, very important.'

'Craig, we know. Don't worry.'

'You see a Serb patrol, you find cover and sit as still as statues. But at the same time I want you to get to Cahan in time to give this to the Special Forces guys. You know who I'm talking about? Do you know an American called Sonnenberg?'

'No. But we will find him. Craig, you can trust us. Okay?'

I send them off with feelings of elation and dread stirred together in a bubbling broth.

I operate throughout the day, concentrating intensely to avoid thinking of the patrol and praying for its success. When the last casualty is cleared, I walk purposefully up to my dugout and prepare myself for the wait. If the coordinates got through, the bombs will fall tonight exactly where they're supposed to. Or that's what I'm hoping for. I wish I could say that I will be filled with remorse when the bombs come down. I wish I could say that it is only with the greatest regret that I have implicated myself in all these imminent deaths. But I can't. I'm thinking of a garrotted child dead in its mother's arms; of comrades blown apart; of bodies that I must now concede were probably those of Shkumbin and Rukije in a heap of corpses on the mountainside. I'm thinking especially of the laughing paramilitaries putting to death the women and children and old men of that village. My better angels may rebuke me in the years to come. But for now, let it be.

Chapter 29

It's pitch dark when the rumble of the NATO planes jolts me out of a trance. I sit upright and strain my ears to catch the sound again. The fact that the planes have come later than usual is a good sign, maybe. It could mean that my coordinates required a fresh briefing for the pilots and crews. It could mean nothing. This may just be a pipe dream, fuelled by desperation and fatigue.

Excited soldiers wander up to my dugout, attracted by the roar of the engines.

'Doctor, they are coming.'

'Yes, I know.'

'Do you think they have the numbers you made?'

'Don't know.'

The first explosions are louder, stronger, more violent than any aerial bombing I've heard here before. The flashes burn in the darkness like an orchestrated pyrotechnic display on New Year's Eve, and in such rapid sequence. The soldiers around me whoop and cheer in a near-ecstasy of approval. Impossibly, the smile on my face broadens even further. I'm slapped on the back again and again, phrases of congratulation in English, German and Albanian are shouted into my ears.

'Craig, see!'

'I thank God for this!'

'Your numbers, Doctor! Your numbers have made this happen!'

Maybe they have. At this point in time I don't know what to think, but my heart is hoping they're right. It's said that revenge is a dish best served cold, but oh no, no, that isn't right; revenge is best served up when the loathing that cries out for it is burning in your chest like a coal from a furnace. I've reflected in disgust on the culture of vengeance that has dominated the Balkans for a thousand years. But I'm not disgusted now. I know exactly what it's all about.

I glance to my left and right at the fire of the bombs lighting the faces of the soldiers around me. They look like kids at a carnival who have been promised a good time, promised so much, and all that they were promised is being exceeded.

The ground beneath our feet is trembling with the fury of the bombardment. The mountain itself is shaking. I'm watching the weeks and weeks of anguish we've endured transformed into a drama of fire and sound; as if the roar of the engines were the thunderous voice of an enraged God: 'Did you think you could murder innocent women and children and never face the wrath of heaven?'

We watch for hours as wave after wave of bombers fly in from Italy and lay to waste the entire eastern sector of the Pastrik front. Way past midnight, the bombardment still unfolding, I sink down to the floor of my dugout and into my bedding. Many of the soldiers watching the drama intend to enjoy every last minute of the spectacle, but a great tiredness has taken hold of me. My body and soul are spent, empty. Not even the shouts and hurrahs and shrieks of delight of the soldiers can keep me awake.

Curled in an awkward arc at the bottom of my hole in the ground, I open my eyes to the brilliance of an enormous blue sky. I wriggle my left arm free of the bedding and hold my wrist up to check the time. It's 8a.m. Any other morning but this one, Serb artillery and mortars would be pounding the mountain top to high heaven. Now, the only sound I'm aware of is that of birds. I grind my hands into my face, shake my head, climb to my feet and scan the sky and the wrecked remains of trees for the source of the birdsong. Crows, swallows – birds that have been in hiding in my time here – have reclaimed the peak of this blood-soaked mountain. High above, I can make out what I think must be a kestrel hanging almost motionless on a thermal.

Could it be that what the bombing was meant to achieve has been achieved? I don't know. It may all be coincidence. I may never know. We who were hunted mercilessly are still alive, the remnants of us, at least; those who hunted us, those who sought our deaths, are themselves dead. I am glad in an immediate way, but the sheer delirium of last night has faltered. A more persistent part of me is already whispering. I doubt very much that the great sense of accomplishment I experienced when the bombs were falling and the Serbs were dying will prevail for long. I recall a story of Jewish prisoners in a death camp who remained alive, just barely, at war's end. When the Americans liberated the camp, the prisoners were offered the chance to shoot the vile guards who'd tormented them. The guards were ill, famished, too slow in making their escape. They waited for death when rifles were put into the hands of the skeletal Jews. But the Jews declined. They did not want revenge to constitute the first act of their newly restored liberty. It may not mean anything truly bad about you if you mete out punishment for dreadful wrongs but by the same token, it doesn't mean anything good about you if you live for the rest of your life with a smile on your face recalling the hammer blows of vengeance.

I heave myself out of my hole in the ground, a hole deeper than many of the graves in which I've buried boys, young men, young women over the past few weeks. Walking back to my cave with my rifle in my hands, I pass soldiers standing in the open air, smiling in a hesitant way, as if this calm and stillness is too new to be entirely trusted. I am greeted with quiet phrases. I am glad of the more subdued mood of the morning. My appetite for triumphant high fives is gone for good.

Then a strange thing happens. A soldier runs across the clearing, contradicting the slow, almost tender mood that has prevailed up to now. He stops in the midst of a cluster of his comrades and within seconds the mountain top is transformed. Soldiers who looked so shy, so abashed a minute earlier are now throwing their heads back and shrieking. I stand baffled, reluctant to involve myself in anything that requires me to smile and shout. Two soldiers I know by name, Enver and Florim, break from a group and sprint towards me.

'Craig, Craig! The war is over! The war is finished!'

The last remaining morsel of elation still dwelling within me responds, and I throw my arms around these two men who have breathed and sweated and fought beside me.

'It's true?' I ask. 'Not just a ceasefire?'

'Not a ceasefire!' says Florim. 'Milosevic is fucked! He signed a truce this morning!'

'Peace!' says Enver. 'Do you believe it, Craig? Peace!'

Other soldiers run over and join us. We're bouncing up and down with our arms entwined, throwing our heads back to broadcast our laughter to the skies.

'Peace! Peace! Thank God for peace! Thank God!'

Finally I break from the group, taking my leave with a repeated round of hugs and slaps on the back. I betray nothing, but my heart is behaving dangerously, swollen with competing emotions. Peace is wonderful, but all this laughter has jolted something loose within me and I am only a whisper away from falling to my knees and sobbing myself to death. The scene of the massacre of two nights ago returns unbidden and is playing itself out in astonishing detail. I can see again the Serb soldiers switching their rifles to fully automatic, I can see the muzzles dipping in preparation for murder. I am desperate to avoid watching all over again what happens next, and that is why I had to get away by myself. And now the killing has started in my head, and the bursts of rifle fire sweep across the huddled shapes in the glare of the headlights. Then the boy, that poor darling boy in my arms on that final journey to his grave. This hurts most. This hurts deep, deep within. I want it to stop, but it won't stop, no power on earth or in heaven can make it stop and the tears spring from my eyes and bathe my face.

I stumble down the track towards my cave, praying that I don't meet anyone on the way. And this prayer, at least, is answered. I catch my breath outside the cave and dry my face. I think it's over, this tempest of tears, but the images start again, the boy in my arms, the tall shapes of the soldiers sweeping their muzzles back and forward over the doomed people of that village, the three children clutching at their mothers.

It takes some minutes for me to regain control of my emotions. I take a series of deep breaths, counselling myself to get a grip. Then I walk the last few metres to the cave.

It's empty, my cave. No wounds to clean, no limbs to amputate, and all the dead have been carried away to burial sites. I prop my rifle against the stone wall and sit in the mouth of this tunnel to the underworld and gaze out over the valley.

Dear God, what a mess I've made of myself. If I ever recover, if I'm ever put back together, it will take a miracle.

What a mess. Dear God, what a mess.

I'm going to take my grenades and hand them in at the weapons depot then start the long walk down the mountain to Cahan. At Cahan, I'll catch some sort of transport to Krume. Then to Kukes, and then to Tirana, a ferry to Italy, a flight to Rome, another flight to Sydney, a final flight to Adelaide. The only image I can employ to shield my brain from those persistent flashes is that of my wife and son waiting in the arrival lounge when I emerge from that other tunnel, the one that joins the aircraft to the airport.

Up above, the kestrel continues its slow, deliberate circling in the sky. Gazing down from that height, its eye must take in so much more than mine. It can see this ruined mountain top, it can see the jubilant soldiers embracing each other, it can see me, no doubt, this broken figure sitting as still as stone at the mouth of a cave. It can see the surviving Serbs at the base of the mountain, dragging bodies and body parts from the debris of last night's bombardment. The hunter in the air with his eye everywhere.

I get to my feet, aching in every place an ache can find, head, heart, body, soul. I let my gaze linger one last time on the green valley, glance up at the bird circling in the sky, then start for home.

Epilogue

The war in Kosovo officially ended on 10 June 1999 with the ratification of UN Security Council Resolution 1244. The end of this war came with all the trappings of a modern Balkan conflict. Reprisal killings and forced expulsions of Kosovar Serbs by Kosovar Albanians were not uncommon in the months after the war's end, the aftermath of which was a Kosovo sharply divided along ethnic lines. Through fear and insecurity, many ethnic Serbs fled to neighbouring Serbia, leaving fewer than one hundred thousand in Kosovo by the end of 2007.

Milosevic was indicted in 1999 by the International Criminal Tribunal for the Former Yugoslavia on sixty-six charges, including genocide and crimes against humanity. After his arrest in 2002, he spent the next four years representing himself in a protracted legal battle in The Hague that was due to end in late 2006. His death in custody on 13 March 2006, before a formal conviction had been reached, deprived his victims of justice and raised him to martyrdom in the eyes of many Serbs.

Kosovo finally achieved nationhood of sorts when her Albanian-dominated parliament declared independence on 17 February 2008. The US and most European countries (with the notable exception of Russia and Serbia) promptly endorsed this declaration. Though a long time coming, Kosovo has finally achieved the independence the majority of her population had sought. She has finally reached a peace, which, though far from perfect, will allow her to develop as a modern European nation.

For me, the years after the war in Kosovo were busy with work and helping to raise a family. I qualified as a cardiothoracic surgeon in 2000, and went on to have two more children, Harrison in 2003 and Liam two years later. They are now at school and my eldest son, Jackson, is currently at the senior end of secondary school. My wife Donna trained in Intensive Care medicine and, after having our two children, continued with Anaesthetic training. Encouraged by many of my colleagues in the defence force, I joined the Australian Army in February 2006. Since then, I have served in East Timor and Afghanistan and continue to participate in the training of defence force health personnel.

Although it has taken me nearly ten years to accept it, my experiences in Kosovo did have a profound influence on my life and on my relationships with family and friends. Within a year of my return, I became aware that it would take little provocation for me to fly off the handle, a simmering anger never far from the surface. Coincident with this, and literally days after starting my career as a fully qualified cardiothoracic surgeon, I became embroiled in a messy legal battle with two of my previous surgical mentors. Though they were charged and subsequently penalised for anticompetitive conduct, the whole affair was very drawn out and stressful, particularly for Donna, an intensive care trainee in the same hospital at the time.

I assumed that my mood change was related to the combined stresses of starting a new career and fighting off vindictive ex-colleagues, and that my erratic sleeping patterns and hypervigilance were a result of long working hours and fatigue. Despite these issues, I put on a brave face and buried myself in my work and family. With the birth of Harrison in 2003, my mood lifted enormously and for the first year of his life I was the happy-go-lucky guy his mother had married five years earlier. My eldest son Jackson was doing well in school and sport, and our relationship grew stronger. With work busier than ever, and the legal battle in full swing, Liam was born in early 2005. His first few months were quite a concern for Donna and I as he suffered from a form of neonatal apnoea, where he would intermittently stop breathing. In fact, Donna had to resuscitate him herself in her hospital bed only twenty-four hours after he was delivered by Caesarean section. For the next year we nursed him on an alarmed mattress, wary that he may stop breathing anytime he fell asleep.

It wasn't until late 2005, more than six years after the Kosovo conflict, that my memories of the war became more pervasive and intrusive. One night whilst preparing a talk on trauma surgery in war zones, I searched the internet for some statistics on the number of civilian casualties from the Kosovo conflict. During my search I came across a NATO report on the Serb casualties of its bombing campaign in Kosovo. The report stated that the bombing at the front on 8–9 June 1999 had resulted in the highest Serb casualty rate of the entire war. In the northeast sector, the position on which I provided coordinates, about four hundred Yugoslav regular army and Serb paramilitary troops had been killed by a combination of standard high-explosive and cluster munitions. Several artillery pieces, armoured vehicles and mortar emplacements were also destroyed in the attack. The report claimed that the actual number of dead might well have been higher, as many bodies were incinerated in the attacks. Yugoslav officials put the number of dead as high as six hundred.

This report, in front of me in black and white, brought home the brutal horrors of the campaign. At the time my actions appeared noble and the victory sweet but with the consequences of my actions now clear, the triumph seemed far less palatable. My hatred of those responsible for the atrocities I witnessed had not abated, but I couldn't help but wonder how many innocent men died during the bombardment on those two days. War distorts one's sense of reason, one's judgement and insight. The decisions taken in battle are based on reasons that seem alien to those removed from it. One's judgement is influenced by the intense mix of fear, physical and emotional stress and camaraderie that pervade the battlefield. These factors interact to distort one's insight and sense of self, resulting in actions which most would construe as reckless and irresponsible: some call this bravery and sacrifice.

Throughout my time in the Balkans, my overriding focus was the delivery of relief to those in need. I convinced myself that circumstance and fate intervened to dictate how I would provide that relief, and that the nobility of the cause transcended all responsibility.

Despite these abstract justifications, feelings of guilt and remorse for many of my actions came to the fore. Before long, the dreams became more vivid, and sleep became something I gave into only when completely exhausted. At times it became hard to distinguish dream from memory; my time at the front playing back in my mind like an old newsreel. After a while I learned to live with this new reality and coasted on, taking one day at a time. My intense sense of duty to my patients and the sense of worth I obtained in providing my service prevented these personal issues from affecting my work. My practice and research activities flourished and in an effort to keep my mind preoccupied, I took on extra responsibilities. Despite these efforts, the joy I gained from my children seemed to be dampened by the fog of my past. My relationship with my wife, too, suffered; she could tell that something had changed, and despite her insistence that I talk to someone about my issues I continued to live on in denial. Worse than that, I joined the army!

With a poorly timed sense of patriotism and an ill-conceived idea that treating more war wounded would somehow correct the wrongs of my past, I enlisted as a captain in the Royal Australian Army Medical Corps in February 2006. Three months later I was in East Timor working in support of Australian Special Forces during Operation Astute. Eighteen months after returning from Timor I again farewelled my family, this time for Afghanistan during Operation Slipper between February and April 2008. I now hold the rank of major. My family suffered terribly during these absences.

I was determined to make a fresh start in life and clean out the ghosts of the past on my return from Afghanistan. The coping skills I had developed were not just ineffective, but selfish and destructive. My time in Afghanistan gave me a chance to reflect on my performance as a husband and father over the years since Kosovo. My team spent many long hours operating on Afghan men, women and children, and Coalition soldiers, all casualties of the war against the Taliban. I saw the brutality of war yet again, but this time I was determined to use this experience to improve the way I approached similar issues from my past.

Our team was actively involved in training some of the Special Forces medics in Tarin Kowt and on a few occasions we were invited to their camp for dinner and a presentation. The answer to my dilemma came to me one night after presenting my stock standard, no emotions-attached talk on the Kosovo war to a team of Special Forces medics. At the end of the talk, one of the medics told me that he thoroughly enjoyed the presentation and that he understood what I had been through at the front. He strongly recommended that I sit down and write a book about my experiences, saying that it would be therapeutic and serve as a record of what really happened. This young medic had seen a lot in his two tours of Afghanistan, and I owed it to him to at least think about his suggestion.

On returning to Australia and yet another tearful reunion with my family, I decided that enough was enough. With a renewed vigour and outlook on life I started recording my memories of my time in Albania and Kosovo. With the aid of my field notebook, maps and photos, many of which I hadn't looked at for nearly ten years, I laboriously wrote down the events as they occurred, day by day. As I did this, the fog that had been clouding my daily existence for so many years started to lift. Sleep was no longer a dark journey that had to be endured, and dreams, once graphic replays of horrific past events, turned to pleasant reminders of happier times. As I continued writing, my mood lifted and my whole outlook on life changed.

I had known all along that I was suffering from some degree of post-traumatic stress disorder, but I was not willing to admit to it. Too many people relied on me for strength. Too many looked to me for support and guidance. Any sign of weakness in the eyes of those around me may have brought into question my ability as a surgeon, as a leader, and as a father. Or so I thought. To this point in time my coping strategies, though imperfect, had allowed me to function perfectly well from a professional viewpoint. Socially, too, I managed to continue without arousing the suspicion of anyone but Donna. But my wife and my children, my family and friends deserved more than this. I deserved more than this. These realisations, and the will to move beyond the horrors of my time on Mt. Pastrik, led me to the point at which I find myself now; at peace, and at ease with the decisions and actions of my past.

The book was completed in late February 2010 and within days of its imminent release being made public it was a front-page story in *Illyria*, an Albanian-American newspaper with wide circulation in New York and many other US cities. I found myself doing radio interviews with Radio Television Kosovo (RTK), and before long the story was being reported worldwide. I began receiving hundreds of emails daily, amongst them one from my old friend Florim Lajki from the Atlantic Battalion. Soon thereafter I was contacted by many of the men and women I had served with on Mount Pastrik. I was thrilled to learn that some were now fathers and mothers living normal lives in the US, Europe and the UK. Florim, now a successful businessman in New York, read the book along with Gani Shehu, the former commander of the battalion on Pastrik. They appreciated that the true story of what happened on Pastrik would finally be told. Through the medium of Facebook, I heard from hundreds of former soldiers, refugees and young Kosovars just wanting to say thank you. I was truly overwhelmed by the flood of correspondence.

One night, 6 March 2010 to be precise, I was up late uploading photos from my time at the front onto the Atlantic Battalion veterans' website. Tired, I switched off my laptop and went to bed. With so much writing behind me, the memories of my time in Kosovo were again at the forefront of my thoughts. I lay there in an uneasy state, tossing and turning, unable to get to sleep. Not wanting to wake Donna, I got up and went to the kitchen. I reopened my laptop to check my emails one last time before giving sleep another try, and could scarcely believe my eyes. Could it be true, after all this time? This is what I read:

From: *Shkumbin*
Subject: *Greetings from Prizren*
Date: *6 March 2010 11:30:39 PM*

Craig, thanks for puting in the book those days and good blesing you what you have done for the soldiers. I was with my wife in Cahan, Krume and we had a lot discussion about War medicine even you stayed for short in Cahan. Me and my wife were exalted when we heard about the book and the film even it will be difficult to describe everything from that time. If this message arrives to you, all the best to you end your family.

P.S.
Maybe you are still married !!!!

Prizren, Kosovo

It was true. Shkumbin and Rukije were alive, and living in Kosovo. An incredible end to a story with few happy endings. We intend to meet and talk and share coffee once more, and they will visit me and swim in the pool we all dreamed of that day in Cahan! Whoever said miracles never happen?

A good portion of the potential joy of the past ten years had been lost because of the effect of a comparatively short time of misery. This cannot be recovered but I can make sure that I enjoy every last minute of my time with my family and friends. Most other women would have left me by now, but not Donna. This book is a testament to her love and resilience, without which I would not have made it through Kosovo or the ten years since.

Many memories, however, will stay with me forever. Though far less painful now, they still act to strengthen the love and devotion I have for my family. As a father I will never forget the pain of holding the lifeless body of that little boy in my arms. I will never forget those long nights in the cave, sleeping beside the bodies of young men taken in the prime of their lives. Time cannot and should not erase the tale of their suffering. These memories serve as a monument to their sacrifice.

To this day, when I sleep, they sleep with me.

Glossary

AK-47, Kalashnikov

The Avtomat Kalashnikova is the most widely used assault rifle in the world. First developed in the Soviet Union by Mikhail Kalashnikov, it was put into mass production in 1947, hence the abbreviation, AK-47. It was one of the first true assault rifles and, due to its low production cost and extreme durability, it remains the most popular and ubiquitous assault rifle in the world today. It uses the 7.62 x 39mm round and has a magazine capacity of 30 rounds. It can be fired in semi-automatic (one round per trigger pull) or fully-automatic (continuous fire whilst trigger held) mode.

Alfresco's

A family-owned café in Rundle Street, Adelaide. My local haunt since the age of seventeen, it is a popular spot for locals, tourists and is a microcosm of the greater city. I wrote the original manuscript here whenever I had a moment to spare.

Barrett bolt action .50 calibre sniper rifle

Designated the M95, this is a bolt-action .50 calibre (12.7 x 99mm) sniper rifle manufactured by Barrett Firearms Company in the US. It has a 5-round magazine set behind the trigger ('bull-pup' design). If the telescopic sight was correctly set up and the rifle correctly sighted in, a target could be hit at up to 2.2 kilometres.

Beretta 92 model

One of a series of semi-automatic pistols designed and manufactured by Beretta in Italy. The 9mm calibre pistol was adopted as the standard sidearm by the United States military in 1985 and given the designation M9. It is a particularly durable and reliable pistol and considered by many to be one of the finest pistols in use by any military force.

CIA

Central Intelligence Agency. A civilian intelligence agency of the US. It is an independent agency for providing national security intelligence to the American administration. It conducts covert operations and paramilitary actions, and exerts foreign political influence through the Special Activities Division.

Czech CZ 9mm pistol

A semi-automatic pistol made by Ceska Zbrojovka Uhersky Brod in the Czech Republic.

Debridement

The surgical removal of dead, damaged or infected tissue to allow healing of the remaining healthy tissue. Most blast injuries, as described in this book, have a significant amount of dead and contaminated tissue associated with the injury and the rapid and thorough removal of this tissue is crucial to the prevention of overwhelming infection and possible death.

Djakova

A small city in the west of Kosovo, near the Albanian border, with a population of 25,000.

Dragunov 7.62 x 54mm semi-automatic sniper rifle

In service in the Soviet Union since 1963, it is a durable, accurate and easy-to-use rifle with a 10-round capacity. It is light and its mechanism is very similar to the AK-47.

DUSHKA

DShK .50 calibre anti-aircraft/ anti-personnel gun. This is a Soviet heavy machine gun firing a 12.7 x 108mm round. It takes its name from its designers, Vasily Degyaryov and Georgi Shpagin, and is sometimes nicknamed Dushka ('sweetie' in Russian) from the abbreviation.

Field compass

A navigational instrument for determining direction relative to the Earth's magnetic poles. It consists of a magnetised pointer marked on the North end which aligns itself with the Earth's magnetic field. Modern military and recreational compasses (field compasses) use a magnetised needle in a fluid-filled capsule, and have an integrated protractor with its own magnetic needle. The rotating capsule has a transparent base marked with map-orienting lines, and the whole compass-protractor is mounted on a transparent baseplate with a direction of travel indicator on one end to be used for taking bearings directly from a map.

Full metal jacket round

This is a bullet consisting of a soft core (usually lead) encased in a shell of harder metal (cupronickel or a steel alloy). The jacket allows the bullet to travel at a faster velocity than a bare lead ('soft-point') round without depositing significant amounts of lead ('fouling') in the rifling (grooves) of the bore (barrel). Their main advantage is that, as the jacket prevents the bullet from expanding, they are very effective at piercing armour.

G8

The Group of Eight (formerly known as Group of Six) is an informal forum, created by France in 1975, for the eight major industrial powers: France, the United States of America, the United Kingdom, Russia, Canada, Germany, Italy and Japan.

Gigli amputation wire

A very strong wire saw used to cut through bone, particularly the long bones of the arm and leg in amputation procedures.

Gorjunov SGM

A Soviet medium machine gun introduced in 1943. It uses the 7.62 x 54mm round and is mounted on small steel wheels. It requires two operators.

Goya, Francisco de (1746–1828)

A famous Spanish painter and printmaker. His series of aquatint prints titled *The Disasters of War* depicts disturbing scenes from the Peninsular War of 1812–15 between France and Spain over the Iberian peninsula. His macabre depiction of the horror of the battlefield represents an outraged conscience in the face of death and destruction. Considered too graphic for their time, they were not published until 35 years after his death.

Grid reference

Grid references define locations on maps using Cartesian co-ordinates. These co-ordinates specify each point on a map by a pair of numbers which are the distances from two fixed perpendicular directed lines (measured in the same unit of length). The grid references or co-ordinates can be used to accurately identify a point on the ground to within 10 square metres on most military maps, but even greater accuracy is now possible with satellite-dependent global positioning systems or GPS.

Hershey's

The famous Hershey Food Corporation produces candies and chocolate bars which have long been issued to US military personnel on deployment in overseas operations.

IMC

A global humanitarian non-profit organisation dedicated to health care training and relief and development programs. Founded in 1984, it has responded to most major civil and natural emergencies and has delivered nearly one billion dollars of assistance to millions of people in over 50 countries.

Katyusha rocket

A rocket fired from a multiple rocket launcher mounted on the rear of a military truck. They can deliver a devastating amount and concentration of explosives to a target area quickly. Originally used by Soviet forces in World War Two, troops gave it the nickname 'Katyusha' from Mikhail Isakovsky's popular wartime song about a girl longing for her absent love, who is away at war.

LAR 'Grizzly' .50 calibre sniper rifle

A .50 calibre sniper rifle with a single shot capacity, but a recoil system that results in minimal 'kick-back' when fired. Produced by LAR Manufacturing Inc. in the US.

Marcaine

The trade name of the local anaesthetic drug Bupivacaine.

MEDEVAC

Abbreviation for medical evacuation. In this instance it involved military ambulances and armoured vehicles with or without transfer to a helicopter.

Mortar

A muzzle-loading indirect fire weapon that fires shells at low velocities, and high-arcing ballistic trajectories. Simple and easy to operate, it consists of a tube into which gunners drop a shell. A firing pin at the base of the tube detonates the propellant and fires the shell. The tube is usually set at an angle of between 45 and 80 degrees to the round, the higher the angle the shorter the firing distance. A mortar can be carried by one or two people, and can be operated by one person. The Serb forces had a small (80mm) and a heavy (120mm) mortar.

NATO

North Atlantic Treaty Organisation. Intergovernmental military alliance based on the North Atlantic Treaty of 1949. It is a system of collective defence whereby its member states agree to mutual defence in the event of an attack by any external party. On 24 March 1999 it saw its first ever large-scale military engagement, Operation Allied Force, an 11-week bombing campaign against the Federal Republic of Yugoslavia (FRY). The aim was to stop the Serbian-led expulsion of ethnic Albanian civilians from Kosovo, a province of the FRY.

Operation Allied Force was mandated by UN resolution 1244, authorising an international civil and military presence in Kosovo under interim UN administration.

NGO

Non-governmental organisation. A civil society organisation – no government representation or participation. In this instance, relief agencies.

NORWAC

Norwegian Aid Committee

Pinzgauer

An all-terrain four-wheel-drive military utility vehicle manufactured in Surrey, U.K., by BAE Systems Land Systems. Originally developed in Graz, Austria, and named after an Austrian breed of horse.

Pristina

Located centrally, the capital of Kosovo is also its largest city with a population of 500,000.

Prizren

Located in the southwest of Kosovo, Prizren is the second largest city with a population of 110,000 prior to the ethnic cleansing campaign of 1999.

SKS

A Soviet 7.62 x 30mm calibre semi-automatic carbine designed in 1945 by Gavrilovich Siminov. It was used in service by the Soviet Union for a short period but was quickly replaced by the AK-47. It is currently used as a ceremonial arm in Russia. It was widely exported and produced throughout former Eastern Bloc nations and China. It has a 10 round fixed magazine and is renowned for its durability and reliability.

Thoracotomy

The incision in the chest wall used by surgeons to enter the thoracic cavity. It varies in size depending on the surgeon and the indication, but can extend from behind the shoulder blade, passing under the tip of the shoulder blade down to a position below the nipple of that side. In trauma situations, a large posterolateral thoracotomy (as described here) is most commonly used as it gives the surgeon excellent access to the lungs, heart, aorta and oesophagus. The surgeon can also open the diaphragm (the muscle separating the chest from the abdomen) allowing examination of the abdominal contents.

Tramadol

A centrally-acting analgesic developed in the late 1970s, useful for the treatment of moderate to severe pain.

UNHCR

United Nations High Commissioner for Refugees. Established in 1950 to assist in the voluntary repatriation, local integration or resettlement of refugees.

VJ

Vojska Jugoslavije is Serbian for the Yugoslav People's Army.

Western Front

A term used during the First World War to describe the contested frontier between the lands controlled by Germany to the east and the Allies to the west.

Wilfred Owen (1893–1918)

A Welsh poet and soldier. His shockingly realistic poetry put to verse the true horror and futility of trench warfare. He was killed in action in the Battle of the Sambre exactly one week before the Armistice of 11 November, 1918, which saw an end to the bloodiest conflict in human history. His best known works – many of which were published posthumously – include 'Anthem for Doomed Youth', 'Dulce et Decorum Est', 'Strange Meeting' and 'Futility'. The preface he intended to use for a book of poems to be published in 1919 contains well-known phrases 'the Poetry is in the pity' and 'War, and the pity of War'.

Hard News, Heartfelt Opinions

FORT WAYNE JOURNAL-GAZETTE
FORT WAYNE INDIANA

Hard News, Heartfelt Opinions

A History of the *Fort Wayne Journal Gazette*

Scott M. Bushnell

Indiana University Press
Bloomington and Indianapolis

071.7274
Bus

This book is a publication of

Indiana University Press
601 North Morton Street
Bloomington, IN 47404-3797 USA

http://iupress.indiana.edu

Telephone orders   800-842-6796
Fax orders   812-855-7931
Orders by e-mail   iuporder@indiana.edu

Published with the support of the *Fort Wayne Journal Gazette.*

© 2007 by The Fort Wayne Journal Gazette
and Scott M. Bushnell

All rights reserved

No part of this book may be reproduced or utilized in
any form or by any means, electronic or mechanical,
including photocopying and recording, or by any
information storage and retrieval system, without
permission in writing from the publisher. The
Association of American University Presses' Resolution
on Permissions constitutes the only exception to this
prohibition.

The paper used in this publication meets the minimum
requirements of American National Standard for
Information Sciences—Permanence of Paper for Printed
Library Materials, ANSI Z39.48-1984.

Manufactured in the United States of
America

Library of Congress Cataloging-in-Publication Data

Bushnell, Scott M.
    Hard news, heartfelt opinions : a history of the Fort Wayne Journal Gazette / Scott M. Bushnell.
        p. cm.
    Includes bibliographical references and index.
    ISBN-13: 978-0-253-34920-0 (cloth)
    1. Ft. Wayne Journal-Gazette. 2. Journalism–Indiana–Fort Wayne–History. I. Title.
    PN4899.F6175F67 2007
    071'.7274–dc22
2006102468

1 2 3 4 5 12 11 10 09 08 07

To the memory of reporters, editors, proofreaders, compositors, stereotypers, pressmen, advertising staff, and circulation crews whose legacy is still found in the pride of producing a newspaper that honestly represents its community every day of the week.

The path of sound credence
is through the thick forest of skepticism.

George Jean Nathan (1882–1958),
dramatist and essayist, born in Fort Wayne

Contents

ACKNOWLEDGMENTS ix

Introduction xi
1. Scoundrels in Paper and Ink 1
2. The *Gazette* 13
3. The *Journal* 41
4. The Acquisition 71
5. After Andy 91
6. Depression and War 125
7. Under One Roof, but Still Independent 143
Epilogue 183

NOTES 185
BIBLIOGRAPHY 191
INDEX 195

Acknowledgments

One of the great pleasures in completing this book is the opportunity to thank the people whose counsel, support, and encouragement were important. Chief among them were Julie Inskeep, publisher of the *Journal Gazette*, and her parents, Dick and Harriett Inskeep. Their desire to produce a comprehensive history of the newspaper was the driving force behind the book. There were many other members of the newspaper staff, past and present, who gave generously of their time and insights. Among them were Tom Pellegrene, Tracy Warner, Craig Klugman, Sylvia Smith, Larry Hayes, Evan Davis, Barbara Olyenik Morrow, Bob Englehart, Steve Sack, Justin Baer, and Griffith and Patricia Kelsey Watkins. Ed Breen and Dean Musser played pivotal roles in securing and reproducing the images. Two members of the Journal Gazette Company, Jerry D. Fox and Sandra Pollom-Boruk, made certain the writer had a place from which to work in the old newspaper building on Main Street.

Many shared their memories and offered greater insight into the newspaper and its community. Of particular note was Thomas D. Logan, whose material on his grandfather, Thomas Bresnahan, was a delightful discovery. Sam and Joel Hyde went to great lengths to find obscure works on Fort Wayne and Indiana from their most valuable bookstore on Wells Street. The times that John Beatty of the Allen County Public Library's Historical Genealogy section solved problems were innumerable; he is one of the great assets of this community, as anyone who has undertaken research here can attest. All of the library staff, especially Alice Barva and Stanley McBride in the microfilm reference area, were considerate, helpful, and interested in helping track down missing pieces of information. Significant contributions also were made by Andrew Downs, director of the Mike Downs Center for Indiana Politics at Indiana University–Purdue University Fort Wayne, and Dana Owen of the Warsaw Community Public Library. Thoughtful guidance was offered by Ladonna Huntley James, Betty Stein, and Vince Robinson.

The staff at Indiana University Press has been kind, considerate, and instructive. This book would not have come to fruition without the assistance of editors Linda Oblack, LeeAnn Sandweiss and Brian Herrmann, and the keen, thoughtful copyediting it received from Elaine Durham Otto.

Four other people had significant influence in the preparation of this book: Michael Hawfield for instilling a love for Fort Wayne and its history; Professor Clifford Scott of Indiana University–Purdue University Fort Wayne for demonstrating the rigor one should bring to local history research; curator Walter Font for the many times he dug through the Allen County–Fort Wayne Historical Society's collection in search of answers to obscure questions; and Ian M. Rolland for his leadership in his business and the community that drew me to Fort Wayne in 1989.

The largest measure of appreciation goes to Barbara Weir Bushnell for her love, patience, and gentle encouragement to "rewrite until it's right." No one could ask for a better partner in life.

Introduction

On the eve of the state's centennial, historian Meredith Nicholson described Indiana as "a typical American State." Much has changed since that observation was made in 1915, in both the landscape and the populace of Indiana. Once lauded as the heartland of America and then pitied as part of the Rust Belt, Indiana is now underappreciated. Its agricultural community is among the nation's most productive, but this influence is dwindling. The engineering knowledge and sheer grit that made Indiana a dynamo in America's great automotive industry have lost their luster in the glow of computer technology.

Fort Wayne's story runs with the currents of the nation, with its growth, success, and disappointments similar to other small cities in the United States. Founded at the confluence of two rivers whose waters reach Lake Erie and beyond, the area was a center for Native American transportation and commerce when Europeans arrived. Fort Wayne flourished in the nineteenth century and blossomed in the twentieth century. Once touted as "the Wonder City of the American Midwest," Fort Wayne failed to diversify its industrial base and lost its economic momentum. It continues to look for a rebirth.

From the time of its settlement, Fort Wayne has been a heterogeneous mixture of peoples: in the beginning, Native American, French, and North American British, later Scots, German, and Irish, and today Spanish-speaking and Southeast Asian immigrants. This admixture of cultures brought different beliefs and expectations to the fertile lands surrounding the St. Mary's River and the St. Joseph River, which join to form the Maumee River. From the period before the Civil War until today, there have been divergent views on the best way to govern Fort Wayne and provide for the welfare of its residents. Whether it concerned abolitionism, monetary policy, prohibition, or municipal development, there seems to always have been a raft of opinion working its way into newspapers of various political persuasions.

One newspaper in particular has a rich heritage and a history of pursuing what it sees as important and honest news for its readers. Drawing from a contentious start during the Civil War, the *Fort Wayne Journal Gazette* has championed causes that were not always welcome. Its positions have frequently been at odds with the prevalent public opinion. The men and women who worked for the *Journal Gazette* have been dedicated to putting important issues before the community. That commitment continues today.

Over the years, a great deal of research has concerned Indiana, but little of it about Fort Wayne. For example, Muncie gained renown when it became the first U.S. community to be systematically examined by sociologists Robert S. and Helen Merrell Lynd in the 1920s and 1930s. The first of their two books on the community, which they called "Middletown," has never been out of print, and Muncie remains a focal point of research today. The volumes about Indianapolis fill bookshelves, perhaps befitting the belief that the state capital is truly representative of a state. Indiana's second-most populous city is unlike the governmental center of the state or any of the cities with one predominant industry, like Gary. Instead, Fort Wayne resembles many U.S. cities born with a shared belief in progress and now facing an accumulation of contemporary urban problems. Fort Wayne as a small American city deserves more critical attention. This examination of the relationship of the community and the media that helped shape its aspirations, its achievements, and even its prejudices is an effort in that direction.

Hard News, Heartfelt Opinions

FORT WAYNE GAZETTE.

THE MORNING JOURNAL.

FT. WAYNE JOURNAL=GAZETTE.

THE FORT WAYNE JOURNAL-GAZETTE.

FORT WAYNE JOURNAL-GAZETTE

FORT WAYNE JOURNAL-GAZETTE

THE JOURNAL-GAZETTE

The Journal-Gazette

Journal Gazette

1

Scoundrels in Paper and Ink

During the Civil War years the people of Indiana were in the grip of factional frenzy which their prosaic descendants find hard to understand.

—G. R. Tredway, *Democratic Opposition to the Lincoln Administration in Indiana*

When David W. Jones turned north toward Fort Wayne in 1863, hauling his printing equipment and his personal belongings in a wagon, the risks he faced were greater than the opportunity. The fifty-mile journey from the small community of Jonesboro in Grant County to the thriving town along the old Wabash and Erie Canal in Allen County would offer him a chance to be more than a job printer. His goal was to start a daily newspaper that would support the policies of President Abraham Lincoln. Jones was not oblivious to the dangers in such an endeavor: the Fort Wayne and Allen County area was known for its tenacious allegiance to the Democratic Party.

The largest county in Indiana in terms of size, Allen County was third largest in population, with 29,328 residents in the 1860 census. The foreign-born population represented 23.4 percent, more than half of whom were from German-speaking lands. There were few African Americans (63) and fewer Native Americans (22).[1] The population of Fort Wayne, the county seat, exceeded 15,000 residents and was growing rapidly. The railroads, which first arrived in the 1850s to supplant the canal, were the engine of economic growth and would remain so well into the next century.

The newspaper that David Jones wanted to produce would espouse unwelcome ideas in Fort Wayne. It would endorse the call-up of more young men for the Union army and civil rights for former slaves. Such a newspaper would only heighten the tempest that had raged in print in Fort Wayne for twenty years.

The attitudes in Allen County in the antebellum period were consistent with Indiana's divided loyalties. The northern and southern sections—the separation perhaps best delineated by the National Road, which crossed Indiana from Richmond in the east through Terre Haute in the west—had their roots in the attitudes of the pioneers from two distinct regions. The southern portion of Indiana had a familial attachment to the states where slavery was legal, particularly Kentucky. The northern section's settlement had followed the migration from New England, New York, and New Jersey and later from Ireland, Scotland, and the German states. Indiana had a common bond, though, and that was a pronounced patriotic sentiment. Many families, north and south, could proudly claim fathers and grandfathers who had fought in the Revolution.

The residents in Fort Wayne and elsewhere in the state watched with growing apprehension the increasingly bitter national debate over slavery in the 1850s. Indiana's citizens were alarmed by the growing strength of the slaveholding states and their threat of secession. At the same time, most were opposed to those who would abolish slavery. This was true in Fort Wayne, located in the northeastern part of the state, which was far more conservative than communities further south, such as Richmond, which were strongholds of abolitionism.

There were two established newspapers in the late 1850s in Fort Wayne whose opinions inflamed political passions. The *Fort Wayne Weekly Sentinel* was begun in 1833 by Thomas Tigar and Smallwood V. B. Noel, who were persuaded to move from Indianapolis to what was then a town on the Wabash and Erie Canal, which was still under construction. The newspaper was published irregularly until 1837 because Tigar couldn't find a reliable source of newsprint. It had begun as a neutral paper because Noel was a Whig, but after he retired in 1834, Tigar made it a Democratic organ. Through the years it remained a champion of the Democratic Party and its candidates. The other newspaper was the *Fort Wayne Times*, operated in the 1850s by John W. Dawson, a phlegmatic political figure and often scurrilous editor. While Tigar was stoutly partisan, Dawson changed his allegiances. Both the *Sentinel* and the *Times*, however, agreed on one issue: slavery was a legal, acceptable condition.

In 1860, Tigar and Dawson's position on abolitionism was consistent with the racial prohibitions of Indiana's new constitution. Granted statehood in 1816, Indiana had been settled by pioneers who by definition were self-reliant and individualistic, cutting their livelihood from a wilderness.

Subsequent settlers were looking for a fresh start, whether they were leaving their past along the Atlantic seaboard or somewhere in Europe. Those who had emigrated from Europe where class distinctions were inescapable traded a few years of indentured service—often in Pennsylvania or Ohio—to have the opportunity to own their own land, homes, farms, and businesses in Indiana. They were among the loudest proponents of an individual's rights in the United States. At the same time, they brought their racial biases with them. The majority of citizens in northeastern Indiana in 1860 did not find it inconsistent to be antislavery and anti–African American. While the first constitution in 1816 prohibited slavery, Hoosiers did not want African Americans—whether fugitive or freed—settling within the state's boundaries. A law passed in 1831 required African Americans wanting to settle within the state to register with county authorities and post a bond as a guarantee of good behavior and economic self-sufficiency. The growing turmoil in the nation and the fact that Indiana bordered on a state that permitted slavery—Kentucky—prompted the new constitution in 1851 to bar any more African Americans from coming into or settling in Indiana with its notorious Article XIII entitled "Negroes and Mulattoes." Anyone employing or encouraging African Americans to settle in Indiana faced a fine of $10 to $500.[2] When combined with other legislation, antebellum Indiana denied blacks the right to vote, prohibited them from attending public schools, barred them from serving in the military, and ruled inadmissible any testimony they might give in court against white citizens.

This constitutional prohibition did not close Indiana's borders to slaves seeking freedom, nor did it stem the desire of some free African Americans to settle in the state. It did have a measurably chilling effect, however. The Underground Railroad operated through eastern Indiana before and during the Civil War. In 1850 there were 165,286 people in northern Indiana, including 16,919 in Allen County, which was the most populated county in the region. The census in Allen County had recorded 102 African Americans, 37 of whom were born in Indiana.[3] In 1860, the black population in Allen County was 63. It is unclear whether this example represents an accurate numerical reduction or whether fear kept freed individuals away from federal census takers or whether some census takers did not count black residents. However, the county's tenor in the period can be seen in Dawson's comment in an April 1860 issue of his *Fort Wayne Times* that "the negroes are becoming intolerable, and it is full time they were drummed out of town."[4]

Yet Fort Wayne was not a one-dimensional racist community. There were pockets of people who spoke out against slavery. Noted abolitionist Henry Ward Beecher organized the Second Presbyterian Church in May 1844 where his brother, Charles Beecher, was the preacher until 1850. Later, attorney Lindley Ninde had close connections with Levi Coffin of the Underground Railroad.[5] Frederick Nirdlinger's home on Main Street just west of Harrison Street, near the commercial center of the community, served not only as the unofficial house of worship for the city's Jewish inhabitants but also as a stop on the secret conduit helping escaped slaves reach freedom in the North.[6] In the mid-1850s, Fort Wayne even had its own abolitionist newspaper, which daringly presented reports on rescues of slaves as well as arguments against slavery. It was an extreme exception, lasting only one year.

The politics of the community were evident in its earliest newspapers. In the late 1840s and early 1850s, the *Fort Wayne Weekly Sentinel* railed against the Free Soil Party, one of the forerunners of the Republican Party. Tigar championed Senator Stephen A. Douglas in the 1860 election and belittled the candidacy of Abraham Lincoln. The *Sentinel* created great anticipation in the town for a campaign visit by Douglas in early October. The Illinois senator was met at the railroad station by a crowd that paraded by torchlight through the streets to hear an hour-long speech by Douglas. Later a straw effigy of Lincoln was hung and burned at the courthouse, and a large log was hurled into the St. Mary's River from the Wells Street bridge, apparently indicating what the crowd would do to the "Rail Splitter" if they had the opportunity.

While the *Sentinel* hailed Douglas's campaign visit, the other newspaper, Dawson's *Fort Wayne Daily Times*, found the speech by Douglas "neither pleasing nor forcible." Worse was the crowd of Democratic supporters. The Democratic candidate, the *Times* said, was greeted "at the depot by a large crowd of noisy, disorderly men—the conduct of many of whom is by no means a thing which an enlightened community can think of but to deprecate."[7]

It was the *Sentinel*, though, that reflected the community's strong political feelings. Douglas received 3,224 votes to Lincoln's 2,552 in Allen County. Seventy-four other votes were divided between Southern Democrat John C. Breckenridge and Constitutional Union candidate John Bell. As the southern states began to debate secession and the nation teetered toward war, the *Sentinel* called on the president-elect to accede to their demands. It was mildly reproachful of Lincoln as he tried to maintain the Union in the face of creation of the Confederate States of America. The *Sentinel* only changed its position after Confederate guns were turned on Fort Sumter,

South Carolina, on April 12. It was not a wholesale endorsement of Lincoln's policies by any means. Instead, Tigar called for the restoration of the Union—on the South's terms, if necessary. The *Sentinel*'s criticism of Lincoln rarely abated. It asserted that the Union army could not defeat the Confederate army, and when the North began to have success on the battlefield, the newspaper declared the cost of the war to be too high. This position and other antiwar activities endorsed by the newspaper fueled the military's belief that Fort Wayne was a hotbed of Confederate supporters— the "butternuts," or the more derogatory term, the "Copperheads."

However, it was the *Times* with its contrary editor that illustrated the complexity of the issues and sentiments of the time. The career of John Dawson, whose influence stretched over twenty years, showed the admixture of emotions that flowed through Fort Wayne between 1854 and 1865. Occasionally running for political office, Dawson was, in turn, a Whig, an anti-Nebraskan, a Know-Nothing, a Republican, a Democrat, and a Union supporter. His literary artifice and intemperate behavior made him a formidable newspaper editor in his time and nearly cost him his life. The animosities he incurred were long-lasting. Near the end of his life, Dawson was described in the *Sentinel* as having "introduced a species of blackguardism, vulgarity and personalities into Fort Wayne journalism which were never before known in this city, and which have happily never been imitated since."[8]

His beginning was modest. Dawson and Thompson N. Hood leased the *Fort Wayne Times*, a Whig newspaper owned by former mayor George W. Wood, in 1852. Dawson bought the newspaper two years later, and as its editor he used it as a platform to become a leader in the Fusion, or People's, Party in Indiana. The *Times* was a progressive newspaper, stoutly opposed to the Kansas-Nebraska Act, which opened new territory to slavery. It was also virulently outspoken in its dislike of abolitionists.

It became evident early that its editor was not above slanderous personal attacks on the competition. In 1854, when the American, or Know-Nothing, Party was playing on the fears that foreigners were taking over the country, Dawson claimed Tigar supported non-native-born residents because of his "passion for Dutch girls, lager beer, saur krout [*sic*] and sausages." He then went on to imply that the *Sentinel* editor had an illegitimate child by a Dutch girl.[9]

There were other Fort Wayne newspapers serving smaller audiences during the 1850s. The German-language *Indiana Staatszeitung* began its nearly seventy-year run when Gustavus J. Neubert published the first weekly edition in 1858. Another German-language weekly, the *Demokrat*, had briefly preceded it in 1856. The *Jeffersonian*, which was known as the "Zebra" because of the striped letters on the masthead, was printed from 1856 to 1858 by R. D. Turner.[10] Other newspapers were begun to support presidential candidacies, such as the first *Weekly Journal*, which backed Republican nominee John C. Frémont in 1856.

More controversial was the *Standard*, first published as a weekly on June 1, 1854. A daily edition was added in 1855 by publisher Daniel W. Burroughs. Perhaps the most radical newspaper in the city's history, the *Standard* called for an end to slavery and equal standing for African Americans as U.S. citizens. Its motto, which was printed beneath the nameplate in every issue, read: "Error Ceases to Be Dangerous When Reason Is Left Free to Combat It." In the turbulent 1850s, the national debate over slavery, especially in the new territories, grew in shrillness and eventually became violent. The Kansas-Nebraska Act of 1854 precipitated the launch of the *Standard*. The act, crafted by Senator Douglas of Illinois, appeased the South and angered the North by dividing the Nebraska Territory into two units, Kansas and Nebraska, and allowing the question of slavery—which seemed to have been barred from the entire territory by the earlier Missouri Compromise—to be decided by the territorial settlers. Signed into law by President Franklin Pierce in May 1854, the act sowed the seeds of bloodshed in Kansas and later in the Civil War.

Despite the general sentiment against abolitionism, there was an audience for Burroughs's beliefs in Fort Wayne and the surrounding area, as evidenced by his adding a daily edition after five months in existence. There may have been two reasons for this. First, unlike many communities of its size in Indiana, Fort Wayne did have a small African American population, indicating a level of tolerance among the residents. The 1850 census put Fort Wayne's population at 6,500. Allen County reported 102 African Americans, and very likely most of them lived in the city. Second, there were individuals in the city with high-profile connections to the abolitionist movement and the Underground Railroad. Among them were attorney Charles Case, who tried and won a fugitive slave case in Fort Wayne and who was one of the first editors of the newspaper. Another was Isaac Julian, from a prominent abolitionist family in Indiana. Both of these men, who were recognized in the national abolitionist movement, served as editors of the *Standard* and raised its prominence during its brief existence.

Daniel W. Burroughs had come to Fort Wayne as a Baptist pastor in 1848, but two years later he resigned his position to open a printing business. He was reputed to be an operator of the Underground Railroad, and his newspaper had some financial backing from like-minded individuals in the Fort Wayne community. In contrast to the other newspapers in the city, the *Standard* devoted considerable news and editorial space to the injustices of slavery as well as reports on rescues and escapes of fugitive slaves, some even occurring in northern Indiana. The newspaper covered the 1854 campaign that saw the Fusion Party oust the Democrats. The party's congressional candidate, former Whig Samuel S. Brenton, was elected from the Tenth District, which included Fort Wayne.[11]

In the summer of 1855, Burroughs halted the printing of the weekly *Standard* in order to focus on the daily edition. He came under increased attacks from the paradoxical Dawson. The positions advocated by the editor of the *Times* often opposed the expansion of slavery; however, his paper attacked those who would give freedom and parity to the slaves. Initially he had welcomed the *Standard*, since both newspapers supported the Fusion Party candidates. However, as Burroughs refused to relinquish or modify his abolitionist opinions and as the *Standard* gained national attention, Dawson turned a venomous pen against the newspaper and its publisher. In December 1855, Burroughs suffered a hand injury while operating his press. A few months later he halted the publication of the *Standard*, closed his printing business, and left Fort Wayne.

This did not halt those opposed to the expansion of slavery from seeking their own newspaper. Peter P. Bailey began the *Fort Wayne Weekly Republican* in May 1858. It was in his "prospectus" for the newspaper—which resembled a masthead, outlining its objectives and listing its subscription costs—published on February 22, 1860, that Bailey predicted that the issue of slavery would "be fought at the ballot boxes in 1860. This will be a contest in which every man from necessity must take sides. The democratic party has gone over to the southern side, and will fight against the North. The Republican party will do battle for the North and in that service this paper is enlisted to serve during the war. To make its purpose available it requires patronage. All who are willing to aid the cause in which it is engaged are invited to subscribe to it." Bailey was among the first editors to recognize the appeal of the party's unexpected presidential nominee, printing a summary of the man's qualities under the front-page headline "Abram Lincoln," using a report from the *Chicago Press and Tribune*. This insight, however, did not bear fruit for the struggling Fort Wayne newspaper in early 1860. The February 2 issue called in vain for Republicans to support the newspaper through additional subscriptions. The *Weekly Republican* came to a curious end in late March at the hands of John Dawson.

A fire in the predawn hours of March 24, 1860, destroyed four build-ings on the northeast corner of Columbia and Clinton streets, one of which housed the *Times* office on its third floor. Dawson's records, print-ing equipment, and four presses were lost. Bailey, who had been described as an "imbecile" by Dawson in the previous day's edition of the *Times*, ex-pressed sympathy for his counterpart in the March 24 story about the de-structive fire. "Of our contemporary, Mr. Dawson, the loss is especially severe. His whole office is gone and that without a cent of insurance." Bailey offered the use of the *Republican*'s offices to Dawson and gave him a front-page column in the same issue to address the patrons of the *Times*.

What transpired in the next ten days is unknown, but on April 2 Daw-son's *Fort Wayne Daily Times* resumed publication with the notice that Dawson had bought the *Weekly Republican*. Its subscribers would now re-ceive the *Times* instead. He wrote that Bailey had been troubled by the "unprofitableness" of the *Weekly Republican*. Dawson said he heeded the advice of the businessmen of Fort Wayne who felt there were too many newspapers in the community to support and opted to buy the entire printing operation. Bailey did not have an opportunity to publish his thoughts in the *Times*.

There were some changes in Dawson's newspaper. Before the fire, it had carried a motto below the nameplate that read: "A Whig Journal,—Perfectly Independent; With Courage to Do Right, Scorning to Do Wrong." This did not appear after the closing of Bailey's newspaper. In addition, the *Daily Times* before the fire carried the listing of the state Democratic ticket for the 1860 election below its masthead. In its newer form, it printed the 1860 state Republican ticket. However, one status quo was again in place: Fort Wayne and northeastern Indiana were without a real Republican newspaper.

The battle of words in the Fort Wayne newspapers was not unusual. The debate over the South's right to control its own destiny and retain slavery sparked passionate discourse throughout Indiana. Often there was little civility in expressions of public opinion. As one historian has noted, "There was considerable opposition to administration policies among the people of the North, with more of it in the Old Northwest than in any other section, and more in Indiana than any other state."[12] The 1860 cam-paign in Indiana was particularly acrimonious. For example, the Demo-crats linked the Republicans to miscegenation and charged that they were the enemy of the workingman, since its abolitionist policies would pro-mote African American immigration to Indiana, leading to fewer jobs and lower wages for white workingmen and farmers. The start of the Civil

War caused most newspapers in Indiana to mollify their opposition to Washington, but only briefly.

Historians argue that most Hoosiers who supported the war saw it as a means of restoring the Union, not as a way to revolutionize the nation's race relations. Initially, Republicans in Indiana seemed to agree with this twofold position, at least in private. The conduct of the early war, the Confederacy's early victories, the draft law and subsequent national discontent, and the administration's actions to suppress dissent all served to reignite the Democrats' opposition.

Fort Wayne was viewed as a center of the opposition, so much so that it was a political and military concern for the Lincoln administration. As the 1864 election approached, the *Sentinel* advocated the beliefs of the Peace Democrats and continued to attack Lincoln's handling of the war. The newspaper did not withdraw from its position that the Union was wrong in invading the South and that there was a constitutional right of property in slaves. The vehemence of the *Sentinel*'s opposition to Lincoln grew, and it was seen as a link to treasonous groups like the Sons of Liberty.

In contrast to the *Sentinel*'s steadfastness of political beliefs was the mercurial behavior of John Dawson. In return for his support of Lincoln in 1860, Dawson apparently demanded a political appointment and was named to the post of governor of the Utah Territory, which he was awarded in 1861. He sold his newspaper to W. S. Smith and I. W. Campbell and said he was accepting the governorship in full knowledge of the problems that lay ahead. Using an Odyssean metaphor that reflected his grandiose style, Dawson said he would "seek to steer between the Scylla of fanaticism and the Charybdis of secession" in the territory.[13] In unusually conciliatory fashion, the fiery editor made many fine comments about the community as he departed, most of which he would later retract. Dawson received in return plaudits to his personal attributes from the competition. The *Daily Sentinel* noted that it had had "some bitter controversies with Mr. Dawson" but that "since the commencement of our national difficulties [he] has been eminently wise and patriotic." The *Sentinel* was sympathetic to what it called Dawson's "bold conservative position" against the abolitionists and applauded Lincoln on November 13 for making what it saw as an appointment aimed at appeasing the president's opposition.

Dawson's assignment in Utah proved to be brief and painful. The territory carved out of the wilderness by the Mormon followers of Brigham Young did not want to be controlled by Washington, especially since

Congress had passed a law against polygamy. The leadership certainly did not like the idea of Dawson being their governor. Brigham Young reportedly said that anyone who had been a newspaper editor for fifteen years "must be 'a jackass.'"[14] There were, Dawson wrote late in his life, intense feelings against those sent to administer the laws.

In fact, Dawson's tenure lasted only three weeks in December 1861. His speech to the territorial legislature calling for the Mormons to pay $26,982 in federal taxes to help finance the cost of the Civil War fell on deaf ears. The governor then vetoed a popular plan for securing statehood for the territory, which resulted in someone firing five shots at Dawson in front of his quarters on Main Street. Dawson suddenly departed Salt Lake City on New Year's Eve, reputedly after propositioning a Mormon widow. The stage carrying the governor was stopped by a gang of vigilantes who beat Dawson viciously and may have tried to castrate him. Dawson survived the attack and returned to Fort Wayne. When he had recovered sufficiently, Dawson repurchased his newspaper and changed its loyalties to the Democratic Party. He became an extreme "Copperhead," regularly referring in print to the president as a tyrant. Ironically, if not for Dawson's newspaper, no one would have known that Lincoln once stopped in Fort Wayne. It was only five lines in length and read: "Hon. Abe Lincoln and wife came from the west this morning at 1 o'clock, on the T.W. & W.RR, and changing cars at this city, went East. 'Old Abe' looks like as if his pattern had been a mighty ugly one."[15] After reaching Fort Wayne on the Toledo, Wabash & Western Railroad, Lincoln apparently caught the 1:12 a.m. Pittsburg, Fort Wayne & Chicago Railroad train to New York City where the future president gave his famous speech at Cooper Union and then went on to tour New England. The woman accompanying him was not Mrs. Lincoln, however, but Elizabeth Dorian Smith, a relative of Mary Todd Lincoln's through the marriage of one of her sisters. The woman's toddler, Dudley, was also on the train.[16]

In the fall of 1862, the political landscape changed when Lincoln indicated he would issue the Emancipation Proclamation on January 1, 1863, freeing the slaves in the Confederate states. This, Indiana Democrats feared, would bring "a black wave surging across the Ohio that would cause Indiana to support a horde of black paupers, idlers, and thieves."[17] The *Sentinel*'s reaction on October 4 was even less tolerant. "This project, besides being unconstitutional, is manifestly absurd and impolitic, impossible of execution, and can only have the effect of still further exasperating the Confederates and uniting them to a more determined and persistent defense of what they consider their rights."

It became evident that many Republicans supported the Emancipation Proclamation in public but found it objectionable in private conversation. It took Indiana's powerful wartime governor, Oliver P. Morton, to sway his Republican brethren at a large rally in Indianapolis in January 1863 with the argument that the Emancipation Proclamation was a necessary war measure, not solely a humanitarian one. Morton castigated the Democrats who had been elected in the fall of 1862 on pledges of support for the war but who now opposed it because of the president's intention to free the slaves in rebel territory.[18]

It was into this atmosphere that the first edition of the *Fort Wayne Gazette* came off David Jones's press on May 2, 1863, with a weekly edition published two days later. The defeat at Fredericksburg had cost the Union army dearly. The confrontation at Stones River near Murfreesboro, Tennessee, was bloody and inconclusive, although Lincoln saw it as "a hard-earned victory which, had there been a defeat instead, the nation could scarcely have lived over."[19] The Emancipation Proclamation had taken effect, and people watched for its impact. Very few people believed a Republican newspaper could survive in Fort Wayne. In general, newspapers were not a satisfactory investment at midcentury in the Midwest. As Bessie Keeran Roberts pointed out in her collection of vignettes, the *Gazette*'s founding represented the seventeenth newspaper started in Fort Wayne since the *Sentinel* was begun thirty years earlier. Of that total, only three were publishing in 1863.[20] After a promising beginning, the *Gazette* proved to be similarly challenged, as it had eight publishers in its thirty-six years of independence.

FORT WAYNE GAZETTE.

THE MORNING JOURNAL.

FT. WAYNE JOURNAL=GAZETTE.

THE FORT WAYNE JOURNAL-GAZETTE.

FORT WAYNE JOURNAL-GAZETTE

FORT WAYNE JOURNAL-GAZETTE

THE JOURNAL-GAZETTE

The
Journal-Gazette

The Journal-Gazette

Journal Gazette

2

The *Gazette*

In Indiana, politics is "a passion as strong as religion."
—Jacob Piatt Dunn, Jr.

It may be forgotten now, but it was the Civil War that created an unprecedented appetite for news among the American people. The so-called popular press had arisen twenty-five years earlier for the masses, but mostly in the major cities. For regions like the Old Northwest and its states of Ohio, Indiana, Illinois, Michigan, Wisconsin, and Iowa, local newspapers printed testimonials about "miracle" patent medicines, advertisements for local dry goods stores, political editorial opinions, and legal notices. News items were often clipped from other newspapers and typeset, occasionally with the local editor's comment. Many daily newspapers were also printing weekly editions, selecting stories from each day's newspaper, for readers in outlying areas.

The years leading up to the Civil War saw a dramatic change in the nature of the press as it became a vehicle for inflamed partisan passions. Newspapers affiliated with political parties became prone to vituperative attacks, such as the *Cleveland Leader* advocating that all "Copperheads" be treated as assassins.[1] The advent of war gave greater meaning to the community, too. Whereas the news in many of the earlier newspapers had been focused on reprinting "news" from Europe that was days or weeks old, the publications in the time of the Civil War were printing information with substantive and timely local impact. Regiments were raised in communities, and their experiences in battle were of vital interest. There were often letters and, after clashes, reports of casualties. After the war, accounts of heroism in combat proved exceedingly popular and helped hundreds of veterans advance their political ambitions.

How the *Fort Wayne Daily Gazette* began in May 1863 is of some question. Printer David W. Jones's daughter, Martha Pierce, said in 1938 that her father had started the paper and then invited Isaac Jenkinson to join. In an article in the *Gazette* in 1897, Jenkinson said he began the paper and convinced Jones to relocate his printing operation to Fort Wayne. Yet that recollection differed from a front-page story on June 30, 1868, when Jenkinson recounted that Jones issued the first editions and two weeks later he "entered into the business as a full partner." However the events unfolded, there was the likely involvement of a third individual, Indiana governor Oliver P. Morton.

The most powerful political figure in Indiana during and after the war, Morton needed a newspaper in northeastern Indiana to support the Union cause, raise more troops, and reelect Lincoln in 1864. Moreover, Indiana was one of the "early states" that went to the polls for the president in October. Morton's was a daunting task. The 1862 elections saw Democratic majorities sent to both chambers of the state legislature. This blocked the Republicans from launching an investigation into the pro-Confederacy secret political societies in the state, even though it was rumored that the Knights of the Golden Circle were planning to assassinate the governor. In the wake of the Emancipation Proclamation taking effect, Democratic conventions throughout the state passed resolutions calling for a halt to the war and opposition to the draft. On January 31, 1863, a Democratic meeting in DeKalb County, just north of Allen County, voted to "not give one cent, nor send one single soldier to the present contest, while it is conducted for its present unholy purpose." Lincoln's signing of the national draft act in March 1863 further inflamed partisan passions. In August, Allen County Democrats offered strong objections to the draft and carefully phrased a call for armed resistance: "that the proposed draft was the most damnable of the outrages perpetrated by the administration, and that the honor, dignity, and safety of the people demanded that they should give to themselves that protection which usurpation and tyranny denied them."[2]

Morton was one of the founders of the Republican Party in Indiana, but he disagreed with the abolitionist wing led by George W. Julian. He knew Fort Wayne and had supporters there. While campaigning in Fort Wayne in 1860 for the Republican Party as its candidate for lieutenant governor, Morton called slavery a "local and municipal" issue, but denied the South's claim that there was a "general principle of law enabling one man to hold another as a slave." He denounced the expansion of slavery into territories and endorsed the right of the national government to stop it. He opposed the Dred Scott decision that allowed for the recovery of

David W. Jones, one of the
founders of the *Fort Wayne
Daily Gazette* in 1863.

fugitive slaves from the North. "Five slave-holders sitting on the bench of
the Supreme Court can not settle forever vital questions of freedom
against eighteen millions of people in the free states."[3] He knew Isaac
Jenkinson and had appointed him enrolling and conscription agent in
1862. A year later, Jenkinson was needed to defend more than the draft,
since the outcome of the war remained in great doubt and threatened
Lincoln's reelection. In addition, the radical wing of the Republican Party
saw Lincoln as incompetent, and Salmon P. Chase was secretly seeking
the 1864 Republican nomination despite being in Lincoln's cabinet. The
Ohioan had many admirers in Indiana. Some Republicans in the German
American community supported John Frémont for the nomination, and
the *Freie Presse* was quoted as saying, "We dare not vote for Lincoln unless
we are willing to participate in the betrayal of the Republic."[4] A Republican newspaper in Fort Wayne was viewed as a means of lessening the opposition to Lincoln.

The man who brought his printing equipment to Fort Wayne in a
wagon to start the newspaper was more than just a printer. David Jones
came to Indiana as a boy from Raleigh, North Carolina, and was appren-
ticed to a printer in Marion. He was the son of Obediah Jones, a farmer
and one of the pioneers of Indiana's Grant County.

His politics were in evidence in his printing work, and his sister told

Isaac Jenkinson, who set the Republican tone of The *Fort Wayne Gazette* from its earliest days.

the story of the Knights of the Golden Circle—a secret society formed in Kentucky in 1854 to create a Confederacy extending into Mexico and the Caribbean with active chapters in the Midwest during the Civil War—laying an ambush for Jones and his brother in Marion that they were able to escape. Jones studied the law through which he apparently became acquainted with Isaac Jenkinson.

Jenkinson had practiced law for a dozen years when the *Gazette* was started. He claimed to have given the first Republican speech he ever heard in 1854 and had been among the party's leaders from its birth in Indiana. The nephew of Major Joseph Jenkinson, the commander of the military's Fort Wayne in 1813 and 1814, he served as city treasurer in 1853. He ran unsuccessfully for mayor in 1854, losing to Charles Whitmore. Two years later, he served as editor of the short-lived *Weekly Journal*, which supported Frémont.[5]

In 1860, when Indiana chose Abraham Lincoln over his rivals (Lincoln received 139,033 votes to 115,509 for Stephen A. Douglas, 12,295 for Vice President John C. Breckenridge, and 5,306 for John Bell), Jenkinson was the northeast Indiana district's Republican elector for the formal reporting of the ballot count. In a dramatic pick-a-name-from-the-hat competition, Jenkinson was chosen to travel to Washington to deliver Indiana's results to Breckenridge, the president pro tempore of the Senate. Jenkinson knew Schuyler Colfax, a Republican congressman from South Bend, who introduced him around the capital. Among the introductions was Senator Andrew Johnson, Democrat of Tennessee, on the steps of the Capitol one afternoon. During the conversation, Jenkinson recalled forty-nine years later, President James Buchanan walked past just as Johnson was vehemently denouncing Buchanan's lack of response to the southern states' threats following the election. Jenkinson said Buchanan ignored the tirade. It was a lesson in diplomacy, as well as the lack of it, for the young Indiana Republican. It was also an example of the behavior that would undo Johnson six years later as president at the start of Reconstruction.

In an interview published on April 16, 1897, almost thirty years after the event, Jenkinson offered this recollection of the newspaper's origin. "There was then not a union paper in the district, except in Noble and Lagrange counties. I needed a paper to assist in my work, and a man named Jones from Jonesboro moved his printing office here to do the mechanical work. The *Gazette* soon had a larger circulation than any other newspaper, because of the fierceness of the fight it waged for the Union. Democrats took it to see what it had to say of them. Most of the young Republicans of those days were at the front, and Democrats were bitter. But the questions that then disturbed our peace are settled, and the people of Allen are as loyal as any in the state."

Whoever proposed the original concept, Jenkinson and Jones operated in a partnership that was founded on their mutual beliefs and that effectively used their respective talents. They were joined by Jones's brother Harvey, who one day would win a competition for the fastest typesetter in the United States.[6]

Early in its existence, the *Gazette* boldly endorsed Lincoln's appeal for additional troops. The national conscription act passed by Congress in March 1863 was deeply resented by Democrats in Indiana. The *Fort Wayne Sentinel*, for example, called the National Conscription Act "a death blow to all State Rights." In a reference that seemed to be aimed at the men who emigrated from Prussia to escape military conscription after 1848, the newspaper said the new law left people "no better than serfs under a military dictatorship."[7]

The seriousness of the opposition to Lincoln in Fort Wayne and the surrounding region was viewed by some state and national officials as a prelude to another rebellion and act of secession, with portions of the Old Northwest possibly forming a "Northwest confederacy." An article in the *Fort Wayne Sentinel* implying that resistance to conscription would be justified and a quote attributed to Dawson's *Daily Times* in which disobedience was advocated led Morton and other state officials to limit the stockpiling of government arms and munitions in Fort Wayne.[8] This suspicion should not be interpreted to mean that a majority of young men in the county evaded the draft. Fort Wayne and Allen County provided almost 5,000 men for the Union army, with about 10 percent dying during the war. Some Allen County men volunteered just days after the firing on Fort Sumter and enlisted in Company E, Ninth Regiment of Indiana Volunteers. Among the officers in the regiment was a young lieutenant from Elkhart named Ambrose Bierce who later became one of the generation's best known writers. The troops from Fort Wayne fought bravely at Shiloh, Chickamauga, Vicksburg, Lookout Mountain, and Atlanta. This level of valor was consistent with the rest of the state. Despite the explicit opposition to invading the South and freeing the slaves, Indiana provided the second-highest percentage of soldiers per capita for the Union army. Only Delaware had a higher percentage per capita.

The *Gazette* demonstrated the intensity of the local partisanship shortly after it began printing when it reported on a bloody fight in Fort Wayne over the wearing of butternut pins. A symbol of Democratic opposition, butternut pins were made from the nuts of the white walnut tree. The term also referred to the color of home-dyed clothing worn by its rustic members. It was more than just a term of disdain for the "party of the people," as Democrats liked to call them. It was also the color of the uniform most often associated with Confederate soldiers. Still, "butternuts" was much preferred over the term *Copperhead*, which referred to the region's detested poisonous snake known to strike without warning or reason. Wearing the butternut pin provoked fights and violence almost anywhere—meetings, bars, even funerals. In mid-May, one such confrontation erupted into a prolonged battle in which many Republican supporters were badly beaten. An appeal to the state government for help was ignored. Other confrontations saw different outcomes. These incidents raised apprehensions in the community, adding to the fears that growing partisan violence would result in the arming of a population that could be used against the Union army. There were rumors of many weapons being gathered for an uprising that would lead to parts of Indiana and Ohio suing for peace with the Confederacy.

Jenkinson's approach in his newspaper was in keeping with the times: He was very pointed in his criticism of the opposition, particularly the *Sentinel.* An 1864 editorial is a prime example of the sword that lay hidden in his pen. Titled "Stand by the Cause," Jenkinson's May 18 editorial drew a parallel between the Civil War and the American Revolution. He saw those who opposed the Union as the Tories of the time. "History is repeating itself, patriots are battling for their country and their liberties, while the Tories and traitors are again earning for themselves an unending need of condemnation and contempt." To make certain the readers knew to whom he was referring, Jenkinson termed the *Sentinel* twelve days later as "our Tory neighbor." In a country that revered—and in some cases remembered their fathers' role as—Revolutionary War heroes, few terms were more denigrating. It questioned not only one's motives of the day but also one's patriotic parentage. Jenkinson was unafraid of tackling the *Times*, either. At the end of 1864 he labeled the *Times* as the acknowledged organ of the Copperhead Party in Allen County. This denigrating term bore special vindictiveness, since it came at a time when the Union was closer to defeating the Confederate army.

The *Gazette* struggled, even though it had a mechanical advantage over its competition. Jones had purchased "a new cylinder printing press, which was powered by a portable steam engine."[9] Its first edition appeared on October 20, 1863, and was said to be the first newspaper produced on a steam press in Fort Wayne. There had been accounts, however, of Daniel Burroughs suffering a badly injured hand on a steam-powered press four years earlier. Whether this press was being used to produce Burroughs's abolitionist journal is unknown. The 1864–65 edition of *Williams' Fort Wayne Directory* carries a sizable advertisement for the "New Steam Printing House" of Jones and Jenkinson, publisher of the *Fort Wayne Gazette*.

"Those were emphatically the days of small beginnings," Jenkinson wrote on June 30, 1868. "With little means and less encouragement and patronage, the *Gazette* still struggled manfully for existence, barely able to maintain its being."

In March 1864 Jones sold his stake in the newspaper to Homer C. Hartman. Jones continued his business as D. W. Jones and Son and printed the *Gazette* for four more years. After the war, Jones published another newspaper, the *Dollar Weekly*. There are no known copies of that 1867–68 publication.

One possible reason for Jones's departure from the *Gazette* masthead was his interest in history. According to his son, Jones contributed "a large portion of the text" of Wallace A. Brice's *History of Fort Wayne* in 1868.[10] Printed and bound by Jones, the book was the standard history text for the community for half a century. Jones also was the principal underwriter of the book, and as a result he lost a considerable amount of money when it did not sell well.

The *Gazette's* editorial operation continued under Jenkinson's direction, while Hartman "labored earnestly for nearly two years to establish the business."[11] It was an unusual team, with one member experienced in newspapers and the other not. Yet it was the inexperienced partner who provided the foundation for the *Gazette*'s survival in 1864.

A real estate and insurance agent in the firm of Hartman and Bossler, Homer Hartman enlarged the newspaper's format to seven columns and financed additional dispatches from the Civil War. A special telegraph service was secured to provide daily reports on the Union army, some from the battlefield to Secretary of War Edwin Stanton. The content provided by this connection was unparalleled in Fort Wayne. While the *Sentinel* was printing outdated news clipped from out-of-town newspapers, the *Gazette*'s articles were more immediate and sometimes more accurate. The *Gazette*'s front-page reports of the war under the standing headline "Latest by Telegraph" were often days ahead of the other Fort Wayne newspapers.

These military reports made the *Gazette* office a very popular gathering site. Hugh McCulloch, among the foremost political figures in Fort Wayne's history, recalled that the early newspapers in the city printed news from "the sea-board [that] was from ten to twelve days old—that which came from the other side of the Atlantic was fifty or sixty."[12] Now the news from war was only a day or two old. This new measure of value—that news needed to be recent in origin—changed the nature of journalism throughout the nation. It also changed Fort Wayne. For a young city with a population of more than ten thousand, the immediacy of war news was exhilarating. The discussions it prompted made Fort Wayne seem more urbane, less a part of the frontier, to its citizens.

Not everyone was happy with the situation, however. The *Sentinel* disputed the veracity of the news printed in the *Gazette*. More than two weeks after the battle at Gettysburg, the *Sentinel* announced, "The accounts sent by telegraph of great victories are notoriously unreliable. This has been especially the case in relation to the late battle between Gens. Meade and Lee at Gettysburg. Our successes and Lee's losses have alike been grossly exaggerated. It seems to be a part of the Administration's programme studiously to keep the truth from the people, and feed them with hopes that are seldom realized. No good can arise from this system of deception. The truth must sooner or later be known."[13]

The proximity of the newspaper offices fueled the competition, too.

It wasn't Fleet Street in London, but the area around Columbia Street was Fort Wayne's center of journalism in the 1860s. The five-block street was the principal commerce area from the time of the opening of the Wabash and Erie Canal. It served as home to mills, shops, hotels, theaters, and saloons as well as newspaper offices during its heyday. The *Sen-*

tinel, the *Times*, the *Staatszeitung*, and a second German newspaper—the *Indiana TriWeekly* and *Weekly Demokrat*, edited by C. G. Jahn—were all within two blocks of each other in the commerce district, while the *Gazette* fronted on Columbia Street. The compact business area undoubtedly contributed to the intense competition among the reporters and the frequent attacks on each other found on the editorial pages.

The *Gazette* was typical of the newspaper design of its day. In its beginning, the front page was filled with advertising and the national and international news and commentary were consigned to page two. Editorials and city miscellany were found on page four. This was the page that attracted the most interest, since the *Gazette* was liberal in its criticism of the opposition newspapers in town. Editorial commentary in 1864 disputed the accuracy of the *Times* and chastised the *Sentinel* for its position that freeing the slaves would destroy the country. The *Sentinel* and the southern sympathizers it supported would exult in a victory when they had "stabbed the government daily in its most vital part," the *Gazette* charged on May 6, 1864. The Republican newspaper wasn't shy in its partisan comments about General George McClellan, the Peace Democrat candidate opposing Lincoln in 1864, whom it referred to as "Littlemac" in its commentary. They found the former Union commander-in-chief unfit for the presidency, claiming the Union's defeats in the early years of the war were caused by what it called McClellan's "criminal failures."

The *Gazette*'s popularity can be seen in one anecdote from its pages. On May 15, 1864, after (what proved to be exaggerated) reports of Grant's success at the Battle of Spotsylvania were received and printed, the newspaper claimed that crowds of Union supporters gathered at the *Gazette*'s office to read the reports, "snatching sheets from the forms as they were printed." The newspaper then added in its column, "On to Richmond!" It proved to be too optimistic, since the war would rage for another eleven months. But by 1865, Jenkinson and Hartman were able to advertise that the afternoon daily had the largest circulation in the city.

The *Gazette*'s editorial efforts, though, produced minimal political success. While the Republicans defeated the incumbent Democrat for the district congressional seat, Lincoln fared worse in the 1864 election in Fort Wayne than he had four years earlier. Despite the Union army's progress in the war, Lincoln lost Allen County, receiving 2,244 votes, while Democrat George McClellan received 4,932. Lincoln's portion of the vote had decreased from 39.2 percent in 1860 when there were four candidates to 31.3 percent in 1864 when there were only two. However, Lincoln captured Indiana's electoral votes with a margin of 20,189 votes.

The end of the war did not bring a return to normalcy for the nation, primarily because of Lincoln's assassination in April 1865. When all but one of the former states of the Confederacy rejected the Fourteenth Amendment, Congress passed the Reconstruction Act, which placed the South under military control. The *Gazette*, like other Republican newspapers, followed the issues with conflicting emotions, sometimes outrage and sometimes regret.

Hartman sold his interests in the *Gazette* to Jenkinson in 1866 and returned to his real estate and insurance practice. He was one of the leading residents who petitioned the county to incorporate South Wayne as a town in 1872. This effort initially failed because of Fort Wayne's opposition; however, it succeeded in the next decade and, in the wake of a state supreme court decision, set the precedent in Indiana for annexation by cities. Hartman also served as deputy clerk to the first U.S. District Court when it was established in Fort Wayne in 1879.

For Jenkinson, the burden of editing the newspaper, serving as a conscription officer, and providing leadership in the Republican Party must have been wearying. W. J. Taylor was hired as the first "local editor" of the *Gazette* in 1866, but he contracted tuberculosis and departed in May 1868 for Omaha, where it was thought he would benefit from a better climate. He died in 1871 at age 29. Whether losing the talented young Taylor contributed to Jenkinson's decision is unknown, but in June 1868 he added two equal partners, James R. Willard and Amos W. Wright. Jenkinson retained general editorial control, while Willard and Wright made plans to build the business. "The new firm propose, as soon as the necessary arrangements can be made, to greatly enlarge the whole establishment, and its capacity for business," Jenkinson wrote on June 30, 1868. He noted that the two young men had already contracted for a new building expressly for the *Gazette* office in a central part of the city.

The newspaper was given a more readable appearance and printed on a better quality of paper, and plans were laid to increase the news content. Whether the new partners had youthful, unrealistic expectations for future growth or did not understand the underlying economics of the business is unknown, but they quickly found themselves in difficult times. While the *Gazette* maintained double the circulation of any competitor in the city, and its weekly edition's subscription list was greater than any other paper's in northern Indiana, the newspaper's advertising patronage was not robust enough to support Willard and Wright's plans.

By mid-July the *Gazette* was carrying front-page editorials about its improvements being apparently unappreciated by the citizenry. Expenses had doubled, but readership had not. The new owners noted on July 16 that they had added Associated Press dispatches "at a heavy cost to ourselves, but without any additional expense to subscribers," and that they were committed to filling its columns "with the freshest and spiciest articles of general interest." They appealed to community pride in calling for more support. "It has been a mortifying fact that Fort Wayne, though recognized as the second city in the State in population and commercial importance, has never been properly represented by her press. While other cities, inferior in every respect to our own, have possessed organs reflecting credit and prosperity on them, Fort Wayne has been forced into comparative insignificance for want of a medium through which to urge her claims for popular fame. This deficiency we shall do all in our power to supply."

As one would imagine, the opposition newspaper took exception to the *Gazette's* assessment about the effectiveness of the city's journalists. The *Fort Wayne Daily Democrat*, whose most influential owner was Circuit Court Judge Robert Lowry, mocked the *Gazette's* new owners as "college-bred youths."[14] The *Gazette*, in turn, noted that Lowry wanted to run for Congress and ought to step down from the bench to eliminate any conflict of interest. That position prompted this response on August 27 to those it called the "juveniles of the *Gazette*": "You are only one of those little creatures, whom God, for some inscrutable purpose, permits to edit a majority of the Republican papers."

Throughout this period of internal change and community controversy, the *Gazette* remained steadfast in its position on the national drama coming to a conclusion in Washington. It supported the impeachment and removal from office of President Andrew Johnson, and it endorsed the presidential candidacy of Ulysses S. Grant. The *Gazette*, like many Republican newspapers, had soured on Johnson, the War Democrat from Tennessee who was Lincoln's second-term vice president. Johnson wanted to follow what he saw as Lincoln's intention to restore the South to the Union, while southerners wanted to return to the antebellum status quo. Radical Republicans were not willing to allow Johnson to dictate the future policy of the country or to let the Confederacy's supporters go unpunished. The president and Congress also differed greatly about the timing of full suffrage for African American men. Johnson was a former slave owner, and he advocated a paternalistic approach that would require education and training for the former slaves before they could vote, while the Republicans led by Senator Thaddeus Stevens of Pennsylvania wanted the right to vote conferred immediately.

Jenkinson had been busy throughout Johnson's presidency. He had written positively of Johnson's visit to Fort Wayne in October 1864. The *Gazette* ran wire service stories on, and editorialized about, the president's impetuous nature and the Republicans' distrust of his background as a slave-owning Southern Democrat. The struggle over control of the defeated Confederate states by military governors ignited into the impeachment conflict when Johnson sought to remove Secretary of State Edwin M. Stanton. As this developed into a political brawl, the *Gazette* joined in the campaign to make Ulysses S. Grant the next Republican presidential nominee. Johnson dismissed Stanton against the wishes of the Radical Republicans and named Grant as interim secretary. Using its recently enacted Tenure of Office Act, the Senate overruled Johnson's move in early 1868, and Grant stepped down. Johnson was furious, believing that Grant had promised not to relinquish the War Department back to Stanton. The two men exchanged angry letters that were printed in full in newspapers around the nation, including the *Gazette*, which sided with Grant. Jenkinson used the front page in April to disavow Johnson and what he called "his wicked career," saying that the charges in the president's trial had been proven without a doubt and that he should be ousted from office.

When Johnson's trial in the Senate fell one vote short of the two-thirds majority needed to convict him, the *Gazette* carried wire service reports of alleged conspiracies in the chamber that prevented the president's removal. The focus of the news then moved to the national election, and Indiana's importance in the race became evident when the Republican Party selected Schuyler Colfax from South Bend as its vice presidential candidate. The *Gazette* found particular favor in Colfax when the candidate rebuffed charges that he was Radical. His slogan of "better a Radical than a Rebel anytime—a Radical for right against wrong" also seemed to sum up the *Gazette*'s position.

The *Gazette* worked diligently for Grant's election. It devoted most of its October 5, 1868, edition to reporting on the community's "Grand Republican Rally" with lists of marchers and speeches by notables. The newspaper participated in the parade with a wagon carrying a press in full operation that printed leaflets which were then handed out as the march wound through Fort Wayne's streets.

The election outcome, however, was not "grand" for the Republicans in Allen County. Although Grant won Indiana and the other "early" states, he lost the county to the Democratic ticket led by New York governor Horatio Seymour. Grant received only 35.2 percent of the votes cast in Allen County, slightly better than Lincoln four years earlier. It appeared, as Judge Lowry argued in his newspaper, that the area's voters were not interested in Civil War issues now. It also implied that new leadership might be needed in Fort Wayne to promote the Republican Party.

On October 12, 1868, Isaac Jenkinson departed from his newspaper with a simple "Good Bye" headline atop the second column of the front page. He applauded the efforts of his partners, Willard and Wright, and thanked the citizens of Allen County for their support. In the spring of 1869, Jenkinson's efforts on behalf of the Republican Party were rewarded when President Grant appointed him U.S. consul to Scotland in Glasgow. A few years later, Jenkinson returned to the newspaper business when he became publisher of the *Richmond Palladium* in eastern Indiana and made it a daily newspaper. Jenkinson's impact on Indiana continued into the twentieth century. He served on the board of trustees for Indiana University for forty-one years and was board president from 1889 to 1906.

In 1869, Willard and Wright moved the *Gazette* office from Columbia Street to a three-story building at 54 Calhoun Street. They invested in a new eight-horsepower steam engine to run its four steam presses, two of which were large drum cylinders. They proudly announced that their third-floor news department and composing room were "well lighted and warm and supplied with every convenience and comfort." It even featured speaking tubes connecting the departments. From their subsequent commentary in the newspaper, the owners were proud of the fact that the *Gazette* did not suspend publication to make the move to the new building.

Wright became the sole proprietor in late 1869 and converted the *Gazette* into a morning newspaper. This was an unusual move, since most newspapers at the time were evening editions. Another unusual aspect was the publisher's role in the community. Unlike John Dawson and Robert Lowry, Wright was not driven to seek political office. He served as president of the Kekionga Base Ball Club when the team became a charter member of the National Association of Professional Base Ball Players. In an era when bylines on local news stories were uncommon, Wright promoted the "local editor" by listing him on the front page. Among those holding the position during Wright's ownership was Benjamin D. Skinner, who established a professional, if perhaps unplanned, practice for nineteenth-century newspapers.

The lead editorial on page four on October 17, 1868, was signed by Skinner and began: " 'The *Gazette* has a d——d secessionist for a Local Editor' was an expression used in our office this morning." Skinner had been "outed" as a Democrat, a venal sin on a stalwart Republican newspaper. In his editorial, Skinner admitted having been a Democrat, but indicated he had not yet cast a ballot for one of its candidates and proclaimed his support for the Grant-Colfax ticket.

As a result, Skinner took steps to state a clear philosophy of separation between political opinion and local news. Partisanship, he wrote on October 17, has no place in a "Local Department." This area of the newspaper "is the organ of the citizen; it gives city news; it corrects city abuses; it praises city improvements; it aims to be authority in city matters. It cannot be all this and a partizan [sic] column, for it demands the support and cooperation of all the citizens." Skinner concluded, "I shall endeavor to keep my politics on the first page of the paper." The local editor then announced he was instituting a policy of refusing to consider unsigned letters for publication. Newspapers were notorious for publishing slanderous allegations carried in letters that were unsigned or that used a pseudonym. The *Gazette* fought that trend.

The aftermath of Johnson's impeachment trial and Grant's election left a divided opposition to the dominant Democratic Party in Allen County. The coalition created by Lincoln's candidacy in 1860 was rendered, and in December 1868 those who disagreed with the *Gazette* started the *Fort Wayne Weekly Journal*. The *Journal* was weaker, but its competition for circulation and advertising revenue put additional financial strain on the *Gazette*, and a period of changing ownerships began for the latter.

In 1871 the *Gazette* was purchased by Robert G. McNiece and De Alva Stanwood Alexander, who served as the principal owners but formed a joint stock company known as the Gazette Publishing Company. Other principal investors were Martin Cullaton, John N. Irwin, J. S. Grafton, and James Bain White.

Both owners were destined for distinguished careers beyond their three years operating the *Gazette*. McNiece, who was a graduate of Dartmouth and Princeton Seminary, traveled to Utah in 1877 to lead the Presbyterian mission to the Mormons. Instrumental in the formation of Westminster College, McNiece was highly regarded for his essays and lectures on the differences between Mormon and Christian doctrines. Alexander, who had enlisted in the Union army in 1862 at the age of 15, came to Fort Wayne after graduating from Bowdoin College in 1871. When he left Fort Wayne, Alexander became the Indianapolis correspondent for the *Cincinnati Gazette*. Later he moved to western New York where he was U.S. attorney. A staunch Republican, Alexander was then elected to seven terms as congressman from Buffalo. However, at the time they were overseeing the

James B. White, merchant extraordinaire, briefly a
publisher and then a contested congressman.

Gazette, neither Alexander nor McNiece was treated with respect in the
opposition newspaper. The *Daily Democrat* pointedly disliked them, calling
them "two Yankee schoolmarms" publishing a newspaper that was "dying
from a dysentery of blackguardism and a constipation of good taste."[15]

Of the other investors, only Cullaton's name recurs in Fort Wayne's
early newspaper history. He was a longtime printer and sometime editor
of newspapers. The only highly prominent name among the investors was
James Bain White, the most successful businessman to have control—albeit briefly—of the *Gazette*. His experience a decade later at the hands of
the *Fort Wayne Journal* may have made him wish he had kept his stock in
the *Gazette*.

White came to the United States from Scotland in 1854 and established himself in Fort Wayne as a dry goods merchant. He served in the
Civil War as a captain in the Thirtieth Regiment of Indiana Infantry,

joining shortly after the start of the war. He was wounded at the Battle of Shiloh in April 1862. He resigned his commission but remained with the army as a sutler—or supplier of goods—primarily for the Eighty-eighth Regiment of Indiana Volunteers. White was captured twice by Rebel troops near Chattanooga, Tennessee, but paroled both times. He returned to Fort Wayne in 1864, where he became a U.S. citizen through the sponsorship of Isaac Jenkinson. He established the White Fruit House, which grew from a fruits and groceries store to one of the most successful dry goods businesses in the region. In 1871 he was credited with being the first merchant to mark his goods with a plain price tag. In addition, all business transactions were conducted on an immediate cash payment basis, which was said to be rare for a grocery at the time.

White was thorough and analytical in his sales practices, and he departmentalized his store in order to make shopping convenient. The store grew to employ between 75 and 100 people and reported annual sales of $500,000 in the 1890s. His practice of systematically arranging the merchandise for sale in his store was reportedly studied and adopted by stores in major cities, such as Wanamaker's in Philadelphia. In 1872 White and his son founded White Wheel Works, manufacturer of carriage and wagon wheels. It became a significant enterprise, employing 130 men and contributing to Fort Wayne's growing reputation as an industrial center. The Whites managed the business until 1892, when it was sold to the American Wheel Company.

In 1875 White owned all of the stock of the Gazette Publishing Company, but he apparently decided to focus on his other business operations, and in that year he sold control of the newspaper to Reuben Williams and Quincy A. Hossler, printers in Warsaw, Indiana. Williams, a brevetted brigadier general for his service with General William T. Sherman's army in the Carolinas campaign, had established the *Northern Indianan*, a weekly Republican newspaper in Warsaw in 1856. Williams and Hossler, who had joined in publishing the *Indianan* in 1866, assumed control of the *Gazette* "upon the urgent solicitation of prominent Republicans in the city of Ft. Wayne."[16] In December 1875 Williams was appointed deputy second controller of the treasury. Hossler carried on alone, but eventually he sold the Fort Wayne newspaper. Williams and Hossler resumed their partnership in Warsaw in 1876 and, in addition to the weekly newspaper, established the *Warsaw Daily Times* in 1881.

The sale placed the *Daily Gazette* and its weekly edition in the hands of two brothers, Frederick W. and David S. Keil, in July 1876. The Keils, who came to Fort Wayne in the fall of 1865 to operate a wholesale bookstore and stationery with two other brothers, demonstrated their business skills in the operation of the *Gazette*. During their ten-year ownership, the Keils built the weekly edition in size and circulation. It reached nearly every town and hamlet in the area and every Republican homestead in the county with "all the reading matter of the *Daily* not purely transient, and a carefully digested summary of the news of the week, stories, miscellaneous reading selection from the best sources or contributed; and an agricultural department prepared exclusively for this edition."[17]

At the outset, Frederick Keil was the publisher, while David Keil served as associate editor. Born and raised in Hamilton, Ohio, Fred Keil was a decorated Civil War veteran and prominent Republican. A graduate of Wittenberg College, he practiced law until the outbreak of the war when he joined the first Ohio unit formed in April 1861 as a private. He later served in the Third Ohio Regiment and was a lieutenant at the Battle of Shiloh. He led his company as a captain in the battles of Perryville, Atlanta, and other campaigns. He came to Fort Wayne after the war to resume the practice of law, but was persuaded to join another brother, Jacob, in the store. In April 1877, nine months after purchasing the *Gazette*, Fred Keil was named postmaster of Fort Wayne by President Rutherford B. Hayes. He held the position for eight years before being dismissed by President Grover Cleveland on the charge of being "an offensive partisan," presumably because Keil was a Republican and the *Gazette* attacked the Democrat's policies.

It fell to David Keil to run the *Gazette* when his brother received the patronage appointment. He was a farmer before following his brother to Wittenberg College at the age of 23, and after graduating in 1860 he taught school in Warren, Illinois. It was in this small town in the northwestern corner of the state near the Wisconsin border that David Keil had his first taste of journalism when he was part-owner and editor of the *Warren Independent*. He later served in the Union army during the Civil War and arrived in Fort Wayne to study law with his brother. At the bookstore Keil served as the traveling salesman, a difficult responsibility because he had to compete with representatives of prestigious companies from much larger cities. His competitiveness proved to be the key for the *Gazette*'s unusual success.

It was David Keil's decision as managing editor to enter the newspaper syndicate business, a publishing method that revolutionized first the rural and then the urban press in the mid-nineteenth century. When newspapers in smaller communities in the Midwest found themselves without trained printers during the Civil War, they began using preprinted sheets of news from larger publishers. For instance, a small weekly would order full sheets with war and other national news printed on one side and then print local news and advertising on the reverse. A Baraboo, Wisconsin, printer named Ansel N. Kellogg established the first independent newspaper syndicate in 1865 and offered preprinted sheets with a story and various items of miscellaneous interest for country weeklies. By 1866, he was serving more than 70 papers, including some in Indiana. When Kellogg died in 1886, his service was a $200,000 company serving nearly 1,400 newspapers.

The syndicate newspaper business grew rapidly with many entrants in the field. Some were called "newspaper unions," although they did not operate in any cooperative or cross-ownership manner. By 1875, nearly one-third of all country weeklies were using a syndicated service in the form of printed sheets.[18] Improvements in stereotyping—the process of producing metal printing plates by making an impression of a page of type or images into a pliable paper mold that could be cast in molten lead—brought greater growth to the business. Soon newspaper unions were supplying a broader range of news—agricultural, children's reading, general religious, wit and humor, short sketches, and home circle items—not only to rural weeklies but also to urban papers. In 1883, Kellogg began supplying a daily plate service to daily newspapers. This business, which gave rise to the pejorative term *boiler plate* because of its non-time-sensitive material on stereotype mats, was not limited to a few large players.

The owners of the *Gazette* recognized the syndicates' potential and established the Fort Wayne Newspaper Union in 1877. Eventually it supplied "patent sides" for 150 rural newspapers in the region. So successful was this cooperative that the Keils' five power presses were said to be continually in operation. One indication is that in 1881 the Gazette Publishing Company had sixty-six employees with an annual payroll of $35,000.

It was not an easily won victory, however. The competition from other newspaper unions was fierce, and they drastically reduced prices in an effort to kill off their Fort Wayne rival. It wasn't until David Keil died that the syndicate business was sold to the Chicago Newspaper Union. An office for this syndicated news operation remained in Fort Wayne into the first decade of the twentieth century.

Few editors in the history of Fort Wayne newspapers were admired as much as David Keil. He was respected for honesty, moral standards, and gentlemanly conduct. When he died suddenly in late October 1886, Keil was eulogized in all of the local newspapers. The pallbearers at Keil's funeral included publishers and editors from the *Gazette*, the *Journal*, the *Sentinel*, and the *Indiana Staats-Zeitung*.

· Even though Fred Keil remained active in the family's bookstore for the next twenty years, the *Gazette* was put up for sale upon his brother's death. His sojourn into political office from the ranks of newspaper ownership was common in the nineteenth and early twentieth centuries. Records show that three other Fort Wayne newspaper owners were appointed Fort Wayne postmaster and three more were elected as mayor during that period.

An example of the relationship between politics and newspaper publishing in the agitated antebellum period can be seen in the career of George Wood, who came to Fort Wayne in 1836 at the age of 27. In 1840 Wood had succeeded Thomas Tigar as publisher of the *Sentinel* and changed it from a Democratic to a Whig Party newspaper. Fort Wayne was then a newly incorporated city with an elected office of mayor, and Wood decided to run for the post. His victory proved to be bittersweet. Fort Wayne lacked a building to house the mayor's office, and the job paid only a nominal salary. So Wood established the mayor's office in a rented room at the newspaper. It must have been a thankless task because when he was elected to a second one-year term, Wood resigned and then sold the *Sentinel*, which reverted to its Democratic Party backing. He started the *Fort Wayne Times* in 1841, only to sell it to Henry W. Jones. Three years later Wood returned to the newspaper business, printing the *People's Press* in support of Henry Clay's unsuccessful Whig candidacy for president. This newspaper also was bought by Jones, who in 1844 published the combined papers as the *Times and People's Press*. When one of the subsequent owners of the *Fort Wayne Times* retired in 1849, Wood once again became a publisher. He operated the newspaper until 1854, selling it to John Dawson. Ironically, at the end of the Civil War, the newspapers once controlled by Wood were bought by W. H. Dills and I. W. Campbell in separate transactions and merged into the *Fort Wayne Times and Sentinel*.

A more successful combination of politics and publishing in the mid-nineteenth century was found in Schuyler Colfax, whose career as congressman, speaker of the House, and vice president of the United States had its roots in his serving as publisher of the *St. Joseph Valley Register* in South Bend. After the Civil War it became commonplace for publishers of Indiana newspapers whose cities or counties delivered a sizable plurality to the victor in federal elections to be named to postmaster positions by the White House. Others ran for Congress, council positions, and clerkships—a practice that seems unthinkable in today's world when a high degree of nonpartisanship is demanded of reporters, editors, and, to some degree, publishers.

It was during the Keils' ownership that the newspaper was briefly renamed the *Morning Gazette* and its masthead carried the slogan "Official Paper of the City." More interesting was the front-page nameplate with a large engraving of the frontier-era military post at Fort Wayne in the center. The engraving depicted a large, square fort with farmers and Native Americans outside the structure and soldiers inside. The representation makes the fort appear larger and more formidable than it apparently was when it was completed in 1816 by Major John Whistler. The new front-page appearance seemed to curry little appreciation among the competition, however. The *Fort Wayne Weekly Sentinel* carried a front-page item on Wednesday, November 1, 1882, that demonstrated how crude the competition among newspapers was becoming.

> As a citizen was coming down town this morning he found an acquaintance leaning in a very despondent way against a lamp post, while the territory in that vicinity gave evidence that the man had been vomiting and was badly broken up.
>
> "What's the matter?" asked the sympathetic citizen.
>
> "I'm sick," said the lamp post leaner.
>
> "What ails you?" continued the citizen.
>
> "Been—reading the—*Gazette*," said the unfortunate, as he went off into another fit of violent retching, while the citizen proceeded, satisfied that the only remedy for such a thoughtless act was to let it wear off in the natural way.

The decade during which the Keils directed the *Gazette*'s growth was a tumultuous time for the city, state, and nation, all of which contributed to increased interest in newspapers. When they assumed control of the paper, Reconstruction was nearing its bitter end, Fort Wayne had reached a population of about 25,000, and Republican Rutherford B. Hayes and Democrat Samuel Tilden had just been nominated in what was to become the most contested presidential election in the nation's history. When Fred Keil sold the newspaper in 1886, Fort Wayne was a robust manufacturing community with more than 40,000 residents.

The *Gazette* had one special note of distinction during the Keils' tenure—the hiring of the first woman reporter in Fort Wayne. Carrie M. Shoaff wrote "special letters" from New York City where she was living, at the invitation of Silas B. McManus, local editor for the newspaper. Her letters were, in fact, reporting on interviews with people she found interesting or Fort Wayne residents visiting New York. Shoaff later gained

The first female reporter for the *Gazette*, Carrie M. Shoaff.

renown for inventing a method of manufacturing imitation Limoges ware, using a blue clay common to the Maumee River and her own glaze. A sketch about her was included in one of the first books in the United States devoted to women in art and industry. McManus, too, gained acclaim as a "Hoosier dialect poet," a form made popular by James Whitcomb Riley.

Still, while the *Morning Gazette* claimed that its eight-page edition costing five cents was "the largest, newsiest and best paper published in northern Indiana," it was averaging only two to two and a half pages of advertising. This demonstrated that a Republican newspaper in a strongly Democratic region was at a financial disadvantage. Advertising dollars, even more than readership, were often influenced as much by partisan preferences as by economic conditions.

The two men who bought the *Gazette* apparently overestimated the support they would receive and were unable to meet the financial terms of the sale. B. M. Holman and Theron P. Keator bought the newspaper in an effort to aggressively campaign against Democratic candidates in 1886, an off-year election. Keator, the editor, wanted to run for Congress in 1884 and perhaps wanted to use the newspaper to launch another campaign. Their failure to capitalize on the opportunity of having the *Gazette* as Keator's campaign vehicle proved beneficial to one of its former publishers, James B. White, who ended up with the seat in Congress, albeit at a great personal expense.

In addition to being a successful businessman, White was an ardent Republican whose political experience began in the 1856 presidential campaign of John C. Frémont. In the early 1870s, White had been elected to two terms as a city councilman, and he also had run unsuccessfully for clerk of the circuit court. White could not be described as a savvy politician, however. According to contemporary accounts, his political philosophy was the same as his approach to business: honest, sincere, and forthright. His Democratic opponent for Congress in 1886, Judge Robert Lowry, was the two-term incumbent and accustomed to political gamesmanship. The battle for the House seat from the Twelfth District—which at that time had never elected a Republican—was hotly contested, and the Democrats opted for political entrapment. Two of Lowry's supporters, Andrew J. Moynihan and Robert C. Bell, learned that there wasn't any record of Scots-born White's naturalization on file in the courthouse. They withheld this information—knowing that if White were not a U.S. citizen, he could not be elected to Congress—until the week before election. As reporters for the *Sentinel,* they arranged a meeting with White and asked if he had been naturalized. White declared that he was and that Isaac Jenkinson was by his side when the oath of citizenship was administered at the courthouse. Moynihan and Bell had their story and published it a few days before the election. The two reporters asserted that White was not a citizen and therefore was ineligible for office. With little time to respond, White printed handbills in rebuttal and managed to defeat his opponent by about 2,500 votes. Lowry, however, wasn't finished. He brought his case before the U.S. House of Representatives. Naturalization law at the time was a two-step process: a person was sworn in as a citizen and then had to file a form attesting to the fact. Apparently, the second step was a formality that many new citizens overlooked or disregarded. The filing was never completed in White's case, or it was lost. Lowry pointed out that Indiana law allowed only fully naturalized citizens to hold office, and the lack of a final filing was White's undoing. Lowry asked the House to give him the seat White had won. The House referred the dispute to the Committee on Elections, which heard the case in executive session on January 17, 1888. The committee voted along straight party lines to recommend to the full House that White be declared ineligible. However, with only one dissent, the committee refused to recommend the seating of Lowry. After much maneuvering over what constituted admissible evidence, the House debated the White-Lowry matter for three days before bringing the issue to a vote on February 6, 1888. At the conclusion, the vote was 184 to 105 in favor of seating White, with 47 Democrats joining the Republicans. It was a victory for Republicans, but White's two-year term was cut in half by the prolonged legal fight. Bitterness prevailed among Fort Wayne Democrats. On February 7, 1888, the *Weekly Sentinel* acknowledged it was now "Congressman White" but would not allow that the action was constitutional.

White's term in Congress saw him propose a minimum wage bill for workers and defend a protective tariff. When he ran for reelection in 1888, he was narrowly defeated by Judge C. A. O. McClellan of Auburn.

While the fight over the congressional seat raged, Holman and Keator defaulted on their payments for the *Gazette*, and the Keils sued to have the newspaper put into receivership. Judge Edward O'Rourke of the Allen County Circuit Court named John W. Hayden as receiver, who sold the newspaper to Nathan R. Leonard and his son, Frank M. Leonard, in 1887. The Leonards returned the *Gazette* to a sound financial position.

A teacher and scientist, Nathan Leonard was 57 and in his "third career" by the time he assumed ownership of the *Gazette*. Growing up in Iowa, Leonard was graduated from Kossuth College in 1857, and he then studied mathematics and astronomy at Harvard University. In 1860, he

Nathan R. Leonard, *Gazette* publisher. *Allen County–Fort Wayne Historical Society.*

returned to Iowa and became a member of the mathematics faculty at the University of Iowa, a chair he held for twenty-seven years. By the end of his career, he had been the dean of the faculty and president of the university. He also served as the Iowa state superintendent of weights and measures, and he wrote numerous articles on astronomy for scientific journals. Leonard was elected a fellow of the American Association for the Advancement of Science.

He came to Fort Wayne in 1887 to join his brothers in a business enterprise but opted to try to revive the *Gazette* instead. Leonard's impact on the newspaper was evident within the first year. In a bold move for a small city newspaper, he sent a reporter to Chicago in November 1887 to cover the execution of four anarchists convicted of the Haymarket Square bombing six months earlier. The story, which included graphic details on the anarchists' final words, appeared on page one on Saturday morning, November 12, with the rare headline reading only "Hanged." One of the drop headlines read: "Full Particulars of the Affair as Gathered by a *Gazette* Reporter on the Ground." On page two under the masthead, the *Gazette*'s editor touted the fact that his paper had its own report, calling it "a fuller and better account of the execution of the Anarchists than any other paper." Then, in a jab at other newspapers in Fort Wayne that had published drawings of the execution supplied by syndicates, he wrote that his newspaper chose not to "weary its readers with stale pictures of the Anarchists or cuts of the execution scene, made . . . many days before the nooses were drawn."

The *Gazette* article offers an interesting comparison to the news stories of today. First, in keeping with the style of the time, none of the first names of the anarchists are given. August Spies, Albert Parsons, Adolph Fischer, and George Engel are only identified by their last names. Second, there isn't any reprise, or explanatory, paragraph on the events leading to their execution. There are no references to the bombing, the arrests, the protests, the court proceedings, or the suicide of one of the other conspirators. There is only one mention of the Haymarket, and it is near the end of the sixty-inch account. Perhaps the absence of these details reflects the editor's belief that the May 4, 1886, Haymarket Square bombing was well enough known by the readers. Lastly, the name of the reporter is unknown. He was among the 250 newspapermen viewing the hanging with other witnesses that included the jurymen who convicted the anarchists. It was a well-written story, including detailed information about the anarchists' final hours—how they slept, what they ate, what they said, and how they prepared for the gallows. Their final words and deaths were graphically described, including the executioner's hurried act that cut off Parsons's attempt to speak. The prolonged agony of each man is recounted as they strangled to death, rather than dying of a broken neck as was customary in state hangings.[19] The *Gazette* report admired the bravery with which the four men met their deaths and emphasized the calmness of Chicago despite the sensational stories of expected riots that it said were the product of eastern newspaper reporters.

Leonard's son, Frank, left the *Gazette* after two years, but apparently not before developing a love for journalism. He later served as editor of the *Inter-Mountain* in Butte, Montana. Another of Nathan Leonard's sons, Levi, served as editor and proprietor of the *Anaconda Review* in Montana.

While he understood his readers' growing interest in sensational news, Nathan Leonard was not always on the same page with community interests. In 1895 he campaigned strongly against building the Allen County Courthouse. He complained that it was a project with an extravagant price tag, and he wrote editorials about the "Million-Dollar Court House" and the "Palace of Justice." Now considered to be a national architectural treasurer, the courthouse was dedicated in 1902, and Leonard's opposition to the construction did not escape mention and ridicule.

Charles R. Lane, Marion E. Beall, and Amos Walter purchased the *Gazette* from Leonard in April 1897 and proceeded to make improvements and add equipment. Walter, who served as president of the company, was a Civil War veteran and a prominent grocer in the city. Beall, listed as secretary and treasurer, was a prominent Presbyterian minister and had been

Charles R. Lane, the last
publisher of the *Fort Wayne
Daily Gazette. Allen County-Fort
Wayne Historical Society.*

a missionary to Mexico. At one point he was the U.S. consul to San Luis
Potosi, a state in central Mexico. Lane, however, had had a distinguished
newspaper career before coming to Fort Wayne. He began his career in
Richmond, Indiana, and then moved to the *Dispatch* in St. Paul, Minnesota. Lane worked for seven years on the *Indianapolis Journal* before becoming part-owner and managing editor of the *Fort Wayne Daily Gazette.*
In a dissertation by Willodeen Price on the history of Fort Wayne's newspaper industry, Lane is described as "one of the most scholarly newspaper
writers that Fort Wayne ever had, and during his connection with the
Gazette it was most ably conducted editorially."[20] This is an interesting
opinion, but what really set the *Gazette* apart was Lane's decision to buy
two new Mergenthaler Linotype machines in the late spring of 1897. This
was a remarkable and costly move for a small city daily. The Linotype,
which had been invented in 1896, set a line of type from a keyboard instead of each letter being set by hand. It operated at twice the speed of the
old process and produced a cleaner, more attractive product. The number
of pages increased, but Lane and his partners were unable to make the
newspaper profitable. They tried a number of approaches to maintain the
circulation, such as offering the *Gazette* through the mail to subscribers
away on vacation at the same price as home delivery. They sold the business at auction in 1899 for $10,050. Lane went on to be the editor of the

Fort Wayne Daily News from 1902 through 1907. He remained active in civic affairs, too, running for Congress unsuccessfully in 1912 and 1914 and serving as secretary of the Fort Wayne Council of Patriotic Services after the outbreak of World War I. Lane also played a key but unrecognized role in preserving the area's history. When Bert Griswold died in March 1927, his tribute to leaders of industry and commerce was incomplete. *Builders of Greater Fort Wayne* was originally planned to include biographies of 300 eminent citizens. Griswold only finished 189 interviews from which he wrote 150 sketches for the book. Lane finished the research, wrote almost half of the book's sketches, and preserved an unparalleled view of the region's development without claiming any authorial credit.[21]

Lane died in 1932, remembered as the last owner of the *Daily Gazette* and as the man who upset Fort Wayne's newspaper world by selling the historically Republican *Gazette* to its archenemy, the now Democratic Party–controlled *Fort Wayne Journal*.

FORT WAYNE GAZETTE.

THE MORNING JOURNAL.

FT. WAYNE JOURNAL=GAZETTE.

THE FORT WAYNE JOURNAL-GAZETTE.

FORT WAYNE JOURNAL-GAZETTE

FORT WAYNE JOURNAL-GAZETTE

THE JOURNAL-GAZETTE

The Journal-Gazette

The Journal Gazette

3

The *Journal*

Andy Moynihan "believed in filling his newspaper with lively copy and his editorial page with barbed steel."

—Robert Adams, Fort Wayne newsman

The Reconstruction era was one of the most tormented times in the nation's history. The brutal cost of the Civil War was followed by a period when almost no element in the conflict was satisfied with the outcome. White southerners wanted to return to their prewar status quo, Radicals in the North wanted to punish those who led the secessionist movement, moderates wanted a peaceful postslavery nation, and African Americans wanted economic freedom and the right to vote. None of these groups realized their dreams. For the era known as Reconstruction and beyond, the North and South remained in ideological conflict about the rights of African Americans.

Fort Wayne reflected the divisions in the nation that were attributed to the turmoil of the Reconstruction period. Democrats were still dominant in Allen County, especially since the coalition that built the Republican Party a decade earlier was in tatters. Lines were drawn around such issues as what was required for readmitting Confederate states into the Union and securing full suffrage for African Americans. There was a difference of opinion about President Andrew Johnson and how he performed his duties after his impeachment and trial. There was controversy over the nation's financial condition and whether the plan to restore the monetary system to the gold standard should be actively pursued. There were few moderates on these issues. Even the most respected Republican in the region, Treasury Secretary Hugh McCulloch of Fort Wayne, was frustrated by the Radical Republicans' demand for immediate suffrage for African Americans and, at the same time, outraged at Johnson's political behavior. Named the nation's first comptroller of the currency in the spring of 1863, McCulloch was appointed secretary of the treasury by Lincoln two years later. He chose to remain in the latter post under Johnson out of a desire to put the nation's financial house in order by retiring the "greenbacks," or fiat money, authorized in 1862 to finance the war. While they were legal tender, the greenbacks were not backed by gold in the treasury. McCulloch's efforts to withdraw enough greenbacks to make their remaining number on a par with gold contributed significantly to a postwar recession and then deflation. Even though Congress may have agreed with McCulloch that contraction was the right course of action, they barred any further reduction in greenbacks in January 1868 when public outcry rose.[1]

These issues contributed to the desire to launch a second Republican newspaper, the *Fort Wayne Weekly Journal*, in December 1868. The *Daily Gazette* was in its sixth year of operation, but the guiding force of Isaac Jenkinson was gone. There had been other changes among Fort Wayne's newspapers as well. The *Sentinel* had been sold four times before being merged with the *Fort Wayne Daily Times* in 1865. The combined *Times and Sentinel* was sold again in January 1866 to Englebert Zimmerman and Eli Brown and renamed the *Fort Wayne Daily Democrat*. In the first edition on January 15, 1866, associate editor H. S. Knapp announced that the *Daily Democrat* was intended to be "a new and independent press, untrammeled by any of the prejudices, passions or other personal feelings and interests that may have impaired the success, or weakened the influence of the *Times* and *Sentinel* during their separate existence or after their consolidation." It was still Democratic in policies, though, and in 1868 it became more partisan when the newspaper came under the influence of Judge Robert Lowry.

There was another significant change in the newspaper business: the rise of the German-language publications to serve the growing immigrant population. While William Eichelsdorfer's *Indiana Volksfreund* and *Fort Wayne Anzeiger* were popular in the 1870s, it was a man of rare intellect who had the greatest journalistic impact on German readers in northeastern Indiana. John Sarnighausen, who came to the United States at age 40, had assumed editorial control of the *Indiana Staatszeitung* in 1860 and purchased it three years later. Sarnighausen had had a remarkable career as a theologian and hymnologist in Göttingen, Germany, compiling the first standard German Lutheran hymnbook from nine regional hymnals in 1855 after several years of work. When he arrived in Fort Wayne in 1860, it was said that 60 percent of the city's population came from Germany. Sarnighausen, who hyphenated the newspaper's name, built the *Staats-Zeitung*'s circulation rapidly and in 1867 increased its frequency from each Wednesday to three times a week. A decade later, it was a daily. Sarnighausen remained its sole owner, publisher, and editor-in-chief until his death in November 1901 at the age of 83. He was elected to two terms in the state senate, where he served with distinction. Notably, the *Staats-Zeitung* had as many readers as any of its English-language competitors in the 1880s.

Amid these changes the *Gazette* found itself increasingly in unpopular positions. While its circulation was strong, its advertising revenue was not. Further, political patronage printing was the domain of the party in power, which in Allen County meant the Democratic Party. The *Daily Gazette* alluded to this economic fact of life in May 1869 when it maintained that the practice of giving lucrative government printing contracts to a printer associated with the party in power should be stopped. A city government's official printing should be given to the lowest bidder regardless of party affiliation. That being said, the *Gazette* editor wrote, "A paper cannot live without patronage and trade no more than any other branch of business. If Republicans want to have a live organ, they should remember that to publish a paper requires money, and that the better the paper the more it costs, and give it their hearty support accordingly."[2]

There were other factors weakening the *Gazette*'s reputation. Its political ties made it unacceptable to the German immigrant population, which was ostracized by the xenophobic American (or Know-Nothing) Party of the mid-1850s that was a forerunner of the Republican Party. Second, its early support of abolitionism remained an unpopular position in a region whose citizenry saw African American suffrage as a political tool to build Republican power in the South. The *Gazette* found it impossible to rebut the criticism over "carpetbaggers" and their activities in the South after the war. Another factor in the German American suspicion of the Republican Party—and, by association, the *Gazette*—was the abolitionist movement's roots in prohibition and temperance, an issue that would be magnified at the turn of the twentieth century.

The *Gazette*'s weakness was even evident in its failure to make a modest impact on the 1868 presidential election when, despite having a northern Indiana "native son," Schuyler Colfax, as his running mate, Civil War hero Ulysses S. Grant lost in Allen County by almost 2,600 votes. The significance of this margin is seen in the statewide results in which Grant defeated the Democratic candidate, former New York governor Horatio Seymour, by more than 9,500 votes. Partisan newspapers that failed to deliver victories in elections were rarely favored with government print-ing contracts. The effort in Congress to legislate universal black male suf-frage through the Fifteenth Amendment to the U.S. Constitution didn't help the *Gazette*'s acceptance in the community either.

On December 14, 1868, the first issue of the *Fort Wayne Weekly Journal* appeared from the printing press of Thomas S. Taylor, with Samuel T. Hanna serving as the financial backer. The newspaper's stated objective was to become the official organ of the Republican Party in the county. However, neither Taylor nor Hanna was well suited for his role. Hanna's participation, while short-lived, was indicative of the party's growing differences with the *Gazette*. Hanna was the fourth of eight sons of Fort Wayne pioneer businessman and civic leader Samuel Hanna. A graduate of Hanover College, Samuel T. Hanna was 34 when the *Journal* began. He was a Republican with a great admiration for Abraham Lincoln. In January 1865 he took his wife and her two bridesmaids on a wedding trip to Washington, where they were entertained by then-comptroller of the currency Hugh McCulloch and other Indiana politicians. In her journal, his wife, Martha, recorded their attendance at a White House reception where they met Lincoln. After some dancing, the Hannas "passed into the reception room again, when Lincoln, towering above those around him, spying us, and beckoning called loud enough for all around to hear, 'Come here, you Fort Wayne people! I want to shake hands with you again. You truly loyal people from that Copperhead place!' We went again and shook hands, Mr. Hanna saying, 'Well, we furnish you with a comp-troller, anyway!' We had a little talk with Lincoln, which I will always treasure in my heart," she wrote.[3]

In financing the start of the *Journal*, Hanna demonstrated a business-man's distrust of prolonging the sectional conflict in the nation. The eco-nomic opportunity, especially to an investor like Hanna, was paramount. With its railroad-linked foundries and manufacturing, Fort Wayne was poised for growth as it had never been before. Whether the newspaper business was too controversial or too unprofitable for Hanna is unknown, but he sold his interest in the newspaper in 1872, the year he was elected to the city council. Hanna made a fortune in railroad investments and was one of several local businessmen who organized the Fort Wayne Street Railway Company. But subsequent financial panics and government scan-dals left him impoverished, and Hanna died of a heart attack at age 53 in 1887.

The *Weekly Journal* was Thomas Taylor's second experience with newspaper publishing. In 1867 he had briefly printed the *Fort Wayne Ad-*

vertiser before it folded. He apparently struggled to produce the *Weekly Journal* in 1869, prompting some Republicans to seek a more experienced editor, and Clark Fairbank was persuaded by his sister's husband to move from Boston to Fort Wayne later that year.

A native of New Hampshire, Fairbank had an impressive professional background. After attending school, he had learned the printing and publishing business in Lowell, Massachusetts, and later in Boston. During the Civil War, Fairbank was a field reporter for a Boston publisher, providing "graphic descriptions of the battle between the *Monitor* and the *Merrimac*, the battles of the Wilderness, and the final entrance of federal troops into Richmond."[4]

Fairbank and Taylor were joined by Taylor's brother, Charles, who was listed as the "local editor." Thomas Taylor left the printing business when he gained a position with the post office, where he worked for thirty-five years, mostly in charge of the dead letter office. Fairbank assumed control of the newspaper with Judge Samuel S. Ludlum and remained editor until 1878 when he resigned to enter the insurance business. In 1880, he married the daughter of former mayor Franklin P. Randall and went on to a successful business career, becoming the first president of the Northern Indiana Life Underwriters Association.

It was during Fairbank's tenure that the biggest national news event since the Civil War reached Fort Wayne. The "Great Strike of 1877" presented a serious challenge to city authorities and also tested the skills of the city's newspapers. The strike began in mid-July when railroad workers in Martinsburg, West Virginia, walked off their jobs rather than accept a second salary reduction in a year from the Baltimore & Ohio Railroad. The strike rippled westward through the railroads, prompting sympathy walkouts in other industries. There were violent confrontations between strikers and militia in Pittsburgh and Baltimore, Ohio, and to a lesser degree elsewhere. Fort Wayne held its breath as it waited to see if the strike would reach its railroad yards.

On Saturday evening, July 21, five days after the strike began, a freight train of the Pittsburg, Fort Wayne and Chicago Railroad arrived for a fresh crew, water, and coal.[5] When it came time to hitch the engine to the freight cars, the brakemen walked off the job. It was then learned that the switch allowing the engine out of the rail yard had been spiked and all the pins linking the freight cars had been removed. A crowd gathered, composed mostly of nonrailroad employees who "freely proffered unsolicited advice of an inflammatory nature" until police arrived.[6] The dreaded strike had arrived.

The strikers in Fort Wayne forced the railroad shops to close, including the foundry. Mayor Charles Zollinger and other city leaders feared a riot that would lead to property being destroyed as had occurred elsewhere in the strike, but the Fort Wayne strikers patrolled the rail yards around the clock, preventing any vandalism to the roundhouse and other buildings. They also asked the city to close saloons near the depot to prevent any drunken violence, and they intercepted a trainload of trackmen intent on reaching Fort Wayne for a show of force. While passenger trains carrying U.S. mail operated freely on the railroads and the Wabash Railroad, which was in receivership, did not participate in the strike, the freight blockade had a rapid impact. By July 24 there were 1,200 workers idled in the city. Perishable goods sat in freight cars on sidings. Wholesalers in the city told their salesmen not to take orders for immediate delivery, and some firms told their traveling salesmen to come home. Zollinger wired Governor J. D. "Blue Jeans" Williams for troops to break the strike, but the governor declined. The only major confrontation occurred when Zollinger, the sheriff, and two railroad officials commandeered a locomotive and tried to remove a coach car and caboose that the strikers were using as their headquarters at the Calhoun Street crossing. The strikers quickly resumed control without bloodshed.

The strike ended gradually along the railroads as company officials persuaded the workers to return to their jobs. The strikers had to accept the reduced pay in exchange for promises that they would not be discharged or discriminated against at their jobs. Fort Wayne's railroad firemen and brakemen followed suit, voting by a bare majority to end their twelve-day walkout on August 1. The following day, federal troops unexpectedly arrived from Toledo, only to learn that their show of force was unneeded.

Fort Wayne's newspapers both struggled with and benefited from the strike. Chronicling the local events and handling the many wire stories about riots from Buffalo, New York, to Reading, Pennsylvania, taxed the small staffs on the *Morning Gazette*, the *Daily Sentinel*, the *Daily News*, and the *Weekly Journal*. On some days, it meant four or five editions. At the strike's end, the *Gazette* acknowledged that its circulation averaged more than 1,600 extra copies for the final ten days of the strike. Since the *Journal* was a weekly, Fairbank had the advantage of bringing more perspective to his coverage and was less prone to print false rumors.

While the strike and the threat of mayhem created a sense of collegiality among the various reporters, the competitive warfare among the newspapers continued. The *News* was accused by the other two dailies of stealing special dispatches that arrived by telegraph for the *Sentinel* and the *Gazette*. The *News* retorted that it did receive special dispatches of its own, and if any were meant for the other papers, it was the messenger "selling" the Western Union pieces to the paper who should be blamed. The individual denied this, and the *News* declined to produce any Western Union receipts for the special news items it printed about the strike.

The strike also demonstrated the lack of perspective among the local newspapers. None of the editors wondered whether the cutthroat competition among the different railroads contributed to their poor earnings and the need to slash the workers' pay. All of them agreed that the strike was illegal, although they praised the restraint and responsible actions of the men in Fort Wayne. They agreed with the *Sentinel*'s observation: "We trust that the relative failure of this strike, the greatest on record, in regard to the number of men engaged and the area of territory affected, has so completely demonstrated the folly of such movements that we shall hear no more of them in the future."[7] It wasn't the last, as this was just the beginning of two decades of labor strife in the United States.

The *Weekly Journal* was initially located in Taylor's printing business on Main Street between Calhoun and Clinton, but in the mid-1870s it moved above the post office on Court Street between Main and Berry Streets. Even with its politically advantageous location, the newspaper remained a weekly with little advertising for its first sixteen years.

From its earliest issues, the *Journal* was involved in a national controversy that elicited some of the worst racist writing in the city's newspaper history. Even before the end of the Civil War, Radical Republicans had followed in the footsteps of the abolitionists by calling not only for land reform in the South but also for equal voting rights for African Americans. After the war's end and Lincoln's assassination, President Johnson refused to support immediate suffrage for African Americans. This was not out-of-step with a good deal of the country. There was similar sentiment in the North where African American suffrage referenda had failed in Connecticut, Minnesota, and Wisconsin in 1865. At the end of 1868, African Americans could not vote in eleven of the twenty-one northern states and all five of the border states.[8]

If it were not for an organization dedicated to terror, the Fifteenth Amendment prohibiting federal and state governments from depriving any citizen of the right to vote on racial grounds might not have been enacted. The secret Ku Klux Klan was formed in Tennessee in 1866, led by Nathan Bedford Forrest, who drew support from numerous other former Confederate generals. Two years later, the hooded-and-robed Klansmen were murdering Republican leaders and voters in the South in its crusade to preserve white supremacy. In response to the intimidation of African American voters, the "lame duck" Congress that served after the 1868 election and before Grant's inauguration in March 1869 approved the Fifteenth Amendment. Indiana's congressional delegation voted along party lines: seven Republicans supported the amendment and four Democrats opposed.

Throughout the nation, Democrats objected strenuously but had little hope of blocking the amendment, since Republicans controlled twenty-five of thirty-three state legislatures and thereby could secure ratification without state referenda.[9] That did not inhibit Indiana's Democratic lawmakers from one of the more bizarre acts in the nation's legislative history. The Fifteenth Amendment was submitted to the Indiana legislature near the close of the session in March 1869. After a caucus, seventeen Democratic state senators and thirty-seven Democratic representatives resigned, thus eliminating the necessary quorum of two-thirds of the members in each house.

In the special election that followed to fill the vacancies, the members who resigned were all reelected. A special session of the legislature was convened on April 8 for the ostensible purpose of securing the necessary state appropriations. The Fifteenth Amendment was brought up in the state senate on May 13. Several Democratic senators spoke against the measure; however, unlike the earlier attempt, the Democrats did not walk out. Instead, ten senators declined to vote, and only one opposed the amendment. Later the ten claimed they had resigned but had not filed an official notification. The following day the Democratic members of the state house of representatives again resigned. This time, the house leadership determined that the two-thirds requirement for a quorum did not apply to this legislation, and the remaining lawmakers approved the amendment.

In response, the *Fort Wayne Daily Democrat* launched a wave of vile editorials about the threat of African Americans having the right to vote. The "farce" of the Indiana legislature ratifying the amendment, the *Daily Democrat* declared on May 18, 1869, would mean:

Negroes at the ballot-box;
Negroes in the jury box;
Negroes in our offices;
Negroes in our public schools;
Negro judges, negro lawyers, negro policemen;
Negroes crowding white men out of workshops;
Negroes competing with white laborers in the field;

Negro outrages committed by negro thieves, paupers, and plunderers;
Negroes everywhere, filling our cities, strolling through the country, degrading
   labor and reducing it to starvation prices.

In subsequent editions, the *Daily Democrat* reported such inflammatory items as seeing "strange black faces on our streets every day" now
that the Fifteenth Amendment had been passed.

The Republican newspapers dismissed such commentary but were
noncommittal on the rights of African Americans. At the time of the ratification of the Fifteenth Amendment, African Americans were excluded
from voting in Indiana by the state constitution. Furthermore, the constitution forbade them to come into the state. It was not until 1881 that
amendments were made to the state constitution to remove these prohibitions and make Indiana law consistent with the U.S. Constitution.

Another issue began to overshadow the political turmoil. In 1870 Fort
Wayne was beginning to experience the industrial boom of the nation in a
manner that was previously unimaginable by the citizenry. The city had a
population of 19,460 people, with twenty-two churches, a college, a high
school, a training school, nine other schools including those conducted in
German, and three private Catholic schools. There were five major
banks, ten bakeries, thirty-six boarding houses, twelve hotels, twelve cigar
manufacturers and tobacconists, and five photographers. The Gas Works
served 606 customers along thirteen miles of streets, and the community's
pride was evident in H. S. Knapp's assertion, "There is probably no establishment, either in Europe or America, which contains in its management so large a degree of science and intelligent business skills as that
which, chiefly under Mr. H. H. Edgerton, secretary of the company, controls the Fort Wayne Gas Works."[10] The city also was the home to the
Fort Wayne Steel Plow Company, whose thirty-five employees produced
10,000 plows annually. Within the city limits there were four sawmills,
producing six million feet of lumber annually. The factories also produced steam engines, tubular and fluid boilers, and tanks.

The city's cognizance of its rapid growth and good fortune was captured in a passage by H. S. Knapp: "The person who, even twenty years
ago, would have suggested that an establishment for the manufacture of
the heaviest iron machinery would one day spring up at where was the
small town of Fort Wayne, and ship this work to the Atlantic States,
would have been considered but a small remove from insanity. Yet the fact
exists, and to businessmen of their stamp is the city of Fort Wayne largely
indebted for its unexampled prosperity."[11]

Amid the growth, a major change occurred in Fort Wayne's newspaper community, one that would have a lasting impact. The *Gazette* had not deigned to comment on the launch of the *Fort Wayne Weekly Journal* in 1868; however, critical comments flowed between the two newspapers as they vied for the Republican mantle. This competition took a very different complexion four years later.

In 1872, the *Journal* was sold to a stock company that included not only the current Republican owners Taylor and Fairbank but also two notable Democrats, Judge Samuel Ludlum and Robert Lowry. Ludlum was judge of the Allen County Circuit Court and a leading member of the Democratic Party. Lowry, an Irish immigrant who came to Fort Wayne in 1843 to practice law, was among the most powerful political figures in northeast Indiana for thirty years. Elected to the city council two years after his arrival, he was a circuit court judge in 1852. He was nominated by the party to run for Congress in 1856, but lost by a close vote. He served as president of the Indiana Democratic State Convention in 1860 when it endorsed Illinois senator Stephen A. Douglas for president. While he was part-owner of the newspaper, Lowry was named to the Indiana Supreme Court in 1877 and then became the first president of the Indiana State Bar Association in 1879. By 1880, Lowry had sold his share in the *Journal* but retained its full support. He was elected to the U.S. House of Representatives in 1882 and reelected in 1884. Two years later he became involved in the contentious political battle that saw him lose his reelection bid to James B. White.

Unlike its birth, the change in the *Journal*'s politics did not go unnoticed. For years the political differences were the subject of repartees and rejoinders in the city's newspapers. An allusion in the January 4, 1882, editor's column of the *Daily Gazette* was typical of the bitterness: "A man up in Michigan is lecturing on 'Lying & Liars.' It seems that men will persist in going round the country talking about democratic editors."

It was the next owner who brought renewed energy to the *Journal* and made it into a very Democratic newspaper. Thomas J. Foster was an ardent Democrat who served as a drummer boy in the Forty-first Ohio Volunteers in the Civil War. With about a year of formal education, he learned the printing business at a cousin's firm. Foster was an industrious young man. At age 23, he purchased the *Monroeville Democrat*, a weekly newspaper in a small town southeast of Fort Wayne, on credit in 1870. Within a year, he had erased his debt, editing and composing the newspaper by himself. Foster continued the Monroeville newspaper after moving to Fort Wayne in 1871 and founding the *New Haven Palladium*, a weekly described as independent but not neutral. In addition, he published between eight and ten patent newspapers before selling the Monroeville and New Haven properties in 1879. In addition, Foster published a newspaper in support of Charles O'Connor, the Straight Democratic candidate for president in the 1872 campaign.

Foster was elected to the state house of representatives in 1876 and to the state senate in 1878, but his love was newspapers. In 1880 he purchased the *Journal* and started its daily edition in January 1884. Whether the life of a politician or the strain of publishing a daily and a weekly edition led him to become an alcoholic is unknown. His death from a self-inflicted gunshot wound to the head in June 1884 shocked Fort Wayne "like a thunderbolt from the sky," according to the *Fort Wayne Daily Gazette*. The newspaper said Foster had brooded over his "terrible appetite" and had broken his vow of abstinence from five months earlier. James C. Beeks, the editor of the *Daily Journal*, told the coroner that he knew of no cause other than "temporary insanity caused by excessive use of intoxicants" in Foster's death. Thomas Foster was 37.

There may have been financial worries for Foster, too. The economic situation of the *Journal* could not have been good. The next owner was Charles H. Eyansides, whose tenure was so ineffectual that, according to a rival newspaper, he had to borrow money to get out of town. The tide, however, was changing for the *Journal*.

Newspapers were a growth industry in the final decades of the century. While the population of the United States doubled between 1870 and 1890, the number of daily newspapers quadrupled and circulation grew sixfold. A great deal of this growth occurred in urban areas where the number of residents tripled. The number of English-language general circulation dailies rose from 489 in 1870 to 1,967 in 1900. The number of weeklies, which may better reflect the non-urban growth, increased from 4,000 nationally in 1870 to more than 12,000 thirty years later.[12]

This trend was certainly evident in Fort Wayne, where the appetite for news grew and the newspaper owners tried different ways to accommodate the readers' demand. There was a brief attempt by the *Daily Democrat* to become a morning paper and challenge the *Gazette*, but this "proved to be a grief on the business office,"[13] and the paper returned to its evening publication. In 1873 William Fleming bought the newspaper and restored its name to the *Fort Wayne Sentinel*. The *Fort Wayne Daily News* was established in June 1874 by William D. Page and Charles F. Taylor as an afternoon newspaper. Page had worked as superintendent of the mechanical department at the *Gazette*. With a smaller size design, the

News was aimed at the workingman whose interests might not be as "high-brow" as its competitors. It was said to be unwelcome in many respectable households because of the "racy" news it printed. The *News* said it was an independent newspaper, but sided with Republicans at election time. The city editor was A. V. D. Conover. Page gained sole control of the *Daily News* from Taylor in 1887 and managed the newspaper until he was appointed postmaster in 1902. C. F. Bicknell bought the paper, making it strongly Republican. Jesse Greene served as editor.

The *Sentinel*, meanwhile, experienced a series of owners. The most noted were two Fort Wayne men who became formidable figures elsewhere in the newspaper industry. William Rockhill Nelson and Samuel E. Morss bought the *Sentinel* in April 1879 with Nelson in control of the business and advertising while Morss, a former *Gazette* editor, oversaw the editorial operation. They sold the newspaper in August 1880 and moved to Kansas City, where they founded the *Kansas City Evening Star*. Nelson built the *Star* into a powerful entity, but poor health caused Morss to leave the newspaper after a year. In 1888 Morss returned to Indiana and purchased the *Indianapolis Sentinel*, which became the state's leading Democratic newspaper. It was there that Morss helped develop the career of Claude Bowers, one of the finest editors in the history of Fort Wayne newspapers and a nationally respected leader in the Democratic Party.

The *Fort Wayne Sentinel* was restored to fiscal health in 1880 when it was purchased by Edward A. K. Hackett, who remained its publisher until his death in 1916. Other newspapers begun in this period focused on special audiences, such as the *Fort Wayne Dispatch*. This weekly edited by James Mitchell and first supporting the National Greenback Party and then other labor and agricultural causes operated from early 1878 until 1901. Another German-language paper was founded in 1888 by Otto Commerow. The *Freie Presse* was published for twenty years until it was consolidated with the *Staats-Zeitung*.

Still, owning a newspaper in the late nineteenth century was not without serious financial risk. Paper—then made from rags and not wood pulp—was disproportionately expensive. It was reported, for example, that the *Chicago Evening News* with its 400,000 circulation faced a daily expense of $30,000 to $40,000 for paper alone. Advertising revenue was the means to profitability, but newspapers such as those in Fort Wayne had difficulty in securing enough ads to cover their costs. In addition, smaller merchants like those in the Fort Wayne market were more prone to going out of business without paying their newspaper bills than retailers in larger cities. The *Daily Gazette* once described its business manager as someone "who will be satisfied if others do as they are done by." Even subscribers were a problem in those days, as many flatly refused to pay their bills. It may be an apocryphal story, but it was said that an editor in nineteenth-century Vermont found an ideal way to deal with the problem: he printed an obituary notice about a delinquent, but still living, subscriber. When the subject came to the newspaper office to protest about the erroneous report of his demise, the editor confronted him with their overdue bill. In that way, it was said, the editor was able not only to bring readers back to life but also to restore their financial respectability.

The *Journal* had a different problem: how to replace the dynamic Thomas Foster. Attorney Martin Van Buren Spencer purchased the *Journal* in late 1884 and formed a joint stock company with several leading Democrats. Among the co-owners were Col. Charles A. Zollinger, who was in his sixth of seven terms as mayor; Allen Zollars, an attorney, former state lawmaker, the first Allen County Superior Court judge, and Indiana Supreme Court justice from 1883 to 1889; Charles F. Muhler, Fort Wayne's mayor-elect; Dr. Lycurgus S. Null, a physician and former state representative; businessman Samuel Miller; and cigar manufacturer Frederick C. Boltz.

The number of backers needed to keep the *Journal* afloat attests to the fact that Spencer's acquisition was viewed as a risky investment. Although there aren't any circulation figures from the time, the *Journal's* sales must have been less than the others. While the Keils were promoting the *Gazette* as "one of the brightest and most popular family journals published in the state," Spencer advertised the *Journal* as "the cheapest morning daily in northern Indiana."[14] The *Journal* was publishing a four-page edition, Tuesday through Sunday, and all contained scant advertising. The new owners hired professionals to manage the newspaper with G. W. Lunt as business manager and George F. Shutts as editor.

There was a salvation for the *Journal*, though, and it was in the form of one of the stockholders who lacked any knowledge of the newspaper business. Samuel Miller was orphaned at an early age in Wells County and lacked any formal schooling. He was, however, an emphatically self-made man. Miller managed to buy a small farm near New Haven, Indiana, and raise enough capital to go into business selling wooden pumps. Other business opportunities developed, enabling him to invest in the *Journal*. Miller replaced Lunt as business manager, and in 1885 Miller purchased all of the shares of the other stockholders. He published the newspaper, which then carried the phrase "Official Paper of the City" in its masthead, until his death in January 1887. "When he took charge of the paper it was

Samuel Miller, who is credited with saving the *Fort Wayne Journal*. *Allen County–Fort Wayne Historical Society.*

heavily encumbered, had a weighty floating debt, had no credit, and was apparently on its last legs," the *Journal* reported in its owner's obituary. "In less than eighteen months, Mr. Miller had paid off the indebtedness, had purchased a large amount of new material, had established a first-class financial credit for the paper, and had money to its credit in the banks."[15] The strain of running a daily newspaper and trying to restore its fiscal health undoubtedly contributed to Miller's heart attack on Christmas Day 1886. He died three weeks later at age 37. The *Journal* was not printed on the Tuesday that he was buried.

Out of office for the first time in more than a decade, Zollinger purchased Miller's stock in 1887 and operated the newspaper for about a year. His experience with the *Journal* was only part of a remarkable political career, one in which he understood the opportunity afforded by the press. Born in 1838 in Wiesbaden, Germany, Zollinger came to the United States in 1848 and eventually settled in New Haven, Indiana, where he became a blacksmith. Zollinger served with two regiments in the Civil War and was elected to the rank of colonel during his time with the 129th Regiment of Indiana Volunteers. After the war, Zollinger was elected sheriff of Allen County in 1870, and three years later he was elected mayor of Fort Wayne, a position he would hold until 1885 and again in 1893. During his years in office, Zollinger saw the city realize many municipal improvements, including extensive paving of city streets, a complete overhaul of the fire department, the establishment of the trolley system, and the construction of the reservoir and new water works system. Zollinger's successes were newsmakers, and he made certain that they were so treated in his newspaper. The grandiose City Building—now the Old City Hall Museum—on Berry Street was constructed during his last term. He died December 28, 1893, while in office.

While Zollinger was a remarkable politician and used the *Journal* to advance his legacy, he was not focused on running the newspaper operation, and it was the next owner who made it more businesslike. Christian Boseker, who was publisher of the newspaper for about eighteen months before selling it in 1889, managed to increase its circulation and advertising lineage. An immigrant from Saxony, Boseker arrived in Fort Wayne in 1846 at age 5. He trained as a carpenter, and after serving with the Thirtieth Regiment of Indiana Volunteers in the Civil War, he established himself as a contractor. In the course of three decades he built a number of notable buildings in the region, including the Wells, Adams, and Defiance (Ohio) county courthouses, the First Presbyterian Church in Fort Wayne, the city hall in Fort Wayne, and the U.S. government building at

Clinton and Berry Streets. Boseker sold the newspaper to brothers William Wright Rockhill and Howell C. Rockhill and Andrew J. Moynihan on June 10, 1889.

This change represented a cultural shift for the newspaper. The new owners had a strong Irish heritage in contrast to many years of owners with a German background. The party politics were the same, if a bit more stridently Anglophobic. The individual powerbrokers and candidates were not the same, however. In addition, the ownership change coincided with the unparalleled period of "yellow journalism." It was to be a dynamic time for Fort Wayne newspapers, and the *Fort Wayne Journal*, now with the largest morning circulation, had the most dynamic of owners.

The Rockhills were the sons of one of Fort Wayne's renowned pioneers, but it was W. W. Rockhill who was an unrepentant partisan. A devoted Democrat, he exercised the power of elective office well before he became part-owner of the *Journal*. In 1881 he was regarded as the best choice for city clerk, recognized as a young man with a reputation above any reproach. He was praised for his performance at city council meetings where his perception and intelligence were cited as materially adding to the council's effectiveness. Rockhill won reelection in 1883 on Mayor Zollinger's slate.

This was the era of patronage, and Rockhill learned the methods of favoritism and reward from his elders. His errors of omission or commission were tolerated by the Democratic councilmen, who fondly called him "Rocksy." Like most any political person, he accumulated opposition as his years in office grew, in part because of his manner of doing business. When it came time for a third term, one opponent said Rockhill had promised to step aside and support him for the clerk's office. The opposition newspapers printed the candidate's allegations that Rockhill's own business had failed and that he had not paid his creditors. The implication was clear that Rockhill ought not to be trusted with public funds as the city clerk. Despite these and other attacks, Rockhill won the party nomination and then a third term.

Opposition was greater for a fourth term in 1887 when Rockhill was criticized for being part of the "Lowryites." Again Rockhill overcame the opposition, but apparently he had had enough. He did not run in 1889, the year that he led the acquisition of the *Journal*.

The acquisition did not put him outside the political arena. In 1892 Rockhill achieved greater political power by being elected to the Democratic State Central Committee. Rockhill's use of his political advantage caused opposing newspapers to attack him and the *Journal*. Special print-ing contracts and legal advertising were at stake, especially in election years. "Ever since the Hon. W. W. Rockhill assumed management of the *Journal*, he has sought to injure the *Sentinel* in every way he could and has not hesitated to misrepresent, misquote, and adopt other means, however disreputable, to do so," the *Sentinel* wrote in July 1892 when Rockhill pub-licly charged that the newspaper had caused Fort Wayne to lose the op-portunity to host the Democratic State Convention. "The prosperity of the *Sentinel* makes Mr. Rockhill jealous—in fact his jealousy sometimes reaches the point of madness—and then he breaks out with an attack on the *Sentinel* that is as untrue as it is malicious. Perhaps the principal cause of losing the convention was that the *Journal* advocated holding it in this city. Some men's support is worse than their opposition. This may be true of the *Journal*."[16]

Despite the rancor in the press, Rockhill and his Allen County ma-chine delivered a 4,500-vote plurality to Grover Cleveland in the 1892 presidential election, "the largest majority ever given a candidate by any Indiana county," according to the *Indianapolis Sentinel*.[17]

In keeping with political tradition, Rockhill expected to be awarded the Fort Wayne postmaster position, and he was not very modest about it. He sought the support of Congressman William McNagny, a Democrat from Columbia City, who apparently wanted to appoint Billy Meyer, an-other Fort Wayne man. Those opposing Rockhill mounted a campaign to block him, even to the extent of calling for a change in federal law so that the Fort Wayne postmaster's position would become an elected office. For nearly five months, the city's newspapers were filled with rumors, in-nuendo, and reports about the controversy. At one point in April, the other candidate believed he had secured the nomination and, after order-ing a round of drinks at a saloon, sauntered over to the *Journal* office to "rub it in." Meyer's confrontation with Rockhill wasn't pleasant, as Rock-hill just smiled at him, according to one report, and Meyer walked away shaken. Six days later, it was announced that Rockhill would get the post. The *Morning Times* said, "Everybody was for Meyer and if the men were pitted against each other at the polls, Mr. Rockhill wouldn't get enough votes to necessitate a recount."[18]

The *Gazette*, while acknowledging that the new postmaster was prob-ably qualified for the job, commented that Rockhill's "cold, cynical, calcu-lating smile" had grown more pronounced.[19]

However, C. R. Higgins, the incumbent postmaster, refused to relin-quish his position, claiming his appointment was initially delayed and that he should serve until January 1894. When Rockhill asked him personally to step down, Higgins declined. Throughout the struggle, the sniping at Rockhill and the *Journal* continued. The *News* said that Rockhill's confronting the postmaster was "in execrable taste" and hoped it would endanger the appointment. Critics claimed that Rockhill and Moynihan were being greedy in their operation of "a paper which demands all the city and county pap in sight."

President Cleveland, apparently wearying of the delay, officially nominated Rockhill on June 29, 1893, and the incumbent resigned three weeks later. Still, the controversy wasn't over. Rockhill was not accustomed to the new civil service procedures. In August, he fired three carriers, an act that the *News* labeled "a travesty." One of the carriers went to the Civil Service Commission and was reinstated in November. Rockhill dismissed the man again. In February 1894, the Civil Service Commission reprimanded Rockhill as a result of repeated complaints of partisan manipulation of the Fort Wayne Post Office. The commission described Rockhill as "a man of good standing in the community, liked by his fellow citizens and in his business dealings honest. But he is one of those officials . . . who think that the ordinary rules of fair-dealing do not apply in politics." The commission concluded that "he cares nothing for the Civil Service law and admits he does not understand it."

In the operation of the *Journal,* W. W. Rockhill served as president and business manager until he became postmaster. Howell Rockhill, who served as account business manager, succeeded his brother before leaving the newspaper business in 1905. Moynihan, who was secretary-treasurer and editor at the outset, pooled his resources with his wife and brother, Martin, and bought the Rockhills' share of the business in 1907.

If there was an archetypical newspaper character in Fort Wayne history, his name was Andrew Joseph Moynihan. Like James Bennett Gordon, who founded of the *New York Herald,* Moynihan was as colorful in real life as the language was in his newspaper. Like Joseph Pulitzer of the *New York World,* he had strong opinions and was committed to printing them as the news. Like William Randolph Hearst of the *San Francisco Examiner,* Moynihan never lacked for sensationalism or heated editorial opinions. And like all of the publishers named above, Moynihan had an extraordinary ability to know where every dime was being spent within the newspaper operation.

Moynihan was never known to shy away from the power of the printed word in the political arena. "No Democrat ever strayed far from what the Irish editor believed to be the reservation," was the way one newsman de-

The *Fort Wayne Journal* staff poses in this 1897 image. The gentleman in white hair and moustache in the center at the counter is W. W. Rockhill. To the right is editor Andrew Moynihan with the black mustache and, next to him, Thomas Bresnahan, looking into the camera.

scribed Moynihan's influence, adding, "No Republican politician ever felt like taking off his armor or relaxing as long as Andy Moynihan was editor."[20] Another recalled, "Only a man of great courage or a half-wit ever dared to incur the ill-will of Moynihan."[21]

Born in County Kerry, near Killarney, in 1856, Moynihan arrived in the United States at age 8. In 1866 he came to Fort Wayne, where he learned the printing trade. He attended Rush Medical School to become a physician, financing his education by working vacations as a printer and then as the local editor at the *Fort Wayne Sentinel*. The newspaper work proved more attractive than the medical studies, and Moynihan worked at the *Sentinel* from 1883 to 1889 before joining in the purchase of the *Journal*. His commitment to Democratic principles was unimpeachable. But so was his commitment to printing the truth. Despite his reasons for "timing" the release of the news about James B. White's legal status as a citizen in the 1886 election, Moynihan was accurate in his reporting: White did not qualify under the law to be elected to Congress.

The stories about Moynihan's temper are legion, and his skill with the word or phrase was unmatched in his time. Moynihan delighted in showing his disdain for the *Gazette* in his pages. When the opposition made light of the Irish editor's writing style in early 1890, Moynihan sniffed, "The *Gazette* ought to style its editorial department, 'Looking Backward.'" He later described the *Gazette* as "clinging to its ancient and venerable style of editorial writing: It is a sort of puzzle column to its remaining readers and robs its contemporaries of a rival in the newspaper field."[22] Moynihan had a particular dislike for one highly educated editor of the *Gazette*, Nathan Leonard. On June 5, 1890, he published two editorials. In one, he lampooned Leonard as an Iowan who "did missionary work in a college out there until he discovered that the people of Hoosierdom needed redemption and by intuition and the approbation of the entire community in which he moved out there, the professor drifted to Fort Wayne." In the other, Moynihan linked Leonard and the *Gazette* to an illegal lottery and the appointment of a crooked deputy U.S. marshal. "This is the newspaper whose editor folds his hands in prayer, takes on an elongated face and raising his voice to high heaven exclaims: 'I thank Thee, O Lord, that I am not as other men.'"

Moynihan was one of those journalists who lived to work. He never lived far from the newspaper office in his fifteen years with the *Journal* and the *Journal-Gazette*, preferring to board in nearby hotels or rooms. Only in 1906 did he buy a house on West Berry Street, a five-block walk to his office.

With his intensity and a keen sense for what constitutes news, Moynihan created a deep loyalty among his reporters. They tolerated his dramatic outbursts, acerbic tongue, and Irish humor. They were loyal to him and told stories about him long after his death. Moynihan didn't tolerate laziness and barely accommodated those who had a penchant for alcohol. Although he hated the telephone and claimed he couldn't hear what was being said to him, Moynihan wasn't shy about calling the local saloons and screaming for the barkeep to send his reporters back to the office. Many years after the event, newsman Cliff Ward related the story about a reporter named Baron Long who would get very drunk with regularity, a fact that would spark a loud tirade from Moynihan. On one occasion, Long had been discovered by two colleagues in an advanced stage of intoxication. They managed to get him sober and into a fresh set of clothes. "Then," Ward recalled, "Baron strolled into the office, opened his desk, and started to work. Everyone who was in on the situation was tense. This would be the most dramatic firing in history. Andy looked up. 'Hello, Baron,' he said mildly, 'where are you working now?' "[23]

Moynihan's wry humor encompassed his profession and its idiosyncratic concerns. For example, Sheriff Aaron M. Reichelderfer presented a problem for the newspaper editor. Quite simply, his name was too long. When there was a news story about an arrest made by the sheriff, it was a real challenge to write a headline for it. Since headlines are constrained by the size of type and the narrow width of a newspaper column, the use of "Reichelderfer" was nearly impossible. "What this county needs," an exasperated Moynihan was heard to say to his city editor, Tom Bresnahan, "is a sheriff named Kelly."[24]

The little known aspect about Moynihan's fiery outbursts and unpredictable behavior was that he was epileptic. Times of prolonged tension and/or high excitement were said to precipitate an attack.

Throughout the 1890s, the strength of the *Journal* grew. Its reporting of local news attracted new readers, and it proclaimed that it had the largest morning circulation in northern Indiana. Moynihan's reporters often beat their competitors to major fires and train accidents, providing better and more graphic firsthand accounts. In a four-day period in February 1893, the *Journal* carried detailed descriptions of a collision between two freight trains that left three railroad men dead in Monroeville south of the city and a passenger train crash to the west of Fort Wayne near Columbia City that left one man dead and twenty-seven injured. In the latter tragedy, the *Journal*'s front-page story pointedly noted that its reporter "was the only newspaperman at the scene of the wreck."[25] The story described how the locomotive's right front drive wheel broke in two as it crossed the Eel River Bridge en route to Fort Wayne. The accident sent the two rear passenger coaches careening down a twenty-five-foot embankment. Using interviews with passengers and other witnesses, the story went into great detail about the injuries suffered by the passengers and their rescue. It was the style of journalism that won readers in the 1890s.

While the *Journal* maintained its stream of criticism of the *Gazette* and gained more subscribers, there was one very sore issue for the newspaper at 43 East Main Street—the wire service it received. The Associated Press and United Press were cooperative associations that arose in the nineteenth century for the purpose of rapidly and impartially collecting and disseminating the news over leased telegraph wires to subscribing newspapers. The Associated Press began in New York in 1849, and regional associations followed, such as the Western Associated Press serving midwestern dailies. However, there were more newspapers wanting access than the member-only AP could provide, and United Press—which is not related to the modern UPI—was formed in 1882. The competition was significant with individual newspapers touting their service. The *Journal*, for example, ran a front-page story on Sunday, January 15, 1893, about the "Peerless United Press" with a sketch of Walter P. Phillips, the UP general manager. The trouble, though, was that Moynihan wanted the Associated Press service for his newspaper, and the *Gazette* was not about to let it go. In February 1894, the United Press was reportedly collapsing after the Associated Press obtained exclusive news contracts with European news agencies. The *Gazette* ran a lengthy story extolling the advantages of reading a newspaper served by the Associated Press, but Moynihan turned the tables on the other Fort Wayne newspaper by noting that it had missed wire service stories on the speeches made by ex-president Benjamin Harrison and Ohio governor William McKinley. The *Gazette*'s "Republican subscribers were compelled to seek out a copy of the *Journal*" to keep abreast of the news, Moynihan noted. This "is only another in the long list of humiliating scoops on the Associated Press, and the local organ that depends on this freight train method of getting its news."[26] This was sour grapes on Moynihan's part, of course, and when the AP service became available later, he moved quickly to acquire it.

Moynihan also developed the *Fort Wayne Weekly Journal* into a more diversified and readable compilation of the week's news, relying heavily on the use of news features with oversized illustrations. As the nation's militarism grew in the 1890s, the nameplate was changed to include a large engraving of General Anthony Wayne, and the newspaper often ran full-page illustrated stories on the buildup of the U.S. Navy. When the Spanish-American War broke out, the *Weekly Journal* expanded to sixteen pages. In 1899, when U.S. soldiers were fighting in the Philippines, the weekly newspaper reached twenty-four pages. Subscriptions remained one dollar a year.

Not all the local news was local. Indiana was still a pivotal state in national elections, as evidenced by the number of Hoosiers selected as presidential and vice presidential candidates between 1876 and 1896. The Democratic candidate for vice president was from Indiana in three consecutive elections: in 1876 and 1884, former governor Thomas A. Hendricks; and in 1880, former Indianapolis mayor William English. In the following two elections, Benjamin Harrison, who moved to Indianapolis at the age of 21, was the Republican nominee for president, winning in 1888.

Fort Wayne was a frequent campaign stop for national candidates for more than a century after the Civil War. Presidential nominees and hopefuls were given grand parades and rousing rallies in Fort Wayne, speaking before thousands in great halls, from the balconies of hotels and from specially built platforms at railroad stations. Some of the political visits were controversial. James G. Blaine, who had campaigned for Rutherford B. Hayes in Fort Wayne in 1876, experienced a notorious campaign stop in his own election bid in late October 1884. The Republican nominee for president tried to make his address from the balcony on the north side of the Aveline House. The Democrats, however, staged a simultaneous rally on the courthouse steps opposite the hotel, and the competing cheering made it impossible for Blaine to speak. The Republicans moved their event to the library hall at Lewis and Calhoun streets, where Blaine delivered an extended open-air address on the tariff question. For years, though, Republican journals embellished on the event to make Fort Wayne seem a rude, inhospitable community. Sixteen years later, U.S. senator Charles Fairbanks characterized the city as politically intolerant when he said in a speech that "James G. Blaine was denied a hearing in Fort Wayne a few years ago."[27] Yet Blaine did not fare poorly in the 1884 election. Grover Cleveland's margin of victory in Indiana was only slightly more than his margin of victory in Allen County. In addition, Blaine was held in high regard in the area. The stalwart Democratic *Fort Wayne Journal* devoted most of its front page in tribute to Blaine's legacy when the former Republican senator and secretary of state died in January 1893. "The nation has developed great men, but none greater" than Blaine, Moynihan wrote in an editorial. For such a partisan newspaper, it was very unusual for the *Journal* to conclude: "Presidents come and presidents go, but Mr. Blaine will live forever and receive, which he did not in life, the glorious crown of his countrymen as the foremost and best representative American of his age."[28]

However, if there was one candidate who captured the imagination of Fort Wayne, it was William Jennings Bryan. In each of his three campaigns for the presidency, Bryan carried Allen County while losing in Indiana overall. Bryan's margin of victory in Allen County was larger in 1900 than in 1896, despite facing a popular incumbent president, and it was even larger in 1908 when he was facing a popular candidate handpicked by another incumbent president. While the Fort Wayne area was considered a Democratic stronghold in presidential elections,[29] Bryan did not find similar levels of support in other partisan regions.

Fort Wayne's love of Bryan has its roots in the *Journal*'s coverage of the candidate. His nomination at the Chicago convention in July 1896 prompted scorn from the Republican-supporting *Gazette* and the *Fort Wayne News*. "Billy Bryan" was the top headline in the *News* on July 10. Calling him "a briefless lawyer," the *News* reported "the young man wins with his silver tongue," in reference to Bryan's famous "Cross of Gold" speech. The *Gazette* was more acerbic on July 11: "The nomination of Bryan was received in Fort Wayne with all the enthusiasm manifested at a funeral. Not [a] cheer or even a ripple of applause greeted the announcement of the result of the final ballot."

The *Journal* saw Bryan's nomination differently, as might be expected from a newspaper that reported his speech: "But when William J. Bryan, of Nebraska, handsome, vigorous and magnetic, and not unlike McKinley in voice, inflection and facial expression, concluded the effort of his life in support of the free coinage platform, there occurred one of those scenes which send the blood coursing fast through the veins of even the most passive spectator and remain fixed in the memory of a life-time. Like the terrible premonitory rumbling that gives warning of the approach of ten thousand cattle stampeded, delegates and spectators began the ovation to the young Nebraskan."[30]

Despite the acclaim, the 36-year-old Bryan apparently was unrecognized when he disembarked at the Nickel Plate Railroad station in Fort Wayne a month later. Harry Williams, who later became one of the city's fabled editors, was a young reporter doing the typical morning rounds when he found the signature of "W. J. Bryan" on the register at the city's finest hotel, the recently renovated New Aveline House. Not believing that it could be the "Boy Orator of the Platte" who had overwhelmed the convention, Williams strode upstairs and knocked on the door of Bryan's hotel room. When it opened, Williams found himself face to face with the Democratic Party's candidate for the presidency. Realizing there had been a major political faux pas, Williams introduced himself before rushing down the stairs and into the street to round up some of the party faithful to serve as a welcoming committee for Bryan. Subsequently, Williams saw his efforts culminate in a "Bryan Day" that attracted thousands of people to Fort Wayne to see and hear the candidate in late October.[31]

Bryan brought an unprecedented level of politicking to the 1896 election, which is considered to be the first modern presidential campaign. While William McKinley, the Republican nominee, remained at his home in Ohio, Bryan delivered thousands of speeches, crisscrossing the nation by train several times. To counteract the effect of the Panic of 1893 on urban workers and rural farmers and ranchers in the West, Bryan advocated restoring silver-backed currency, placing an income tax on the wealthy, and reducing tariffs. He promised that the increased money supply, freer trade, and less concentration of capital among the wealthy would benefit the majority of the people. Farmers, he said, would be freed from the pincers of lower crop prices and higher transportation costs. Urban workers would be able to find jobs and be paid higher wages. It was a radical message, delivered by the most intriguing political figure in decades. It also was a complex message, drawing upon two decades of debate on the national economy. While Bryan spoke to thousands throughout the nation, his issues were not embraced by the electorate. It seems in retrospect that it was the candidate and not the message that was the attraction.

Bryan's capacity for campaigning became legendary. His October 22, 1896, visit to Fort Wayne concluded a long day of campaigning in Indiana with a large rally at the city's Princess Rink and a speech at Saengerbund Hall. Bryan's address became a yardstick by which future political appearances were measured, even his own. When Bryan came to Fort Wayne three years later, slightly hoarse from a severe cold, his voice appeared ready to fail him. "As he progressed, however, his voice cleared and ere long the matchless resonance that has stirred millions to enthusiasm was there, and the peerless eloquence of William Jennings Bryan carried the great crowd in a torrent of ecstatic delight that recalled the memorable days of 1896."[32]

It was the role of editorials, not elocution, that was influential in the 1896 election, however. In endorsing Bryan, the *Fort Wayne Journal* was in the distinct minority. In fact, the number of newspapers backing Bryan in the nation was the fewest any major party candidate had received up until that time. In New York City, only the *Journal* supported him. There weren't any papers endorsing Bryan in Chicago, and the *Detroit Free Press* abandoned the Democratic Party for the first time in its history. Another statistic with long-term significance was that 503 of 581 German-language newspapers in the United States endorsed McKinley. This was a dramatic change in voter allegiance. Since the mid-1850s, German Americans, particularly in the Midwest, had been solidly Democrat. The Republicans' campaign portrayed Bryan as moving away from Democratic principles and McKinley as being more sympathetic "to a commonly shared concern with 'prosperity.'"[33] This change went unrecognized by the *Fort Wayne Journal*.

The *Journal* never seemed to address the reasons for Bryan's loss in 1896 or why Indiana and the other states of the Old Northwest voted with the East. In a November 3 editorial, the *Journal* argued that electing

Bryan and his "free coinage of silver" policy would mean "an era of rising prices for all farm produce and as all general prosperity is conditioned in the prosperity of agriculture the benefit must be distributed to every producing class and to all mercantile classes." It did not recognize that the farmers' predicament lay not so much with national fiscal policy as it did with progress. While Bryan and his supporters advocated an increase in the money supply, the main reason for lower commodity prices was overproduction, brought on by the westward development of arable land and improved efficiency through farm mechanization. The business failures that began in the 1893 depression left thousands out of work in the cities, reducing the demand for the farmers' products. The *Journal*'s other arguments proved unsubstantiated. For example, it maintained that McKinley's promise to remain on the gold standard would impoverish the country because of the precious metal's scarcity. "There cannot be enough gold thrown into our coinage to increase the circulating medium at a ratio equal to the increase of population." Of course, the newspaper could not anticipate new methods for extracting gold from surrounding ore that made such an argument moot.

The *Journal*'s opinions about Bryan's positions were convincing to Allen County's rural voters, however. Bryan captured more than 58 percent of the ballots cast in the county's townships outside of Fort Wayne, compared with slightly more than 40 percent for McKinley. This was in contrast to the rest of Indiana. Although a state with a large agricultural base, Indiana did not identify with the problems experienced by the western farmers. One of Bryan's assumptions was that all farmers shared similar concerns. It was not so. Some lacked access to capital while others lacked access to markets. Some farmers in the Old Northwest resented the advantages of their counterparts in the West who benefited from government-granted lands. Indiana gave McKinley a plurality of more than 18,000 votes, but Allen County supported Bryan by a 1,442-vote margin. The election results show Bryan winning Fort Wayne by only 72 votes of 10,979 votes cast.

Bryan's results did not affect other Democratic candidates on the ticket in Allen County. Benjamin Shively outpolled Republican James Mount in his unsuccessful bid for governor, while James M. Robinson upset the incumbent Republican congressman, Jacob D. Leighty. Another indicator of Democratic strength was that the Republican effort to defeat Bryan avoided Fort Wayne, including many of the young Republican orators who would play a large role in twentieth-century Indiana politics—notably Albert J. Beveridge, Charles W. Fairbanks, J. Frank Hanly, and James E. Watson.

There was one aspect to the reporting of the 1896 election that caused an uproar in Fort Wayne. The *Journal* printed several "extra" editions as wire service stories speculated on the outcome of the national election. One edition on November 4 featured claims by Democratic national chairman James K. Jones that certain states had been won by Bryan, giving him the election. These statements were false, prompting other newspapers to accuse the *Journal* of trying to profit from incomplete results. "Our compliments to the *Journal* company," the *Fort Wayne Gazette* wrote in its column of editorial comments on November 5. "They have created a demand for papers this morning that will not inure entirely to their profit. When people buy newspapers, they would like to buy one that will at least attempt to give genuine news, instead of bogus dispatches." In another comment on the same page, editor Nathan Leonard alleged, "The flurry started by the Bryanites last evening, asserting that Bryan was probably elected, is open to the charge of being started for the purpose of giving those who had lost heavily on the elections a chance to recoup themselves. It is said that some relatively poor people out in Frenchtown were so carried away that they were betting 5 to 1 on Bryan." The *Fort Wayne Daily News* made similar comments, saying the story was tantamount to knowingly printing false returns.

The *Journal* took umbrage at the pointed remarks on November 6. Moynihan said the newspaper was showing its "characteristic enterprise" in issuing the Wednesday evening special edition. "The claims made by Chairman Jones were current as rumors in every city of the land and the *Journal* met the popular demand for the news by printing an extra that furnished all there was to be known at that hour about the matters in question. If anyone was ill-advised enough to wager money on information so meagre in the face of overwhelming indications to the contrary he cannot hold the *Journal* extra at fault." Then, in keeping with the decorum—or lack of it— of the day, Moynihan then vented his spleen at the editor of the *News*, Jesse Greene. "As to any effort on our part to falsify the returns we pronounce the charge made by the *News* as a deliberate lie. We took occasion a few days ago to inform the editor of the *News* that he is a wanton and unconscionable liar. That he may not now, as he did then, charge that political effect is sought, we repeat it. He is a liar, and he daily gives proof of it."

In his three presidential races, Bryan never lost Allen County or won Indiana. He received 53.2 percent of the total presidential votes cast in the county in 1896, 55.7 percent in a rematch against McKinley in 1900, and 53.9 percent in 1908 against William Howard Taft. Bryan's strength remained in the rural area, particularly in the rematch with McKinley in 1900 when he received almost 60 percent of the ballots cast. On May 8, 1899, the *Fort Wayne Journal* called Bryan "the People's Idol, the American Champion of

Popular Rights." It was an apt term since his fame, perhaps more than his politics, attracted great crowds throughout his career. "Many who had no idea of voting for Bryan came through mere curiosity to hear him."[34]

During the 1890s, Moynihan continued to build and train an exceptional staff of reporters and editors at the 43 East Main Street offices. Among them was Thomas Francis Bresnahan, "one of the keenest minds that ever wrote a line for a linotype in this city."[35] Bresnahan had a flair for writing about politics. He was not opposed to "muckraking," but he was more comfortable with capturing the life of the city. He wrote stories about elections, strikes, and baseball, in addition to his editorials. Fluent in French and German and able to read Greek and Latin, he was the best educated of his colleagues. In a May 26, 1896, letter to his sister, who was away in Chicago, Bresnahan showed his reporter's nose for news, his writer's ability to craft a story, and his editor's discretion for what could be made public in print:

> After the thunder storm, I learned that Dr. McCausland had taken some bandages from Doellering's[36] drug store, but hadn't said where he was going. This was Sunday evening. I had previously learned that Harry Beyerle had fallen down stairs and cut his throat on broken beer bottle. I wasn't quite able to see the whichness of the wherefore, and went to his boarding place, at Moran's, and had a rather exciting interview with Mrs. Moran, who told me he had cut his throat 'accidentally while shaving.' There is a sensation behind the published account of the affair, but it is a dangerous matter to handle. Mrs. Moran is a delusion and a snare, and she has a dog about four sizes larger than a dog with a peaceful mission should grow.

Even though Bresnahan was a favorite of Moynihan's, he could not escape the owner's wrath when it came to money. Once when Moynihan was away, Bresnahan decided that the repair of a typewriter couldn't wait for the editor's return and authorized it be done immediately. When Moynihan found a 50-cent invoice from the repairman, he asked Bresnahan to show him the repaired typewriter. Bresnahan, who knew that nothing good could come from this situation, ushered his boss to the machine in the City Room. Moynihan examined it carefully, picked it up, and "then nestling the machine to his waist, walked out onto the middle of the street and there threw the machine violently to the ground, saying, 'There, Bresnahan, you'll have something more to fix!' "[37]

Yet this was an editor who was said to have spared no expense in getting a story and making certain it was accurate. If A. J. Moynihan wanted a story in the *Journal*, it got there. The same held true for photographs, and he used them increasingly over the years.

Moynihan hired experienced newsmen with strong personalities. William P. Cooper culminated a remarkable newspaper career as managing editor of the *Journal* in 1895. Cooper's parents had settled in Fort Wayne when it was little more than a Miami village, and his father, Henry, was the first schoolteacher in Allen County. William Cooper had served as city editor for the *Gazette* before leaving to attend Dartmouth College. After graduating in 1873, he spent a year at Columbia University studying law before coming back to Fort Wayne to prepare for the bar with local attorneys. However, before taking his exams Cooper chose to return to journalism as city editor of the *Fort Wayne Daily News*. He was later city editor for the *Sentinel*, then the *Gazette* again, and finally the *Journal* before being hired by the *St. Louis Post-Dispatch* in 1888. Named a national correspondent, he reported on many major events, including political conventions, before Moynihan hired him. As might be inferred from his being the only individual to serve as city editor of all of Fort Wayne's four English-language daily newspapers, Cooper was said to be a man of robust convictions. He was widely respected for his simple and direct writing style, his literary tastes (he had been the class poet at Dartmouth), and his sense of humor. Yet there must have been some friction with Moynihan because Cooper's tenure as managing editor was brief and he left the profession to become an agent of New York Life Insurance Company, a position he held until his death at 70 in 1922.

Moynihan's principal foe in the newspaper business was the editor and part-owner of the *Fort Wayne News*, Jesse Greene. Known for vitriolic writing, Greene was a match for Moynihan, and the editorial exchanges between the two men in print were said to make men laugh and women blush. But it was not in jest; rather, it was a bitter enmity. One of the most notorious comments came from Moynihan in his column about his counterpart undergoing surgery for appendicitis at St. Joseph Hospital. The doctors' opening up Mr. Greene yesterday, Moynihan reported, explained the stench in that area of town. Clifford Ward, who was hired as a reporter by Greene in 1923, said Greene was small in stature with a "reverential face" and gray hair. The editor's grit, however, was much more sizable, and he made the *News* into a formidable Republican newspaper before it purchased the *Sentinel* in 1918. Greene died of Bright's disease in October 1923 at the age of 56.

As one commentator on the history of the city's newspapers remarked, it was a time when one didn't have to be crazy to be an editor, but it was not an occupational handicap.[38]

FORT WAYNE GAZETTE.

THE MORNING JOURNAL.

FT. WAYNE JOURNAL=GAZETTE.

THE FORT WAYNE JOURNAL-GAZETTE.

FORT WAYNE JOURNAL-GAZETTE

FORT WAYNE JOURNAL-GAZETTE

THE JOURNAL-GAZETTE

The Journal-Gazette

The Journal Gazette

4

The Acquisition

All successful newspapers are ceaselessly querulous and bellicose. They never defend anyone or anything if they can help it; if the job is forced on them, they tackle it by denouncing someone or something else.

—H. L. Mencken

To the public, the sale of the *Gazette* to the *Journal* occurred unexpectedly. The former's worrisome financial situation was known in the community, but the 1890s had been difficult for all business with an economic downturn, labor strife, and farmer discontent. The *Journal*, in fact, had made an overture a year earlier to combine the newspapers so they could share access to the Associated Press news service. The *Gazette* refused and maintained its exclusive rights to the AP in Fort Wayne. When the *Gazette* was put up for auction in the late spring of 1899, the *Journal* hired a proxy to pursue the property. To do otherwise would have attracted other buyers who would have tried to block the *Journal*'s bid and raise the purchase price. Still, it was a spirited auction until C. C. Miller raised his bid by $50 to $10,050 and Thad Butler, publisher of the *Huntington Herald*, dropped out. Later it was learned that Miller was acting on behalf of the Rockhills and Moynihan.

Occurring almost ten years to the day after the purchase of the *Journal*, the acquisition of the *Gazette* on June 13, 1899, was a major coup for the Rockhill brothers and Moynihan. A major competitor was removed from the marketplace, and there was one less Republican newspaper with which to struggle for public opinion.

The owners of the new combined newspaper scrambled to produce the initial edition for the morning of June 14. First they called Melville K. Stone, the general manager of the AP, to secure the morning newspaper rights to use the wire service. Then they quickly redesigned the front-page nameplate, using an abbreviation for the city name and hyphenating the combined name—"*Ft. Wayne Journal-Gazette*." There apparently was

FT. WAYNE JOURNAL=GAZETTE.

This is the first nameplate of the combined newspapers. Note that the hyphen is actually an equals sign.

some difficulty with the type font that the new owners had on hand, since an equals sign was substituted for the hyphen between *Journal* and *Gazette*. In addition, a period was added to the end of the name. When it came to the masthead on page four, they reversed the order of the names, placing the older *Gazette* on top of the *Journal*. The editorial below the masthead pledged to provide northern Indiana with a newspaper equal to the Midwest's metropolitan newspapers, noting that the *Journal* had recently installed a Cox 6000 duplex press. At the conclusion of the editorial, Moynihan acknowledged the political shift that the acquisition represented for the Republicans in Fort Wayne, Allen County, and northern Indiana. "A great percentage of the readers of the *Gazette* have all along been readers of the *Journal*," he wrote. "Perhaps we have not been as mindful of their feelings as a newspaper should be, but we feel sure that the kindly relations that have existed between the *Journal* and its republican friends will not be disturbed by the *Journal-Gazette*."

It was a generous statement, perhaps as generous as Moynihan could offer. The truth was that there wasn't any appointed Republican newspaper in the region. Both the *Sentinel* and the *Staats-Zeitung* were Democratic, and the *News* was independently minded as was the *Freie Presse*. Not until 1906 would there be a formal Republican standard-bearer in the pages of the *Fort Wayne Daily News*.

Given the man and the times, Moynihan's conciliatory posture toward Republican readers could not last. Both the partisanship of the *Journal-Gazette* and the political tensions of the day were evident in the visit of Theodore Roosevelt to Fort Wayne on October 10, 1900. "The rough rider colonel came, saw and went away again" was a thinly veiled attempt to equate Roosevelt and Caesar that the newspaper used in its lead paragraph about the previous day's series of speeches and street parades. The reporter took exception to the militaristic display that accompanied the visit, noting that previous political rallies had been "purely civic demonstrations in the old democratic way."

As might be expected from a newspaper that endorsed William Jennings Bryan in the 1900 rematch with William McKinley—and in a community that favored Bryan over McKinley four years earlier—the *Journal-Gazette* treated the Roosevelt visit in a somewhat disdainful tone. An examination of the editions on the days preceding the visit fails to show any advance notice of the event. In fact, neither the front page nor the inside news columns of the October 10 *Journal-Gazette* had any mention of when Roosevelt would arrive that day or where his speeches would be given. Instead, the front page included an obligatory story on the Bryan campaign and a local story on the Democrats' Sixth Ward meeting that was so well attended that it was too large for its hall.

The ten-page edition on October 11 seemed entirely devoted to Roosevelt. A two-column sketch of "Governor Roosevelt" dominated the front page. The main headline read, "Crowds See Roosevelt," with the drop headline "Addresses Three Large Audiences during the Evening— The Street Parades Both Failures in Point of Attendance." The main story occupied two full columns on page one and nearly four columns on page two, with extensive verbatim passages from Roosevelt's speech. But there was not one mention that Roosevelt was the Republican vice presidential candidate. All the references used the title of colonel or governor, and it was not until deep into the page two continuation of the story that there was a mention of the Republican ticket, albeit a reference to "McKinley-Roosevelt songs."

While there was substantial reporting on Roosevelt's response to recent Bryan charges and his defense of the military action in the Philippines, the October 11 *Journal-Gazette* found an opportunity to cast doubt on the New York governor under the heading "Rebukes Young America." During some applause for Roosevelt, there was some shrill whistling that affronted the speaker. "In every Fort Wayne audience, there is found the boy who whistles when others applaud, and speakers have always taken this feature good naturedly. Not so the doughty, pugnacious Colonel Roosevelt. At this point in his address, turning in the direction whence the sound came, with a scowl on his face, he declared he wanted 'no hoodlums' to interrupt him while he was talking and asked someone to stop the boy. The colonel dignified the occurrence by making it the occasion of a discourse on fair play and good manners."

There was another controversial incident that brought condemnation onto Fort Wayne. En route from the railroad station to the Princess Rink, where the first rally was held, Roosevelt's party had been struck by some stones. The incident was likely the work of boys, but it infuriated those with Roosevelt, even though the candidate laughed it off. Colonel Curtis Guild Jr. of Boston, who was in the entourage of officials arriving in Fort

Wayne with the candidate, confronted Thomas Bresnahan, the *Journal-Gazette* reporter at the press table, and said that he and Roosevelt had been attacked "with a shower of stones from a crowd of roughs." Guild produced a small stone that he said had wounded him in the face. The reporter noted there didn't seem to be any wound, but he went to investigate. In a two-column separate story on page one beneath Roosevelt's sketch, the reporter related his findings: He had a conversation with the driver of the carriage who said a stone was thrown but no one was hit. The police captain in charge of the escort said there were about fifteen officers walking with the carriage and that three objects were tossed into the carriage but not thrown with any force. The police captain said it was the work of some very small boys.

The *Journal-Gazette* said that Guild and other Republicans seemed too anxious to report the story. The newspaper warned that "in scores of cities to-day people will read of the attack of a wild rabble upon Governor Roosevelt in the streets of Fort Wayne. The city's name will be dragged in the mire and Fort Wayne will be made to appear a den of rowdies and the abode of the scum of creation." Save for the literary hyperbole, the writer was prescient. The initial Associated Press story from Fort Wayne said that Guild had been seriously wounded. It was later corrected after Bresnahan sought out the AP writer with the actual information. While the *Fort Wayne Daily News* pooh-poohed the *Journal-Gazette*'s concerns on October 11, out-of-town newspapers embellished on the incident. The *Chicago Times-Herald* called the incident "a discreditable outbreak, similar in some respects to the attack made upon him at Victor, Colo." U.S. senator Charles Fairbanks, who was in the Roosevelt party, told the Associated Press from Marion he had been told there was "a carefully laid plot on the part of the rough element of the Fort Wayne democracy to break up the meeting as they did in 1884 when Blaine came here to speak. They succeeded then, but this time they were discovered." Harry S. New, a Republican national committeeman from Indiana and future U.S. senator, told the wire service that he saw the rocks thrown and described the man who was the assailant to the police immediately.[1]

It was "yellow journalism" at its apparent best, and the *Journal-Gazette* used the incident to advance its causes. Subsequent editorials criticized Roosevelt's retinue, Republicans in general, and the reporting of other newspapers. Yet the newspaper's criticism of Roosevelt's militarism was more a matter of political, rather than philosophical, difference. In the months leading up to and during the Spanish-American War, the *Journal* had filled its pages with stories, illustrations, and the jingoism that made

Roosevelt and the Rough Riders famous. It contracted with a correspondent with the U.S. Army for stories from Manila on the Philippine insurgency in 1899. When the *Fort Wayne Weekly Journal-Gazette* made its debut on Thursday, June 15, 1899, the sixteen-page and sometimes twenty-four-page newspaper regularly featured full-page illustrated stories about military events. The difference in 1900 was the *Journal-Gazette*'s support of William Jennings Bryan, whose campaign focused on the evils of American imperialism.

The *Journal-Gazette*'s success was more than just the tandem of Moynihan and Bresnahan. The editor had an instinct for identifying talented young men and training them. Edwin C. Hill was a teenager when he went to work for Moynihan at about the time of the merger. Hill left Fort Wayne in 1901 after becoming the newspaper's first industrial editor, and he went on to become a famed national radio reporter whose peers included Edward R. Murrow and HV Kaltenborn as World War II approached. Karl Detzer was a reporter on the *Journal-Gazette* from 1907 to 1916. He was a screenwriter and technical director in Hollywood in the mid-1930s and an editor of the *Reader's Digest* from 1939 to 1942. After World War II, he became publisher of the *Enterprise and Tribune* in Leland, Michigan. His account of Fort Wayne at the turn of the century, "Myself When Young," is redolent with memories of the Gilded Age.

Not all of Moynihan's reporters achieved acclaim in the newspaper industry. Baron Long, the reporter whose drinking habits incurred his editor's wrath, went on to become the leading racetrack and hotel operator in southern California.[2] Ford C. Frick rose from the lowest spot in the *Journal-Gazette* newsroom to the baseball's Hall of Fame. Frick, who was born in Wawaka, Indiana, in December 1894, attended Fort Wayne's International Business College when he worked as the *Journal-Gazette*'s office boy and occasional police reporter in 1910. He also served as its correspondent while earning a degree at DePauw University in Greencastle, Indiana, in 1915. Frick moved to Colorado, where his reporting on the 1921 devastating floods led to a job with the *New York American*. In August 1923, he moved to the *New York Evening Journal*, where he covered baseball's New York Yankees. On that beat, Frick developed a close relationship with Babe Ruth and was the ghostwriter of the Bambino's autobiography. In 1934, Frick was elected National League president, where he was instrumental in the founding of baseball's Hall of Fame. Frick's greatest contribution, though, was his support of Jackie Robinson's heroic integration of the national pastime. In 1951, Frick was elected the third commissioner in the history of Major League Baseball, and he held the post until retiring in 1965. He was elected to the Baseball Hall of Fame in 1970 and died in 1978 at the age of 83.

While Moynihan was exceptional in identifying and developing talented newsmen, he also was savvy when it came to business. He convinced Carl J. Suedhoff to return to Fort Wayne from the *Kalamazoo Gazette* to become his advertising manager. Suedhoff's innovations and persistence enabled the newspaper to gain a larger share of the advertising market. One idea that benefited the community as well as the newspaper was his suggestion that retailers hold a cooperative, semiannual Dollar Day sale. This became the biggest retail shopping event in downtown Fort Wayne in the 1920s. Suedhoff later founded the Inland Chemical Corporation as well as one of Indiana's earliest advertising agencies.

Moynihan's impact on Fort Wayne's newspapers was not only producing an opinionated newspaper and heaping criticism on the competition. In a way, he also played a role in the success of the *Fort Wayne News-Sentinel*, although certainly not intentionally. Moynihan hired Oscar Foellinger in 1905 in the business department. Foellinger helped build the *Journal-Gazette* at the expense of the *News* and the *Sentinel*, rising to the post of business manager.

One example of his success was a promotional campaign in 1909 to celebrate Fort Wayne's industrial growth and link the *Journal-Gazette* to the improved business climate. In one year's time Fort Wayne's number of business and industrial firms had grown 3.6 percent to 1,329. In addition there were almost 300 manufacturing and wholesale establishments within the city. Growth like this, it was thought, warranted the city having a slogan, much like Chicago's "I Will" and Kalamazoo's "We Do." As business manager of the *Journal-Gazette*, Foellinger worked with the Fort Wayne Commercial Club to stage a contest through the newspaper with a $50 prize for the best slogan describing the city. Considerable hoopla generated hundreds of entries. The winning slogan came from Jennie Wilson, a young woman in South Whitley who had composed more than five hundred songs and hymns, although she could not read music. Paralyzed by a spinal disease, she had visited Fort Wayne a few years earlier, and she had drawn upon those memories for her entry. In the interview announcing her award on June 6, 1909—complete with large images of the $25 checks from the Journal-Gazette Company and the Fort Wayne Commercial Club across the top of page one as well as above a smaller photo of the winning contestant—Miss Wilson said she had originally thought of "Fort Wayne, Thrift and Beauty," but had discarded it because it wasn't poetic enough. Instead, she said the idea of

"Fort Wayne—With Might and Main" struck her fancy and apparently the judges' as well. The phrase "with might and main" was an idiom dating from medieval times that meant with all one's strength. The slogan was used extensively through mid-1917, and every edition of the *Journal-Gazette* carried "Fort Wayne—With Might and Main" in its front-page nameplate.

Despite successes like the slogan campaign, Foellinger found it difficult to work for Moynihan. A final blowup came when Foellinger and Frank G. Hamilton, a reporter, developed a plan to reuse the illustrations from local advertising by selling them to businesses in other cities. The reasoning behind such a scheme was simple: an artist's rendition of a young man in a new suit that was published in the *Journal-Gazette* as part of an advertisement could be used by another men's clothing store in another town for another newspaper. This would save the distant store the cost of having its own illustration prepared, and it would provide some additional cash for the two Fort Wayne men. If this was an error in editorial judgment, a greater mistake was made in not telling Moynihan. He fired them both, claiming that Foellinger was stealing his money and Hamilton was stealing his time. Foellinger moved to the West Coast, but in time both he and Hamilton were working for the *Fort Wayne News*, which purchased the *Sentinel* in 1918. When publisher C. F. Bicknell died in 1920, Foellinger became president and general manager of the *News and Sentinel*, which he built into the dominant newspaper of the region. His death on a hunting trip in October 1936 did not impair his newspaper, as his daughter, Helene Foellinger, proved to be a very capable publisher.

While progress was clearly evident in the growth of Fort Wayne in the early 1900s with its new businesses, new residents, and new municipal services, it did not halt one of the scourges of the city: fire. The community's early history was pockmarked with major conflagrations that swept through its business district and neighborhoods.

One of the worst fires occurred in 1908, testing the ability, stamina, and quality of the region's newspapers. In the early morning hours of May 3, as the presses were running with the *Journal-Gazette*'s Sunday edition, Fort Wayne's finest hotel suddenly became an inferno. Flames roared through the five-story Aveline Hotel, leaving twelve people dead and dozens injured. Built during the Civil War and located prominently at Calhoun and Berry streets, the hotel's clientele included opera stars, nationally touring actors, and presidential candidates as well as wealthy businessmen who used the fashionable rooms as a residence and travelers seeking the best accommodations. The fast-moving fire trapped many

AVELINE HOTEL FIRE FT WAYNE IND, MAY 3" 1908.   LONGS NOVELTY HOUSE
2+8

The worst fire in the city's history swept through the fashionable
Aveline Hotel in the early morning hours of May 3, 1908. *Allen County–
Fort Wayne Historical Society.*

guests, some of whom flung themselves from upper-story windows to escape what the county coroner later called "a veritable deathtrap, a hell."

The *Journal-Gazette* staff worked through the night and into midday
Sunday, publishing four extra editions with updated information and photographs. The stark horror of the fire and its toll was fully evident in the
fifth and final edition, whose lead story began, "The Aveline hotel today is
a tomb." Typical of the era, the news pages were filled with short items
from the fire scene, including descriptions of people screaming for help,
only to disappear back into the flames. The news stories sifted through
conflicting reports on the sequence of events and the names of victims or
missing guests.

The newspaper played more than a reportorial role in the Aveline
tragedy. Employees of the *Journal-Gazette* on their way home from work
spotted the fire and alerted the fire department. After assisting in the rescue effort, they returned to the newspaper to work on the extra editions.
Members of the editorial and composing room staff worked an unbroken
stretch of forty hours, finishing Sunday's editions and Monday morning's
newspaper. In the final hours of the marathon effort, the composing room

superintendent was reported to have collapsed and been carried home to recover.

While tragedy has been a dominant subject of newspapers throughout the nation's history, there has been another favorite enterprise in the business: advancing or ending the careers of politicians. Few, however, have played as significant a role as the *Journal-Gazette* did with Thomas Riley Marshall.

Columnist Louis Ludlow first raised the possibility of Marshall's being a good candidate for governor of Indiana, but it was Moynihan and the *Journal-Gazette* who propelled the modest, relatively unknown Hoosier onto the national political stage. In 1908, Moynihan asked his managing editor, Tom Bresnahan, to go to Columbia City's law firm of McNagny and Marshall and interview William McNagny in the belief that the former congressman should receive the Democratic nomination for governor. "Mr. Bresnahan reported that he had seen both members of that important law firm and that it was not McNagny but Marshall that ought to have that nomination." Bresnahan reasoned that McNagny "strictly had a legal mind and not a political one. On the other hand, Marshall was a magnetic personality with a vein of humor that gave him charm entirely lacking in his able partner."[3]

Moynihan had his editor invite Marshall to the newspaper for an interview. It was in Bresnahan's office that a reporter for a Republican newspaper found Tom Marshall, as he was generally known then.

> "Hello, Tom," said the caller. "What are you doing here?"
> With a sort-of guilty smile, Marshall replied: "I am announcing myself as a candidate for the Democratic nomination by the state convention for governor."
> "Go to it," said the caller. "If we have to have a democratic governor, you suit us better than anybody else, and we republicans would just as leave beat you in November as anybody."[4]

Marshall prevailed in securing the nomination when he was the compromise candidate between two party factions. The November gubernatorial election pitted the polished congressman James E. Watson against the down-home, commonsense Marshall. The national tickets were led by Republican William Howard Taft, endorsed by President Theodore Roosevelt, who did not then want a second term, and William Jennings Bryan. The outcome in Indiana was very Republican in 1908. Marshall went to bed on election night believing he was defeated. His wife, Lois, thought otherwise and awoke him the next day with the news that he was governor-elect. While the Republicans swept almost all of the national and state races in Indiana, Marshall was seemingly unaffected by it. His 10,000-vote victory over Watson was in sharp contrast to Taft's nearly 15,000-vote margin at the top of the ticket.

The Republican landslide didn't reach Allen County. The Democratic candidates for president, governor, congressman, state senator, and state representatives all won handily. Marshall won every ward in Fort Wayne and sixteen of nineteen townships in the county.

Rarely if ever genteel in his criticism, Moynihan was hardly ever reserved in his praise. On November 5, two days after the election, the front page of the *Journal-Gazette* was dominated by two-column sketches of President-elect Taft and Vice President-elect James Sherman. But beneath them was a headline in bold type: "Thomas R. Marshall for President in 1912." Without a single day in statewide office, Marshall was being touted as a national figure. The governor-elect, the Indianapolis-datelined story maintained, "possesses qualities which make him peculiarly available as a presidential candidate. He has not been conspicuous in politics and is not hampered by factional enmities."

Moynihan was not one to dwell on the past, either. The comments in the editorial column on November 5 included a tribute to Bryan ("He has been the foremost man of his generation and an apostle of righteousness") and a call to "Start the Marshall boom now."

Marshall's election was a bitter pill for many Indiana Republicans, whose party had held the governorship for a dozen years. The incumbent governor, J. Frank Hanly, at first refused to even attend Marshall's inauguration. Marshall, known for his wit, wrote later that his predecessor seemed assured "that my election would blight the crops, blot out the churches, and destroy the civic sense of justice in the state."[5] His term of office wasn't that onerous, but Marshall found himself under frequent attack. The *Journal-Gazette* supported Marshall and touted him as a potential favorite-son national candidate. In 1912, the newspaper began printing "For President—Thomas R. Marshall, governor of Indiana" below the page four masthead.

The early 1900s have been called the golden age of editorial cartoonists,[6] and the *Journal-Gazette*, while not in the same league as the *Chicago Tribune* and the *Washington Star*, joined the trend. Moynihan hired Emil G. Hoefel in 1904, using his work in a very political manner. Hoefel's page one editorial cartoons often attacked the Republicans and the *Fort Wayne News*. The drawing was harsh and the message harsher. It was common for Hoefel to have two large panels, separated by an explanatory paragraph or story from the *News*. The issue of February 4, 1904, titled

One of the earlier editorial cartoons by Emil Hoefel that was critical of the Republican response to an outbreak of typhoid fever in connection with impure city water in 1904. Note the cartoonist's signature bird with the pointer.

"Before and after Taking," concerned an outbreak of typhoid fever. The top panel re-created the *News'* reporting on Republican promises for clean municipal water in 1903 while the lower panel showed a skeletal Grim Reaper driving a hearse pulled by a monstrous creature labeled "Typhoid Bacilli." The editorial comment beneath simply read: "How the Republicans fulfill their promises to the people." Hoefel's cartoons often included a bird caricature with a hooked bill and one glaring, judgmental eye. Hoefel, who also produced sketches of the city neighborhoods in the 1904 floods for the front page of the newspaper, seems to have spent only one year in Fort Wayne. Phil Porter was another apparently local political cartoonist whose work appeared in the *Journal-Gazette* in 1908, but not thereafter.

Edgar F. Schilder's work appeared in the *Journal-Gazette* in 1914 and 1915. His works were often studies, such as a little boy labeled "The American Youth" staring up at a portrait of Lincoln in a front-page editorial cartoon titled "His Ideal" in the *Fort Wayne Weekly Journal-Gazette* on the anniversary of Lincoln's birth in 1914. He also contributed to a page one feature in the daily newspaper entitled "Someone You Know." The series of articles, which anchored the lower left portion of the front page, introduced a recognizable, but not prominent, individual in the community. The format was a head-and-shoulders photo of the individual with the background drawn by Schilder. His editorial cartoons disappear from the *Journal-Gazette* after 1915, and his name does not appear in subsequent city directories.

The approach of the 1912 presidential nominating conventions prompted the *Journal-Gazette* to carry a front-page story almost every day on how Marshall would handle key issues if elected president of the United States. For twenty-nine ballots, Indiana's delegation cast its vote for Marshall. On the thirtieth ballot, its decision to transfer its support from Marshall to Woodrow Wilson gave the New Jersey governor the lead in delegates over House Speaker Champ Clark of Missouri. When Wilson won the nomination on the forty-sixth ballot, he wanted House Majority Leader Oscar Underwood of Alabama as his running mate. The congressman refused, however, and Marshall was selected to be the Democratic vice presidential candidate. He never forgot the support from Fort Wayne and Moynihan, whom he later recalled as "the most loyal soul who ever lived on earth."[7]

While the 1912 election presented a pivotal choice on the nation's economic policy, a Democratic victory in the race for the White House was foreordained by the rupture in Republican relations. Roosevelt had denounced Taft for being too conservative, and he tried to wrest the Republican nomination away from him at the party's national convention in June. But the president and the Republican National Committee thwarted his effort and Roosevelt bolted the convention to start his own party. Known more commonly as the Bull Moose Party because of Roosevelt's comment early in the campaign that he felt healthy as a moose, the Progressive Party captured a sizable portion of the Republican Party base. But even with California governor Hiram Johnson as his running mate, Roosevelt could not overtake Wilson. Roosevelt finished second in November with 4.12 million votes (88 electoral votes) to Wilson's 6.28 million votes (435 electoral votes). Taft was a distant third with 3.48 million votes (8 electoral votes).

Allen County followed the same order: Wilson 8,659 votes, Roosevelt 4,246 votes, and Taft 3,423 votes. The surprising local result in 1912 was that Socialist Party candidate Eugene V. Debs received 1,152 ballots, more than the total number of votes he received there in his three previous presidential candidacies combined. If there was one point of agreement among all of Fort Wayne's daily newspapers—Republican, Democrat, and German—it was that they despised the socialist from Terre Haute.[8] Debs, however, received more of the national vote (6 percent) than any previous socialist candidate for president.

The *Journal-Gazette* had barely finished saluting Wilson and his Hoosier vice president at their inauguration in March 1913 when, as artist and historian Bert Griswold wrote, "somebody tipped over the entire year's supply of rainfall and for a time it looked as if the rushing waters would flush us off the map."[9] A storm of unprecedented proportions swept over the city, sending the rivers into the neighborhoods, leaving 6 dead and more than 15,000 homeless. From its earliest settlement, Fort Wayne had been vulnerable to spring flooding. The St. Mary's River rises in Ohio and flows north-northwest to join the St. Joseph River, which originates in Michigan and flows westward. The two rivers wind together through Fort Wayne with relatively small natural embankments before forming the Maumee River, which reaches Lake Erie.

The massive size of the 1913 storm system (it was once described as making a vast inland ocean from Illinois to Pennsylvania), combined with the limits of communication at the time, made the flooding a difficult story to capture in the daily newspaper. The storm system began on Easter Sunday, March 23, 1913, with seven violent tornados in Nebraska and Iowa. It moved quickly across the Mississippi River and into the upper Midwest. Fort Wayne was inundated. Almost five inches of rain

HIGH WATER ALONG
ST. JOE BLVD. LAKESIDE
FT. WAYNE, IND
MARCH. 25. 1913
STANDISH, PHOTO

A massive storm flooded the Midwest in late March 1913, including Fort Wayne. A day after this photograph was taken, the earthen dike along St. Joe Boulevard broke, sending water into the neighborhood and residents fleeing for their lives. *Allen County–Fort Wayne Historical Society.*

were recorded between 7:25 a.m. March 23 and 9:45 p.m. March 25. Three inches of snow fell on March 26 as the St. Mary's and St. Joseph rivers continued to rise. The Maumee River rose twelve feet in a day and crested at twenty-six feet, one inch on March 26, still a record. Water covered the Nebraska and Bloomingdale neighborhoods as well as the Spy Run area. In the middle of the night, the earthen dike along St. Joe Boulevard broke in two places, causing many residents in the Lakeside section to flee. When it was discovered that the swollen St. Mary's River had driven the occupants of the Allen County Orphanage to the second floor, a rowboat was dispatched the morning of March 26 to ferry the children to safety. But in one of the trips, the current spun the boat and dumped three young girls into the river. Their bodies were found three days later. Three other fatalities were recorded, including a four-year-old boy who fell into the river on March 29.

The frantic feeling that prevailed in the city is visible on the front page in the *Journal-Gazette.* The March 25 "Extra" had three streamer headlines, with one above the nameplate reporting that the flood had shut down the city's power plants, "plunging the city into stygian darkness." Four photographs of the city's flooded streets and homes were on the front page, along with wire service stories on the death toll in Omaha, Nebraska, and Terre Haute, Indiana. The March 26 edition showed the confusion in the catastrophe. The main headline read, in part, "300 Dead at Peru"; however, the story in the left-hand column was topped with three stacked bulletins giving conflicting versions of the situation. More than half of page two was filled with random vignettes: earthen dikes giving way, the railroad using handcars to transport passengers from the east side of Fort Wayne to the depot, and hospitals turning away patients because of a lack of potable water.

The front pages concerning the 1913 flood made extensive use of local photographs, unlike the 1904 flood for which the *Journal-Gazette* used images prepared by an artist. Many of the photographs are dark, reflecting the fact that the morning newspaper was trying to provide the latest images as night fell on the stricken city.

This is an interesting aspect to all of the reporting in the 1913 flood. Unlike newspaper reports of flooding in a later era when there were fewer, more focused stories, the 1913 editions with their haphazard accounts and stark photography are still vibrant. There is drama in the writing about rescues as well as nuance in the details of people's reactions. There aren't any long quotes from elected officials; instead, the sources of the information are those individuals in harm's way, like policemen, street workers, and store owners. It reads today as if it were new, as if it were still news.

The breakneck pace and extraordinary demands placed on the newsroom by the flood may have strained Moynihan, for within three years he would be so weakened that he had to give up his beloved *Journal-Gazette*. There was another issue, though, that required attention and would bring about great changes: the gathering war clouds in Europe.

Fort Wayne, a Chicago newspaper once stated with the authoritarian manner of big city newspapers examining smaller communities, was "a most German town." At the time of its writing, the assertion was seen as a compliment to the cultural state of the community. As the United States was pulled into World War I, the statement became a negative.

The German influence in Fort Wayne and Allen County was substantial in the early twentieth century. Henry Rudisill and his wife were the first German-born settlers in the town of 150 people in 1829. The town rapidly attracted farmers, craftsmen, and tradespeople. The political turmoil across Europe in 1848 and the growing dominance of Prussia among the German states contributed to another exodus, particularly young intellectuals. Nearly 35 percent of the immigrants to the United States in the 1850s were German-speaking men and women. Those who settled in Fort Wayne were from towns and farms in Baden, Hanover, Württemberg, Prussia, Bavaria, Saxony, and Hesse-Cassel. Many were Lutherans from Catholic-dominated areas, and the backwoods of Indiana attracted many missionaries. The Reverend Friedrich C. D. Wyneken, who arrived in Fort Wayne in 1838, is credited with organizing the Lutheran Church west of the Appalachian Mountains. "His letters from America, which were published in Germany between 1838 and 1842, did more to awaken the German Lutherans to the spiritual needs of their American brethren than any other message or effort."[10] Wyneken's successor in Fort Wayne, the Reverend Dr. Wilhelm Sihler, helped form what is known today as the Missouri Synod at a meeting in Fort Wayne in July 1846.

The great migration of German-speaking people to the United States is often dated from 1870 to 1890 when more than 2.1 million immigrants were registered as "German." This represented 27.5 percent of the total immigration to the United States in those two decades. However, the fact that the German influx in the Fort Wayne area began earlier can be seen in the federal census. In 1860 Allen County recorded 4,150 German residents, second only to Vanderburgh County in southern Indiana. Twenty years later, the size of the German-born population is the dominant segment among immigrants. The 1880 census found 3,782 residents, or 41.1 percent of the immigrant population, were German-born. More than 38 percent of those German-born reported they were from Prussia.[11] In 1910, the census reported 5,599 of Allen County's 62,177 residents were born in Germany, which was the third highest in the state, trailing Marion and St. Joseph counties. The German American influence is not fully represented in these figures, since they do not take into account the thousands born in the United States of German heritage who were residing in Fort Wayne and the rest of Allen County.

Another indicator of the substantial presence of German-speaking citizens was the number of newspapers that were viewed as "a trusted and benevolent guide in a bewildering new country."[12] There were at least three started in Fort Wayne before the Civil War, and at least six more appeared after 1870. Among them was the *Freie Presse*, operated by Herman Mackwitz, which would buy the *Staats-Zeitung* and advertise in 1915 that the circulation of its six-day evening paper was 4,152, adding that "Fort Wayne's 78,000 Population Is Sixty per Cent. German."[13]

German Lutherans were in the majority, with German Catholics second. There were other German Protestant groups, notably in the Reformed Church and the Presbyterian Church. German-born politicians were dominant, and the names of some of Fort Wayne's mayors in the late nineteenth and early twentieth centuries speak clearly to the political influence of the German American community: Zollinger, Muhler, Berghoff. This meant that most political appointments in the city were awarded to Democrats of German heritage. Some classified advertisements for jobs in downtown Fort Wayne stores stated that only German-speaking men would qualify as applicants. The political foundation of the Democratic Party in the city and the county was built upon the anti-British sentiments of the German American and Irish American communities. For example, the *Journal* in early 1890 was quick to point out in its editorial column that the new chancellor of Germany, Leo von Caprivi, "traces his lineage back to Irish blood."[14] In the same vein, there were public rallies and lengthy articles supporting the Boers in their war with Great Britain in South Africa. When the North American Gymnastic Union—formally known as the Turnerbund—brought about 50,000 participants to Fort Wayne for its quadrennial competition in May 1897, the *Gazette* printed the front-page story's headline in German.[15]

It would be hard to overestimate the impact of the German American–owned and –operated factories, stores, hotels, and restaurants on Fort Wayne. The economic influence was matched by the cultural influence found in the theaters, the social clubs, and grand settings such as Germania Park. In the first decade of the twentieth century, it was possible "in Fort Wayne to grow up into adulthood in an almost pure German culture."[16]

There was resistance to assimilation within the national and local German American community. In 1903, Fort Wayne formed a chapter of the National German American Alliance whose goal was to bring together "citizens of German descent to participate in traditional German activities, and to protect these activities from nativistic attacks."[17] The growing prohibitionist movement reflected Anglo-American mores and sparked a widespread denunciation of German beer drinking on Sundays. In 1911, the Indiana legislature passed the Proctor Laws, which allowed individual towns to vote on banning the public sale of liquor. Full prohibition in Indiana followed seven years later, putting many skilled brewery workers and tavern keepers of German heritage out of work in Fort Wayne.

The advent of World War I in Europe in 1914 brought a government-enforced suppression of the German character and culture. President Wilson's stance of neutrality angered German Americans who saw the

French and British as the aggressors. In April 1917, the government declared that all German-born men were to be considered "enemy aliens," regardless of the length of time they had lived in the United States. They were required to register with federal authorities and to surrender any firearm, implement of war, aircraft or wireless apparatus, and any form of cipher code. This edict was widely ignored, forcing Wilson to issue a second edict requiring all German-born men to register at their local police headquarters. The *Journal-Gazette* urged the German American populace to comply, calling the Wilson proclamation reasonable. It noted that the surrender of any weapon would not be publicized. It was an unpopular position. According to one historian, Allen County was reputed to have the largest percentage of registration dodgers in the state.[18] In May 1918, Wilson added German-born women to the regulation edict. The result was greater indignation among German residents, yet this also caused more to pursue the naturalization process that led to U.S. citizenship.

The war brought more pressure on the German-speaking institutions. Churches were encouraged to halt the use of the language in liturgy and sermons. The German wording for the Stations of the Cross was removed from German Catholic churches in 1917. Lutheran teachers were forced to halt mandatory instruction in the German language in 1918, ending almost a half-century tradition in their Fort Wayne parochial schools.

The *Journal-Gazette* had a history of skepticism about attempts to "Americanize" the entire population of the nation. The *Gazette* had chastised the *Fort Wayne Daily Democrat* in 1868 for "continued and unjustifiable defamation" of the city's German citizens whose main "crime" was apparently favoring Republican candidates. In 1889 Wisconsin's passage of the Bennett Law, which mandated the teaching of English reading and writing in parochial schools, sparked a national campaign aimed specifically at German schools. German Americans in Fort Wayne joined in the denunciation of the law. The *Journal* sided with the German American position, in sharp contrast to the position taken by the *Gazette*.

News reports at the outset of World War I drew cries of protest from German Americans in Fort Wayne. The *Journal-Gazette* was sympathetic to the early complaints that the news from the war was one-sided. It pointed out that its stories were clearly labeled as dispatches via London or via Paris and that a bias should be assumed. An editorial on August 14, 1914, entitled "Censorship in This Country, Too?" explained how British and French forces controlled the cables and their censors determined what war news would be released. Later developments in the war—such as the occupation of Belgium and France as well as the indiscriminate sinking of ships by German submarines—made the newspaper less sympathetic.

The antagonism of the German American population in Fort Wayne and Allen County upset the political balance of power, sending traditional German Democrats into the Republican ranks. An analysis of the 1890–1914 elections by Clifford H. Scott, professor of history at IPFW, indicates that about 60 percent of the local German American voting population cast their ballots for Democratic candidates, whereas about 30 percent supported Republicans and 10 percent voted for independent or socialist candidates. The election of 1916 was a clear indicator that there had been a change in the political makeup of Allen County.

But in 1916, the time of change had arrived at the *Journal-Gazette*, too. Moynihan suffered a nervous breakdown and was advised by his doctor to quit his job. He called upon Lewis Ellingham in Indianapolis and said, "I've had it in my mind that when I quit you should take up my work and go on with it. Would you like to own the *Journal-Gazette*?" Ellingham responded that it "would be the dream of my life" to operate the Fort Wayne newspaper, and the deal was completed in June.[19]

After an unprecedented twenty-seven years as editor, Moynihan moved to California, where the climate was expected to be better for him. Less than a year later, however, he died of a heart attack in Long Beach at the age of 61. The so-called "Allen County Bosses" of 1890—Zollinger, Rockhill, and Moynihan—were all gone. While still supporting the Democratic Party, the *Journal-Gazette* entered a trying time in its existence.

FORT WAYNE GAZETTE.

THE MORNING JOURNAL.

FT. WAYNE JOURNAL=GAZETTE.

THE FORT WAYNE JOURNAL-GAZETTE.

FORT WAYNE JOURNAL-GAZETTE

FORT WAYNE JOURNAL-GAZETTE

THE JOURNAL-GAZETTE

The
Journal-Gazette

The Journal-Gazette

The
Journal Gazette

5

After Andy

History is the torch that is meant to illuminate the past, to guard
us against the repetition of our mistakes of other days. We cannot
join in the rewriting of history to make it conform to our comfort
and convenience.

—Claude G. Bowers

Lewis G. Ellingham was 48 when he assumed control of the *Fort
Wayne Journal-Gazette* in 1916. He was not a novice to the newspaper
business or to the world of politics. Ellingham had operated a smaller
newspaper and been elected to state office earlier in his career. He was
among the best prepared owners for taking control of the *Journal-Gazette*,
as an anecdote in a book promoting the municipality indicated:

In 1898, Ellingham was the sole proprietor of the *Decatur Democrat*.
One morning he turned to a new reporter and asked for the story about
the fire that had occurred the previous evening.

"What fire—the one that burned up the livery stable, the grocery
store, and the shoe shop last night?"

"Yes," Ellingham said. "Where is it?"

"Why," said the young reporter, "everybody in town was watchin' 'em
burn up, so I couldn't see any sense in wasting any space tellin' 'em about
it."[1]

That was not the answer Ellingham wanted, and the story was written
thoroughly. Born in Wells County on February 23, 1868, to a couple who
emigrated from Scotland to Indiana, Ellingham was raised in Bluffton and
worked on the town newspaper while in school. At age 19 he managed to
buy the Geneva, Indiana, *Herald*, which he operated for three years. The
cost was $300. Ellingham sold the Geneva newspaper and bought the
Winchester Democrat and operated it for three years before starting the *De-*

catur Democratic Press. He purchased the competing *Decatur Weekly Democrat* in 1896 and combined the newspapers under the name *Decatur Daily Democrat* in January 1903. Ellingham's prominence in the party rose. In 1896 he was a delegate to the Democratic National Convention, where he heard Bryan's "Cross of Gold" speech. He served as Eighth District chairman in 1906 and 1908.

With Marshall as governor, Ellingham ran for secretary of state in 1910 and surprisingly led the ticket, winning by 13,000 votes. He was reelected in 1912 by a greater margin. At the end of the second term, Ellingham looked for other alternatives, and Moynihan invited him to come to Fort Wayne in 1916. He saw the *Journal-Gazette* as a "splendid exponent of the city's progressive character" and purchased the newspaper with Edward G. Hoffman, an attorney who rose from Democratic precinct committeeman to member of the national committee.

It was a contentious time to jump into a new community. The national presidential campaign was a closely contested affair, and feelings were strong in Fort Wayne. Most Americans opposed entering the war. President Woodrow Wilson emphasized his efforts to maintain U.S. neutrality, even though he had doubts about continuing that position in the face of continued attacks on U.S. shipping by German submarines. The Republicans nominated the respected and conservative Charles Evans Hughes, who stepped down from the U.S. Supreme Court to run for the presidency. His position on Germany was probably similar to Wilson's, but he was eventually seen as the "war candidate" because of a third individual who was not even running for president. Theodore Roosevelt had turned down the Progressive Party's nomination in order to try to reunify the Republican Party, which he had torn asunder four years earlier. Roosevelt campaigned for the United States to become involved in the war. "Col. Roosevelt Scores the Germans. No Room in This Country for Anything but Real Americans" was the *Journal-Gazette* headline on November 4, 1916. Ironically, it would be one of Roosevelt's protégés who would decide the election.

Unlike other presidential elections in which the *Journal-Gazette* was supporting the trailing candidate, the newspaper acknowledged that Wilson was in trouble. The editors also knew why—the disaffection of the voters with a German background. The leader of the Democratic Party in Indiana, Senator Thomas Taggart, was told that men of German heritage who had been Democratic voters were "not only against him [Wilson] but so much so that I am sure they cannot be turned back."[2] The *Journal-Gazette* warned its German American readers, who resented Wilson's treatment of "enemy aliens" after war broke out in Europe, that they were being deceived by the Republicans. Hughes didn't really support an arms embargo, as he had claimed, the newspaper asserted in its editorials. This argument was to little or no avail.

The newspaper focused on what it saw as inconsistencies in other parts of the Republican candidate's campaign. Hughes's visit to Fort Wayne in late September prompted a series of blistering editorials. *Cowardice* was the term the *Journal-Gazette* applied to Hughes for failing to address a key issue for the railway center of Fort Wayne. In August as a national railroad strike loomed, Wilson signed the Adamson Act, which provided an eight-hour workday and time-and-a-half overtime pay for all railroad employees. Hughes, after a week's period, declared the Adamson Act was "a step in the pathway of disaster and pregnant with a threat of civil war" for the nation. The *Journal-Gazette* argued on September 23 that Hughes should have shown his presidential caliber by explaining his position during his Fort Wayne stop. "Here was the place to tell the railroad brotherhoods that they bludgeoned the government of the United States. Here was the place to tell the workingmen that their eight-hour-day propaganda was evil. He did not do it. He feared to do it."

On the final weekend before the 1916 election, Wilson asked the vice president to campaign in Indiana. While Marshall attracted thousands to a Saturday night rally at the Palace Theatre in Fort Wayne, it too was to no avail in Allen County. Hughes and his running mate, Charles Fairbanks of Indiana, defeated the incumbent president in the county by 1,441 votes. It was only the second Republican presidential victory in Allen County in the fifteen presidential elections since 1860. Hughes won Indiana by less than 7,000 votes—the first time Indiana had not voted for the winning presidential candidate since 1876.

Nationally, the race between Wilson and Hughes came down to the votes in one state, California. The early editions of the *Journal-Gazette* went to press before the tally was completed in the West and featured a front-page portrait of Hughes and Fairbanks with the overline "Probable Victors in National Election." An extra edition off the press after 5 a.m. replaced the engraving with one of Wilson and Marshall. Beneath a banner headline with the story's text set seven columns wide, the Associated Press reported that Wilson had been reelected. It was correct if a bit premature. The election was finally decided in California where Governor Hiram Johnson, who had been Roosevelt's vice presidential candidate on the Progressive Party ticket in 1912, was running for the U.S. Senate. Hughes slighted Johnson in the campaign, and with a Roosevelt-like pique, the Californian delivered the state—and the presidency—to Wilson by 4,000 votes.

In Allen County, however, the die was cast. The Democratic Party's past powerhouse in presidential elections was wounded, and subsequent developments would spell its end.[3] The declaration of war by the United States against the Central Powers on April 6, 1917, cemented the change in the county's political composition. The Republican Party was in the driver's seat, and so was patriotism. More than 40,000 were said to have participated in a parade and rally in downtown Fort Wayne two weeks after the nation entered the war. The propaganda was hardly subtle. A full-page Red Cross advertisement seeking $1 memberships appeared on December 17, 1917, with the headline "Which Are You For?" Beneath it were two drawings, one with a nurse spoon-feeding a wounded U.S. soldier with the caption "The Angel of Mercy" and the other with a German soldier strangling a young woman as a child looks on with the caption "or The Fiends of Hell." The text read: "Every loyal man, woman and child in all America is on the side of justice and mercy and against the hideous barbarities that the Kaiser has instructed his men to commit."

An incident in December 1917 was indicative of the community's attitude. A man was seen walking along the alleys of downtown and making sketches of buildings. A number of citizens became alarmed and called the police, who arrested the man on a charge of being a German spy. When news of this circulated through downtown, a crowd gathered outside the police department with the intent of making certain the "spy" was summarily punished. Mayor William Hosey intervened and had the individual brought to his office. The suspect explained that he was employed by a fire insurance firm in Chicago and that his maps were used for determining the risk presented by the buildings and the premiums that businesses would pay for coverage. He was released, and Hosey calmed the crowd by praising their patriotic vigilance and encouraging them to continue their good work.[4]

The two daily newspapers covered the war as best as they could, selecting from often conflicting wire service reports and commentaries. The *Journal-Gazette* editors were proud that it did not print the news of the "false Armistice" about two weeks before the actual cessation of the war. They did not want to miss the real story and maintained a crew round-the-clock to produce an edition when the war ended in 1919. At 1:50 a.m. on November 11, the AP wire machines began ringing their bells with the "Flash" that the war was over. Factory whistles blew throughout the city, and people rushed from their homes to celebrate. By 3 a.m., ten

Thanks to the timing of the armistice, the *Journal-Gazette* was able to publish the news of the end of the war long before the competition.

hours before any other newspaper in the area, the *Journal-Gazette* was on the street with a special edition that featured a three-and-a-half-inch-high headline in red ink reading, "HUNS QUIT!" The next day's edition captured the city reaction with its headline: "Joy Reigns When News Brings Peace."

During the war, Ellingham refined the newspaper, adding features, including columnists covering national topics. He began to de-emphasize the *Fort Wayne Weekly Journal-Gazette*, and it was discontinued after 1919. Ellingham hired skilled writers and editors. Few men who came into the editor's chair at the *Journal-Gazette* had the political experience of Claude G. Bowers. Fewer still went on to national and international prominence than this native of central Indiana.

When Bowers arrived in Fort Wayne in 1917 at the age of 38 to be the editorial writer for the *Journal-Gazette*, he already had had an enviable career in journalism and politics. Growing up in the 1880s in Whitestown, about twenty miles northwest of Indianapolis, Bowers was raised in a very active political community, one that was overwhelmingly Democratic. Nearly seventy years later he recalled being among the 10-year-olds packed in a wagon cheering for the candidacy of Grover Cleveland. But it was in Indianapolis, where Bowers lived from 1891 to 1903, that he gained his political education. He remembered being a newspaper boy for the *Indianapolis Sentinel* and being thrilled "through and through" upon reading William Jennings Bryan's "Cross of Gold" speech from the 1896 Democratic National Convention. He developed his rhetorical skills by observing some of the best orators of the era in Indianapolis, including a former president, Benjamin Harrison; a future governor, U.S. senator, and biographer, Albert J. Beveridge; and a former candidate for vice president and later a U.S. senator, John W. Kern. Bowers said it was Bryan's speech that set his course for life: "From that hour I thought in terms of politics."[5]

At age 21, Bowers was hired as an editorial writer for the *Indianapolis Sentinel*, the newspaper of the Democratic Party. He had written two articles on Jefferson and Hamilton for an obscure magazine and received rave reviews for a political speech in Lebanon, Indiana. Reports of the speech reached Jacob Piatt Dunn, one of the leading men of political letters in the Progressive era, who apparently was weary of being the sole editorial writer on the *Indianapolis Sentinel* and hired Bowers in order to take a vacation. Dunn was soon thereafter appointed city comptroller and, as Bowers recalls in his posthumously published memoirs, "I got his editorial job with the understanding that if the Democrats won the city election I would remain, otherwise he would return."[6]

Claude Bowers, editor, author, political pundit, and U.S. ambassador. *Vigo County Historical Society.*

There was no attempt to conceal the partisan nature of newspapers in the late nineteenth century. As Ray Boomhower noted in his biography of Dunn, the newspapers' role was to be the primary source of information about politics for the citizenry. The *Indianapolis Journal* was the Republican newspaper, and the *Sentinel* was staunchly in the Democratic camp. To be informed, a citizen read both but usually believed one or the other. As Bowers pointed out, "These papers did not pretend to political impartiality, and their news stories, while colored, deceived no one. With papers representing both parties, the public had the advantage of a debate, so important in a democracy."[7] Later Bowers would lament the demise of partisan newspapers. In the 1950s he worried that "the mass media of communication were passing into the possession of one school of thought and economic group."[8]

Bowers was not a natural writer at first. In his memoirs he notes that he would take his ardently written editorials to the *Sentinel*'s owner and editor, Samuel Morss. Invariably, Morss would read them, chuckle, and say, "Well, I don't know exactly what you're trying to say, but they sound all right, so send them down" to the composing room.[9]

In 1903, Bowers left Indianapolis to work for the *Terre Haute Gazette*, and when that paper was sold, he joined the *Terre Haute Star* as an editorial writer. It was here that Bowers became friends with Eugene V. Debs, the leader of the Socialist Party in the United States, and with novelist Theodore Dreiser. It is also in Terre Haute that he was nominated to run for Congress on the Democratic ticket in 1904. The campaign was an education, since some communities in the district were so strongly Republican that Bowers feared for his safety when he campaigned in them. For seven weeks, Bowers spoke every afternoon and evening, reaching every township in the seven-county district. He also maintained his newspaper job, writing nonpolitical editorials for the *Star* each night after the last meeting. Although he was defeated in the Republican landslide, Bowers was unanimously renominated for the congressional race in 1906. He lost again.

The campaign for U.S. senator in 1910 pitted John Kern against Albert Beveridge. Kern was known for his campaigning, while Beveridge was renowned for his eloquence. Years later Bowers would write the biography of each man. Kern emerged victorious and surprised Bowers by asking him to be his secretary in Washington. While planning to serve only a year, Bowers remained with Kern throughout the senator's six-year term, which coincided with the Democratic Party's revival under Woodrow Wilson. In doing so, Bowers had an opportunity to learn from the great debaters of the time. He gained a national prominence in the party, especially since Kern was the majority leader who struggled to move Wilson's programs through the Senate in the period before the United States entered World War I.

Kern was defeated for reelection in 1916; however, before Kern's term was completed Bowers was offered a post with the *Fort Wayne Journal-Gazette*, probably at the urging of his friend Ed Hoffman. Bowers described the *Journal-Gazette* as the foremost Democratic paper in Indiana at the time, "and so, without regret, I left Washington and turned back to my native state."[10]

At the *Journal-Gazette*, Bowers's position was officially listed as editorial writer, but as he stated in his memoirs, "since I selected my own subjects and treated them in my own way without consultation, it was more nearly that of an editor in chief."[11] He joined the staff a few days before the United States entered the war, which became the primary focus of his early work in Fort Wayne. Later he became a vigorous advocate for the League of Nations.

Bowers's political expertise also was tapped by the party during his Fort Wayne period. The party's state convention in 1918 was among the earliest in the nation, and Bowers was asked to be chairman of the platform committee. As such, he was asked to incorporate resolutions dealing with postwar policies and was told that the request came from the president himself. Also at that convention, Bowers was offered the nomination for secretary of state, which he declined.

Bowers continued to play significant roles for the Democratic Party, particularly in support of Wilson's policies. His Sunday columns—under the heading "Kabbages and Kings," a reference to a poem in Lewis Carroll's "Through the Looking Glass"—provided an unusually insightful perspective into Washington affairs at a level of sophistication that was rare for a small midwestern newspaper. The column was part commentary on contemporary politics and part lesson in political history. It often ran more than fifty inches in length, covering several national and international issues. Bowers wrote six to fourteen editorials daily, and after dinner with colleagues at Dutch Heine's tavern or indulging in fried chicken at the YMCA cafeteria, he would read proofs until 8 p.m.

It was during this period "in a tiny, dusty room on the ground floor of the *Journal-Gazette*, writing to suit myself and without serious concern about a publisher, I wrote 'The Party Battles of the Jackson Period' after the paper had been put to bed."[12] The book was a lengthy examination of Andrew Jackson's political history, very much in keeping with Bowers's appreciation of the principles of Jefferson and Jackson. Bowers argued for much of his adult life that Alexander Hamilton and then later the Republican Party had advocated a government that served those with money and that Jefferson and Jackson had advocated a government that served the people. The original manuscript was lengthy, and Houghton Mifflin wanted it condensed to one volume, a request to which Bowers acceded, much to his lasting regret.

The book was popularly received, and it changed the course of Bowers's career. The reviews drew the attention of the *New York World*, the famed liberal newspaper begun by Joseph Pulitzer, and its editors (including Frank Cobb and Herbert Bayard Swope) began reading the *Journal-Gazette* closely. Bowers was invited to a meeting in Indianapolis where he was offered a job as editorial writer on the *Evening World*. He accepted the offer to start in New York on December 1, 1923, with some misgivings, thinking that it would be an abandonment of all political activities and the state he knew so well.

Bowers was wrong in this assessment, especially with regard to politics. He developed great friendships while with the *World*, from politicians to playwrights to philanthropists to presidents. Bowers published his second book at this time, a study of Jefferson and Hamilton and their dispute over the country's direction at its founding. He was the keynote speaker of the Democratic National Convention in 1928. He became a close friend of Franklin Delano Roosevelt, who named him ambassador to Spain shortly before the outbreak of the Spanish Civil War. In 1939 he was named ambassador to Chile, a post he held for fourteen years.

Bowers's reputation has been diminished over the years because of his partisanship and because of his racist perspective in the one book that he thought was his masterpiece, *A Tragic Era: The Revolution after Lincoln*, published in 1929. Bowers was a product of his time with deep racial biases. His book, which was in keeping with his efforts to heal the differences between northern and southern Democrats that dated back to the antebellum era, condemned the role that the Radical Republicans played in the Reconstruction era, using terms such as "pillaging the South" to describe their actions. Bowers ridiculed Republican leaders like Thaddeus Stevens for advancing African American suffrage, using racial slurs in reference to the capabilities of African Americans. In Bowers's opinion, the Fourteenth and Fifteenth Amendments to the Constitution were primarily means for Republicans to enlarge their voter rolls. This came from a man who wrote editorials condemning lynchings and the Ku Klux Klan. But it was also from a man with limited personal exposure to other races.

A Tragic Era was well received. The *New York Times* declared that the "chapters on Reconstruction conditions in the South are masterpieces."[13] For decades it set the tone for historians' writings on Reconstruction. The book's lasting imprint on Americans' views can be seen in the fact that it was cited in the arguments by lawyers defending school segregation before the Supreme Court in 1954.

However, *A Tragic Era* did not receive a universally favorable reception. His unrestrained style and opinions—for example, he refers to Senator Oliver Morton of Indiana as "bloodthirsty"—earned the criticism of some historians. One reviewer of the book in 1929 was prescient when he wrote that Bowers's oeuvre "would be much sounder, live longer, and do less harm had he understood that it is not so much the business of the historian to blame and praise, as to explain the political leaders. Neither is it the chief business of the historian to drive his own interpretations into the minds of his readers with the most forceful English that he can command, but instead to present the truth clearly, leaving his readers free to form their own conclusions in the presence of the evidence impartially stated."[14]

In the newspaper business, though, Bowers was very respected. His influence in Fort Wayne was heightened by one of the reporters he had trained. Holman Hamilton returned to his native Fort Wayne in 1932 after earning a degree in English at Williams College in Massachusetts. Hired as a reporter at the *Journal-Gazette*, Hamilton became friends with Bowers, who encouraged and helped develop his appreciation of history. Hamilton resigned from the newspaper in 1934 to do independent historical research. He returned to the newspaper in the spring of 1935 as editor, a position he held, with the exception of service in the army during World War II on the staff of General Douglas MacArthur, until 1951. Even while editor of the newspaper, Hamilton maintained his dedication to history. In 1941 he published his first volume of the biography of Zachary Taylor. The second volume was published in 1951, when Hamilton left the *Journal-Gazette* to enter graduate school at the University of Kentucky at 41. He completed his doctorate in three years, became a renowned professor of history at the university, and wrote seven books. He retired from teaching in 1975. At the time of his death in 1980, Hamilton had completed drafts of about half of the Bowers biography.[15]

Toward the end of Bowers's tenure with the *Journal-Gazette*, the newspaper was confronted by an unprecedented challenge. While the history of newspapers in Fort Wayne has always been a very competitive one, there is only one case of an outright "war" in the news business. A competitive businessman by training, Oscar Foellinger chafed at the *Journal-Gazette* having the only Sunday edition in the region. He decided to launch a Sunday *News-Sentinel* in 1921, making his newspaper a seven-day-a-week publication and challenging the *Journal-Gazette*'s exclusive Sunday morning market. The outcome was a solid, workmanlike Sunday newspaper that could serve the *Sentinel*'s larger number of readers. The twenty-eight-page newspaper was made more attractive by a Photogravure section that included photographs of elegant Fort Wayne homes and fashions.

Infuriated, the *Journal-Gazette* management retaliated, setting off a two-year battle that challenged the *News-Sentinel*'s stronghold, the evening edition. Ellingham assembled a group of men to design a modern-looking product. They also carefully laid out a modern marketing campaign. The first issue of the *Fort Wayne Evening Press* appeared Monday, April 11, 1921, with thirty-two pages, at a cost of two cents. The lead editorial did not acknowledge any motive other than that its inception was "in response to what had appeared a widespread and imperative call. . . . The people of this city and of this section of the state have wanted and were in full readiness to receive an afternoon paper that should have the character it is resolved the *Evening Press* shall have." The first issue was a clear example of its direction. The newspaper's front-page design focused on late-breaking news, similar to afternoon papers in metropolitan areas. There was a streamer headline across the top of the page, above the nameplate, referring the reader to an inside story. The main headline was often for a sensationalized topic and ran seven columns. The far left-hand column was reserved for noted national columnist Arthur Brisbane. Titled "Today," Brisbane's column was among the most-read daily opinion pieces in the world. Known for a writing style that emphasized punchy leads and short sentences, Brisbane is best remembered today for his key role on Hearst's *New York Journal* when it whipped up a national fever for war against Spain in 1898. His column was seen as a coup for the 1921 *Evening Press*, which crowed that its front-page review of the world news was "by one who has the unique distinction of being the highest salaried editorial writer in the world." The first issue included a stack of "Bulletins" on the front page, a feature that was moved in later issues to page two, where most of the continuations were located. The newspaper proudly billed itself as "First with the Latest."

The inside of the newspaper was organized by topics, clearly headlined as "Daily Magazine Page for Everybody," "*Evening Press* Pictorial Page," and "*Evening Press* Page of Sport News and Comment." The magazine page carried the serialized novels that were still popular in newspapers, while the page of photographs was from the International News Service. There also were feature pages, such as one on dressmaking that included an eight-column-wide mat illustration on frocks. The back page was dedicated to comic strips.

From the outset, the *Evening Journal* had the look and feel of a well-planned modern newspaper. In a front-page "Appreciation" in the first issue, Ellingham said the public had afforded the new newspaper a "wholesome reception" since it had been announced eleven days earlier. "There are not many instances on record where a circulation has been built before a single paper was issued," Ellingham wrote. In a reference to other newspapers' shady efforts at pumping up circulation figures by including free copies, he stated: "The *Evening Press* only goes to a bona fide list of subscribers, those who have ordered and expressed a desire to be readers of the publication."

The publisher promised to print the circulation figures the following day, which he did on the front page: 15,070 in Fort Wayne via carriers, newsstands, and street sales, and 5,142 suburban. "We take pride in the fact that 8,627 copies of the *Evening Press* were delivered to Fort Wayne homes," he wrote, adding that the number was greater on Tuesday. But Ellingham wasn't about to overstate the "circulation score" for the newspaper. "Our street sales developed into an avalanche due in part to the fact it was the first appearance of the *Evening Press*. We hardly expect to duplicate our first day's sales, at least not soon."

The amount of display advertising in the first week's issues was another indicator of the planning and marketing that went into the newspaper. The launch of the *Evening Press* coincided with the annual spring sale of the city's major department store, Wolf & Dessauer, and its advertisements covered several pages throughout the first week. The second section front was consumed by a six-column advertisement for Topper's, a women's store. More advertising was evident as the newspaper gained momentum.

The *Evening Journal* was not meek in its self-promotion, either. A full-page advertisement trumpeted its securing George McManus's cartoon, "Bringing Up Father," calling it "The Greatest Comic Drawn in the World." The advertisement included an interview with the illustrator of "Jiggs" and "Maggie." Later, a full-page advertisement encouraged readers to "watch for the *Evening Press* Money Man." This promotional effort included an individual "going all over this city calling at the homes of the *Evening Press* readers and if they have the previous issue of the *Evening Press* he will leave a new crisp one dollar bill." The advertisement promised that the "money man" would be making his rounds for many weeks.

Not everything in the newspaper was as sophisticated as it may have seemed. The local feature stories often used a flowery writing style of pneumatic proportions. "Fort Wayne also has the distinction of having given birth to a pretentious array of musical genius, which has been spreading the fame and name of musical Fort Wayne throughout various parts of the country."[16] Another example was that the women's page was overseen by Ignota B. White, whose title was published as "Society Editress."

By May 11, the *Fort Wayne Evening Press* was even claiming that it was "the miracle of Journalism." For the period ending April 30, the newspaper reported that its average circulation was 17,708 and that it was being delivered to more than 50 percent of the homes in Fort Wayne. The increase, it predicted in a clear call to advertisers, will continue as "more and more people appreciate the good qualities of this clean, newsy home paper."

This, however, was superficial wishing. The *Evening Press* only appeared to have a promising future, since it was not a good time to be engaged in a newspaper war. The nation was still suffering from a postwar recession with manufacturers' inventories too high and consumption flat.

Falling wages, unemployment, and bankruptcies were news items. The competition between the *Journal-Gazette* and the *News-Sentinel* was draining their respective resources, and by mid-1922 it was clear that it could not continue. On August 29, 1922, the front page of the *Evening Press* included a box with the headline "An Announcement." With little other fanfare, the *Evening Press* and the Sunday *News-Sentinel,* by mutual agreement, said they would cease their publication in three days. The editorial in final edition of the *Evening Press* on Saturday, September 2, was not as stoic: "It has come about that wisdom dictates to the publishers that the *Evening Press* suspend, leaving an army of readers who like and desire it, abandoning a field which had been fairly won, deserting a position in which it had served. As this newspaper came into existence in response to a call that could not be mistaken, it yields to circumstances that have become plain to common sense and business considerations."

Fort Wayne returned to its previous condition: the *Journal-Gazette* seven mornings a week and the *News-Sentinel* six evenings a week. If there was a victor in the newspaper war, it was the *News-Sentinel,* whose Saturday edition became a much stronger weekend edition in the aftermath. The competitive fires had been banked, but as events a decade later would show, they were not out.

There was a positive outcome for the *Journal-Gazette,* though, when Ellingham retained some of the *Evening Press* staff. Among them was Harry M. Williams, who succeeded Bowers in the editor's chair, and Robert A. Reed, who would become a legend as the newspaper's sports editor from the 1920s into the 1960s. Others, like city editor William M. Kellogg, moved on to major newspapers such as the *Indianapolis News.*

Harry Morton Williams was called the Boswell of Fort Wayne as the city rapidly grew at the beginning of the twentieth century. It was a metaphor well meant and well earned. Williams spent more than forty years in Fort Wayne newspapers, serving as typesetter, reporter, editorial writer, and editor. He is the only man to serve as top man in the newsroom—either editor or managing editor—of the three modern Fort Wayne dailies during his career. In addition, he was elected state senator and served as secretary to a congressman.

Born in 1866, Williams had a remarkable heritage. His mother's family settled in Massachusetts in 1630. His paternal grandfather was an American officer in the Revolution, and his grandmother was descended from a prominent Quaker family who arrived in Pennsylvania with William Penn. His father, William Williams, was a decorated battlefield surgeon for the Union army in the Civil War. Promoted to colonel for his work tending the wounded at Shiloh, Willams's father was seriously wounded at Stones River, taken prisoner, and incarcerated at Libby Prison in Richmond, Virginia, before being released in an exchange of prisoners.

Harry Williams gained his first newspaper experience as a schoolboy in Albion, Indiana, serving as a printer's apprentice for the weekly newspaper. He left Michigan State after three years of study to teach school and work as a printer. Among his early ventures was the establishment of a weekly newspaper in Milford which he published for a year before selling it and becoming a journeyman printer.

Williams arrived in Fort Wayne in 1890, working for two years as a typesetter before becoming managing editor of the *Morning Press*, a publication that folded in 1893. That summer he went to Chicago as a printer, reporter, and freelance writer during the World's Columbian Exposition.

He returned to Fort Wayne where over the next fifteen years he became city editor of the *Morning Journal*, editor of the *Evening Times-Post*, city editor of the *Morning Gazette*, political and editorial writer for the *Morning Journal*, and managing editor of the *Evening Sentinel*.

Williams left newspapers for about a year to serve as secretary and publicity director for a movement launched by Theodore F. Thieme, a Fort Wayne manufacturer and civic leader, for the reform of municipal government in Indiana. As a result, Williams became an authority on municipal affairs in his later newspaper writing.

He returned to the *Evening Sentinel*, but in 1916 he was hired by Lewis Ellingham to be editor of the *Journal-Gazette*. A year later, he assumed editorial charge of the *Sentinel* for Mrs. E. A. K. Hackett. This change caused Ellingham to begin the national search for a replacement that led to the hiring of Claude Bowers. In 1918, Williams was promoted to news editor of the newly merged *News* and *Sentinel*, a post he left in 1921 to serve as editor of the *Evening Press*. Williams became editor of the *Journal-Gazette* in November 1923.

In 1930 Williams ran for the state senate and received an unusual front-page endorsement signed by Ellingham. Williams had never run for political office, although he was an active participant in Democratic Party politics. He ran a modest campaign, citing his belief that an income tax ought to be enacted to relieve the tax burden on real property, particularly on farm land. Williams asserted he was "no reformer," offering instead to "render sane, practical service to the people of my county." Ellingham went further: "We doubt if there is a citizen better equipped or qualified to represent this city and county in the highest law-making body in the

State of Indiana. He knows government and its needs. He knows the political quack and knows his game."[17]

Williams was elected to the state senate by a margin of 4,244 votes. He left the *Journal-Gazette* in 1933 to join the public relations department for the General Electric Company, where he was editor of the *GE Works News*. He also served as secretary to Congressman James I. Farley, a Democrat and former president of the Auburn Automobile Company who had been elected to the first of three terms in Congress in 1932. Williams retired in 1937 because of ill health and died at age 75 in June 1942.

Fair, logical, and a champion of sound principles of government and economics, Williams has been described as a Jeffersonian Democrat. Perhaps his greatest influence as an editor was achieved in the 1920s when he used the editorial columns of the *Journal-Gazette* to campaign against the intolerance of the period.

> [T]he sooner we get back to the notion that America cannot be made an instrumentality of medieval hate and prejudice, and back to the good old days when men fought their honest differences in the open, and, forgetting the differences of origin and religion, and remembering only our common devotion to a common flag, march all one way—the sooner shall we forget that there ever was a time when the philosophy of hate was preached and practiced that a few men might make personal fortunes on the gullibility of the many.[18]

In its editorial eulogizing Williams, the *Journal-Gazette* noted his "phenomenal memory and an encyclopedic mind. It seemed to his associates that he never forgot anything he had read, seen, or heard. There was a common saying about the *Journal-Gazette* office to this effect: 'If it isn't in the dictionary, or the encyclopedia or the histories, ask Harry Williams.' And Harry always came up with the right answer."[19]

The other extraordinary journalist hired by Lew Ellingham was Bob Reed, the consummate sports writer of his era. When he began as sports editor of the *Evening Press*, Fort Wayne had two high schools, no actual basketball court, one golf course, and one small bowling alley. Reed's sports pages contributed to the *Evening Press*'s successes, even if it was short-lived. The sports news was compartmentalized and clearly labeled. Reed filled the pages with columns by national writers like Walter Camp and photographs—usually from mats obtained through the mail—as well as news of local events, leagues, and athletes. Unlike many other afternoon newspapers, the *Evening Press* was unafraid of putting a baseball game (since they were all day games at the time) in the late news column.

Longtime sports editor Robert Reed.

Reed brought the same aggressive approach to the *Journal-Gazette* when its afternoon paper folded in 1922.

This is not to say the *Journal-Gazette* had a history of ignoring or underplaying sports. The earliest newspapers in Fort Wayne carried reports on the baseball clubs, as they were described in the late 1800s. Games between the Fort Wayne Kekiongas and the renowned Cincinnati Red Stockings in 1869 received lengthy stories. Horse racing and boxing matches often were included in the early newspapers. Seven of the eight columns of the front page of the January 26, 1894, edition of the *Fort Wayne Journal* were devoted to the championship fight between James J. Corbett and Charles Mitchell. The only portion of the front page not about the bout was a column of advertising. While at first glance it seems extreme, the coverage of boxing was significant at the time. Corbett, who was in the midst of his five-year reign as heavyweight champion of the world, was rumored to be willing to stage a bout in Fort Wayne, and this was the subject of considerable speculation for weeks.

There was little gentility in the manner in which sports writers treated athletes in the papers. A baseball game in June 1899 saw Fort Wayne lose to Mansfield in the Interstate League when an infielder named Tim Flood made two errors in the final innings. The June 14 *Morning Journal-Gazette* headline read: "Well! Well! Timothy." The drop head added:

"Your Presence Yesterday Gave Mansfield the Game." The text spared the 21-year-old player even less, deprecatingly describing him as "once the idol of local base ball enthusiasts." The sports writer was apparently a poor judge of talent as Flood went on to play three seasons in the National League.

Even Reed's own approach to writing sports was different. He used a byline at a time when few writers, other than columnists, put their names atop stories. In 1927, when the New York Yankees played an exhibition game in Fort Wayne, "By Robert A. Reed" was atop the *Journal-Gazette* story while the *News-Sentinel*'s report carried the byline "Onceover." Reed had a higher profile by traveling to sporting events and reporting on them, rather than using wire service stories. The first World Series he covered was in 1926 when the Yankees played the St. Louis Cardinals, and he didn't miss another one until his retirement. There was more to his interests than baseball, too. Reed started the Fort Wayne Golden Gloves Tournament and organized the Downtown Quarterback Club, which featured a weekly businessmen's luncheon during the football season. Reed was well known in the sports world, which came in handy on occasion. When baseball commissioner Kenesaw Mountain Landis came to Fort Wayne for the funeral of baseball statistician Louis Heilbroner in 1933, the *Journal-Gazette* managed to get an exclusive story by using a bit of subterfuge on the part of its sports editor. Judge Landis, who knew Reed from his coverage of baseball, was told upon his arrival in the city that the *Journal-Gazette* sports editor was ill. Landis felt he needed to visit his friend before granting any interviews, and Reed—in his pajamas—chatted at home with the commissioner until it was time for Heilbroner's funeral. Landis left Fort Wayne afterward, and the *Journal-Gazette* got the story it wanted. When Reed retired in 1962, his successor was another veteran sports writer, Carl F. Wiegman. Beginning with the *Journal-Gazette* in the spring of 1943, Wiegman served as sports editor until his death in May 1977.

The blossoming of sports in Fort Wayne in 1920s was a manifestation of the city's unprecedented growth. In 1920, Fort Wayne's population reached 85,549, surpassing Evansville and making it Indiana's second most populous city. This represented an 89.6 percent growth since the turn of the century, while the entire state was experiencing a 16.4 percent growth in population in the same period. There was a building boom in the city, with three new elementary schools, two annexes, and a new high school being erected along with the First National Bank, the Lincoln National Life home office, and the Mizpah Shrine temple in a five-year period.

The city's industrial growth was highlighted by its successful bid for the International Harvester Truck Company in 1922. Twenty-six other cities, many much larger than Fort Wayne, were in the competition for the "world's greatest truck plant," as it was billed. The Fort Wayne bid was engineered by the Greater Fort Wayne Improvement Corporation, sometimes known as the "Million Dollar Committee" and composed of several business leaders. The committee's effort exhibited the exuberance of the post–World War I era in the United States. The committee promised amenities that larger, more traditional cities would not—or could not—match. The land they proffered wasn't even within the city boundaries and had to be annexed as the Harvester Park Addition. The company wanted housing for its workers, powerful and reliable utilities to run its operations, and transportation for its goods and people. All of this was guaranteed by the committee, which raised the money through a subscription drive for the promised home sites, streets, electric and water service, and railroad and street car services to the new manufacturing site. When it opened, International Harvester was the community's largest employer, a position it would hold for more than fifty years.

The truck plant, along with the world's largest manufacturer of fine copper wire (the Dudlo Corporation), a new hosiery knitting mill (Thieme Brothers), and the presence of two prominent pump manufacturers (Tokheim and Wayne) made it easy for Fort Wayne to tout itself as a progressive city and for boosters to proclaim it "a veritable Wonder City." The *Journal-Gazette* promoted this message in every Sunday's edition and often used its news columns to preach continued municipal improvements, such as printing photographs of dilapidated buildings under the headline "Why Tolerate This Ugly Spot?"

There was a major impediment to the city achieving its full potential, one that ironically was also its lifeblood. The railroads that made Fort Wayne a center of commercial activity were also guilty of blocking future growth. It was an issue that the *Journal-Gazette* would fight for almost a half-century.

In the 1920s and 1930s, there was a movement in cities across the nation to improve safety by eliminating "at-grade" railroad crossings by building overpasses to carry the rail beds. Fort Wayne was like many cities where passenger and freight trains—moving and stopped—blocked streets at railroad crossings, often for extended periods. Many motorists were killed or badly injured when their vehicles collided with trains. Newspapers frequently reported the discovery of bodies of pedestrians who had been walking on the tracks or trying to cross between cars of a stopped train.

In Fort Wayne, the danger was magnified by the layout of the railroads. The east-west routes of the Pennsylvania and Wabash railroads blocked access to the downtown district from the south side until the 1920s. The Nickel Plate Railroad through the center of the business district was a formidable barrier to commercial growth of the northern portion of the city and would remain so until the 1950s.

Two factors came into play that enabled Fort Wayne to solve this problem. One was the late-nineteenth-century development of new methods using Portland cement as the binder for an aggregate of sand and gravel to create a high-early-strength concrete. When used with steel reinforcements, this construction became the standard for building railroad elevations over thoroughfares with earthen fill used as the transition between the streets. The second factor was the rare technical ability and dedication of one mayor, William J. Hosey. A self-educated man, avid reader, and railroad machinist, Hosey ran for mayor in 1905 at age 51 after serving one term on the city council. A Democrat with a Progressive's perspective on municipal government, he generated controversy. He was, after all, a worker and not a business leader in the community. While the *Journal-Gazette* endorsed him, the *News* forcefully opposed him in favor of businessman Edward White of the White Fruit Company. Karl Detzer recalled that his mother, who was well read and hosted family and friends in her parlor on Sunday afternoons, would often spark a verbal donnybrook by asking their opinion on "whether Machinist Bill Hosey of the Pennsy Railroad Shops would make a good mayor."[20]

In his first of four nonconsecutive terms (state law forbade mayors of large cities to succeed themselves at the time), Hosey demonstrated he was not the typical mayor. His ability to comprehend engineering issues in great detail benefited the city not only with the elevation of the railroads but also in the construction and operation of the municipal utilities, street improvements, and flood prevention. He also was an opponent of patronage and graft. His opposition to the exploitation of the city by the privately owned interurban lines was a rare stand for a mayor at the time. The mayor's determination in negotiating with the railroads cannot be underestimated. One of Hosey's successors was inclined to accept a Pennsylvania Railroad offer to trade an apparent $100,000 worth of property for a $2,000 cash settlement in 1912, a proposal that incurred the wrath of the *Journal-Gazette*, which said it produced "a stench to honest men."[21]

It is not known how Hosey's career with the Pennsylvania Railroad was affected by his political life, although he was able to return to his job between terms as mayor. However, the newspapers didn't seem to see any conflict of interest, and Hosey showed no apparent favoritism for the railroads in his role as mayor. In fact, Hosey was a determined advocate for Fort Wayne's battle with the railroads in the state legislature. He fought legislation that would be detrimental to the cities. In 1907 he testified before a joint House-Senate committee in Indianapolis to force the railroads to pay a portion of the elevation construction costs in cities throughout the state. Although Governor J. Frank Hanly signed the bill, the railroads proved unwilling to negotiate. Hosey reached an agreement with the Wabash Railroad to raise the crossings at Calhoun Street, Fairfield Avenue, and Broadway in 1907, but found that financial negotiations for payment of the construction were incomplete when he began his second four-year term in 1914. This intransigent behavior on the part of the railroads would continue.

Hosey managed to negotiate for more elevated crossings until World War I, when a steel shortage halted such projects. In his third term, which began in 1921, agreements were reached with the Wabash and Pennsylvania Railroads, whose efforts had to be coordinated because their trackage was interconnected. The Nickel Plate Railroad through downtown Fort Wayne was a different matter.

The city and the railroad dickered for thirty-two years over raising the rail bed and another twenty years to pay for it. "The amount of negotiations, renegotiations, threats, haggling, conferences, public meetings, plans, plans scrapping, false hopes, plus false starts was staggering," reporter Jerry Huddleston wrote in 1955. A 1923 city council resolution to elevate the crossings and evenly share the costs with the railroad led to the passage of a $300,000 bond issue by the electorate, 9,026 votes to 849. The Nickel Plate stalled the project by examining whether it should reroute its tracks around downtown Fort Wayne rather than incur the expense of an elevated rail bed. When the railroad ruled out this alternative, it just ignored the city's resolution. Threats of mandating the construction and forcing the railroad to pay 65 percent of the costs in 1930 were dismissed by the railroad. The Depression prevented any further consideration of the issue, although the railroads did manage to get the Indiana legislature to pass a law limiting their exposure in such construction to a maximum of 20 percent of the cost. A proposal to undertake the project was approved by the Nickel Plate management in 1941, but World War II took precedent before the work could be planned. In 1947 a contract was signed, but the work was never begun because of disputes over lands around the tracks. After more years of haggling over the cost of the work, a $5.75 million bond issue pushed the project into reality in 1953. The final ground-level train went through the north end of the city on October 15, 1955, and the elevated tracks went into service.

The *Journal-Gazette* campaigned for years to have the project completed. News stories, editorials, photographs, and advertising campaigns hammered away at the issue, emphasizing the economic advantages it would offer and the public safety it would improve. The newspaper demonstrated that the trains endangered the lives of the citizenry in an emergency, whether it was police or fire personnel responding to a fire or accident or an ambulance transporting injured and sick people to the hospitals. In the spring of 1951, the *Journal-Gazette* launched a campaign to involve the citizenry in convincing the railroad to undertake the project. "No More Wait— Let's Elevate the Nickel Plate" appeared regularly on the newspaper's front page with the opinions of Fort Wayne's community leaders, men and women, young and old. The message was to the point: "Fort Wayne is completely fed up. The people have had enough, in fact, more than enough. They want elevation. They want it now. They want it completed in 1951."[22]

There was another obstacle to Fort Wayne's success in the mid-1920s, and it was national in scope. When the Ku Klux Klan reared its hooded head in the 1920s, most Indiana newspapers skirted the organization's philosophy of racial and ethnic hatred. Instead, most editors were satisfied to reflect Indiana's overwhelming acceptance of the Klan's positions and report on it like any other mainstream organization. The *Fort Wayne Journal-Gazette* was not among them. Its editorial pages openly campaigned against the Klan, its intolerance, and its candidates. "When race is arrayed against race, and religion against religion, when neighbors become enemies because they worship in different churches, and when our people cease to be a people and become a miserable hotchpotch of quarreling factions, we cease to be the America that was born of the Revolution," the *Journal-Gazette* wrote on November 20, 1923.

It was a time when the nation was caught up in a groundswell of xenophobia in the wake of World War I, increased immigration, and the rise of communism. Also, the concept of a "return to normalcy" as articulated by the Republicans in the 1920 presidential campaign implied restoring what were seen as the values of the nation's founding: moral decency, honesty in government, public education, honest law enforcement, regular church attendance—all associated with white Protestant male-dominated society. Prohibition was another factor, viewed as the proper removal of a vice that had prevented American society from realizing its potential. Violation of the Volstead Act was seen as the work of foreigners, and some Klan supporters advocated expulsion, rather than imprisonment, of those

The *Journal-Gazette* campaigned for five decades to have the railroad tracks through the center of Fort Wayne elevated to reduce traffic congestion and safety concerns. The final sections of the Nickel Plate elevated tracks in the downtown business district were finally put in place in 1955.

convicted of making or selling alcoholic beverages. The Klan movement capitalized on all of these factors. With its professed hatred of Catholics, blacks, and Jews and with its emphasis on morality and family values, the Klan captured a large portion of the populace's favor. This was especially true in Indiana where between 25 percent and 33 percent of all native-born white men became Klansmen in the 1920s.[23] It enabled the Klan to take control of the Republican Party in 1924, electing a governor and a majority in both legislative chambers.

The support for the Klan was across the board, in small towns and large cities and in rural as well as urban areas. It seemed to be strongest in areas that had been changed by the growth of industry. Yet, of all the major cities in Indiana, Fort Wayne had the smallest percentage of Klan members among native-born white men. According to Klan records recovered in 1925, only 7 percent of the native-born white men in Allen County were Klansmen. This compared with 33 percent in Madison County (Anderson); 31 percent in Vigo County (Terre Haute); 27 percent in Marion County (Indianapolis) and Delaware County (Muncie); 26 percent in Elkhart County; and 20 percent in Lake County (Gary, Hammond, and East Chicago).[24]

Even with the relatively small number of members, the appearance of hooded-and-robed Klansmen in Fort Wayne was disturbing. A 1924 photograph of Klansmen distributing literature among the crowd at the interurban depot remains a chilling reminder of an intolerant time. The coverage of the Klan also sparked the competition between the Fort Wayne newspapers. The *Journal-Gazette* scolded the *News-Sentinel* for its decision to print a seven thousand–word speech by Klan Imperial Wizard Hiram Evans in 1923 on the same day it allocated only forty words to Senator Hiram W. Johnson's announcement that he would be a candidate for the Republican Party's presidential nomination.

The outcome of the national and state elections in 1924 were probably a foregone conclusion, but the *Journal-Gazette* waged an intense, sustained effort to foil the Klan's influence on the nomination of candidates, the campaign, and the vote itself. The presidential campaign pitted Republican president Calvin Coolidge against Democrat John W. Davis and the U.S. Progressive Party's Robert M. LaFollette, Sr. Coolidge had succeeded Warren G. Harding, who had died in August 1923 as the illegal leasing of naval oil reserves to a private company known as the Teapot Dome scandal rocked the Republican administration. While the scandal offered some faint hope of a Democratic victory, the party self-destructed in its national convention. A struggle over whether to condemn the Klan

The Ku Klux Klan was a powerful force in Indiana in 1924 as this photograph of two robed Klansmen at the Interurban Depot on West Main Street indicates. The *Journal-Gazette* opposed the Klan and warned of it taking control of the Republican Party in the state. *Allen County-Fort Wayne Historical Society.*

by name in a resolution led to a marathon nominating process that ended with Davis selected on the record 103rd ballot. A respected lawyer who was anti-Klan, Davis was little known to the voters. The divisive convention must have been particularly painful for the party faithful in Fort Wayne, since the Democratic national chairman at the convention was Edward G. Hoffman, until early 1923 part-owner of the *Journal-Gazette*. The weakness of the Democrats was so obvious that the Republican vice presidential candidate, Charles G. Dawes, paid no attention to them in a speech in Fort Wayne on October 3, 1924. Instead, Dawes focused solely on what he called "the red menace" posed by LaFollette.

Coolidge was victorious in Allen County—although by a smaller margin than Harding's in 1920—with LaFollette a distant third. The order of the finish was the same in Indiana; however, the decisiveness was much different. Coolidge crushed Davis in the state by more than 310,000 votes, a margin of victory that was more than two-and-a-half times greater than Harding's four years earlier. The voter turnout in Indiana was a disappointing 67.6 percent in 1924, indicating many voters didn't care for any of the candidates.

The gubernatorial campaign was much more problematic. The Klan, led by D. C. Stephenson, secured control of the Republican Party by backing two-term secretary of state Ed Jackson in a primary. Similar to the national party, Indiana Democrats were in turmoil, as some leaders wanted to ignore the Klan issue and others favored a moderate anti-Klan position. When a primary proved inconclusive, the state nominating convention selected Dr. Carleton McCulloch to run for governor. It also passed an anti-Klan plank, although the party leaders advised McCulloch to dodge the issue as much as possible.

Jackson, too, was coy about the Klan in public. The Republican candidate said he supported "liberty of conscience and freedom of worship," but he would not condemn the tenets of the Klan that were to the contrary. The *Journal-Gazette* wrote editorials against Jackson on a daily basis, calling him a "klux-Republican." In early October it wondered why the steadfastly Republican *News-Sentinel* had not endorsed Jackson. "Is it passing strange that the Republican candidate for governor of Indiana should have entrée to every page of that newspaper save the editorial page?" The fact of the matter was that the Coolidge-Dawes campaign was giving wide berth to Jackson. Near the end of the campaign the *Indianapolis Times*—which won a Pulitzer Prize for public service in 1928 for exposing the corruption in Indiana government—published KKK records showing that Jackson was a Klansman. While it was too little too late, the information might not have made a difference if it had been proven earlier. Jackson received 53.4 percent of the state vote in the Republican landslide. He did not win in Fort Wayne, however. McCulloch defeated Jackson by 1,675 votes out of more than 44,000 votes cast. It was the Democratic candidate's only urban victory.

The *Journal-Gazette*'s only comment after the election appeared on November 8: "Gov.-elect Jackson announces that he is going to be everyone's governor, but we suspect he will soon learn of a considerable body of his late supporters who will insist that he guess again." At a reception after Jackson's inaugural, Stephenson was seen standing by the governor's side, making certain he recognized Klansmen and Klanswomen who supported the Republican.

Yet the *Journal-Gazette* had been prophetic in 1923 when it wrote that "many have been enticed into the sheets and hoods, but most of these, five years hence, will not be proud of the association."[25] In November 1925 Stephenson was convicted of second-degree murder in the rape and suicide of a 28-year-old woman who was a state employee. He apparently expected a pardon from the governor; but when that didn't occur, Stephenson testified before a grand jury that indicted Jackson. At the trial, Stephenson revealed he had given illegal contributions to Jackson and that both men had tried to bribe Governor Warren McCray.[26] While Jackson was spared and able to complete his term of office because the statute of limitations for his crimes had expired, the Klan's stranglehold on Indiana's government was broken.

There was more somber news for the newspaper in 1925. Former vice president Thomas Marshall died in Washington on June 1 after an ill-advised trip to Indiana to deliver commencement addresses at Columbia City High School and Manchester College. As might be expected, the tributes printed in the *Journal-Gazette* were extensive for the man who was known to millions as "Tom" and who preferred to be thought of as "just a plain everyday average American citizen."[27] The memorial on the editorial page emphasized his honesty, plainness, and quaint humor. "He had come to be the nation's great apostle of kindliness and common sense."[28] There was scant mention of accomplishments and only a general reference to "his quaint and subtle sense of humor, which the pall of senatorial dignity failed to dampen."[29] Neither was there any mention of Marshall's isolation from the White House, even as Wilson lay incapacitated by a stroke during their second term in office.

Less than two months later, another champion of the *Journal-Gazette* died in Dayton, Tennessee. William Jennings Bryan died five days after serving as the prosecutor and most noted witness at the "Scopes Monkey Trial." Defense attorney Clarence Darrow's aggressive questioning of Bryan at the trial over the teaching of evolution made headlines throughout the country and weakened the former presidential candidate in the summer heat. A political progressive but a religious conservative, Bryan had campaigned against the theory of evolution since 1921. The *Journal-Gazette* had supported Bryan in his three presidential bids, but it parted ways with him over evolution.

During the 1920s an editorial cartoonist was hired whose work had considerable impact on the *Journal-Gazette*. Edmund "Eddie" Gunder produced memorable—sometimes haunting—images of local, state, and national issues in both the *Evening Press* and the *Journal-Gazette*. At times Gunder's cartoons were alternated with works by the acclaimed *New York*

World cartoonist Rollin Kirby. His work promoted the city's growth, as in the opening of a new company headquarters or the erection of a sky-scraper. On occasion there was a gentle mocking pointed at the newspaper and himself. One 1927 cartoon showed a somewhat worn-down editorial cartoonist dreaming of a "vacation week" amid a pile of assignments for a variety of weeks, such as "Music Week," "Thrift Week," and "Smile Week." The caption read, "The week we're waitin' for."

Gunder produced a series of promotional cartoons in 1922 for the *Evening Press* and Sunday *Journal-Gazette* that were very popular in the community. The "Know Fort Wayne" contest featured a cartoon puzzle from which readers had to guess which street it represented. For example, a Robin Hood–like character shooting at a bull's-eye with a bow and arrow represented the city's "Archer Avenue." Others were more difficult, such as a character in the form of a capital letter *D* sitting atop a brick wall and looking down at another capital letter *D* represented DeWald (dee-wall-ed) Street. In addition, each drawing had a compass in it, and contestants had to indicate the direction in which the street traveled. There were six puzzles in each of three weekly contests, with prizes of $15, $10, and $5 as well as theater tickets awarded in each contest. The contest was a success, with thousands of readers clipping the cartoons and entering their answers. There were also hundreds of complaints as people disputed the results.

However, Gunder's strongest work came during the Depression when he was able to capture some of the fear and despair of the time. A haunting image appeared in the December 22, 1931, issue of the *Journal-Gazette* with a little bedraggled boy and his smaller, equally bedraggled sibling, holding hands and staring at the items in the toys section of a department store. A woman behind the counter is looking down kindly at him as he replies, "No, Ma'm. We're just lookin'."

Another cartoonist in the 1920s whose evocative work was found in the *Journal-Gazette* was George Spayth. His work had a homespun detail and could be very moving, as in his haunting sketch of a one-legged doughboy on crutches, published on the day that veterans of the Great War raised funds by selling forget-me-not flowers. The background spells out "Forget me not" in the shape of the flowers. Spayth also produced a memorable cartoon critical of the Lincoln Highway shortly after the first coast-to-coast road reached northern Indiana. The June 16, 1921, front-page cartoon from the Sunday *Journal-Gazette* showed a car being pulled through the hubcap-high mud by a team of horses, with the Lincoln Highway sign indicating the scene was between Fort Wayne and Chu-

Eddie Gunder was the *Journal-Gazette*'s editorial cartoonist for years. His work often promoted the growth of the city, as in this depiction of the impact of the Lincoln National Bank skyscraper, which opened for business in November 1930.

rubusco. The cartoon captured a perennial problem for the highway, and the ironic caption read: "Indiana's Monument to the Great Emancipator."

There was another major "passing" in the same period of time, one that had a more lasting local impact: the end of the last remaining German-language newspaper in Fort Wayne. The reason for closing the *Freie Presse–Staats-Zeitung* cited by publisher Herman Mackwitz was the city's decision to widen Clinton Street and set back the newspaper's building by ten feet. The changes in the operation that this would require were too expensive, he said. Mackwitz had been publisher of the newspaper for thirty-two years, a period surpassed only by his editor, Anselm Fuelber, whose career encompassed forty-six years on three German-language newspapers in Fort Wayne.

There were other factors, too. The number of German-speaking people immigrating to the United States was far less than a half-century earlier. The World War, as it was known then, had brought about a greater assimilation of German-speaking citizens into the American culture. The number of non-English-reading German Americans had significantly declined. In 1914 there were approximately 700 German-language newspapers operating in the United States. By the end of the war in 1919, there were 230. "Between the time the immigrants left the good influences of the fatherland and the time they were able to seize the ideals of America, it was the German newspapers which filled the gap by reminding them of the ideals which they understood—ideals which were much the same whether written in German or in English."[30]

In a lengthy tribute to Mackwitz and the newspaper on January 30, 1927, *Journal-Gazette* reporter Frank Roberts noted, "During the World war when passions were aflame everywhere, the publishers of the *Freie Presse–Staats-Zeitung* showed a judgment, patience and moderation which many people on both sides of the controversy failed to match." The newspaper had been an influence for the good in the city. "It preached in its columns for 70 years those virtues which made the German immigrant such a powerful force in the building of a strong and sturdy nation." In a style of writing not usually found on the front page in 1927, Roberts reminisced about the heyday of the German-language newspapers, even though he was too young to remember them:

> They represent "the good old days" to many. Life was more leisurely. Home and family meant more than they do today. No real man ever smoked a cigaret. The old curved stem pipes were strong enough to shoulder a two-bushel sack of wheat. Men strained their beer through their mustaches. It was nothing unusual to pass a building and hear a mannerchor singing the night away. Every week was thrift

The Journal-Gazette Building at Clinton and Main Streets as it appeared in 1930.

week. Pleasure was cheaper than now. Pleasure and a free lunch could be had for five cents. The fire station was more of a community center. Hardly anyone knew what blasé or sophisticated meant and no one had ever heard of psychoanalysis. Parents did not try to "sublimate" the child's desire to be mean, but a paddle consisting of a big fat hand was an aid to the Ten Commandments in teaching growing boys the difference between right and wrong.

The expansion of Clinton Street to handle more automobile and truck traffic had a more positive effect on the *Journal-Gazette* than it did on its German-language brethren. The newspaper was located in the south end of the Bass Building at the southeast corner of Clinton and Main, leasing space that Moynihan had secured in 1908. By moving the *Journal-Gazette* from 43 East Main Street to the larger structure, Moynihan not only gained more space for his operation but also raised the profile of the newspaper in the business community. It was now in a central location and more inviting to the general public. The structure was built in 1880 by industrialist John Bass, whose world-renowned foundry produced railroad car wheels, stationary engines, iron abutments for bridges, and many types of heavy castings.

In 1927 Lew Ellingham purchased the entire building, razed it, and had a new structure erected by March 1928. In a feat of engineering derring-do, the two printing presses remained in the south two bays and operated during the fourteen months of demolition and construction around them. At its dedication in 1928, the building was described as being the most appropriately designed newspaper plant. Ellingham had asked his architect, Charles Weatherhogg, to design something more than a functional newspaper building. Now viewed as a prime example of early-twentieth-century Romantic Revival commercial architecture, the new building was praised in 1928 for its handsome look. It featured two shining copper canopies, the architect's trademark, on Clinton Street. Weatherhogg included several distinctive architectural elements, including cast-iron columns with Doric capitals and bases, parapets carved from Oolitic Indiana limestone, and arched windows. The interior featured intricately stamped metal pan ceilings and cornices as well as decorative plaster work. A final touch was to install a picture window in the press room so passersby could watch presses run.

The *Journal-Gazette* operated from this building at 701–713 Clinton Street until 1950.

FORT WAYNE GAZETTE.

THE MORNING JOURNAL.

FT. WAYNE JOURNAL=GAZETTE.

THE FORT WAYNE JOURNAL-GAZETTE.

FORT WAYNE JOURNAL-GAZETTE

FORT WAYNE JOURNAL-GAZETTE

THE JOURNAL-GAZETTE

The Journal-Gazette

Journal Gazette

6

Depression and War

There is a mysterious cycle in human events. To some generations
much is given. Of other generations much is expected. This
generation has a rendezvous with destiny.

—President Franklin Delano Roosevelt, 1936

The story of the Depression in Fort Wayne is not the standard
textbook history of the period. For a few years the community was able to
resist the economic abyss precipitated by the stock market crash in October 1929. Fort Wayne's prosperity in the 1920s provided insulation against
Wall Street's speculation-induced disaster. Fort Wayne's population had
grown from 86,500 in 1920 to 115,000 in 1930. The value of its manufactured products rose from $76.7 million to $121.6 million in the same period, a remarkable 58.5 percent increase.[1] The city's banks were less affected by the stock market plunge than larger cities' financial institutions
because a sizable portion of their investments were in local companies instead of in dubious speculative ventures. The April 20, 1930, edition of the
Journal-Gazette gave the impression that the economic downturn would
be another brief recession, limited in its scope.

But while Fort Wayne thought it was insulated; it wasn't a fully self-
sustaining community. The products from its factories were sold nationally, and their markets were drying up. The local unemployment rate rose
to 5 percent in mid-1930, mostly from construction workers. Some
thought that consumer spending could bring the economy out of its
downward spiral, and in April 1930 the *Journal-Gazette* campaigned for
tenants of rental units to consider buying a new home. "Spend Now" was
the movement endorsed by the city leaders and the newspapers. The
Journal-Gazette donated full-page advertisements calling for people to respond as they did when they bought Liberty Bonds in support of the war.

The advertisements asserted that the underlying problem was essentially "a nation-wide buyers' strike" that required readers to "spend just one more dime each day and help drive the hard times away."

The inescapable lapping of the ocean of Depression at Fort Wayne's shore was viewed with growing alarm by some leaders in the community, though. As early as November 9, 1928, Arthur F. Hall, the president of the Lincoln National Life Insurance Company, had written to one of the largest banks in the city to assure them of the insurer's solvency. "You no doubt have a very considerable amount of money loaned to local people with stock of Lincoln Life as collateral," he wrote to Samuel M. Foster, chairman of the Lincoln National Bank, reassuring him that the insurer's stock was sound. A year later, Hall moved to protect his company and his employees. In a November 13, 1929, memo to his employees noting that some banks were calling for all or partial payment of outstanding loans, Hall offered to intercede: "If you find yourself in difficulty over a loan on Lincoln Life stock, please take the matter up with me."

Conditions worsened in the winter of 1930–31 as industry after industry felt the impact. A citywide survey brought to light deplorable conditions among residents—a lack of food, clothing, fuel, and even simple medicinal remedies necessary to withstand the cold weather. A "Hooverville" of shacks began to grow in the area north of the business district. Still, the underlying pride of the community made it resist outside help, especially from the federal government. An Allen County Emergency Unemployment Committee (ACEUC) was formed to raise money for the needy in December 1930. Not tied to any political entity, the relief effort raised $360,000 for its first year of operation. The wealthy and the worker alike donated to the effort. At Lincoln Life, on December 13, Hall asked employees earning between $50 and $100 a month to give half a day's pay each month for the three-month drive. Lincoln Life employees making more than $100 a month were asked to donate one day's pay per month.

If some thought that this effort would suffice and that the economy would return to normal, they were wrong. A second volunteer effort was launched for 1932 with a goal of $385,000. It failed to reach that mark. Yet government-supplied relief was an anathema in Fort Wayne. The *News-Sentinel* on November 12, 1931, campaigned against direct payments to the impoverished, declaring that they "contravene the spirit of Anglo-Saxon traditions, encourage laziness, and create a class of permanent dependents." Mayor Hosey, a progressive but not radical Democrat, favored federal aid in 1932, but the *Journal-Gazette* warned against this "dangerous" possibility. By 1933 there were said to be more than five thousand families on relief in the city. Allen County had created a scrip currency for use with hundreds of local merchants, including the two newspapers as well as doctors and dentists.

The *Journal-Gazette* was not impervious to the Depression's effects either. The newspaper reported a net paid daily circulation of 44,837 in 1930, about 10 percent less than the *News-Sentinel*'s. The Sunday newspaper circulation was nearly 33,000. By the time Franklin Delano Roosevelt was sworn in as president of the United States, advertisements were far fewer than before, and the daily *Journal-Gazette* was fourteen pages selling for three cents.

Roosevelt's sweeping victory over President Herbert Hoover saw him carry Allen County by more than 11,000 votes. The newspaper coverage of the 1932 campaign devoted more attention to the issue of possibly repealing Prohibition than to national economic policy.[2]

There were doubters in northeast Indiana about the necessity of Roosevelt's "New Deal," but this changed as banks collapsed under the weight of bad loans and mortgages. There were twelve banks in Fort Wayne before the Depression and only two avoided being reorganized: The Lincoln National Bank and the Peoples Trust & Savings Company. The initial collapse was the First and Tri-State National Bank in June 1931, and it was a test of Fort Wayne's mettle. The city's financial leaders learned at a suddenly called evening meeting that the bank was insolvent, that its capital surplus was gone. The bank's directors pledged $1.4 million, and after quite a bit of discussion, another $1.1 million was promised by the directors from Lincoln Life, Lincoln National Bank, and Old National Bank, which assumed control of Tri-State, as well as some trust funds from Chicago and Indianapolis institutions. When Roosevelt declared the national bank holiday on March 3, 1933, the First and Tri-State went into receivership and emerged afterward as the Fort Wayne National Bank.

The main good news in 1933 was the repeal of Prohibition, which was welcomed in Fort Wayne. Evidence that "dry" was not a favored political position can be seen in the thirteen presidential elections between 1884 and 1932 when no presidential candidate on the Prohibition Party ticket ever received more than 602 votes in Allen County. Since Fort Wayne's brewers were very successful before Prohibition in 1918, the area's residents looked forward to the reopening of the Centlivre and Berghoff breweries. It meant more than a bottle of beer or ale; it also resulted in the revival of hundreds of jobs in the production and distribution of the product. The old *Journal-Gazette* editor, Harry Williams, wrote a lengthy reminiscence about the city's pre-Prohibition saloons and taverns. It was an assignment that Williams savored, recalling establishments like the White Elephant with its porcelain pachyderm on the plate glass front window. Williams noted that one owner after another went broke running the establishment, perhaps because they were held in such high repute for the quality of its beer and for the free lunch. There also was a maudlin aspect to Williams's report as it recalled the "old Fort Wayne" that could not be re-created. There had been unique characters in the city then, such as the proprietor of a drinking establishment, Jimmie Summers. Williams maintained that Chicago newspaperman Peter Finley Dunne's famous fictive observer of mankind, Mr. Dooley, did not compare favorably with Jimmie Summers, whose tavern was located on the northwest corner of Calhoun and Baker streets.

"One day when Mr. Summers was not in the barroom, but near at hand," Williams wrote in the April 11, 1933, edition of the *Journal-Gazette*, "his bartender called to him.

'Mr. Summers, is Dinny Martin good for drink?'

'Has he it?'

'He has.'

'He is.'

"Probably no momentous affair of business was ever negotiated and concluded with words so few," Williams observed. With the Depression weighing down on the community, it did not seem the observation could be repeated, especially since so few businessmen could afford to run a tab.

The economic difficulties were being felt by the newspaper, too. Whether construction costs associated with the new building or some bad investments in the company portfolio precipitated the concern, Ellingham worried that the newspaper might become bankrupt and be silenced by creditors. The desperation can be surmised from the plan that was launched: change the daily *Journal-Gazette* from a morning to an afternoon newspaper and go toe-to-toe with the *News-Sentinel*. The Sunday edition remained unchanged.

Confident that his newspaper was a better product, Ellingham and his son, Miller—now assistant publisher—announced on May 21, 1933, that the *Journal-Gazette* would "pass into the ranks of the evening papers" on May 23. Their decision was influenced by rapid "social and industrial changes" that brought about "changes in the reading time and habits of our subscribers." They promised a late edition would roll off the press at 8:30 p.m. with the latest markets and news and still be able to reach the rural areas of the county.

With a style reminiscent of the launching of the *Evening Press* a decade earlier, the *Journal-Gazette* marketed the change diligently. Full-page ads assured readers that popular columnists like Will Rogers, Arthur Brisbane, and Edgar Guest, local features such as the Woman's Page, and syndicated comic strips and crossword puzzles would continue in the *Evening Journal-Gazette*. The *Journal-Gazette* wasn't about to change its politics, though. The front page of the first afternoon edition featured a congratulatory letter from President Roosevelt and an assurance from the party's national chairman, Postmaster General James A. Farley, that the newspaper would continue as "a Democratic lighthouse in northeastern Indiana."

While the change was seen as a dramatic step in Fort Wayne, the *Journal-Gazette*'s move to an afternoon paper was in keeping with national trends. The publication of morning newspapers was being abandoned in much larger cities than Fort Wayne. "The whole picture of daily journalism in the United States has changed or is changing from what it was a short quarter of a century ago," was the editorial page comment on May 21. As might be imagined, the *News-Sentinel* publisher criticized the move and bemoaned the loss of a morning paper from the market. The *Journal-Gazette* publishers answered in-kind, and the battle was engaged.

By mid-1934, the *Journal-Gazette*'s dire financial straits were publicly known. Its losses were growing with little relief in sight. The company had defaulted earlier in the year on its first scheduled debt payment and seemed likely to do so again at the next scheduled payment. The *Journal-Gazette* decided to seek bankruptcy protection from its creditors. The existing capitalization of the business included 1,000 shares of preferred stock with a par value of $100 and 4,000 shares (1,991 of which were issued) of common stock at $100 par value. Under the reorganization plan approved by U.S. District Judge Thomas Slick in September, secured creditors were paid more than $80,000 and new debentures were issued for the unsecured creditors. These bonds were issued January 1, 1935, and were due January 1, 1950. New shares of preferred stock and two layers of common shares were also issued. Three prominent Democrats bought the reorganized business: James Fleming, Virgil Simmons, and Paul McNutt.

Their first operational decision was to return the newspaper to a morning publication as of December 3, 1934. The new owners positioned the change as "answering an almost unanimous call to service from the readers of Fort Wayne and northern Indiana."[3] They promised "a militant, but fair, Democratic newspaper," supporting the principles of Presi-

There was more to deliver than newspapers for *Journal-Gazette* drivers at Christmas in 1940. The Christmas baskets program was an annual effort to help the needy at the holidays.

dent Roosevelt. "December 3 will mark the beginning of a New Deal by the *Journal-Gazette*—Fort Wayne's New Deal Newspaper."

At the same time, Roosevelt named Lew Ellingham postmaster of Fort Wayne, a post he held until his death in 1939. One of Ellingham's final personnel moves at the *Journal-Gazette* had been to appoint Frank Roberts as managing editor in 1933. Roberts, who would play a leadership role in the newspaper for the next forty years, was indicative of the men and women Ellingham hired to make the newspaper more urbane and more committed to the modern standards of journalism, namely, greater objectivity and greater understanding of the community. Men like Roberts, Cliff Milnor, and Bob Reed set the tone of the *Journal-Gazette* for many years. Lew's son, Miller Ellingham, who joined the newspaper after graduating from Columbia University in 1924, would spend thirty-seven years with the *Journal-Gazette*.

The search for a publisher presented an interesting problem for the owners of the *Journal-Gazette*, since none of them could take on the responsibilities. At the time Paul McNutt was governor of Indiana, the first Democrat to hold that office in sixteen years and a rising star in the party nationally. McNutt viewed the ownership of the Fort Wayne newspaper as crucial for the party, since the lack of Democratic newspapers was "the greatest problem the party has faced in the last half century."[4] His perception was reminiscent of his Civil War predecessor, Oliver Morton, except that Morton had been bemoaning the lack of a Republican newspaper, not a Democratic one.

Simmons, who directed McNutt's gubernatorial campaign in 1932, held an appointed office in the state and couldn't undertake the responsibility of running a daily newspaper. The third co-owner, James Fleming, was a federal prosecutor. So McNutt turned to his former roommate at Indiana University, William A. Kunkel Jr., and asked him to be the *Journal-Gazette* publisher in 1934. Simmons and Fleming remained as co-owners, and Kunkel—whose other roommate at IU was Wendell C. Willkie—became president of the corporation in October 1935.

Like Ellingham, Kunkel gained his first newspaper experience as a youth at the *Bluffton Banner.* Born February 20, 1895, in Wells County, Kunkel was graduated from Bluffton High School and earned a bachelor's degree at Indiana University in 1916. A year later he received his law degree from Harvard University and entered the navy as an ensign during World War I.

Kunkel had a breadth of business experience, including service as a receiver for three banks, president of an interurban line, consultant on oil production and financing, and officer of a hotel company before joining the *Journal-Gazette.* He was committed to improving the newspaper and was the first publisher in Indiana to add Associated Press Wirephoto Service to his newspaper. This made news photographs available in the same time frame as the wire service's news copy. Kunkel's interests weren't limited to the printed word. In 1947 he established radio stations under the call letters WKJG and WKJG-FM. The KJG stood for "Kunkel Journal Gazette."

Kunkel's civic interests were varied, too. He was on the first board of directors of the Fort Wayne Musical Society, the forerunner of the Fort Wayne Philharmonic. He was a member of many Indiana University alumni groups and had a deep interest in sports, not only at the collegiate level but also at the professional level. He was instrumental in bringing professional minor league baseball back to Fort Wayne in 1948 when the Fort Wayne Generals were granted a franchise in the newly reorganized Central League.

It is rare that anyone—let alone a publisher—has the opportunity to watch his former college roommate run for president of the United States. Kunkel did in 1940 when Wendell C. Willkie won the Republican Party nomination. Energetic and idealistic, Willkie was very attractive to those wanting to block Roosevelt from having an unprecedented third term and from the United States entering the war in Europe. Willkie's background as a president of a large utilities holding company and opposition to the New Deal made him attractive to businessmen throughout the nation. While it must have been tempting to join the other Indiana supporters of the Hoosier-born candidate, the *Journal-Gazette* did not. It continued to warn of the Nazi onslaught in Europe and believed that FDR was the man who should be in the White House if the United States went to war. But Willkie never came close to winning the presidency. With a record turnout of more than fifty million voters, Roosevelt defeated him by five million votes. The Electoral College vote was overwhelming—449 for Roosevelt to 82 for Willkie. In Allen County, Willkie beat Roosevelt by more than 10,000 votes, contributing to his 25,000-vote margin of victory in his home state of Indiana.

The *Journal-Gazette*, like most of Indiana's newspapers, had a fondness for Willkie. This admiration grew after the election as Willkie worked for the Allies' victory in the war and his book *One World* set the stage for the creation of the United Nations. When he died unexpectedly in 1944, the newspaper's editorial page praised him as "a true statesman." His efforts for world peace left an "imprint permanently upon the thinking of this generation," the newspaper wrote.[5]

The role of the United States in the European conflict was the subject of a strong editorial disagreement between Fort Wayne's two newspapers. The *News-Sentinel* became one of the strongest supporters of the nation's isolationist policies, as one might expect of a Republican newspaper at the time. The *Journal-Gazette*, meanwhile, endorsed President Roosevelt's efforts to sustain Great Britain in the face of Adolf Hitler's Nazi war machine. The *News-Sentinel* did not see any benefit in the nation becoming involved in European wars. It certainly was against any cooperation with the Soviet Union and "Bloody Joe Stalin," as it regularly referred to the Russian dictator. On the other hand, the *Journal-Gazette* favored the weakening of the Neutrality Act, the strengthening of the Lend-Lease program with England, and the right of American ships to protect themselves.

The *News-Sentinel* was among the stoutest supporters of the America

First movement and championed the membership efforts of the local committee. As a result, Colonel Charles Lindbergh was invited to make a major speech in Fort Wayne in October 1941. The wildly adored hero of the first solo flight from America to Paris in 1927 was the leader of the America First campaign, convinced that war did not make any sense and that conflict with Hitler must be avoided. He criticized Roosevelt, claiming the president deceived the American people in early speeches about the nation maintaining its neutrality. By the time of his Fort Wayne appearance, Lindbergh was losing his popularity. In a speech in Des Moines on September 11, 1941, he said the British, the Jews, and the Roosevelt administration were the three main agitators pushing the United States into the war. This caused a small firestorm of criticism around the county, which puzzled Lindbergh somewhat, since he believed "the entire audience seemed to stand and cheer"[6] when he made the accusation. In an entry in his journal on September 15, Lindbergh added: "It seems that almost anything can be discussed today in America except the Jewish problem. The very mention of the word 'Jew' is cause for a storm." Lindbergh's supporters agreed with him privately, but feared he had gone too far and that any further speeches might be suppressed by the opposition or by the Roosevelt administration. In the weeks leading up to the Fort Wayne speech, the *News-Sentinel*'s editorials defended Lindbergh against what it called a "smear" campaign. It ominously warned of potential disruptive tactics by the opposition at future America First events.

Lindbergh traveled to Fort Wayne from New York on October 2, 1941, noting in his journal that he was going to be the guest of an exceptionally good American First chapter due to the efforts of the chapter secretary "and to the fact that one of the local papers has been giving us support. We have become so accustomed to an opposition press that it is a strange and pleasant experience to pick up a local paper which carries friendly headlines and editorials."[7] The *Journal-Gazette* covered the arrival in its October 3 edition with a photograph on page one of Lindbergh being welcomed by Mayor Harry Baals and American First representatives, along with a short article about the United Auto Workers chapter stating that the visit was an "unwelcome event." The photograph's caption noted that William J. Gross, editorial editor, and Clifford B. Ward, managing editor, of the *News-Sentinel* were among the welcoming committee but that they had declined to pose for the *Journal-Gazette* photographer. The editorial column led with a poem entitled "Knight of the German Eagle." In part, it described Lindbergh as

> A man who speaks Hitler's language,
> Whose counsel is: Wait and pay:
> Pay with the blood of your young men;
> Pay the full price of defeat:
> Wait for your friends to be vanquished,
> Then die here at home—or retreat.

The October 3 edition of the *News-Sentinel* put the event in perspective when it wrote that "the eyes of the nation will be on Fort Wayne tonight," since Lindbergh's speech was to be broadcast by the NBC Blue Network. It called again upon the opposition not to disrupt the proceedings at the Gospel Temple on Rudisill Boulevard and to allow Lindbergh to be heard. Lindbergh noted in his journal that the *Journal-Gazette* carried a full-page ad in which "statements are attributed to me which I never made. As far as the 'war party' is concerned, what I actually say seems to be of little importance."[8] He apparently did not notice that the full-page ad that reprinted a scathing editorial from the New Bedford, Massachusetts, *Standard Times* also appeared in the *News-Sentinel.*

Lindbergh's speech was not disrupted by any of the feared demonstrations. The interpretations of the speech and the people's reactions differed greatly in two Fort Wayne newspapers on Saturday, October 4. The eight-column headline in the *Journal-Gazette* read, "Lindbergh Stands on Record," with a three-column drop headline noting that the speaker did not disavow his anti-Jewish statements. A second drop headline added: "America First Spokesman Tells Audience 1942 Elections Endangered by President; Decries Administration's Anti-Nazi Efforts." A complete version of Lindbergh's speech was printed on page twelve. The newspaper noted that Senator Champ Clark, who had been billed as one of the speakers, was replaced by the Reverend John A. O'Brien of the University of Notre Dame. In addition, the front page carried a story that Wallace W. Kirkland, photographer for *Life* magazine, was barred from the speech. Kirkland was denied credentials in the afternoon, and when he tried to enter the Gospel Temple, he was dragged from the building upon the orders of the America First committee. No reason was given for the action.

The Saturday evening *News-Sentinel* story focused on Lindbergh's concern that he would be silenced in the days ahead by the government. "Free Speech Gag May Be Government's Next Step, Lindbergh Says" was the October 4 headline. "Address Here Possibly His Last, Hero Tells America First Rally" was the drop headline on page one. Lindbergh's speech was set in an easy-to-read two-column format on page one.

In his remarks Lindbergh warned that the United States was about to enter a period of dictatorship and foreign war. He said that going to war against "the greatest military power the world has ever known" would require "turning this country into a military state on standards similar to those of Germany herself." Lindbergh predicted America would have to raise an army of ten million men and "that every family in America will have its wounded and its dead." There would be further costs, he said. An invasion of Europe by U.S. troops would be devastatingly costly to the American way of life. "There is not a chance for freedom, moderation, tolerance, and idealism to emerge from a prolonged war," Lindbergh said.[9]

While the reporting in the two newspapers captured Lindbergh's message, they differed on the size of the audience and its reaction. Emery Applegate, Jr., of the *News-Sentinel* described a cheering crowd of 10,000, with 5,500 inside and 4,500 or more outside. Phil Nicar of the *Journal-Gazette* said the city fire chief estimated the crowd inside at 4,200 and at more than 2,000 outside. Nicar, unlike his counterpart, went into detail on how those in the reserved seat section behind the podium were directed to heighten the crowd's reaction to Lindbergh's comments. "At the conclusion of Lindbergh's comments the crowd stood and there was a long cheer, staged largely by the group that occupied the speakers' platform," Nicar wrote.[10] Lindbergh was pleased with the reception, having been told by the mayor that extra seats had been added so that the hall held 8,000 people. "The crowd was with us from the beginning," Lindbergh wrote in his journal. "There was no opposition during the entire meeting. (As a matter of fact, I think some opposition is a good thing.)"[11]

There were different interpretations in subsequent editorials from the two newspapers, too. The Sunday *Journal-Gazette* said the people of Fort Wayne listened but did not cheer the Lindbergh speech. "They were curious about you, Mr. Lindbergh. Men and women, who formerly admired you with a genuineness you no longer deserve, hoped you might take back some of the prejudicial remarks spoken or written by you. . . . They were disappointed, Mr. Lindbergh. Those who had not been previously disillusioned were disillusioned Friday."[12]

On the editorial page Monday evening, the *News-Sentinel* was ecstatic. "After that Lindbergh rally, can there be any question in any sane mind as to the anti-war sentiments of, not 80, but at least 90 percent of the people in this community?" the editorial writer asked rhetorically. "The rally was a great outpouring of representative citizens of a typical American community, who with spontaneous enthusiasm stood and cheered and shouted to Colonel Lindbergh their wish to continue to ride that new 'beam' of support accorded him by all those millions who, whatever may be their incidental differences with him, are in full sympathy with the Lone Eagle's central purpose of opposing this country's needless participation in other peoples' wars."[13]

While Lindbergh worried that his speech in Fort Wayne would be his final one, Washington did not silence him. Lindbergh spoke before a very large crowd inside and outside Madison Square Garden in New York on October 30, 1941. Five weeks later, though, the Japanese attack on Pearl Harbor made the issue of the United States remaining out of the war moot, and Lindbergh eventually found a role in the fighting.

The war brought challenges to Fort Wayne and to its newspapers. The number of young men entering the service from the community was significant. The War Manpower Commission monitored industrial areas such as Fort Wayne in which 48-hour minimum work weeks were compulsory for essential industries. Every four months the commission classified each area's labor supply as critical, strong, adequate, or plentiful. Fort Wayne was listed as critically low from the fall of 1943 to the spring of 1945.[14] Rationing had an impact on reporters, advertising, and circulation. As the war wore on, the shortage of newsprint forced the newspaper to temporarily eliminate all advertising from the Saturday and Monday editions.

In late October 1944, one of the most stirring campaign rallies in the city's history took place in the downtown area. Franklin Delano Roosevelt, said to be looking tanned and fit, made an informal appearance and presentation at the Harrison Street railroad elevation on his way to the party's nominating convention in Chicago. A sea of humanity—estimated at between 30,000 and 35,000 people—crowded into the plaza below the station to see the president. During the long wait before Roosevelt's arrival, little impatience was shown by the crowd. "The people wanted to see their war leader and didn't mind the exhaustion that standing in one place can produce," *Journal-Gazette* reporter William J. Sweeney wrote.

When he arrived, Roosevelt spoke for only ten minutes, rebutting some of the charges leveled by his Republican opponent, Thomas E. Dewey. Roosevelt praised productivity of the region's workers, especially farmers and railroad employees, for their war efforts. He urged them to vote, saying that he wanted to win or lose by a big margin. Winning or losing by a small margin "wouldn't spell democracy."

When Roosevelt finished "and was on his way back to his chair in the last car of the train the majority of the crowd stayed where it was,"

A weary Franklin Delano Roosevelt addresses a crowd during a brief
stop in Fort Wayne in October 1944. FDR was en route to the
Democratic Party National Convention, which would nominate him
for an unprecedented fourth term as president.

Sweeney wrote. "They wanted to look at the famous Roosevelt wave of
farewell."[15]

FDR won his fourth term in November, but Dewey defeated Roosevelt in both Allen County and the state. In five more months FDR
would be dead.

There were some bright spots in Fort Wayne in 1945. One was the arrival of an All-American Girls Professional Baseball League team that
would capture the hearts of the community for decades to come. The
league was conceived by chewing gum magnate and Chicago Cubs owner

Philip K. Wrigley in 1943 as a way to boost attendance during the war. In 1945 a team was assigned to Fort Wayne, but it lacked a nickname. As the start of the season neared, the league featured some delightful names: the Grand Rapids Chicks, the Rockford Peaches, the Racine Belles, the South Bend Blue Sox, and the Kenosha Comets. The local team was only listed as the "Fort Wayne Girls Team." The *Journal-Gazette* stepped in and sponsored a contest to name the team. Two days before the season opened, the name "Daisies" was selected from more than 100 entries. Appropriately, the first prize of a season's pass was awarded to a woman, Jeanmarie Hackman.[16] The Fort Wayne Daisies became the darlings of the city during the life of the league. Forty years later a movie, *A League of Their Own*, paid tribute to the AAGPBL players and rekindled the community's appreciation of the women who were pioneers in professional sports.

The end of the war in Europe was a moment of triumph for the *Journal-Gazette* newsroom, but the day that Japan surrendered was not. The newspaper was well prepared for a special edition once the Germans surrendered in May 1945. Jim Lovette, who joined the newspaper in 1937, was the news editor at the time. He remembered that an entire newspaper, filled with previously written wire service copy and advertising, had been made up in advance and cast in plates for the presses. "Each night after the morning's regular edition was run, these war extra plates were put on the press. All Page One needed was the war lead bulletin and it was ready to go. The last week of the war, I think I slept on a settee in the photo studio, just waiting to get this one on the road," he said in an interview with reporter Dell Ford in 1977. While the VE Day extra was a success, VJ Day was not. Both the *Journal-Gazette* and the *News-Sentinel* were shut down by a printers' strike.

In September 1945, one of the most popular newspaper writers in the history of Fort Wayne launched his column. For the next twenty-seven years, Cliff Milnor's "Lines and Angles" would entertain readers with his understated midwestern humor. The column gathered anecdotes from throughout the area that made readers smile and appreciate their community. When Milnor retired on October 10, 1972, *Journal-Gazette* reporter Dell Ford wrote that Milnor's wit and style "provided the sugar for many a cup of morning coffee."

A native of Rome City, Indiana, Milnor began his career at the *Goshen Daily Democrat* after graduating from Indiana University in 1930. He joined the *Journal-Gazette* in 1933 and worked as a copy editor, state editor, city editor, and acting managing editor before beginning his column.

Its immediate popularity didn't surprise Park Williams, who remembered that Milnor was the most popular staff member during the local newspaper strike. Although there wasn't a newspaper printed for distribution during this period, staff members produced news releases on the strike and posted them in the windows of the Journal-Gazette Building. "It was Cliff's duty to hang the comics each day," Williams recalled, referring to the syndicated strips that arrived in the mail, "and he was the only staff member to collect an advance crowd."[17]

The cessation of the fighting brought to a gradual close the front-page stories of area men killed, wounded, or missing in action in World War II. An examination of copies of front pages of the morning newspaper from 1942 through 1945 shows a seemingly ceaseless series of news stories about the casualties, usually accompanied by a small photograph of a serviceman in uniform. While the return of the GIs promised a new prosperity ahead, the economic conditions of the *Journal-Gazette* were not ideal. William Kunkel's death of a heart attack in his office on October 7, 1948, thrust the responsibility of running the newspaper on the remaining partners, Virgil Simmons and James Fleming. Simmons was elected president of the corporation on January 4, 1949. The cost of operating the radio stations and other corporate amenities was proving to be too much of a burden. Simmons and Fleming decided to sell the radio stations, eliminate a private automobile service for top management, drop the country club membership perks, and halt the operation of a private dining room on the top floor of the *Journal-Gazette* building. They also sold a building across Clinton Street that had served as a garage for the maintenance of corporate-owned vehicles.

From his experience with state government during the Depression, Simmons knew how to cut costs. Born in Bluffton in 1893, Simmons was a graduate of Indiana University and a lawyer, earning his law degree at IU in 1918. He served as assistant U.S. district attorney in Indianapolis after graduation before joining his father as a member of a law firm in Bluffton. Simmons entered politics in 1931 when he was elected to the General Assembly. A year later, he earned statewide recognition for his efforts on behalf of McNutt's gubernatorial candidacy. The new governor rewarded his former college roommate with an appointment in 1933 as chief administrative officer of the State Conservation Department, where Simmons used the new federal programs of President Roosevelt—particularly the Civilian Conservation Corps (CCC)—to revitalize Indiana's state parks. Under his direction, forty-two CCC camps were established whose participants built shelters, picnic areas, trails, and roadways. In addition,

Simmons oversaw extensive water, drainage, and erosion control projects as well as numerous educational programs.

His public service career continued in Washington, D.C., in 1940, first as an administrative assistant in the Federal Security Agency. After World War II began, Simmons was appointed to the powerful War Manpower Commission. His final public post was as a member of the board of trustees for the U.S. Virgin Islands, an appointment made by President Harry Truman.

When Kunkel died in late 1948, Simmons returned to Fort Wayne to serve as president as well as co-publisher with Fleming. Known to his friends and family as "Skitz," Simmons shepherded the *Journal-Gazette* into a new era of newspapers in Fort Wayne.

FORT WAYNE GAZETTE.

THE MORNING JOURNAL.

FT. WAYNE JOURNAL=GAZETTE.

THE FORT WAYNE JOURNAL-GAZETTE.

FORT WAYNE JOURNAL-GAZETTE

FORT WAYNE JOURNAL-GAZETTE

THE JOURNAL-GAZETTE

The Journal-Gazette

Journal Gazette

7

Under One Roof, but
Still Independent

If a free society cannot help the many who are poor, I cannot save
the few who are rich.

—John F. Kennedy

When the *Journal-Gazette* and the *News-Sentinel* announced the
signing of a joint operating agreement on March 13, 1950, for the production and distribution of their newspapers, it was greeted with shock, disbelief, and even anger in the community. Compounding those reactions
was a general misunderstanding of what the agreement meant. Most
people assumed that it was a good deal for the *News-Sentinel*; many believed that the afternoon paper would gain even more influence in the
community; and some thought it would mean the eventual demise of the
morning newspaper.

It may never be known whose idea it was to merge the non-news portions of the newspapers. Helene Foellinger, the publisher of the *News-
Sentinel*, apparently told associates she realized that the *Journal-Gazette*
was in financial difficulty again and needed to be rescued. That could have
been true with the expense of the radio stations; however, net paid daily
circulation had reached 69,000 in 1949 while the Sunday paper's circulation topped 85,000. The *News-Sentinel*'s circulation was 81,417. Virgil
Simmons, who was running the day-to-day operations, apparently read
about a similar operating agreement in Tucson and brought the suggestion to Miss Foellinger. The *News-Sentinel* invested the necessary capital
to start the new company, Fort Wayne Newspapers, Inc.

The concept of an agreement allowing separately owned newspapers
to consolidate services without violating antitrust laws is more common

today than in 1950, when it was a radical idea. The Fort Wayne joint operating agreement creating Fort Wayne Newspapers required federal legislation which Congressman E. Ross Adair sponsored. It gave the control of decisions affecting all the operations outside of the newsroom to a three-person board. That board was composed of two representatives from the *News-Sentinel* and one from the *Journal-Gazette*. While it lowered the operating costs for both newspapers by eliminating redundant jobs, there was a built-in decision bias for the majority owner, the *News-Sentinel*. The *Journal-Gazette*, for example, was prevented from having sufficient staff for a seven-day news operation. Any decision to add news staff to the *Journal-Gazette* resulted in a greater addition to the *News-Sentinel* staff so that the six-day evening newspaper had more reporters, editors, and photographers than the seven-day morning newspaper. Reportedly, the new combined circulation department limited the *Journal-Gazette*'s growth in circulation by requiring an equal or greater growth in the number of *News-Sentinel* subscribers.

The fact was that the 1950s were a struggle for both newspapers. The *Journal-Gazette*'s average net paid daily circulation fell from 67,519 in 1950 to 63,867 in 1959. The *News-Sentinel*'s corresponding circulation numbers were 81,729 and 75,968, respectively. While both dailies' sales were down, the Sunday *Journal-Gazette*'s increased 12 percent, from 87,589 to 97,391. The *News-Sentinel*'s circulation rose through the mid-1960s when it almost reached 78,500. Since then, the afternoon newspaper's average has fallen steadily, dropping to 28,994 in 2006. The *Journal-Gazette*'s average net paid daily circulation dropped below 60,000 in 1981 and hovered around that figure until 2002, when it jumped 11.8 percent. In 2006, the *Journal-Gazette*'s circulation was 70,004. Meanwhile, the Sunday newspaper passed the 100,000 circulation mark in 1980 and in 2006 averaged more than 121,000 copies sold each week.

In 1970 Congress passed the Newspaper Preservation Act in the wake of several daily newspaper closures. According to the Newspaper Association of America, the law was "created to preserve a diversity of editorial opinion in communities where the market no longer supported two competing daily newspapers." There have been fewer than thirty joint operating agreements, and only twelve remain in operation. Some are in large metropolitan areas, such as Cincinnati, Detroit, Denver, and Seattle. Others are located in York, Pennsylvania, Charleston, South Carolina, Birmingham, Alabama, Las Vegas, Salt Lake City, and Albuquerque. The Fort Wayne agreement is among the oldest; it is located in one of the smallest populations and has been renewed twice.

The Mergenthaler typesetting machine in the old Journal-Gazette building.

This photograph was part of a series in 1950 showing how the newspaper was produced. Here, a compositor is placing type in a form for a news page.

The signing of the joint operating agreement in 1950 meant one significant physical change for the *Journal-Gazette*: its staff had to move. The agreement kept the news-gathering departments separate and competitive, but they—like the consolidated production operation—could be housed under one roof. The logical site for the new arrangement was the *News-Sentinel* building at East Washington Boulevard and Barr Street. That building, which was erected under the direction of publisher Oscar Foellinger in 1925, was three stories with a handsome lobby. The editorial department for the *Journal-Gazette* was located on the third floor while the *News-Sentinel's* newsroom was on the second floor.

The move from "the old homestead" on Clinton Street, as columnist Cliff Milnor called the building, was not without some remorse. The building had been the *Journal-Gazette's* home for fifty-two years, and it held generations of memories. In a column titled "Lights Out at 701," Milnor remembered the lamps that hung from long cords over the editing desk, with their large green glass shades on which Bill Kellogg would tap out "Assembly" with a copy pencil; the .45-caliber bullet in the baseboard of the morgue where a young reporter had debated whether he needed a gun to go out on a vice raid with police and accidentally fired the weapon; and the time Andy Moynihan was so upset with a poor connection on the telephone that he ripped it off the wall, carried it to the street, and flung it into the gutter. In many ways, the building held memories of an industry now disappeared.

The executive offices of the Journal-Gazette Company remained at the Clinton Street building. It was remodeled into multi-tenant office space in 1951. As would be expected, the structure aged appreciably over the years because of the constant truck and automobile traffic along the major thoroughfares as well as the soot from trains passing two blocks away. When the city promoted a revitalization of the Central Business District in the early 1980s, *Journal-Gazette* publisher Richard Inskeep put into action a plan to renovate and restore the Journal-Gazette Building to its original beauty. The concept of the renovation undertaken in 1982 by Archonics, Inc., was to create an "atmosphere of harmony and openness" inside the structure through a blend of old decorative design elements and contemporary features. A striking glass-covered atrium allowed light into the building's interior, providing a central organizing feature while eliminating corridors to individual offices. The ornamental stamped metal pan ceilings were uncovered as were beam and cornice details in the atrium's mezzanine area. The exterior was cleaned, and the original stonework was repaired. Weatherhogg's original copper canopies had been damaged over the years and were replaced with copies developed from artist renderings and photographs of the original structures. The brick arched windows were restored, some segmented with double arched wood infill panels. Decorative copper-spandrel panels were added in the ground floor windows. As a result, the Journal-Gazette Building was named to the National Register of Historic Places in late December 1982.

It did not take as much work to restore the community's understanding that the *Journal-Gazette* was still an independent news operation, although it did take some time. Public reaction to the announcement of the joint operating agreement in 1950 was confused. Some thought the morning newspaper's editorial independence was going to be silenced. The Allen County Democratic chairman told a luncheon meeting of the party faithful that it was an "unconstitutional monopoly" and that the *Journal-Gazette* had abandoned the Democrats. Fort Wayne, Jim Kelley said, was now a one newspaper town. In another moment of political hyperbole, Kelley charged that co-publisher Jim Fleming had "sold his soul to the Republican Party."[1]

The "soul," if you will, of the *Journal-Gazette* newsroom had not changed, even if it was in new quarters. Miller Ellingham, tall, distinguished, and unsmiling, was the executive editor. Frank Roberts, now with a shock of white hair, was the managing editor. Jim Lovette, who encouraged reporters to develop good story ideas, was the news editor. Columnist Cliff Milnor circulated among the staff, catching up on the news and sometimes finding items for his "Lines and Angles." Nick Plasterer, who would later write a classic journalism textbook, was the graying, mild-mannered city editor. Claude Nichens was still a fixture on the copy desk, wearing one of the industry's hallmarks, a green eyeshade.

Even Helen May Irwin was still writing for the *Journal-Gazette*. Although she was officially retired as the church editor, Helen May—as she was called—wrote long, long stories about Christmas and Easter services. Almost painful in their attention to detail, the stories covered several pages which, when pasted together for the copy desk, measured several feet in length. She was a short, stout, and very devout woman who always dressed in black and reportedly huffed and puffed up the three flights of stairs to deliver her copy to the newsroom. As with most newsrooms, the *Journal-Gazette* had its share of near-legendary stories about reporters and editors, and one concerned Helen May. It seemed she had submitted a lengthy Easter story to Park Williams, who was managing editor during the early days of World War II. Williams sent her back to cut it. Helen May took a black pencil to it, crossed out a few details, and resubmitted it.

Again, Williams sent her back to cut it. Again, she made some minor deletions. At the third submission, Williams looked up at her from his copy desk chair. "Helen May, when I tell you to cut your copy," he said, reaching for the long shears used to cut news copy off the wire service printers, "this is what I mean." And he lopped off half of her copy and let it drop into the wastebasket. Helen May was still writing lengthy stories on church life in the early 1950s, and it didn't appear to some members of the staff that Park Williams's message had left any impression on her.

The only major transformation in the design on the newspaper occurred in August 1952 when the editorials were set in a more readable two-column format. There was a bigger change going on, though. One day the Society editor received a call from a woman who wanted to know if the *Journal-Gazette* accepted colored pictures. The editor answered, "Yes, but we prefer black and white," and ended the conversation. In a few minutes, she realized the real nature of the question as a young African American woman, who must have been calling from the lobby of the building, brought in her engagement photo. The *Journal-Gazette* ran the photograph and notice, but the rarity of an African American woman appearing in the Society's pages made it so memorable that Pat Kelsey Watkins, a staff writer who was there, remembered it fifty years later. Unlike some southern newspapers at the time that printed births, weddings, and obituaries of African Americans only as paid notices, there were no racial prohibitions for the *Journal-Gazette*. There were occasional photographs earlier in the century of African Americans, often to illustrate news items about organizations such as the Phyllis Wheatley Social Center. These were rare, though, and it was a form of invisible segregation that was to be overcome.

There wasn't anything silent about political shenanigans in Fort Wayne. Accusations and allegations about elected officials had existed since the town was settled, but in November 1950 a grand jury investigation really rocked city hall. Tabloid-sized headlines led the story about the mayor, police chief, police captain, a city councilman, a city purchasing agent, and the president of a coal supply company being named in a fifty-two-count indictment. The charges surrounded an alleged conspiracy to overcharge the city by two dollars a ton for the coal to supply its power plant. The mayor and the police chief were charged with several counts of conspiracy, while the police officials were charged with perjury. The coal company president was charged with bribery, and the councilman was indicted for accepting bribes.

Today the story seems vague, as it fails to convey the significance of the charges. Interestingly, copies of the Sunday newspaper after the arrests have not been preserved. The absence of an edition in the 1950s microfilm is an unusual occurrence, raising questions about what editorial commentary or political fallout was reported in that issue. Charges against Mayor Henry E. Branning Jr. and the others were dismissed in May 1954 because state law protected public officials from prosecution when compelled to testify about public contracts. Branning's mayoral career was over by that time, as he was defeated in the 1951 Democratic primary by Paul Mike Burns. It was only after another mayoral scandal that the 1950 case was reexamined and placed in a political context. The president of the coal company had been the county Democratic Party chairman during Branning's 1947 mayoral campaign. The person who sparked the grand jury investigation was Burns, who learned of the scheme from the supplier of coal to the city during the administration of Republican mayor Harry Baals. Burns lost the 1951 election but finally became mayor in 1960.

The coverage of the coal scandal in 1950 should have demonstrated to the community that the two newspapers' staffs were independent. Even though they were in the same building (but on different floors), competition remained intense. Even the "schools beat," as it was called then, was an area where a scoop counted. The managing editor for the *News-Sentinel* was a leader in the Fort Wayne Catholic Diocese, and naturally the newspaper's schools reporter, Dick Smith, received many news items first from the bishop. This was a sore spot with Griff Watkins, his counterpart on the *Journal-Gazette*. On one occasion, the bishop was announcing plans for a fund-raising campaign associated with new Catholic high schools. The intent was to make this announcement in the diocesan weekly newspaper, *Our Sunday Visitor,* published in Huntington. The *News-Sentinel* had the entire story in advance, whereas the *Journal-Gazette* had not even been contacted. But the *Journal-Gazette* had a stringer in Huntington who happened to work at *Our Sunday Visitor.* He called Watkins with the information, and the *Journal-Gazette* ran the story before the *News-Sentinel.* The bishop was furious and complained that his priests should have the news first from their own paper, which happened to coincide with the *News-Sentinel*'s news cycle. Watkins met with him to explain the *Journal-Gazette* position, and the bishop agreed to share future announcements. When the next major story was about to break, however, the bishop fell back into the old habit of not notifying the *Journal-Gazette.* The Huntington stringer alerted Watkins, who went to the Fort Wayne Post Office where he persuaded a worker to let him come

Columnist Cliff Milnor.

in to read from the edition of *Our Sunday Visitor* and to take notes. The *Journal-Gazette* ran the story the next morning and attributed the information to the diocesan weekly.

Not all of the news that was fit to print in the *Journal-Gazette* in that period was of a serious nature. With Cliff Milnor on the staff, there was always a bit of levity, even to the point of poking fun at his own industry. In late 1957 he wrote "Know Your Newsmen" with his typically deft touch. The column—it actually was spread over two issues, October 1 and 7, because of its length—provided some basic information to readers about the newspaper operation while also letting some air out of certain colleagues whose titles inflated their egos. Today it offers an insight into the newsroom of the 1950s:

> This is Newspaper Week. Last week was Dog Week. There is no plausible explanation for the proximity of the two observances as far as we know.
>
> The longer one remains in the business the more he is impressed by how little the general public knows (or cares) about what goes into a newspaper, and how it gets there.

For those who don't know and do care, we have prepared a sort of glossary defining the functions of various departments and persons who make up the newsroom of a newspaper.

(The newsroom has been described by cynics as the department which fills the spaces between advertisements. Efforts to eliminate news from newspapers have been unsuccessful thus far.)

REPORTERS: There are more of these than any other kind of person. They are the ones who make contact with the public more often. They gather the news and write it. They have friends and enemies in high-up and low-down places. Their job is regarded as the softest touch on the paper.

COPY READERS: These are the mist men of the profession. The public seldom sees them or hears their names. Their job is to read the reporters' copy and make cuts and corrections. Then they write a headline on it. You should meet more copy readers; their stuff is widely read.

Copy readers are sometimes accused of being intellectuals because they have been known to pull a volume of Proust from a drawer during a lull. More often it is a ham on rye from a lunch bucket. They regard themselves as craftsmen. Reporters call them murderers of deathless prose. Their job is considered by everyone else as the softest on the paper.

WIRE EDITOR: He sorts out the freshest, most pertinent stories coming in on the wire service teletypes and deals them out for editing to other copy readers. His evaluation of the wire news from Indianapolis to Istanbul is reflected on the front page. He also writes headlines and often has the outline of a novel at home. He knows the names of every French Cabinet member, but he can't find his way home from Calhoun and Washington.

CITY EDITOR: The fall guy. He cracks his whip over reporters, gives them assignments, points out their mistakes, and makes suggestions for improvement. He also must strive for harmony on his staff, keeping in mind that everyone can't have Christmas and Arbor Day off.

His is the thankless task of trying to mollify a committee from the Yakkity Benevolent Society whose officers' pictures got squeezed out by a hurricane. Sometimes he can be overheard in the small hours of morning saying, "I don't care what you think you heard on the radio. We have nothing on Princess Margaret's elopement with Aly Khan."

MANAGING EDITOR: Another fall guy. He is the policy carry-outer. Here is the buffer between his staff and the public. You take your troubles to him and he'll listen, then forget them because he has plenty of his own. He must soothe the disgruntled advertiser and protect his staff from attacks by offended persons. (What he tells his staff behind closed doors is nobody's business.) Few people covet his job.

EDITORIAL WRITER: The ivory tower dweller who finds himself forming opinions about everything he reads and sees. These people are noted for sniffing out trends. Editorial writers often are the most learned men in the building. It is easier to ask them how to spell a word than to seek it in an unabridged dictionary.

SOCIETY DEPARTMENT: These are females who are concerned with social events and women's interests. If they ever get all the weddings written, they'll attend some meetings in person. These gals are useful about the office. They decorate a small Christmas tree and always are getting candy and cookies.

SPORTS DEPARTMENT: A group of men headed by a sports editor who get to attend all athletic events and write about them. The sports editor attends the most important games. This department is a fount of wisdom for thick-voiced telephone callers who "wan' a li'l bet settled." They are a source of many passes for co-workers. Considered by everyone else the softest job on the paper.

OFFICE BOY: Purveyor of coffee and sandwiches, filler of pastepots and late mail sorter, this lad is here because he wanted to work his way into the newspaper business. After a year or more he will wrap his experience into an application blank and enter the public relations field. He'll be president yet.

COLUMNIST: This is regarded as the softest touch of all by everyone in the newsroom, including the columnist. Job usually filled by someone too weak to work, too mean to starve. The name "columnist" is derived from the length of his daily output, which, if he has judged the length of his copy correctly, should make about one full column of type. That is what he had in mind when he started this thing.

CARTOONIST: A white-collar worker with dirty fingers. Spends long hours gazing at blank drawing board with blank expression, then with bold strokes presents an opinionated picture of his mind. These men are true artists, and they detest an average-looking person. They want features they can caricaturize. A craggy brow can be sinister or benign, according to which faction its owner belongs.

PHOTOGRAPHERS: The brassiest guys in the business because they have to be. They are suckers for gory scenes and kids-with-pets pictures. They have been known to risk life and limb to get a fire shot and run away from a dead snake. Photogs will memorialize the first person to take a group picture without (1) the firing squad lineup (2) two of group shaking hands (3) group looking where someone is pointing. There is a dash of Rembrandt in all good photogs. Some of them spell identifications correctly.

LIBRARIAN: Like whisky, a librarian's value improves with age. Usually a female. She is the keeper of the morgue where cuts (pictures on zinc) are filed along with obituaries, news clips, etc. She may also double as the boss' secretary, so her opinions are valued. She usually is available for helping trim the Christmas tree.

Newspapers like the *Journal-Gazette* serve as the training ground for men and women who make significant contributions in the world of journalism later in their career. Gene Miller joined the Fort Wayne newspaper in 1950 after graduating from Indiana University. He left the newspaper in 1952 when he was drafted into the army. Miller later was a reporter for the *Wall Street Journal* and then won Pulitzer Prizes in 1967 at the *Miami Herald* and in 1976 for reporting that led to the release of people wrongly convicted of murder.

Another alumnus of the newspaper was Ray Scherer, who became NBC's Washington correspondent. A 1942 graduate of Valparaiso University and a veteran of the D-Day invasion, Scherer joined NBC News in

Ray Scherer, right, accepts an award from Fort Wayne Press Club president David Lee as his father, Arnold Scherer, beams in June 1956. Scherer, an NBC White House correspondent during the Eisenhower administration, began his career with the *Journal-Gazette*.

Washington in 1947 and was the first newsman to do a daily radio broadcast from the White House. He covered Presidents Dwight D. Eisenhower, John F. Kennedy, and Lyndon B. Johnson. His father, Arnold Scherer, who was hired in 1906 by Andy Moynihan, retired in February 1968 as assistant secretary of the Journal-Gazette Company and of the auditing department for Fort Wayne Newspapers. Ray Scherer spoke at Hotel Van Orman in June 1956 about his four years covering Eisenhower, relating how Ike had a memory for detail. They were on the 1952 campaign train traveling through Ohio that stopped briefly in Fort Wayne so that local officials could brief the candidate on the city's industrial prowess. After going on and on about pumps, pistons, magnet wire, small motors, and the fact that Fort Wayne was known as the City of Churches, Ike asked if they hadn't forgotten something. No, it didn't seem so. In 1922, Lt. Dwight Eisenhower had brought a convoy through the city and

It was a happy day for both the publishers of the *Journal-Gazette* and
the *News-Sentinel* when ground was broken for the newspaper building
on West Main Street in July 1956. Smiling for the camera were Helene
Foellinger of the *News-Sentinel* and Virgil Simmons and James Fleming
of the *Journal-Gazette*. Mrs. Foellinger's mother, Esther, is second from
right.

stayed two days with a local family. All he heard about then was Johnny
Appleseed this and Johnny Appleseed that. Perhaps, Ike said with a small
smile, the city officials ought to include something about the legend of
John Chapman and his propagation of fruit trees in the 1820s wilderness
in their presentations about Fort Wayne.

By the mid-1950s, the combined operation of the two newspapers was
putting a strain on the News-Sentinel Building. After two years of planning, ground was broken on July 26, 1956, for a new building to house
both newspapers on a three-acre site on West Main Street between Van
Buren and Fulton streets. The Fort Wayne Newspapers building, housing
the *News-Sentinel* on the second floor and the *Journal-Gazette* in a smaller
area at the rear of the first floor, was opened in 1958. Virgil Simmons died
unexpectedly on February 19, 1958, at age 64.

Of the three men integral to the operation of the *Journal-Gazette* for almost forty years—Kunkel, Simmons, and Fleming—it was James R. Fleming who was the oldest by more than a decade. Born in Henry County, Indiana, in November 1881, Fleming earned a law degree from the University of Michigan in 1904. Two years later he was elected to serve as prosecuting attorney for the 58th Judicial Circuit in Jay County in Portland from 1906 to 1910.

Fleming's career in public service began with a two-year term in the Indiana House of Representatives in 1913 and then four years in the Indiana Senate. He was elected a member of the Indiana Democratic Central Committee from 1922 to 1926, a period of turmoil in the party. In 1933, he was named U.S. district attorney for the Northeastern District of Indiana in Fort Wayne, a post he held until 1941. It was from this office that he personally prosecuted some of the more notorious criminals of the 1930s. Fleming played an important role in the community, especially with those activities focused on youth, education, the arts, and business. He twice served as chairman of the Indiana Arts Commission and was named by President John F. Kennedy to serve on the U.S. Advisory Commission on International Education and Cultural Affairs in 1962 and the National Youth Employment Council in 1964. He was one of thirteen prominent U.S. citizens named to UNESCO by Secretary of State Dean Rusk in 1964. Among his business activities was serving as a member of the Indiana Port Authority, which brought the state its first deep-water port facility in Porter County, and promoting the Allen County War Memorial Coliseum.

Fleming focused on the business aspects of the *Journal-Gazette*, letting professionals like Frank Roberts run the news operation. Despite being a tough former prosecutor, Fleming had his sensitivities. When he became fed up with what he believed to be irresponsible criticism of the newspaper in the letters to the editor, Fleming banned them from the *Journal-Gazette*. This policy wasn't reversed until Dick Inskeep ordered their resumption in May 1971. Roberts, on the other hand, was a steady hand at dealing with the public. Among the last of the remaining staff members from the *Evening Press*, both he and his wife, Bessie, came to Fort Wayne to work as reporters for the evening newspaper in 1921. When that newspaper folded, he moved to its morning parent. A native of Chandler, Indiana, Roberts was a high school orator in Boonville and worked summers on the *Boonville Standard* and in Tell City. He attended Indiana University before enlisting in the army during World War I. His early newspaper employment included the *Evansville Courier* and *Evansville Press*. In Fort

Frank Roberts spent fifty-one years with the *Journal-Gazette*, serving as a reporter, editorial page editor, and managing editor before retiring in 1972.

Wayne, he served as courthouse reporter and political writer before being named managing editor of the *Journal-Gazette* in 1933 at the age of 38. He also wrote editorials for the next thirty-nine years until his retirement. He won several Freedom Awards for editorials supporting the American way of life. He was named editor in 1963.

Roberts was what is sometimes called an "old school" newsman. He was in the newsroom every day, flatly refusing to take vacations. His knowledge of history and ability to cite famous quotations were formidable. He was gregarious and talked with a steady stream of visitors to the newsroom. The Roberts household in the 1930s and 1940s was a gathering place for artists, writers, politicians, teachers, and scholars. Poet and Lincoln scholar Carl Sandburg stayed with the Roberts during his visits. Bessie Keeran Roberts was a feature writer and society reporter for the *Journal-Gazette* and became a syndicated columnist whose interviews with famous people offered insights into issues of the times.

While Roberts was respected for being erudite and polite, his tenure on the editorial page carried over into a tumultuous, challenging time. His editorials were balanced, offering both sides of a dispute and more often than not hoping that a just solution could be found. He was informative, not contentiously opinionated like some of his predecessors. The war in Vietnam proved to be an editorial conundrum for the *Journal-*

Gazette, just as it did for many daily newspapers in the nation. News stories of the early actions in the war—such as the so-called Gulf of Tonkin incident in August 1964—received front-page treatment but no comment on the editorial page. The first national "teach-in" in Washington, D.C., was reported on page five on May 16, 1965, whereas an explosion that had killed 21 men at the Bien Hoa Air Force Base was on page one. While not mentioning either event, there was an editorial on May 17 that quoted Homer's Ulysses in relation to the war in Vietnam and the turmoil in the Dominican Republic. It reasoned that while these conflicts were "trying the patience of many Americans," the earlier generations had persevered in war. "Have we weakened?" it asked. "Viet Nam and the Dominican Republic are not something we wished for, but they have to be faced. Americans have borne worse than this." At the end of April 1967, General William Westmoreland told Congress that more combat troops were needed. The *Journal-Gazette* didn't offer its opinion the next day, but printed John T. Wheeler's Associated Press dispatch on the war-torn life of South Vietnamese farmers on the opinion page.

On February 1, 1968, the weather "ear" on the front page said the day would be "Murky." The story from Da Nang said the death toll of the Viet Cong was soaring in the Tet offensive. The headline on the first editorial that day reflected the outlook: "How Long a War?" In the wake of the enemy's desperate fighting, "Americans would like to think that this effort may be the beginning of the end, if it fails to achieve its goal. But that is a rather optimistic theory and may be just wishful thinking." The Tet offensive continued another three weeks, and the newspaper commented editorially that the chairman of the Joint Chiefs of Staff "sees no early end." More troops were being requested and would probably be sent to Vietnam, the editorial noted.

The newspaper's position on the Vietnam War changed over the next ten months. On January 1, 1969, publisher James R. Fleming wrote a front-page New Year's message that included his frustrations about the war. About two-thirds through the message, Fleming wrote:

> After our experience in Vietnam, we must realize that we cannot fight ground wars in either Asia or Africa.
>
> During the past few years more than a half million of our young men have been sent 10,000 miles from home to fight in the jungles of Vietnam against hordes of barbarians whose lives have very little, if any, value to the countries in which they live.
>
> Many have been killed and many more have been seriously wounded.
>
> These boys have been conscripted and taken from their homes, and the life of

every young man in America has been affected and disrupted by this unfortunate war.

Billions of dollars have been wasted with no result in gain.

We have lost the respect and friendship of most foreign nations, and the greater portion of our troubles at home have been caused by our entrance into this most unfortunate war.

But no matter how strongly you might disagree with the policy followed by our administration, as long as our boys are fighting in Vietnam, we must do everything in our power to help them in this struggle with the hope that President Nixon will be able to bring this war to a speedy conclusion.

Then on May 5, the *Journal-Gazette* and every other morning newspaper in the United States carried the story of the students slain by National Guardsmen at Kent State. There wasn't any immediate editorial comment as authorities tried to determine which group prompted the shootings. In a comment prior to the mammoth antiwar demonstrations throughout the nation, the newspaper said that it hoped the protesters would behave with dignity.

The publication of the Pentagon Papers—the top-secret, highly critical study of U.S. involvement in Southeast Asia—by the *New York Times* and the Justice Department's efforts to suppress the news prompted the *Journal-Gazette* to publish a lengthy editorial, "How the Nation Goes to War" on June 17, 1971. While declining to make a prediction on how the Supreme Court would rule on the publication of more of the report, the editorial noted: "What the report does accomplish is to eliminate a widely popular myth that the United States awkwardly, almost innocently, was drawn into an expanded military role in Southeast Asia. There is nothing in the published excerpts of the reports to indicate anything other than a carefully calculated effort to enlarge this nation's military participation in the war without appearing to have changed the basic public policy on the U.S.'s role."

There was a new editor and a new publisher by the time the Vietnam War ended. When Saigon capitulated to the North Vietnamese, an editorial headlined "The War We Lost" was published on May 1, 1975, and it had a bitter edge. While "the temptation to repress the memory is overpowering," the editorial maintained, "it was, in the final analysis, the United States which kept it all going, enriched the fawning supplicants of U.S. military might, and created a horrifying nightmare." It also was critical of "shrill and strident" protests and the violence that followed.

"There were so many things to debate, there was little room left for reason. There was so much to conceal and lie about that successive ad-

Richard Inskeep, publisher
from 1973 to 1997.

ministrations appeared totally cunning and deceitful. And so many died in
Vietnam that their 'honor' had to be defended. The killing had to continue." In a reference that was eerily reminiscent of the first editorials almost exactly ten years earlier, the May 1 editorial referenced the mythic
Ulysses: "So the Vietnam insanity fed on itself. Like a tragic hero, the nation was so steeped in blood that going forth seemed easier than returning."

When Frank Roberts retired in 1972, he had spent fifty-one years with
the Journal-Gazette Company. The newsman who never took a vacation
died less than a year later at age 78. The man who had read his editorials
throughout the years, publisher James Fleming, died four months later at
age 91. His successor was Richard G. Inskeep.

Dick Inskeep was the right man at the right time for the *Journal-
Gazette*. Hired at a time when few could know the fundamental changes
newspapers would face in the rest of the twentieth century, Inskeep
brought a sound, well-balanced approach. He hadn't started at the top;
instead, his first assignment in September 1949 was to create a new plant
ledger, inventorying and describing every piece of equipment in the
Journal-Gazette Building, from editors' pencils to the lead pigs used for
setting type and from the mail room to the mezzanine. It was a challenge
for the army veteran who was graduated from Indiana University on the

G.I. bill, but the experience taught him the workings of a newspaper like few of his peers. It was not "make-work" for someone handpicked to be publisher, either. When Virgil Simmons—who was the bachelor uncle of Dick's wife, Harriett—suggested Dick Inskeep might like to work at the newspaper, it sounded to the young man like an interesting job in accounting, not an offer that might lead to the publisher's position. Also, the *Journal-Gazette* was in the midst of trying to find ways to cut costs, and Inskeep's inventory would be valuable in knowing the nature of the company's assets. It was a pattern of learning-by-doing that continued until the Bluffton native appreciated what it took to publish a newspaper every day. From the distance of being a new employee, he watched as Simmons reorganized the newspaper company's priorities. Inskeep's experience as an infantryman and then as a cash-poor college student made him amenable to what was happening. Fifty years later he was still amazed at the excesses that had grown in the newspaper since 1940, from the free use of automobiles for the executives to the private dining room with its free lunch for department heads and their immediate assistants.

The joint operating agreement with the *News-Sentinel* came to fruition within his first year with the company. In retrospect, Inskeep can see the positives of the consolidated business operations. Yet he still harbors some sadness that the directors of the *Journal-Gazette* advertising and circulation departments lost their jobs. Inskeep believes their success in building the morning newspaper's revenues made the *News-Sentinel* aware of the increased competition it faced and made it willing to consider the joint operation.

Inskeep's education continued in the business office and tours of duty in the circulation, advertising, and composing departments. In the late 1950s, he moved into the editorial department, serving as managing editor. He spent a lot of time observing the operation and listening to the staff, rather than making snap judgments. He traveled with reporters and photographers to cover news events to understand what was involved and how they dealt with the pressures of deadlines. He came away with an appreciation for journalists and "their skill to listen, absorb and write about what they saw or heard in a complete and accurate fashion." His understanding of the newsroom's workload in producing a seven-day-a-week newspaper proved to be a critical factor later.

When Inskeep assumed the publisher's post in 1973, the joint operating agreement with the *News-Sentinel* was nearing its expiration date. His concern about the fairness of the agreement had been growing for several years. For example, the *Journal-Gazette* needed more staff, but it was blocked by the *News-Sentinel*'s majority on the Fort Wayne Newspapers board. The advertising rates were skewed against the *Journal-Gazette*. In addition, some of its subscribers were forced to receive their morning newspaper by mail rather than through home delivery.

When negotiations began to renew the operating agreement, Inskeep wanted thirteen changes made to produce a level of parity for the two newspapers. Each of Inskeep's proposals was rejected by a vote of two to one. It was time, Inskeep decided, to consider another alternative: Build a *Journal-Gazette* printing plant and end the operating agreement. A parcel of land on Interstate 69 was purchased while negotiations continued. A building designer, engineer, and construction managers were hired. A press was ordered and converted to offset to handle the *Journal-Gazette*. A groundbreaking was being planned when the *News-Sentinel* decided to sell its operation to the Knight-Ridder group. The sale was completed in 1980, and an operating agreement was signed between Knight-Ridder and the Journal-Gazette Company. Alva Chapman, then chief executive officer of Knight-Ridder, emphasized that the corporation wanted a profitable operation and would not impede the growth of the morning newspaper.

In 1980, the national trend in U.S. newspapers was evident. The number of daily morning newspapers had risen by 65 since 1950, while the number of daily evening newspapers had fallen by 62. There were 186 more Sunday newspapers in 1980 than thirty years earlier. The change in demographics—population, housing, education, television—was making the American stereotype of Dad and Mom reading the evening newspaper at home after supper an anachronism in many cities across the nation. It wasn't as severe in Fort Wayne, but the trend was visible.

The net paid circulation for the *News-Sentinel* averaged 71,088 in 1980, down from 81,729 in 1950. The *Journal-Gazette*'s average net paid circulation had dropped from 67,519 in 1950 to 60,369 in 1980. Sunday circulation averaged 105,666 in 1980, as compared with 87,589 in 1950. In 1985, the *Journal-Gazette* surpassed the *News-Sentinel* in net paid daily circulation.

When Frank Roberts retired, Inskeep promoted Larry Allen to editor and ushered in the modern design era of newspapers. For decades, most newspapers were gray and text-heavy. Long columns of type ran beside blocks of stodgy advertising. The front page was crowded with stories that continued on inside pages. The advent of new methods of setting type and reproducing images brought new concepts in layout for newspapers, especially from newspaper designers like Edmund Arnold. Stories were displayed in horizontal fashion and set in wider formats for easier reading. Photography and graphics became more prevalent, and color began to appear. Some days it was hard to distinguish the front page from another section front in the newspaper.

One of Inskeep's first steps as publisher was to change its political inclination. No more would the *Journal-Gazette* be the mouthpiece of the Indiana and Fort Wayne Democratic Party. The newspaper was still committed to issues like civil rights, school desegregation, and equal rights for women. Its positions would be liberal but not party-bound. Inskeep and his editors proved to be more determined about their positions than before. Their support of gun control, a woman's right to have an abortion, and affirmative action were unpopular in the conservative environs of Fort Wayne, and the newspaper's circulation suffered. From 1981 through 1985 and again in 2000, the *Journal-Gazette*'s circulation fell below 60,000, only to rebound to nearly 80,000 in 2004.

Allen, who had joined the *Journal-Gazette* in 1965 after graduating from Indiana University, was one of the staff's most polished reporters. He had covered local, state, legislative, and campaign issues, and he had written editorials since 1970. In his role as editor, Allen brought about more changes to the editorial page. It was by chance, however, that he revived a long dormant position of editorial cartoonist.

Despite its proud heritage, the *Journal-Gazette* chose to use editorial cartoons from syndicated artists until Larry Allen hired Bob Englehart.[2] Now one of the nation's leading editorial page cartoonists, Englehart sold his first cartoon to the *Journal-Gazette* in 1973 for twenty dollars. A native of Fort Wayne, he was graduated from South Side High School with a full scholarship to the American Academy of Art. After working for eight years in the art department of the *Chicago Today*, an evening newspaper, Englehart moved back to Fort Wayne where he owned a freelance art studio. His work in the *Journal-Gazette* increased from three cartoons a week to five. His first cartoon concerned the school board, which was planning on putting cameras in the high school bathrooms to stop smoking. Englehart's cartoon was in opposition to the plan, and congratulatory letters poured in. In 1975, Englehart began working full-time for the *Journal-Gazette* for $15,000 a year. He remembers Larry Allen saying, "Bob, there are people who have been working here for 20 years that aren't making that much money."[3] Englehart's work on the Nixon White House was remarkable, although it had an ironic ending. With its pronounced jowls and dark, baggy eyes, Englehart's Nixon was a classic political cartoon figure. Englehart produced a stream of cartoons as the Watergate scandal

When the U.S. Supreme Court ruled on July 25, 1974, that President
Richard Nixon must turn over the White House tapes regarding the
Watergate break-in, Bob Englehart drew this striking cartoon about
constitutional powers and who must obey them.

intensified. Yet the *Journal-Gazette* cartoonist was on vacation when the
president resigned, and he did not get to draw what might have been a
coup de grace. Englehart moved to the Dayton, Ohio, *Journal Herald* for
five years and then in 1980 to the *Hartford Courant*, where he has won
many awards.

In 1978 Allen hired Steve Sack, whose drawings of Richard Nixon
("here's a man you can't trust") and former mayor Win Moses ("cute like
a chipmunk") were memorable. Sack's national work was very pointed,
but it was his depictions of Fort Wayne attitudes that are still remembered. One cartoon chided then-candidate Moses for promising to spend
a day in various city departments to learn how the city runs. With chip-
munklike cheeks, the Moses character is equipped with a multitude of
cartoonish contraptions to help with garbage collection, snow removal,
the police department, the zoo, and abandoned car removal. A sickly cat
on the back of the equipment was labeled "mayoral assistant and rat control." In the bottom corner was a small wagon marked "desk calender [*sic*]
in case he wants to squeeze in some time to be mayor." In 1981 Sack

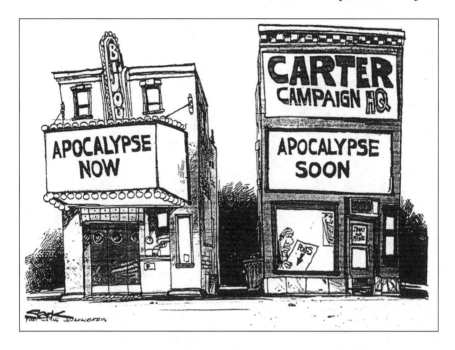

This classic editorial cartoon from the pen of Steve Sack is typical of the provocative work during his three years with the *Journal-Gazette*.

moved to the *Minneapolis Tribune*, which was later merged with the *Minneapolis Star*. He has become a prominent syndicated cartoonist whose work occasionally appears in the *Journal Gazette*.[4]

The third cartoonist in the newspaper's recent history was Dan Lynch, whose work at times was outrageous but more often outrageously funny. His topics were national and local. When Lincoln National announced it would move its corporate headquarters to Philadelphia in 1999, Lynch drew a cartoon of a modern-day news conference with Abraham Lincoln at the podium and one of the reporters in the foreground saying to another, "Sure he says the rest of the company will remain in Fort Wayne, but after Bill Clinton, who's EVER going to believe a President again?" In late September 2001, Lynch suffered a stroke and could no longer draw. For many admiring readers, the *Journal Gazette* was not the same without his work.

Another addition to the *Journal-Gazette* editorial page during Larry Allen's tenure was one of the most committed editorial writers in the region's history, befitting his early dream of being a preacher. Larry Hayes

Dan Lynch was equally adept at making the reader stop and think about one of his cartoons, whether it concerned a national or local issue. In this case, youth violence was a problem in Fort Wayne as well as Washington, making this cartoon especially poignant.

brought a busload of intensity to his editorials, especially those which involved people thought to be the underclass of society. Raised in Defiance, Ohio, Hayes was graduated from Great Lakes Bible College and attended a seminary. He taught high school English in Kentucky before joining the *Journal-Gazette* in 1973. In a community with very conservative views, Hayes fought long and hard for a fourteen-year-old Huntington girl who set a fire that killed her mother and sister. By Hayes's own admission, Donna Ratliff was a repulsive subject.[5] But he was incensed that the judicial system was intent on imprisoning the teenager as an adult and for failing to provide the therapy she needed. For nine years, Hayes pursued Ratliff's case, writing editorial after editorial, irritating officials, winning awards, and making a difference. In the late 1980s Hayes became a determined supporter of school desegregation. He retired in 2000, but remained passionate about social issues in the community.

Economic issues have plagued Fort Wayne for more than two decades, especially after International Harvester closed its mammoth plant. Once the career path for generations of workers—good-paying jobs for fathers

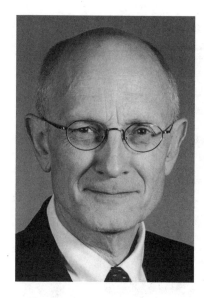

Larry Hayes, crusading
editorial writer.

meant good-paying jobs for their sons—the Harvester demise depressed
the community not only economically but also emotionally. While a
major strike by the United Auto Workers Local was seen as precipitating
the Harvester decision to close the Fort Wayne facilities, the problems
dated back further. The decision by Harvester to start producing a four-
wheel drive vehicle called the Scout was among several major investments
in the 1960s that were affected by the recession and energy crisis a decade
later. The Scout was discontinued in 1980 in an effort to save money. In
July 1982, Harvester announced it would close a truck plant either in Fort
Wayne or in Springfield, Ohio. The latter was chosen in September, and
the Fort Wayne assembly line shut down in July 1983. The *Journal-
Gazette* followed the story extensively, recording the impact of the Harvester shutdown on the smaller firms that supplied the plant. It also reported on the impact on workers who chose to ride a bus to work in
Springfield each day—a 125-mile journey—in order to have a job and preserve their retirement pensions.

The deregulation of banks leading to a dearth of locally owned
lenders and investors further eroded the economic base. Older city residents lament the disappearance of owner-operated shops and stores that
made downtown a vibrant place. Another generation was perplexed by
the failure of one of the first giant malls south of the city. Throughout
the downward slide, the newspaper has treated the Fort Wayne economy
as its most important story. Business editors like Frank Gray, Tom Pelle-

The last International Harvester Scout rolls off the production line in October 1980. The closing of the International Harvester plant was a severe blow to the area's economy.

grene, Donna Rogers, and Lisa Green Newhouse have assigned, compiled, and edited hundreds of stories about closings, lost jobs, government plans to attract new firms, and volunteer initiatives trying to foresee what can be done. With new developments seeming to occur every day, it is a work-in-progress.

The editorial page of the *Journal-Gazette* has been graced with many excellent writers in the past twenty years who have been encouraged to focus on specific topics of interest, rather than serve as a stable of general opinion writers. George Neavoll was among the first writers who wrote knowledgeably about the environment on these pages. Barbara Olenyik Morrow moved to the area from Louisville, Kentucky, where she had been a reporter on the *Courier-Journal* and won awards for her work on Fort Wayne education topics. Later, Evan Davis joined the staff and wrote incisively and knowledgeably about the city's controversial annexation of adjoining territory. Davis also drew attention to preventing child abuse and identifying at-risk children. The freedom of this team to pursue areas of interest was attributed to Dick Inskeep's management style. Unlike other newspapers where publishers often dictated what topics

Frank Gray has been writing a thrice-weekly column in the *Journal Gazette* since 1998. His preferred mode of transportation keeps him ahead of the issues and close to the people of the community.

An army of journalists and onlookers surround Mayor Win Moses as he explains the status of the investigation into the shooting of Vernon Jordan in Fort Wayne in 1980.

should be covered in the editorials, Inskeep asked pertinent questions at the morning editorial meetings and rarely scotched a subject.

There were many other men and women in the newsroom who made the newspaper an important part of the community. Reporters like Sandy Thorn Clark, Nancy Vendrely, and Dell Ford wrote about people and events in their distinctive styles. Young reporters like Jim Risen—who went on to win two Pulitzer Prizes with the *New York Times*—brought fresh energy to the staff. Others made their careers in Fort Wayne and used their experience to benefit the community, such as Frank Gray, who joined the newspaper in 1982 as a reporter, later served as business editor, and since 1998 has written a thoughtful, compassionate column on life in the city.

The day-to-day business of reporting the news has had its unexpected developments. In 1980, Fort Wayne suddenly found itself as front-page news across the country. Civil rights leader Vernon Jordan Jr. was shot in an assassination attempt in a hotel parking lot after a speech before the Urban League. It was the nation's first shooting of a major civil rights leader after the assassination of Martin Luther King, Jr., in 1968, and it brought a flood of media into the city. The incident received inflammatory attention because Jordan was driven to the hotel by a white woman who had attended the speech. He was shot in the back by a rifle after exiting her car. President Jimmy Carter, NAACP director Benjamin Hooks, and Senator Edward F. Kennedy were among the officials coming to see Jordan in the hospital and to make statements about the racial hatred in America in general and in Fort Wayne in particular. The initial investigation by local authorities was fragmented and confused, arousing public anger. It took Mayor Winfield Moses and local Urban League director Robert Williams to maintain the city's calm and urge the investigation forward. In the end, it was learned that Joseph Paul Franklin, a 45-year-old man with white supremacist beliefs, was the one who shot Jordan as part of a string of murders and violence that began in 1977. He was charged with the Jordan shooting in 1982, but acquitted by a jury in South Bend. After being sentenced to six life sentences for other murders, Franklin told the *Indianapolis Star* in 1996 he had come to Fort Wayne from Chicago after failing to stalk and kill Jesse Jackson. He shot Jordan because he saw him with a white woman, and he said he felt no remorse over his crime.

The newspaper staff was challenged again in March 1982 when the area was inundated by another flood. On March 4 a heavy rainstorm combined with a melting snow pack to send both the St. Mary's and the St. Joseph rivers to flood stage simultaneously. The Maumee River crested at 25.9 feet, and a large portion of the central city was flooded. President Ronald Reagan flew over the city as part of the disaster relief assessment effort. The *Journal-Gazette*'s reporting was solid and focused, providing detailed analyses of the flooding and the efforts of the emergency workers and volunteers. But it did not compare with the work of the *News-Sentinel* staff. The afternoon newspaper won a Pulitzer Prize for its coverage.

Craig Klugman succeeded Allen as editor in July 1982, bringing a wealth of practical and academic experience to the *Journal-Gazette*. He had spent eleven years with the *Chicago Sun-Times* as city editor, telegraph editor, and assistant managing editor for features. From 1978 to 1982 he had been an assistant professor and director of undergraduate studies at Medill School of Journalism at Northwestern University in Evanston, Illinois. A native of Fargo, North Dakota, Klugman was graduated from Indiana University in 1967 with a bachelor's degree in journalism and political science. At a time when there have been more changes in newspapers than any previous twenty-year period, Klugman was the right choice by Inskeep. Not only is the technology vastly different—laptops, computers for designing news pages, cellular phones, ad infinitum—but the news itself is different. Reporters are writing about issues and events that were

The 1982 flood at its height.

not publicly discussed when Klugman started at the *Sun-Times*. A story about testicular cancer was not even within the realm of possibility at a daily newspaper in 1975, for example. Two decades later, such stories were more commonplace. The role of a newspaper editor has changed, too. Management issues and strategy are more important, requiring different competencies. The *Journal-Gazette* also has to try to reach a younger cadre of readers.

The issue of same-sex unions was one of the new challenges before the newspaper. When gay couples began publicizing their weddings in San Francisco, the *Journal-Gazette* decided it would handle all weddings the same manner. The first test, though, came a decade earlier in the form of an obituary notice. Klugman insisted that it would not be a problem to list a same-sex companion as long as the name was used, just as in any other obituary. It was a different time, but a newspaperman or newspaperwoman still has to have a sense of fairness and skepticism to go along with talent and determination.

The city was rocked by another mayoral scandal in late October 1984 when Win Moses and four others were accused of violating the state's campaign financing act. Unlike 1950, when another Fort Wayne mayor made headlines by being arrested, this was a full-scale media event with television crews, radio reporters, and photographers. Those charged with crimes were shown entering the City-County Building for booking. While an editorial on October 30 called it "Fort Wayne's dark day," the *Journal-Gazette* was careful to point out that those charged "have not been tried and convicted for their alleged offense, and they are entitled to the presumption of innocence." The charges seemed frivolous, but in the wake of the Watergate scandal, all political misbehavior took on a heightened newsworthiness. The popular Democratic mayor and his associates were charged with making undocumented contributions to a candidate seeking the 1982 Republican primary for sheriff. In a 1985 plea bargain, Moses pleaded guilty to a misdemeanor charge instead of a felony and stepped down as mayor. He was also fined and given a suspended sentence. If convicted of the felony, he could have faced a maximum sentence of more than thirty years in prison.

The plea bargain also enabled him to begin campaigning to regain the mayor's office. Moses won a Democratic caucus, but lost in the election. He later was elected to the Indiana House of Representatives.

The changing nature of news coverage—and the election of another Indiana man to be vice president of the United States—led to the creation of a Washington bureau in the summer of 1988. Dan Quayle's nomination as George H. W. Bush's running mate sparked a wave of media coverage, much of it unfavorable to Quayle. The *Journal-Gazette*'s coverage area included Quayle's former congressional district, so he was considered a hometown boy, although perhaps less so than Thomas Marshall in 1912. The possibility of the Bush-Quayle ticket winning in November made it seem imperative that the *Journal-Gazette* have its own coverage of issues, both national and local. Sylvia Smith was then assistant managing editor for news, responsible for the late-breaking news, the design of the first page, and the entire newspaper going to press on time. When Klugman came to her and asked who might be a candidate for the Washington bureau, she ticked off the needed skills: had to be a self-starter, had to know about politics, and had to understand Indiana. No one jumped to mind, and she returned to the tasks at hand. A few weeks later, managing editor Tim Harmon took Smith to dinner and said the editors wanted her to take the job.

A graduate of Michigan State University where she majored in journalism, Sylvia Smith opened her office in the National Press Building in early January 1989. Her first interview was with former Indiana governor Otis Bowen, the new secretary of health and human services. It was a 90-minute interview with Bowen, with only a press aide sitting alongside to take notes. She returned to her office and, since she didn't have any furniture, perched her computer on a stack of District of Columbia telephone books and sat on the floor to write her story. Despite the working conditions, it was an auspicious beginning for her. It was the only one-on-one interview Smith has ever had with a cabinet secretary in Washington. After six months in Washington, she was asked to start writing a column for the Sunday newspaper.

Not all of Smith's experiences were so positive, though. For two years she was denied access to Senator Dan Coats of Indiana. Coats's press secretary was Tim Goeglein, a Fort Wayne native later named to a post in George W. Bush's White House, who refused in January 1997 to deal further with Smith because of an article she wrote. Smith had reported that two months before Coats decided to abandon a 1998 reelection campaign, a poll by a Virginia-based Republican firm showed him trailing Governor Evan Bayh in every area of Indiana except suburban Indianapolis. Her story included a quote by Goeglein that the poll had no bearing on Coats's decision. Goeglein was incensed and wrote to Klugman that Coats would not communicate through Smith. For the next two years, Smith's in-person coverage of Coats was his Senate committee hearings, since they were conducted in a public venue from which she could not be barred. Otherwise, she had to rely on other reporters faxing the senator's news releases to her. When Coats had a news conference in his office, other Indiana reporters would take along Smith's tape recorder. When he did a telephone news conference, she went to another Indiana journalist's office to listen to the senator on a speaker phone.

In 1995 Fort Wayne found itself facing a massive environmental issue. The Adams Center Landfill, Indiana's only collection site for commercial hazardous waste, came under attack for allegedly failing to conform to environmental requirements. A citizens' environmental group wanted the site, operated by Chemical Waste Management, closed down. Business—especially the chemical plants, foundries, and steel mills that brought hazardous waste to the site—wanted it to remain open. In the wake of the Love Canal environmental expose, the Adams Center Landfill was an emotional issue with a vocal environmental group trying to get their concerns heard. It was also a complex matter to explain in the newspaper. The rules governing its operation and the environmental science surrounding hazardous waste products forced the *Journal-Gazette* to find ways to supplement its reporters' understanding of the issues. Reporter Glenn Hall, whose business beat included environmental issues, covered the story in the early 1990s before leaving for an assignment in Germany

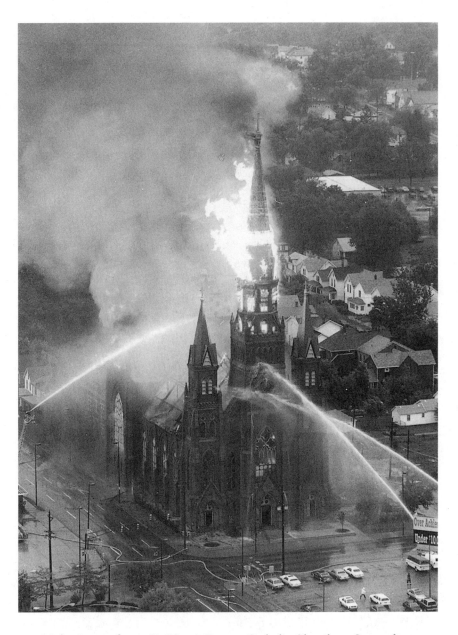

Lightning set fire to St. Mary's Roman Catholic Church on September 2, 1993, destroying one of Fort Wayne's treasured landmarks. Dramatic photography such as this has been a hallmark of the *Journal Gazette*'s history.

for Bloomberg Business News. Anne Marie Obiala followed, as did Ron Shawgo, Jay Margolis, and Terri Hughes-Lazzell. While the technical issues posed challenges, most of the coverage evolved from old-fashioned reporting on meetings, hearings, trials, documents, and interviews. While a political battle developed over annexation of the property by the city of Fort Wayne, the landfill was eventually closed and capped in 1998. Chemical Waste Management is responsible for monitoring the site until 2028 for potential leakage.

Justin Baer is another *Journal Gazette* alumnus who has used his Fort Wayne experience to advance his career. He joined the newspaper in 1997, covering insurance, manufacturing, and labor news. Baer's biggest story was the decision by Lincoln National Corporation, a Fortune 100 company that was founded in Fort Wayne in 1905, to move its headquarters to Philadelphia. From his perspective the story transcended business news into an event in which everyone in the community had an interest or felt the impact. Baer's several months of intensive reporting on the Lincoln National story led to his being offered a position with Bloomberg Business News in New York where his assignments included daily coverage of the telecommunications industry and the nation's money centers.

Not every story in a newspaper's life concerns problems outside the newsroom; sometimes the newspaper itself becomes news, and it can be painful. For eleven years the *Journal-Gazette* found itself in the courts because of a mistake in a headline. The legal struggle turned out to be one of the most important freedom of press issues in Indiana history.

An article published October 6, 1988, reported that the Fort Wayne–Allen County Board of Health had decided to close a restaurant after an inspector's report showed evidence of insects and rodents. The headline read: "Health Board Shuts Doors of Bandido's; Investigators Find Rats, Bugs at North-side Eatery." The inspector's report said nothing about rats, and the headline writer apparently didn't consider that the rodent species includes a range of small gnawing mammals, including mice and squirrels. The *Journal-Gazette* ran a story on October 7 that included a retraction and an apology. The restaurant wasn't satisfied and sued the newspaper, alleging it libeled the business by printing a headline it knew to be false or demonstrating a reckless disregard for whether it was true.

In 1994 a Noble County jury found in favor of the restaurant and ordered the *Journal-Gazette* to pay $985,000 in damages. The newspaper appealed. In November 1996, the Indiana Court of Appeals overturned the award, reasoning that the restaurant had failed to prove that the *Journal-Gazette* published the headline with malice or with reckless disregard for the truth. "While the Journal may well have been extremely careless in printing the subheadline . . . there is not sufficient clear and convincing evidence to demonstrate that the paper had knowledge that the headline was false or that the paper entertained serious doubts as to the truth of the headline."[6] The restaurant was not satisfied and pursued an appeal to the Indiana Supreme Court where a 3–2 decision also overturned the 1994 award and supported the newspaper's position. The case was then taken to the U.S. Supreme Court. In mid-November 1999, the nation's highest court allowed the appeals court ruling to stand.

The significance of the case is in its defense of freedom of the press and Indiana's application of libel law with regard to private individuals. The U.S. Supreme Court's landmark decision on libel in the media, *New York Times Company v. Sullivan* in 1964, established that actual malice or reckless disregard for the truth must be proved in a libel or defamation lawsuit brought by public officials. However, in a later case, the U.S. Supreme Court left it up to the states to determine their own standards of libel for defamation of private individuals.

In the 1970s, the Indiana Court of Appeals ruled that the state would apply the *Times v. Sullivan* principles in cases involving private individuals in matters of public interest—that is, individuals have to prove that the offending material was published by a newspaper that either knew it was false or showed a reckless disregard for the truth.[7]

The Indiana Court of Appeals reaffirmed this decision in overturning the jury verdict against the *Journal-Gazette*. The attorneys for the restaurant did not agree, pursuing an argument that private citizens should only have to prove negligence on the part of the newspaper, a standard used by many other states. The U.S. Supreme Court's decision to not hear the appeal indicated that it was comfortable with the higher Indiana standard.

There were other issues regarding the newspaper's image, some substantive and some cosmetic. The rapidly growing Latino population in Fort Wayne presented a pressing challenge: how to provide news and information to an audience whose first language is not English. According to a study by the Community Research Institute at IPFW, Hispanics constituted 2.7 percent of Fort Wayne population in the 1990 census. The Hispanic population in the 2000 census was reported at 5.8 percent, a total that many believe was undercounted. There was a precedent for the *Journal-Gazette* with regard to reaching an audience whose first language was not English. In the nineteenth century the city's newspapers occasionally printed headlines, and less often entire news stories, in German to reach the non-English-speaking populace. The *Journal-Gazette* printed a tabloid-size holiday gift guide in Spanish, using its own staff, in December 2002. It published a Spanish-language translation of an editorial on programs for students for whom English is a second language. Other news items published in both English and Spanish included a business story about the local realtors making home-purchase agreements available in Spanish and a human-interest story on an effort to raise funds for victims of earthquakes in El Salvador. All these efforts—especially the gift guide—taught the editors two lessons. First, there were multiple issues outside the newsroom to resolve, including advertising and distribution. Second, there were not enough bilingual staff members in the newsroom to produce a long-term regular publication. The newspaper, though, remains committed to finding ways to engage Hispanic readers.

Another example of the newspaper's changing environment appeared at the top of the front page in 1994. While newspapers often go through a redesign process to improve their readability, this change represented a break from the past when Craig Klugman proposed that the 95-year-old hyphen be dropped from the newspaper's name. What had served to signify that the two distinct, often warring newspapers were working together was no longer germane. "The Journal and Gazette merged in 1899, and it is no longer two merged papers, but one paper," the editor wrote when the new design was unveiled on November 28. For a seemingly minor cosmetic change to outsiders, this was tantamount to sacrilege for some traditionalists in the newsroom. For others, it was not. If it were not for Klugman's published explanation, it might not have attracted much public notice. As it was, one wag in the newsroom responded to the internal controversy by cutting small pieces of black paper into one-quarter-inch pieces and putting them in a box at the reception desk for those going through "hyphen withdrawal."

Throughout the tumult, Dick Inskeep kept the newspaper going forward. He found working with Knight-Ridder in the joint operating agreement an amenable process. He also was becoming the dean of Indiana publishers and was inducted into the Indiana Journalism Hall of Fame in 1991. Blessed with a wonderful wife, Harriett, who was active in the community effort to desegregate Fort Wayne's schools, Inskeep maintained a steady course for the newspaper. He also realized that one of their three children had developed a love for the newspaper business. Julie Inskeep joined the editorial board in 1984 and was named assistant publisher six years later. With two degrees from Indiana University as well as experience in social work, she brought an understanding of community issues that individuals trained solely in journalism lacked. Her executive

The *Journal Gazette* editorial board meets on a daily basis to discuss issues and positions the newspaper may want to take on the Perspectives page. From left are editorial writers Julie Creek and Karen Francisco, editor Craig Klugman, publisher Julie Inskeep, Perspectives page editor Tracy Warner, and editorial writer Stacey Stumpf.

training at Northwestern's Newspaper Management Center helped prepare her further to succeed her father as publisher when he retired in 1997.

The previous year Dick Inskeep had won the First Freedom Award from the Hoosier Press Association for the newspaper's commitment to the freedom of expression. The *Journal Gazette* was praised for its willingness to take stands of conscience, even when not popular. During his tenure, it had sued for the release of public information from courts, police, and school boards. Its stand on abortion rights withstood a circulation boycott.

"In an era when most newspapers are loath to give offense, when diversity of opinion is celebrated more in theory than practice, Dick Inskeep has preserved a different kind of newspaper, with its own heartfelt opinions about society, government, and business," the tribute concluded.

Julie Inskeep has developed her own style of management: give the newsroom the tools it needs to do the job, and get out of its way. She has overseen a redevelopment of the editorial page under the direction of Tracy Warner to include a more balanced approach to opinions. New staff has been added, and the Perspective section now features more in-depth examination of issues, supplemented by better graphics and statistical information. There have been staff additions elsewhere in the newsroom, and the size of the newspaper has grown.

She has enhanced the *Journal Gazette*'s reputation by serving on the boards of the Associated Press, the Newspaper Association of America, and the Hoosier State Press Association. She has also served as board president of the United Way of Allen County, the Fort Wayne Community Foundation, and the Neighborhood Health Clinics.

While technology changes the production and delivery of the news, some elements of the *Journal Gazette* business do not change. One is the care and concern the newspaper holds for its community. As was evident during the Depression, the concept of corporate philanthropy to benefit the local community is well ingrained in Fort Wayne. After he became publisher in 1973, Richard Inskeep began to plan for a more organized approach to corporate giving for the Journal-Gazette Company. From 1978 through 1984, the company made contributions totaling $464,095. In 1985 Inskeep created the Journal-Gazette Foundation, whose objective was to be more effective in reviewing and granting funds to community organizations. In December of that year, the company's board of directors authorized an allocation of 10 percent of the company's net income to the foundation. Serving on the board since its inception are Richard Inskeep, Harriett Inskeep, and Julie Inskeep. Thomas Inskeep joined the board in 2003. By the end of 2006, the Journal-Gazette Foundation was contributing a half-million dollars a year to charity, and total gifts exceeded $8 million.

Stephen Inskeep, a chartered financial analyst in Atlanta formerly with AT&T, had joined the Journal-Gazette Company's board in 1993. He was also named vice president of finance, and in 2000 he assumed his father's seat on the Fort Wayne Newspapers board, serving with his sister, Julie.

In 2002, the *Journal Gazette* and Knight-Ridder began another round of negotiations concerning the joint operating agreement, with Julie and Steve Inskeep representing the *Journal Gazette* interests. The yearlong process resulted in an extension of the contract until 2050 that sustains the local ownership of the morning newspaper and its independence. Knight-Ridder gained a greater share of the jointly owned business operation, with its incentive for greater profits resting in part on the continued growth of the *Journal Gazette*. To achieve that growth, the contract guaranteed additional resources to the *Journal Gazette* for its news operation. The new agreement also addressed issues that were never contemplated

Artist's rendering of the Fort Wayne Newspapers printing plant
scheduled to be operating in 2007.

in the 1980 agreement, such as ownership and control of Web content. One of the developments in the wake of the agreement was Fort Wayne Newspapers' decision to build a $35 million press adjacent to the current building in downtown Fort Wayne. The 46,000 square foot facility, which will include a pressroom, newsprint storage, and work areas, represents a significant investment not only in the newspaper's future but also in downtown Fort Wayne. The project is expected to be completed in late 2007.

Julie Inskeep and editor Craig Klugman recognize that the new challenges in the marketplace are formidable. The new generation of readers is not turning to newspapers as often as their parents and grandparents did. Part of the reason is that access to other sources of news and opinion has grown exponentially. Another is the ability of the Internet to convey news and images with a breathtaking immediacy, one that ignores the traditional deadline. Other challenges reach to the core of newspapers. Studies show that readers are more prone to be skeptical of bias in the media. The public also appears to be less concerned with First Amendment rights and access to government decisions and documents.

The *Journal Gazette* Web site (www.journalgazette.net) has become an increasingly important part of the newspaper's delivery of news and advertising content. The newspaper also has a news reporting relationship with WPTA-TV and WOWO radio. With the television station, newspaper staff regularly report via a camera in the newsroom. Partnerships appear to be where the business of news is headed as the journalism of the twenty-first century takes form. But the partnership that will be the most beneficial to the newspaper's future will be the one it has with good journalism. It is in this area that newspapers are uniquely positioned to ensure that accurate, balanced news and information are disseminated in the digital world.

The concern that newspapers will be driven out of the future's hyper-digital world seems without foundation. When VCRs and movie videotapes entered the market, some observers said it was the end of movie theaters. It was not the case. Neither did radio nor television bring about the demise of newspapers and magazines. If the Internet is faster, television more visual, and radio more personal, a newspaper has to exploit its strengths: detail, investigation, and analysis, leavened with humor, graphics, and color. The challenge will be not only in making the newspapers' reportage available on the Web to those who want their news delivered that way but also in repackaging the news in a manner that is interesting to them.

This is not to minimize the risks ahead. The *Journal Gazette* has been the Inskeep family's life work for more than a half-century, yet never before have the challenges been so unremitting. Success depends not only on innovation and technology but also on the health of Fort Wayne's economy. Leadership that is imaginative, compassionate, and dedicated to the best practices of daily journalism will be the linchpin in the operation.

But the *Journal Gazette* has survived greater threats. Born in the dark days of the Civil War, the *Journal Gazette* has printed the news through social upheaval, depressions, mergers, boycotts, lawsuits, politically motivated owners, and nasty competition to become the dominant newspaper in northeast Indiana. And there it stands but does not rest.

Epilogue

The Fort Wayne newspaper market has always been a dynamic entity, so it should come as no surprise that the newspaper landscape changed after the writing of this book was completed.

In November 2005, three of Knight-Ridder's largest stockholders demanded that the company be put up for sale, citing poor stock performance. Four months later, it was announced that the nation's second-largest newspaper company—and the *Journal Gazette*'s partner for twenty-six years in the Fort Wayne joint operating agreement—was indeed to be sold.

The McClatchy Company of Sacramento, California, agreed to acquire Knight-Ridder and its thirty-two daily newspapers. However, upon reaching that deal, McClatchy disclosed its intention to divest twelve of those newspapers, saying they did not reflect its high-growth goals or presented antitrust concerns. One of those "unwanted" papers was the *Fort Wayne News-Sentinel*.

On June 7, it was announced that Ogden Newspapers of Wheeling, West Virginia, had made the winning bid for the *News-Sentinel* and the 75 percent share of Fort Wayne Newspapers, the entity that provides advertising and business operations for the *Journal Gazette* and the *News-Sentinel* under the joint operating agreement. Ogden Newspapers is a privately held, family-owned multimedia company that has published newspapers since 1890 and owns thirty-nine newspapers in ten states. The Journal Gazette Company and a minority partner, Jerome Henry, Jr., of Fort Wayne, were among the unsuccessful bidders.

The acquisition of the *News-Sentinel* and the majority share of Fort Wayne Newspapers is part of the American experiment with public versus private ownership of newspapers.

At the time Knight-Ridder bought the *News-Sentinel* from the Foellingers, many observers praised the acquisition as heralding a better day for local newspapers. It was part of a national trend whose rationale was that the corporate discipline of public ownership would mean access to more capital and more efficiently run businesses.

The net expected result was to be better newspapers.

A quarter of a century later, corporate discipline had become corporate demands. That was evident when the *News-Sentinel* was put up for sale. Compelled by the stock market to focus solely on growth and a high level of return on investment, the public corporations ignored Fort Wayne. Wall Street showed little interest in Main Street. A private company saw things differently. Ogden Newspapers is intensely private, just like the Journal Gazette Company.

In a way, things have come full circle: Once again, two private companies control the destiny of newspapers in Fort Wayne. The community, which has benefited from having different—often divergent—newspaper voices for nearly 175 years, will continue to have that option.

Notes

1. Scoundrels in Paper and Ink

1. Robert M. Taylor Jr. and Connie A. McBirney, eds., *Peopling Indiana: The Ethnic Experience* (Indianapolis: Indiana Historical Society, 1996), 650, 654–56.

2. The money collected from such fines was to be used for the colonization of African Americans who were living in the state before the 1851 constitution and who would be willing to emigrate.

3. Elfreida Lang, "An Analysis of Northern Indiana's Population in 1850," *Indiana Magazine of History* 49, no. 1 (March 1953): 17.

4. Emma Lou Thornbrough, *The Negro in Indiana: A Study of a Minority* (Indianapolis: Indiana Historical Bureau, 1957), 132.

5. Peggy Seigel, "The *Fort Wayne Standard:* A Reform Newspaper in the 1850s Storm," *Indiana Magazine of History* 97, no. 3 (September 2001): 170–71.

6. James M. Schaab, *The Streets of Fort Wayne*, vol. 1, *The Streets of West Central* (privately printed, 1991), 64.

7. Bessie Keeran Roberts, *Fort Wayne's Family Album* (Fort Wayne: Cummins Printing Company, 1960), 15.

8. *Fort Wayne Weekly Sentinel*, August 18, 1875.

9. *Fort Wayne Times and Press*, September 21, 1854.

10. John W. Miller, *Indiana Newspaper Bibliography* (Indianapolis: Indiana Historical Society), 6.

11. Seigel, "The *Fort Wayne Standard*," 171.

12. G. R. Tredway, *Democratic Opposition to the Lincoln Administration in Indiana* Indianapolis: Indiana Historical Bureau, 1973), xiii.

13. *Dawson Daily Times*, November 19, 1861

14. *Salt Lake Tribune*, December 30, 2001.

15. Dawson's *Fort Wayne Daily Times*, February 23, 1860.

16. Harold Holzer, *Lincoln at Cooper Union: The Speech That Made Abraham Lincoln President* (New York: Simon and Schuster, 2004), 61.

17. Tredway, *Democratic Opposition*, 9, quoting the *Jasper Courier* of February 27, 1861.

18. Wood Gray, *The Hidden Civil War: The Story of the Copperheads* (New York: Viking Press, 1942), 140.

19. James M. McPherson, *Ordeal by Fire: The Civil War and Reconstruction* (New York: Alfred A. Knopf, 1982), 311.

20. Roberts, *Fort Wayne's Family Album*, 163. Most of the defunct newspapers had been tied to political candidates.

2. The Gazette

1. William E. Huntzicker, *The Popular Press, 1833–1865* (Westport, Conn.: Greenwood Press, 1999), 126.
2. William Dudley Foulke, *Life of Oliver P. Morton*, 2 vols. (Indianapolis and Kansas City: Bowen-Merrill, 1899; reprint, New York: AMS Press, 1974), 1:382n, 383n.
3. Ibid., 1:71, 78.
4. William Zornow, "Indiana and the Election of 1864," *Indiana Magazine of History* 95, no. 1 (March 1949): 15–16.
5. John W. Miller, *Indiana Newspaper Bibliography* (Indianapolis: Indiana Historical Society, 1982), 6.
6. *Fort Wayne Journal-Gazette*, July 24, 1938.
7. Kenneth M. Stampp, *Indiana Politics during the Civil War* (Indianapolis: Indiana Historical Bureau, 1949; reprint, Bloomington: Indiana University Press, 1978), 202–3.
8. Tredway, *Democratic Opposition*, 71. The only other Democratic locality receiving such treatment was Dubois County.
9. Robert S. Robertson, *Valley of the Upper Maumee River* (Madison, Wisc.: Brant and Fuller, 1889), 320.
10. Bert J. Griswold, *The Pictorial History of Fort Wayne, Indiana*, 2 vols. (Chicago: Robert O. Law, 1917), 1:486.
11. *Fort Wayne Daily Gazette*, June 30, 1868, 1.
12. Hugh McCulloch, *Men and Measures of Half a Century: Sketches and Comments* (New York: Charles Scribner's Sons, 1888; reprint, New York: Da Capo Press, 1970), 491.
13. *Fort Wayne Weekly Sentinel*, July 18, 1863.
14. Others in the ownership, known as R. D. Dumm & Co., were Robert D. Dumm and John W. Henderson.
15. *Fort Wayne Daily Democrat*, January 25, 1872.
16. *Biographical and Historical Record of Kosciusko County, Indiana* (Chicago: Lewis, 1887), 223.
17. *Polk's Directory, 1882–1883*, n.p.
18. Elmo Scott Watson, *A History of Newspaper Syndicates in the United States, 1865–1935* (Chicago: privately printed, 1936), 27.
19. James Green, *Death in the Haymarket* (New York: Pantheon Books, 2006), 270.
20. Willodeen Price, "Newspapers of Fort Wayne," 26.
21. Rex M. Potter, *The Historiography of Fort Wayne: The Contribution of Bert Griswold* (Fort Wayne: Allen County–Fort Wayne Historical Society, 1958), 8.

3. The Journal

1. McPherson, *Ordeal by Fire*, 202, 540.
2. *Fort Wayne Daily Gazette*, May 17, 1869, 4.

3. *Fort Wayne Journal-Gazette*, February 12, 1912. The news item was excerpted from "Downer's History of Williamstown, N.J., and Its Descendants" in an article on the anniversary of Lincoln's birth.

4. *Fort Wayne Journal-Gazette*, August 15, 1908.

5. Formed in an 1856 consolidation of several lines, the *Pittsburg* spelling reflects that the railroad was formed before the *h* was added to the city's name.

6. *Fort Wayne Daily Gazette*, July 23, 1877.

7. *Fort Wayne Weekly Sentinel*, August 8, 1877, 4.

8. McPherson, *Ordeal by Fire*, 545.

9. Ibid.

10. Robertson, *Valley of the Upper Maumee River*, 392.

11. Ibid., 394.

12. Edwin Emery and Michael Emery, *The Press and America*, 5th ed. (Englewood Cliffs, N.J.: Prentice Hall, 1984), 231.

13. *Fort Wayne News-Sentinel*, June 16, 1926

14. *Fort Wayne City Directory, 1883–84* (Fort Wayne: R. K. Polk, 1883).

15. *Fort Wayne Journal*, January 15, 1887.

16. Scrap Book of Wright W. Rockhill.

17. *Indianapolis Sentinel*, November 26, 1892.

18. Scrap Book of Wright W. Rockhill, citing *Monday Morning Times*, April 1893.

19. *Fort Wayne Daily Gazette*, April 20, 1893.

20. Clifford Ward, "Journalistic Memoirs," n.d., 18, at Allen County Public Library. Ward was editor of the *News-Sentinel* from 1941 to 1966.

21. Robert Adams, "Hoosier Professional Backgrounds: Newspapers," *Old Fort News* 23, no. 1 (1960): 43.

22. *Fort Wayne Journal*, March 27, 1890.

23. Herbert G. Bredemeier, *Colorful Journalism in Fort Wayne, Indiana* (Fort Wayne: Fort Wayne Public Library, 1966), 21.

24. Karl Detzer, *Myself When Young* (New York: Funk and Wagnalls, 1968), 151.

25. *Fort Wayne Journal*, February 23, 1893, 1.

26. *Fort Wayne Journal*, February 15, 1894.

27. *Fort Wayne Journal-Gazette*, October 25, 1900.

28. *Fort Wayne Journal*, January 28, 1893.

29. Allen County favored the Democratic nominees in ten of the eleven presidential elections between 1872 and 1912.

30. *Fort Wayne Journal*, July 10, 1896, 1.

31. Roberts, *Fort Wayne's Family Album*, 21.

32. *Fort Wayne Journal*, May 28, 1899, 1.

33. Paul Kleppner, *The Cross of Culture: A Social Analysis of Midwestern Politics, 1850–1900*, 2nd ed. (New York: Free Press, 1970), 368.

34. Charles Roll, *Indiana: One Hundred and Fifty Years of American Development* (Chicago and New York: Lewis, 1931), 2:357.

35. *Fort Wayne News-Sentinel*, June 19, 1926.

36. This was a typographical error in the letter. It was actually Moellering's.

37. Ward, "Journalistic Memoirs," 23.

38. Bredemeier, *Colorful Journalism*, 23.

4. The Acquisition

1. These three news items were printed or commented upon in the October 12 edition of the *Fort Wayne Journal-Gazette*.

2. John Ankenbruck, *Twentieth-Century History of Fort Wayne* (Fort Wayne: Twentieth Century Historical Fort Wayne, 1975), 312.

3. *Fort Wayne News-Sentinel*, June 19, 1926.

4. Ibid.

5. Thomas R. Marshall, *A Hoosier Salad: Recollections of Thomas R. Marshall, Vice President and Hoosier Philosopher* (Indianapolis: Bobbs-Merrill, 1925), 174.

6. Emery and Emery, *The Press and America*, 440.

7. Marshall, 154.

8. Detzer, *Myself When Young*, 235.

9. Griswold, *Builders of Greater Fort Wayne* (Fort Wayne: Hoosier Press, 1926), 260.

10. Charles R. Poinsatte, *Fort Wayne during the Canal Era, 1828–1855* (Indianapolis: Indiana Historical Bureau, 1969), 165.

11. Ibid., 150–51.

12. Oscar L. Bockstahler, "The German Press in Indiana," *Indiana Magazine of History* 48, no. 2 (June 1952): 19.

13. Bert J. Griswold, *Griswold-Phelps Handbook and Guide to Fort Wayne, Indiana, for 1913–1914* (Fort Wayne: Griswold and Charles A. Phelps, 1914), 96.

14. *Fort Wayne Journal*, March 27, 1890, 4.

15. *Fort Wayne Gazette*, May 7, 1897. The headline read:

Groszer Auszug
Von Turnerbund Mitglieder Bei St. Louis
Das Fest War Gestern Eroefnet-
Fuenfzig Thausend Fremden Sind in Der Stadt

16. Mark A. Rogers, "'Wir Trinken und Tanzen' in Germania Park: Fort Wayne German-American Society and the National German Alliance during World War I" (History Studies Seminar, Indiana University–Purdue University Fort Wayne, Spring 1994), 3.

17. Ibid., 4.

18. Clifford H. Scott, "Fort Wayne German-Americans in World War I: A Cultural Epidemic," *Old Fort News* 40, no. 2 (1977): 5.

19. Bert J. Griswold, *Builders of Greater Fort Wayne* (Fort Wayne: Hoosier Press, 1926), 101.

5. After Andy

1. Griswold, *Builders of Greater Fort Wayne*, 148. Griswold's book was promotional in nature, as its subtitle would indicate: "A collection of portraits of the men of today who are carrying on the work of the fathers in the making of 'The Wonder City of Midwestern America.'"

2. James Philip Fadely, *Thomas Taggart: Public Servant, Political Boss, 1856–1929* (Indianapolis: Indiana Historical Society, 1997), 149.

3. In Allen County, Republican candidates for president defeated the Democratic candidates in nineteen of twenty-two elections between 1920 and 2004. The only exceptions were Franklin Delano Roosevelt in 1932 and 1936 and Lyndon B. Johnson in 1964.

4. Scott, "Fort Wayne German-Americans in World War I," 10.

5. Claude G. Bowers, *My Life* (New York: Simon and Schuster, 1962), 44.

6. Ibid., 40.

7. Ray E. Boomhower, *Jacob Piatt Dunn Jr.: A Life in History and Politics, 1855–1924* (Indianapolis: Indiana Historical Society, 1997), 45.

8. Bowers, *My Life*, 41.

9. Ibid..

10. Ibid., 90.

11. Ibid., 91.

12. Ibid., 103.

13. Peter J. Sehlinger and Holman Hamilton, *Spokesman for Democracy: Claude G. Bowers, 1878–1958* (Indianapolis: Indiana Historical Society, 2000), 121.

14. William O. Lynch, "Review: *The Tragic Era: The Revolution after Lincoln* by Claude Bowers," *Indiana Magazine of History* 25, no. 3 (September 1929): 247–48.

15. Peter J. Sehlinger, professor emeritus of history at Indiana University Indianapolis, edited and completed the manuscript, using Hamilton's notes and collected material. The book, *Spokesman for Democracy: Claude G. Bowers, 1878–1958*, was published in 2000 by the Indiana Historical Society.

16. *Fort Wayne Evening Press*, April 2, 1922, 9.

17. *Fort Wayne Journal-Gazette*, November 2, 1930, 1.

18. *Fort Wayne Journal-Gazette*, November 20, 1923.

19. *Fort Wayne Journal-Gazette*, June 3, 1942, 4.

20. Detzer, *Myself When Young*, 85.

21. *Fort Wayne Journal-Gazette*, February 12, 1912, 4.

22. *Fort Wayne Journal-Gazette*, April 9, 1951.

23. Leonard J. Moore, *Citizen Klansmen: The Ku Klux Klan in Indiana, 1921–1928* (Chapel Hill: University of North Carolina Press, 1991), 11.

24. Ibid., 58.

25. *Fort Wayne Journal-Gazette*, November 20, 1923.

26. Moore, *Citizen Klansmen*, 182.

27. *Fort Wayne Journal-Gazette*, June 2, 1925, 1.

28. *Fort Wayne Journal-Gazette*, June 3, 1925, 4.

29. *Fort Wayne Journal-Gazette*, June 2, 1925, 1.

30. *Fort Wayne Journal-Gazette*, January 30, 1927, 1.

6. Depression and War

1. Iwan Morgan, "Fort Wayne and the Great Depression: The Early Years, 1929–1933," *Indiana Magazine of History* 80, no. 2 (1984): 124.

2. Ibid., 140.

3. *Fort Wayne Journal-Gazette*, November 22, 1934.

4. James H. Madison, *Indiana through Tradition and Change: A History of the Hoosier State and Its People, 1920–1945* (Indianapolis: Indiana Historical Society, 1982), 349.

5. *Fort Wayne Journal-Gazette*, October 10, 1944.

6. Charles A. Lindbergh, *The Wartime Journals of Charles A. Lindbergh* (New York: Harcourt Brace Jovanovich, 1970, 542.

7. Ibid., 543.

8. Ibid., 544.

9. *Fort Wayne News-Sentinel*, October 4, 1941.

10. *Fort Wayne Journal-Gazette*, October 4, 1941.

11. Lindbergh, *Wartime Journals*, 544.

12. *Fort Wayne Journal-Gazette*, October 5, 1941.

13. *Fort Wayne News-Sentinel*, October 6, 1941.

14. Hugh M. Ayer, "Hoosier Labor in the Second World War," *Indiana Magazine of History* 59, no. 2 (June 1963): 9.

15. *Fort Wayne Journal-Gazette*, October 29, 1944.

16. *Fort Wayne Journal-Gazette*, May 22, 1945.

17. *Fort Wayne Journal-Gazette*, October 10, 1972.

7. Under One Roof but Still Independent

1. *Fort Wayne Journal-Gazette*, April 26, 1950.

2. The *Journal-Gazette* published sketches from community life by an artist named Rozella Z. Hinton in 1951, but they were not editorial page material.

3. Interview with Bob Englehart, January 14, 2005.

4. Interview with Steve Sack, January 19, 2005

5. Larry Hayes, *Monday I'll Save the World: Memoir of a Heartland Journalist* (Fort Wayne: LifeQuest, 2004).

6. *Fort Wayne Journal-Gazette*, November 27, 1996.

7. *Aafco Heating & Air Conditioning Co. v. Northwest Publications, Inc.*, 162 Ind. App 671, 321 N.E.2d 580 (1974).

Bibliography

Adams, Robert. "Hoosier Professional Backgrounds: Newspapers," *Old Fort News* 23, no. 1 (1960): 43.

Ankenbruck, John. *Twentieth-Century History of Fort Wayne.* Fort Wayne, Ind.: Twentieth Century Historical Fort Wayne. 1975.

Ayer, Hugh M. "Hoosier Labor in the Second World War." *Indiana Magazine of History* 59, no. 2 (June 1963).

Bartholomew, H.S.K. "Editor John B. Stoll." *Indiana Magazine of History* 28, no. 2 (June 1932).

Bates, Roy M., and Kenneth B. Keller. *The Columbia Street Story.* Fort Wayne: Fort Wayne Public Library, 1966.

Biographical and Historical Record of Kosciusko County, Indiana. Chicago: Lewis, 1887.

Bockstahler, Oscar L. "The German Press in Indiana." *Indiana Magazine of History* 48, no. 2 (June 1952): 19.

Boomhower, Ray E. *Jacob Piatt Dunn Jr.: A Life in History and Politics, 1855–1924.* Indianapolis: Indiana Historical Society, 1997.

Bowers, Claude G. *A Tragic Era: The Revolution after Lincoln.* Cambridge: Houghton Mifflin, 1929.

———. *My Life: The Memoirs of Claude Bowers.* New York: Simon and Schuster, 1962.

Bredemeier, Herbert G. *Colorful Journalism in Fort Wayne, Indiana.* Fort Wayne: Fort Wayne Public Library, 1966.

Brice, Wallace A. *History of Fort Wayne from the Earliest Known Accounts of This Point to the Present Period.* Fort Wayne: D. W. Jones and Son, 1868.

Detzer, Karl. *Myself When Young.* New York: Funk and Wagnalls, 1968.

Emery, Edwin, and Michael Emery. *The Press and America,* 5th ed. Englewood Cliffs, N.J.: Prentice Hall, 1984.

Fadely, James Philip. *Thomas Taggart: Public Servant, Political Boss, 1856–1929.* Indianapolis: Indiana Historical Society, 1997.

Foner, Eric. *Reconstruction, 1863–1877.* New York: Harper and Row, 1988.

Fort Wayne City Directory, 1883–84. Fort Wayne: R. K. Polk, 1883.

Foulke, William Dudley. *Life of Oliver P. Morton.* 2 vols. Indianapolis and Kansas City: Bowen-Merrill, 1899.

Gray, Ralph D., ed. *Gentlemen from Indiana: National Party Candidates, 1836–1940.* Indianapolis: Indiana Historical Bureau. 1977.

Gray, Wood. *The Hidden Civil War: The Story of the Copperheads.* New York: Viking Press, 1942.

Green, James. *Death in the Haymarket.* New York: Pantheon Books, 2006.

Griswold, Bert J. *Some Fort Wayne Phizes.* Fort Wayne: Archer Printing Company. 1904.

———. *The Griswold-Phelps Handbook and Guide to Fort Wayne, Indiana, for 1913–1914.* Fort Wayne: Griswold and Charles A. Phelps, 1914.

———. *The Pictorial History of Fort Wayne, Indiana.* 2 vols. Chicago: Robert O. Law, 1917.

———. *Builders of Greater Fort Wayne.* Fort Wayne: Hoosier Press, 1926.

Hall, Arthur F. Correspondence files. Fort Wayne: Lincoln Life Insurance, 1928, 1929.

Hanna, Robert B., and Harry M. Williams. *The Fort Wayne Year Book for 1906.* Fort Wayne: Archer Printing, 1906.

Hawfield, Michael C. *Here's Fort Wayne, Past & Present.* Fort Wayne: Personal Marketing Systems, 1988.

Hayes, Larry. *Monday I'll Save the World: Memoir of a Heartland Journalist.* Fort Wayne: LifeQuest. 2004.

Helm, T. B. *History of Allen County, Indiana.* Chicago: Kingman Brothers, 1880.

Herschell, William M. *Recollections of Isaac Jenkinson.* Fort Wayne: Allen County–Fort Wayne Historical Society. 1962.

Holzer, Harold. *Lincoln at Cooper Union: The Speech That Made Abraham Lincoln President.* New York: Simon and Schuster, 2004.

Huntzicker, William E. *The Popular Press, 1833–1865.* Westport, Conn.: Greenwood Press, 1999.

Kleppner, Paul. *The Cross of Culture: A Social Analysis of Midwestern Politics, 1850–1900.* 2nd ed. New York: Free Press, 1970.

Knapp, H. S. *History of the Maumee Valley.* Toledo: Blade Mammoth Printing. 1872.

Lang, Elfreida. "An Analysis of Northern Indiana's Population in 1850." *Indiana Magazine of History* 49, no. 1, March 1953.

Lindbergh, Charles A. *The Wartime Journals of Charles A. Lindbergh.* New York: Harcourt Brace Jovanovich, 1970.

Lynch, William O. "Review: *The Tragic Era: The Revolution after Lincoln* by Claude Bowers." *Indiana Magazine of History* 25, no. 3 (September 1929).

Madison, James H. *Indiana through Tradition and Change: A History of the Hoosier State and Its People, 1920–1945.* Indianapolis: Indiana Historical Society, 1982.

Marshall, Thomas R. *A Hoosier Salad: Recollections of Thomas R. Marshall, Vice President and Hoosier Philosopher.* Indianapolis: Bobbs-Merrill, 1925.

May, Richard L. "Notes on the Formation of the Republican Party in Fort Wayne, Indiana, 1852–1858." *Old Fort News* 30, no. 1 (Winter 1967).

McCulloch, Hugh. *Men and Measures of Half a Century: Sketches and Comments.* New York: Charles Scribner's Sons, 1888.

McPherson, James M. *Ordeal by Fire: The Civil War and Reconstruction.* New York: Alfred A. Knopf, 1982.

Miller, John W. *Indiana Newspaper Bibliography.* Indianapolis: Indiana Historical Society, 1982.

Moore, Leonard J. *Citizen Klansmen: The Ku Klux Klan in Indiana, 1921–1928*. Chapel Hill: University of North Carolina Press, 1991.

Morgan, Iwan. "Fort Wayne and the Great Depression: The Early Years, 1929–1933." *Indiana Magazine of History* 80, no. 2 (1984): 348–78.

———. "Fort Wayne and the Great Depression: The New Deal Years, 1937–1940." *Indiana Magazine of History* 80, no. 4 (1984): 122–45.

Phillips, Clifton J. *Indiana in Transition: The Emergence of an Industrial Commonwealth, 1880–1920*. Indianapolis: Indiana Historical Bureau and Indiana Historical Society, 1968.

Poinsatte, Charles R. *Fort Wayne during the Canal Era, 1828–1855*. Indianapolis: Indiana Historical Bureau, 1969.

Potter, Rex M. *The Historiography of Fort Wayne: The Contribution of Bert Griswold*. Fort Wayne: Allen County–Fort Wayne Historical Society, 1958.

———. *Politics in Allen County, 1884–1892*. Fort Wayne: Allen County–Fort Wayne Historical Society, 1968.

Price, Willodeen. *Newspapers of Fort Wayne, Yesterday–Today*. New York: Columbia University School of Library Science, 1937.

Public Library of Fort Wayne and Allen County. *Art Souvenir of the Fort Wayne Gazette, 1894*. Fort Wayne, 1955.

———. *Captain James B. White, Fort Wayne Soldier, Merchant, Banker*. Fort Wayne, 1957.

———. *Colonel Robert S. Robertson, 1839–1906: Soldier, Public Officer, Historian, Social Arbiter*. Fort Wayne, n.d.

———. *William J. Hosey: Fort Wayne's Dedicated Mayor*. Fort Wayne, n.d.

Roberts, Bessie Keeran. *Fort Wayne's Family Album*. Fort Wayne: Cummins Printing Company, 1960.

Robertson, Robert S. *Valley of the Upper Maumee River*. Madison, Wisc.: Brant and Fuller, 1889.

Rockhill, Wright W. Scrap Book (1881–89). Allen County Public Library, Fort Wayne, n.d.

Rogers, Mark A. "'Wir Trinken und Tanzen' in Germania Park: Fort Wayne German-American Society and the National German Alliance during World War I." History Studies Seminar, Indiana University–Purdue University Fort Wayne, Spring 1994.

Roll, Charles. *Indiana: One Hundred and Fifty Years of American Development*. 5 vols. Chicago and New York: Lewis, 1931.

Roseboom, Eugene H. *A History of Presidential Elections*. New York: Macmillan, 1957.

Sarnighausen, Hans-Cord. "Johannes Diederich Sarnighausen (1818–1901): From Hymnologist in Göttingen to State Senator in Fort Wayne, Indiana." *Old Fort News* 64, no. 2 (September 2001).

Schaab, James M. *The Streets of Fort Wayne*, vol. 1, *The Streets of West Central*. Privately printed, 1991.

Scott, Clifford H. "Fort Wayne German-Americans in World War I: A Cultural Epidemic." *Old Fort News* 40, no. 2 (1977): 3–17.

Sehlinger, Peter J., and Holman Hamilton. *Spokesman for Democracy: Claude G. Bowers, 1878–1958*. Indianapolis: Indiana Historical Society, 2000.

Seigel, Peggy. "The *Fort Wayne Standard:* A Reform Newspaper in the 1850s Storm." *Indiana Magazine of History* 97, no. 3 (September 2001).

Slocum, Charles Elihu. *History of the Maumee River Basin.* Indianapolis: Bowen and Slocum, 1905; Bowie, Md.: Heritage Books, 1997.

Stampp, Kenneth M. *The Era of Reconstruction, 1865–1877.* New York: Vintage Books. 1965.

———. *Indiana Politics during the Civil War.* Indianapolis: Indiana Historical Bureau, 1949; reprint, Bloomington: Indiana University Press, 1978.

Taylor, Robert M., Jr., and Connie A. McBirney, eds. *Peopling Indiana: The Ethnic Experience.* Indianapolis: Indiana Historical Society, 1996.

Thornbrough, Emma Lou. *The Negro in Indiana: A Study of a Minority.* Indianapolis: Indiana Historical Bureau, 1957.

Tredway, G. R. *Democratic Opposition to the Lincoln Administration in Indiana.* Indianapolis: Indiana Historical Bureau, 1973.

Ward, Clifford. "Journalistic Memoirs." Carbon copy of typescript for presentation to Quest Club. Fort Wayne, Allen County Public Library, 1950.

Watson, Elmo Scott. *A History of Newspaper Syndicates in the United States, 1865–1935.* Chicago: privately printed, 1936.

Williams' Fort Wayne Directory, City Guide, and Business Mirror, for 1864–65. Fort Wayne: N. P. Stockbridge, 1865.

Zornow, William. "Indiana and the Election of 1864." *Indiana Magazine of History* 95, no. 1. (March 1949).

Index

Adair, E. Ross, 144
Adamson Act, 93
Alexander, D. S., 26–27
Allen, Larry, 162–163, 171
Aveline Hotel, 64, 77–79, *78*

Baals, Harry, 133, 150
Bailey, Peter P., 7–8
Beall, Marion E., 37
Beecher, Charles, 4
Beecher, Henry Ward, 4
Beveridge, Albert J., 66, 96, 98
Bicknell, C. F., 52, 77
Blaine, James G., 63; campaigns in Fort
    Wayne and, 63
Boltz, Frederick, 53
Boseker, Christian, 55–56
Bowers, Claude, 52, 96–101, *97*, 105
Bresnahan, Thomas, *59*, 61, 68, 74, 75,
    79
Bryan, William Jennings, 63–66, 72, 79, 92,
    96, 117
Burroughs, Daniel W., 6–7, 19

Campbell, I. W., 31
Case, Charles, 6
Civil War journalism, 13–22
Colfax, Schuyler, 16, 24, 31, 43
Cooper, William P., 69
"Copperheads," 5, 18
Cullaton, Martin, 26–27

Dawes, Charles G., 115; campaigns in Fort
    Wayne, and 115
Dawson, John W., 2, 4, 5, 7, 9, 10, 25, 31; as
    governor of Utah Territory, 9–10
Debs, Eugene, 83, 97
Depression, 125–130, *130;* collapse of First
    & Tri-State Bank and, 127
Detzer, Karl, 75, 110
Dills, W. H., 31

Douglas, Stephen A., 4, 16; campaigns in
    Fort Wayne and, 4
Dunn, Jacob Piatt, 96

Ellingham, Lewis, 89, 91–92, 96, 102, 105,
    122, 130
Ellingham, Miller, 128, 148
Englehart, Bob, 163–164, *164*
Emancipation Proclamation, 10–11, 14
Eyansides, Charles H., 51

Fairbank, Clark, 45, 50
Fairbanks, Charles, 63, 74, 93
Fleming, James, 129, 139–140, *155,* 156, 158,
    160
Flood of 1913, 83–85, *84*
Flood of 1982, 172, *172*
Foellinger, Helene, 77, 143, *155*
Foellinger, Oscar, 76–77, 101
Fort Wayne Daisies, 137–138,
Fort Wayne Evening Press, 101–104
Fort Wayne Evening Journal-Gazette, 128–129
Fort Wayne Newspaper Union, 30
Foster, Thomas J., 50–51
Frick, Ford, 75–76

German influence, 85–89, 92–94
German-language newspapers, 5, 21, 42–43,
    52, 86, 120–121; *see also* Herman Mack-
    witz
Grant, Ulysses S., 23, 24, 43, 48
Gray, Frank, 167, *169*
Great Strike of 1877, 45–47
Greene, Jesse, 52, 69
Gross, William J., 133
Guild, Curtis, Jr., 73–74
Gunder, Edmund, 117–118, *119*

Hackett, E. A. K., 52
Hall, Arthur, 126
Hamilton, Frank G., 77

Hamilton, Holman, 100–101
Hanly, J. Frank, 66, 80, 111
Hanna, Martha, 44
Hanna, Samuel T., 44
Hartman, Homer C., 19–22
Hayes, Larry, 165–166, *167*
Hill, Edwin C., 75
Hoefel, Emil, 80–82, *81*
Hoffman, Edward G., 92, 98, 115
Holman, B. M., 34–35
Hosey, William, 94, 110–111, 126
Hossler, Quincy A., 28
Hughes, Charles Evans, 92–93; campaigns in Fort Wayne and, 93

Inskeep, Julie, 178, *179*, 181
Inskeep, Richard, 147, 150, *160*, 161–163, 178–180
Irwin, Helen May, 148–149

Jackson, Ed, 116–117; *see also* Ku Klux Klan
Jenkinson, Isaac, 14, 15, *16*, 17–19, 21, 24–25, 28, 35
Johnson, Andrew, 16–17, 23–24, 41, 47; campaigns in Fort Wayne and, 24
Johnson, Hiram, 83, 93
joint operating agreement, 143–144, 147
Jones, David W., 1, 11, 14 -17, *15*, 19
Jones, Harvey, 16–17
Jordan, Vernon: assassination attempt, 170–171, *171*
Journal Gazette Building, 121–122, *121*, 147–148
Journal Gazette Foundation, 180
Julian, Isaac, 6

Keator, Theron, 34–35
Keil, David, 28–30
Keil, Frederick, 28–29
Kellogg, Ansel, 30
Kellogg, William, 104, 147
Kern, John W., 96, 98
Klugman, Craig, 171, 178, *179*, 181
Knight Ridder Company, 180, 183
Knapp, H. S., 42, 49
"Know Your Newsmen," 151–153
Ku Klux Klan, 47, 112–117, *115*
Kunkel, William A., 131–132, 139

Lane, Charles R., 37–39, *38*
Leonard, Frank M., 35, 37

Leonard, Nathan R., 35–37, *36*, 60, 67
Lincoln, Abraham, 4, 7, 16, 21; in Fort Wayne, 10
Lindbergh, Charles, 133–136
Long, Baron, 60, 75
Lovette, James 138, 148
Lowry, Robert, 23, 25, 34, 50
Ludlum, Samuel, 45, 50
Lynch, Dan, 165, *166*

Mackwitz, Herman, 86, 120–121
Marshall, Thomas R., 79–80, 82, 92, 117
McClatchy Company, 183
McCulloch, Hugh, 20, 41–42, 44
McManus, Silas, 32, 34
McNagny, William, 57, 79
McNiece, Robert, 26–27
McNutt, Paul, 129, 131
Miller, Gene, 153
Miller, Samuel, 53–55, *54*
Milnor, Cliff, 130, 138, 147, *151*. See also "Know Your Newsmen"
Mitchell, James, 52
Morss, Samuel E., 52, 97
Morton, Oliver, 11, 14
Moses, Win, 170–173, *170*
Moynihan, Andrew, 34, 56, 58–63, *59*, 67–72, 75–76, 79, 82, 85, 92, 121, 147
Muhler, Charles, 53

National Conscription Act, 17–19
National Newspaper Preservation Act, 144
Nelson, William Rockhill, 2
New, Harry S., 74
Nichens, Claude, 148
Nickel Plate Railroad. *See* railroad elevated crossings
Noel, Smallwood V. B., 2
"Northwest confederacy," 17–18
Null, Lycurgus, 53

Ogden Newspapers, 183–184

Page, William D., 51–52
Pierce, Martha Jones, 14
Plasterer, Nick, 148

railroad elevated crossings, 109–112, *113*
Reed, Robert A., 104, 106–108, *107*, 130
Roberts, Bessie Keeran, 11, 156–157

Roberts, Frank, 120, 130, 156–157, *157*, 160

Rockhill, Howell C., 56, 58, 70

Rockhill, William Wright, 56–58, 59, 70

Roosevelt, Franklin Delano, 100, 127, 129; campaigns in Fort Wayne and, 136–137, *137*

Roosevelt, Theodore, 72–74, 79, 82, 92–93; "attacked" in Fort Wayne, 73–74

Rudisill, Henry, 85

Sack, Steve, 164–165, *165*

Sarnighausen, John, 42–43

Scherer, Ray, 153–154, *154*

Schilder, Edgar F., 82

Shoaff, Carrie M., 32–34, *33*

Shutts, George F., 53

Simmons, Virgil, 129, 171, 139–140, 143, *155*

Skinner, Benjamin D., 25–26

Smith, Sylvia, 173–174

Spayth, George, 118–120

Spencer, Martin V. B., 53

Standard, 6–7

Stephenson, D. C., 116. *See also* Ku Klux Klan

Suedhoff, Carl J., 76

Taylor, Charles, 45, 47, 50

Taylor, Charles F., 51

Taylor, Thomas S., 44–45

Taylor, W. J., 22

Tigar, Thomas, 2, 5, 31

Vendrely, Nancy, 170

Vietnam War, 157–159

Walter, Amos, 37

Ward, Cliff, 60, 69, 133

Watson, James E., 66

Weatherhogg, Charles, 122

White, James Bain, 26–28, *27*, 34–35, 50

Williams, Harry M., 63, 104–106, 127–128

Williams, Park, 139, 148–149

Willard, James, 22, 25

Williams, Reuben, 28

Willkie, Wendell, 131–132

Wilson, Jennie, 76–77

World War I, 94–96, *95*

World War II, 136–139

Wood, George W., 5, 31

Wright, Amos, 22, 25

Zollars, Allen, 53

Zollinger, Charles, 46, 55

Scott M. Bushnell is a seasoned journalist who began his career as a sports writer in his hometown of Poughkeepsie, New York. From 1977 through 1984, he worked for the Associated Press as a reporter, sports writer, and then news editor in the Connecticut bureau. He directed the media relations efforts at two Fortune 100 companies (Travelers and Lincoln National Corp) from 1985 to 1999. Based in St. Joe, Indiana, Bushnell is coauthor with Pete Eshelman of *Roanoke: The Renaissance of a Hoosier Village* (Emmis Books, 2003).

Contents

Foreword   v

Introduction   vii

Part I: Ethical and Philosophical Dimensions
     Associated with Alternative Education   1

Chapter 1   Why Offer Alternative Education?   3

Chapter 2   Who Are These Students?   9

Part II: A Practical Guide   15

Chapter 3   Mission Statement   17

Chapter 4   Assembling a Great Team   23

Chapter 5   Getting Organized and Providing Structure   29

Chapter 6   Providing a Quality Curriculum in a Flexible Manner   37

Part III: The Assessment Piece   49

Chapter 7   General Characteristics of a Quality Program   51

Chapter 8   Indicators of a Quality Program   55

Chapter 9   A Case in Point   65

Chapter 10   Conclusion   101

About the Author   109

Foreword

There are as many different types of alternative schools as there are communities to support them. Fifteen years ago, when we started the T-S-T Community School, there were almost no templates or guidelines for developing an alternative school for students at risk for dropping out. There were very few schools that dealt, exclusively, with our type of student. Today, educators have an advantage we did not have. They can find out how others have done it by reading the *Alternative Network Journal*. Now, with the publication of *Breaking the Cyle of Failure*, there are even more guidelines for establishing a successful program. Read it carefully.

In my meetings with those who want to establish a new alternative school, the first action I suggest is to talk. Talk with teachers, with parents, with students, with school administrators, with representatives of the courts and social service agencies. Your success in establishing a new program is almost always directly related to the amount of support that can be generated, especially from a few influential, key players. When we were planning the T-S-T Community School, we found a very supportive judge who set up a meeting and personally invited the leaders from schools as well as probation, mental health, and social service agencies. When a judge calls a meeting, people attend. We listened to needs and suggestions and began our school with broad support to address the stated needs. With either keen intelligence and foresight or just dumb luck, we designed the school to conform to most of the characteristics in quality alternative schools. But a successful start is just that—a start.

Your success in the long haul depends on constant change and evolution to meet changing needs and regulations. It is essential for an alternative school working with at-risk students to have a high-quality program as measured by student academic outcomes. That is the only way legitimacy is earned in the eyes of the public and traditional school personnel. We did this by having a top quality staff who wanted to work with our kind of student and were willing to put in the extra time and effort that requires. Notice that I wrote *staff* and not *teachers*. The entire staff—teachers, aides, secretary, childcare workers in our teen-parent daycare, and I—work with our students and wants to be here. This is emphasized in this book and is essential. We meet almost daily, after students leave, to discuss the students and program. The staff is wonderful and dedicated and keeps us moving.

To start your own alternative school or to improve an existing one, read, visit, and talk. Read *Breaking the Cycle of Failure*, read the *Alternative Network Journal*, read about other programs and the latest research in learning. Visit other programs. Talk to staff and students. It is easier to borrow than create.

Finally, keep in mind what it is all about—developing a school that is a real alternative—one that fosters the development, intellectually and socially, of future citizens. Enjoy!

Gerald S. Friedman, Ph.D.
Principal, T-S-T Community School
Ithaca, NY

Introduction

The same assumptions of crisis and failure
that have fueled every other recent reform debate
are being invoked . . . by our favorite myths:
that there was once a golden age,
an era when schools maintained rigorous
academic standards, when all children learned,
when few dropped out and most graduated on time.
— *Schrag*

Most of us recognize this statement for what it is, merely a myth. There has been no golden age of education. Like every other dynamic sector of society, education constantly faces challenges as time marches ahead. Today's challenges include the expectation that a greater range of students is expected to graduate from high school, dealing with the raging pace of technology, and the burdensome task of changing a huge bureaucratic structure.

Over the past 20 years, the proportion of children attending high school has risen markedly. Before then approximately 20% of males, especially, left school after 8th or 9th grade and worked in family businesses or sought employment in what has been traditionally called "blue collar" fields. And this was quite acceptable. Today, fewer of these opportunities are available and many employers demand a more highly specialized workforce.

Few people seem to consider that the profile of the average high school student has changed considerably during the last 20 years, but many listen to news reports from employers who decry the lack of appropriately trained employees. Full employment and changes in welfare laws have exacerbated the situation. Individuals are in the workplace today who have never worked before. Predictably, education is struggling under the weight of these issues.

In the face of accusations of educational ineptitude, the government has welcomed innovative educational practices from a variety of sources. The result is the advent of a number of initiatives such as "choice programs," national charter school legislation, and legislation either proposing or supporting alternative learning centers and/or programs. Now, more than ever, it is acceptable for parents to choose how their child is to be educated. "Parent and student empowerment" is becoming a byword of our day.

Other legislation has granted variances in the qualifications for teaching credentials. Big business and several corporations are offering to assist schools in their educational training programs. Some schools are even run by management corporations rather than the traditional educational administrative group. There are a number of "alternative ways" to providing education for certain groups of students emerging that vary from how "it's always been done."

This book addresses the topic of alternative education, because the number of alternative schools is rising rapidly, yet there are few guidelines to determine the establishment or assessment of these programs. Some well-meaning school boards and school administrations are opening alternative schools that are becoming "dumping grounds" for the least desirable elements of the school population, with less and less evidence of academic achievement. These dumping grounds are old, substandard buildings with few facilities and, often, poor teachers. Their students suffer from a myriad of behavioral and emotional disorders that make it difficult for them to find success in the regular school setting. It doesn't need to be this way. There are standards and procedures that can be followed to ensure that alternative schools do not become expensive dumping grounds. But first we should establish what we are talking about when we use the term *alternative education*.

Alternative Education: What Is It?

Alternative education, like traditional education, is based on the belief that all children can learn. However, in alternative schools it is assumed that not all students are able to learn in all school environments, or without the school having the ability to adapt to some of these students' needs.

The first schools to be called alternative schools emerged in the 1960s, primarily in urban and suburban areas across the country. The urban model was aimed at making school work for those who were not succeeding in school— minority and poor children. In the suburbs, the programs tended to be more innovative.[1] "The term itself was most often used to describe schools that were alternatives to existing public schools."[2] During the 1970s alternative schools were "co-opted into a broader political agenda as they were incorporated into much larger desegregation plans."[3] A 1972 report by the President's Commission on School Finance called for an increase in options in the form of alternative education.[4] As a result, the number of alternative schools increased from 464 in 1973 to 5,000 in 1975.[5] The term *magnet* replaced the term *alternative* in some states, and parents were given a choice of public school for their children. Since then, the "choice movement," which gives parents a greater choice in controlling their children's education, has grown markedly. Alternative, magnet, and charter schools have joined the traditional choices of public, private, or parochial schools.

Since the 1980s, alternative schools have regained their original identity. According to the New Jersey Department of Education, alternative education is defined as: An education program that embraces subject matter and/or teaching methodology that is not generally offered to students of the same age or grade level in the traditional school settings, which offers a range of educational options and includes the students as an integral part of the planning team.[6]

Put more succinctly, the Virginia Department of Education defines alternative education as "providing learning opportunities that accommodate the needs of students not optimally served by the regular program, alternative education aims for student success through varying degrees of departure from standard school organization, programs, and environments."[7]

Although there is no typical model of an alternative school, there are some common structures and processes. These include collaborative, site-based management, small school size, small class size, extended roles for teachers, cooperative roles for students, voluntary membership, student involvement in governance, and the absence, or minimization, of tracking, ability grouping or other kinds of labeling. In many cases, students are not given letter grades but accrue points towards graduation through coursework, independent study, and internship or service learning activities.[8]

The degree of departure from standard school organization, programs and environment depends, in large part, on the mission of the alternative program. Each purpose shapes each alternative school in a unique way.

The Need for Change

Educating our youth has been an important aspect of American life since the birth of the American nation. How this is to be accomplished, and for what purpose continues to be a matter of debate which should not be surprising to us, especially at the close of the 20th century. America continues to be an increasingly dynamically complex society.

The plethora of pedagogies would suggest that the educational system should be in an amoebic state, growing and re-shaping to fit current standards and needs, but this is not so. The subjects that are taught and the way in which information is presented to students is similar to the way they were presented one hundred years ago, despite the fact that the background of the average American student has changed dramatically. There have been some additions to these subjects and a variety of teaching methods utilized in some schools, certainly, but few significant changes have occurred.

Up until this point, education has been an effective tool for preparing the majority of students for the world ahead of them. It must be remembered that we are now taking children from a vast array of backgrounds and attempting to educate them at a level of sophistication that has never been considered before. The high incidence of foreign-born children living in America today makes this an even greater challenge. Few people predicted the explosion of technology and the impact it would have on our world.

With a growing sense of urgency to educate as many children as possible, the time is ripe to try new, innovative strategies that are sensitive and responsive to the cultural and affective needs of local student populations. Alternative Schools have come to the forefront as pioneers in meeting these needs. This book will help guide you in either beginning or improving upon a program in your area.

The Organization of This Work

Part I deals with the ethical and philosophical dimensions associated with alternative education. Chapter 1 addresses the issue of why alternative education should be offered at all within the purview of the public education system. Chapter 2 looks at the types of students who function best within the alternative school setting.

Part II contains the practical guide to establishing an alternative school/ program. Chapter 3 is the most important chapter. It explains the importance of determining a mission statement before addressing the details of opening an alternative school. Chapters 4 through 6 cover the day-to-day issues themselves.

Part III can be used as an assessment tool. Chapter 7 is a discussion of the characteristics of a good program. Chapter 8 contains a list of quality indicators that should be present in a quality alternative education school/program. Chapter 9 is a review of a study I conducted in 1999 comparing alternative education centers in the state of Minnesota. It illustrates how different quality programs can have different profiles of significant quality indicators. It also contains an example of a program that could not be considered as being a quality program.

Notes

1. Raywid, M. A. (1998, October). The journey of the alternative schoolmovement: Where it's been and where it's going. *The High School Magazine*. 10–15.

2. Bauman, A. (1998, April/May). Finding experts in unexpected places: Learning from those who have failed. *The High School Journal*. p. 258.

3. Bauman. Finding experts in unexpected places. p. 259.

4. Stewart (1993) in Katsiyannis, A. & Williams, B. (1998, September/October). A national survey of state initiatives on alternative education. *Remedial and Special Education*. 276–283.

5. Katsiyannis, A. & Williams, B. (1998, September/October). A National survey of state initiatives on alternative education. *Remedial and Special Education*. 276–283.

6. New Jersey Department of Education. (1994) in Katsiyannis, A. & Williams, B. (1998, September/October). A national survey of state initiatives on alternative education. *Remedial and Special Education*. 276–283.

7. Virginia Department of Education. (1994) in Katsiyannis, A. & Williams, B. (1998, September/October). A national survey of state initiatives on alternative education. *Remedial and Special Education*. 276–283.

8. Neuman, W. L. (1994). Social research methods. Boston: Allyn and Bacon. Office of Educational Research and Improvement (1996). URL: http://www.ed.gov/.

Part I

Ethical and Philosophical Dimensions Associated with Alternative Education

1

Why Offer Alternative Education?

Change is not synonymous with progress. Sometimes preserving
good practices in the face of challenges is a major achievement,
and sometimes teachers have been wise to resist reforms that
violated their professional judgment . . . actual reforms have typically
been gradual and incremental—tinkering with the system.
It may be fashionable to decry such changes as piecemeal and inadequate,
but over the long periods of time such revision of practice, adapted to local
contexts, can substantially improve schools. Tinkering is one way of
preserving what is valuable and reworking what is not.
— *Tyack and Cuban*

The American education system is touted as being one of the best in the world. And for many people it is. However, for approximately one million students each year it is actually untenable. They drop out of school. Others stay in school but perform well below their ability level and become "in-school" dropouts. What happens to these "out-of-school" dropouts? Where do they go? What do they do? What are the economic and social costs of all of these dropouts? In a nation that was founded on liberty and justice for all, is the deprivation of opportunity that faces these students acceptable to us?

Do we even care?

Thankfully, the answer is yes, we do care about these students. The rapid rise in the number of alternative schools in some states, professional organizations, and the launching of the new *Alternative Network Journal* are proof of this. They are proof that "tinkering with the system" works. We are listening to students who are telling us, loud and clear, that the traditional way of education is not working for them. But they do want to be educated.

In 1989 there were 894 public alternative schools in America. By 1995, this number had increased to 2,640. Since that time there has been a literal explosion in the number of public and private alternative schools and programs opening around the country.

3

This "explosion" is exemplified by statistics provided by the Department of Children, Families and Learning in the state of Minnesota. In 1989, 4,050 students were enrolled in alternative education centers/programs in that state. This number mushroomed to 81,332 in 1998. With the addition of "targeted (after school) services" to elementary-aged students in 1999, the number further increased to 133,520 students, a staggering 15% of the school-aged population. In the state of Minnesota alone, 133,520 students who are considered at risk for dropping out of school are constructively involved in the education process.

Our Changing Society

Our rapidly changing, pluralistic society is placing unprecedented demands on the educational structure. Although it may be fashionable to criticize education for not responding rapidly enough, it is also important to put this viewpoint into perspective. "In evolutionary terms, education has worked well over the past 100 years. Although many people have fallen through the cracks and numerous inequities have occurred, the model of education has been a good 'fit' for the industrial age. Large numbers of people have been equipped to function in industry. And education and industry have been perceived through the same larger lens. What is now happening is that the world itself is changing, and the lenses through which we have peered are being replaced. As this happens in other larger spheres of life, a point is reached where education must follow suit."[1]

The lenses, through which we now find ourselves looking, are tinted with hues of greater pluralism and technological advancements. We are looking out onto a world where the size and location of the workforce is changing markedly, and employees should expect to change careers several times in their lives. Educating students for their first, and possibly only, job is no longer sufficient. Students must be educated to learn how to learn in order to acquire new skills and change jobs with some fluidity and thus remain viable in the global job market. The question of the day is, of course, how can this end be achieved? "Changing our thinking is the first thing we have to do both individually and collectively, because without that change we cannot possibly change what we do on a day-to-day basis. Regardless of what new "method" or latest technique is attempted, the mind/brain will always choose to reduce such practices to fit entrenched assumptions and beliefs."[2]

Rather than attempting to change a huge, bureaucratic structure, perhaps small-scale innovations are the best vehicles for change. Logically, it would seem appropriate to address students who are not optimizing their abilities in the present school structures before making whole-scale changes for students who are doing well in the present system. "Keep that which has worked well. Change is not synonymous with progress. Sometimes preserving good practices in the face of challenges is a major achievement, and sometimes teachers have been wise to resist reforms that violated their professional judgment . . . actual reforms have typically been gradual and incremental—tinkering with the system. It may be fashionable to decry such changes as piecemeal and inadequate, but over the long periods of time such revision of practice, adapted to local contexts, can substantially improve schools. Tinkering is one way of preserving what is valuable and reworking what is not."[3]

The Economic Impact of Dropping Out of School

Until recently, a certain percentage of students dropping out of high school was considered inevitable and natural. For the most part, dropping out was not viewed as being either positive or negative. Schools merely sorted those who were successful academically from those who were not. Those who graduated from high school filled jobs requiring higher levels of skills. Those who did not were relegated to unskilled jobs. Before the days of advanced technology, a sufficient supply of unskilled/moderately skilled jobs was available. However, many of these jobs have disappeared from the American labor market at a time when the traditional pool of new workers is shrinking.

Dropping out of school is now considered to be a major socio-economic problem. David Kearns, former head of Xerox Corporation, commented that, "Public education has put this country at a terrible competitive disadvantage. The American work force is running out of qualified people. If current demographic and economic trends continue, American business will have to hire a million new workers a year who can't read, write or count. Teaching them how and absorbing the lost productivity while they're learning will cost industry $25 billion a year for as long as it takes. And nobody knows how long that will be."

The world around us is changing rapidly; educational reform is not. According to news reports, education is approaching a stage of crisis and despair. However, a closer look at "what is really going on" paints a different picture.

An article written by Peter Schrag, that appeared in the *Atlantic Monthly*, reminds us that we are trying to take children from an unprecedented array of ethnic and cultural backgrounds, many of them speaking little or no English, and educate them all to a level of sophistication never imagined for so large a proportion of any population.

"Juxtapose relatively stable achievement together with improving test scores among minorities and the poor, with changes from 1950 to the late 1980s in social conditions that could be expected to lower the academic performance of pupils: a tripling of the percentage of children living in single-parent families; an increase in teenage pregnancy; catastrophic unemployment rates for young blacks; soaring arrest rates for youth under eighteen and high rates of drug abuse and violence. Would it not be reasonable to applaud the success of educators in holding steady in the face of so many impediments?"[4] The answer to this question is both yes and no. Those students staying in school are doing well. Those dropping out are not. And dropouts have become a luxury that, according to David J. Kearns, the economic well-being of the country can ill afford.

The Social Impact of Dropping out of School

More than one million students drop out of school each year, resulting in one-third of young people entering adult society without a high school diploma. There are some serious issues associated with dropping out, not only for the individual but also for society as a whole. American society needs an educated and trained work force in order to compete in world markets, and some consider a high school education a "minimum survival kit for coping with today's world."[5] Statistics from juvenile court records indicate that dropouts are more likely to engage in criminal activities and in some states, 75 percent of youth appearing in juvenile court have dropped out of school.

A U.S. Office of Education report links welfare dependency to poor achievement in school. In 1992, 17 percent of those receiving welfare from the ages of 18–24 were high school dropouts, compared to 6 percent of high school graduates. In a report prepared by the Educational Testing Service, three-fourths of welfare recipients performed at the lowest two levels of literacy (out of a possible five). These welfare recipients cannot consistently perform . . . such tasks as writing a letter to explain a billing error, entering information into an automobile maintenance form, or calculating miles per gallon using information given on a mileage record chart.[6] This means that a large percentage of those on welfare will not be employable in today's high-skill workplace nor have the background to benefit from training programs designed to prepare them for employment.

The Emotional Impact of Dropping Out of School

Dropping out of school is a very difficult, even if inevitable, decision for individuals to make at a very vulnerable time of their lives. Research has found that dropouts are desperately trying to escape failure. They have already decided that they are beyond help. They have suffered daily indignities by being told in various subtle and direct ways that they are not good at anything. For some it is due to academic failure; for others it is conflicts with peers or adults, loneliness and isolation and a general lack of success in anything valued by the school or their peer group.[7]

No adolescent should have to endure suffering daily indignities and feelings of isolation and loneliness.

There are even some serious implications for the children of dropouts, apart from the sad fact that they are more likely than their peers to drop out of school. Many dropouts maintain a lifelong grudge against the education system, which in their view has failed them. Most who drop out leave behind a history of humiliation, indignation and repeated failure and frustration.[8]

So the question becomes, who are these dropouts and what should be done about them?

Notes

1. Caine R., & Caine G. (1997). Education on the edge of possibility. Virginia: ASCD.

2. Fullan, M. (1993). Change forces. London: Falmer Press.

3. Tyack, D., & Cuban, L. (1995). Tinkering towards utopia. Cambridge: Harvard University Press. p. 5.

4. Schrag, P. (1997). The near-myth of our failing schools. *Atlantic Monthly.* 71–82.

5. Roderick, M.R. (1993, Winter). Grade retention and school dropout: Investigating the association. *American Education Research Journal.* 729–59.

6. *The Education Digest*, November, 1995. p. 72.

7. Wehlage, G., et al. (1989). Reducing the risk: Schools as communities of support. London: Falmer Press.

8. Grossnickle, D. (1986). High school dropouts: Causes, consequences and cure. Bloomington, Indiana, Phi Delta Kappan Educational Foundation.

2

Who Are These Students?

Give me your tired, your poor, your
huddled masses yearning to breathe free.
The wretched refuse of your teeming shore,
Send these, the homeless, tempest-tossed to me:
I lift my lamp beside the golden door.
— *Emma Lazarus*

These words, written by Emma Lazarus in the early 20th century, refer to the many immigrants flocking to America for a better life. Even after many years in the United States, a number of these immigrant families are still tired and still poor. They may find themselves tempest-tossed by drug and alcohol addiction, social or emotional problems, inadequate housing or a poor fit between the education offered in the mainstream classroom and learning style. More children than ever are finding themselves homeless. Whatever the reason, too many children are not able to access the American dream because they are undereducated.

In 1980 there were 5.9 million undereducated youth in America, 58 percent of whom were majority White males, 17 percent African-American, and 16 percent Hispanic. They constituted 28.1 percent of their peer group. Since that time these numbers have improved, but neither proportionately nor significantly for all groups.

The average youth not enrolled in school and who is not a high school graduate is still a majority White male born in the United States into a monolingual English-speaking family with income above the poverty level. Before dropping out of school he completed at least nine grades and lived in an urban area. However, due to the differences in raw numbers, factors such as poverty, race and country of birth tell a very different story. Poor minority youth are particularly susceptible to dropping out of school.

- 41% of Hispanics,
- 40% of Native Americans, and

- 28% of African Americans living below the poverty line drop out of school.[1]

An analysis of a national sample of high schools in 1989 found that 5 percent of males and 37 percent of females gave "family-related problems" as the reason for dropping out of school. Eight percent of the young women in their study had to help support their families, 31 percent left to get married, and 23 percent left because they were pregnant.[2]

Reasons for dropping out of school vary greatly. According to Thomas Koch there are two root causes for the urban dropout: many students from disadvantaged homes are never able to catch up, and many others arrive at school with physical and emotional problems so severe as to make learning impossible.[3] Dropouts desperately try to escape failure. In their minds it is too late for them to get help.[4] By fourth grade the average grades of early grade dropouts are significantly lower than those of their classmates, and over one half of the students have been retained. These students' grades often decline significantly following a transition from one school to another.[5]

Clearly, all of these students are on the "At-Risk Merry-Go-Round"[6] with no hope of getting off.

Some common early warning signs are poor attendance, truancy, tardiness, consistently low grades, lack of basic skills (especially reading), home problems, poor communication between home and school, poorly developed organizational skills, history of school transfer and family moves, poor social adjustment, failure to see relevance of education, inability to relate to authority figures, having an older sibling or a parent who is a dropout, and low self-esteem.[7]

Canaries in the Coal Mine?

Alternative school students may not be as unique a population, as one might think. Some believe that only a fine line separates these students from the rest of the student population, especially in the inner city. As a group they are more challenging than the rest of the student population and that is why they are more dependent on a good education. The reason why alternative education works for these students is that it reflects many of the current reforms touted in educational pedagogy. Practices such as pursuing a theme, making a school a community, empowering staff and authentic assessment were pioneered by alternative schools. "Alternatives are the clearest example we have of what a restructured school might look like."[8]

THE AT-RISK MERRY-GO-ROUND

Negative school experiences for marginal students are mutually reinforcing: one negative experience leads to another. As these experiences accumulate, students come to believe that "school is not for me." Finally, the combination of concrete problems and students' perceptions of themselves and their potential for success at school results in them dropping out.

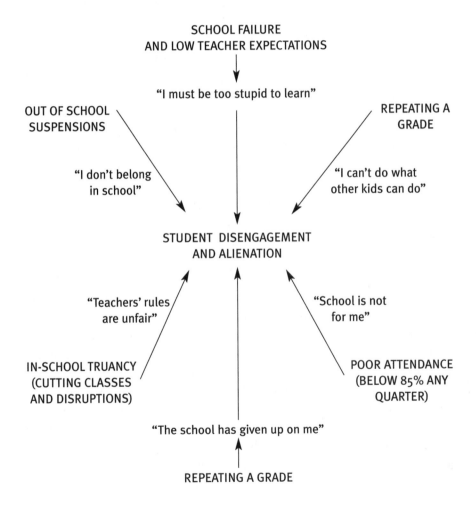

— Anne Wheelock

Source: Haasch, Patricia. (1990). *Changes in Minnesota Public Alternative Education, 1980–1990,* Unpublished master's dissertation, Bemidji State University, Bemidji, Minnesota.

Or a Different Breed of Cat?

On the other hand, a study of 50 at-risk junior and senior high school students in four alternative schools in 1996 revealed a different picture. The authors adopted Comb's definition of at-risk students as "those with the potential for displaying academic, behavioral and social problems." It applied Douglass' nine factors representing at-risk youth. The nine factors are a record of poor academic achievement, family backgrounds of low socioeconomic and cultural status, poor school achievement, truancy, no membership in school extracurricular activities, verbal abilities inferior to non-verbal abilities, record of repeated norm-violating disruptive behaviors, a peer group composed of similar students, and a negative attitude towards school. The group reflected five of Douglass' nine at-risk factors: poor achievement (grades) in school; truancy; no participation in extracurricular activities; records of repeated norm-violating behaviors; and a negative attitude towards school.[9]

Two personality tests were also administered as part of the study, the Minnesota Multiphasic Personality Inventory-Adolescent (MMPI-A) and the Behavior Assessment System for Children (BASC). A factor analysis isolated six factors: defensiveness/hopelessness; attention seeking; antisocial disorders; conduct disorders; interpersonal problems; and family relationship problems.[10]

It was concluded that these at-risk students did have a specific profile. This profile suggests that these students often present an array of circumstances that makes finishing high school extremely difficult for them, if not just a remote possibility. The authors suggested that alternative education students need an integrated curriculum with specific academic program goals, vocational program goals, social skills development goals and personal development goals.[11]

This research is supported by the 1996 Minnesota Student Survey, conducted by the Minnesota Association of Alternative Programs. Students in alternative learning centers were found to be twice as likely to have come from homes with family substance abuse; to have been physically or sexually abused; to have witnessed physical abuse or to have attempted suicide. Reports of sexual activity, anti-social behavior, and substance abuse were reported to be significantly higher than in mainstream high schools.

Another interesting study was conducted in1998. It examined the coping strategies at-risk students reported using when facing challenges in their lives. 264 high school students from three midwestern communities were studied. This number included an equal number from alternative schools and traditional high schools.[12] The students were given The Adolescent Coping Orientation for Problem Experiences and the Behavior Health Inventory Adolescent Symptom Checklist.

Research has suggested that those children who cope effectively with tasks utilize many of the behaviors associated with active coping and demonstrate an ability to maintain high levels of motivation, persistence and concentration in problem solving. In contrast, research has viewed the avoidance of a problem situation to be the result of a primary appraisal of threat and a secondary perception of insufficient resources to meet the demands of the situation.

Alternative school students in this study reported utilizing avoidance coping strategies (staying away from home, using drugs/alcohol) to a greater degree than those students enrolled in a traditional high school. They also reported a significantly greater preference for developing self-reliance. This may reflect the tendency on the part of alternative education students to fail to seek out sources of help, instead choosing to avoid the stressor itself.[13] These students are unable to find a relevant connection, or ally, in their world of significant adults. Rather, they see most adults as either intrusive or ineffective, at best. It seems to them that they have little choice but to drop out of this "ineffectual-adult dominated" world.

It is my contention that "the true" alternative education student is a "different breed of cat." Lack of skills, support structure and coping strategies make these students easy prey to a cycle of dejection and failure within the mainstream setting. These students desperately need small school size, small class size, extended roles for teachers, cooperative roles for students, voluntary membership, student involvement in governance, and an absence or minimization of tracking, ability grouping or other kinds of labeling.

Notes

1. Waggoner, D. (1991). Undereducation in America: The demography of high school dropouts. Westport, Connecticut. Auburn House.

2. Fine, M. (1991). Framing dropouts: Notes on the politics of an urban high school. State University of New York Press.

3. Koch, T. (1992, October 5). Reasons for dropping out of school. *U.S. News & World Report.* 42.

4. Grossnickle, D. (1986). High school dropouts: Causes, consequences and cure. Bloomington, Indiana, Phi Delta Kappan Educational Foundation.

5. Roderick, M. R. (1993, Winter). Grade retention and school dropout: Investigating the association. *American Education Research Journal.* 729–59.

6. Haasch, P. (1990). Changes in Minnesota Public Alternative Education, 1980–1990. Unpublished master's dissertation, Bemidji State University, Bemidji, Minnesota.

7. Grossnickle, D. (1986). High school dropouts: Causes, consequences and cure. Bloomington, Indiana, Phi Delta Kappan Educational Foundation.

8. Raywid, M. A. (1994, September). Alternative schools: The state of the art. *Educational Leadership*. 26–31.

9. Fuller, C. & Sabatino, D. (1996, April/May). Who attends alternative high schools? *The High School Journal*. 293–297.

10. Fuller, C. Who attends alternative high schools?

11. Fuller, C. Who attends alternative high schools?

12. May, H. & Copeland, E. (1998, April/May). Academic persistence and alternative high schools: Students and site characteristics. *The High School Journal*. 199–208.

13. May, H. & Copeland, E. Academic persistence and alternative high schools.

Part II

A Practical Guide

3

Mission Statement

On a group of theories one can found a school;
but on a group of values one can found a culture,
a civilization,
a new way of living among men.
— *Ignazio Silone*

A common complaint, voiced by alternative education students, about their experience in a traditional high school is, "No one cared about me." Despite the presence of excellent teachers (as reported by many other students) and well-developed curriculum, these students were unable to thrive. They complain, probably correctly, that the emphasis was on academics and not on individual differences and needs, which is so important to them. As a result, they found themselves unable to relate to the culture of the school. It doesn't help that high school buildings are large and seen as being impersonal.

At the same time, other high school students find a sense of belonging in after-school sports and clubs. For whatever reason, the popularity of these groups increases the feeling of alienation these alternative students experience. Alternative education students rarely belong to school organizations, yet they still need to feel a sense of belonging. They need to feel connected but are unable to do make the connections themselves. They are looking for "a new way of living among man."

The primary goal of an alternative school program is to first make connections with each student, and then be sure to maintain these connections. They often do this by providing a "family-like" atmosphere and do, indeed, become surrogate families. An inordinate number of students in alternative schools come from homes that are dysfunctional for a variety of reasons, such as poverty, substance abuse, divorce or mental illness. These factors render parents unable to adequately nurture their children. Alternative educators find themselves providing emotional support and social skills that are traditionally provided by the family unit.

Once this has been established, the secondary (academic) goal may be addressed. It is important to note here that emphasizing connectedness does not diminish the role of academic progress. In fact, once connections have been made, students should be more able and willing to learn.

Three Distinct Missions

The first mission is to be innovative and seek to make these schools challenging and fulfilling for their students. They are schools of choice and are usually popular. They sometimes resemble magnet schools. They may be called *popular innovation* schools. The second mission is to provide last-chance programs for students who are at risk of dropping out of school, have dropped out or been expelled. This is their last chance to graduate and some students are given no other choice than to attend this program. These may be known as *last chance* schools. The third mission is to provide a remedial focus for students who need academic and/or social-emotional remediation, and are recognized as *remedial focus* schools.[1]

Alternative schools in large cities and those designed for a very specific population (for example, new immigrants who do not speak English) are often classified as one of these types, but in rural and some suburban areas they are more often an amalgam of all three.

A number of features found in alternative education are reflected in what we have learned about dropouts. Dropouts should be taught by caring teachers, but the individuality of each student should be reflected in the teaching technology used. Dropouts also need to acquire vocational skills, but first they need to learn to read in a learning environment that does not resemble a traditional classroom. In addition, dropouts should work, but the experience from the work sites should be used as pedagogical reinforcement in a classroom component that is clearly connected to the job.[2]

Local Culture

It has been suggested that the key decision-makers in providing a free, equal education for all children should be at the local school district level, unless they prove inadequate for the task. Schools need to be community-based, reflecting the realities and needs of the local community in order to succeed. At this level, the mores and customs of the students can be taken into account when making key decisions. Specific problems can also become a determining factor. Some schools are currently struggling with refining their constructivist strategies, while others are more concerned about poor attendance, poverty and crime.

Knowledge of the local culture and population may call for a markedly different approach to educating students. Aspects such as school calendar, teaching days, time of day and organization of subject matter are similar in many districts across the country, but do they need to be? There are alternatives. For example, there is a cultural compatibility approach that is meliorist—it uses a least change model. This approach would require schools to make the least changes possible to achieve the desired results. Culturally compatible approaches to teaching and learning recognize that schools and homes serve different socializing functions and that all children experience some kind of discontinuity when they go to school. One of the best examples of this model is the Kamehameha Early Childhood Project (KEEP) based in Hawaii. This program incorporates a valued aspect of Hawaiian culture, the "talk story," into school practices. The "talk story" is a style of discourse in which several people talk at once to produce a story, which is in sharp contrast to the usual teacher-led discussions found in other schools. Hawaiian children are typically kept in groups according to age and so are not used to being addressed by adults. In order to accommodate this trait the teachers developed their attentional value by manipulating the incentives for listening in the classroom. Teachers found out rather quickly that Hawaiian children value the qualities of being either nice or tough, with little in between, and adjusted their teaching style accordingly.

An attempt to repeat this successful experiment on a Navajo reservation failed dismally. Navajo children do not value the two qualities of niceness or toughness, and most Navajo groups are sex-specific. It is only on rare occasions that girls and boys are mixed together in one group.[3]

In retrospect, insensitivity to local core values and traditions in this cross-cultural experiment seem ludicrous, at best. But it serves as an excellent example of how crucial local mores and customs, not the mores and customs of others, can be in developing a successful program.

Although other successful models of Alternative schools have something to offer in the creation of a new program, the most important thing to remember is that every program should be developed to meet the unique needs of the local population.

Developing "Your" Mission

Despite the fact that smaller programs, especially in rural areas, tend to be an amalgam of the different types of alternative programs, it is rarely appropriate to develop a mission statement whose goal is to provide education to every student who has not been reached in the traditional high school setting. As heartbreaking as it may be to knowingly omit a certain sector of the population from a new alternative program, trying to be all-things-to-all-people is unrealistic and a sure sign of failure. Students whose basic needs stem from English being their second language, and others whose basic needs stem from severe behavioral disorders are, for example, very difficult to educate together in a small setting. Successful programs are good ambassadors for adding more programs, poor ones are not. Additional alternative programs can be added at a later date. School board philosophy statements often refer to the education of all students, and this tenet may be an appropriate one for a vision statement for alternative education throughout a district. It just isn't appropriate for one small setting. However, certain attributes of students can be combined successfully, such as poor basic skills due to lack of ability and poor basic skills due to poor attendance.

There are four basic steps involved in developing a mission statement for an alternative education program:

1. *Develop a vision statement*
   If anything were possible, what would be your vision for students who are either dropping out of high school or potential candidates for doing so? This statement should be much more thoughtful than, "to have 100% of students graduate from XYZ School." It should include a statement about your core values and beliefs. Hopefully, these values will transcend the realm of the school day into teaching the value of lifelong learning, teaching independent learning skills and providing students with the evaluative tools to "think for themselves."

2. *Determine the availability of funds*
   At this point you know what you want to do, but now is time for a reality check—how much is possible?
   • What start-up funds are available?
   • What will be your ongoing sources for funding?
   • What is the likelihood of securing special grants and additional monies?
   • What materials and supplies will be available to you at little or no cost? These may be supplied by local school districts or non-profit agencies.

- What other "people" resources are out there? College volunteers? Senior citizens? Community experts?
- What are your staffing needs?
- What are your building needs?
- What are your materials and supplies needs?
- What "special" needs are there for your specific population?

3. *Develop a mission statement*

This is the tricky part. You have a number of students who are addressed by the vision statement, but you can't serve them all in this program. How do you determine which sector of the population you are going to serve, and how do you justify the sector of the population you are not going to serve? This process may take several months of meetings with various stakeholders, and still not result in consensus. However, it is crucial to craft this statement carefully before moving forward. It may be tempting to move ahead and address less contentious issues, but this would be a mistake. A mission statement is a statement of commitment to a certain group of students. It is also, by default, a lack of commitment to other groups of students at this point in time. It is a morally taxing endeavor.

In order to develop the mission statement, several factors need to be taken into account, such as:

Grade levels to be served/age of students—Is the program for high school students, middle/junior high aged students and/or adults?

Basic skills needs—Is the population to be served lacking in basic skill instruction? This may be due to one or more factors: lack of ability, poor attendance, English as a Second Language or social/emotional issues? The root source of the problem will have a great effect on the way the program is designed.

Prerequisite skills—Do students have the prerequisite skills for the classes they need to graduate from high school? Do they have the necessary background in American history, for example, to take a high school American History class? If not, is this due to poor attendance in the past, cultural factors or other issues?

Extended opportunities—Are the students to be served quite bright, but merely disenchanted with the traditional high school setting? Are they looking for a different mode of instruction or emphasis in a particular area, such as art?

Cultural factors—Is the population to be served a minority population, either by federal definition or local culture? Should cultural issues help determine how, when and what classes are offered?

Social/emotional issues—Is the primary reason the target population needs an alternative setting their particular social/emotional needs? A program for students with severe behavioral problems will look very different than one designed for pregnant teens.

Specific issues—Is the program designed for students with one specific issue, such as teen pregnancy or recovering addicts?

External factors—Are there external factors that determine the population? For example, is the program one for adjudicated youth?

4. *Regularly review the vision statement and the mission statement*
   Once the program is in place do not let down your guard! Is the program meeting its mission statement? Is the mission statement still consistent with the vision statement? These are questions that should be asked on a regular basis.

A review of these factors, and others peculiar to your setting, should result in a specific mission statement that will allow you to move forward in a productive manner and begin the planning process.

Notes

1. Raywid, M. A. (1994, September). Alternative schools: The state of the art. *Educational Leadership*. 26–31.

2. Hahn, A. (1997, December). Reaching out to America's dropouts: What to do? *Phi Delta Kappan*. 256–263.

3. Trueba, H., Spindler, G. & Spindler, L., eds. (1989). What do anthropologists have to say about dropouts? London: Falmer Press.

4

Assembling a Great Team

I've never met a kid I liked.
— W. C. Fields

W. C. Fields would not have been a good employee in an alternative school, or any other school for that matter. The difference is that in an alternative school, he would have done much more damage.

Although alternative education programs may seem like microcosms of larger school systems from the outside, a closer look will not support this view. A quality alternative school will have been designed for a specific population of students. As a result, it requires a specific population of adults to work with these students.

The single, most important criteria for staffing an alternative school is to ensure that these people want to be there. Alternative students tend to have more academic and social/emotional needs than equivalent school populations. Placing teaching and/or support staff in these programs because they are not succeeding elsewhere is a recipe for disaster. Just one disgruntled staff member can be enough to destroy any program. Typically, students attending an alternative program have experienced rejection for many years. They don't need to be exposed to any more rejection or inappropriate teaching styles. Fledgling programs are particularly vulnerable to the destructive nature of this type of employee.

There are some general characteristics that apply to all staff working in an alternative school.

General Characteristics

1. *A positive outlook*
   All staff members need to have a positive outlook on life. This is not a good place for the half-empty society.

2. *Common vision*

    A common vision is an essential component of a small, specialized staff
    such as this. Everyone needs to understand and respect the unique
    needs of each student and be willing to respond enthusiastically. This
    common vision will come about through training and the many planned
    and incidental conversations that occur during the day. Pedagogical
    renegades are common in programs such as this, but at least they
    should all be tilting at the same windmills.

    It is also important for this vision to be shared by top administrators
    in supervising school districts. After all, the overall objective is to pro-
    vide a quality education for all students. Superintendents may not com-
    pletely understand how to accommodate the needs of students in an al-
    ternative setting, but they should have faith in their staff to provide this.
    Alternative Schools are perfect sites to allow leaders to take calculated
    risks and explore new and innovative ideas.

3. *Team players*

    The small confines of the typical alternative school demands that its
    employees are good team players. The renegades can renegade in their
    own space, but they need to be able to work harmoniously with other
    employees in the shared spaces. And, above all, everyone needs to re-
    spect everyone else. This does not mean that conflict will never occur.
    However, it can be excellent modeling for students to observe quite dif-
    ferent people being respectful and resolving conflict peacefully.

4. *Flexibility*

    The ability to be flexible is crucial with this population of students.
    Their self-defeating attitudes and behaviors will not change overnight.
    Possibly more than anything else, they need to learn how to face a prob-
    lem situation, re-group and, when necessary, re-group again. Many of
    them have responded to problem situations by simply walking away
    from them, regardless of the consequence.

    Alternative schools are fertile ground for individuals with leadership
    potential. There are often lots of good ideas about lots of good things.
    These "bright eyes and bushy tails" and removed location may tempt
    district administrators to take a "hands-off" approach in this setting.
    However, before doing so a number of things need to be taken into con-
    sideration.

Leadership Staff

The majority of alternative programs open their doors with few staff members. As a result, it is typical for one staff member to wear at least two hats, teaching and administration. This person is often known as the *lead teacher*. Although small in size, these programs still require the same array of administrative duties required in larger programs. Setting up the program, facilitating changes in the program, interviewing staff and students, developing and overseeing the budget, curriculum development, communicating with appropriate school district personnel, maintaining close ties with parents and social service agencies, and being responsible for discipline are but a few of the tasks expected of the lead teacher. These duties take time and energy, and it is not realistic to expect someone to maintain a full teaching load whilst also performing these tasks. It is very important to provide release time for the lead teacher so that these duties can be performed adequately and in a timely manner.

As a result of the fact that lead teachers are often primarily classroom teachers, they usually do not have any formal training in administration. It is important for the lead teacher to know how to access administrative files that are pertinent to the site, are privy to administrative decisions that pertain to the site, and have a good command of the budget process. It is most helpful if one administrator is assigned to the lead teacher to provide this important information. The lead teacher and the assigned administrator can then work together to ensure that the best decisions are made for individual students at the alternative school.

Everyone a Leader

One of the most empowering aspects of a small, vibrant organization, such as an alternative school, is that there is ample room for leadership development at all levels. Not only are there opportunities for leadership, but each of the jobs requires it. The lead teacher will be more than occupied with his/her duties. Therefore, some crucial elements of the program will naturally default to other staff members. It is important that this leader can share the reins of control. In an environment where there are few hands and many tasks, control can be shared so that the person with the most skills for a particular task will adopt that task. But responsibilities also need to be shared, (something that will follow when the mission is shared) and care must be given that tasks not fall just to those willing to do them.

The small teaching staff may become completely responsible for curriculum development in alignment with local, state and federal requirements. The small support staff may become completely responsible for the day-to-day running of the program. It is important that everyone receives adequate training to do their respective jobs on an ongoing basis.

Alternative school staffs often resemble "leadership teams" more than a "hierarchy of staff members." It is important for them to have the latitude to make important decisions about their site, especially in the areas of curriculum development and staffing.

Teaching Staff

Teachers at alternative schools need to be selected carefully. It is not realistic to expect teachers to be licensed in all areas they are required to teach in an alternative setting. However, a math-certified teacher could reasonably be expected to teach science and math. Similarly, a social studies-certified teacher could reasonably be expected to teach social studies and language arts. A teacher with an avocation for woodworking, metalworking, baking or sewing could realistically be considered competent to offer classes in these areas. And many do so. However, it is important for teachers to be licensed at the appropriate level they are teaching. For example, high school-level teachers should have a secondary teaching license when working with students in subjects at this level. However, in a number of instances, students may be reading and writing at an elementary level and an elementary trained teacher would be more suitable.

If an unrequested transfer occurs at an alternative learning site, it is usually a member of the teaching staff. It cannot be emphasized enough what a terrible mistake this is. Teaching staff should either apply to teach at an alternative school or request a transfer to teach at an alternative school. School districts hate to terminate teaching contracts during times of fiscal crises, but transferring a teacher to an alternative learning site, rather than lay that person off, is not appropriate. No one should be given the choice of being laid off or transferring to an alternative school.

Teachers also need to feel comfortable with a variety of teaching and assessment techniques that can be tailored to the learning style/needs of the students.

Instructional Aides

The presence of skillful instructional aides can be the difference between a successful, quality program and one that struggles. Working under the direction of a certified teacher, these aides can provide a cost effective way of achieving an appropriate staff:student ratio. Many quality programs function extremely well with a 1:10 ratio of staff to students, including instructional aides. It is important to recognize, however, that these aides often do not have a teaching license and thus should not be expected to plan and deliver whole units of curriculum. After working repeatedly with small groups of students in one particular class, they will become very skillful and invaluable. But this takes time and assistance.

A survey of instructional aides/support staff at the 2001 Minnesota Association of Alternative Programs Conference revealed that one of the most important elements to their success was receiving adequate training in what they were expected to do.

Another advantage of these aides is that, due to the size of the program, they may also need to be the office help as well, and can function in that capacity. It is only larger programs that can usually afford to hire instructional aides and support staff.

Clerical Staff

Being a good, independent problem solver, willing to do whatever is needed to be done in a cheerful manner is probably the hallmark of a good alternative school employee. It applies to the clerical staff as much as to the teaching staff. And every adult in these programs needs to be prepared to be a counselor and confidante. As a long-time secretary in a well-established alternative school stated, "If you're not prepared to be a day mom, don't take the job."

A staff of competent, positive, enthusiastic, flexible players is an unbeatable team.

5

Getting Organized and Providing Structure

Many at-risk students occupy socially marginal status positions in society,
and are bordering upon feelings of alienation and estrangement.
These students frequently thrive
when they are provided a school alternative which grants them
personal respect, responsibility and support.
Most of us would ask no less for ourselves and our children.
— Johnston and Wetherall

Program organization and structure refers to issues that reflect the basic organization of the program, as well as activities that directly affect student learning. A well organized program with ample flexibility within the structure is one of the hallmarks of a quality program.

One of the strongest forces driving adolescent behavior is the need to belong. A history of rejection creates in the student an expectation of future rejection. And so it is very important that these students feel that they have "come home" and will be nurtured and supported in an alternative setting, irregardless of their problems and needs. The most important factor here is that students feel safe, both physically and emotionally. Typically, they did not feel safe or have a sense of belonging in their previous environment, especially emotionally. Other students, staff and family members may have subjected alternative education students to feelings of insecurity and inferiority. Students have to feel they are free from physical and verbal harassment. They need to feel secure that their goals are going to be realized. Students need to feel comfortable enough to both succeed and, yes, sometimes fail.

Some alternative programs are called "last chance" programs, meaning that if a student cannot succeed in this setting there may be no more chances for a high school diploma. Although this may technically be true, the term "last chance" is very unfortunate because it does not support the concept of a nurturing atmosphere that is essential for vulnerable students to succeed. It may be the first barrier that is to be overcome when students enroll in an alternative school. Students primary concern should not be that if they are not successful they will have to drop out of a system—again—and admit they are a failure—again.

The overall organization and structure will address the following issues:

- Facilities
- Program structure
- Procedural issues
- Scheduling/calendar
- Delivery of curriculum
- Instructional materials

Facilities

First impressions are important. We judge people and places immediately upon our first contact with them. Further contacts are often determined by the perceptions made during the first contact. This may be especially so with individuals who have been/felt rejected by the status quo and are desperately seeking another opportunity to succeed. An old abandoned building with a leaky roof and no heating will do little for the self-esteem of a student who has felt rejection and failure in a multi-million dollar high school.

This philosophy was clearly understood by the founders and organizers of Boys' Town, Nebraska. Boys' Town takes 500 of the poorest, toughest, sometimes crime-ridden, drug addicted children in the country. These children have known poverty, violence and despair firsthand. Yet at Boys' Town they are housed with families in beautiful, large homes with manicured lawns, on a campus with its own school, huge gym and two churches with incredible stained glass windows. Many of them have transferred from the ghetto to middle class America, along with all its rights and responsibilities. The message is clear. You are worth all of this. You belong here.

This same philosophy needs to be applied to alternative education. Although different programs have different facilities available to them, there are several important attributes that should be present at each site.

1. *Cheerful and welcoming site*
   It is important for the program site to be cheerful and welcoming. It is not appropriate to place alternative education programs in old aban-

doned buildings with leaky roofs and no heating. A variety of venues, such as storefronts, shopping malls, churches and fellowship halls have all been successfully renovated to provide a cheerful, welcoming atmosphere. The first impression must be one that encourages students and parents to feel "you are worth it" rather than "we are warehousing you away from the rest of the student population until you are old enough to be ejected from the educational system."

2. *Adequate space*
    At the same time, the facility also needs to be large enough to accommodate the student population and program needs. Providing shop classes and history in the same room is bound to doom one or other, or both, of the classes to failure. Temporary lack of space may be acceptable as a program expands unexpectedly, as long as there is a short range plan illustrating how the problem will be solved in the very near future.

3. *Away from regular high school*
    It is preferable for the program site to be away from the regular high school, yet still accessible to any student who chooses to attend. There should be equal accessibility to students who are physically challenged as well as those who are not.

Program Structure

One of the problems alternative education students encounter in regular high schools is the sheer size of the building and student population. They tend to prefer a smaller, family-like atmosphere. For this reason, a quality program should include the following factors:

1. *Appropriate program size*
    Kept to below 200 students at one location.

2. *Appropriate class size*
    Similarly, class sizes should be kept below 15 students per teacher in "seat time" programs. "Seat time" programs are ones where students are expected to complete most, if not all, of their schoolwork at the site of the alternative program. If this cannot be realistically achieved, then

classes should be kept to below 15 students per supervising adult. This would typically consist of a combination of teachers and instructional aides.

3. *Access to off-site classes*
   Despite the fact that it is desirable for alternative programs to be located away from the traditional high school, it is also important to provide opportunities for students to take classes at other sites. These classes may be part of post-secondary options, such as university or vocational school classes, that are not available at the alternative learning site. They may be specialized classes, such as music, foreign language, shop classes or drivers' education that are offered at a high school campus and are not feasible to offer at smaller alternative education sites. Few students may opt to participate in these off-campus classes; but at least the opportunity is there for them.

4. *Structure with flexibility*
   Students entering an alternative learning program are often disenchanted with their past school experiences. However, the traditional school program is the only one they are familiar with and "starting over" in an alternative setting may be threatening and confusing for both them and their parents. Therefore, these programs need to provide a great deal of structure for students in a flexible manner. For example, once clear academic and behavioral standards have been established, students should be able to have input into how these standards will be met.

5. *Clear admissions procedure and orientation session*
   The structure needs to begin with a clear admissions procedure and an orientation session as students enter the program, so they know what to anticipate in their new setting. Typically, transitions are difficult for these students and they do not like to ask a lot of questions until they feel safe doing so. Often, students are interviewed by staff members at the alternative site so they can see what it is like. It is common for alternative education students to conduct tours of their site for incoming students so that "student-oriented" questions can be answered.

6. *Combination of seat time and independent learning*
   Some students function best in a "seat time" program, while others may need to complete work independently. Many may benefit from a combination of the two systems. Problems are inherent in both programs.

Seat time programs are usually more expensive to operate and may preclude students who have to work full time. Students who would opt for an independent study program may find it difficult to stay on task and access resources. A quality alternative education program will have carefully evaluated the need and appropriateness of both options before deciding to offer one or the other, or both. It is usually preferable to offer a choice of options to students, and staff members will counsel students into the program best suited to them. However, there are many successful alternative programs that offer only seat time or independent study.

7. *Support services*
    Support services need to be readily available to students attending an alternative education site. Keeping class sizes low is the first step so that positive relationships can develop between students and staff members. Smaller class sizes help teachers/staff to deal with problems as they arise, while maintaining the academic cadence of the class. Problems may not necessarily need to be discussed during class time. Sometimes just acknowledging there is a problem and making a plan to resolve it is all a student needs to have. Addressing the issue is important, however, as alternative education students typically are unable to set aside personal problems in order to focus on academic studies.

    Guidance counselors are a luxury that few small alternative schools can provide on-site. However, it is important that one is available for students who have issues that need to be addressed by a professional.

8. *Availability of staff*
    It is important for staff to be available to students, parents/guardians and Human Services workers before and after school so that questions and problems can be taken care of in a timely manner.

9. *Access to Human Services*
    County Human Services workers may be assigned to alternative education students. It is important for the staff at the site to facilitate the interaction between students and their workers, and be aware of the services available to students, so that relevant information is passed on to them. In my program, case workers usually visit with my students at school. This allows us the opportunity to share information and solve problems in a family setting.

Procedural Issues

Alternative schools have the luxury of not needing a cumbersome bureaucratic system in order to operate. However, they do need an effective structure in order to function effectively. Some important parts of this structure are:

1. *Students need to apply to the program*
    Students need to apply to enter the program, rather than being transferred involuntarily. Involuntary transfer doesn't work for staff or students. Uncooperative students may be equally disastrous for a program as an uncooperative adult. Students may need to be persuaded that the alternative school is the best option for them. But there definitely needs to be some kind of, at least tacit, consent to being there.

2. *Continuous learning plan*
    Goal setting needs to occur at regular intervals and staff needs to meet regularly to review the progress towards the goals. Students and their parents/guardians need to have input into these goals. It is crucial to conceptualize this in terms of developing and sustaining a plan that reflects individual needs. Many students are in the alternative school because the traditional school could not be flexible enough to adjust to their individual needs.

3. *Orientation class*
    It is helpful if students are offered an orientation class as they enter the program. This class may consist of outlining the rules and expectations of the program plus some assessment of basic skills, learning styles and career aspirations. Typically, these students have attended school somewhat erratically and will each have a unique profile of strengths and weaknesses that need to be addressed.

4. *Attendance policy*
    In order that the weaknesses are not perpetuated, it is essential that attendance is taken in each class throughout the day and the attendance policy enforced. Learning needs to be continuous from one day to another. Attendance has often been a problem for these students, but early follow-up by staff members to report an absence, and working with parents and students should help the situation immeasurably. We can't teach them unless they are present!

5. *Caring, supportive teachers*

A typical alternative education student will report that teachers at their regular school did not care about them. It is essential, therefore, that they see their teachers at the alternative education site as being caring and supportive. Once again, smaller class and program sizes help a great deal in allowing teachers and other staff members to get to know students personally. Academically, these students are very fragile. Any strengths that may have been identified in earlier grades will often have been eroded, along with their self-esteem. Building self-esteem and recapturing these strengths can be achieved by teachers having high/ appropriate expectations for their students and celebrating their achievements on a regular basis.

Calendar/School Day

The calendar should be determined by the needs of the students and staff at each site. It should be remembered that, after all, staff are working with at-risk students who have more problems and needs than students in a mainstream high school. Staff need time to meet regularly for planning and team building activities. They also need time away from teaching duties so they can recoup and energize their batteries.

Some programs may need to be offered on a year-round basis with many smaller breaks during the year. Others may need to operate four quarters a year in order to get students to complete three quarters worth of work. Many alternative schools do not have school five days a week. Many require students to attend four days a week with makeup time on Friday. The time of operation should vary throughout the country depending on local needs and customs. Some programs may be open from early morning until early afternoon. Others may be open late morning until late afternoon. There are some night programs for students who feel they have to work full time. This may be partially determined by the age of the student population. The most important factor is that there is an attendance policy in place and that it is enforced.

Initial program sites are often a major problem for alternative schools. The question becomes, "Is it better to begin a program in a run-down building, or is it better to wait for something big and fancy?" The response has often been to open a new program in a run-down building. However poor the structure, a new coat of paint, some colorful bulletin boards and some ready smiles can look like paradise to a student who feels like "wretched refuse." Indeed, the most important attributes of an alternative learning program is one that grants students personal respect, responsibility, support and the sense that they belong.

6

Providing a Quality Curriculum in a Flexible Manner

How do we tie democratic values, the words of
Shakespeare and Plato, poetry and the arts
to education agendas focused on business functions?
What of love? Of compassion?
What of creativity and the arts?
What of joy and feelings of connectedness
to other human beings, animals and nature?
What happens to our "souls" as human
beings and our soul as a nation?
— Caine and Caine

One of the most important features of an alternative school program is that curriculum is delivered in a manner that is different than at the local high school. This different manner will be driven by the mission that was established for the program in the first place, and students' needs for "joy and feelings of connectedness to other human being." Different could mean different materials, different pacing of instruction, different methods of instruction, different methods of evaluation, etc. The most important thing to remember, once again, is that these decisions must be driven by the mission of the program and the individual needs of each student.

The second most important thing to remember is that the curriculum must hold meaning for students. They have already been exposed to taking subjects "because they were required." And they were not successful in that setting. Now, they need to understand the rationale behind learning specific bodies of knowledge and have that knowledge delivered in a way that holds meaning for them. Constructivist theory encourages students to become intimately involved in the subject matter at hand and manipulate and interpret it in a manner that makes meaning for them. Facts and figures are available, literally, at the push of a button—on an Internet-ready cell phone. Knowing a plethora of facts and figures is not as important in today's world as understanding and knowing how to manipulate them for the task at hand.

In this chapter we will discuss issues such as:

- Basic guiding principles
- Delivery of curriculum
- Elective class offerings
- Instructional materials
- Student assessment

The only common factor about learners in alternative settings is that they did not thrive in their previous setting. Beyond that, they can be very different from each other. Some will be auditory learners, some visual learners, some tactile learners, some kinesthetic learners. The majority of students found in alternative school programs are kinesthetic learners. They learn best when they can experience things. In order to accommodate these learners, it is best to have a variety of experiences available to them during the course of a unit of a study. It is important to establish the learning style of each student before charting their course in the alternative setting.

There are a number of things to take into account when designing curriculum and instruction.

Basic Guiding Principles

1. *Academic standards*
   Academic standards should be established for the program before it begins.

2. *School district requirements*
   The curriculum should keep in line with the graduation requirements of the host or home school district, unless there is a specific need not to do so. These specific needs should be clearly articulated in the statement of academic standards. But the Alternative School must retain flexibility in how those standards are met so that an individualized approach can be maintained.

3. *State and federal guidelines*
   The curriculum should keep in line with state and federal guidelines, unless there is a specific need not to do so. These specific needs should also be clearly articulated in the statement of Academic Standards.

4. *Early diagnosis of basic skills*
   There should be an early diagnosis of basic skills to detect both strengths and weaknesses.

5. *Provision of remedial classes*
   Students who are deficient in reading, writing, math or technology should be provided with classes to remediate these deficiencies. A lack of skill in these areas is a major barrier to the current philosophy of education, to prepare "lifelong learners."

6. *Early diagnosis of learning style*
   There should be an early diagnosis of learning style also. Information about strengths and weaknesses in basic skill areas, along with a determinant of learning style, can be powerful tools when developing a continuous learning plan.

7. *Multiple intelligences*
   Classes should be designed in such as way as to accommodate different intelligences, including emotional intelligence.

8. A *variety of classes*
   A variety of classes should be offered that appeal to different interests, learning styles and intelligences.

9. *Innovative classes*
   Alternative education students are risk takers. They enjoy seeing their teachers also take risks. Try a new class, new materials or even add a different twist to an old class. This is the population where you can safely "let down your hair" and try something you have always wanted to try!

10. *Ethnic pride*
    This is an ideal opportunity to offer classes that reinforce knowledge and pride in students' ethnic backgrounds.

11. *Cultural awareness*
    It is also an ideal opportunity to provide cultural awareness and sensitivity classes for all students. The change in ethnic makeup of the United States, and its role in the global economy, make knowledge and understanding of other cultures a necessity for coping successfully in today's world.

Delivery of Curriculum

Seat time programs can offer instruction in a variety of ways, and should be determined by each student's learning style and preference. If several students need to take a particular class, for example math, it may be wise to offer this in a small-group, teacher-directed setting. However, if a student or two would like to work alone or in pairs, that option should be available, also—as long as the student/s make/s sufficient progress. After all, the goal of allowing flexibility is to accommodate each student's learning style. Some students may choose to work with a friend and then spend more of class time talking about social issues than assigned tasks. Frequent, authentic assessment should reveal this problem and provide the teacher with a solid reason why this work group may not be the best choice for either student. Basic skills instruction should be offered in a variety of settings, including computer-assisted, individual and small group, depending on the age of the students and availability of materials.

Elective Class Offerings

Elective classes at the high school level often prove to be challenging for Alternative Schools, especially small ones. The small number of staff requires those involved to sometimes be quite ingenious. It often involves the adage, "It takes a village to educate a child!" And involves a lot of planning and preparation. The following options might be considered:

1. *Cultural programs*
   This is the perfect opportunity to provide cultural enrichment and cultural sensitivity programs for students.

2. *Software programs*
   Software packages such as Adobe Photoshop, iMovie, Office Suite (Word, Excel and Powerpoint), Dreamweaver, Visual Basic, CAD Design and many more can be offered independently with minimum supervision from individuals on or off campus. There are even training programs that can be purchased for some of this software.

3. *On-line classes*
   A number of thematically oriented classes are now offered on-line. The ones that I have seen lend themselves superbly to students at the middle level. They are high quality and can be easily augmented by using local

materials. National Geographic and OnlineClass are two such sites. They can be used equally as effectively at other levels where the work is thematic in nature.

4. *Staff members' avocations*

Developing units of study around a staff member's avocation, such as woodworking, sewing, metalworking, cooking, genealogy etc. can be rewarding for both staff and students.

5. *Guest speakers*

The world is full of teachers! Many people who have chosen careers in other fields, such as business or services, often express an interest in sharing their knowledge with school-age students. These people can provide authentic, first-hand information about a wide variety of topics. For example, a unit of study about healthy living could involve speakers from human services and local emergency services agencies. This takes a lot of time and coordination but can be extremely effective.

6. *Off-campus classes*

Allowing students to take classes at a local high school campus should always be an option. Typically, subjects such as driver education and foreign language are unavailable in alternative schools but readily available at local high schools.

7. *Senior options*

More capable senior students should be able to exercise the option of taking classes on local university and vocational college campuses. This is an excellent way to encourage them to pursue further education. Because alternative school students are classified as part of an "at-risk" population in some states, special funds and waivers of registration deadlines are often available to them.

8. *School to work*

Alternative education students have difficulty with transitions, and so providing school-to-work activities should be considered essential. A variety of learning style and career aptitude tests are available to help students focus on their future. Some students may come from homes where "steady work habits" were not modeled and so would benefit from any work placement, paid or unpaid. Other students would benefit greatly if they could gain some experience in a setting that was identified by their career aptitude assessments.

9. *Student input*

The purpose of elective classes is to allow students to pursue classes that are of interest to them. Rather than try to come up with all the ideas, allow students to tell you what they would like to study. Then, develop a curriculum unit for it.

10. *Team teaching with senior citizens*

Baby boomers have begun to retire in record numbers! They are young, talented and have plenty of time on their hands. Some may find team teaching small groups of students a dream come true.

11. *Community mentors*

Students can be paired with members of the community with common interests to pursue a unit of study. It is very important to establish parameters in situations such as these to protect the student and community member, and give academic credence to the unit of study.

Allowing a number of students to pursue a variety of options can be like herding cats! One way to keep control is to require that a form such as the following is completed before a class begins. It ensures that students/mentors have given some thought to the goals, planning and assessment for the unit of study.

Instructional Materials

The program site also has to be adequately equipped with materials for students to accomplish the tasks set for them. Technology needs to be at least as good as that available at their mainstream high school. There should be sufficient other supplies such as notebook paper, trade books, calculators, pens and pencils for all students. It may be appropriate to supply all or some of these items. It may be equally as appropriate to have some of these items available for students to purchase.

Shoddy, hand-me-down materials that have been discarded by area schools can be equally as damaging to alternative education students as the building with the leaky roof. Unfortunately, the two often come together. These students may have already failed classes using these materials when they were considered up-to-date. Using them again probably won't work—again.

The selection and application of instructional materials should be driven by the mission of the program. High functioning students in a sobriety program

INDEPENDENT STUDY PLANNING SHEET

Students can accrue either one half or 1 full credit depending upon the duration and intensity of the course of study. This document has to be filed with Dr. Mottaz before beginning the independent study.

Student: _____

Mentor: _____

Advisor: _____

Name of Project: _____

Goals to be Achieved: _____
   1. _____
   2. _____
   3. _____

Weekly Planner: (approximately 6 hours per week)
   1. _____
   2. _____
   3. _____
   4. _____
   5. _____
   6. _____
   7. _____
   8. _____
   9. _____
  10. _____

How will goals be assessed?
   1. _____
   2. _____
   3. _____

Plan approved by: _____ Date: _____

Final grade: _____ Date: _____

Concluding Comments:

will require quite different materials than students for whom English is a second language.

Software Options

With the advent of computers, many alternative programs are looking to software packages to strengthen their course offerings. Some companies claim to offer entire curriculum packages, while others are designed to supplement existing materials. Surprisingly, there are a number of good, specific skill programs that are inexpensive and can be purchased at local computer outlets.

I have tried a number of institutional packages with varying degrees of success. They are: Skillsbank, Learning 2000, Plato and NovaNet. Before purchasing any major packages such as these, I highly recommend that you pilot them at your site. This will usually involve paying a training fee to the company, but is much more cost effective than purchasing software that does not meet the needs of your students. Even visiting other sites that use these software packages can be of limited value. I am often surprised to hear "great things" about packages that my students found hard to work with or boring.

My students love using technology as a resource tool, but they do not particularly enjoy receiving the bulk of their instruction via the computer.

Print Materials

These come in many shapes and forms, and should be purchased according to the group of students being served. Some alternative learning programs simply adapt materials being used at the local high school. Skillful adaptations can be very effective although they also tend to be very time consuming.

Certain companies cater to students with specific learning needs, such as a deficiency in the area of reading. One such company that I use extensively is American Guidance Service, Inc. (*www.AGSnet.com*). This company produces full-text books in each of the major required high school classes, at a readability level of 4th to 6th grade. These books are accompanied by a series of study guides, workbook and activity pages, and tests, all on a compact disk. The study guides are particularly helpful for students working independently or semi-independently so they know what the major points are in each chapter. The company also offers smaller, soft cover books that cover key concepts and serve as a foundation for other classes.

Having found success with American Guidance Service early on in my alternative education career, I have not pursued other options. There are a number of other choices available today.

Some alternative schools choose to use Graduation Equivalency Diploma materials and then award students a GED rather than a high school diploma. This is a well established set of materials that is easy to administer. However, it is a far cry from a full high school curriculum and should only be used after it has been determined that the target population is unable to achieve a high school diploma.

In reality, most alternative schools may eventually include each of the print materials options in their repertoire of offerings.

Other Materials

The presence of adequate access to computers is more important today than ever before. They provide vast resources of materials that would otherwise be unavailable to the majority of people. Links to primary sources, organizations, library catalogs, on-line encyclopedias, maps, etc. provide "up-to-the-minute" information and are invaluable in a small setting with few teachers.

The amount and variety of materials available from different organizations is quite astonishing. They are often available in amounts that lend themselves to their dispersal at an alternative learning site, but not in large school system. Every area of the curriculum has related informational, advocacy and educational materials that can prove to be valuable, current resources for the alternative school classroom. The trick is to access these groups. This can be achieved by conducting an extensive internet search, consulting State Departments of Education and local organizations.

Student Assessment

The alternative school nemesis! As a whole, alternative school students do not do well on standardized achievement tests. This may be due to a number of reasons. Poor attendance is particularly hard on developmentally sequential subjects, such as math and reading. Kinesthetic learners do not excel in "lecture-type" classes that are common in many high schools. Rote learning holds little value for many students today.

But, accountability is an important aspect of any program that has goals and objectives. It is crucial to know if goals are being met. Assessment tools should have certain characteristics. They should:

1. Reflect the goals established in the continuous learning plan

2. Be ongoing

3. Contain data from other sources in addition to standard paper-and pencil tests, such as:
   - student portfolios, both print and electronic
   - demonstrations
   - speeches
   - role re-enactment
   - classroom conversation

4. Include progress in thinking skills and participation

5. Document progress towards a vocational goal

6. Include progress in personal development skills

7. Reflect growth in basic skills areas

There are a variety of basic skills and criterion reference assessments available on the market for times when a traditional test situation is appropriate. Both can be taken in print form or on the computer. The choice of assessment should be driven by its purpose. At the beginning of each year I have opted to require students to take a paper and pencil basic skills test so that I know immediately what their skill level is. Tests such as the TABE (Test of Adult Basic Education) have optional self-scoring answer sheets that save time and provide a lot of good information. Both methods have advantages and disadvantages.

Providing high quality instruction to students who feel connected with their curriculum and school site is the goal of all good alternative schools. It takes time and expertise, but it is already happening. There are many quality programs in existence around the country. Terry Lydel, of the Minnesota Association of Alternative Programs, describes these programs as being "Learning Centered" after a term used in the Malcolm Baldrige Quality Award program. According to this program, "Education organizations exist primarily to develop the fullest potential of all students, affording them opportunities to pursue a variety of avenues of success. A learning centered organization needs to fully understand and translate market place and citizenship requirements into appropriate curricula and developmental experiences . . . setting high developmental expectations and standards for all students . . . understanding that students learn in different ways and at different rates."

In referring to alternative education in Minnesota, Terry goes on to say, "That sounds like us."

Part III

The Assessment Piece

7

General Characteristics
of a Quality Program

There is nothing wrong with short-term quantitative results,
nor are they necessarily antithetical to long term qualitative results.
Some of the best organizations in the world
understand that balance and practice it daily.
The trouble is, not many of them are in the United States.
— *W. Patrick Dolan*

If the purpose of a good alternative school is to provide high quality instruction to a "specific" group of students, who feel connected to their curriculum and school site, then every program "should look" somewhat different.

Despite the fact that no two alternative programs are the same and that they deal with idiosyncratic populations, some key characteristics of good programs have emerged. They are linked to what Raywid[1] describes as three sets of factors that account for the success of alternative schools. The first two she credits to Wehlage et al.[2] The third is her own.

- First, these schools generate and sustain a sense of community.
- Second, they make learning engaging for the students.
- Third, they provide organization and structure to make the first two factors possible.

Three studies have been conducted that address this issue. Some attributes are the same, and others are unique to the particular study site.

Raywid conducted the first study in 1994. She identified eleven features that mark alternative programs in general:

1. They were small;
2. Both the program and organization were designed by those who were going to operate them;

3. They took their characters, themes, or emphases from the strengths and interests of the teachers who conceived them;

4. Their teachers all chose the programs, with subsequent teachers selected with the input of present staff;

5. Their students and families chose the programs;

6. A teacher-director administered each program;

7. Their small size denied them much auxiliary or specialized staff, such as librarians, counselors or deans;

8. All the early programs were housed as mini-schools in buildings that were dominated by larger programs;

9. The superintendent sustained the autonomy and protected the integrity of the mini-schools;

10. All of the programs were relatively free from district interference, and the administration also buffered them from demands of central school officials; and the continuity of leadership has been considerable.

Kellmayer,[3] a veteran principal of an alternative school for at-risk youth, has developed ten key characteristics of effective alternative programs, which he describes as follows:

1. *Size*—try to keep class and program size small, 1–15, with small group and individual activities.

2. *Site*—the richer the site the better. At a minimum, students should have access to computers, other forms of technology, science laboratories, counseling and employment services and recreational facilities.

3. *Voluntarism*—participation should be voluntary on the part of the students and the teachers.

4. *Participatory decision making*—allow students and staff to have a real voice in day-to-day decision making. Parents and the community should be involved in program planning and operation.

5. *Curriculum*—try to achieve as many academic goals as in the regular program, but curriculum should be student centered, and instruction should be related to students' academic and personal concerns.

6. *Separate administrative unit*—effective alternative programs usually have their own administrative unit.

7. *Distinctive mission and family atmosphere*—there should be a clear mission and a specialized program to meet the needs of the unique population.

8. *Flexible teacher role and program autonomy*—teachers, counselors and administrators who work in successful programs accept a broader and more flexible role.

9. *Access to Social Services*—preferably, these services should be available on site.

10. *Use of technology*—students should have at least as much access as students at regular high schools.

A study by Dugger and Dugger (1998) of a successful high school for dropouts in Peoria, Illinois, identified seventeen key characteristics of a good alternative program:

1. Teachers had high expectations, employed positive discipline and established a rapport with the students.

2. The school was located away from other high schools and was within reach of public transportation.

3. The curriculum was individualized and emphasized hands-on learning.

4. All students attended school half a day and either worked the other half of the day or volunteered for half a day.

5. Enrollment in the school was limited to 100 and the staff-student ratio was 1:12.

6. All staff members considered student counseling to be part of their job.

7. Staff worked hard to create a family atmosphere.

8. Goal setting was a regular part of the curriculum. Formative, summative and self-evaluation were an important part of the program.

9. The faculty met for two hours each Friday to discuss the progress of each student.

10. The alternative school worked closely with other community agencies.

11. Daily follow-up was made on all students who were tardy or absent.

12. There was an extensive extrinsic reward system to promote attendance and academic achievement.

13. Staff development for teachers was ongoing and comprehensive.

14. There was an individualized process of transitioning from school to work.

15. Staff members modeled the kind of behaviors they were trying to elicit from students.

16. The program was both highly structured and extremely flexible.

17. All students were able to apply to the program and no student was forced to attend.[4]

Most of these characteristics were reinforced by my study of Minnesota Alternative School employees in 1999.

Notes

1. Raywid, M. A. (1998, October). The journey of the alternative schools movement: Where it's been and where it's going. *The High School Magazine*. 10–15.

2. Wehlage, G., et al. (1989). *Reducing the risk: Schools as communities of support.* London: Falmer Press.

3. Kellmayer, J. (1998, October). Building educational alternatives for at-risk youth: A Primer. *The High School Magazine*. 26–31.

4. Dugger, J. & Dugger, C. (1998, April/May). An evaluation of a successful high-school. *The High School Journal*. 218–228.

8

Indicators of a Quality Program

The prevailing paradigm is highly mechanistic.
It is built on the idea that the world
can be controlled like a big machine.
The problem is that schools are much more complex;
in reality, they have more in common with the weather.
When we think of a school as a weather system.
Our perspective changes.
— *Caine and Caine*

The basic problem with attempting to validate quality, idiosyncratic programs, such as alternative schools, is that they are difficult to quantify. However, a 1999 study of Minnesota Alternative School staff discovered that, although difficult, this was possible (Mottaz, 1999).

The results of this study clearly indicate that people working in the field of alternative education in the state of Minnesota do have an extensive list of characteristics they feel are important for a quality program. From an exhaustive list of 126 quality indicators, practitioners identified over half of them as being significant. This extensive list is supportive of, and supported by, current research reported in chapter 7.

These characteristics are not identical for all programs. Rather, they reflect the needs of the local student population as perceived by key people at each site.

What is very clear is that in order for alternative educators to have an excellent program, they need to have a shared perspective with the majority of other alternative educators. This shared perspective translates into successful programs having the vast majority of significant quality indicators identified by their peers. However, this shared perspective does not result in a standardized "look" to all alternative programs. The goal is not to find "the one" program on which all other programs should be modeled. As Mary Anne Raywid noted in her recent article in *Phi Delta Kappan*, "There's no single formula yielding a model that is an ideal 'school for the unsuccessful.' "[1] Rather, the significant quality indicators should be viewed as objectives that can be met in a number of ways. The important thing is not the way each significant quality indicator is achieved, but that it is achieved, according to how key people at the site interpret their world.

The following list of quality indicators can be used as a "check-off" for both programs already in place and programs currently being planned. It is not realistic to believe that a program will have every significant quality indicator. Some may choose not to incorporate some items due to the idiosyncrasies of the program. However, as was stated above, the more indicators present in a program, the higher quality the program can be judged to be.

72 Significant Quality Indicators

Rank order of significant quality indicators

1. Students feel physically "safe" at school
2. Students feel "emotionally" safe at school
3. Students view teachers as caring, supportive adults
4. Teachers are able to deal with problems as they arise during class time
5. Teachers have high/appropriate expectations for their students
6. The program site is cheerful and welcoming to students, staff and parents
7. The program site is large enough to accommodate the student population and program needs
8. There are enough resources for all students (desks, chairs, computers, calculators etc.)
9. An orientation meeting before/as students enter the program
10. Staff at the site make decisions about curriculum issues
11. Clear admissions procedure
12. There is some clerical/secretarial help on-site
13. Support services are available from community agencies such as probation and social services
14. Students apply to enter the program, i.e., they are not placed without their consent

15. A counselor is available to students

16. Students have adequate access to technology (Internet, computer stations)

17. Early diagnosis of weaknesses in basic skills

18. Availability of individual instruction

19. A variety of classes are offered

20. Class size is kept below 15 students per teacher at "seat time" programs

21. There is some clerical help available

22. Students have input into the continual learning plan

23. Teachers/staff volunteer for the program (i.e., no unrequested transfers)

24. A selection of activities is provided for each unit of study (e.g., reading out of book/magazine, watch video, interview someone, computer testing, etc.)

25. Instruction maximizes student's learning style

26. Early diagnosis of social/emotional areas of need

27. Career skills training is available

28. Attendance policy is in place and enforced

29. The program site meets building codes

30. All students have academic program goals

31. There is a "family" atmosphere

32. Academic standards established for the program

33. Students are assessed in a variety of ways

34. Attendance is taken in each class throughout the day

35. The structure of the program is closely tied with the needs of the local student population

36. Program provides a great deal of structure for students in a flexible manner

37. Class size is kept to below 15 students per supervising adult at "seat time" programs

38. Students are required to "demonstrate" their knowledge, where appropriate

39. All students have personal development goals

40. Curriculum keeps in line with the graduation requirement of the host or home school district

41. Staff receive staff development at least twice a year

42. Teachers are readily accessible to students before and after regular school hours

43. Students are given immediate feedback about their daily work and progress towards a goal

44. Students are given the opportunity to graduate at the program site

45. Teachers/staff meet weekly to discuss student performance

46. Teachers are readily accessible to parents/guardians before and after regular school hours

47. Learning and assessment tasks involve student production instead of reproduction of knowledge

48. Post-secondary options are available

49. Staff at the site make decisions about staffing at the site

50. Program has a purposeful mission statement

51. Hands-on activities are available in all classes

52. The location is accessible to any student who would like to attend the program

53. Program has a director/release time for a director

54. Students are given the opportunity to graduate at a mainstream high school graduation ceremony

55. Goal setting occurs at regular intervals

56. Audio visual materials are readily available

57. Learning tasks aim for depth of understanding rather than superficial exposure

58. Total size of "seat time" program is kept below 200 students at one location

59. All students have an individualized, continual learning plan

60. Teachers are qualified in the level (i.e., secondary) they are to teach

61. Interdisciplinary units where appropriate

62. Constructivist techniques used in class settings (construction of knowledge, disciplined inquiry and value beyond school)

63. Science lab equipment available for science classes

64. Location is away from the regular high school

65. All students have vocational program goals

66. Students can take classes outside of alternative learning program/center

67. Choice of an independent study, all "seat-time" or a combination of both programs available

68. Parents/guardians have input into the continual learning plan

69. There is an orientation/introductory class

70. All students have a service learning experience before they leave the program

71. Teachers also perform counseling duties

72. Staff belong to a professional organization, such as the Minnesota Association of Alternative Programs

Significant Quality Indicators Broken Down by Category

A breakdown of these significant quality indicators into categories looks like this:

# of Items	Category
15	Student Support
2	Governance
14	Program Structure
19	Program Organization
4	Program Support
18	Curriculum and Instruction

Although it may be tempting to dismiss the category of Governance due to the low incidence of items, it would be foolish to do so. In talking with practitioners around the state, I discovered that autonomy is extremely important to them. Autonomy in the areas of staffing and curriculum allows the staff at each site to develop a unique program that caters to their perceived needs of the local population.

The total list of significant quality indicators, broken down by category is as follows.

Program Organization

- The program site is cheerful and welcoming to students, staff and parents
- The program site is large enough to accommodate the student population and program needs
- An orientation meeting before/as students enter the program
- Clear admissions procedure
- Class size is kept below 15 students per teacher at "seat time" programs
- Teachers/staff volunteer for the program (i.e., no unrequested transfers)
- Attendance policy is in place and enforced
- The program site meets building codes
- Class size is kept to below 15 students per supervising adult at "seat time" programs
- Students are given the opportunity to graduate at the program site
- Post-secondary options are available
- Program has a purposeful mission statement
- The location is accessible to any student who would like to attend the program
- Program has a director/release time for a director
- Students are given the opportunity to graduate at a mainstream high school graduation ceremony
- Total size of "seat time" program is kept below 200 students at one location
- Location is away from the regular high school
- Students can take classes outside of alternative learning program/center
- Choice of an independent study, all "seat-time" or a combination of both programs available

Governance

- Staff at the site make decisions about curriculum issues
- Staff at the site make decisions about staffing at the site

Program Structure

- Teachers have high/appropriate expectations for their students
- There are enough resources for all students (desks, chairs, computers, calculators, etc.)
- Students apply to enter the program, i.e., they are not placed without their consent
- Availability of individual instruction
- A selection of activities is provided for each unit of study (e.g., reading out of book/magazine, watch video, interview someone, computer testing, etc.)
- All students have academic program goals
- Attendance is taken in each class throughout the day
- All students have personal development goals
- Teachers/staff meet weekly to discuss student performance
- Goal setting occurs at regular intervals
- All students have an individualized, continual learning plan
- Teachers are qualified in the level (i.e., secondary) they are to teach
- All students have vocational program goals
- There is an orientation/introductory class

Curriculum and Instruction

- Students have adequate access to technology (Internet, computer stations)
- Early diagnosis of weaknesses in basic skills
- A variety of classes are offered
- Instruction maximizes student's learning style
- Career skills training is available
- Academic standards established for the program
- Students are assessed in a variety of ways
- Students are required to "demonstrate" their knowledge, where appropriate
- Curriculum keeps in line with the graduation requirement of the host or home school district
- Students are given immediate feedback about their daily work and progress towards their goals

GOVERNORS STATE UNIVERSITY
UNIVERSITY PARK
IL 60466

- Learning and assessment tasks involve student production instead of reproduction of knowledge
- Hands-on activities are available in all classes
- Audio visual materials are readily available
- Learning tasks aim for depth of understanding rather than superficial exposure
- Interdisciplinary units where appropriate
- Constructivist techniques used in class settings (construction of knowledge, disciplined inquiry and value beyond school)
- Science lab equipment available for science classes
- All students have a service learning experience before they leave the program

Student Support

- Students feel physically "safe" at school
- Students feel "emotionally" safe at school
- Students view teachers as caring, supportive adults
- Teachers are able to deal with problems as they arise during class time
- Support services are available from community agencies such as probation and social services
- A counselor is available to students
- Students have input into the continual learning plan
- Early diagnosis of social/emotional areas of need
- There is a "family" atmosphere
- The structure of the program is closely tied with the needs of the local student population
- Program provides a great deal of structure for students in a flexible manner
- Teachers are readily accessible to students before and after regular school hours
- Teachers are readily accessible to parents/guardians before and after regular school hours
- Parents/guardians have input into the continual learning plan
- Teachers also perform counseling duties

Program Support

- There is some clerical/secretarial help on-site
- There is some clerical help available
- Staff receive staff development at least twice a year
- Staff belong to a professional organization, such as MAAP

This list is certainly not exhaustive and will, hopefully, change over time. It is a good starting point for school districts that would like to initiate a new alternative education program, measure the effectiveness of a program in place, or identify weaknesses in a program that does not appear to be effective.

Notes

1. Raywid, M. A. (2001, April). What to do with students who are not succeeding. *Phi Delta Kappan.* 582–584.

9

A Case in Point

Faith in the power of education
has had both positive and negative consequences.
It has helped to persuade citizens to create
the most comprehensive system of public schooling in the world.
But overpromising has often led to disillusionment
and to blaming the schools for not solving problems beyond their reach.
— *Tyack and Cuban*

It may be helpful at this point to make a comparison between some alternative programs in order to illustrate how different quality programs can have different profiles of quality indicators.

For this purpose, three Alternative Learning Centers in the state of Minnesota have been chosen to represent two quality programs and one moderately successful program. Two of these centers have been described as "excellent" by the Department of Children, Families and Learning. Glory Kibbell, the highly respected Enrollment Options Specialist for the Department, describes them as follows, "These programs are very student-centered yet hold students accountable. Both are always looking for new programming ideas and concepts that work with "at-risk" students. Additionally, both are involved in various initiatives. Above all, their primary motivation is to provide strong programming that meets the various needs of the students they serve."

These two programs are compared to a third Area Learning Center that I would describe as being moderately successful. This Center has significantly fewer quality indicators, many of which are out of control of the people working there.

Information gathered from these three sites was part of a study to determine what people working in Alternative Schools in Minnesota identify as quality indicators of alternative school programs and whether different, effective alternative programs can have their own unique profiles of quality indicators (Mottaz, 1999).

Table 9.1: Instructions for Questionnaire

Please place a number, from 0 to 5, in front of the quality indicator according to how important you believe the indicator is to alternative education. This should be a personal response rather than an assessment of your program. Thank you.

0 = not important at all	3 = moderately important
1 = slightly important	4 = very important
2 = of some importance	5 = extremely important

A questionnaire was sent to a stratified random sample of practitioners in the field (directors, teachers, counselors, instructional aides) throughout the state of Minnesota asking respondents to identify quality indicators they believe are important for any alternative education program. Seventy-eight percent of the questionnaires were returned and yielded a total of 72 quality indicators identified as being significant, i.e., extremely important or very important.

Instructions for completing the questionnaires can be found in table 9.1.

The case study technique was applied to two Alternative Learning Centers identified as being excellent by the Department of Children, Families and Learning and one site that was considered to be moderately successful. These sites were observed in order to note the number of significant quality indicators evident at each site. The two excellent Alternative Learning Centers exhibited 90% of the significant quality indicators identified by the statewide sample. However, there were some distinct differences. The moderately successful alternative learning center exhibited only 58% of the significant quality indicators identified by the statewide sample.

This study would suggest there are specific indicators of quality alternative programs as they are defined in the state of Minnesota. However, they are not identical. Different, effective alternative programs can have their own, unique profiles of quality indicators.

The two excellent programs are in the suburbs of the St. Paul/Minneapolis, Minnesota metropolitan area. One is on the south side of the cities and the other is on the north side. For ease of identification, the one on the south side will be referred to as South High Alternative Learning Center (ALC); the one on the north side will be referred to as North High Alternative Learning Center (ALC). The moderately successful program will be identified as West Alternative Learning Center (ALC).

A Day in the Life of South High ALC

But First a Little Background Music

South High opened its doors in 1987 as a response to a significant number of dropouts in the cooperating districts that it was to serve. The introduction to the proposal presented to the school board on January 26, 1987 acknowledged that "Students with school related problems are having difficulty surviving in the school and often infringe on the rights of other students' learning." The Mission Statement advised school board members that this program would be an extension of the high school and would focus on basic and survival skills, career development, citizenship and personal development.

Program Organization

The first location for South High ALC was a storefront. It had 35 students and four teachers. It is currently housed on the third floor of an up-scale office building in an office park across a highway from a fairly large strip mall. The host district rents the space for $20,000 a month. It consists of seven full-sized classrooms, a shop/classroom, a photographic darkroom, a commons area, a kitchen, a conference room, a general office, eight faculty offices and an office for itinerant specialists.

The rooms are large and bright with windows along the length of each outside wall. The commons area is home to a bank of 25 computers. The computers are available to all classes for research and word processing projects. They are all hooked up to the Internet. There is a separate, smaller computer lab with several sophisticated software packages loaded on the computers. The Art room is one of the largest rooms and appears to have adequate supplies for the projects students were engaged in. The photography teacher reports that the darkroom is also adequately equipped, although there was "always more" equipment he would like to have. The main office is quite large and, in keeping with the building, looks more like an up-scale business office than a school office.

Students who would like to attend South High ALC may apply at any time. They are required to complete a comprehensive application form that includes attendance and makeup policies and an ALC guidelines contract for students to sign. It also includes a request for permission for the student to transport him/herself between school sites during the school day and access to the Internet for independent study projects. These have to be signed by a parent or guardian. The first page of the application form consists of a checklist to ensure that students do provide all necessary information. The final step in the application procedure is a mandatory informational meeting for prospective students and their parents. Information relating to this meeting is stapled to the front of the application form so that students and parents/guardians are aware of it before they begin completing the forms. Once students are accepted into the program, they are given a calendar and advised of the first day of the new term when they will be able to attend South High ALC. The school district provides transportation to and from school each day.

One hundred sixty seven students were registered for the 1999 spring session, and there were 11.5 teaching positions. The staff:student ratio of the host district is 1:22 students and the approved staff-student ratio of South High ALC is 1:20. This is one aspect the ALC Director, Jean, has tried to change for some time, but she is quick to note, "This is one point the district won't budge on." Jean teaches part of the day and has administrative release time the rest of the day. The staff is also supplemented with four office personnel, a nurse two hours a day, a half-time counselor, a special education specialist two days a week, and a school psychologist one day a week.

South High ALC has a year-round calendar that is broken into seven, six-week sessions with a week in between all of them except for the summer session. The typical summer session follows one week after the second spring session with a break of two weeks before the first fall session. Students register for one session at a time.

The school day runs from 8:30 A.M. until 1:45 P.M. with five minutes between classes, Monday through Thursday. As students enter the building they register by placing their identification cards in an electronic card reader in the office. As students do this they are often greeted personally by one of the office staff or the teachers. Students are also required to "check out" at the end of the day, and attendance is taken in each class throughout the day.

Students who register for the consumer economics class are responsible for planning and preparing lunches. Students order lunch at the beginning of the day, and the consumer economics students deliver meals to the classrooms. Lunch is eaten during class time.

Students who attend South High ALC may take classes outside of the program, but few take advantage of this opportunity. The ALC program itself offers several classes "away from the building" such as Auto Maintenance, Building and Cross Country Skiing and Snow Shoeing. Last year the students built a day care center for the host city.

At this time students do not have a choice of programs; the only one available to them is the "seat-time" program. Jean is not a proponent of independent study programs. She claims that her students have difficulty motivating themselves to complete academic tasks. Many have often experienced years of frustration and failure according to Jean. As a result, South High ALC doesn't assign homework because it is generally felt that students won't complete it. However, Jean has added a unique independent study program. Jean's rationale for doing so is to keep students engaged in school as many days as possible. She designed the program to, "provide an opportunity for students who aren't able to stay in their mainstream school but miss our application deadline. It's a bridge to our daytime program."

Jean is extremely proud of the fact that, to date, over 800 students have graduated from her program. Students have a choice of either going back to their mainstream school to graduate with their peers there or attending the ALC graduation ceremony. A very nice ceremony is held at the local Civic Center twice each year for graduates of South High ALC.

Governance

A faculty meeting discussion revealed that the staff at South High ALC feel strongly about staffing at the site. Each of them applied to teach in this program, and some of them had to wait until a position became available. The staff as a whole decides what teaching skills the program needs and hires someone accordingly.

Continued discussion revealed that the staff believe the curriculum should keep in line with that offered at the local high school, especially in the area of basic skills requirements. One teacher who had taught in the local school district for 15 years before transferring to South High ALC commented that, "We teach the same subjects they do at the high school but in a very different way. We know that sitting and listening doesn't work for these kids. We have to get them involved in what is going on in our classes. Here, we can do what we know works for kids."

Program Structure

The majority of students who apply to South High ALC do so under their own volition. However, there are a few who are persuaded to do so by their parents, school administrators or the court system. For students who have been suspended or expelled, this may be their last chance of obtaining a high school diploma.

As part of the registration process, students' transcripts are reviewed with the student and parent/s, and goals are set. Every student has a continual learning plan (as required by state statute) that includes academic, vocational and a personal development goal. As implied by the name, each continual learning plan is unique, designed to address the individual needs of each student. As each student travels through the program, this continual learning plan is tailored to meet the changing academic, vocational and personal needs of each student.

Each of the classes offered at South High ALC has a scope and sequence and certain requirements that must be met in order for a credit to be awarded. Classes are scheduled for Monday through Thursday with Friday as a makeup day. All students are assigned advisors who meets with them every Thursday and reviews their progress that week. A fairly sophisticated computer program provides each student with a weekly printout of the classes being taken, the percentage of points accrued towards the credit to be earned, the number of absences and number of hours owed. This information is shared at the weekly staff meeting, and interventions are planned for the following week.

All of the teachers teaching at South High ALC are qualified in the level they teach, i.e., secondary education.

Curriculum and Instruction

The curriculum offered at South High attempts to mirror that found in the host district, but it is presented in a different way. Jean teaches an Orientation class to students as they enter the program. It includes an explanation of the rules and procedures along with a career inventory and some learning styles and aptitude assessment. By the spring 1999 session Jean had taught this particular class 48 times. She has found that at least 80% of her students, and possibly closer to 90%, are kinesthetic learners, and she wants the curriculum in her ALC to reflect this learning style. These students learn best by "doing." Students are currently offered a wide choice of 33 different classes, including Art, Auto Maintenance/Body, Consumer Economics, Building, Service Learning, Shakespeare, History of Flight, Project Holocaust and Weather. All but two of these classes are interdisciplinary, and several are team-taught at some time during the term. Classes run for 50 minutes per day unless they are scheduled for multiple blocks of time. Career Math, Orientation, Photography, Weather, Community Involvement, the Brain, The 60s, Physical Education and Project Holocaust are each scheduled for two blocks each term. Auto Maintenance/Body and Building are scheduled for a triple block. A Social Studies class is offered at the end of the regular school day from 2:30–4:30 P.M. and a Work Experience credit is offered to those students holding a job at the end of the school day.

During the course of study nine different classes were observed: Orientation, The Brain, Pagemaker, Current Events, Mystery, Geometry, Health, MAAP Stars and 9th Grade Project—Holocaust. The day of observation in the Orientation class, students were processing the results of the "Kaleidoscope Profile: A Tool to Discover a Student's Learning and Working Style" they had completed the day before. It included a discussion about what kind of learners most high school classes serve, and compared this information with the kinds of learners in the room. Of the 18 students in this class, 14 were kinesthetic and 4 tactile learners. None of the students were either visual or auditory learners. It was generally agreed that most high school classes lend themselves to visual and auditory learners. In the 100-minute class period the type of activity changed several times. It began with a review of the Kaleidoscope test completed the day before, after which students self-scored the Kaleidoscope Profile, with guidance from the teacher, and then they discussed the results. One part of the discussion centered on students being responsible for their own schedules, according to their learning and/or life styles. They were admonished, for example, that if they smoked and had difficulty at the end of the day, they should take a class where there is a lot of movement or an activity they find particularly engaging. Classes are often offered a couple of times a day to suit students' learning/lifestyles. This discussion led nicely into the next activity. Directions were given for a group project that involved students sketching on a large piece of butcher paper. Students worked in these groups until five minutes before the end of the period when they returned to their seats and a summary of the day's activities was given together with a plan for the next class period.

In addition to understanding their learning styles, students also learn about the attributes required of a good employee in this class. A large portion of the class is devoted to employability skills.

The Orientation class also includes an assessment of basic skills. Students who enter the program with a Special Education IEP (Individual Educational Plan) receive Special Education services twice a week.

In the Pagemaker class students were developing their own desktop publication using a variety of features from the Pagemaker software program. On the day I visited the skill emphasis was on importing pictures from the Internet and manipulating them on the page. This period was the lunch period, and students continued working as they ate their lunch at the computers. One student, in particular, "caught on" to today's skill very quickly and was proudly helping other students in the class.

The Brain class was team taught by two teachers, one because she was certified to teach science and the other because he was interested in finding out what a brain looks like. Students had previously learned about the function and anatomy of the brain. Once students got used to the smell of the formaldehyde, they settled down and appeared to be fascinated with what they were seeing. Lunch was not served during this class.

The Current Events class began with a discussion about the war in the Yugoslavia region of Kosovo. The teacher asked the students what they had heard about it. Typically, some students knew quite a lot about the topic and others knew, or were willing to share, very little. This was followed by a short videotaped speech given the evening before on the same topic. At the conclusion of the tape an oral quiz was given. The questions ranged from strictly factual to interpretive, with "one question thrown in to make sure everyone was watching." The question was, "Is that Ted Koppel's real hair?" A lively debate ensued after each of the questions was presented to the class. The one about Ted Koppel's hair came at the end of the hour and students continued that debate as they left the classroom!

The Mystery class was observed the last day of term. Students were watching the "Shawshank Redemption" as a culminating activity. The students were very attentive.

The topic for the day in the Geometry class was the perimeter and area of a triangle. The teacher announced that she would review the concepts before students received their worksheet. This was met with some protests from several of the students who insisted they knew all there was to know about this topic and didn't need a review. They wanted to get straight to work! This challenge was met with a counter-challenge from the teacher who invited the students to demonstrate what they knew, which they did. Their skill level was not quite as proficient as they had thought, but the conversation achieved the teacher's original objective very nicely. However, when the teacher changed topics to the practical uses of knowing the perimeter and area of a triangle, the objections rose once again. She negotiated with the students for "just seven minutes." Apparently, this is something that happens regularly because they further complained that she had trouble telling time because when she asked for five or ten minutes it always ended up being more. I was asked to be the official timekeeper, and she did indeed finish her discussion within her allotted seven minutes. "Finally" (chorused half the class) they were given their worksheet and settled right down to work. This friendly banter reflected a very warm relationship between the students and their teacher. Both sides seemed to enjoy their "victories" immensely!

The observation of the Health class occurred towards the end of the term. Students had been studying a variety of health issues and were now engaged in completing a report on one of a variety of health issues they had chosen. They had been given an outline and were working in pairs or by themselves. Students were using a variety of resources spread around the room. While the students were working, the teacher took the opportunity of visiting with all the students to review their progress in this class. She referred to a study sheet she kept for each student with the assignments required for this class and the ones that she had signed as being complete. She reminded students with missing work what the assignments looked like and suggested ways they could be completed. Students stopped by each other's tables when they got up to look for resources and were, for the most part, attentive to their tasks and making good progress.

MAAP Stars is a program organized by the Minnesota Association of Alternative Programs. Students can choose to attend an annual conference and participate in a number of events. One of the events, MAAP Stars, is a competition to see which team knows the most answers to a set of 200 question called Lifesmarts. These questions are taken from a variety of general knowledge areas, and this class prepares students for the competition. It was gratifying to note that the end of term was drawing near in this class also because the students knew a number of answers that I did not. In answer to a remark I made about not knowing some of the answers a boy replied, "Don't worry about it. We've been working on these questions for a long time. You'd soon catch on." I was touched by this comment.

The final class I visited was the 9th Grade Project class. This is a required class for all ninth grade students and focuses on basic skills. It is an interdisciplinary class team taught by a social studies and English teacher. The topic this term had been the Holocaust. Students had learned about it, written about it and were now watching *Schindler's List*. Several bean bags were on the floor in the front of the room and a number of the students were reclining in them. Other students were sitting on the floor or at their tables. They were all extremely attentive. Occasionally a student would make a comment about the class having read or talked about a certain aspect of the movie.

A striking feature about the classes observed at South High ALC is that they all included frequent interactions between the teacher and the students. Sitting in the back of the room and doing nothing did not appear to be an option. Students were expected to be either working on an activity or taking part in a class discussion. There was much evidence of students demonstrating the knowledge they had accumulated in each class. And no two classes looked alike or appeared to be taught exactly the same way two days in a row.

The assessment procedures for each class vary greatly according to the nature of the class. Some classes require ongoing assignments, others have worksheets, tests and quizzes, others have culminating projects, and most have a combination of assessment procedures. At the end of each term the staff plan an activity to bring together the whole student body. At the end of the first spring term, the students and staff hosted an art show of their work. The quality and diversity was impressive, ranging from traditional painting to jewelry making, photographs displayed in a variety of ways and some sculptures. The artwork was sorted by genre and displayed in several of the classrooms. Hors d'oeuvres, made by some of the students with the help of one of the male teachers, were served in the commons area. Students and teachers meandered through the rooms looking at the artwork and nibbling on their hors d'oeuvres. As this was the last day of the term, several of the students had graduated from the program and were planning on attending the graduation ceremony the following day. One young man appeared reluctant to leave. He returned three times to say goodbye to Jean, even returning after all the other students had left to thank the staff for everything they had done for him.

Service learning is also an important part of the South High ALC program. Students are encouraged to participate in school-wide service learning opportunities, as well as to participate in activities of their own choosing.

Student Support

Comments made by students in response to the question, "What do you like about coming to this school?" reflect the safe, caring atmosphere valued by educators in alternative education throughout the state. The most common response was a variation of, "People accept me the way I am" and "The teachers care about me here. In my old school no one cared about me." Another comment, offered by one of the girls in the Health class and supported by many of the other students in the class was, "I feel comfortable here. Nobody gets on my case. They just leave you alone here so you can learn." When asked to explain the last part of this comment, students were quick to add that in their old school, teachers and administrators were "always on their case," wanting to know what was wrong with them because they didn't come to school, were late, didn't have an assignment completed or seemed depressed. Another common complaint about their old high school was, "They expect you to do work, but no one explains anything to you. If you ask one of the teachers to explain something they'll tell you you're supposed to listen the first time." One of the boys who had attended South High ALC for three years added, "Yea, they write stuff down for you here so you don't forget it, and then they remind you if you do. I have to come in on Fridays sometimes to make up some time but that's okay; it's better than being kicked out of school. This place just works for me."

In two of the classes observed, personal student problems were raised during a class discussion. On both occasions the teacher acknowledged the problem, made a sympathetic statement suggesting a temporary solution and then continued with the class discussion. One suggestion was to stay after class to discuss the problem in more detail, and the other was to go and see Jean after school. In both cases the students appeared to accept the suggestion and settled back into the routine of the class.

The daily availability of a counselor and nurse at South High ALC gives students the opportunity to address their social/emotional needs in a timely manner. Students can elect to visit one of the specialists, may be recommended by a concerned advisor or parent or may be referred as a result of the weekly staff meeting.

The physical arrangement of the school allows for high visibility of staff members. Before or after school, teachers are either in their first hour class or in their offices. The teachers' offices are arranged along the wall of the main office where students check in each morning. By merely glancing across the main office or taking a few steps to look down a hallway, students can see if teachers are in their offices.

Program Support

The clerical/secretarial help at South High ALC is one of the most important aspects of the cheerful, welcoming atmosphere. The secretary appears to know every student by name and feels comfortable engaging in "friendly bantering" with those students she knows well. She attends the weekly staff meetings, adding a wealth of information about student attendance and contacts with the home.

All of the teachers are encouraged to attend the MAAP meeting, at least for part of the time. The Director, Jean, has been active in this organization for a number of years and is a Board Member.

When asked to describe her program in one sentence, Jean replied, "We all enjoy coming here; we have fun teaching and the kids have fun learning."

An Analysis of Significant Quality Indicators Observed at South High ALC

Sixty-seven (93%) of the 72 quality indicators were observed at South High ALC. All of the Governance, Curriculum and Instruction and Program Support significant quality indicators were in evidence. 16 (84%) of the 19 Program Organization significant quality indicators were evident. Of the 14 significant Program Structure quality indicators, 13 (93%) were also evident at South High ALC. A similar proportion of Student Support scores were evident with 14 (93%) of the 15 being identified.

Table 9.2 shows the significant quality indicators that were not observed at South High ALC.

The staff-student ratio remains an issue that Jean continues to address. Unfortunately, according to Jean, her high graduation rate and student/parent satisfaction with her program does not support her argument that she needs more staff.

Table 9.2: Significant Quality Indicators Not Observed at South High ALC

SIGNIFICANT QUALITY INDICATOR	STATEWIDE RANK
Program Organization	
Class size is kept below 15 students per teacher	20
Class size is kept below 15 students per supervising adult	37
Choice of independent study, seat time or combination	67
Program Structure	
Goal setting occurs at regular intervals	55
Student Support	
Parents/guardians have input into continuous learning plan	68

Even though there is an independent study component to the South High ALC program, students do not have the choice of selecting it. As mentioned above, it is a unique way to keep students engaged in their education until the next term begins.

While the formal task of "goal setting" was not evident, neither was a need for it demonstrated. Goals tended to be global in nature, for example, outlining academic goals for the term ahead. The weekly advisor-advisee meeting appeared to be most effective in keeping students "on track" with their goals or providing appropriate modifications.

The significant quality indicator, "Structure of program is closely tied with needs of local student population," was extremely difficult to observe. Conversations with Jean and several of her staff indicated that they value this indicator. A common reply was given to the question: "How is the program structured to meet the needs of the local student population?" Several of the teachers gave a variation of the response, "Each kid is different, and each group that comes through has different needs. You just take them where they're at and go from there."

As students enter the program an initial goal setting meeting is held with school personnel and their parents. Parents may not be invited to revisit these goals in the form of a continual learning plan unless the initial plan becomes untenable.

Significant Quality Indicators Identified by Staff at South High ALC

As can be seen from table 9.3, 14 (74%) of the 19 significant Program Organization quality indicators were identified by South High staff members. Both

Table 9.3: Categories of Significant Quality Indicators Ranked by Average Score for South High ALC

# OF ITEMS	CATEGORY	AVERAGE SCORE
3	Program Support	4.72
14	Program Organization	4.54
13	Student Support	4.45
12	Program Structure	4.37
2	Governance	4.25
16	Curriculum and Instruction	4.20

Table 9.4: Significant Quality Indicators Not Identified by South High Staff

Significant Quality Indicator	South High Average	Statewide Average Score	Statewide Rank
Program Organization			
Post secondary options available	3	4.03	48
Program has a purposeful mission statement	3.67	4.03	50
Program has director/release time for one	3.67	4.02	53
Students can graduate from mainstream school	3.67	4.01	54
Students can take classes outside ALC	2.83	3.87	66
Program Structure			
Goal setting occurs at regular intervals	3.5	4.01	55
All students have a continuous learning plan	3.67	3.98	59
Curriulum and Instruction			
Learning tasks aim for depth of understanding	3.17	4	57
Students are required to demonstrate knowledge	3.67	4.23	38
Student *Support*			
Parents have input into continuous learning plan	3.17	3.82	68
Teachers also perform counseling duties	3.67	3.78	71
Program Support			
Staff belongs to a professional organization	3.5	3.77	72

of the significant Governance quality indicators were identified by the South High staff. Of the 14 significant Program Structure quality indicators, 12 (86%) were also considered significant by South High staff members. Apart from the significant Governance quality indicators, there was the greatest agreement in the category of Curriculum and Instruction. Of the 18 significant quality indicators, 16 (89%) were identified by the staff at South High ALC. Student Support scores were close behind with 13 (87%) of the 15 being identified. Lastly, 75% (3 of the 4) of the significant Program Support scores were identified by members of South High ALC.

Four of the significant quality indicators received a perfect average score of 5 from South High ALC staff members: students feel physically safe at school; students feel emotionally safe at school; the program site is large enough to accommodate the student population and program needs; and there is some clerical/secretarial help on site.

Table 9.4 illustrates which of the significant quality indicators were not identified by the sample from South High ALC and the average score accorded each one.

There is a 10% difference between the number of significant quality indicators observed at South High ALC (93%) and those identified by the sample of staff who returned the questionnaires (83%). The top 19 significant quality indicators identified by the statewide sample were observed and identified as being important. And if the class size issue could be resolved, the number would increase to 37, half of the total number of significant quality indicators identified by the statewide sample.

A Day in the Life of North High ALC

But First a Little Background Music

North High opened its doors in 1992, also as a response to the significant dropout rate in the district in which it is housed. There were already other alternative learning programs in the district but the lead teacher of North High had a different vision for his program. In the initial proposal presented to the school board in the winter of 1992 the purpose of the program was given as follows: "Many students who are currently dropping out of the regular school system are capable of obtaining a high school education. We know the circumstances under which these students have not been successful, and we have designed this proposal to change these things that research says works for the 'at risk' population, i.e., length of day, class size, increased technology, connection with school, etc." The unique element proposed to the board was that the program was to be run in a storefront property like a "one-room school house with a twentieth century twist." The designer, Wesley, believed that his concept of the "Two-room Schoolhouse is rooted in the belief that "at-risk" students will stay on task and function much better educationally in very small school situations." Their motto is, "Small equals friendly, friendly equals success."

Program Organization

North High ALC is located in a small strip mall along a very busy highway. The two main rooms that face the front of the building are bright and sunny. There is a teacher work station in each of these rooms. The room of the lead teacher, Wesley, takes up approximately one fifth of the space. It contains his desk, several work tables for students and two computer stations with some very sophisticated desktop publishing, computer graphics and Adobe software packages. The room directly behind Wesley's room contains five TV/VCR stations and an extensive library of videotapes. Almost one half of the space on the opposite side of the facility is Jane's domain and houses her desk and a bank of 12 computers with a large variety of educational compact disks. There is a small storeroom behind Jane's room. Between these two areas is an office space for the secretary, bathrooms and a utility room. All of the rooms are an adequate size for the number of students present at any one time.

Students who would like to attend North High may apply at any time. They are required to complete a simple application form and attend an individual orientation meeting with their parents or guardians before entering the program. Once students are accepted into the program they can start as soon as a place becomes available. On average, there is a two–three month waiting period. All students are required to document that they are holding jobs for a minimum of 15 hours per week, as part of a school-to-work transition.

The number of students attending North High stays constant at 60, with graduates and dropouts being replaced instantly by students on the waiting list. There are two full-time teachers and two part-time teachers to cover the three daily "shifts." Two teachers work each shift. There is no release time for the lead teacher. A school psychologist is available to this program upon request.

North High ALC has the same calendar as the local high school with no summer component. Students may opt to go to another ALC in the district for credits during the summer.

Students have a choice of one of three times to attend the program: 8 A.M.–11 A.M., noon–3 P.M. or 5–8 P.M. Each session is broken down into four 45 minute periods with a brief break between each period and runs for four days each week. An additional seven hours of independent study research is assigned each week. The combination of 12 hours in school together with 15 hours at work and 7 hours of independent study equals a normal time commitment for students at the local high school. Twenty students attend each session which gives a staff-student ratio of 1:10.

As students enter the building they are greeted by one or both of the teachers and their presence is noted in an attendance book. In order for students to be counted in attendance they need to be "on-task" at all times. If students are noted to be "off-task" for an extended period of time they are either fined a certain portion of their time for the day or asked to leave.

At this time students do not have a choice of programs; the only one available to them is the combination of "seat-time" and "independent study" unless they choose to attend another ALC in the district.

Wesley is extremely proud of the fact that 95% of the students who have attended this program have received enough credits to receive their high school diplomas. Students have a choice of either going back to their mainstream schools to graduate with their peers or attend a special graduation ceremony for alternative education students hosted by the school district.

The school district will provide transportation to and from school for the two daytime programs, but students are responsible for their own transportation in the evening.

Governance

Discussions with Wesley and Jane indicate they have very strong opinions about governance at the site. They opened this program together in 1992 with a clear vision of what they wanted it to look like: a two-room schoolhouse. They attach great importance to the fact that they have been able to hire their part-time teachers themselves, thus retaining their control of the program. As with South High ALC, this program offers a curriculum that is aligned with the local high school, but presented in a different manner.

Program Structure

All of the students who apply to North High ALC do so under their own volition. There are several alternative learning centers in this district from which students can choose. As part of the registration process, students' transcripts are reviewed with students and their parents, and goals are set. Every student has a continual learning plan that includes academic and vocational goals. The small size of the program and lower teacher-student ratio facilitates the continual modification and reinforcement of these goals.

North High ALC adopts the scope and sequences of classes offered at the mainstream high school, and develops its own for classes that are unique to this site. The work to be completed for each of these classes is broken down into units so that students know exactly what requirements have to be met in order for a credit to be awarded. Each week a new goal is set for the following week. Students are expected to meet 80% of their weekly goal. This includes 80% attendance, work completed, accuracy of work and test scores. Tests may be retaken until a score of 80% is achieved. During the course of this study it was noted that students often asked few questions while they completed work assignments the first time, but were eager to discuss an assignment or test that did not meet the 80% standard. Students who are unable/unwilling to meet the 80% standard are given two weeks in which to make up the requirement. If this is not done, or students are deficit two weeks in a row, they are dropped from the program and their names are put at the bottom of the waiting list. According to Wesley, almost all of the students who are dropped from the program choose to be placed on the waiting list and continue successfully upon re-entry into the program.

All of the teachers teaching at North High ALC are qualified in the level they teach, i.e., secondary. However, Jane was originally an elementary teacher and feels strongly that her elementary background has much to offer the program, especially in the area of basic skills remediation.

Curriculum and Instruction

The required classes offered at North High ALC follow the scope and sequence of classes found at the local high school. Jane facilitates the learning of the basic skills of reading, writing and math. The primary tool students use is the Learning 2000 computer software package. This program has an assessment portion that indicates the appropriate level where each student should begin. Students log into the program using their own names and continue their work from the day before. Jane supplements the writing portion with required essay writing three times a week that becomes a student's writing portfolio. The reading portion is supplemented with additional reading assignments from books, magazines, etc. The math portion is supplemented with a large selection of compact disks.

The remaining required classes are divided into units taken from the most current textbooks being used at the local high school. Students are assigned a variety of activities to achieve the goals for each unit. This may include, for example, reading a selection from the textbook, completing a map or graph with information taken from the textbook, watching a related video, completing a related computer program, giving an oral report and/or taking an end of unit test. Computer related tasks are completed in Jane's classroom, and other activities are completed under Wesley's direction.

There is no science equipment at North High ALC. Both Wesley and Jane believe that the same experiences can be gained via the interactive computer software they offer to their students.

Wesley offers a selection of technology credits including Microsoft Office and Adobe Photoshop. He is an accomplished photographer and has designed some photo-enhancing classes that students were enjoying immensely. One boy demonstrated his proficiency in scanning in an old photograph that had been badly damaged, enhancing it using Adobe Photoshop and "repairing it" to almost perfect condition. This was a very skillful operation that took a lot of patience and care.

In order for students to receive work credits they must document their employment hours and take a class at North High ALC on career skills. This class addresses issues such as how to look for a job, how to dress for an interview, skills employers are looking for and handling conflict at the work site.

As students enter the building they are greeted by one of the teachers. Typically, Wesley suggests where they should begin their "day" and they are given the necessary materials. After 45 minutes students return their materials or check out of their computer programs, take a brief break and move on to their next "class." The independent nature of this program allows teachers to confer with students constantly, monitoring progress, making suggestions and "making connections" with the students.

The assessment procedure for each credit varies greatly according to the nature of the class. The basic skills classes taken via the Learning 2000 software have an assessment component. The other required classes have a variety of required activities and an end-of-unit paper and pencil test. The technology credits have an authentic assessment element where students have to demonstrate progress on their unit as well as time on task.

Service learning is also an important part of the North High ALC program. Students are required to perform 40 hours of community service. In addition, students have the opportunity to earn a full elective credit of community service. Most of the service learning opportunities are established by Jane, but students are also encouraged to find opportunities that are of interest to them. Jane keeps an impressive scrap book of students engaged in service learning activities.

Student Support

Due to the independent nature of the program at North High ALC it was possible to interview several students and ask them about their experiences at North High. Six questions were posed to each student:

1. Why do you come here to school?
2. How does it compare to the high school you used to attend?
3. What do you like about this program?
4. Do you have to set goals for yourself? What are they?
5. What is the best thing this program has done for you?
6. If you had to recommend this program to someone else, what would you say about it?

In answer to question number one, half of the students replied that they could work and get a high school diploma at the same time. One student mentioned that she had got so behind at her old high school, she knew she could never get caught up there. All of the students commented that they liked the small size, they could work at their own pace, it was easier to get help and the teachers were nice to them. They liked the fact that they knew everyone and everyone knew them. "Everyone cares about you here," was a comment made by one young man.

One particularly vociferous young woman summarized many of the answers given by other students to question number two. She stated that she considered her "old" high school too crowded, she didn't like going from classroom to classroom, she hated carrying all of her books all day and 20 minutes was "way too short" for lunch. She is a single mother and she felt that the teachers at her "old" high school had been very judgmental of her. At North High ALC she reported that everyone is treated as an equal, it is easier to get along with people and she feels more motivated to learn. A boy added that he liked the lack of lectures and the accessibility of all the computer "stuff." Several comments were made about the availability of getting either 1-on-1 attention or immediate help if a problem arose with a unit of study. The greatest difference, according to a young man who had attended several high schools, was that there are fewer rules here.

One thing all the students liked about the program was the teachers. Answers varied from, "They're really cool here" to "Wesley and Jane know who I am, and I know they like me. In my old school none of the teachers knew the names of half the kids" to "They're not always so serious here." The second most common answer, from all of the senior students was, "The trips." An important part of Wesley's philosophy about "making connections" with the kids is to share a major travel experience with each of them before they graduate from the program. To achieve this goal he takes a small group of approximately eight students to Europe each year. Photo-collages of past trips decorate the wall of Wesley's room. One of the observation sessions as part of this study occurred two weeks after a recent tour to France and Germany. The students, literally, could not say enough good things about the trip. Not only did they enjoy the experience of flying and visiting a foreign country, but they truly appreciated the fact that a teacher would take his own time to accompany them on such a marvelous adventure. For some of them this experience was probably an opportunity of a lifetime, never to be repeated. The anticipation of this experience appeared to be a powerful motivator for the younger students. While the recent travelers were sharing details from the collage, younger students were making comments such as, "I'll be able to go next year," or "I'm going my senior year as a graduation gift." The sense of anticipation, accomplishment and joy truly filled the room.

Goal setting occurs at the beginning of each quarter. Students are required to write an essay describing their goals, and this dialogue is negotiated into a plan of action. Each of the students shared a global and an academic goal with me. The global goal was either to graduate as soon as possible or "stick with the program." The academic goals reflected a good understanding of what was going on in their academic lives at the time, such as, "Finish my Social Studies credit," "Move on to eleventh grade English," or "Finish one more credit." One student was adamant that she wanted to get 100% on all of her assignments.

The answer to the question about the best thing this program has done for you reflects the fact that these students care about their education and graduating from high school. They all mentioned the importance of being able to stay in school and graduate with a high school diploma. This has been accomplished, according to one young lady, by the fact that she doesn't mind coming here and it has changed her attitude towards education. She was going to graduate soon and thought that she might like to go on in school some time in the future.

All the students at North High ALC would recommend this program to other students. They would tell students that the teachers are great, the program is small, it's easy to get help when it's needed, no one is judgemental and it's easy to get along with the other kids. They would also tell other students that the program is laid back but focused, students can work at their own pace and work on computers a lot. The most important thing one young lady would like to tell prospective students is that this program "helps you deal with life. You work on practical things here that are going to be useful later on."

The two room schoolhouse philosophy gives students great access to teachers before and after school. Parents are invited to call at any time with questions and/or concerns.

Program Support

There is a part-time secretary at North High ALC. The staff members are required to attend district in-service activities, and they both belong to MAAP.

An Analysis of Significant Quality Indicators Observed at North High ALC

Sixty-four (89%) of the 72 quality indicators identified as being significant were evident at North High ALC. All of the Governance and Program Support significant quality indicators were in evidence. Sixteen (84%) of the 19 Program Organization significant quality indicators were evident. Thirteen (93%) of the 14 significant program Structure quality indicators were evident at this site. Of the 18 significant Curriculum and Instruction quality indicators, 16 (89%) were also evident at North High ALC. A slightly lower percentage of Student Support scores were evident with 13 (87%) of the 15 being identified. Table 9.5 shows the significant quality indicators that were not identified as being significant to staff at North High ALC.

Continuous entry results in students being able to finish their credits at any time during the year. This factor, plus the small location, would make a formal graduation at this site difficult. Possibly because less emphasis is placed on the "importance of a graduation ceremony," most of the students did not express a preference for whether they would want to "walk through the line" or not.

If interactive computer software is considered a hands-on activity, then this was very much in evidence at this site. The purpose of hands-on materials is to allow students to observe the results of the manipulation of certain materials. While interactive computer software does not yet have a smell, taste or physically tactile component, it does require the manipulation of materials vicariously. It would be of interest to discover whether the combination of working with compact disks and individually watching videotapes of experts per-

Table 9.5: Significant Quality Indicators Not Observed at North High ALC

SIGNIFICANT QUALITY INDICATOR	STATEWIDE RANK
Program Organization	
Program has a director/release time for a director	53
Students are able to graduate at the program site	44
Choice of independent study, seat time program or both	67
Program Structure	
Teachers/staff meet weekly to discuss student performance	45
Curriculum and Instruction	
Interdisciplinary units where appropriate	61
Science lab equipment available for science classes	63
Student Support	
A counselor is available to students	15
Early diagnosis of social/emotional problems	26

forming experiments achieves the same goals and objectives as having students work with their own hands.

The units of study observed during the course of this study did not involve any interdisciplinary units of traditional high school classes. Once again, however, it is difficult to work with interactive computer software and not be involved in more than one skill area. Adobe Photoshop, for example, involves reading directions, working with proportions and other geometric functions and being somewhat artistic.

According to Wesley, the relatively short duration of seat-time prohibits students leaving to see a counselor. When students enter the program he presumes they have social/emotional issues that prohibited them from succeeding in the mainstream high school. Rather than taking the time to have these problems individually analyzed, he prefers to offer students what he says he knows works, a small, storefront setting that allows for continual, positive interactions with students. However, if students appear to be particularly troubled and need specific help, he will facilitate the access of support services from community agencies. Students are then expected to pursue these services outside of school time.

Conferences are held quarterly at North High ALC and many phone conferences are held between times as the need arises. During the course of this study the end-of-third-quarter conferences were observed. Each conference began with students explaining the current or past few weekly report sheets. Those students who were regularly meeting their target performances were praised by both parents and teachers alike and the discussion moved on to the topic of graduation. One student had not met his target performance two weeks in a row and was in danger of being dropped from the program. Wesley began the conference by telling the student that he and Jane really wanted to see him stay in the program, and they needed his help in understanding what was going on. The boy explained his perception of the problems he was having at the moment, but concluded optimistically that he thought he "had things straightened out" now. He related some problems he was having at work and, in particular, with his girlfriend. The initial goals were reviewed and all parties agreed that they were still patent. Wesley "cut the student a deal" whereby he would allow him to have an extra week to make up hours and work if there were no more absences during this time frame. The student and parents left happy and satisfied. On the way out the student's mother made the comment, "That's why we like this program. It gives the kids another chance when things go wrong. I didn't graduate from high school because I never had second chances when I screwed up." This review of current performance and initial goals allows parents some very important input into the continual learning plan for their children.

Significant Quality Indicators Identified by Staff at North High ALC

Two teachers at North High ALC received and returned a questionnaire. Their profile of responses was markedly similar to the profile of responses from South High ALC, with the exception of one category, Student Support. Fifty seven (79%) of the significant quality indicators identified by the statewide sample were also identified by this group.

As can be seen from table 9.6, 14 (74%) of the 19 significant Program Organization quality indicators were identified by South High staff members. Both of the significant Governance quality indicators were identified as significant by the North High staff. Of the 14 significant Program Structure quality indicators, 11 (79%) were also considered significant by North High staff members. Apart from the significant Governance quality indicators, there was the greatest agreement in the category of Curriculum and Instruction. Of the 18 significant quality indicators, 16 (89%) were identified by the staff at North High ALC. Interestingly, Student Support scores are the lowest category with 11 (73%) of the 15 being identified. Lastly, 75% (3 of the 4) of the significant Program Support scores were identified by members of North High ALC.

# OF ITEMS	CATEGORY	AVERAGE SCORE
	Table 9.6: Categories of Significant Quality Indicators Ranked by Average Score for North High ALC	
2	Governance	5
11	Student Support	4.86
3	Program Support	4.83
14	Program Organization	4.75
16	Curriculum and Instruction	4.53
11	Program Structure	4.45

Unlike South High ALC, many of the significant quality indicators received a perfect score of 5. As can be observed in table 9.7, a total of 35 quality indicators were given an average score of 5. The largest number (9) of these were assigned to the category Program Organization. They are the following: the program site is cheerful and welcoming; the program site is large enough to accommodate the student population and program need; an orientation meeting is held; there is a clear admissions procedure; class size is kept below 15; an attendance policy is in place and enforced; the program site meets building codes; the total size of the program is below 200 students; and the location is away from the mainstream high school.

Both significant Governance quality indicators received a perfect score of 5, as did 8 significant Program Structure indicators. These quality indicators included: teachers have high/appropriate expectations; there are enough resources for all students; there is the availability of individual instruction; a selection of activities is provided for each unit of study; all students have academic program goals; attendance is taken in each class throughout the day; all students have personal development goals; and all students have an individualized continual learning plan.

Of the 16 significant Curriculum and Instruction quality indicators, 6 received a perfect average score of 5. These quality indicators are: students have access to adequate technology; a variety of classes is offered; academic standards are established for the program; the curriculum keeps in line with the graduation requirements of the host or home school district; students are given immediate feedback about their daily work; and learning tasks aim for depth of understanding rather than superficial knowledge.

Table 9.7: Significant Program Organization Quality Indicators Receiving a Perfect Score of 5 — North High

Program Organization

4.58 (5) The program site is cheerful and welcoming to students, staff and parents

4.57 (5) The program site is large enough to accommodate the student population and program needs

4.54 (5) An orientation meeting before/as students enter the program

4.48 (5) Clear admissions procedure

4.37 (5) Class size is kept below 15 students per teacher at "seat time" programs

4.36   Teachers/staff volunteer for the program (i.e., no unrequested transfers)

4.33 (5) Attendance policy is in place and enforced

4.32 (5) The program site meets building codes

4.23   Class size is kept to below 15 students per supervising adult at "seat time" programs

4.07   Students are given the opportunity to graduate at the program site

4.03   Post-secondary options are available

4.03   Program has a purposeful mission statement

4.02   The location is accessible to any student who would like to attend the program

4.02   Program has a director/release time for a director

4.01   Students are given the opportunity to graduate at a mainstream high school

3.99 (5) Total size of "seat time" program is kept below 200 students at one location

3.88 (5) Location is away from the regular high school

3.87   Students can take classes outside of alternative learning program/center

3.82   Choice of an independent study, all "seat-time" or a combination of both programs available

Although relatively few significant Student Support quality indicators were identified at this site, the majority[8] that were identified, were given a score of 5. The quality indicators are: students feel physically safe; students feel emotionally safe; students view teachers as caring/supportive adults; teachers are able to deal with problems as they arise in class; there is a family atmosphere; the structure of the program is closely tied to the needs of the local popula-

Table 9.8: Significant Quality Indicators Not Identified by North High Staff

Significant Quality Indicator	North High Average	Statewide Average Score	Statewide Rank
Program Organization			
Students can graduate at program site	2.5	4.07	44
Post secondary options available	3.5	4.03	48
Program has director/release time for one	2	4.02	53
Students can graduate at mainstream site	3.5	4.01	54
Choice of independent study, seat time or both	3.5	3.82	67
Program Structure			
Teachers/staff meet weekly	3	4.06	45
Teachers are qualified in level they teach	2	3.97	60
Introduction/orientation class	3	3.81	69
Curriculum and Instruction			
Hands-on activities in all classes	3.5	4.03	51
Science lab equipment for Science classes	2	3.93	63
Student Support			
Support services from community agencies	2.5	4.48	13
A counselor is available	0	4.45	15
Early diagnosis of social/emotional needs	2.5	4.34	26
Parents have input into continuous learning plan	3	3.82	68
Program Support			
Staff belong to a professional organization	35	3.77	72

tion; the program provides a great deal of structure for students in a flexible manner; and teachers also perform counseling duties.

Finally, of the 3 significant Program Support quality indicators, 2 of them were given a perfect score of 5. These quality indicators are: There is some clerical/secretarial help on site and there is some clerical help available.

A comparison of these perfect average scores of 5 and the statewide rankings reveals an interesting pattern, especially in the category of Program Support. In this category, the top two significant quality indicators also received a score of 5. In each of the other categories a group of items receiving a perfect score of 5 are clustered towards the top and then "sprinkled" throughout the rest of the quality indicators.

Table 9.8 illustrates which of the significant quality indicators were not identified by the sample from North High ALC and the average score accorded each one.

Once again there is a 10% difference between the number of significant quality indicators observed at North High ALC (89%) and those identified by the sample of staff who returned the questionnaire (79%). If the items relating to students getting specialized help for social/emotional issues are disregarded, the top 43 significant quality indicators identified by the statewide sample were either observed or selected.

A Day in the Life of West High ALC

Program Organization

West High ALC is housed in an old condemned building. There are several safety concerns and the roof leaks. It does not meet building codes. It is not large enough to accommodate the student population or its program needs. It is not welcoming or cheerful.

Some staff members have been transferred to this program involuntarily and one, in particular, is very resentful of this fact. There is an attendance policy but there was no evidence that it is strictly enforced. This lack of enforcement keeps the class sizes to less than 15 students per staff member on most days, but the population is not consistent from day to day or class to class.

Students attend this program all day, five days a week. There is no choice of independent study, all seat time or a combination of both.

Governance

One person has been unofficially designated lead teacher. It was not clear how this had occurred, but she is responsible for scheduling classes and she has some release time for these duties. She appeared to make most of the decisions for the site with the help of a handful of other teachers. One teacher complained that she was not in the "in group" and her opinion was never sought. Conversations with other staff members gave the impression that the governing structure was oligarchic in nature. Although the unofficial lead teacher made many decisions about the building, this was obviously not true as far as staffing is concerned. She made a comment that, "Staff were sent to her."

Program Structure

The area in which staff at this site appear to be struggling the most is the area of academic standards. The classes observed appeared to have markedly lower academic standards than would be considered acceptable in most high schools. The lead teacher claimed that all the students passed the eighth grade graduation test before they graduated from the program. However, almost all of the students in a language arts class talked the entire time the teacher was teaching the lesson. When the assignment was given on a poorly reproduced worksheet, over half the students claimed they had no idea what the worksheet was about. Several offers of help to different groups around the room revealed that these students were unable to read the simple worksheet about nouns. Rather than complete the worksheet, some students talked among themselves until one of the other students finished their worksheet, and then copied it. When asked about the virtue of doing this they claimed that they did it all the time. "You don't expect me to do that s--t do you?" asked one of the boys.

Curriculum and Instruction

It was not clear to what extent this was attributable to the extreme lack of resources available at this site. No audio-visual equipment was available to teachers despite the fact that one of the classes offered to students was designed to be presented audio-visually. The teacher of this particular class remarked that she watches the videos at home and teaches the information she has gleaned the next day. The lack of resources also appeared to have a deleterious effect on the variety of activities available in each class. Students were using outdated textbooks that had been donated to the program when another school bought new ones. There were no computers for students to use.

The program at West High ALC includes two discipline rooms where students are sent if they are uncooperative in class or commit acts of violence. One room keeps students in isolation and the other room is more of a "cooling off" area where students complete a plan stating the problem they had and how to resolve it. One of the students cooling off had been a fairly good student at his mainstream high school except that he had been caught smoking several times. He had heard that students at West High ALC could smoke, so he planned on getting a semester of failing grades in order to attend West High ALC. He had been sent to the discipline room for making comments about the work assigned in class. He complained bitterly about the boring work at West High ALC, claiming that he had completed "stuff like this" in elementary school. He was distressed that he was learning nothing new at West High, and was planning on going back to his mainstream high school the following semester.

The learning tasks appeared to be designed to address superficial knowledge rather than any depth of understanding. Constructivist techniques were conspicuously absent and no interdisciplinary units were in evidence.

The location of the program does not lend itself to the pursuit of vocational goals for students. No career education was evident in the current classes being offered. Service learning was not referred to in any of the conversations held with students or staff.

Student Support

It would appear that the majority of students who attend West High ALC choose to do so because they have experienced physical and emotional safety issues in the past. A conversation in the stairwell at lunchtime revealed that students like coming to this program because they feel safe here. No one ridicules them for the way they look or what they can't do (academically). And intimidation is absolutely forbidden. Many kind comments were made about the teachers at West High ALC, especially the lead teacher. One interesting set of comments pertained to the lead teacher "taking care" of them. When tentatively asked about the copied assignments in the language arts class, one student offered the comment that Elizabeth (the lead teacher) would make sure they were ready to leave West High ALC "before she boots us out." "Boots us out" referred to graduating from the program. A small group of older boys expressed concern about leaving the program at all, not knowing if they could cope "on the outside" without Elizabeth.

Academic shortcomings aside, almost all of the staff at West High ALC interacted positively with the students and seemed to care about them a great deal.

Program Support

None of the teachers at West High ALC belong to any professional organizations, except for Elizabeth. The most common answer when questioned about this was, "Those organizations don't have much in common with what we do here at West High." None of them belong to the Minnesota Association of Alternative Programs or have ever attended one of their conferences.

An Analysis of Significant Quality Indicators Observed at West High ALC

Forty-two (58%) of the 72 quality indicators identified as being significant on the statewide sample of questionnaires were evident at West High ALC. Table 9.9 illustrates this data by noting the significant quality indicators not observed at this site. Thirteen (68%) of the 19 Program Organization significant quality indicators were in evidence. Only 1 (50%) of the 2 Governance significant quality indicators were applicable to this site. Faring just slightly better, 8 (57%) of the 14 Program Structure significant quality indicators were in evidence. By far the lowest category of significant quality indicators is Curriculum and Instruction with 4 (22%) of 18 being evident. In contrast, the proportion of significant Student Support quality indicators, 13 (87%) is similar to the results found at the two excellent sites. This is also true of the significant Program Support quality indicators, where 3 (75%) of the 4 indicators were evident.

No questionnaires were returned from West High ALC so that data was not available for this study.

Summary

Practitioners in the field of alternative education in the state of Minnesota identified 72 quality indicators they believe are significant for the success of an alternative education program. These items were almost equally divided between organizational/academic issues and affective/social-emotional issues.

The question of whether these significant quality indicators are evident at all alternative program sites was dispelled with a comparison between two sites described as excellent by the Department of Children, Families and Learning and a site that was described as moderately successful. At the two excellent sites, South High ALC and North High ALC, 93% and 89% of significant quality indicators were observed respectively. These numbers are in stark comparison with a mere 58% of significant quality indicators being observed at the moderately successful site, West High ALC. A further look at these sites reveals that, of the top half of significant quality indicators identified by the statewide sample, 97% and 94%, respectively, were observed at South and North High ALCs. This is in comparison with just 58% at West High ALC. At West High ALC, 21 of the top 36 significant quality indicators were observed. Twelve of these were from the category of Student Support, leaving just 9 from the other five categories combined. See table 9.10.

Table 9.9: Significant Quality Indicators Not Observed at West High ALC

SIGNIFICANT QUALITY INDICATOR	STATEWIDE RANK
Program Organization	
Program is cheerful and welcoming to parents and students	6
Program site is large enough to accommodate students and programs	7
Teachers/staff volunteer for the program	23
Attendance policy is in place and enforced	28
Program site meets building codes	29
Choice of independent study, seat time or combination	67
Governance	
Staff at site make decisions about staffing at the site	49
Program Structure	
Teachers have high/appropriate expectations for their students	5
There are enough resources for all students	8
A selection of activities is provided for each unit of study	24
Goal setting occurs at regular intervals	55
All students have vocational goals	65
There is an orientation/introductory class	69
Curriculum and Instruction	
Students have adequate access to technology	16
Instruction maximizes student's learning style	25
Career skills training available	27
Academic standards established for the program	32
Students are assessed in a variety of ways	33
Students are required to demonstrate their knowledge	38
Curriculum keeps in line with the graduation standards	40
Hands-on activities are available in all classes	51
Audio visual materials are readily available	56
Learning tasks aim for depth of understanding	57
Interdisciplinary units where available	61
Constructivist techniques used in class settings	62
Science lab equipment available for science classes	63
All students have a service learning experience	70
Student Support	
The structure of the program is closely tied with the needs of the local student population	35
Program provides a great deal of structure in a flexible manner	36
Program Support	
Staff belong to a professional organization such as MAAP	72

At both North and Sough High ALCs there was the most disagreement between observations at the sites and the statewide sample in the area of Program Organization. At West High ALC there was the greatest disagreement in the are of Curriculum and Instruction, followed by Program Organization.

The evidence gleaned from South High ALC and North High ALC would lead one to believe that these two sites would be strongly supported by practitioners in the field of alternative education in Minnesota. There is a high correlation between significant quality indicators observed and those selected by the statewide sample. The same could not be said for West High ALC. Although there is a strong social/emotional dimension to the program there, it is academically deficient. A strong social/emotional component is obviously advocated at the two excellent sites and throughout the state, but not at the expense of a solid academic program.

Table 9.10: Significant Quality Indicators Observed at Each Site

SH	NH	WH	
			Program Organization
X	X		The program site is cheerful and welcoming to students, staff and parents
X	X		The program site is large enough to accommodate the student population and program
X	X	X	An orientation meeting before/as students enter the program
X	X	X	Clear admissions procedure
	X		Class size is kept below 15 students per teacher at "seat time" programs
X	X		Teachers/staff volunteer for the program (i.e., no unrequested transfers)
X	X		Attendance policy is in place and enforced
X	X		The program site meets building codes
	X		Class size is kept to below 15 students per supervising adult at "seat time" programs
X			Students are given the opportunity to graduate at the program site
X	X	X	Post-secondary options are available
X	X	X	Program has a purposeful mission statement
X	X	X	The location is accessible to any student who would like to attend the program
X		X	Program has a director/release time for a director
X	X	X	Students are given the opportunity to graduate at a mainstream high school
X	X	X	Total size of "seat time" program is kept below 200 students at one location
X	X	X	Location is away from the regular high school
X	X	X	Students can take classes outside of alternative learning program/center
			Choice of an independent study, all "seat-time" or a combination
			Governance
X	X	X	Staff at the site make decisions about curriculum issues
X	X		Staff at the site make decisions about staffing at the site

SH	NH	WH	
			Program Structure
X	X		Teachers have high/appropriate expectations for their students
X	X		There are enough resources for all students (desks, chairs, computers, calculators, etc.)
X	X	X	Students apply to enter the program, i.e., they are not placed without their consent
X	X	X	Availability of individual instruction
X	X		A selection of activities is provided for each unit of study (e.g., reading out of book/magazine, watch video, interview someone, computer testing, etc.)
X	X	X	All students have academic program goals
X	X	X	Attendance is taken in each class throughout the day
X	X	X	All students have personal development goals
X		X	Teachers/staff meet weekly to discuss student performance
	X		Goal setting occurs at regular intervals
X	X	X	All students have an individualized, continual learning plan
X	X	X	Teachers are qualified in the level (i.e., secondary) they are to teach
X	X		All students have vocational program goals
X			There is an orientation/introductory class
			Curriculum and Instruction
X	X		Students have adequate access to technology (Internet, computer stations)
X	X	X	Early diagnosis of weaknesses in basic skills
X	X	X	A variety of classes are offered
X	X		Instruction maximizes student's learning style
X	X		Career skills training is available
X	X		Academic standards established for the program
X	X		Students are assessed in a variety of ways
X	X		Students are required to *demonstrate* their knowledge, where appropriate
X	X		Curriculum keeps in line with the graduation requirement of the host or home school
X	X	X	Learning and assessment tasks involve student production not reproduction of knowledge
X	X		Hands-on activities are available in all classes
X	X		Audio visual materials are readily available

SH	NH	WH	
X	X		Learning tasks aim for depth of understanding rather than superficial exposure
X			Interdisciplinary units where appropriate
X	X		Constructivist techniques used in class settings
X			Science lab equipment available for Science classes
X	X		All students have a service learning experience before they leave the program

Student Support

SH	NH	WH	
X	X	X	Students feel physically "safe" at school
X	X	X	Students feel "emotionally" safe at school
X	X	X	Students view teachers as caring, supportive adults
X	X	X	Teachers are able to deal with problems as they arise during class time
X	X	X	Support services are available from community agencies
X		X	A counselor is available to students
X	X	X	Students have input into the continual learning plan
X		X	Early diagnosis of social/emotional areas of need
X	X	X	There is a "family" atmosphere
X	X		The structure of the program is closely tied with the needs of the local student population
X	X		Program provides a great deal of structure for students in a flexible manner
X	X	X	Teachers are readily accessible to students before and after regular school hours
X	X	X	Teachers are readily accessible to parents/guardians before and after regular school hours
	X	X	Parents/guardians have input into the continual learning plan
X	X	X	Teachers also perform counseling duties

Program Support

SH	NH	WH	
X	X	X	There is some clerical/secretarial help on-site
X	X	X	There is some clerical help available
X	X	X	Staff receive staff development at least twice a year
X	X		Staff belong to a professional organization, such a MAAP

10

Conclusion

Every child must be encouraged to get as much education as
he has the ability to take. We want this not only for his sake
but for the nation's sake. Nothing matters more to the future
of our country: not military preparedness—for armed might
is worthless if we lack the brain power to build a world of peace;
not our productive economy—for we cannot sustain growth
without trained manpower; not our democratic system
of government—for freedom is fragile if citizens are ignorant.
— *Lyndon B. Johnson, president of the United States, 1963–1969*

Indeed, why build glorious, first class cities if the inhabitants do not feel like glorious, first class citizens? We have too many examples of shiny, brand new buildings being erected and paid for with excessive amounts of tax dollars—for the purpose of incarcerating wretched, second class citizens. Surely, it makes more sense to spend this money to prevent as many individuals as possible from embarking on a life of enduring daily indignities and feelings of isolation and loneliness—and, too often, incarceration.

Meeting this challenge requires making a specific commitment to students who become disenfranchised within the halls of mainstream education: a commitment of funds as well as a commitment of philosophy. But, rather than attempting to change a huge, bureaucratic structure to accommodate these students, small-scale innovations are the best vehicles for change.

One of the most powerful examples of small-scale innovation is the alternative school. Alternative education, like traditional education, is based on the belief that all children can learn. However, in alternative schools, it is assumed that not all students are able to learn in all school environments, or without the school having the ability to adapt to some of these students' needs.

Although there is no typical model of an alternative school, there are some common structures and processes. These include collaborative, site-based management, small school size, small class size, extended roles for teachers, cooperative roles for students, voluntary membership, student involvement in governance, and the absence, or minimization, of tracking, ability grouping or other kinds of labeling. In many cases, students are not given letter grades but accrue points towards graduation through coursework, independent study, and internship or service learning activities.

The degree of departure from standard school organization, programs and environment depends, in large part, on the mission of the alternative program. Each purpose shapes each alternative school in a unique way.

It is my contention that "the true" alternative education student is a "different breed of cat." Lack of skills, support structure and coping strategies make these students easy prey to a cycle of rejection and failure within the mainstream setting. These students desperately need small school size, small class size, extended roles for teachers, cooperative roles for students, voluntary membership, student involvement in governance, and an absence or minimization of tracking, ability grouping or other kinds of labeling.

The most important step in establishing an alternative school is to determine the Mission Statement for the program. Despite the fact that smaller programs, especially in rural areas, tend to be an amalgam of the different types of alternative programs, it is rarely appropriate to develop a mission statement whose goal is to provide education to every student who has not been reached in the mainstream setting. As heartbreaking as it may be to knowingly omit a certain sector of the population from a new alternative program, trying to be all-things-to-all-people is unrealistic and a sure sign of failure. Students whose basic needs stem from English being their second language, and others whose basic needs stem from severe behavioral disorders are, for example, very difficult to educate together in a small setting. Successful programs are good ambassadors for adding more programs, poor ones are not. Additional alternative programs can be added at a later date. School board philosophy statements often refer to the education of all students, and this tenet may be an appropriate one for a vision statement for alternative education throughout a district. It just isn't appropriate for one small setting. However, certain attributes of students can be combined successfully, such as poor basic skills due to lack of ability and poor basic skills due to poor attendance.

The primary goal of an alternative school program is to first make connections with each student, and then be sure to maintain these connections. They often do this by providing a "family-like" atmosphere and do, indeed, become surrogate families. An inordinate number of students in alternative schools come from homes that are dysfunctional for a variety of reasons, such as poverty, substance abuse, divorce or mental illness. These factors render parents unable to adequately nurture their children. Alternative educators find themselves providing emotional support and social skills that are traditionally provided by the family unit.

Once this has been established, the secondary (academic) goal may be addressed. It is important to note here that emphasizing connectedness does not diminish the role of academic progress. In fact, once connections have been made, students should be more able and willing to learn.

Schools need to be community-based, reflecting the realities and needs of the local community in order to succeed. At this level, the mores and customs of the students can be taken into account when making key decisions. Specific problems can also become a determining factor. Some schools are currently struggling with refining their constructivist strategies, while others are more concerned about poor attendance, poverty and crime.

Knowledge of the local culture and population may call for a markedly different approach to educating students. Aspects such as school calendar, teaching days, time of day and organization of subject matter are similar in many districts across the country, but they do not need to be that way.

Although alternative education programs may seem like microcosms of larger school systems from the outside, a closer look will not support this view. A quality alternative school will have been designed for a specific population of students. As a result, it requires a specific population of adults to work with these students.

The single, most important criteria for staffing an alternative school is to ensure that these people want to be there. Alternative students tend to have more academic and social/emotional needs than equivalent school populations. Placing teaching and/or support staff in these programs because they are not succeeding elsewhere is a recipe for disaster. Just one disgruntled staff member can be enough to destroy any program. Typically, students attending an alternative program have experienced rejection for many years. They don't need to be exposed to any more rejection or inappropriate teaching styles. Fledgling programs are particularly vulnerable to the destructive nature of this type of employee. There are some general characteristics that apply to all staff working in an alternative school, such as having a positive outlook, a common vision, being a team player and being flexible.

The majority of alternative programs open their doors with few staff members. As a result, it is typical for one staff member to wear at least two hats, teaching and administration. This person is often known as the lead teacher. Although small in size, these programs still require the same array of administrative duties required in larger programs. Setting up the program, facilitating changes in the program, interviewing staff and students, developing and overseeing the budget, curriculum development, communicating with appropriate school district personnel, maintaining close ties with parents and social service agencies, and being responsible for discipline are but a few of the tasks expected of the lead teacher. These duties take time and energy, and it is not realistic to expect someone to maintain a full teaching load whilst also performing these tasks. It is very important to provide release time for the lead teacher so that these duties can be performed adequately and in a timely manner.

As a result of the fact that lead teachers are often primarily classroom teachers, they usually do not have any formal training in administration. It is important for the lead teacher to know how to access administrative files that are pertinent to the site, are privy to administrative decisions that pertain to the site, and have a good command of the budget process. It is most helpful if one administrator is assigned to the lead teacher to provide this important information. The lead teacher and the assigned administrator can then work together to ensure that the best decisions are made for individual students at the alternative school.

One of the most empowering aspects of a small, vibrant organization, such as an alternative school, is that there is ample room for leadership development at all levels. Not only are there opportunities for leadership, but each of the jobs requires it. The lead teacher will be more than occupied with his/her duties. Therefore, some crucial elements of the program will naturally default to other staff members. It is important that this leader can share the reins of control.

The small teaching staff may become completely responsible for curriculum development in alignment with local, state and federal requirements. The small support staff may become completely responsible for the day-to-day running of the program. It is important that everyone receives adequate training to do their respective jobs on an ongoing basis.

Alternative school staffs often resemble "leadership teams" more than a "hierarchy of staff members." It is important for them to have the latitude to make important decisions about their site, especially in the areas of curriculum development and staffing. A staff of competent, positive, enthusiastic, flexible players is an unbeatable team.

A well organized program with ample flexibility within the structure is one of the hallmarks of a quality program. First impressions are important. We judge people and places immediately upon our first contact with them. Further contacts are often determined by the perceptions made during the first contact. This may be especially so with individuals who have been/felt rejected by the status quo and are desperately seeking another opportunity to succeed. An old abandoned building with a leaky roof and no heating will do little for the self-esteem of a student who has felt rejection and failure in a multi-million dollar high school.

One of the most important features of an alternative school program is that curriculum is delivered in a manner that is different than at the local high school. This different manner will be driven by the mission that was established for the program in the first place. Different could mean different materials, different pacing of instruction, different methods of instruction, different methods of evaluation, etc. The most important thing to remember, once again, is that these decisions must be driven by the mission of the program and the individual needs of each student.

The second most important thing to remember is that the curriculum must hold meaning for students. They have already been exposed to taking subjects "because they were required." And they were not successful in that setting. Now, they need to understand the rationale behind learning specific bodies of knowledge and have that knowledge delivered in a way that holds meaning for them. Constructivist theory encourages students to become intimately involved in the subject matter at hand and manipulate and interpret it in a manner that makes meaning for them. Facts and figures are available, literally, at the push of a button—on an Internet-ready cell phone. Knowing a plethora of facts and figures is not as important in today's world as understanding and knowing how to manipulate them for the task at hand.

The only common factor about learners in alternative settings is that they did not thrive in their previous setting. Beyond that, they can be very different from each other. Some will be auditory learners, some visual learners, some tactile learners, some kinesthetic learners. The majority of students found in alternative school programs are kinesthetic learners. They learn best when they can experience things. In order to accommodate these learners, it is best to have a variety of experiences available to them during the course of a unit of a study. It is also important to establish the learning style of each student before charting their course in the alternative setting.

Seat time programs can offer instruction in a variety of ways, and should be determined by each student's learning style and preference. If several students need to take a particular class, for example math, it may be wise to offer this in a small-group, teacher-directed setting. However, if a student or two would like to work alone or in pairs, that option should be available, also—as long as the student/s make/s sufficient progress. After all, the goal of allowing flexibility is to accommodate each student's learning style. Basic skills instruction should be offered in a variety of settings, including computer-assisted, individual and small group, depending on the age of the students and availability of materials.

The program site also has to be adequately equipped with materials for students to accomplish the tasks set for them. Technology needs to be at least as good as that available at the mainstream high school. There should be sufficient quantities of other supplies such as notebook paper, trade books, calculators, pens and pencils for all students. It may be appropriate to supply all or some of these items. It may be equally as appropriate to have some of these items available for students to purchase.

The selection and application of instructional materials should be driven by the mission of the program. High functioning students in a sobriety program will require quite different materials than students for whom English is a second language.

As a whole, alternative school students do not do well on standardized achievement tests. This may be due to a number of reasons. Poor attendance is particularly hard on developmentally sequential subjects, such as math and reading. Kinesthetic learners do not excel in "lecture-type" classes that are common in many high schools. Rote learning holds little value for many students today.

But, accountability is an important aspect of any program that has goals and objectives. It is crucial to know if goals are being met. There are a variety of basic skills and criterion reference assessments available on the market for times when a traditional test situation is appropriate. Both can be taken in print form or on the computer. The choice of assessment should be driven by its purpose.

Despite the fact that no two alternative programs are the same and that they deal with idiosyncratic populations, some key characteristics of good programs have emerged.

The basic problem with attempting to validate quality, idiosyncratic programs, such as alternative schools, is that they are difficult to quantify. However, a 1999 study of Minnesota Alternative School staff discovered that, although difficult, this was possible.

The results of this study clearly indicate that people working in the field of alternative education in the state of Minnesota do have an extensive list of characteristics they feel are important for a quality program. From an exhaustive list of 126 quality indicators, practitioners identified over half of them as being significant. These characteristics are not identical for all programs. Rather, they reflect the needs of the local student population as perceived by key people at each site.

What is very clear is that in order for alternative educators to have an excellent program, they need to have a shared perspective with the majority of other alternative educators. This shared perspective translates into successful programs having the vast majority of significant quality indicators identified by their peers. However, this shared perspective does not result in a standardized "look" to all alternative programs. The goal is not to find "the one" program on which all other programs should be modeled. As May Anne Raywid noted in her recent article in *Phi Delta Kappan*, "There's no single formula yielding a model that is an ideal 'school for the unsuccessful.'" Rather, the significant quality indicators should be viewed as objectives that can be met in a number of ways. The important thing is not the way each significant quality indicator is achieved, but that it is achieved, according to how key people at the site interpret their world.

It is with gratitude and relief that the answer to the question, "Do we even care about students who are disenfranchised within the education system?" is a resounding "Yes." There is still an open invitation to new and current huddles masses to become part of the American dream. There is still someone who is willing to hold the lamp high for these children beside the golden door.

This gratitude can be keenly felt in the comments made as students graduated from the Cass Lake, Minnesota Alternative Learning Center:

- "I'm really glad I came to the ALC. It is such a great place to come and do your work, one to one with a teacher, get caught up inschoolwork and get to know new great people. The staff is likeanother family. I'm really going to miss seeing them every day."

- "It was fun, but it was also a learning experience and it helped me reach a goal I thought I wouldn't reach before my baby was born."

- "My experience here would have to rate the highest because it expects the most out of you and in turn does not ask that it be rushed or crammed into a little time, because work takes time. I would like to thank the ALC staff for its cooperation and help in developing my needs to move on to college, and for giving me the confidence to go for my goals."

About the Author

Carole Mottaz was born and raised in London before moving to River Falls, Wisconsin, where she currently lives with her husband Cliff, whom she credits as her "greatest source of support." Having taught every grade level on three continents, she now finds herself drawn to alternative education because she believes that in the right setting . . . every child can learn and become a productive member of society.